National Intelligencer Newspaper Abstracts 1855

Joan M. Dixon

HERITAGE BOOKS
2008

HERITAGE BOOKS
AN IMPRINT OF HERITAGE BOOKS, INC.

Books, CDs, and more—Worldwide

For our listing of thousands of titles see our website at
www.HeritageBooks.com

Published 2008 by
HERITAGE BOOKS, INC.
Publishing Division
100 Railroad Ave. #104
Westminster, Maryland 21157

Copyright © 2008 Joan M. Dixon

All rights reserved. No part of this book may be reproduced or transmitted in any form or by any means, electronic or mechanical, including photocopying, recording or by any information storage and retrieval system without written permission from the author, except for the inclusion of brief quotations in a review.

International Standard Book Numbers
Paperbound: 978-0-7884-4771-6
Clothbound: 978-0-7884-7474-3

NATIONAL INTELLIGENCER NEWSPAPER
WASHINGTON, D C
1855

TABLE OF CONTENTS

Daily National Intelligencer, Washington, D C, 1855: pg 1

Appointments & Transfers-10th Regt of Infty-Riflemen: 117; 123
Appointments by the President: see index.
Appropriations-2nd Session of 38th Congress: 191-196
Army appointments & Promotions: 437-439
Army General Orders: 281-294
Blood of the Butlers: 402

Cadets appointed at large by the President: 104
Cadets appointed to West Point: 166-167
Capitol Dome: 331
College of William & Mary: 315
Colonel Aaron Burr: 471

Commencements: Academy of the Visitation, near Balt, Md: 266
                              Academy of the Visitation, Gtwn, D C: 270-271
                              Medical Dept of Gtwn College, D C: 112
                              St Mary's, Charles Co, Md: 306

Court of Claims attorneys: 263-264
Death of Dorothy Wordsworth: 90
Death of Emperor Nicholas: 135-136
Death of John W Maury: 58
Death of Madam Sally S Wood-authoress: 28
Death of Margaret Jane Johns: 7

Dogma of the Immaculate Conception: 14
East India Squadron casualties-[1855]: 397-398
Finger rings: 10
Fire in Alexandria: 431
Glenwood Cemetery: 233
Henry VIII: 478
I O O F Officers: 153

John Quincy Adams' monument: 5-6
Kansas pro-slavery: 297
Marine Corps promotions: 387
Maryland Agricultural Society: 414-415
Mason & Dixon Line: 248
Medical Alumni of Gtwn College, D C: 208
Methodist Episcopal Church appointments: 125; 475
Military Appointments: 96
Monument between U S & Mexico: 123
Mount Vernon Ladies Association: 403
Naval Appointments: 83
Naval Board Surgeons: 159
Naval Intelligence: 425
New Hampshire Veterans: 467-468
N Y C Railroad disaster: 336-338; 341; 342; 344; 347; 351; 384
Nominations for Wasington City officers: 178
Norwich-1792-1793: 328-329

Officers of the:	Arctic: 212; 220; 389
	Congress: 273
	Constitution: 17
	Mississippi: 161
	Potomac: 224
	Porpoise: 210
	Preble: 237; 328
	Release: 220
	St Louis: 148

Opening of the Saut Canal: 249
Oregon & Washington Territories: 457
Origin of the Alden family: 474
Paintings in the Rotunda of the Capitol: 78; 84
Portraitures of Washington: 440-442
Promotions in the Navy: 158; 373-376
Public School teachers-Washington: 233
Retired Naval Officers: 363-370
Revenue Marine Service: 113
St Louis railroad disaster: 416; 421
Sioux Expedition Headquarters-Gen Harney's report: 379-380
Soldiers of the War of 1812: 3; 13
The Tent of Washington: 189
Treasury Dept clerical changes: 249
U S Agricultural Society: 93-94
U S brig Porpoise disaster: 210

War Dept: 228
Washington City-Jurors: 99; 235; 451
Washington City tax sale: 29; 41
Washington Corp Councils: 217
Washington Corp-Mayor nominations: 252-253
Washington National Monument Society: 173
Washington Navy Yard: 384
West Point: 214-215; Graduating class: 258
William Jennens: 131-132

Yellow Fever deaths-[Includes deaths in Norfolk & Portsmouth, Va]: See index

Dedicated to the memory of my uncle:
Franklin Joseph Neff
b.1880 Wash, D C d. 1977, Wash, D C.
Married 1st: Annie C Warring,
b. 1890, Wash, D C d. 1911, Wash, D C
Married 2nd: Ruth Deatley,
b 1898, Wash, D C d. 1973, Wash, D C

PREFACE
Daily National Intelligencer Newspaper Abstracts
1855
Joan M Dixon

The National Intelligencer & Washington Advertiser is hereafter the Daily National Intelligencer. It was the first newspaper printed in Washington, D C; Samuel H Smith, the originator. The same was transferred to Jos Gales, jr on Aug 31, 1810; on Nov 1, 1812, the paper was under the firm of Jos Gales, sr, & Wm W Seaton. The Library of Congress has microfilm of the paper from the first issue of Oct 31, 1800 thru Jan 8, 1870, the final paper. The Evening Star Newspaper of Jan 10, 1870 reports: The Intelligencer is discontinued: the proprietor, Mr Alex Delmar, says that having lost several thousand dollars, & being in poor health, he has resolved to discontinue its publication.

Included in the abstracts are advertisements; appointments by the President; Hse o/Rep petitions; passed Acts; legal notices; marriages; deaths; mscl notices; social events; tax lists; military promotions; court cases; deaths by accident; prisoners; & maritime information-crews. Items or events which might be a clue as to the location, age or relationship of an individual are copied.

No attempt has been made to correct the spelling. Due to the length of some articles, it was necessary to present only the highlights of same. Chancery and Equity records are copied as written.

The index contains all surnames and *tracts of lands/places*. **Maritime vessels** are found under barge, boat, brig, frig, schn'r, ship, sloop, steamboat, tugboat, yacht or vessel.

ABBREVIATIONS:

AA CO	ANNE ARUNDEL COUNTY
CMDER	COMMANDER
CMDOR	COMMODOR
ELIZ	ELIZABETH
ELIZA	ELIZA
MONTG CO	MONTGOMERY COUNTY
PG CO	PRINCE GEORGES CO
WASH	WASHINGTON
WASH, D C	WASHINGTON, DISTRICT OF COLUMBIA

BOOKS IN THE NATIONAL INTELLIGENCER NEWSPAPER SERIES: 1800-1805/1806-1810/1811-1813/1814-1817/1818-1820/1821-1823/1824-1826/1827-1829/1830-1831/1832-1833/1834-1835/1836-1837/1838-1839/1840/1841/1842/1843/1844/1845/1846/1847/ 1848/1849/ 1850/1851/1852/1853/1854/1855. SPECIAL: CIVIL WAR 2 VOLS, 1861-1865

NATIONAL INTELLIGENCER NEWSPAPER
1855

MON JAN 1, 1855
House of Reps: 1-Cmte on Naval Affairs to inquire into allowing to Cmder Wm F Lynch, during the time he was engaged in the exploration of the Dead Sea, the same pay that has been allowed to Lts Herndon & Gibbon during the time they were engaged in the exploration of the Amazon. 2-Cmte on Public Lands: bill for the relief of Henry H Marsh: committed. 3-Bill for the relief of Joshua Chamberlain: referred to the Cmte on Revolutionary Claims.

The corner-stone of the Free College at Shamokin, Pa, was laid on Fri by Gov Bigler. The college is to be endowed by Judge Helfenstein, & indigent & worthy students will be educated free of charge. Judge H proposes to dedicate forever a valuable & productive coal estate, in the Shamokin coal basin, for the benefit of the destitute poor of N Y, Phil, Balt, Lancaster, & Carlisle.

Chancery sale: by decree of the Circuit Court of Wash Co, D C, in the cause wherein Jas Adams is cmplnt & Richd Patton is dfndnt: public auction on Jan 24, of lots B & H, being lots 1 & 30, in square 693, Wash City, with improvements thereon.
-W Redin, trustee -Green & Scott, aucts

Redemption of Va 6% debt: redeemable on Mar 8, 1844, & afterwards within a period not exceeding 15 years. Apr 1, 1855, set to redeem the said certificates at the Treasury of the Commonwealth aforesaid. The holders are to surrender the same at the ofc of the Second Auditor; &, whether surrendered or not, the interest thereon will cease on that day.
1825
Jan 19: Baring, Brothers & Co: $10,000
1827
Jul 1: Edw Meyler, of Islington, Middlesex Co, England: $5,000
1831
Apr 20: Robt Viner, of Gantby Hall, Lincoln Co, England: $9,000.
Dec 29: Smith, Payne & Smiths, of London, bankers: $10,000
1842
Nov 21: John Ferguson, of Irvine, in North Britain: $20,000
1843
Aug 23: Johanna Schaer, of Germany: $2,000
Aug 26: Mrs Jane L Graham, of Wash City: $250
1844
Jan 16: Miss Catharine Hays, of Richmond: $1,000
Jan 20: Saml Ford, of Richmond: $10,000
Feb 21: Jos Jackson, of Richmond: $250
May 21: Thos Cotterill, a present residing at Birmingham, Eng: $1,000

1846
Sep 21: Most Hon Richd Seymour Conway, Marquis of Hartford, Great Britain: $35,000
1849
Jan 30: L Nunnally: $100
May 31: Jas Haskins, Cmte of John Haskins, of Brunswick: $200
Aug 20: John Ferguson, of Irvine, in Great Britain: $10,000
Dec 16: Haxall Brothers & Co, Richmond: $2,000
1851
Jul 12: Alfred Lewis, No 102 Picadilly, London: $10,000
1852
Feb 7: Tazewell Taylor, exc & trustee under the will of Upton Beall: $800
Feb 9: Arthur A Morson, special com'r in the suit of Hicks vs Morris' administrator: $1,000
Mar 9: A A Morson & R T Daniel, as com'rs for the Circuit Court of Chancery: $350
Mar 18: Jane E Clopton, of Gloucester: $500
Mar 18: E A J Clopton, of Richmond: $200
Mar 19: Robt R Carter, U S Navy: $4,000
Mar 19: Hill Carter, of Shirley: $450
Aug 3: E A J Clopton, of Richmond: $2,000
1853
Feb 3: Saml Reeve, trustee of Mrs Ann Howard: $650
Feb 3: Miss Harriet E Tate, of Richmond: $650
Feb 4: Edw Berkeley, trustee for Mrs Ann B Berkley: $200
1843
Nov 23: Pres & Dirs of the Firemen's Ins Co of Balt: $3,000
1844:
Jan 18: Miss Mgt Wilson, of Norfolk: $1,000
Jan 12: Portsmouth Provident Society: $600
Aug 21: Norfolk Provident Society: $1,000
1845
Sep 5: Portsmouth Provident Society: $1,500
G W Clutter, Auditor Public Accounts
S H Parker, Register
Geo W Munford, Sec Commonwealth. The Com'rs of the Sinking Fund.

Died: on Dec 21, at the residence of his son, Frank H Stockett, in the city of Annapolis, after a protracted illness, Jos Noble Stockett, of Anne Arundel Co, Md, in his 76th year.

Mrd: on Dec 26, by Rev John Thompson, Wm H White, of Wash City, to Miss Kate Gibson, of Kent Co, Eastern Shore, Md.

Mrd: on Dec 28, at St James' Church, N Y, by Rev P McKenna, Pastor, Wm J Fitzpatrick, of Wash, to Kate, daughter of Chas Foal, of N Y.

Mrd: on Dec 26, at the residence of D Spaulding, Gloversville, N Y, by Rev H M Robertson, of Wisc, Francis H Pierpont, of Fairmont, Va, to Miss Julia Augusta, daughter of Rev Saml Robertson, of Wisc.

The trial of Geo W Green, a wealthy citizen of Chicago, for the murder of his wife, is now absorbing the attention of the people of Chicago. The trial has been in progress several days. [Jan 6th newspaper: Geo W Green has been convicted of murder in the first degree. A motion has been made for a new trial.] [Jan 12th newspaper: new trial has been granted-competent evidence was excluded from the jury.] [Feb 21st paper: Geo W Green is reported to have hung himself in his cell on Sunday morning.] [Feb 26th newspaper: Geo W Green died worth from $50,000 to $100,000. He made a will in his cell, leaving his property to his youngest son, cutting off the 2nd eldest entirely. The will is to be contested on the ground that no sane man would commit suicide.]

In the county court sitting at New Haven, Ct, Jesse W Rose, being on trial for assault with intent to murder, was defended on the ground of insanity; & while Judge Blackman, the counsel for the prisoner, was examining a witness to prove the defence, Rose suddenly raised his arm & with a back-handed blow knocked his own lawyer over. Such a practical demonstration of mental imbecility was conclusive upon the Court & the State's Atty, who immediately withdrew the case, & Rose was remanded to jail to be taken care of as an insane person.

A small girl, daughter of Riley Ashley, living in Jasper Co, Ohio, was shot in the forehead by a traveler, who was amusing himself by shooting at game along the way.

Hon Saml A Peters died in Colchester, Conn, on Dec 19, aged 85 years. He was probably the oldest member of the legal profession in the State. For many years in succession he was a member of the House of Reps & of the Senate of his native State, & for a considerable period a judge of the New London Co Court.

The printing establishment, known as the Manchester Print Works, in Smithfield, R I, owned principally by & under the entire control of Theodore Schroeder, was entirely destroyed on Dec 21.

In Newark, N J, a lady named Rachel has recovered a verdict of $500 damages against Wm A Francis for alleged slander.

<u>Soldiers-1812.</u> Nat'l Convention of the Soldiers of the War of 1812-Army, Militia, & Navy: to be held in Washington on Jan 8, in the Presbyterian Church on 4½ st, near Pa ave.
Cmte of Arrangements: -Jno P Dickinson, Sec
Geo McNeir   Wm Jones   Jas A Kennedy
G W P Custis   Tobias Watkins
Jas L Edwards   Jno S Gallaher

Hon John Hastings, formerly a member of Congress from the Columbia district, Ohio, died at his residence on Dec 9.

The Com'rs of Holmes Co, Ohio, offer a reward of $2,000 for the arrest of John M Shrock, Treasurer of said county, with the public funds, with which he has absconded, or the sum of $1,000 for his arrest without the public funds, so that he may be had for trial on a charge of forgery now pending against him in Holmes Co. He left Millersburg, Holmes Co, Dec 2, & was last heard of in Cleveland, Dec 5. He is a full-faced, heavy set man, aged about 50 or 55, is 5 feet 9 inches high, weighs about 175 pounds, dark complexion, dark straight hair mixed with gray, reads, speaks, & writes both English & Dutch, writes a smooth fine hand, & is remarkably lame in the left hip.

TUE JAN 2, 1855
Ex-Govn'r Jas T Morehead, of Ky, died at Covington, Ky, Dec 28, age 59 years. He filled many responsible ofcs, from member of the State Legislature to U S Senator.

Died: on Jan 1, after a short illness, Mr Michl Cavenagh, in his 38th year. He leaves a widow & 7 small children to deplore their loss. His funeral is this evening at 3 o'clock, from his late residence on H st, between 2nd & 3rd.

Died: Called to Heaven: L Rebecca, wife of Thos G Clinton, & daughter of the late Thos Johns, born 1828, married & died 1854. Her funeral services will be solemnized at St Matthew's Church, [Rev Fr Donelan,] at 1 o'clock P M, Jan 2. The corpse will be transferred to St Matthew's from the residence of her family, E st, near 10th.

Boston Advertiser: Jos E Spear, a clerk in the post ofc of that city, has been detected in purloining letters containing a large amount of money. He confesses his guilt, & says he has been committing his peculations for 6 or 7 months. He has restored $841.50 of money thus unlawfully obtained by him.

Saml D Scoville, the defaulting ofcr of the Marine Bank Agency of Macon, Ga, has, it is said, made a full confession of delinquency, & manifests a proper spirit of resignation to the fate that awaits him. Gambling victimized Scoville, as it has done a plenty of others.

The Jackson Mercury of Dec 9 says: Houston Taylor, son of the late Smith Taylor, went before Mayor Fletcher on Friday last & voluntarily stated that he had shot Mr R D Shackelford in the late deplorable tragedy in this city. The mayor discharged him, under the statute, as having acted in defence of the life of his father.

Mr John Jones, formerly of Augusta, accidentally lost his life at Alexandria, Burke Co, Geo, on Wed last. Whilst he was riding a race with a friend, & when at full speed, his horse fell & threw him, breaking his neck.

A monument has just been placed in the Unitarian Church in Quincy, Mass, to the memory of John Quincy Adams, by his son, Hon C F Adams. It is composed of highly polished Italian marble, & in size & form very nearly resembles the one erected to the Ex-Pres John Adams, with the exception of the upper part where the bust rests, which is enclosed on both sides by the upper members of the Cornish, that sweeps upwards in graceful lines towards it. It was designed & executed at the Quincy Marble Works by McGrath, Mitchell & Co. The bust which rests upon the top was executed in Italy by the great American sculptor, Hiram Powers. Under the bust is a Latin sentence composed of 2 words, "Alteri Seculo." The following is the inscription on the monument:

Near this place
Reposes all that could die of
JOHN QUINCY ADAMS,
Son of John and Abigail [Smith] Adams,
Sixth President of the United Stated.
Born 11 July, 1767.
Amidst the storms of civil commotion
He nursed the vigor
Which nerves a Statesman and a Patriot,
And the faith
Which inspires a Christian.
For more than half a century,
Whenever his country called for his labors
In either hemisphere or in any capacity,
He never spared them in her cause.
On the twenty-fourth of December, 1814,
He signed the second Treaty with Great Britain,
Which restored peace within her borders;
On the twenty-third of February, 1848,
He closed sixteen years of eloquent defence
Of the lessons of his youth
By dying at his post
In her great National Council.
A son, worthy of his father;
A citizen, shedding glory on his country;
A scholar, ambitious to advance mankind;
This Christian sought to walk humbly
In the sight of his God.

Beside him lies
His partner for fifty years,
Louisa Catherine,
Daughter of Joshua & Catherine [Nuth] Johnson.
Born 12 February, 1775.
Married 26 July, 1797.
Deceased 15 May, 1852,
Aged 77.
Living through many vicissitudes and under
High responsibilities,
As a Daughter, Wife, and Mother,
She proved equal to all.
Dying she left to her family and her sex
The blessed remembrance
Of a "woman that feareth the Lord."
Herein is that saving true, one soweth and
Another reapeth. I sent you to reap
That whereon ye bestowed no
Labor. Other men la-
Bored, and ye are
Entered into their
Labors.

WED JAN 3, 1855
Fatal accidents. 1-John Perry, of Cantwell's Bridge, Delaware, while gunning on Christmas day, was accidentally shot & died the next day. 2-Saml Bush, a son of Mr Chas Bush, of Wilmington, Delaware, was run over by a wagon at Edinburg, Va, on Dec 23, & died the following day.

London, Dec 15, 1854. The death of Lord Fred'k Fitzclarence, Cmder-in-Chief at Bombay, is announced. His lordship was second son of Wm the Fourth & Mrs Jordan, & of course cousin to Queen Victoria. He was 55 years of age. [No death date given-current item.]

Senate: 1-Ptn from Jos Clymer, of Missouri, asking indemnity for losses sustained in consequence of the failure of the Gov't to carry out a contract made with him for the transportation of military stores. 2-Additional documents submitted relating to the claim of Josiah S Lyttle. 3-Ptn from L L Chapman, of Camden, N J, asking a reward for a scientific principle alleged to have been discovered by him, & an appropriation to enable him further to prosecute his investigation. 4-Ptn from Hall Neilson, asking remission of the interest on notes given by him to the U S in payment for land. 5-Cmte of Claims: adverse report on the resolution for the relief of John Donnel & Sons. Same cmte: bill for the relief of Wm P Young.

Died: on Dec 28, in Norwich, Conn, Peter Lanman, aged 83 years. He was a man of extensive travel in early life, of enlarged & cultivated mind, & occupied a high position in the respect & confidence of the community in which he spent his long life.

Obit-died: Mgt Jane Johns, on Nov 22, at **Malvern**, near Alexandria, [the residence of her husband,] the gifted & distinguished woman whose name stands at the head of this article. Mrs Johns was born at Annapolis, Md, & was the eldest daughter of Thos Shaaff, an eminent physician, then a resident of that city. He was twice married. By the first marriage he had 5 children, 2 sons & 3 daughters. Many years ago he removed with his family to Gtwn, D C, where he died, & where his widow & one daughter now reside. By the second marriage he had only a one child, a son, who died in early boyhood. Jane Shaaff, the author of this tribute, was of great beauty both of features & figure united not only with high mental powers, but of character & sweetness of disposition. She did not marry until entering the meridian of life. She became the wife of Rev John Johns, then a resident minister of the Episcopal Church in the diocese of Md, but a few years afterwards one of the Bishops of Va. He was a widower with 5 children, 3 daughters & 2 sons, at the time of his marriage. As a Christian wife, mother, sister, & friend she lived & died without reproach. She was not unlike her near kinsman, the late Frank Key, whom in many traits of character she strongly resembled, & for whom she had the deepest love & veneration. She left on only child, a noble boy, who had been the idol of her heart, & from whom she had never been separated a day & night. Among her requests she asked that he might be committed to the care & guidance of her 2 single & lovely daughters, with the dying injunction that if he lived they would bring him up a Christian. She had suffered with an affection of the heart. She spoke to her husband & children a short time before she expired with calmness & mildness in her tones of voice. She was interred in the **Congressional Grave Yard** near Wash City.

House of Reps: 1-Memorial of Wm B Wood, on behalf of the family of Brevet Maj G W F Wood, deceased.

Dissolution of the copartnership under the firm of Paul & Brown, by mutual consent. –Isaac Paul, Chas H Brown, Gtwn, D C, Jan 1, 1855.

THU JAN 4, 1855
Household & kitchen furniture at auction on: Jan 10, at the House Furnishing Warehouse of Messrs Heartwell & Johnson on Pa ave, between 9th & 10th sts. -Jas C McGuire, auct

Books at auction: on Jan 10, at the ofc room occupied by A D Merrick, on 7th st. -Green & Scott, aucts

Fine furniture at auction on this day, at 10 o'clock, at the residence of Mr Gildemeister, on 4½ st, near the corner of C st. –Green & Scott, aucts

We learn of the death of Hon Jas T Morehead, formerly Govn'r of Ky, & for several years one of her Senators in Congress. [No death date given-current item.]

A wife & mother killed by a drunken husband: at N Y on Monday. Thos Hummonds, who is employed in one of the U S bonded warehouses in West st, abused his wife, kicking & beating her until he killed her. He was arrested & taken to jail. The parties have 3 children, who were taken care of by the neighbors.

Wash Corp: 1-Cmte of Claims: Act for the relief of John Caton: passed. 2-Cmte of Claims: asking to be discharged from the consideration of the ptn of Thos Talbert & others in reference to an alley in square 996: discharged accordingly. 3-The Pres appointed L R Smoot, on the Cmte of Ways & Means & on Police, to supply vacancies occasioned by the resignation of C A Davis. 4-Ptn of Fred'k Iddins & others, asking the grading & gravelling of the carriage-way on N Y ave, between 1st & 7th sts: referred to the Cmte on Improvements.

Public sale of very valuable negroes: by order of the Orphans' Court of PG Co, Md: sale on Jan 30, at O C Harris' Hotel, in Upper Marlboro, PG Co, Md, 17 servants. Among them are some prime plantation hands of both sexes. These negroes belong to the estate of the late Thos Duckett. –C C Magruder, Adm de bonis non of Thos Duckett, Marlboro.

Circuit Court of Montg Co, Md: Nov Term, 1854. In the matter of the ptn of Wm A Cook & others. The return of the Com'rs, with the plat, having been filed on Jul 25, 1853, & no objection being made thereto, it is Nov 17, 1854, adjusted that said report be ratified & confirmed. It is further ordered that the auditor of this Court state an account of the costs & expenses attending this commission, & that the same be paid by the several parties entitled according to their respective shares. –Nicholas Brewer, Circuit Judge. –Jas J Hening, Clerk Circuit Court Montg Co, Md.

Carriages for sale: Wm T Hook, D st, between 9th & 10th sts.

Fatal affray lately in Henry Co, Ga, between John Hilsman & Wm Wyatt, which resulted in the death of the former. Wyatt eloped with & married Hilsman's daughter on the previous day. Hilsman shot at Wyatt, who snatched up a gun & shot Hilsman, who fell mortally wounded & died in a few moments. Wyatt has given himself up & demanded an investigation.

FRI JAN 5, 1854
Mrs Henry Sears, who was severely wounded by burglars on Dec 29 at the house of her husband in Naugatuck, Conn, & whose child was killed by them at the same time, has died of injuries which she received.

Senate: 1-Ptn from Isaac Williams, asking to be remunerated for his property destroyed in Calif in consequence of having been occupied by the troops of the U S during the late war with Mexico. 2-Ptn from Robt C Schenck, asking compensation for his services as Envoy Extra & Minister Pleni on special missions to the Argentine Confederation & the Oriental Republic of Uraguay in the years 1852-53. 3-Ptn from Jno Holohan, asking to be paid for a plaster capitol, executed by him for the U S Capitol extension. 4-Ptn from Col Wm Gates, U S Army, asking that an act may be passed to indemnify him for the loss of all his property on board the steamship **San Francisco**. 5-Ptn from Saml B Porter, asking a pension for injuries received while in the discharge of his duties. 6-Ptn from Purser S P Todd, asking to be allowed an indemnity for loss sustained in consequence of the depreciation of Treasury notes placed in his hands for disbursement during the last war with Great Britain. 7-Ptn from the sole surviving children of Saml Hammond, of the Revolutionary war, asking to be allowed the commutation pay to which he was entitled. 8-Ptn from Jeremiah Moors, asking compensation for services rendered & losses sustained in the construction of a lighthouse on Big Thunder Bay Island, in Lake Huron.

Nearly 3 months having now elapsed since any tidings have been received of the sloop-of-war **Albany**, the conviction increases that she has been lost, leaving none to tell of the fearful scene. She was manned by 18 ofcrs, 23 marines, & 156 seamen. List of her ofcrs: Jas T Gerry, Cmder; Wm W Bleecker, Lt; Montgomery Hunt, Lt; John Quincy Adams, Lt; Henry Rodgers, Lt, Robt Marr, Acting Master; Stephen McCreery, Surgeon; Richd D Cowman, Assist Surgeon; Nixon White, Purser; Bennett J Riley, Midshipman; Wm Jones, Boatswain; Wm Craig, Gunner, Jas Frazer, Sailmaker; Rowland Leach, Carpenter; Belliger Scott, Master's Mate; Wm J Bond, do; Dexter Brigham, do; Nicholas F Morris, Capt's Clerk.

Mrd: in Wash City, by Rev R L Dashiell, Mr John E Febrey, of Fairfax Co, Va, to Mary F, daughter of John Ball, of Wash City. [No date given-current item.]

Mrd: on Jan 3, at the residence of her brother, Richd Oden Mullikin, PG Co, Md, by Rev Mr Rolfe, Frank S Shulze, of Pa, to Miss Alice, daughter of the late Barack Mullikin.

Died: on Jan 4, Mrs Mary, consort of the late Brook Edmunson, aged 78 years, 10 months & 18 days. Her funeral is today at 2 o'clock P M, at the residence of her son-in-law, Mr Jas Towles, on H, between 8th & 9th sts. Her remains will be taken to **Glenwood Cemetery**.

Died: on Jan 3, in Wash City, Rezin Estep, aged 60 years. His funeral is today at 11 o'clock, from the residence of Thos C Magruder, on E st, from whence his remains will be conveyed to **Glenwood Cemetery**.

U S Legation at the Hague, Sep 9, 1854: Mr Belmont to Mr Van Hall. I have the honor to acknowledge the receipt of your note of the 7th instant, by which I see with deep regret that the Gov't of the Netherlands persists in refusing to allow the claim of Capt W M Gibson for the cruel treatment & losses which he suffered at the hands of the officials of Netherlands India. Walter M Gibson, an American citizen, sailing under the flag of his country, has been most cruelly & unjustly imprisoned & despoiled of his property by the authorities of the Netherlands India, & as his rightful claim for indemnity is wholly refused by you it now only remains for my Gov't to take such measures for the enforcement of Mr Gibson's claim as it may deem fit & proper in the premises. –Auguste Belmont

SAT JAN 6, 1855

New Book: The History and Poetry of <u>Finger Rings</u>, by Chas Edwards, Counsellor at Law, N Y, Redfield: N Y, 1855. Love has placed the ring where a vein was supposed to vibrate in the heart. The ethnic Romans were much addicted to rings. In ancient time the fore-finger was emblematical of power, & bore the regal ring. In one of the Egyptian pyramids, the monuments of the mighty but misdirected mind of ancient Misrain, has been found a ring, the ring of Suphis, who built the Great Pyramid for his mausoleum. This valuable relic is now in this country, belonging as it does to the Egyptian collection of Dr Abbott. A cut representing the shape & signet of this most valuable antique ring in the world is given by Mr Edwards. Probably, says our author, the next most important ring is one believed to have been that which was given by Pharaoh to the patriarch Joseph. Upon opening, in the winter of 1824, a tomb in the necropolis of Sakkaha, near Memphis, Arab workmen discovered a mummy, every limb of which was cased in solid gold; each finger had its particular envelope, inscribed with hieroglyphics. "So Joseph died, being 110 years old, & they embalmed him, & he was put in a coffin in Egypt: Genesis, ch 1, v 26. It is necessary to remember that when Pharaoh took off his ring from his hand & put it upon Joseph's hand; & he made him ride in the 2nd chariot which he had, & they cried before him, bow the knee; & he made him ruler over all the land of Egypt. And Pharaoh said unto Joseph, I am Pharaoh, & without thee shall no man lift up his hand or foot in all the land of Egypt; & the Pharaoh called Joseph's name Zaphnath-Paaneah. The seal has the cartouch of Pharaoh, & one line upon it has been construed into Paaneah, the name bestowed by Pharaoh on Joseph. This signifies, in combination with Zephnath, either the Revealer of Secrets or the Preserver of the World. We have much more faith in the genuiness of Shakespeare's signet-ring than we have in the Hebrew Patriarch's. Mr Edwards gives us a fac-simile of the precious relic, a relic which we would not swap for a dozen of Suphis' rings, if we were so happy as to be its proprietor.

Trustee's sale of house & lot at auction: by deed of trust from Wm Peterson & wife to the subscribers, dated Feb 5, 1850, recorded in Liber J A S #12, folios 383 to 389, of the land records of Wash Co, D C: sale of the south half of lot 14 in square 347, with a good dwlg house, fronting on 10th st, between E & F sts. –Walter Lenox, Henry Naylor, trustees -Green & Scott, aucts

Senate: 1-Ptn from Danl Littlefield, one of the heirs of D Littlefield, of the Revolutionary army, asking that the 7½ years' half pay that said Littlefield was entitled to may be paid to the heirs at law. 2-Ptn from Irene G Scarritt, widow of an ofcr of the army, asking a pension.

House of Reps: 1-Bills of the Senate referred: relief of Catharine B Arnold; claim of the late firm of C M Strader & Co; relief of Betsey Whipple; & relief of C E Greneaux. 2-Cmte on Military Affairs: bill for relief of Richd Fitzpatrick: committed. Same cmte: joint resolutions for relief of John Dugan & for relief of Geo W McCerren: committed. 3-Cmte on Public Lands: bill for relief of Theresa Dardenne, widow of Abraham Dardenne, deceased, & their children, with the recommendation that it pass: committed. 4-Cmte on Commerce: bill for relief of E J McLane: committed. 5-Cmte on the Post Ofc & Post Roads: bill for relief of Richd White & Saml Sherwood: committed. 6-Cmte on the Judiciary: bill for relief of J H F Thornton, Lawrence Taliaferro, & Hay T Lawrence, sureties of D M F Thornton, late a Purser in the Navy: committed. Same cmte: bill for relief of Jos Ridgway: committed. 7-Cmte on Private Land Claims: bill for relief of Boswell Minard, father of Theodore Minard, deceased: committed. 8-Cmte on Invalid Pensions: bill committed: relief of Wm Brown; of Jas McIntire; of Solomon La Follette; of Eliz Freeman; of Thos C Ramsey & Ananias O Richardson. Same cmte: adverse reports on ptns of Lydia Andrews, widow of Benj Andrews; of Andrew Lawson, of Tenn; of citizens of Preble Co, Ohio, asking that a pension may be granted to Wm Morris; of Comfort Willey, of Rockingham Co, N H; of John Elwyn; of Thos Poulson, of Pa; of Dudley F Holt; of John Campbell; of Edw Rumery, of York Co, Maine; of Caleb Stover; of March Farrington; of R J Murray; of the children of Jos Dale; of Richd Reynolds; of Henry Young; of Sally Sleyter, of Mich; of Hiram Seat; of Rachael McMillan; of Luther Cole, of Vt; & of Geo F Dunkel, of N Y. Same cmte: bill for the further relief of Isaac Allen, of Turner, Maine; relief of Wyatt Griffith, of Wash Co, Tenn; & a bill to repeal an act for relief of Geo M Bentley, of Indiana: committed. Same cmte: adverse on the ptn of citizens of Henderson Co, Tenn, in behalf of Thos Boatwright; of Thos J Napier; of Ebenezer Hitchcock; & of Wm Sparks. Same cmte: bill for relief of Amos Knapp: recommended that it do not pass: committed. 9-Cmte on Patents: adverse reports on the ptn of Jos S Kite, for the extension of his patent for safety beams in railroad cars; of Aza Arnold for the renewal of a patent; & of Jas H Stimpson, executor of Jas Stimpson, also for the extension of a patent. Same cmte: adverse reports on the ptns of Duke Williams, of Wm Atkinson, of W W Woodworth, adm of Wm Woodworth, deceased, & of Wm Emmons, sr. 10-Cmte on Naval Affairs: bill for relief of the legal reps of Wm A

Christian, & a bill for the relief of Sarah Morris, the only heir of Robt Mitchell, deceased: committed. 11-Bills to be reported to the House with the recommendation that they pass: bill for the relief of the widow & children of Ezra Chapman, deceased, with an amendment striking out the allowance of interest. Relief of the heirs & legal reps of Jos Savage, deceased, with an amendment striking out the allowance of interest, & making the amount appropriated in full of all claim against the Gov't. Relief of the heirs of Thos Parks, deceased, with an amendment similar to the preceding bill, & also providing that the amount appropriated be paid to the legal reps of Parks. Also, bills for the relief of the heirs & reps of Uria Prewitt, deceased; of the legal reps of Jas Erwin, of Ark; for indemnifying Moses D Hogan for cattle destroyed by the Indians in 1842; for the relief of Thos Marston Taylor, with an amendment striking out the allowance for lawyer's fees, & making the amount appropriated in full of all claim against the Gov't; relief of Purser Francis B Stockton, with an amendment making the amount appropriated in full of all claim against the Gov't; relief of Thos Underhill, exc of Thos Underhill, deceased; of Stephen Lutz, of N Y; of John H King; of the heirs of Lt Andrew Finley; & of Andrew H Patterson. 12-Bills laid aside with the recommendation that they do not pass: relief of Conrad Wheat, jr, or his legal reps; & bill to confirm the claim of Wm H Henderson & heirs of Robt Henderson to 500 acres of land in the Bastrop grant.

Lucian Ayer, the enterprising Kansas banker, is a splendid illustration of the genius of age. Without a dollar in his pocket he built a line of telegraph from Troy to Montreal, & for 2 or 3 years kept himself before the people as president of 3 lines of telegraph. His affection for his family led him back to N H, where, under an indictment obtained at the beginning of his career, his glorious energies are to be repressed, cabined, cribbed, confined, within certain gloomy stone walls at Concord. Will it then be his fault if the Kansas Bank fails for want of confidence? Decidedly he ought to be pardoned & go free as Ayer. –Boston Post

The New Orleans Delta announces the death there on Dec 29, of Seth Barton, former Solicitor of the Treasury, & afterwards Charge d'Affaires to Chili, under Mr Polk's administration.

In the case of Geo & Nancy Jones, convicted of murder in the 2nd degree, & then, upon a 2nd trial, of murder in the 1st degree, the Supreme Court of Texas held that the conviction of murder in the 2nd degree was an acquittal of the higher decree, & that the subsequent conviction of murder in the 1st degree was erroneous. They also laid down the rule that in all criminal cases hereafter when it shall appear that ardent spirits were used by the jury, regardless of quantity, the verdict will be set aside.

Mrd: on Jan 2, at Elk Landing, Cecil Co, Md, by Rev Mr Mears, Dr R Covington Mackall, of Savannah, Ga, to Miss Isabel Hollingsworth, daughter of the late Wm Hollingsworth, of the former place.

Soldiers-1812. Order of the Marshal of the Old Soldiers. Soldiers of the War of 1812. On Jan 8, the line will be formed on 4½ st, the right resting on Pa ave. Order of the Line:
Military escort of District Volunteers.
Col Wm Hickey
Lt Col Jno H Riley
Maj Robt Keyworth
Adj L J Middleton
Surgeon Morgan
Assist Surgeon Grimes
Quartermaster McCullum
Pres' Mounted Guards, Capt Peck.
Washington Light Infty, Capt Carrington.
Nat'l Grays, Capt Towers
Montgomery Guards, Capt Key
Nat'l Guards, Capt Tate
Scott Guards, Capt Jameson
Union Guards, Capt Byrne
Union Infty, Capt Lassell
Washington Highlanders, Capt Reese
Boone Riflemen, Capt Smith
Marion Riflemen, Capt Shekel
The Washington Nat'l Monument Society
Chief Marshal & Aids
Pres & Ofcrs of the Convention
Soldiers of the War of 1812
American Flag & Music in the center of the line.

Died: on Jan 1, at his residence in Montg, Md, John White, in his 60th year.

Died: on Jan 5, Charles Thomas, aged 10 years & 5 months, son of Mich & Philippa C French.

Meeting of the Carpenters & Workingman's Friends was held on Jan 3. Meeting called to order by Mr Henry Trine. Mr Robt T Knight chosen to preside & John F Offutt appointed Secretary. Cmte appointed: Messrs Jas A Lovelace, W B Davis, & John F C Offutt. Mr J P Pepper & Mr Bamberger made very able speeches against the hire of convicts in our penitentiaries for any mechanical purposes, so as to place the convicts of penitentiaries on a footing with honest working men.

Orphans Court of Wash Co, D C. Letters of administration on the personal estate of John H Thompson, late of Wash Co, deceased. –Gustavus Waters, adm

MON JAN 8, 1855

Literary notice: Autobiography of Rev Wm Jay, edited by Doct Redford & John Angell James. N Y: published by Carter & Brothers, 2 vols, 12 mo. Sold by Gray & Ballantine. One of the most successful ministers of England, the Pastor of the Independent Chapel of Bath, Eng, near 70 years.

Senate: 1-Bill with no objections with the recommendation that they pass: relief of Chas W Morgan, Wm R Rodman, & Edw Merrill; relief of the reps of Thos D Anderson, deceased, late Consul of the U S at Tripoli; of Wm Duer; of Fred'k Vincent, adm of Jas Le Caze, survivor of Le Caze & Mallet, with an amendment striking out the allowance of interest; relief of Jas Holstin; of Wm Case; of the heirs & legal reps of Wm Weeks; of Francois Cousin; of Susan Coody & others; of Chas J Porcher, acting purser of the brig **Falmouth**; of Jeptha L Heminger; of Thos B Parsons; of Mrs Ann W Angus; & of Lot Davis. Also, bill authorizing the legal reps of Antoine Vasquez, Hypolite Vasquez, Jos Vasquez, & John Colligan to enter certain lands in Missouri. 2-Ptn of Harris Power, praying a pension for wounds received by him in the line of his duty during the late war with Mexico. 3-Ptn of Mrs Sarah Peacock, asking compensation for depredations committed on her property in Florida.

On Tue of last week Col Abner Parker, of Red Mountain, Orange Co, N C, committed suicide by cutting his throat with a razor. He had been deeply afflicted in the loss of all his children by consumption; & to this was added about 12 months ago a severe affliction in the loss of his wife. He was about 61 years of age, & highly esteemed in the county for his intelligence, public spirit, & hospitality.

The **Immaculate Conception**. The addition of a new dogma to the tenets of the most numerous of the religious denominations of Christendom is one of the remarkable events of the day. The Pope has thought fit to collect the opinions of the Bishops of the Catholic Church on the question of the immaculate conception of Mary, the mother of Jesus, & a large majority of their voices being in the affirmative, he has proclaimed, as the doctrine of the church, that the blessed Virgin was conceived without any stain of original sin. [Jan 9th newspaper: the Immaculate Conception of the Virgin is now a fixed fact-a settled dogma of faith in the Roman Catholic Church.]

Mr John Lentz was shot in Charleston, Kanawha Co, Va, recently. On going to bed he hung his coat, in the pocket of which was a loaded revolver, on the bed-post. The coat fell down, & the concussion caused the pistol to go off, lodging a ball in his foot near the heal.

On New Year's evening Mr McCarty, a tinner, left his house with his 14 year old son, & went to Wills' creek to cross on the ice. Mr McCarty fell through the ice & his son ran to help him, & both father & son were drowned. –Cumberland Journal

Mrd: on Jan 2, by Rev F Israel, Edw J Byrum to Miss Mgt A King, all of Wash City.

Died: on Jan 6, Mrs Sally Ann Nuttrill, in her 58th year, daughter of the late Abraham Barnes Thompson & Sarah Annie Mason, of Loudoun Co, Va. Her funeral will be from the residence of her son-in-law, P M Fortier, on 13th st, near G, today at 10 A M.

Died: on Dec 15, at Edinburgh, Scotland, after a short illness, Mr Jas Slight. The deceased was extensively known for his scientific & mechanical acquirements.

Trustee's sale: by deed of trust from Geo W Garrett & wife, dated Jul 6, 1854, [& by direction of Messrs Simonton & Rittenhouse, the parties secured thereby,] the following property will be sold at auction on Jan 8, 1855: part of lot 6 in square 459, in Wash City, known as Lot C on the plan of the heirs of Solomon Drew, with the 4 story new brick dwlg-house thereon. –W Redin, trustee -Green & Scott, aucts

TUE JAN 9, 1855
Trustee's sale: by deed of trust from Messrs Davis & Garrett, dated Aug 17, 1854, to the subscriber, & by the direction of Henry Sothoron, the party secured by such deed, the following property will be sold at auction on the premises, on Feb 12, 1855: part of lot 26 in Rothwell & Naylor's subdivision of square 425, in Wash City, on 7th st, between L & M sts, with an excellent brick dwlg house & other improvements thereon. –W Redin, trustee -Green & Scott, aucts

A young man named Wm Fallan was in the act of changing a belt in the Granite Facotry in Howard Co, Md, when his arm got caught in a loop, & he was drawn around the shaft about 60 times. He was literally crushed to atoms.

Mrd: on Dec 19, by Rev Mr Wilmer, Mr Alfred B Clagett, of PG Co, Md, to Miss Mgt J Hodges, daughter of the late Wm M Hodges, of Chas Co.

For sale: 40 to 50 acres of good land, 4 miles from Wash City. Apply to the subscriber near *Tennallytown*, D C. –Chas R Belt

Orphans Court of Wash Co, D C. Letters of administration on the personal estate of John D Brown, late of Wash Co, deceased. –J C McGuire, adm

For rent: a desirable location for a Physician, a house & lot in the village of *Long Old Fields*, PG Co, Md, for a term of years. Inquire of Thos Dutton, U S Patent Ofc, or by mail to the undersigned, *Long Old Fields* post ofc, post-paid. –R T Brooks

The Atlantic [Geo] Examiner says over 800 bushels of sweet potatoes have been raised by Mr Edw Shepherd on 2 acres of land near Columbus, Ga.

Wm H Lucas was convicted at Middletown, Ct, on Wed, & a 2nd time, for placing obstructions on the Middletown Railroad. On the former conviction he was sentenced to the State prison, but was taken out & granted a new trial, because there were some reasons to believe that a part of the testimony against him had been improperly & untruly given. The second jury confirmed the decision of the first.

N H Gaz [Portsmouth] is in its 99th year. Connecticut Courant is in its 91st year.

WED JAN 10, 1855
Executor's sale, by order of the Orphans Court of Wash Co, D C, of negroes, horses, cows, hogs, corn, wheat, oats, farming utensils, & furniture, at auction, on Jan 29, at the late residence of John Brereton, deceased, on the old road to Bladensburg, 4 miles n e of Wash. -Green & Scott, aucts

Wash City Ordinance: 1-Act for the relief of John H O'Neill: the Register to refund to him the sum of $5.25, amount overpaid by him for improvements not completed until Mar 27, 1854. 2-Act for the relief of Elias E Barnes: the balance of $70.81 be paid to him for grading & gravelling 6th st. 3-Act for the relief of John Considine: Register to pay him $30, that being the amount of fines imposed on him by Justice Thompson for taking sand out of Tiber Creek. 4-Act for the relief of Chas A Davis: the sum of $16.66 be paid to him, being the amount of salary as Sec of Board of Trustees of the Public Schools for the month of Sept last. 5-Act for the relief of Matilda Ann Beall: the fine imposed on Apr 13, 1854, for selling liquor without a license, is remitted, provided she pay the cost of prosecution. 6-Act for the relief of John Caton: the sum of $17.74 be paid to him, the said Caton having been erroneously assessed to that amount. 7-Act to allow Wm H Faulkner to lay a foot pavement along the line of his property on Pa ave; said pavement to be similar to the one laid by J C Rives in reservation 10. 8-Act for the relief of John McGarvey: the sum of $60 be refunded to him for money deposited by him for a license to keep a tavern, which was not granted.

Senate: 1-Ptn from Capts Chas Stewart, H E Ballard, & Archibald Henderson, ofcrs of the frig **Constitution**, asking to be rewarded for the gallantry & good conduct displayed in the capture of the British ships **Cyane** & **Levant** in the last war with Great Britain. 2-Ptn from Isaac Williams & J T Wayne, on behalf of the heirs of Pallo & Jose Apis, asking the passage of an act to authorize the Board of Com'rs to examine Land Claims in Calif to examine into the title under which they claim. [Mr Weller explained that the minors, having no legal rep or guardian to present their claim & prosecute the same before the board within the prescribed time, were in consequence excluded from all the rights & benefits of said act.] 3-Ptn from Mrs Jane McCrabb, widow of an ofcr of the army, asking payment of certain moneys equitably due to her deceased husband for extra official services in the Florida war. 4-Ptn from Dominic Lynch, asking to be allowed pay as master while he acted in that capacity on board the schnr **Shark** in 1840-41. 5-Ptn from Dorcas Carey, widow of a soldier of the war of 1812, asking to be allowed the same amount of pension that was granted to her late husband. 6-Ptn from John Hinkley, grandson of Capt Jno Hinkley of the Revolutionary army, asking compensation for the services of his grandfather. 7-Ptn from Alex'r R Boteler, one of the heirs of Robt Stockton, of N J, asking the passage of an act for the settlement of said Stockton's accounts. 8-Ptn from the daughter of Andrew Crosby, late a purser in the navy, asking that the pension allowed her may be extended. 9-Cmte on Military Affairs: bill for the relief of Lt Jno C McFerran & Saml D Sturgiss, & a bill for the relief of Jacob Dodson. Same cmte: adverse report on the House bill for the relief of Chas H Wilgus. Same cmte: adverse reports on the following memorials: of John Hudry, of La; of Jos T Walker, atty in fact of E Harrelson & others; of Wm Wells & others for loss sustained in the sale of their horses in Mexico, for which they were refused transportation; of Danl Kelley, for remuneration for imprisonment in the Island of Cuba in 1816; of Isaac Hulse, & of Saml Boots. 10-Cmte on Revolutionary Affairs: bill for the relief of the legal reps of Col John H Stone. 11-Cmte on Foreign Relations: bill for the relief of Saml A Belden, & asked the consent of the Senate to consider it at once. 12-Bill for the relief of Ephraim Hunt: passed. 13-Bill for the relief of Francis B Stockton: passed.

The frig **Constitution**, bearing the broad pennant of Cmdor Isaac Mayo, Jno Rudd, commanding, was at Porto Praya, the naval depot, Nov 15, discharging the storeship **Bounding Billow**, of Boston. Ofcrs & men all well. List of her ofcrs: Cmdor, Isaac Mayo; Cmder, Jno Rudd; Lts, S F Hazard, B M Dove, Saml Larkin; Flag Lts, C R P Rodgers, A G Clary, C S McDonough; Surgeon of the fleet, M G Delaney; Passed Assist Surgeon, J L Burtt; Assist Surgeon, J C Coleman; Purser, J H Watmough; Marine Ofcr, Capt & Bt Maj, N S Waldron; acting Master, Colville Terrett; Cmdor's Sec, Llewellyn Boyle; Midshipmen, E E Potter, Wm H Dana, Wm L Bradford, Aeneas Armstrong; Acting Boatswain, E Chamberlain; Gunner, A S Lewis; Carpenter, Lewis Holmes; Sailmaker, Wm Bennett; Cmdor's Clerk, E Cobb; Capt's Clerk, W L Swayze; Purser's Clerk, Richd Reardon; acting Master's Mate, Jno Collins; Hospital Steward, John Sullivan; Purser's Steward, Philip Dillon.

Wm H Williams was convicted yesterday at Newcastle, Del, of robbing the Milford post ofc & sentenced to 4 years' hard labor.

Henry Ruggles, assist postmaster at Northfield, Vt, has been detected in appropriating to himself money letters placed in the ofc to be sent away by mail. The heaviest loss was $600 in bank notes, in a letter there in Nov last. This sum was recovered. The unfortunate man was arrested & committed to prison.

Orphans Court of Wash Co, D C. Letters of administration on the personal estate of Henry Isemann, late of Wash Co, deceased. –A Gross, adm

Mrd: Jan 8, by Rev Dr Hill, Jas Rollings to Matilda Riggs Gaither, both of Anne Arundel Co, Md.

Mrd: Jan 8, by Rev Mr Clarkson, of St Dominick's Church, Mr Saml Wilmer Marsh, of N Y C, to Miss Cordelia E Mattingly, 4th daughter of Mr Geo Mattingly, of Wash City.

Died: on Jan 9, suddenly, from congestion of the lungs, Miss Anne Polk, eldest daughter of Gilliss Polk, deceased, of the Eastern Shore of Md. She was a native of Somerset Co, Md, but for many years a resident of Wash City. Her funeral is on Jan 11, at 12 o'clock, at her late residence, No 23 Pa ave, near Gtwn.

Died: on Jan 9, Mr John Brown, in his 64th year. His funeral is today at 3 o'clock from his late residence on the corner of 6th & E sts.

Died: on Jan 8, after a protracted illness, Mrs Cordelia M Flowers, wife of the late Richd Flowers, in her 45th year. Her funeral is today at 2 o'clock, at her late residence on 6th st, between H & L sts.

U S Patent Ofc, Wash, Jan 8, 1855. Ptn of Jesse Reed, of Marshfield, Mass, praying for the extension of a patent granted to him on Apr 16, 1841, for an improvement in Pumps, for 7 years from the expiration of said patent, which takes place on Apr 16, 1855. –Chas Mason, Com'r of Patents

THU JAN 11, 1855

Senate: 1-Cmte on Naval Affairs: adverse reports on the memorials of Alex'r F Barnard, a pilot on board the U S steamer **Michigan**, & of Justin Spaulding, asking for pay as chaplain. Same cmte: asking to be discharged from the consideration of the memorial of Zelia M Crosby, & that it be referred to the Cmte on Pensions.
2-Cmte on Revolutionary Claims: bill for the relief of Danl Beddinger's heirs; of the heirs of Larkin Smith; & of the administrator of the heirs of Thos Wishart.
3-Bill for the relief of Ephraim Shaler: introduced.

Mrd: on Jan 9, in Wash City, by Rev G W Samson, Mr Henry Fox, lately of Phil, to Miss Eliz S Harris, of Wash.

Mrd: on Jan 1, at *Cassilis*, by Rev Chas E Ambler, Dr Henry P Cooke, son of the late John R Cooke, to Mary E, daughter of Andrew Kennedy, all of Jefferson Co, Va.

Mrd: on Jan 9, by Rev Mr Hodgins, Mr Jas C Brooke to Miss Mary C Perkins, of the District of Columbia.

Orphans Court of Wash Co, D C. In the case of John T Sullivan, adm of Hugh Calhous, deceased: the administrator & Court have appointed Jan 30th, for the final settlement of the estate of the deceased, of the assets in hand.
–Ed N Roach, Reg/o wills

The Manchester [N H] American says that an infant son of Mr Wm Gardner, of Mason Village, was strangled on Dec 25, when the foot of his little sister, who was in the same bed, got entangled in the string of the night dress about the neck of the child, & drew it so tightly as to cause its death.

On Dec 31, 3 children of Mr O McCallen, John, 4, Rosy, 6, & Catherine, 9, went on the river without the knowledge of their parents, when the little boy fell through a hole or cleft in the ice, & his sisters endeavored to save him. They all were drowned.
–Burlington [Vt] Gaz, 2nd

U S Patent Ofc, Wash, Jan 10, 1855. Ptn of Jas M Putnam, adm of Jas R Putnam, deceased, of New Orleans, La, praying for the extension of a patent granted on May 6, 1841, to Jas R Putnam, for an improvement in machines for removing obstructions of bars from the mouths of harbors & rivers, for 7 years from the expiration of said patent, which take place on May 6, 1855. –Chas Mason, Com'r Patents

U S Patent Ofc, Wash, Jan 10, 1855. Ptn of Ebenezer Beard, of New Sharon, Maine, praying for the extension of a patent granted to him on Apr 10, 1841, for an improvement in propellers, for 7 years from the expiration of said patent, which takes place on Apr 10, 1855. –Chas Mason, Com'r Patents

Dissolution of the partnership under the firm of Downs & Hutchinson, by mutual consent. The business hereafter will be carried on by J T Downs.
–John T Downs, Jos Hutchinson, Jan 11, 1855.

Notice of lost land warrants. I placed in the post ofc at Asheville, N C, a package, addressed to S Bulow Erwin, Wash, D C, containing 2 land warrants: No 1,092 for 160 acres, issued to Jacob Wike; the other, No 1,407, for 80 acres, issued to Nathan Coward, both for military services in the Cherokee war, & dated Jan 9, 1854; & said warrants have been lost or mislaid, notice is given that at the proper time I shall apply to the Com'r of Pensions for duplicates of the same. –W W McDowell

FRI JAN 12, 1855
For rent: elegant new brown stone front warehouse on 7th st, one door below Odd Fellows' Hall. Apply on the premises to Henry Thorn, or at his residence, on 8th st, between D & E sts.

Died: on Jan 10, Eugene, infant son of Dr L & Phillippa Dovilliers, aged 6 months. His funeral is today at 12 o'clock, from the residence of his father.

Senate: 1-Ptn from the widow of Midshipman Jos S Cameron, who died of disease contracted while in the service, asking to be allowed a pension. 2-Ptn from Sarah Smith Stafford, only daughter of Jas B Stafford, a Lt in the navy in the Revolutionary war, asking to be allowed the half-pay due her late father. 3-Ptn from Elisha Camp, asking compensation for fencing used by the U S troops for fuel at Sackett's Harbor in 1812, for lead used in making shot, & for the occupation of his property by the said troops as a parade ground. 4-Ptn from Robt McConnell, asking compensation for a negro carried off by the Creek Indians in 1813, & indemnity for other property destroyed by said Indians. 5-Ptn from Jesse Steadman, asking a pension on account of disability incurred during the war of 1812. 6-Ptn from Thos W Tansill, asking for extra pay & bounty land as a private in the Marine Corps, & pay & allowances as a musician in said corps, withheld on account of his inability to procure a legal certificate of his discharge. 7-Ptn from R W Thompson, asking compensation for services rendered by him as atty for the Menomonic Indians. 8-Ptn from Danl Campbell, Marshal Brown, & other citizens of Wash, asking an act of incorporation for the Columbia Wood Gas Light Co. 9-Ptn from Geo P Marsh, asking compensation for his services under the act of Aug, 1848, imposing judicial duties on the minister resident at Constantinople, & for diplomatic services under a special commission to Greece. 10-Ptn from Joel Ware, of Alleghany Co, N Y, asking that the present tariff may be so altered as to give ample protection & encouragement to all the varied productions of the country, so that our nat'l policy may conform to the recently developed sentiment known as American or Know-Nothingism. 11-Ptn from Maj H Day, Lt G H Paige, & other ofcrs of the U S Army, asking to be remunerated for the losses they sustained through the wreck of the steamship **Winfield Scott** on the Pacific coast. 12-Ptn from Dr Wm P Buell, asking compensation for medical services to the 3rd Regt of U S Artl on board the steamer **San Francisco** & the ship **Three Bells**. 13-Ptn from Emma B Thompson, widow of the late Cmder Thompson, asking to be allowed the pension her husband would have been entitled to had he applied for the same. 14-Ptn from Jeremiah Day & others engaged in literary & scientific pursuits, asking that the works of Cmder Wilkes on the exploring expedition may be reprinted by Congress. 15-Ptn from Thos W Powell & E Moore, asking to be released from liability as security for the appearance of Otho Hinton, charged with robbing the U S mail. 16-Ptn from Saml B Sawyer, grandson of Saml, asking to be allowed the commutation pay to which his ancestor was entitled as an ofcr in the Revolutionary war. 17-Ptn of Jane Irwin, asking to be allowed additional pay & bounty land on account of the services of her father. 18-Ptn from Judge Bradford, of the 6th judicial district of Iowa, & others, asking that Johnson Pierson may be remunerated for losses sustained by him in executing a contract for surveying the public lands.

Died: yesterday, in Wash City, in the 84th year of her life, Mrs Mary Jane McHenry, wife of Mr Hamilton McHenry, & oldest daughter of Mr Franklin Edmonston. Her funeral will take place this afternoon at 2 o'clock, from her late residence.

House of Reps: 1-Ptn of John W Caldwell, of Charleston, S C, to change a vessel's name. 2-Ptn of Ruth B Phillips, of Fall River, Mass, praying a pension for wounds received by her deceased husband in the war of 1812. 3-Ptn of Ambrose W Ghier, John Meung, & Solomon Disney, for compensation for services, hardships, & sacrifices rendered & endured while seamen on board the U S sloop-of-war **Peacock** during the shipwreck & loss in 1841. 4-Cmte of Claims: bill for the relief of Medford Caffey, of Tenn: committed.

Jennings Case. A gentleman of this city, in connexion with other gentlemen of standing in the State of Va, has lately spent some time in traveling through several counties of Eastern Va, taking important depositions, searching records, & collecting important items of information, preparatory to establishing the claim of the heirs of a certain John Jennings to an estate valued at over forty millions of dollars, who emigrated or sailed from Whitehaven, England, about Dec, 1751, & settled at Fredericksburg, Spottsylvania Co, Va. He had a brother in England whose name was Jonathan. Brought with him from England his wife & 3 children, whose names were Eliz, Luke, & John; had a daughter living in Va; had a son named Thos Jennings, whom he left in England, & who was adopted by an uncle whose name was Cenhors or Cenhouse Jennings; was supposed to have been sent by his uncle to Westminster school, or some other school bearing a similar name. Thos Jennings, the son, came to Va about 1761 to visit his father & family, but did not return to England. Information wanted of the above named John Jennings & Thos Jennings. Thos Jennings had correspondence with relatives living in England. Information of his correspondents wanted. All parties desirous of obtaining information or having any information to impart are to address H H, post ofc, Wash City, D C.

Olney Whipple, long a resident & estimable citizen of Pawtucket, R I, was found dead on Monday in an out-house near his dwlg. His death was produced by the inhalation of gas arising from a furnace of burning charcoal placed near his person for the purpose of self-destruction. From letters which he left it appears the suicide was deliberate. Mr Whipple was formerly a manufacturer at Central Falls, but of late years he has been unfortunate in his business operations. He was 70 years of age. -Providence Journal

Private sale of valuable real estate. By the last will & testament of Lewis Kemp, late of Fred'k Co, deceased, the subscriber, as exec, offers that splendid country seat, late the residence of said deceased, known as *Prospect Hill*, near Fred'k City, Md, containing 332 acres of land, more or less; with a large & elegant brick mansion, 70 feet by 45 feet, 2 story with basement, & spacious piazza. Also, a large double brick house for a tenant or overseer, & out-houses for servants. Call on Jas L H Duvall or Chas L Kemp, residing on the premises. –Lewis G Kemp, exc of Lewis Kemp, deceased

U S Patent Ofc, Wash, Jan 11, 1855. Ptn of Loring Coes, of Worcester, Mass, praying for the extension of a patent granted to him on Apr 16, 1841, for an improvement in screw wrenches, for 7 years from the expiration of said patent, which takes place on Apr 16, 1855. –Chas Mason, Com'r of Patents

FRI JAN 13, 1855
Hon Moses Norris, a Senator in Congress from N H, died on Thu, in Wash City, after an illness of only 3 or 4 days. He died of an affection of the heart. He has left a wife & family of children. Mr Norris was the son of a Revolutionary soldier. He was born at Pittsfield, N H, in 1799; graduated at Dartmouth College; commenced the practice of law in his native town.

Christopher A Keene, a Southerner, was arrested at N Y on Wed, charged with forging 3 Texas State Bonds, which he offered for sale at the ofc of Fred'k V James, broker in Wall st, for $1,300. Keene was taken into custody. –Journal of Commerce

Mrd: on Jan 11, by Rev Mr Laney, at the residence of her father, in PG Co, Md, Thos J Barclay to Eliz D, daughter of Israel Jackson, all of said county.

Died: on Jan 6, at his residence, at *Ellaville*, PG Co, Md, Douglass Vass, of the Post Ofc Dept, & formerly of Fredericksburg, Va. He was a gentleman much esteemed for his probity & intelligence.

N Y, Jan 12. The Evening Post learns by private letter from Paris that Hon Mr Mason, our Minister to France, was struck with paralysis on Dec 27, & was quite unwell when the letter closed.

A correspondent of the Journal of Commerce, who writes from Callao, under date of Dec 10, tells of the execution of Gen Moran, the defeated cmder of the Gov't troops. He was dragged from the house he has ensconced himself & was shot in the public square. He begged hard for his life. He had been a resident of that city for 30 years, where his wife & 2 daughters then lived.

Centreville [Md] Sentinel: the numerous friends of Mr John Grason, son of Ex-Govn'r Grason, of Queen Anne, who mysteriously disappeared from Balt city about 3 years ago, & from whom no tidings could be had, will be glad to learn that he returned to his paternal home a few days ago in fine health & spirits. We have not heard in what section of the globe he has been since his departure.

Farm at public sale: on Feb 9 next, about 1 mile north of Rock Creek Church: 88 acres, with dwlg house containing 6 rooms. Call on the subscriber at 84 East Capitol st. –Benj Sharbut

MON JAN 15, 1855

Household & kitchen furniture at auction on: Jan 17, at the house of the late Mrs Flowers, on 6th st, near I st. –Rothwell & Brown, aucts

On Thu, as the omnibus running between Manlius & Syracuse, N Y, was coming into the latter city the horses became restive & dashed down the hill, overturning the omnibus. Mr A W Spencer, a merchant of Cassenovia, was instantly killed. Mr Levi Martin, the leader of a band in Syracuse was very badly injured, as was Mr John C Smith, from N Y.

Mr Robt Maywood, formerly an actor of some celebrity, has been sent to the lunatic asylum in N Y. It appears that he has but lately arrived from Trieste, Austria, where he had been living wiht his daughter, Miss Augusta Maywood, who is of some celebrity in Italy & Germany.

Land for sale: a tract of 50 acres in D C, & bounded on the public road which passes **Glenwood Cemetery**. Inquire of Mr Henry Queen, who resides near the premises.

Three brothers, John, Jas, & David Sharp, of Mecklenburg Co, N C, got into an affray last week, in which John was killed. He was literally cut to pieces.

A boy named Geo Belden committed suicide in West Rocky Hill [Ct] on Fri. It appears that the boy was staying with Mr Culver, keeper of the town poor, who, having lost $2, charged the theft upon the lad, & it is asserted that the money was found in his possession. A prosecution was threatened. He was found in the barn hanging by the neck. He was only 14 years of age.

Mr Jas M Roche, the oldest practical printer in Delaware, died at Wilmington on Thu, aged 74 years. He worked at his case almost constantly up to the time of his decease.

On Sat night Patrick Flynn & his wife were suffocated in their room at their residence near Glen Cove, Long Island, by the gas escaping from a furnace full of ignited charcoal.

Died: on Jan 5, at Aldie, Loudoun Co, Va, in his 80th year, Wm Noland, formerly several years Com'r of Public Bldgs at Wash, & previously for many years a leading member of the Legislature of Va.

A burglar, Geo Goins, a stout negro, who had entered the warehouse of Mr Evan Lyons, in Gtwn, on Sat, was discovered, whilst seeking his accomplice, by Mr Jesse Kitchen, one of the night guard, who fired upon him & killed him by a shot in the neck.

TUE JAN 16, 1855

Mr Sherman M Booth was tried last week at Milwaukee, Wisc, before the U S District Court, under the fugitive slave law, for aiding in the escape of a fugitive slave named Glover. The jury found Booth guilty of the charge.

Mr Eli Slifer was yesterday elected Treasurer of the State of Pa.

Mrd: on Nov 30, in Wash City, by Rev G W Samson, Mr Geo W Calvert to Miss Helen B Osborne, all of Wash City.

Died: on Jan 15, in Wash City, Jas N Cochran, aged 24 years. His funeral is on Jan 17, at 10 o'clock, from the residence of his sister, Mrs A V Hevner, 6th st, between E & F sts.

Died: on Jan 15, John H Evens, son of Benj Evens, in his 7th year. His funeral is today at 2 o'clock, from the residence of his father, on 14th st, between H & I sts.

Senate: 1-Ptn from Amos B Eaton, asking to be allowed certain items which were rejected at the Treasury Dept in the settlement of his accounts. 2-Ptn from the heirs of Nathan Hutchins, a Revolutionary ofcr, asking that the commutation pay to which said Hutchins was entitled may be paid to his heirs. 3-Ptn from John W Pray, asking that the commutation pay to which his ancestor was entitled might be paid to the heirs. 4-Ptn from Geo Gerrish & others, residing in N Y & elsewhere, asking that steam ferry-boats may be required to carry one of Thomas' safety cars. 5-Ptn from Eliza Henley, widow of an ofcr of the army, asking an additional pension. 6-Ptn from the heirs of Nathan Steele, asking indemnity for damages on account of being ejected by the U S troops from a valuable tract of land purchased from a half-breed Cherokee. 7-Ptn from John Harman & other soldiers of the war of 1812, asking that a pension may be allowed to the survivors of that war. 8-Ptn from John Foy, of Wash, asking to be reimbursed for damages done to his house by reason of the construction of certain works of the Gov't. 9-Ptn from John C McLemore & other citizens of Calif, asking that a port of entry may be opened at the junction of the Gila & Colorado rivers. 10-Cmte on Pensions: adverse report in the case of Catharine Clark. 11-Cmte on Revolutionary Claims: bill for the relief of the children & heirs of Maj Gen Baron De Kalb: reported back the same without an amendment. 12-Cmte on Public Lands: asking to be discharged from the consideration of the claim of Ornan Randall, & that he have leave to withdraw his papers: agreed to. 13-Cmte on Public Lands: bill for the relief of Mary Felch, widow of Rev Cheever Felch: asked its immediate consideration: passed.

Hon David Johnson, of S C, formerly successively Circuit Judge, Chancellor, Judge of the Court of Appeals, & Govn'r of the State, died on Jan 6, at his residence near Limestone Springs, in his 73rd year.

Obit-died: on Fri, at his residence in Culpeper Co, Va, Hon John S Barbour, of Va. Thirty years ago he was a Rep in Congress, where he served 10 years. He was a member of the Constitutional Convention of Va in 1829-30; was chairman of the Va Delegation in the Democratic Nat'l Convention of 1852. His death was sudden & unexpected. Having taken a cold, it brought upon him a return of neuralgia, which ultimately reached his heart, & he died in a few minutes when neither he nor his family had any reason to believe his life was in danger. He was in his 66th year.

Dr Benj K Hennegan, an ex-Govn'r of S C, died in Marion district on Jan 10. He was elected Lt Govn'r in 1840, & soon afterwards succeeded to the Executive chair, in consequence of the death of Govn'r Noble.

The Cincinnati papers state that Mrs Harrison, the widow of the late Gen Harrison, has nearly recovered from her late severe illness.

Miss Sarah C Bacon committed suicide at Cincinnati on Jan 8. She had deposited near $1,000 in one of the broken banks, &, brooding over her loss, she became insane.

Miss Emma R Coe was yesterday registered at the ofc of the district court as a student of law in the ofc of Wm T Pierce, a member of the Phil bar. Coe will be a good name to go into partnership with after Miss Emma is admitted to practice.

WED JAN 17, 1855
Trustee's sale of house & lot at auction: on Feb 16, by deed of trust from Edw Lockery & Wm T Hook, dated Jul 23, 1850, recorded in Liber J A S No 15, folios 393 thru 395, of the land records of Wash Co, D C: sale of lot 5 in square 378, containing 4,407 square feet, more or less, with improvements appertaining thereto: fronts on north D, between 9th & 10th sts. –Walter Lenox, Henry Naylor, trustees –Green & Scott, aucts

Hon Jas Pollock was yesterday inaugurated Govn'r of Pa.

Wash City Corp: 1-Bill for the relief of Wm Shorter: referred to the Cmte of Claims. 2-Referred to the Cmte of Claims: bill for the relief of Henry Turner; of Wm F Bayly; & of Saml Samestay. 3-Ptn of the legal reps of Richd Holmes, deceased, in reference to the purchase of a certain lot: referred to the Cmte of Claims

Mrd: on Jan 15, in Wash City, by Rev A Steele, Mr Jas H Whaley to Miss Sarah J Hutchison, both of Pleasant Valley, Fairfax Co, Va.

Mrd: on Jan 16, by Rev Jas H Brown, Mr John Adam Snyder to Miss Mary Jane Bell, both of PG Co, Md.

Mrd: on Jan 16, in Gtwn, D C, by Rt Rev Dr McGill, Bishop of Richmond, Lt Jos C Ives, Corps of Topographical Engineers, U S Army, to Cora M, daughter of the late R Semmes, of the former city.

Died: on Jan 16, after a painful & lingering illness, Mrs Virginia, wife of E H Edmonston, in her 24th year. Her funeral is this afternoon at 3 o'clock, from her father's residence, 340 19th st.

Died: on Jan 16, Mr Andrew Reintzell Locke, after a suffering illness of consumption, in his 49th year. His funeral is on Thu at 10 o'clock, from his late residence, 459 10th st, above E st.

Died: on Jan 15, Mrs Dorothy Burke, relict of the late Dennis Burke, in her 74th year. Her funeral will take place from the residence of Mr Richd Stoops, corner of 9th & I sts, this afternoon, at half past 2 o'clock.

Mrd at the Marshall House, in Marshall, Mich, by Rev L H Moore, at a single ceremony, Messrs D M Vaughan, C E Woodruff, & A J Lapham, all of Emmet, & Miss Fanny A Johnston, Betsey A Yarrington, & Mary L Drake, all of Leroy. The public cannot learn from this notice who is married to which lady.
-Rochester American

THU JAN 18, 1855
Household & kitchen furniture at auction on Jan 23, at the residence of Mr Thos J Villard, Gay st, near Wash st, Gtwn. –Hugh Caperton, trustee
-Barnard & Buckey, aucts

Senate: 1-Ptn from Frances B Webster, widow of Lt Col Lucien B Webster, who died of a disease contracted during the war in Mexico, asking to be allowed all immunities & emoluments which the pension laws allow to widows of a lt col. 2-Ptn from Christian F French, asking that a register may be issued for the foreign built barque **The Lily**. 3-Ptn from Capt Fremont, late an ofcr in the U S Army, & one of those wrecked in the steamship **San Francisco**, asking that an act may be passed causing his accounts as regimental quartermaster & commissary to be settled at the Treasury Dept. 4-Ptn from Wm Allen, grandson of Jonathan Allen, an ofcr of the Revolution, asking that 7 years half-pay may be paid to the heirs of said Jonathan Allen. 5-Cmte of Claims: bill for the relief of Jas Pool, with a report: passed. 6-Bill for the relief of Thos Ap Catesby Jones: introduced. 7-Bill for the relief of Sylvester Humphrey & the heirs of Alex'r Humphrey: passed.

From the Wash Territory we have the announcement of the death of Capt Thos J Montgomery, of the 4th Infty, who expired at **Fort Steilacoom** on Nov 22. He served throughout the Mexican war.

Isaac P Davis, whom every body knew & loved, died at his residence in Boston on Jan 13, in his 84th year. He was a connoisseur in art, poetry, & mechanics; a gentleman of the old school. He was one of the 3 surviving original members of the Mass Charitable Mechanic Association, his connexion with that institution was commenced 60 years ago. He was an intimate personal friend of Danl Webster.

Mrs Julia Stanley, wife of Hon Edw Stanely, formerly of N C, died at San Francisco. [No death date given-current item.]

On Monday, Timothy Shaughnessy, employed as a laborer on the farm of Mr Hugh B Sweeney, while engaged in driving a wagon, fell from his seat & was killed by a wheel passing over him.

Obit-died: on Fri last, John P Brintnall. He was the 3rd ofcr of the U S mail steamship **Hermann**, & in the act of going on board on Thu, in company with the 4th ofcr, Mr Herring, he accidentally fell from the gang-plank & was drowned. Mr Herring made every exertion to rescue him, at the peril of his own life, but his efforts were in vain. By his death parents have lost an only son, & sisters an only brother. –B G L

Died: on Jan 16, Mrs Sarah Sack, in her 54th year. Her funeral will take place this afternoon, at 2 o'clock, from the residence of her brother-in-law, Mr R J Pollard, 245 south B st.

Phil, Jan 17. Alex'r Bowman, of Hagerstown, Md, a student of medicine, was fatally burnt in a fire in the boarding house kept by Mrs Edwards, on Chestnut st, near Broad. He was removed to the hospital, where he died shortly afterwards.

Ky Military Institute: directed by a Board of Visiters appointed by the State, is under the superintendence of Col E W Morgan, a distinguished graduate of West Point & a practical engineer, aided by an able faculty. –P Dudley, Pres of the Board

C Warriner, Watchmaker, 339 Pa ave, between 9th & 10th sts, Wash.

FRI JAN 19, 1855
Valuable farm near Wash City at public sale on Feb 1, at my Auction Rooms: the farm known as *Oak Hill*, being part of *Long Meadow*, about 1½ miles east of the Capitol, adjoining the farm of Mr John Douglass, gardener & florist. Contains about 100 acres, with a house that is a well built modern bldg. -Jas C McGuire, auct

Obit-died: the last mail from England brings the intelligence of the death of Rev Dr Routh, the venerable Pres of Magdalen College, in the Univ of Oxford. He was in his 100th year, & had filled the ofc of head of that college for 64 years. –Journal of Commerce

Senate: 1-Ptn from the heirs of Maj Saml Scott, of the Revolution, asking the bounty land due their ancestor by resolution of the Va Legislature, which they were unable to obtain on account of their papers having been mislaid in the Pension Ofc by the Gov't ofcrs, & not being found until the resolution expired by limitation. 2-Ptn from John Vaublancum, a civil engineer, asking an appropriation to test an invention for carrying the mail, which he asserts can readily attain a speed of 500 miles per hour. 3-Ptn from Enoch Moore, late of Calif, asking to be indemnified for the loss of clothing on board the barque **Oriole** in the mouth of the Columbia river, while acting in obedience to the orders of the Gov't. 4-Ptn from W C Fay, asking that a register may be issued for a foreign barque, picked up at sea & sold by the U S & purchased by him. 5-Cmte on the Judiciary: bill for the relief of Wm Case: recommended its passage. 6-Cmte on Military Affairs: bill for the relief of Dr Wm P Buell. Same cmte: bill for the relief of Geo W Torrence.

Died, in Kennebunk, Jan 6, Madam Sally S Wood, at the advanced age of 95 years & 3 months. Mrs Wood was the last person in town retaining the once popular but now obsolete title of Madam. It is supposed she was the first authoress of Maine. Among her novels of many years ago were "Dorval, the Speculator," "Ferdinand and Almira," "Amelia, or the Influence of Virtue," & Tales of the Night." She was the daughter of Nathl Barrell, of York, Maine. She retained her mental powers almost to the last. Madam Wood was for more than 40 years a communicant of the Unitarian Church at Portland, Maine.

Benajah Allen has been arrested in Rensselaer Co, N Y, upon a charge of murder committed 10 years ago. The affair was an incident of the Anti-rent troubles in 1844, when Elijah Smith was shot & killed by one of a party of men disguised as Indians. The discovery now made rests upon the affadavit of Jos A Martin, who, having quarreled with Allen, charges him with the crime.

Died: on Jan 17, after a protracted & painful illness, Mrs Mgt Flanigan, in her 56th year. Her funeral will take place from her late residence on 9th st, between D & E sts, this afternoon, at 2 o'clock.

Orphans Court of Wash Co, D C. Case of Benj K Morsell, adm of John F Bowen, deceased, the administrator & Court appointed Feb 6 next, for the final settlement of the estate of the deceased, of the assets in hand. –Ed N Roach, Reg/o wills

SAT JAN 20, 1855
Senate: 1-Cmte on Military Affairs: bill for the relief of Amos B Eaton. 2-Cmte of Claims: bill for the relief of Mrs Jane McCrabb, widow of the late Capt McCrabb. 3-Cmte on Commerce: adverse report on the claim of Enoch Moore.

Mrd: on Jan 18, by Rev E P Phelps, at Foundry Parsonage, Mr Alex'r T Borland to Miss Mary C Borland, of Wash City.

Wash City property to be sold on Apr 16th next, to satisfy the Wash Corp for taxes due thereon. [Years 1853-1854.]

Allen, Benj
Armitage, Benj
Adams, Chas F, jr
Alexander, Columbus
Addison, Danl D
Adams, Edw & others
Abbott, Geo J
Armstrong, geo B
Atkinson, Geo
Adams, Geo R & Richd
Adrian, Geo W
Atchinson, Geo R
Appleton, Henry
Allen, Mary E
Anderson, R P
Anderson, Saml J
Allison, Susan
Acken, Wm D
Austin, Wm F
Butler, Abraham
Brown, Absalom
Boone, Ann M L
Bowie, Adam
Bates, Ann
Bohrer, Benj S
Beall, Benj
Butler, Benj
Bean, Benj
Bell, Chas
Brown, Chas
Beall, Chas
Bean, Cally
Bomford & Decatur
Burr, Devere
Bell, Danl
Bruce, Danl
Barrett, Eliz
Bett, Eliz
Burford, Eliz
Berg, Fred'k
Barscht, Gregor
Buckey, Geo
Bomford, Geo
Barker, Geo
Brown, Geo
Bergershausen, Geo W
Bauer, Geo
Bryant, Henry
Berrian, Hobart
Barry & Holtzman
Ball, Henry W, jr [1844-54]
Breckenridge, John
Bright, Jesse
Brodbeck, Jacob
Bond, John F
Butler, Jas
Brown, John D
Brereton, John
Bailey, Joh, John Gardner & J Larned
Baltimore, Jos
Boyle, John
Bigelow, Jacob
Boss, Jas H
Boyle, Junius I
Bradley, Jos H
Bradley, Jos H, exc of Robt E Kerr
Boone, John B
Beardsley, Jos
Burche, John C, in trust for Catharine Burche
Baden, J W & T E
Baker, John
Benjamin, Jos D
Beckett, Jos
Brent, John Carroll
Burch, John C
Busher, Jas M, in trust
Buttle, John
Bowen, John
Branat, John D
Baltzer, John
Baltzer, John L
Bower, John
Bower, John G

Barsahlin, John
Bickley, Lloyd
Bate'er, L S
Borremans, Mary Ann
Butler, Mary A
Ball, Martha
Bond, Marie E
Birkhead, Middleton
Bowen, Martha
Barnes, Mary
Bosse, Martin
Bryan, Mary A
Benezett, Maria
Bateman, Nathl C
Bias, Noah
Brooks, Richd, & A Brown, in trust for Eliz Taylor & others
Battle, Sally
Bowen, Sayles J
Brereton, Saml
Burche, Saml Q A
Burche, Saml
Busey, Saml C
Byington, Saml
Baker, Thos E
Brown, Wm, in trust for E & P G Carreco & others
Brown, Wm
Belt, Wm M
Bates, Wm
Bradley, Wm A
Bosce, Wm
Bird, Wm
Boone, Wm
Berry Thos F & F Mohun
Clark, Ann
Carroll, Danl, of Duddington [1851-54]
Colbert, David
Cross, David G C
Chapman, Eliz
Chapman, E & F Dodge, jr
Curtis, Edw
Chester, Elijah
Costigan, Eliza
Clements, Eliza L
Cross, Eli

Bestor, Owen H
Bradley, Phineas
Byrne, Patrick A
Browning, P W
Bradley, Phineas J
Bates, Robt W
Barry, Richd
Briscoe, Richd G
Brent, Robt Y
Boarman, Ralph
Beale, Robt
Barry, Richd
Brooks, Richd
Barnhouse, Richd

Bowen, Thos H
Brown, Thos B
Berrett, Thos J
Blagden, Thos
Byrne, Thos
Barron, Thos H
Burch, Victor M

Clements, B H
Cheever, Benj H
Clements, Chas A
Cox, Clement
Collins, Charlotte & Mary Eliz
Coltman, Chas L
Coddington, Camila
Carroll, David
Conroy, Dominic

Clarke, Edw M
Cudlip, Fred'k
Cross, Francis
Charles, Gregory G
Cochran, Geo W
Cole, Geo
Conolly, Geo
Clarke, Geo W
Coombe, Griffith

Cruttenden, Harvey
Coburn, Jos L
Clark, John Geo
Cathcart, Jas L
Campbell, Jas
Corcoran, John L
Carr, Julian
Carreco, Jas
Corse, J D
Chism, John
Callahan, John
Crome, John
Connolly, John
Cabot, Jos S
Clarke, Jos S & R S Briscoe
Carlisle, Jas M [in trust]
Clarke, Jas T
Cahoe, John T
Callan, Nicholas, in trust for Jane Lynch
Causin, Nathl P
Carusi, Nathl
Callan, Nicholas
Carroll & Prout
Curtis, Patrick
Campbell, Robt G
Clarke, Richd H, in trust for E Hassler
Combs, Robt M
Cochran, Robt
Clarke, Reuben B
Carbery, Thos, & W Jones, in trust for E Mills
Connelly, Thos, of John
Connolly, Thos C
Chandler, Walter S
Clarke, Wm
Collins, Wm
Corcoran, Wm W
Chappin, Wm
Cobb, Wm R W
Cox, Wm
Coxen, Wm H, jr
Carr, Wm Edw
Carker, Wash
Clarke, Wm
Carrico, Wm B

Callan, John F
Clarke, Jos L
Costin, John T
Coombe, Jas G
Crutchett, Jas
Cannon, John
Carreco, Jos M
Costigan, John
Cryer, Jas
Crump, Jas T
Coste_, Letitia, Alice Ann Ferguson
Carrol, Mary
Caton, Michl, use Eliz Holland
Cox, Mary Ann
Cox, Mary Ann & children
Connell, Mary Ann
Craven, Maria

Collins, Sarah
Closkey, Saml
Crown, Saml
Colemen, S S
Clarke, Stephen
Crawford, Thos B
Corcoran, Thos & W W
Cathcart, Thos J
Corcoran, Thos

Cranch, Wm G
Davis, Alex'r McD
Davis, Ari
Dayton, Aaron O
Dent, Bruce
Davis, Chas A & others, in trust
Davis, Chas B
DeSelding, Chas
Delius, Edw
DeKrafft, Edw
Dyer, Edw
Dickins, Francis A
De_ios, Fred'k
Deas, Geo

Davis, Geo M
Donn, Geo W
Dyer, Geo F
Dent, H H
Densley, Hugh
Dickenson, J P
Dewdney, John
Duff, Jas
Donn, John M
Dant, Jas
Downer, Joel
Davis, Jas T
Dixon, John
Dufief, John L
Dixon, Jas
Davis, Jos & G W Garrett
Dement, John E
Day, John F
Dulin, Joshua V
Devlin, John S
Dulany, John
Dalton, John
Disher, Lewis
Digges, Matthew
Davidson, Mgt
Dyer, Mary Eliza, trustee
Dayton, Mary B
Dixon, Martha E
Donohoo, Mary
Dale, Mgt T & Mary L Livingston
Davidson, Nelson
Doyle, Patrick
Duley, Robt W
Doyle, Robt E
Dyer, Robt W, in trust
Daley, Sarah, sr
Douglas, Stephen A
Day, Sarah
Donohoo, Thos S
DeCamp, Sydney
Dant, Thos E
Donn, Thos C
Douglas, Wm
Diety, Wm H

Durr, Wm
Dowling, Wm
Douglass, Wm
Dulin, Wm
Doniphan, Wm
Ellicott, Andrew
Elliott, Bernard
Ellis, Chas F
Edelin, Chas K
Ellicott, Elias
Evans, French S
Erving, Geo W
Eignbrodt, Geo
Ellis, Henry
Espey, John
Ellicott, John
English, Julia
Elliot, Jonathan
Evans, Jos T
Espey, Jas
Edwards, Lewis
Eckel, Mary Ann
Emerick, Peter
Estop, Rezin
Etting, Solomon
Evans, Travis
Easby, Wm
Easby, Wm, in trust
Emmert, Wm
English, Wm H
Elliot, Wm P
Evans, Wm
Ewing, W G & G W
Fletcher, Arthur W & W B Webb
Favier, Agricol
Forrest, Chas W
Fish, Chas B
Fisher, Chas
Flint, C W
Frankenberger, Chas, & A Wittenaur
Fraeler, Chas
Faunce, Conrad
Farragut, David G
Finch, David

Fenwick, Edw
Fugitt, Gerard
Faunce, Geo
Forrest, Henry
Fischer, Harriet
Furse, John
Farrell, John
Fowler, Jas J
Frye, Jos
Fowler, John L
Flemming, John
Fulmore, Mary Ann
Frye, Nathl
Farnham, Robt
Frazier, Simon
Frazier, Thos
Flint, Thos, & others
French, Thos
Fowler, Virginia R
Gibson, Geo, & others, in trust for heirs of H Hunt
Garrett, Geo W, & Jos Davis
Gillies, Groenveldt, Rudolph Mees, & Pieter V W Vollenhoven
Grammer, G C
Garrett, Geo W
Gay, Gamaliel
Goldsborough, Howes
Garnett, Henry T
Gunnell, Helen M, in trust
Garrett, Henry
Guttesnson, John
Gobeens, John T
Goddard, John H
Gordon, Jas A
Greenwell, Jas B
Greenleaf, Jas
Gereche, Lisette
Groff, Michl
Howard, Chas, in trust for Virginia Key
Holmead, Cornelia V
Hendly, Circelia V
Havenner, C W
Hicks, Chas
Hibbs, Chas
Hines, D & C & M

Fletcher, Thos
Fanning, Wm H
Fitzgerald, Wm P N
Force, Wm Q
Franzoni, Virginia & Julia
Franzoni, Virginia & F Jardella
Gladman, Addison B
Grayson, Alice Ann
Green, Benj E
Gaston, Catharine J
Genan, Danl
Gilliss, E J
Gay, Ellen M
Grinder, Eleanor
Goddard, Emma A C
Greenleaf & Elliot
Grindall, Edw
Godfrey, Francis
Gaither, Geo R
Gordon, Geo
Gahan, Michl
Goodwin, Robt
Gibson, Sarah K
Gregg, Saml
Gray, Thos K
Goddard, Wm C
Gallant, Wm
Gadsby, Wm
Gunnell, Wm H
Hoover, Andrew
Hoover, Andrew, & others
Hetzel, A Revere
Humphreys, Anna Maria
Herald, A G
Hart, Bridget

Hall, David A
Hines, David
Homans, Danl
Hall, Edw
Houzam, Fred'k
Horning, Geo D

Hughes, Hugh
Hilleary, Henry
Hines, Henry
Haney, Hugh
Hunt, Henry & B O Tayloe
Hoban, Henry
Henning, Henry N
Hazle, Harriet A
Harrison, John B
Harris, Jos G
Holland, John E
Hurley, Jas W
Haliday, Jas F
Huber, Jacob
Hutchinson, J
Hickman, J L
Herrity, Jas
Hellen, Johnson
Houston, John H
Howlett, John
Hepburn, Jeremiah
Halligan, Jas
Hazle, John Z
Holmead, Jane J
Headley, John P
Hall, Jas
Hampton, Jas W
Hohing, Lewis
Herbert, Wm W, in trust for Amelia J Irwin
Hindman, Wm
Holmes, Wm
Hayman, Wm
Hunt, Wm [1847-54]
Hodges, Wm
Hubbs, Wm
Hollins, Wm
Ingle, John P
Ingle, Wm
Jackson, Apthorpe
Jackson, Alex'r
Johnson, A E H
Jost, Benedict
Jarboe, Benedict
Jones, Chas S

Hall, Lavinia
Hicks, Lloyd
Hunt, Montgomery
Hetzell, Mgt
Hetzell, Margaretta J
Hays, Matilda
Hoban, Marion B & A Diamond
Hoover, Mary Ann
Hanson, Nosh
Hanney, Peter
Hooe, Peter H & others
Harrison, Richd
Harrison, Rachel
Herbert, Rachel
Howe, Rachel & Eliz
Hoffman, Robt H
Harrison, Susan A
Hogan, Sarah
Harkness, Saml
Harris, Saml L
Humphreys, Saphronia G
Hughes, Sarah T & Jos
Harris, Sarah
Howdall, Thos
Hall, Thos
Harris, V & E H
Heron, Walter & J E Doyle

Johnson, Clement & Susan
Johnson, Catharine M
Johnson, Catharine
Jacobs, Cornelius
Jones, David & B Minor
Johnson, Dearborn
Jones, Emily G
Jones, Francis Lee & others
Johnson, Henry
Johnson, Henry D
James, John S
Johnson, Jas
Joy, John jr
Jones, Jas
Johnson, John

Jones, Joel W
Jones, Morris
James, Mary W
Jackson, Milly
Jones, Noah
Jay, Peter A
Jackson, Philip
Jennings, Polly
Johnson, Rachael
Joyce, Richd
Jenifer, Rachael
Johnson, Richd W
Jordon, Richd L
Jackson, Thos
Jenkens, Thos C
Johnson, Wm, of Peher
Johnson, Wm
Jacobi, Wm
Johnson, Wm P
Kelly, Bernard
Keirnan, Chas
King, Elijah
King, Edwin H
Knight, Edw A
Knoll, Francis
Koones, Fred'k
Krafft, G T & J W
King, Geo, of Chas
Key, Henry S
King, Josiah W
Key, John Tayloe
Kuhn, J L
Kelley, Jas
Kraft, John M
King, John
King, John H
King, John F
Kendall, John E
Kedglie, John
Kennedy, John
Kelley, Miles
King, Martin
Key, Philip
Kinney, Patrick

Kurtz, Peter
Krafft, Philip, & others, in trust
Knight, Saml W, & C W Bennett
Kesley, Sarah E
Kelley, Thos
King, Wm
Logan, Ann
Lindsay, Adam
Lefevre, Ann M & others
Lephard, Adolphus
Lucas, Bennet
Lancaster, Basil
Lucas, Eliz [1843-54]
Lawrence, Eliz
Lindsly, Eleazer
Lacey, Edw
Laight, E W
Lee, Ellen
Lewis, Esther M
Lear, Francis D
Lombardi, Francis
Lindsley, Harvey
Lockery, Hugh
Louden, Hubert F
Lee, Jesse
Libbey, Jos
Litle, John
Lare, John G
Laurie, Jas
Lewis, Jos C
Lewis, J C, & E Burnett, trustees
Lodge, Jas
Lockey, Jane
Lanhart, Jacob
Little, John E
Lightell, John
Lewis, Jos S, for assignees of John Frye
Lockey, Jas B
Lear, Louisa
Lenthall, Mary K
Little, Peter, jr
Little, Peter
Lenox, Peter

Leckie, Robt
Latham, R W
Lykes, Semas
Lewis, Saunders
Lazenby, Thos A, in trust for Jeremiah Smith & wife
Lyndall, Thos
Lawson, Thos
Law, Thos
Lewis, Wm B
Larkin, Wm
Lewis, Washington
Miller, August
McIntyre, Arthur L
McWilliams, Ann T
McWilliam, Alex'r
McGee, Bernard
Moxley, B F
Middleton, B F
Milburn, Benedict
Magar, Benj S
Mantz, Casper
McCarty, Chas F
Murck, Christian H
Meehan, Chas H W
McNamee, Chas
Myers, Chas
Mills, Chas C
McLaughlin, Danl
Mudd, Dominic
Mallett, Emily
Mason, Enoch
McCarthy, Eugene
Mantz, Francis
Mohler, Fred'k
Masi, Francis & Vincent
McCarthy, Florence S
Myer, Ferdinand F
May, Fred'k & J M McRae
McGlue, Geo T
Mitchell, Geo W
Miller, Geo
Markwood, Geo W
McKnight, G B & M H
Mason, Geo

Lundy, Thos
Lunt, Saml
Lumpkin, Thos

Myers, Geo
Markell, Geo H
Moran, Horatio
Merryman, Horatio R, in trust
Moscrop, Henry
Morfit, Henry M
Moreland, John H
McCutchen, John H G
McBlair, John h
McBride, john
Mickun, John T
McConchi, John T S
Massey, John H
Mathews, Jas
Moses, Jas S
McClelland, John
Merman, Jane
Miller, John
McChesney, John H
Marlow, John W
Moulder, John A
McCutchen, John, in trust
Maguire, Jas
Maury, John W
Miles, Jane
McGrann, Jas
Miller, Isaac F
McCandless, Juliana
McCormick, Jas
McCormick, Jas M
McCracken, John
McKeon, John B
Martin, John W
Mitchell, Jas
McGee, Jas S
Mackall, Leonard
Martin, Luther J & M J
Morelion, Mary
McCarthy, Michl

McPherson, Mary E
Morris, Maria
McKnight, M H
Martin, Mary & Julia
Milburn, Mgt [in trust]
Mooney, Michl
Morgan, Mary A
Mackey, Philip
Mitchell, Perry A
Marceron, Peter J
Miller, Robt
McPiers, Sarah
Morsell, Saml T G
McKim, Saml A H
Moore, Thos
McMinn, Thos
Nailor, Dickinson, in trust for W C Nailor
Newman, Henry
Naylor, Henry & A Rothwell
Naylor, Henry, in trust for Mrs E J Beale
Naylor, Henry [use E Walls]
Naylor, Henry
Nailor, Joshua S
Norse, Michl
Neale, Ramsay
Nicholson, Sarah C
Newman, Thos A
Nairy, Thos
Noyes, Wm
Nicholls, Wm S
Noyes, Wm
Norris, Wm G
O'Harra, Christopher S
Osborne, Eliz & children
O'Connor, Eugene
O'Ferrall, Jas
Owen, John
O'Donnell, John & Michl
Orme, Thos T & Mary Ann
O'Neale, Wm
Provest, Alex'r
Power, Ann
Pratt, Carey
Peter, David

Maxcy, Virgil
Mosely, Wm H
Markwood, Wm
Morton, Wm
Morrow, Wm
McPherson, Wm S
Marshall, Wm
Macey, Wm
Moreland, Wm A
McFarland, Wm
McKnew, Z W
Mardis, Wm
McPeak, Wm
Nailor, Allison
Nicholson, Augustus A

Nixdorf, Henry

Pancoast, David
Pickrel, E & A H
Parker, Francis E
Page, Geo & Geo Mattingly
Plant, Geo H
Page, Geo
Pratt, Henry & others
Pupo, Harriet
Phillips, John H
Plant, Jas W
Peck, Jos C
Peck, Jos
Phillips, Janett B
Phillips, Jas B
Phillips Jas B
Prout, Jonathan
Pearson, Jos, M Y & A M, [1849-54]
Phelps, John T
Parsons, Jas
Powers, Jas
Perry, Lewis F
Peck, Lewis C
Page, Lucien S
Purl, Mary

Prout, Mary
Payne, Orris S
Pearson, Peter M, in trust for R R Robey
Phillips, Richd, in trust for A D Davis
Prout, Eliz
Payne, Saml
Peugh, Saml A
Platt, S H
Peters, Thos
Plumsill, Thos
Parker, Wm
Perkins, Wm H
Philip, Wm H
Powell, Wm
Philip, Wm H, W C Zantzinger & F Dainese
Patton, Wm
Prout, Wm
Preston, Wm
Pratt, Wm
Phillips, Wm
Quinn, Jas
Rothwell, A
Randall, Emily
Ross, Eliza
Rigdon, Eliz
Rodbird, Ebenezer
Ritter, Fred'k W
Riggs, Geo W
Rider, Geo F
Randall, H K
Remily, John C
Rye, John T
Roberts, John
Rodgers, Johnson K
Sheckells, B O, in trust for Eliza McGuire
Shadd, Bonvsentura
Stott, Chas
Sengstack, C P
Sherman, Chas E
Stewart, Carter A
Schnebley, Danl H
Smith, Danl
Stabler, Deborah H

Prather, Overton J

Riley, Joshua
Reynolds, Jos
Russell, John T
Redman, Jos
Reeler, Jesse
Raley, Jas
Ready, John Y
Ratrie, Jas
Ray, Josiah
Rothwell, Larua E, & Laura M Tree
Ray, Paul
Rodier, P L
Roach, Mahlon
Ross, Robt
Redfern, Saml
Redman, Sarah
Ritchie, Thos
Reid, Thos
Randolph, Wm B
Reading, Wm
Ratrie, Wm, jr
Ruggles, Wm, jr
Ryland, Wm, & others
Schwartz, Andrew
Shepherd, Alex'r
Smith, A Thos
Smith, Archer B
Shorter, Bazil
Sands, B F
Sheckell, B O
Simms, Basil

Smallwood, Dennis
Saunders, David
Silence, Eliz
Stewart, Eveline
Swann, Edw
Selden, Francis
Small, Geo
Seibel, Geo C

Stewart, Geo W
Seitz, Geo
Schaub, Gallas
Semmes, Geo
Sweeny, Geo
Smith, Gerret
Sage, Gustavus A
Simpson, Gilbert
Scroggin, Geo W
Stoke, Geo
Stewart, Hanson
Seifers, Henry
Sweeny, Hugh B
Sibley, Jas
Smith, J B H, trustee
Snowden, John & others
Stewart, Jas E
Smith, Jas
Sharratts, John F
Sharratts, John F & Martha A E
Scrivener, Jas
Sands, Julia M
Shields, Jas W, & McClintock Young
Smith, John T
Scott, John
Smull, Jas T
Scott, Jas W
Stinchcomb, John H
Sauer, John A
Springman, John M
Sisson, John A
Sinon, John
Sufferie, John J
Simms, Lucinda
Smallwood, Lucy
Shanks, Michl
Simms, Mary Ann E
Stoop, Mary Ellen
Sweeny, Mary
Swain, Moses P
Snyder, Nicholas
Sullivan, Patrick
Sewall, Robt
Sommerville, Robt

Smoot, Saml C
Stott, Saml
Stettinius, Saml
Seibert, Selman
Strong, Saml
Scott, Saml
Sewall, Thos
Sweeny, Thos
Sterling, Wm
Speiden, Wm
Stewart, Wm
Stewart, Wm R, Robt H & Mary E
Steiger, Wm T
Sibrey, Wm
Santer, Wenderline
Selden, Withers & Co
Scott, Wm
Swain, Wm H
Southoron, Wm B
Stickney, Wm
Tilghman, Amelia
Thornton, A M & Ann Brodean
Thomas, Anthonis W
Thruston, Buckner
Tayloe, B O
Thompson, Chas
Thomas, Chas
Turner, Christiana
Tucker, Enoch
Thompson, Eliz A
Tighlman, Frisby
Thomas, Geo
Turner, Henry
Thomas, Harriet Ann
Turner, Henry, & others
Toughey, Hugh
Thomas, John Hanson
Toll, Isaac D
Tayloe, John, 3rd
Taylor, John
Thayer, John M
Taylor, John
Thomas, Jas H
Trueman, Josiah

Throckmorton, John A
Taylor, Jos S
Trook, John N
Thorn, Mary Jane, in trust for M J & W H T Thorn
Taylor, Robt
Tweady, Robt
Tomkins, Richd
Tustin, Septimus & Eliza
Travers, Sydney V
Todd, S J
Trook, Susannah C
Tucker, Thos
Taylor, Thos J
Todd, Wm B, & W H Philip
Todd, Wm B
Voorhees, B M
Van Ness, Chas W
Van Paxen, Chas A
Van Ness, Eugene
Van Ness, Edw
Vernon, Henry T]
Vowell, John C
Vecey, J
Van Ness, John P
Van Reswick, John
Vivans, Lewis
Watterston, Geo, [in trust for Mary Sweeny]
Wilson, Harriet & Hannah
Williamson, Harriet
Weeden, Henry A & L Haslap
Wood, Henry F
Whitmore, H O, in trust
Williams, John
Whalen, John
Williamson, John
Williamson, Jos
Williams, J & J
Walters, Jas, sr
Walters, Jas sr, & Theodore
Williamson, Jos
Wheat, Jos H
Wilson, John
Wakefield, Jane W
Wise, Jas Alex'r

Taliafero, Jas M, in trust
Tenney, Mary

Villard, R H L
Wilson, Alex'r
Wadsworth, Adrian R
Waller, A B
Wallingsford, Alfred
Williams, Ann
Washington, Bailey
Wiltberger & Burch
Wise, Berle
Winder, Chas H
Wheelan, Catharine Ann
Wall, Columbus O
Wallach, Chas S
Wiltberger, Chas H
Watson, Chas C & E A
Walker, Dorcas
Wilkes, Chas
Wilkerson, Edw
Wheeler, Eliz [1836-54]
Wood, Ferdinand F
Willner, Geo F H
Willner, Geo & others, in trust

Whitney, Jas O
Walker, John
Wallard, Jas F
Walker, Jonathan T
Ward, Jane
Wimsatt, Jos
Withers, John
Wirt, John L
Wise, John H
Wailes, Isaac H
Wilson, John A
White, John P
Wormley, Jas
Ward, John
Wilkerson, John
Weed, J C & N S
Wilson, Jesse B

West, John	Wood, Saml
Wilson, John H	Welch, Thos
Williams, Lemuel	Waters, Thos
Wright, Louisa	Ward, Ulysses
Winder, Levin H	Worthington, Wm M
Wood, Mary Ann E	Worthington, Wm
White, Martha R & others	Wilson, Wm
Wroe, Mary	Winder, Wm H
Wingate, Mgt G T	West, Wm H
Wilson, Offa	Wroe, Wm
Wilson, Patrick	Woodward, Wm R
Washington, Perrin	Wall, Wm
Whorton, Robt S	Ward, Wm H
Winters, Richd	Wright, Washington S
Wallford, Rebecca	Weaver, Wm A
Walter, Robt	Whitmore, Wm
Wroe, Saml C	Ward, Wm H
Young, Benj, surviving trustee of E & E M Brooke	
Yardella, Francis & V Franzoni	Younger, Sally
Young, Henry N	Young, Susan
Young, Mary A	Yeatman, Thos J
Young, Mgt	Zellers, David

From N Y: the British mail agent at this port, Capt Granby Calcraft, formerly in the Royal navy, died here last night. His loss is much regretted by a very extended circle of acquaintances.

Mrd: on Jan 12, by Rev Dr Cole, Saml H Carlisle to Miss Mary Virginia Griggs.

Mrd: on Jan 18, in Wash City, by Rev G W Samson, Mr Robt V Godman to Miss Mary A Grainger, both of Wash.

Mrd: on Jan 15, in Balt, by Rev E P Phelps, Mr John L Hooff, of Va, to Miss Clara S, daughter of the late Jas H Bennett, of Wash City.

Died: on Jan 19, in Wash City, Col Henry Northrop, in his 78th year. His funeral will be from the residence of Mr Ward, on 6th st, [Island] between D & E sts, on Sunday next, at 3 o'clock P M.

Official, Dept of State, Wash, Jan 18, 1855. Information has been received from Horatio Sprague, U S Consul at Gibraltar, of the death, near that place, of John Fallon, a citizen of the U S. [No other information.]

MON JAN 22, 1855

Appointments by the Pres, by & with the advice & consent of the Senate.
Wm H Endicott to be Postmaster at Navada city, Calif, vice R A Davidge.
Robt E Davis to be Postmaster at Columa, Calif, vice A D Waldron.
Thos Carbery, Lewis Carbery, Nicholas Callan, John D Clarke, Jos N Fearson, John H Goddard, Wm J McCormick, Henry Reaver, Pierce Shoemaker, & Wm Waters, to be Justices of the Peace in the District of Columbia, to take effect from Jan 20, 1855, when their present commissions expired.

Ho John S Wells, appointed by the Govn'r of N H to fill the vacancy in the U S Senate occasioned by the death of Hon Moses Norris, arrived in Wash City on Sat.

Hon Wm H Muse, Sec of State of Mississippi, died at Jackson on Jan 9, after a brief illness. He was a native of N C. Mr E W Rootes has been appointed by Govn'r McRae to fill the vacancy.

Hon John Van Buren, formerly a member of Congress from the Ulster district of N Y, died at his residence in the village of Kingston on Tue last. With a single exception he was the oldest practitioner of law at the Ulster bar.

A statue of Benj Franklin is to be erected in Boston costing $10,000. Greenough, the sculptor, is expected to have it completed in 1856. It is to be of bronze & 8 feet in height. It represents Franklin in citizen's dress, with a cane in his right hand & his cocked hat under his left arm. The entire cost of the statue & bas reliefs will be $18,000.

Petersburg Express: John W Rice, of that city, formerly of Brunswick Co, has been guilty of committing forgeries by which he has swindled the banks of Petersburg out of $20,000 & individuals in the country & N Y out of $30,000 more. He fled from Petersburg last week, & his guilt is known. –Richmond Enquirer

On Monday we witnessed the trial of the new steam-engine constructed at the American Machine Works in Springfield, Mass, for the Mint at New Orleans. Its designer is P B Tyler, & has been honored as one of the best steam-engines, if not the very best, ever built in the U S. –Springfield Republican

Mrd: on Jan 10, at the residence of Jas C Latham, Detroit, Mich, by Rev Bishop McCoskey, Fred'k T Andrews, of Richmond, Va, to Miss Lura Dolsen, 2nd daughter of the late John Dolsen, of Chatham, Canada West.

Mrd: on Jan 16, at the Cathedral, in Balt, by Rev H B Coskery, Mr Edmund J Plowden to Miss Josephine V, only daughter of John D Freeman, all of St Mary's Co, Md.

Died: on Jan 20, after a short illness, John M Degenhart, Sgt U S Marine Corps, in his 42nd year. His funeral will take place this evening at 2 o'clock, from his late residence, between 10th & 11th sts, Navy Yard.

New Orleans, Jan 18. Mrs Gaines has recommenced suit to establish herself as legatee under the will of Danl Clark, her father, in the probate court of New Orleans.

Galena, Jan 19. John J Taylor was hung here this afternoon for the murder of his wife. About 10,000 were present, to whom the criminal spoke for nearly an hour. He protested his innocence at heart, & attributed his crime to intoxicating drink.

Cincinnati, Jan 20. Stephen Short & Wm Hanning were hung at Greenupsburg, Ky, Jan 19, for murder. They confessed their guilt. 6,000 persons witnessed their end.

Boarding & Rooms to let: Mrs R E Wheeler has several rooms to let, if applied for immediately. West side of 4½ st, 3rd door south of Pa ave.

For rent: a large 3 story brick house, on C st, between 4½ & 3rd sts, adjoining the residence of Dr J F May. Inquire of J P Pepper, at Adams & Co's Express Ofc, or of J W Hicks, City Post Ofc, Executors for the heirs.

TUE JAN 23, 1855
Senate: 1-Ptn from Geo Simpton, a captain in the revenue service of the late Republic of Texas, asking to be placed on the same footing as the ofcrs of the Texas Navy. 2-Ptn from Lt Jas Totten, asking to be reimbursed for expenses incurred in selling at auction certain commissary stores of the U S. 3-Ptn from Jacob Kerr, asking compensation for 4 land warrants delivered by him to a U S surveyor for location, & by him converted to his own use. 4-Ptn from Howard & Co, remonstrating against the renewal of the patents granted to Cyrus McCormick & Obed Hussey for improvements in reaping machines. 5-Ptn from J Warren Newcomb, grandson of Gen Warren, who fell at Bunker's Hill, asking to be allowed bounty land. 6-Ptn from Josiah Snelling, for a pension. 7-Ptn from Wm Goff; & of Wm S Oliver, for a pension. 8-Ptn from Thos Coward, a Lt on board the privateer **Chasseur** in the war of 1812, asking a pension on account of wounds received in battle. 9-Ptn from John Heneage, asking the same allowance that was made to other official reporters. 10-Cmte on Pensions: adverse report on the ptn of Mrs Rachael McMilan. 12-Cmte on Indian Affairs: bill for relief of John Rogers. 13-Cmte on Revolutionary Claims: asking to be discharged from consideration of the ptn of Mrs Anne Royal, the petitioner being dead: which was agreed to. Same cmte: bill for relief of Wm A Duer, John Duer, & Beverly Robinson, trustees of the estate of Sarah Alexander, widow of Maj Gen Wm Alexander, commonly known as Lord Sterling, submitted an adverse report on the same: which was agreed to. Same cmte: bill for relief of the legal reps of Saml Prioleau, deceased: passed. 14-Cmte to Audit & Control the Contingent Expenses of the Senate: memorial of Jas W Sheahan for

reporting for one of the select cmtes of the Senate in the case of Geo A Gardner, indicted by the Gov't for fraud, reported a resolution directing the Sec of the Senate to pay out of the contingent fund $286.80, being at the rate of $3 per colums. 15-Cmte on Public Lands: asking to be discharged from the consideration of the memorial of Hall Neilson for remission of interest on notes given the U S, & that it be referred to the Cmte on Finance: agreed to. 16-Cmte of Conference: bill for the relief of Thos Marston Taylor, submitted a report.

St Timothy's Hall, Catonsville, Md: Institution for Young Gentlemen, 6 miles from Balt, Md, has been conducted by the present Rector during the last 10 years. Pupils are received at any time during the year. Terms $250 per annum. For further information address Rev L Van Bokkelen, Rector

Trustee's sale: a Mill & 212 acres of land near Annapolis for sale: by decree of the Circuit Cout of Anne Arundel Co, sitting as a Court of Equity, & passed on Dec 23, 1854, in a cause between B T B Worthington & John Ridout, excs of John Spence, cmplnts, & Alex'r Randall & others, dfndnts: public sale on Feb 3, at the Courthouse door, the property known as ***Spence's Mill***, adjoining the farms of Mrs Ann Dorsey, Jas W Gray, & others. The tenant, Gilbert M Conner, [a skilful & responsible man,] has also bound himself, in addition to the money rent of $135, to keep the mill in repair. –B T B Worthington, trustee

Mr David Thomas, residing in Balt, was married on Friday night & retired to rest. In about an hour afterwards the bride heard him breathing in a singular manner, & on arising found him at the point of death. The jury rendered a verdict of death from organic disease of the heart. The deceased was in the neighborhood of 60 years of age.

At Safe Harbor, Pa, a few days ago, Mrs G W Johnson & Miss Lewis called at the house of Mr Wm Haney, & whilst there he started to fill a fluid lamp, which exploded & set fire to the clothing of the ladies. Mrs Johnson was so badly burnt that she died. Miss Lewis was also much burnt, but is considered out of danger.

Augustus Davis, a middle-aged or elderly man, well known in Wash City, as a market dealer, was found dead near the upper bridge, between Wash City & Gtwn, yesterday. On returning to his home in Wash at a late hour on Sat night, he fell from a precipice at the roadside. His neck was broken by the fall. -Globe

Mrd: on Jan 21, by Rev Henry Slicer, Mr Elias Travers to Miss Mary E Warner.

Criminal Court: on Sat, Geo Shenig & Geo Barnes, youths on the near approach of manhood, were tried & convicted on the charge of setting fire to the stable of Mr G W Hopkins, in the First Ward. There are 3 other indictments pending against the same parties. -Star

Died: on Jan 12, in the town of London, Upper Canada, Mrs Mary Eliz Andrews Jones, widow of the late Dr Thos P Jones, formerly U S Com'r of Patents at Wash. In all the relations & duties of daughter, wife, mother, & friend, she was a shining example, & her heart was the abode of all womanly virtues.

Died: on Fri last, at Balt, in his 68th year, John S Schriver, an old & highly esteemed citizen. At the time of his death he was the active Pres of several steamboat lines.

Died: on Jan 12, at Whitehall, Greene Co, Ill, of scarlet fever, Nannie, eldest daughter of Isaac D & Sarah E Vedder, formerly of Wash City, aged 5 years & 1 month.

WED JAN 24, 1855

Cmder Jolly, late of the British schnr-of-war **Bermuda**, has died on his passage from Jamaica to England. He was transferred at St Thomas from the royal mail steamer **Derwent** to the ship **Atrato**, on Dec 16, in a very precarious state, & died at sea on the 16th. Cmder Jolly was the British ofcr who protested against the bombardment of Greytown by Capt Hollins.

Chas Lewis Bachman, lately arrested at N Y & conveyed to Richmond, on a charge of having robbed Hon Fayette McMullen of $1,700 last Aug, has been committed to jail for trial. He admits his guilt, & that he gave $860 of the money to Jas Howle, who was arrested at Richmond for the robbery, but was discharged for want of evidence. Bachman has visited Germany since the robbery, & appears to have spent all the money. Mr McMullen suffered this loss in consequence of a collision between a regular train of cars & a hand-car, in which he was proceeding to Richmond from the Slash Cottage, where he was accidentally left behind. In the confusion incident to the collision Mr McMullen lost his valise, which was picked up by Bachman & rifled of the money.

Household & kitchen furniture at auction on: Jan 31, at the store & residence of H Lisberger, on Pa ave, near 20th st. -Jas C McGuire, auct

Wash Corp: 1-Ptn of Robt R Rywell, asking permission to erect a livery stable: referred to the Cmte on Police. 2-Cmte of Claims: bill for the relief of Wm Shorter: laid over for futher consideration. 3-Ptn of Solomon Dunmore, for remission of a fine: referred to the Cmte of Claims. 4-Bill for the relief of Henry Turner: passed.

Orphans Court of Wash Co, D C. Letters of administration on the personal estate of Col John H Stone, late of the State of Md, deceased. –Nathl Pope Causin, adm

A fire occurred in Richmond on Sat which destroyed the stable of S S Myers, together with a carriage & 2 fine horses; the stable of Mr Winper, with 3 mules & 2 horses; the dwlg & store of Mr Costa; the dwlg of Mr Ihler, & stable of Mr Bragg.

Senate: 1-Ptn from the widow of Louis Labranche, of Louisiana, asking the confirmation of her title to a tract of land in the Parish of St Chas. 2-Ptn from Caleb Frye, heirs of Nathl Frye, of the Revolutionary army, asking to be allowed commutation pay. 3-Ptn from Silas Stockwell, asking to be allowed to locate a military land warrant issued to one Wm G Shaw, & by him transferred to memorialists. 4-Ptn from Jean Baptiste Faribault & Pelagie Faribault, asking payment of the price agreed upon with the Sec of War for the purchase of an island at the confluence of the Mississippi & St Pierre rivers for a military post. 5-Ptn from John Guest, a lt in the navy, asking compensation for services in surveying the coast between Apalachicola, in Fla, & the Mississippi. 6-Ptn from Solomon Andrews, asking compensation for the use, by the Post Ofc Dept, of his invention of the clam-shell lock for securing mail bags. 7-Cmte on Finance: asking to be discharged from the consideration of the ptns of Harriet Saunders & of Jane M Rudolph: they they be referred to the Cmte on Pensions. 8-Cmte on Pensions: adverse report on the ptn of Raymond Williams: which was agreed to. 9-Cmte of Claims: adverse report on the memorial of John Garvin: which was agreed to.

House of Reps: 1-Bill for the relief of Andrew Jackson Heaton: referred. 2-Cmte on Comerce: bill to change the names of the American built vessel **J H Holmes** & the vessel **Franklin Pierce**: passed. 3-Bill granting a pension to Jos McCormick: referred.

$20 reward will be paid for the apprehension of Bartholomew Hays, who stole $65 & a note of hand for $59.75 on Mr Estwick Evans. Calls himself Bat Hays, is about 5 feet 8 inches high, 19 years of age; weighs about 130 or 140 pounds, rather good looking; an Irish boy, but speaks very little broken. His connexions live in N Y C. -W C Johnson

Mrd: on Jan 23, by Rev Mr Stanley, H M B McPherson to Miss Edith McPherson, daughter of H H McPherson, of Wash City.

Mrd: on Jan 21, in Christ Church, by Rev W Hodges, Jos Grinder to Miss Eliz A Williams, all of Wash City.

Mrd: on Jan 23, at Foundry Parsonage, by Rev E P Phelps, Mr Paul S Evans to Miss Emma Brown, both of Alexandria, Va.

Mrd: on Jan 22, by Rev Mr Hodges, Geo Arnold to Miss Lydia Champion, all of Wash.

Died: yesterday, in Wash City, after an illness of only a few hours, Capt Jas Cryer, of St Mary's Co, Md, but for many years a resident of Wash City, & a clerk in the City Post Ofc, aged 42 years. His funeral is today at 3 o'clock, from his late residence, on 12th st, near the Smithsonian Institute.

Died: on Jan 23, Nora, daughter of John & Nora Tretler, aged 4 months. Her funeral will take place from the residence of her parents today at 3 o'clock.

THU JAN 25, 1855

Trustee's sale of desirable bldg lot on the Island. On Feb 5, on the premises, by deed of trust from Geo Thomas & wife, dated Jan 16, 1854, recorded in Liber J A S No 71, folios 232 & 233, of the land records for Wash Co: subscriber will sell lot 2 in square 288, fronting 25 feet on south F st, between 9th & 10th sts, running back 125 feet to an alley. –Jos C Isaac, trustee -Jas C McGuire, auct

Senate: 1-Ptn from Anthony Phelps, a Revolutionary soldier, & also from Eliza Gibbons, to be allowed pensions. 2-Ptn from Ed D Tippett, asking the appointment of a cmte to examine a plan invented by him for navigating the air & an appropriation to enable him to exhibit it. 3-Ptn from Geo A Magruder, a Lt in the navy, asking to be allowed the pay of a capt during the time he acted in that capacity on board the frig **Columbia**. 4-Additional documents submitted in the case of Mrs Lewright Browning. 5-Cmte on Pensions: adverse report on the ptn of John T Sprague, in behalf of Mgt S Worth. Same cmte: adverse report on the ptn of Chambers C Mullin. Same cmte: adverse report on the ptn of Eliz S R Sailly. Same cmte: adverse report on the ptn of John S Develin; also on the ptn of Sarah Vincent, widow of John Vincent. 6-Cmte on Revolutionary Claims: bill for the relief of Fred Vincent, adm of Jas Le Case, survivor of Le Case & Mallet: passed.

Wm Lecky, found guilty at Pittsburg of selling liquor to an inebriate, has been sentenced to pay a fine of $50, the costs of prosecution, & undergo an imprisonment of 59 days in the county jail. The highest punishment the law demands is 60 days- the court gave Lecky credit for one day to balance one night he spent in prison.

Mrd: on Nov 20 last, in Payta, Peru, in the Church of San Francisco, by Rev Dr Don Jose Manuel Corcuero, Fayette M Ringgold, U S Consul at Payta, to Marcedes Lanas, eldest daughter of Senor Don Jose Lanas, of that place.

Died: on Jan 25, Eliz Webster, wife of John D McPherson. Her funeral is on Thu, at 2 o'clock, from the residence of her husband, on F st, between 9th & 10th sts.

Died: on Jan 23, William Thomas, only child of William & Marcelina Farish, aged 23 months & 1 week. His funeral is this evening at 3 o'clock, from the residence of his grandmother, Mrs Goggin, 400 Penn ave.

FRI JAN 26, 1855

New book recently published in N Y, under the title of the "American Portrait Gallery, containing portraits & memoirs of eminent Americans now living." The extract is taken from "A sketch of the life & public services of Lt Col S H Long," an old soldier, & relates to his expeditions in the far West.

Senate: 1-Pen from John G Watmough, asking a continuation of the pension granted to him in consideration of severe wounds received during the last war with Great Britain, & particularly that received in the storming of **Fort Erie**. 2-Ptn from Huldah Butler, asking to be allowed the commutation pay to which her father was entitled as a Lt Col in the war of the Revolution. 3-Ptn from T B Tilden, asking the purchase by the Senate of Mitchell's Universal Atlas. 4-Ptn from Jas Harper & Robt W Harper, heirs of Jas Harper, asking to be allowed to locate a quantity of land named in the military land warrants issued by the State of Va to their ancestor. 5-Cmte of Pensions: adverse reports on the ptns of Mgt G Hanson & Geo Felker. Same cmte: asking to be discharged from the consideration of the ptn of the heirs at law of Capt Wm Underwood, & that they have leave to withdraw their papers, on the ground that the Com'r of Pensions had informed the cmte the case can be adjusted at that ofc if application be made. 6-Cmte on Pensions: adverse report on the ptn of Oakley H Wright. Same Cmte: bill for the relief of Jeptha L Heminger: recommended its passage. 7-Cmte on Public Lands: bill granting a bounty land to Susan Palmer. 8-Cmte on Commerce: bill for the relief of Jeremiah Moore. 9-Cmte on Pensions: adverse report on the ptn of Harriet H Saunders. Also, on the ptn of Emily L Slaughter, widow of Cmder Slaughter, of the navy; & upon that of John Brown, asking that his pension may go back to the time of disability.

Daring robbery perpetrated on the premises of Mr Peter Otto, in Carroll Co, 9 miles from Emmittsburg, on Jan 17, by 4 men named Parrish, Rowe, Otto, & Haps. They blackened their faces & on Jan 10th they proceeded to the farm of Mr Otto, supposing that he was absent from home, it being his usual day to visit the Balt market. When they found he was present at home, they went the following night. Mrs Otto heard them, &, lighting a candle, went to the window. One of the desperadoes stood with a knife in one hand, a pistol in the other, & commanded her to deliver up to him all the money there was in the house. Fearing she would be murdered, she went into another room & brought out a shot-bag containing silver. She then was compelled to bring them a small bundle of notes, & she declared that there was no more. The robbers left the house. One of the robbers returned to the hotel in Emmitsburg the next morning, his face still black. He received $20 and thought that he had not been fairly treated and informed against the others. They were all arrested and committed to prison to answer for their temerity. Mr Otto states that the whole amount of money obtained was $210, little of which has been recovered. -Balt American

Mrd: on Jan 17, at Canandaigua, N Y, by Rev Dr Daggett, Caleb Brinton, jr, of Pa, to Hattie M Granger, daughter of Gen John A Granger.

Late from Calif: 1-Jas Hogan, the City Marshal, is a defaulter to the amount of $20,000. 2-The Supreme Court have declared that **Sacramento** is to be hereafter the State Capitol.

Died: on Dec 9 last, at the British Consulate in Tripoli, [Bashary,] by Col G F Herman, British Consul-General, [acting under a special warrant from the Queen,] Marcus Junius Gaines, U S Consul-General at Tripoli, to Maggie, youngest daughter of Dr John Dickson, late Surgeon in the British Navy.

Wash City Ordinances: 1-Act for the relief of Saml Curson: the sum of $88.20 be paid to him for grading a public alley. 2-Act for the relief of Wm F Bayly: the sum of $21, assessed on the brick house of Wm F Bayly, on K st, between 11th & 12 sts, is remitted; said house not being tenantable until after Jan 1, 1854. 3-Act for the relief of Jos D Lafontaine: the fine imposed on him for selling ice-cream on Sunday is remitted, said Lafontaine paying the costs of prosecution.

Masonic. A stated communication of St John's Lodge, No 11, will be held on Jan 25, at their new Hall, D & 9th st, at 7 o'clock. –Hopkins Lightner, sec

SAT JAN 27, 1855
Senate: 1-Bill for the relief of Benedict J Heard: advocated the passage of the bill. 2-Bill for the relief of Capt Philip F Voorhees, U S Navy: postponed. 3-Settling the claims of the legal reps of Richd W Meade, deceased: passed over. 4-Bill to adjust the claim of Capt Saml C Reid & other owners, & pay the amount found due, not to exceed $131,000, which was the sum originally demanded from Portugal: it was agreed to.

Mrd: on Thu, by Rev John C Smith, Richd Cruit to Miss Mary Ann Creager, both of Gtwn.

Died: on Jan 26, in Wash City, at the house of her son-in-law, B F Larned, Mrs Eliz H Newman, relict of the late Col Francis Newman, of Md. In a long & useful life her Christian character has shown itself in deeds of charity & benevolence. Her funeral will take place from St Patrick's Church, on F st, on Sunday, at 2 o'clock.

MON JAN 29, 1855
Hon Luther Severance, long & favorably known as the founder & Editor of the Kennebec Journal, died in Augusta, Me, on Jan 25, of cancer, with which he had long been afflicted. He was for 4 years a Rep in Congress, & then Com'r of the Sandwich Island, where he remained 4 years.

Mr Everett, in his memoirs of the late Peter C Brooks, just published in the Genealogical Register, states that Mr Brooks abstained as a general rule from speculative investment.

Cross-Roads Farm & Tavern for sale: it contains 172 acres: it lies on the plank & Union turnpike road, about 9 miles from Wash, in Montg Co, Md.
-Patrick Lyddane, living near Cross-Roads Farm.

The Pittsburgh [Pa] Post says that David Bates was convicted of bigamy at the last term of the Indiana County Court, & sentenced to 22 months' imprisonment in the Western Penitentiary, to which place he was brought the other day. It appears he was committed for the same offence in 1851, & had just got out. He dyed his whiskers, returned to Blairsville & changed his name to David Beatty, & was again married to a young widow, before the same Justice of the Peace who married him before. One of the witnesses on the trial stated that Bates had 7 wives living, or even more.

The steamer brings intelligence of the death of Mary Russell Mitford, the favorite & gifted author. She died in the village of Swallowfield, England, on Jan 10th. She was born in 1789. [Feb 3rd newspaper: Miss Mitford was the author of "Our Village." She was born in Abresford, in Hampshire, in Dec, 1789. She was loved as a sister by Mrs Hemans & Mrs Browning, & in the list of her friends were Talfourd, De Quincy, Wilson, & Wordsworth. –N Y Courier]

On Jan 12 Danl Dufour, aged 86 years & 11 months, died at Vevay, Switzerland Co, Indiana, where he had resided for about half a century. He was one of a numerous family of brothers who emigrated from the Canton Vaud, Switzerland, & who were the first persons, or among the first, that cultivated the grape with the view to the manufacture of wine. Their first experiments were made in Ky; afterwards the older brother & leader, John Jas Dufour, received an entended credit by act of Congress for 24,000 acres of land, on the Ohio river, between Indian creek & Plum creek, on condition of introducing the culture of the vine. On this tract the town of Vevay, 60 miles below Cincinnati, founded by the Dufours is located. They moved from Ky to Indiana at an early date in this century, & there the elder branch, of whom but few remain, resided, honored & respected by all. Their numberous descendants now form a large portion of the inhabitants in & around Vevay. One of the orginal band of brothers, John Francis Dufour, was for many years Postmaster & afterwards Judge of the county. –Cincinnati Times

Died: on Sep 24, on board the U S steamer **Hancock**, near Fou-chou-fou, China, Acting Lt Henry St George Hunter, of the U S Navy, in his 31st year.

Orphans Court of Wash Co, D C. In the case of Florian Hitz, adm of Frederic F Wingenroth, deceased, the administrator & Court have appointed Feb 17, for settlement of the estate of said deceased, of the assets in hand.
–Ed N Roach, Reg/o wills

TUE JAN 30, 1855
Mr Chas H Anderson, Postmaster of Cynthiasa, Ky, was killed on the railroad near that place on Jan 21. He had taken a hand-car, in company with several other gentlemen, to go down the road, when his coat caught in the crank & he was thrown on the track. The wheels passed over his head & neck & he was killed.

The Columbia Times learns by telegraph from Charlotte, that Rev Cyrus Johnson, D D, of that town, died suddenly of apoplexy on Thu in an omnibus, whilst going to the railroad depot. He was on his way to **Fort Mills** for the purpose of marrying a gentleman & lady. He was the 2nd clergyman who had been engaged to perform the ceremony. The Rev A S Watts, who had been engaged for the same purpose, died on the day appointed for the wedding. –Wilmington [N C] Herald

Senate: 1-Ptn from Roger B Ironside, asking compensation for medical attendance on the Shasta Indians in Calif, under authority of the agent for those Indians. 2-Ptn from Wm Leonard, asking indemnity for depredations committed by the Pawnee Indians on his cattle, while journeying to Calif. 3-Ptn from J Williams, asking that the title of a certain tract of land in Calif may be confirmed to him & his minor children who failed to file their claim in time before the Com'rs. 4-Ptn from the heirs of Richd H Kerr, an assist surgeon under Capt Gunnison, asking to be allowed his pay from the time of his death to the return of the expedition, with the expenses incurred by him. 5-Ptn from John Rooney & other pensioners, asking an increase of their pension, & of all those who lost limbs in the war with Mexico. 6-Ptn from Chas W Dennison, late consul for British Guiana, asking reimbursement of expenses incurred in procuring information & collections in agriculture, commerce, mechanics, & science, in South America, for the Patent Ofc. 7-Ptn from Robt Morton, asking that a pension be allowed Abigail Morton as a widow of the Revolution may be paid to her children. 8-Cmte on Pensions: bill for the relief of Ley C Harris. Same cmte: bill for the relief of Mrs Anna W Angus, widow of the late Capt Angus, without amendment. Same cmte: adverse report on the ptn of Hiram Seat. Same cmte: asking to be discharged from the consideration of the ptns of Mrs J J McClelland, Irene G Scarritt, Mary A M Jones, & Frances W Webster, on the ground that these cases were embraced in a general bill. 9-Cmte on Pensions: submitted an adverse report on the ptns of Mrs Jane A Browner & of Myles T Wooley. 10-Cmte on Naval Affairs: asking to be discharged from the consideration of the memorials of Wm H Kennon, of the watchmen of the Navy Dept, of Prof Espy, from that of Henry Ruggles, & from resolutions in Maine in relation to the spirit ration: which was agreed to. 11-Cmte on Revolutionary Claims: bill for the relief of the widow & children of Ezra Chapman, deceased, & for the relief of the heirs of Lt Andrew Findlay, reported back without amendment. Also, from the same cmte, an adverse report on House bill for the relief of Nathl Reddick, adm of Richd Taylor.

Household & kitchen furniture at auction on: Feb 5, at the residence of Mrs Esterly, Pa ave, between 2nd & 3rd sts. -Green & Scott, aucts

Died: on Jan 28, in his 27th year, Edw McCulloh, a resident of Wash City. His funeral will take place from his late residence on Capitol Hill, today at 2½ P M.

Died: in PG Co, Md, in her 70th year, Mrs Sophia Mantle, wife of John Major. Her funeral will take place from her husband's residence, 1½ miles beyond Rock Creek Church, this day, at 2½ o'clock. [No death date given-current item.]

Phil, Jan 29. The coroner is investigating this morning the death of Michl Durkin, who died last night at the hospital from the effects of a blow on the head with a pound weight, inflicted on Thu by Michl Loughney.

WED JAN 31, 1855

The dismissal from the Navy of the U S of Lt Chas G Hunter is announced in the Star of last evening. He was recently in command of the brig **Bainbridge**, on the Brazilian station, &, in consequence of a difference of opinion as to their respective duties between him & the Cmdor of the squadron, he brought his vessel home without orders from his superior. For this act of insubordination the Pres has caused his name to be struck from the rolls of the Navy, which he entered 20 years ago.

Senate: 1-Ptn from Scott Campbell, interpreter & agent of the Sioux Indians, asking payment of an annuity secured by the treaty of 1837 between the U S & the Sioux Indians. 2-Ptn from John Shaw, a soldier of the war of 1812, asking relief by pension or otherwise. 3-Ptn from Christopher Cory, asking the appointment of competent agents for the purpose of testing the discovery of the nature & causes of the potato rot, together with the best mode of treating it. 4-Ptn from O F Johnson, of the U S Navy, asking to be allowed the difference of pay between midshipman & passed midshipman from Jun 8, 1852 to Jun 8, 1853. 5-Ptn from Ebenezer Clark, of Mississippi, asking an act to change the name of the schnr **Henry Plantagenet** to that of the schnr **A G Brown**. 6-Ptn of Fred'k Griffing, asking to be allowed the amount
withheld by the Sec of the Navy of the purchase money of the property at Brooklyn, N Y, between the naval & marine hospitals & navy yard, & sold by him to the U S. 7-Ptn from John Shaw, asking remuneration for losses sustained in furnishing 6 companies of rangers on the Mississippi with ammunition during the late war with Great Britain. 8-Ptn from Hyacinth Riopel, grandson of Ambrose Riopel, asking that the heirs of said Riopel may be confirmed in their titles to a certain tract of land which was surveyed, but the claim not finally acted on. 9-Ptn from Anna Tongue, heir of Col John Stuart, of the Revolutionary army, asking a pension. 10-Cmte on Naval Affairs: bill for the relief of John Guest, a Lt in the U S Navy. 11-Cmte on Military Affairs: memorial of Lt Jas Totten, asking to be reimbursed expenses incurred in selling commissary stores at auction, reported a bill for the relief of Jas Totten, U S Navy.

Trustee's sale of gold watches, chains, & silverware: by deed of trust, dated Aug 17, 1854: sale at the Auction Rooms, 6th st & Pa ave, on Feb 2. –Joshua A G McManners, trustee -Green & Scott, aucts

House of Reps: 1-Bill for the relief of R A Clements, adm of Jas A Mullican: referred. 2-Bill for the relief of Thos B Graham: referred. 3-Bill for the relief of D B Myers: referred. 4-Bill to re-establish *Snow Hill*, Md, as a separate collection district. 5-Cmte on Revolutionary Claims: bill for the relief of the heirs of Philip B Rice, deceased: committed. 6-Cmte on Commerce: adverse report on the ptn of Isaac S Smith. Same cmte: bill for the relief of Geo Dennett, of Portsmouth, N H, with the recommendation that it do not pass. Same cmte: bill for the relief of John R Bowes, the agent in charge of the property of the U S at Michigan City, Indiana: committed. Same cmte: adverse report on the ptn of Atkins Dyer. 7-Cmte on Military Affairs: bill for the relief of Catharine B Arnold: committed. Same cmte: bill for the relief of Wm G Preston, late a capt in the war of the U S with Mexico: committed. Same cmte: Lt John Clark, of Pa, obtained leave for the withdrawal from the files of the House of all the papers in relation to the said case. 8-Cmte of Claims: bill for the relief of Israel Ketcham; of the widow of Wm Irving, deceased; of Wm Haggerty; & of Thos S J Johnson: all committed. 9-Cmte on Revolutionary Claims: bill for the relief of the heirs of Thos Morris: committed. 10-Cmte on Naval Affairs: bill for the relief of Rebecca Winn, widow & excx of the last will & testament of Timothy Winn, deceased, late a purser in the U S Navy: committed. 11-Cmte on Invalid Pensions: bill for the relief of the assignee of bounty land warrant 27,849, issued to Wm Phillips & Sarah Connor, & a bill increasing the pension of Anthony Walter Bayard, of Pa: committed. Same cmte: bill to increase the pension of Patrick C Miles: committed.
12-Cmte on Private Land Claims: bill for the relief of Geo Bush, of Thruston Co, in the Territory of Wash; a bill for the relief of Jas P Roan; a bill confirming a land claim to Elijah White, of the Territory of Wash: committed.

Mrd: on Jan 27, by Rev W Hodges, Isaac Bradley to Miss Frances Broadhead, all of Wash City.

Mrd: Tue, by Rev John C Smith, Hendly Nelson to Miss Eliz Morland.

Mrd: Tue, by Rev John C Smith, Allen G Fox to Miss Martha V Whaley, all of Va.

Wash Corp: 1-Ptn from Patrick Keating for remission of a fine: referred to Cmte of Claims. 2-J F C Offut & others have leave to withdraw their papers from the files of the Board. 3-Ptn of B Guevall for remission of a fine: referred to Cmte of Claims. 4-Ptn from Jacob Kleiber, asking for increase of compensation as Messenger: referred to Cmte on Finance. 5-Ptn of Wm Aiken, for remission of a fine: referred to Cmte of Claims.

$150 reward for runaway negro man, David Young, about 30 or 31 years of age. He has a wife at Sylvester Boone's, relations at Capt John H Gwynn's, Tarleton Berry's, & near Benedict, where his former master, the late Wm Dyer, resided. –Wm H Gwynn, of Thos: living near Brandywine, PG Co, Md.

Circuit Court of Wash Co, D C, in Equity. The United States against Geo Schwartz, Maria Schwartz, Walter C Livingston, Mary L Livingston, Mgt A Dale, Jas Dundas, Clement S Miller, Wm C Cunningham, Jas Cunningham, Chas E Cunningham, Geo F Cunningham, Thos B Cunningham, Rebecca Washington, Robt Morris, John Cosgrove, Eliz Cosgrove, Mary Vanderheuvel, Henry W Morris, Caroline Stark, Harriet Morris, Emily Morris, Wm W Morris, Joshua L Husband, Mary M Husband, Henry Morris, Amelia S Morris, Robt Morris, Wm S Morris, Charlotte S Morris, Sallie Morris, Robt M Marshall, Jas Marshall, Richd Cary Ambler, Susan M Ambler, John Marshall, Henry M Marshall, Eliz Ninon, Hetty Ninon, John Moss, Emily N Moss, Edw N Waln, & Ellen Cora Waln. The bill, which is a bill of revivor, states that in Nov 1813, a bill of cmplnt was filed in the said Court by Thos Munroe, superintendent, in his own name, but in behalf of the U S, setting forth that Thos Law had purchased of Robt Morris & Jas Greenleaf a large amount of ground in Washington & took a mortgage from them to secure the title; that an agreement was then made between Law, Morris, Greenleaf, & Nicholson & the com'rs, by which the com'rs were to convey to Law 6 squares of his selection from the ground purchased by said Greenleaf & Morris of said com'rs, & Law was to release to said Morris, Nicholson, & Greenleaf 6 other squares of the ground mortgaged to him as aforesaid, & said squares were then to be conveyed to the com'rs to replace the former; that accordingly the com'rs conveyed to Law 6 squares, containing 792,939½ square feet of ground, & Law released squares 465, 468, 469, 470, 495, & 498, in Washington, to Robt Morris & Wm Cranch, as atty of said Morris, afterwards conveyed them to the com'rs; that, there being a supposed defect in said conveyance, one Wm Campbell, who had had an attachment issued against Morris, Nicholson, & Greenleaf, in the State of Md, for a debt, caused it to be levied on said 6 squares as their property, & procured a judgment condemning them for payment of said debt, the validity of which judgment of condemnation was still contested between said Campbell & Henry Pratt, Thos Willing Francis, John Miller, jr, John Ashley, & Jacob Baker, assignees of Morris, Nicholson, & Greenleaf; that said bill denies the validity of said condemnation, or that in any event it could affect more than the equitable title of said parties in said squares, which was nothing; it claims that, to whomsoever the legal title be adjudged, he or they would be bound to convey to the U S; but that if the attachment be sustained Law would be bound to return the ground conveyed to him, the consideration of the agreement to which he was privy failing, or to indemnify the U S out of the property mortgaged to him, or else to pay the balance of purchase money due for the ground conveyed to him from Morris & Nicholson to the U S. The bill of revivor further states that Law subsequently filed an answer to said bill of cmplnt, admitting the agreement set out in the bill, but denying an responsibility for defects in the deed from Cranch; that in Oct, 1815, Wm Campbell filed his answer stating his ignorance of said agreement & his belief that according to it the squares conveyed to the com'rs were intended only to secure payment for the squares conveyed to Law; that two of these were paid for & the rest might have been but for the negligence of the com'rs, wherefore they are not entitled to any lien on the 6 squares conveyed to them; that in Dec 1815, John Miller, jr, filed an answer stating that he is the bankrupt & insolvent assignee of Greenleaf, admitting that Greenleaf conveyed to Morris & Nicholson, but claiming that it was upon conditions & considerations which have failed, whereby the property conveyed, including the 6 squares, has reverted to Greenleaf & become vested in respondent, or at least ought first to indemnify him for the failure of Morris & Nicholson to perform their agreement, & denying that Greenleaf was privy to the agreement aforesaid, & that the conveyance to Law was the consideration of the 6 squares, & insisting that Greenleaf's lien for puchase money is paramount to any claim of the com'rs. The said bill of revivor further shows that on Jun 21, 1826, orders were passed in said cause giving each party leave to take out commissions & directing an audit of the accounts between the U S & Morris, Greenleaf, & Nicholson & of the claim of the cmplnt on the 6 squares, & that no further proceedings have been since had in the cause. It further shows that all the dfndnts to said original cause are dead; that no one has been substituted for John Miller, jr, as assignee of Greenleaf; that Greenleaf's heirs-at-law are Maria Schwartz wife of Geo Schwartz, Mary L Livingston wife of Walter C Livingston, & Mgt A Dale, a widow; that the assignees of Morris & Nicholson by survivorship & mesne conveyances are Jas Dundas, & Clement S Miller; that the heirs-at-law of Wm Campbell are Wm C Cunningham, Jas Cunningham, Chas E Cunningham, Geo F Cunningham, Thos B Cunningham, & Rebecca Washington; that the heirs-at-law of Robt Morris are Robt Morris, Eliz Cosgrove wife of John Cosgrove, Mary Vanderheuvel, widow, Henry Morris, Caroline Stark, a widow, Harriet Morris, Emily Morris, Wm W Morris, Mary M Husband wife of Joshua L Husband, Henry Morris, Amelia S Morris, Robt Morris, Wm S Morris, Charlotte S Morris, Sallie Morris, Robt M Marshall, Jas Marshall, Susan M Ambler wife of Richd Cary Ambler, John Marshall, Henry M Marshall, Eliz Ninon, Hetty Ninon, Emily N Moss wife of John Moss, & Ella Cora Waln wife of Edw N Waln. It further shows that none of said original parties or their heirs have interfered with the property in question or asserted title to it since the suit commenced otherwise than by their answers aforesaid, & that Greenleaf expressly disclaimed all title. It prays that the suit may be revived against said heirs & assigns, & that the heirs of Robt Morris may be required to convey the 6 squares above mentioned, in Washington, to the U S. It further states that all of said parties dfndnts are non-residents. Said parties to appear in Court on or before the first Monday of Jun next. –Jas Dunlop -Jno A Smith, clerk

THU FEB 1, 1855

Wash City Ordinances: 1-Act for the relief of Saml Samsctag: the fine of $20 is remitted: Samsctag to pay the costs of prosecution.

Governess wanted in a private family, who is capable of giving instruction in music on the piano & all the usual branches of female education. Compensation: a salary of $200, with board as one of the family in all respects. A member of the Protestant Episcopal Church would be preferred. Address Dr W H Briscoe, Leonardtown, St Mary's Co, Md.

Senate: 1-Ptn from C F French & A J Meincke, asking to be allowed to take out a register for the Russian ship **Aina**, purchased by them in the port of N Y at a sale by a U S Marshal. 2-Ptn from Lorin Blodget, asking Congress to direct an equitable hearing & adjustment of his claims against the Smithsonian Institution, for services rendered & expenses incurred while in the employment of said Institution. 3-Cmte on Pensions: adverse reports on the ptns of Wm Goff & Thos Dinsmore. 4-Cmte on Revolutionary Claims: adverse reports on: act for the legal reps of Henry Hoffman; of Thos Underhill, exc of Thos Underhill, deceased; & of the legal reps of Edw Meade.
5-Cmte on Naval Affairs: bill for the relief of Oscar F Johnson; & adverse report on the memorial of Thos W Tansill. 6-Bill for the relief of Jacob Dodson: passed.

Mrd: on Jan 30, at Foundry Parsonage, by Rev E P Phelps, Mr Jacob Slingland to Mary E Kennedy, both of Alexandria, Va.

Dissolution of copartnership, by mutual consent. Chas Haskins will settle the accounts. –J H Adams, jr, Chas Haskins.
+
Chas Haskins, Architect, Pa ave, between 10th & 11th sts, will continue the business.

U S Patent Ofc, Wash, Jan 31, 1855. Ptn of Chas Davenport & Albert Bridges, formerly of Bridgeport, Mass, praying for the extension of a patent granted to them on May 4, 1841, for an improvement in the manner of constructing railroad carriages so as to ease the lateral motion of the bodies thereof, for 7 years from the expiration date of May 4, 1855. –Chas Mason, Com'r of Patents

FRI FEB 2, 1855
We announce the decease, on Feb 1, at his residence in Wash City, after a lingering illness, of Senor Don Felipe Molina, Minister Plenipotentiary of Costa Rica, Guatemala, & San Salvador. His death is sincerely regretted.

N Y papers: Hon Herman Knickerbocker died on Jan 30, at the residence of his son-in-law, in Wmsburgh, in his 76th year. He was a descendant in the 3rd generation of the first emigrant of that name from Holland to the then colony of N Y. Inheriting an ample fortune, he entered the political field at an early period of his life & in 1810 was elected to the Federal party to the U S House of Reps from the Rensselaer district. Diedrich Knickerbocker, in his preface to his history of N Y, alludes to Judge K as his "cousin the Congressman."

Hon Junius Hillyer, of Ga, & Hon Roland Jones, of La, have declined being candidates for re-election to Congress.

Mrd: on Jan 30, by Rev J B Spottswood, Lloyd Tilghman, of Centreville, Md, to Miss Mary M, daughter of Chancellor Johns, of Newcastle, Delaware.

Senate: 1-Ptn from Edw Riddle, asking reimbursement for expenses incurred as agent of the American contributors to the Industrial exhibition in London in 1851. 2-Ptn from Wm M F Magraw, contractor for carrying the mail from Independence, Mo, to Salt Lake, in Utah territory, asking compensation for losses & expenses in consequence of Indian hostilities. 3-Ptn from Alfred G Benson, asking indemnity for losses sustained in consequence of the failure on the part of the Peruvian Gov't to fulfill an agreement entered into between that Gov't & the U S in relation to Guano. 4-Ptn from the heirs of Edw Rogers, asking reimbursement of money advanced by their ancestor for the public use during the Revolutionary war. 5-Cmte on Commerce: bill for the relief of Ferdinand Clark: recommended its passage. Same cmte: asking to be discharged from the consideration of the memorial of John Thomas, asking an examination of a marine railway: which was agreed to. 6-Cmte on Pensions: bill for the relief of Lot Davis: reported back without amendment. 7-Cmte on Public Lands: bill for the relief of Jas Hodges Gale: passed. 8-Bill for the relief of Mrs Anna W Angus be recommitted to the Cmte on Pensions: agreed to. 9-Cmte on Retrenchment: asking to be discharged from the consideration of the ptn of memorial of Wm G Ridgely, chief clerk in the bureau of yards & docks, & that it be referred to the Cmte on Naval Affairs: agreed to. Same cmte: adverse report on the memorial of John Heneage, a reporter. 10-Cmte of Claims: bill for the relief of Lt Col Edw R S Canby. Same cmte: bill for the relief of the heirs of Jabez R Rooker. Same cmte: bill for the relief of Jos Loranger. Same cmte: bill for the relief of Jas T B Thompson. 11-Cmte on Revolutionary Claims: bill for the relief of the heirs of Col Wm Grayson: reported back with an amendment. Same cmte: bill for the relief of the legal reps of Richd Kidder Meade. 12-Cmte on Pensions: bill for the relief of Pamelia Slavin, wife of John Blue, deceased: reported it back without amendment. From the cmte was referred the bill for the relief of Thos T Russell, of Florida, submitted an adverse report on the same. 13-Cmte on Printing: in favor of printing the memorial of Aaron V Palmer: which was agreed to.

The undersigned have associated themselves under the firm of Hutchenson & Munro, for the purpose of carrying on the Fancy Business, & have taken the new store next to Harper's, 310 Pa ave, between 9th & 10th sts, & will open on Feb 5. –Jos Hutchenson, Jas B Munro

Mrd: on Jan 31, by Rev Mr Boyer, Alex'r J Dallas, U S Marine, to Frances V Masi, daughter of S Masi, of Wash City.

Died: on Jan 31, Stephen Pleasonton, Fifth Auditor of the Treasury Dept of the U S, in his 79th year, after an illness of 10 days. His funeral will be from his late residence, 385 west 21st st, on Sat at 12 o'clock, to proceed to the *Congressional Cemetery*. [Feb 3rd newspaper: Mr Pleasonton discharged his duties as Auditor for 50 years, & was retained in the place he so ably filled by 12 Presidential administrations.]

Died: on Thu, His Excellency Senor Don Felipe Molina, Minister of Costa Rica, Guatemala, & Salvador. His funeral will take place on Feb 3, at 12 o'clock. The cortege will leave the residence of the deceased, corner of 15th & G sts, & proceed to St Matthew's Church, where the body will be deposited. [Feb 3rd newspaper: the funeral cortege of the late Senor Molina, will move from his late residence, 15th & G sts, at 11 o'clock, this forenoon.]

House of Reps: 1-Cmte on Revolutionary Claims: reported adversely on the ptns of Mrs Barbara Rall, widow of Thos Rall, deceased; & of A S Jordan & B Jordan, sons of Thos Jordan.

SAT FEB 3, 1855
The city of Washington has just sustained a severe loss in the death of a most valued citizen, John W Maury, who died yesterday, after an illness of 5 or 6 days, of intestinal inflammation or derangement, as we understand. He had filled with honor the Chief Magistracy of Wash City, & the native nobility of his character, his kindness, liberality to the poor, public spirit & usefulness, & his domestic & social virtues, had combined to win for him the affection & respect of all classes of men. Mr Maury was in his 46th year, & leaves a widow & 12 children, 5 sons & 7 daughters, the eldest a son 22 years old & the youngest a daughter between 2 & 3 years old. He was born in Caroline Co, Va, where his parents still reside, & he came to Wash City when he was 17 years old, & acted in the capacity of clerk. He was Pres of the Bank of the Metropolis of Wash City at the time of his death. He was aware for 12 hours before his death that he must die in a few hours, & met death calmly & willingly. [Feb 5th newspaper: yesterday the remains of John W Maury were conveyed to Trinity Church in the afternoon, where Rev Dr Cummings read the impressive funeral services of the Episcopal Church.]

The South Carolina papers announce the death of Rev Wm Capers, D D, Bishop of the Methodist Episcopal Church South. He died suddenly on Jan 29, of disease of the heart, at his residence in Anderson. Dr Capers was born in St Thos Parish, on Jan 26, 1790: received the degree of M A from the S C College; received into the annual Conference of native State as a traveling Minister in 1808; in 1828 he was sent to England as Rep of the American Meth Episc Church to the British Conference, & for several years he was one of the general Missionary Secretaries. He was elected Bishop in 1846. –Charleston Courier

Senate: 1-Bill granting bounty land to Susan Palmer, widow of Lt Junio B Palmer: passed. 2-Cmte of Claims: bill for the relief of the heirs of Jos Gerrard: passed.

House of Reps: 1-Bill for the relief of Dr Wm F Sherrod: introduced. 2-Cmte on Invalid Pensions: bills committed: relief of Kennedy O'Brian; of Joel Collins; of Wm Bullock; of Salvador Accardi; of Abner Merrill; and a pension to Chas Connor.

Same cmte: adverse reports on the ptns of Dr Richd W Stockton; of Thos Hendrickson, of Jasper Co, Ky; of E F Gilbert; of John Henry; of Mrs Ann Nippins; of Martha Swain, daughter of Jas Swain; of Jas Harrington; of Jane M Rudolph, widow of Thos C Rudolph; of Jas B Langdale; of Maurice K Simons; of Saml Butler; of Wm Pool; of J W Knipe, of Pa; of Jas Simmons, of Green Co, Tenn; & of F A Heisley. 3-Cmte on Military Affairs: bill for the relief of Richd Fitzpatrick: committed. Same cmte: bill for the relief of Mrs Isabella Crough, mother of the late Lt Michl P Doyle, of the 15th Regt U S Infty: committed. Same cmte: adverse report on the ptns of Mgt & Eliz Clapsdale, heirs of Hohn Jost Hess, & of Jacob Rudolph. Same cmte: joint resolution for the relief of Joel Henry Dyer: committed. 4-Cmte on Private Land Claims: bill for the relief of Lewis Benedict; bill to confirm the title of Ruhama Whitaker & Rebecca Whitaker to certain lands in the State of Louisiana; & a bill for the relief of the legal reps of John Erwin, deceased: committed. Same cmte: adverse reports on the ptns of C G Hunter & of Gaston Turner Raoul; on the joint resolution of Washington Territory, relative to a confirmation of a land claim to Edw Giddings, jr; & a bill of the House for the relief of Nathl Ewing, assignee of the interest of H Richard: laid on the table. 5-Cmte of Claims: bill for the relief of Isaac Swain: committed. Same cmte: joint resolution in favor of Wm Monagan: passed. 6-Cmte on Comerce: adverse report on the ptn of John P Norton. Same cmte: adverse reports on the ptns of Henry Smalley, of Troy; of Thos C Cardwell; on ptns of Wm Harper, of Miles Castin, & of citizens of Galveston, Texas, relative to the superintendence of the pier-lights in that harbor. 7-Cmte on Public Lands: bill for the relief of Willis Bennefiel: committed. Same cmte: adverse report on the bill of the Senate granting bounty land to Eliz Summers: laid on the table. Same cmte: adverse reports on the ptns of Sylvanus L Henderson; of Eunice Fairbanks, widow of Elisha Howard; of John Barrett; & of the citizens of White Co, Ark, in behalf of Hugh Reed. 8-Cmte on the Judiciary: discharged from the consideration of the ptn of G B Lamar, of N Y; of Abelard Guthrie; of J B Woodfin; of Jos Mahan; of Enoch Honeywell; & the opinion of the Supreme Court of R I in the case of Thos W Dorr. 9-Cmte on Revolutionary Claims: adverse reports on the ptns of Clement Sewell; & of the heirs of Capt Fred'k Schoonmaker. Same cmte: adverse reports on the ptns of the heirs of Wm Curry, deceased; of John T Hargrave & the other heirs of Alex'r Rose, deceased; & of John W Wilder, adm of Stephen C Graham, deceased. Same cmte: bill for the relief of Caroline Fierer, deceased, the sole surviving residuary legatee of Chas Fierer: committed. Cmte on the Post Ofc & Post Roads: bill for the relief of Jos Carr, of Iowa. 10-Cmte on Foreign Affairs: bill for the relief of Henry S Sanford: committed. 11-Cmte on Naval Affairs: adverse report on the ptn of Jas C McCormick, assignee of Robt A Parker. 12-Cmte on Revolutionary Claims: adverse report on the ptn of Alan Mead, Walter Mead, & Mary Ann Sniffin, & on the ptn of Willis Wilson. 13-Cmte on Revolutionary Pensions: bill increasing the pension of Mrs Frances Smith, of S C: committed. Same cmte: bill for the relief of the heirs of Judith Worthen, deceased: committed. Same cmte: adverse reports on the ptns of Matthew Vandiver; of Avis Ennis, of Newport, R I; of John C Finckel, only surviving son of Dr Philip Finckel; & of Peter Guise. Same cmte: adverse reports on the ptns of the heirs & legal reps of John Cotton & of Tabitha Lester. Same cmte: adverse report on the ptn of the heirs of Saml Tibbald. 14-Cmte on Public Expenditures: bill for the relief of Jos C G Kennedy: committed. 15-The following bills were appropriately referred: relief of: Ephraim Hunt; of Mary Felch, widow of Rev Cheever Felch, deceased; of Capt Thos Ap Catesby Jones; of Jacob Dodson; of Jas Hodges Gale; & of Saml A Belden & Co. 16-Bill laid aside with a favorable recommendation: relief of: don B Juan Domercq, a Spanish subject; of Henry H Marsh; of E J McLane; of John Dugan; of the legal reps of Wm A Christian; of Jos Ridgway; of Wm Brown; of Jas McIntire; os Solomon La Follett; of Thos C Ramsey & Annanias O Richardson; of Isaac Allen, of Turner, Maine; of Geo M Bentley, of Indiana; of Wyatt Griffith, of Wash Co, Tenn; of Geo W McCerren; of Medford Caffey, of Tenn; of Paul S Ridgway; of Jas Hughes; of Fred'k Griffing; of the heirs-at-law of Wm Van Wart, deceased; of Catharine B Arnold; of the widow of W Irving, deceased; of the heirs of Thos Morris, deceased; of Wm Haggerty; of Rebecca Winn, widow & excx of the last will & testament of Timothy Winn, deceased, late a purser in the U S Navy; of Thos S J Johnson; of the assignee of bounty land warrant 27849, issued to Wm Phillips & Sarah Connor; of Wm G Preston, late a capt in the war of the U S with Mexico; of Geo Bush, of Thurston Co, Wash Territory; of Jas P Roan; of John R Bowes, agent in charge of the property of the U S at Michigan City, in Indiana; increase the pension of Patrick C Miles; of Anthony W Bayard, of Bellfont, Pa; pension to Jos McCormick; bill for the benefit of the heirs of Philip R Rice, deceased. Bill for the relief of Geo Dennett, of Portsmouth N H, laid aside: with the recommendation that it do not pass.

Died: on Feb 2, at his residence in Wash City, in his 46th year, John W Maury. The ardent devotion of a large family, the recorded honors of high & delicate official trust, & a large fortune, the product of his industry & enterprise, were the rewards that blessed his years. The funeral of Mr Maury will take place on Sunday afternoon, at 3 o'clock, from his late residence.

Mrd: on Feb 1, at **Cool Spring Farm**, near Wash City, by Rev Mr Leachman, Mr Geo W Dawson, of Wm, of Logan Co, Ky, to Miss Frances A Isherwood, daughter of the late Robt Isherwood.

Mrd: on Feb 1, in Wash City, by Rev J M P Atkinson, Geo Lowry to Eliz D, eldest daughter of the late Geo Johnson, all of Wash City.

The Maine Giant: her name is Silva Hardy, a native of Wilton, Franklin Co, & is 7 feet 6 inches in height, is rather lean than fleshy, yet weighs 330 pounds, is nearly 30 years of age, & is still growing; maintaining herself in the capacity of a nurse. Her mother is said to have been below medium size & her father not above it. She was a twin, & at birth weighed but 3½ pounds; her mate did not live. –Portland Argus

MON FEB 5, 1855

Mrd: on Jan 31, 1855, at Quantico, near Dumfries, Va, by Elder John Clark, Henry F Williams, of San Francisco, Calif, to Eliz Dunnington, only daughter of Dr R W Wheat.

Died: on Feb 4, at his residence near Wilmington, Lt Robt E Johnson, of the U S Navy, aged about 46 years. He was a native of Warren Co, N C, & entered the navy in 1827. As an ofcr he was faithful & energetic, & as a man his life was honorable. He has left an affectionate wife & many relatives & friends to mourn his loss.

Died: on Sat last, in Wash City, Mrs Eliz Davis, relict of the late Chas B Davis, in her 79th year. Her funeral is this day at 3 o'clock, from the residence of her son, Geo A Davis, 9th st, near M.

Died: on Sat, in Wash City, Mrs Mary E Cochran, of New London, Conn, wife of John W Cochran, of N Y, in her 23rd year. Her funeral is this morning at 11 o'clock, from her late residence on F st, opposite the Patent Ofc.

House of Reps: 1-Private bills passed: relief of: Thos C Ramsey & Ananias O Richardson; of John R Bowes, agent in charge of the property of the U S at Michigan City, Indiana. The former bill was amended by including within its benefits Jas McLaughlin, of Va, & the latter was amended by the addition of a section for the relief of Isaac S Smith, of Buffalo, N Y. 2-Recommended that the bill for the relief of Geo Dennett do not pass. 3-Cmte on the Judiciary: bill for the relief of Jos Nourse, deceased: committed.

Govn'r Gardner, of Mass, has issued an official order discharging Col Benj F Butler, of the 5th Regt of light Infty, from the militia service, in consequence of his refusal to execute the order commanding him to disband a foreign company attached to his regt. Col Butler is a lawyer of some eminence, & denied the Govn'rs authority to act in the summary manner that he did, & threatened to bring the question to a legal issue. Mr John Mitchell, in an address to the disbanded companies, recommends that for every musket given in to the State armory three be purchased forthwith.

Capt Simeon Hicks, the last of the Americans who were in the battle of Bennington, died at the residence of his grandson, Maynard Knight, in Sunderland, Vt, on Jan 24, aged 99 years, 5 months & 2 days. He was born in Mass, Aug 22, 1755, & was the eldest of 22 children. Capt Hicks served in the Revolutionary army, first under Washington at Cambridge & afterwards under Stark in 1777.

Phil, Feb 3. This afternoon, as large crowds were skating on the Schuylkill river, above Fairmount, the ice broke, & Mr Earle F Shinn, druggist, & a Miss Russell, his wife's sister, were drowned. Mr Shinn belonged to one of our oldest & most respectable Quaker families.

Died: on Feb 4, Mr Thos Jarboe, in his 46th year. His funeral will take place this day at 3 o'clock, from his late residence, near the corner of 6th st & Mass ave.

Wm Thompson, who has been confined to his bed by rheumatism for about 14 years, during which time he had not been able to walk one step, nor even to sit up in his bed, was married on Jan 17 to Miss Mgt Morris, of Smyth Co, Va.

Circuit Court of Wash Co, D C-in Chancery. Mary Hoffman, adm & heir at law of Thos Moore, deceased, vs Hannah Moore & Jas Moore, heirs at law of said Thos Moore, deceased. The bill states that the cmplnt, Mary Hoffman, as admx upon the personal estate of said Thos Moore, late of the County & District aforesaid, deceased, has fully administered said personal estate, & that the same is not sufficient for the payment of the debts of said Thos Moore & has become exhausted; that the said Thos Moore died seized of certain real estate, being all that piece or parcel of ground lying & being in Wash City, D C, known as square 303, with bldgs, improvements, & appurtenances, & leaving the said Mary Hoffman & the dfndnts, Hannah Moore & Jas Moore, his sisters & nephew, his only heirs at law; that said cmplnt & dfndnts are now joint owners & tenants in common of said parcel of ground, & that the same produces little or no income, is subject to taxation, & depreciating in value; that a sale thereof is necessary for the payment of the debts of said Thos Moore, & would be greatly to the interest & advantage of the said cmplnt & dfndnts, heirs at law of said Thos Moore; & that said dfndnt, Hannah Moore, resides out of D C & the jurisdiction of this Court, in England, in the kingdom of Great Britain. The object of the bill is to procure a decree for the sale of said piece or parcel of ground & premises, & the appointment of a suitable person as trustee to make such a sale for the payment of said debts of said Thos Moore. Absent dfndnt, Hannah Moore, to appear in this Court on or before the second Monday in June next. –Jas Dunlop, Assist Judge -Jno A Smith, clerk

TUE FEB 6, 1855
Orphans Court of Wash Co, D C. In the case of Thos C Magruder, adm de bonis non, with the will annexed, of Thos Boothe, dec'd, the adm & Court appointed Feb 27, for final settlement of the estate, of assets in hand. -Ed N Roach, Reg/o wills

Senate: 1-Ptn from the administrator of F Burt, dec'd, late Govn'r of Nebraska, asking reimbursement of the traveling expenses incurred by the deceased in proceeding to Nebraska to enter upon the duties of his ofc. 2-Ptn from Wm Jones & others, of Barney's florilla, in the war of 1812, asking to be included in the benefits of the bounty land bill now pending before Congress. 3-Addition testimony in the case of the cognizors of Otho Hinton: referred. 4-Ptn from Louisa W Tutwiler, asking the renewal of certain lost certificates of forfeited land scrip issued in the name of her father. 5-Ptn from Jos Wandestrand, asking the confirmation of a title to a tract of land in Louisiana. 6-Ptn from Jno Derelin, asking an appropriation to enable him to defray the expense of the publication of a new system of astronomy. 7-Ptn from Danl Doland, a soldier in the war with Mexico, asking a pension. 8-Ptn from Theodore Adams, asking indemnity for loss occasioned by the annulment of his contract for bldg an appraiser's store at San Francisco. 9-Ptn from Aaron Livingston & other settlers in good faith on the Bastrop grant, asking that their titles may be confirmed. 10-Ptn from Mariano G Vallejo, asking to be compensated for the use of his property at Sonora by troops of the U S. 11-Ptn from Starr G Spalding, a paymaster's clerk in the war with Mexico, asking bounty land & his traveling expenses. 12-Ptn from Boyd Reilly, asking a renewal of his patent for a portable apparatus for the convenient & safe application of gaseous & other vapors; & also from the same, asking further compensation fo his invention of the same.

I hereby warn & forewarn all person from crediting any one on my account, as I will pay no more debts contracted without my written order. –W P Faherty
-Ed N Roach, Reg/o wills

Orphans Court of Wash Co, D C. In the case of John T Cochran, adm of David Cordery, deceased, the adm & Court have appointed Jan 27, for the final settlement of the estate of said deceased, of the assets in hand. –Ed N Roach, Reg/o wills

Mrd: on Feb 4, by Rev Stephen P Hill, Wm W Hedley to Alice Beecher, all of this District.

Died: on Feb 5, Mary Buford, only daughter of Lewis & Mary C Waring, aged 3 years & 3 months. His funeral is today at 12 M, from the residence of Maj Scott, H st, & 20th.

Died: on Feb 4, in Wash City, Andrew J Davidson, in his 10th year, son of John B & Mary A Davidson, & grandson of the late Richd Rock, of Alexandria. His funeral will be this afternoon, at 2 o'clock, from his father's residence, corner of 12th st & Md ave.

Lost, one piece of Bounty Land Scrip, No 5,541, for 62½ acres, issued Sep 6, 1854, on warrant No 9,553, by the Com'r of the Gen Land Ofc at Wash, in favor of Martha J Goddin, one of the heirs of Edw Digges, deceased, a captain in the Va State Line, & forwarded by mail Oct 27, 1854. Unless heard from within 6 weeks application will be made for a duplicate. –Wm Sumner, agent

Loudon Land & Iron Ore Mine for sale: under a decree of the Circuit Court of Loudoun Co, pronounced on Oct 13, 1854, in the case of Sarah Ann Dawson, widow & excx of Saml Dawson, deceased, & others, cmplnts, against Andrew Ellicott & others, dfndnts, the undersigned will, on Mar 24 next, offer at the Court-house in Leesburg, Loudoun Co, Va, at public auction, a tract of land in said county containing about 59½ acres, known as **The Iron Ore Field**. –D Hixson, com'r

Concord, Feb 5. Rev John Moore, late the Know-Nothing candidate for Govn'r, died suddenly yesterday.

Marshal's sale: by writ of fieri facias, the property of Roger C Weightman, being part of lot 7 in square 491, & next adjoining lot 8, fronting 20 feet on Pa ave, with the bldgs & improvements thereon, in square 491, in Wash City, D C. Seized & levied upon as the property of Roger C Weightman, & sold to satisfy judicials No 3 to Mar term, 1855, in favor of Mary E Barney, by Maxwell Woodhull, her next friend. –J D Hoover, Marshall for D C

WED FEB 7, 1855
Senate: 1-Documents presented in support of the claim of Martha Scott, widow of a Revolutionary soldier. 2-Ptn from Wm H French, in behalf of the widow of J S K Reeves, late of the army, for a pension. 3-Additional documents presented in relation to the claim of G R Drake. 4-Ptn from Robt Graham, asking the confirmation of a title to certain lands sustained in consequence of the falling of the iron bridge at Little Falls, Potomac river, for the bldg of which he had contracted. 5-Ptn from Sarah Larabee & others, widows of soldiers of the war of 1812, asking that where a woman is a widow of 2 husbands that may have served in that war she may be allowed a pension in each case. 6-Ptn from Geo H Gordon, wounded in the war with Mexico, asking a pension. 7-Ptn from Horatio J Petty, asking compensation for services rendered & expenses incurred while acting as charge d'affaires of the U S to Spain. 8-Ptn from R S Patterson & other citizens of Washington, asking an appropriation for the improvement of East Capitol st. 9-Ptn from the administrator of Calvin Read, asking payment for lumber supplied by him for the erection of a fort at Mandarin bay. 10-Additional documents presented relating to the claim of the heirs of Edw Rogers. 11-Cmte on Private Land Claims: bill for the relief of Richd Albritten. Same cmte: asking to be discharged from the consideration of the memorial of Jacob Kerr, & that it be referred to the Cmte of Claims: which was agreed to. 12-Cmte on Military Affairs: joint resolution for the relief of John Dugan: recommended its passage. 13-Cmte of Claims: bills from the House-recommended their passage: relief of: Gilbert C Russell; the widow of Wm Irving; & of Thos S J Johnson, of the Territory of New Mexico. 14-Cmte on Military Affairs: bill for the relief of Jas Huges: reported it back without amendment.

Same cmte: adverse report on the memorial of Wm Read, asking pay for difficult services performed when the early settlers of Tennessee were about being overrun by hostile Indians. 15-Cmte of Pensions: bill restoring Joshua Mercer to the roll of invalid pensioners. 16-Cmte on Naval affairs: adverse reports on the memorials of Wm B Scott, late Navy Agent at Wash, D C, & on that of R Piermont & others, asking compensation for saving the U S ships **Raritan** & **Vandalia** from fire in 1847. 17-Cmte on Pensions: bill for the relief of the heirs of Simon Smith. Same cmte: adverse report on the ptns of Sarah Griff, & of Danl Littlefield. Same cmte: asking to be discharged from the consideration of the bill for the relief of Mrs Anna

W Angus: which was agreed to. 18-Cmte on Foreign Relations: bill for the relief of Saml A Belden & Co: passed. 19-Cmte on Indian Affairs: asking to be discharged from the consideration of the memorial of Wm Walker: which was agreed to. 20-Cmte of Claims: bill for the relief of Franklin Chase: passed. 21-Bill for the relief of John Steene, to place him on a pension roll: passed. 22-Bill for the relief of the heirs of Larkin Smith. The Cmte on Revolutioanry Claims had stricken out the interest, & Mr Hunter moved that the Senate concur: passed. 23-Bill for the relief of Brev Brig Gen John B Walbach, of the U S Army, was agreed to & passed.

While Mr Richd B Marchant & Capt Jonathan Worth, of Edgartown, were on a clamming cruise down the harbor at that place, on Tue, the boat was met by a squall & overturned, & they were drowned. They both were about 52 years of age.

Frank May, the absconding cashier of the Farmers & Mechanics' Bank of Indianapolis, writes from Crestline, Ohio, to Mr A May, his uncle, & owner of the bank, that he only took $7,000, & regrets his course extremely; that he did not contemplate leaving 2 hours before he departed, & has not the nerve to return. Mr A May says that amount exceeds $7,000, & the 2 hours part is false, as Frank gave orders the night before to be aroused earlier than usual.

Mr Lyon & Mr Egan were killed when they were sent with others to free the wheels of the steamer **Ottawa**, when ice accumulated on the wheels. While engaged, by misunderstanding, the engine was started and precipated them into the water.

Wash City Ordinance: 1-Act for the relief of Henry Turner: to be refunded $31.50 for taxes assessed to & paid for the year 1854 on the brick houses erected by him on lot 13 in square 345, 3 of said houses not being tenantable until afer Jan 1, 1854. 2-Act for the relief of Nicholas Funk: pay to him $11.16, for assessment on part of lot 24 in square 101, on the books of this Corp in the name of F A Wagler, for paving the alley in said square, the lot not touching on the alley.

The Newburyport Herald reports the death of Orlando B Merrill, of that city, at age 92 years, probably one of the oldest ship-builders in the country. He built the U S ship **Pickering** in 1783 & the U S sloop-of-war **Wasp** in 1813. He appeared quite vigorous & well at the celebration in Newburyport on Jul 4th last.

Died: on Feb 6, after a long & painful illness, Mr Bernard Parsons, in his 82nd year, a native of St Mary's Co, Md, & for the last 60 years a resident of Wash City. He was industrious, honest, charitable, kind to the widow & orphan, a good father, & a worthy citizen. His funeral will take place on Thu, at 10 o'clock, from his late residence on 6th st, & proceed to St Peter's Church, Capitol Hill, where high solemn mass will be offered up.

Died: yesterday, in Wash City, after a few hours' illness, the only child of Rev Dickson Lewis, a rep of the Choctaw nation to this Gov't. His funeral is this afternoon, at 3 o'clock, from the residence of Mrs Clark, 387 9th st. Friends of Mr Lewis & family are respectfully invited to attend.

The London papers brought by the last arrivals mention the deaths of Sir Jas Kempt & Sir Andrew Barnard, two of the most distinguished of Wellington's ofcrs. Sir Jas Kempt entered the army so long ago, that he had attained the rank of lt colonel before the commencement of the present century. Sir Barnard has been 14 years in the service. [No death dates given-current item.]

THU FEB 8, 1854
Senate: 1-Ptn from Thos Cahill, asking to be remunerated for expenses incurred by him in relieving his brother, who died from injuries received at the Phil navy yard. 2-Ptn from Wm W Martin, asking to change the name of the steamboat **Fanny Fern** to **Thos H Stuart**. 3-Ptn from the widow of Chas Duffy, killed at the Phil navy Yard, asking an appropriation for her support. Also, from Mary Putnam, who husband was killed at said yard. 4-Cmte on Naval Affairs: House bills-recommended their passage: relief of-Rebecca Winn, widow of & excx of Timothy Winn, deceased; of the legal reps of Wm A Christian; & of Sarah Morris, only heir of Robt Mitchell, deceased. Same cmte: asking to be discharged from the consideration of the memorial of Wm G Ridgely, chief clerk in the bureau of docks & yards. 5-Cmte on the Judiciary: asking to be discharged from the consideration of the ptn of memorial of L Blodget in relation to a claim against the Smithsonian Institution, & that it be referred to the Cmte of Claims: which was agreed to. 6-Cmte on Pensions: discharged from the further consideration of the ptn of Wm Wood, asking that a pension be allowed the widow of Geo W F Wood, who died of yellow fever while in the discharge of his duty, on the ground that a general bill had been reported providing for applicants of that class, & placing widow of ofcrs of the army on the same footing as those of the navy. Same cmte: asked to be discharged from the consideration of the ptn of Mgt Williams & Maria Wendell, & that it be referred to the Cmte on Revolutionary Claims: which was agreed to. Same cmte: bill for the relief of Michl Hennessey. 7-Cmte on Private Land Claims: land claim to Elijah White of the Territory of Wash; act for the relief of Geo Bush, of Thruston Co, Wash Territory. 8-Cmte of Claims: joint resolution for the relief of John Y Laub, a clerk in the ofc of the 1st Comptroller: passed. 9-Cmte on Pensions: bill for the relief of Catherine Dickerson, the lady being now 90 years of age: passed. Same cmte: bill for the relief of Mrs Nancy Weatherford, widow of Col Wm Weatherford, of the 1st regt of Ill volunteers in the Mexican war, reported it without amendment. Mrs Weatherford was the relict of a very gallant ofcr, who died from injuries received in the Mexican war. 10-Cmte on Pension: adverse reports on: John G Watmough, asking increase of pension; of Eliza Gibbons, mother of Thos Gibbons, who died while in the navy; & of Geo Middleton, for remuneration for services in the war of 1812.

Balt Patriot of last evening: Col Standifer, U S Army, a gentleman of Cambridge, Eastern Shore, of Md, died at that place last week. He was a veteran in the service, & had been long afflicted with a severe wound in his leg, which terminated his life.

Thos Carbery elected Pres of the Bank of Metropolis, to succeed J W Maury, deceased.

Letters testamentary on the personal estate of Stephen Pleasanton, late of Wash Co, deceased, having been issued to the subscriber, all persons having claims against the estate are to present them for settlement. –Hopkins Lightner, exc, of the ofc of the Treasurer of the U S.

Mrd: on Jan 11, by Rev S A H Marks, Mr Chas G Gripenschutz to Mrs Ann Davis.

Mrd: on Feb 6, by Rev S A H Marks, Mr John W Murphey to Miss Drucilla C Martin, daughter of Mr Saml Martin, all of Wash City.

Law of the U S passed at the 2nd Session of the 33rd Congress of the U S: Act to change the names of the American built schnr **J H Holmes**, now owned by Henry Gordon & Carston Nohrden, citizens of Charleston, S C, to the schnr **Effort**. The steamer **Franklin Pierce**, an American built vessel, owned by L T Murdock & W W Witherbury, citizens of Cincinnati, Ohio, name changed to the steamer **Texans**.

Circuit Court of Wash Co, D C-in Chancery. Thos Sewall et al vs Basil Sims' administrator & heirs. The trustee reported the sale by him of the real estate of the late Basil Sims, on Jun 21, 1852, Eliz Travers was the purchaser of lot 8, in subdivision of lots 4 & 5 in square 791, in Wash City, for $125; that Mary Tate was the purchaser of part of lot 4 in square 576, for $250; that Eliz Travers & Washington Ingram, to whom Mary Tate hath since assigned her interest in said purchase, hath each complied with the terms of sale. –Jno A Smith, clerk

FRI FEB 9, 1855
Rev John Moore, pastor of the Universalist Society of Concord, N H, was between the depot & his residence when he dropped down dead. His complaint was an affection of the heart.

Senate: 1-Memorial lately presented from Mr Aaron H Palmer, of Wash, a gentleman who by travel & study has aquired extensive knowledge of the riches & commercial capabilities, & political & social condition of the Asiatic countries, humbly prays that the Sec of the Senate may be authorized to pay him such sum of its contingent fund for those services as to your honorable body should seem just & equitable. –Aaron H Palmer, Wash, Jan 18, 1855 [A lengthy history of his travels can be found in the Feb 9th newspaper.] 2-Ptn from Wm C Dennis, engaged in the manufacture of salt at Key West, asking that a specific duty be imposed on foreign salt. 3-Ptn from Rebecca Halsey, widow of an ofcr of the Revolution, asking to be allowed a pension. 4-Cmte on the Judiciary: memorial of Thos W Powell & E More, asking to be released from their liabilities as bail for the apperance of Otho Hinton, charged with robbing the mail of the U S, submitted a report, accompanied by a joint resolution for the relief of Rebecca Hinton, wife of Otho Hinton, & asked its immediate consideration: passed. Powell & More gave $10,000 for his appearance; the wife Rebecca, having a separate estate of $9,000 in the hands of a trustee for her separate use for her life, with the remainder to her daughters, joined with her daughters & said trustee in conveying it to bail as security to release the husband from jail; the husband fled beyond the jurisdiction of the U S, thus forfeiting the bail bond & depriving his wife & daughters of their estate, not derived from the husband, but from her relatives, who had made the provision for herself & children; they had no other object in view but to enable the husband to prepare his defence & to appear for trial. 4-Cmte on Private Land Claims: bill for the relief of Hyacinth Reopel & others, heirs & assignees of Ambrose Hyacinth. 5-Cmte on Naval Affairs: joint resolution for the relief of Lt J C Carter, with an amendment limiting the amount to $1,869: passed. 6-Cmte on Pensions: bill for the relief of Wm S Oliver. 7-Cmte on the Dist of Columbia: adverse reports on the memorials of John Foy, & of B F Watson.

House of Reps: 1-Cmte on the Judiciary: adverse report on the ptn of Thos Woodward for relief on account of services as coroner of Wash Co, D C.

Accident on Sat, says the Newburyport Herald, in Bradford, when the up train ran into a wagon in which Mr Moses Johnson, age about 60 years, was riding, injuring & killing him.

Mrd: on Dec 28, 1854, in San Francisco, Calif, the residence of Hon Wm M Gwin, by Bishop Kip, Hon J S K Ogier, Judge of the U S District court for the southern district of Calif, to Miss Anna Kiger, of Falmouth, Va.

Mrd: on Feb 6, at Foundry Parsonage, by Rev E P Phelps, Mr John Boreland to Miss Eliz S Miller, all of Wash City.

Died: on Feb 8, Mary R, daughter of the late John & Mgt Keith, in her 21st year. Her funeral will take place from the residence of her uncle, John Tretler, on 9th, between G & H sts, this evening, at 3 o'clock.

Died: on Feb 7, after a painful illness of 2 weeks, Mr John Hutchinson, of Wash City, in his 35th year. His funeral is at 2 o'clock this afternoon, from his late residence, near the southern basin of the canal

SAT FEB 10, 1855
Circuit Court of Wash Co, D C–in Equity. John G Robinson & Eliza his wife, & others, vs Wm Gunton, Ellen Friend, Solomon Friend, Wm Venable, Chas Venable, John W Venable, Thos Venable, Jos Venable, Lemuel Friend, Richd Friend, Geo Friend, Jos Friend, Wm S Friend, Josiah O Friend, Saml K Friend, Simon Burnham & Sally his wife, Jas Merchant & Mary his wife, Martha Watson, Fred'k Norwood & Eliza his wife, Franklin Friend, & Sally Friend, dfndnts. The bill states that the cmplnts, as the heirs at law, & as purchasers from said heirs at law of Richd Charles, late of Wash City, deceased, are entitled to a piece of ground on square south of square 825, in said city, improved by 2 tenements, of which said Richd Charles died seized & possessed to him & his heirs; that after the death of said Richd Charles, by arrangement between Eliza Charles, his widow & admx, made with Jas Friend in his life, to whom said Charles died indebted, & the said property having been sold in 1826 by the Corp of Washington for arrears of taxes, & purchased by Wm Gunton for $70, by which said arrangement said Friend entered into possession of said property agreed to redeem it from said Gunton for the benefit of the heirs of said Richd Charles, to pay the taxes & repairs, to receive the rents & income until he was fully repaid all his outlays for the redemption, taxes, & repairs, & also his own debt, & then to surrender it to the said heirs; that accordingly he redeemed it from Gunton, took an assigment of the certificate of the tax sale, & remained in possession & received the rents till his death; that his widow Ellen survived him, & likewise continued in possession, & received the rents during her life; that after Friend received the said assignment from Gunton he assigned the same certificate to Chas Venable without consideration; Venable received the deed from the Corp & afterwards conveyed the property to Friend without an consideration; that Ellen Friend, the widow, has rendered an account of the outlay to 1845, but has refused to charge herself with the rents; that the rents have far exceeded the whole amount of the debt, & the property ought to be released; that Jas Friend & Ellen Friend are both dead; & Solomon Friend, Lemuel Friend, Richd Friend, Geo Friend, Jos Friend, W S Friend, Josiah O Friend, Saml K Friend, Sally Burnham, Mary Merchant, Martha Watson, Eliza Norwood, Franklin Friend, & Sally Friend are the only heirs at law of said Jas Friend, & all reside out of D C, & in the State of Mass, & claim the said property. The bill prays that they may be declared trustees of said property, & called upon to account; that the deed from the Corp to Venable, & from Venable to Friend, may be set aside as fraudulent & void; & that cmplnts may be let in to redeem if there is any balance due, & if no balance is due from them that the dfndnts be decreed to release the said property to them. Bradley & Bradley for cmplnts. Absent dfndnts are to appear in this Court on or before the 2nd Monday of Jun next.
—Jas Dunlop, Assit Judge Cir Court D C -Jno A Smith, clerk

Mrs Bridget Morgan, a native of Ireland, aged 18 years, lost her life by accidently falling from the 3rd story of her residence in N Y on Sat last.

Mrd: on Jan 28, by Rev Bishop Rutlidge, Lt Lardner Gibbon, U S N, to Miss Alice R Shepard, 2nd daughter of the late John S Shepard, of Tallahassee, Fla.

Senate: 1-Bills of the Senate passed: relief of Louis Washington, jr; of Geo M Farnum, commercial agent of Port Louis; of Michl Hansen; of Peter Amey, colored man; of Abraham Cutter; of Cmdor Foxhall A Parker, U S Navy; of Geo W Harris; of the heirs of Wm Tervin, deceased; of Lt W D Porter; of Wm Rich; of John P Brown; of Wm C Clark; of Puig, Mir & Co; of Horatio J Perry; of Robt M Walsh; of Geo W Lippitt; of Henry Savage; of J B Holman; of Peter Parker; of Jos Graham; of Ferdinand Coxe; of Betsey W Eve; of Jas H Smith & Chas Stevens; of Chas W Carroll; of Simeon Stedman; of Wm P Young; of John C McFerran & Saml D Sturgis, of the U S Army; of Chas McCormick, assist surgeon in the U S Army; of Dr Wm P Buel; of the heirs of Jabez B Rooker, deceased; of Lt Col Edw R S Canby; of Richd Albritton; of Amos B Eaton, a commissary of subsistence in the U S army; of the assignees or legal reps of Jacques Moulon; of Nancy D Holker, widow & admx of John Holker, deceased; of Parmelia Slavin, late the wife of John Blue, deceased. 2-Bills from the House of Reps finally passed: relief of: Saml McKnight, of Ky; of Wm Wallace, of Ill; of Geo H Paige, U S Army; of John Brown; of John H Hicks, of Ind; of Abraham Ausman; of the legal reps of Lt Francis Ware; of John Cole; of Geo Lynch; of Geo Elliott; of Geo T Rallston; of Wm Gore; of Wm Parker; of Eleanor Hoople, of the Province of Canada; of the legal reps of John Putnam; of Sidney P Pool, of Maine; of Lincoln Bates; of Polly Carner, widow & excx of Nathan Carner, deceased; of Wm Case; of the widow & children of Ezra Chapman, deceased; of Gilbert C Russell; & of Danl Bedinger's heirs. Also, to provide a pension for Oliver Brown, of Chemung Co, N Y; provide a pension for Edmund Mitchell, of Carroll Co, Ky; & grant bounty land to Cornelius Coffey.

House of Reps: 1-Cmte on Naval Affairs: bill for the relief of Cmder G J Pendergrast: committed. 2-Cmte of Claims: bill for the relief of the widow & children of Henry M Shreve: committed. Same cmte: adverse report on the resolution for the relief of John L Smith & Jas McGraw: laid on the table. 3-Bill for the relief of the heirs of Larkin Smith, returned from the Senate with an amendment, striking out the allowance of interest: concurred in. 4-Joint resolution for the relief of Lt J C Carter, retuned from the Senate with an amendment limiting the amount to $1,869: concurred in. 5-Bills of the Senate appropriately referred: bounty land to Susan Palmer; relief of Brvt Brig Gen John B Walbach, U S Army; of Franklin Chase; of John Y Laub; of Mrs Nancy Weatherford, widow of Col Wm Weatherford; of Geo W Torrence; of Jeremiah Moors; & of Mrs Catharine Dickerson. 6-Bill for the relief of Catharine M Hamer, widow of the late Gen Thos L Hamer: referred to the Cmte on Military Affairs.

MON FEB 12, 1855
$20 reward for runaway negro man Sam Carroll. –Warren Summers, near ***Long Old Fields***, PG Co, Md.

Senate: 1-Additional documents from Wm Archer in relation to the Pacific railroad, & also documents in the case of J Cook & A Lockwood: presented. 2-Ptn from Geo H Giddings, asking additional extra compensation for carrying the mail from San Antonio, in Texas, to Santa Fe, in New Mexico; & also from Jas H McFadin, asking compensation for carrying the mail: referred. 3-Ptn from B F Marshall, asking to be paid for beef & other provisions furnished to Indians in Calif. 4-Ptn from the widow of Peter Staff, a soldier in the war of 1812, asking the same rates of pension that have been allowed to the widows of the soldiers of the Mexican war may be entended to her & other widows of ofcrs & soldiers of the war of 1812. 5-Documents relating to the claim of Lucretia Gardner: referred. 6-Cmte on Military Affairs: bill for the relief of Whitemarsh B Seabrook, Jos Whaley, & others, ofcrs & members of the Edisto Island Co of S C. Same cmte: bill for the relief of Sylvester Churchill: passed. Same cmte: bill for the relief of A S Robinson, Cashier of the Bank of the state of Missouri, at St Louis. Same cmte: bill for the relief of the heirs of Col Simeon Knight, late of the U S Army. Same cmte: adverse report on the claim of Starr G Spalding. 7-Cmte on Naval Affairs: bill for the relief of Lt Fred'k Chatard, U S Navy. 8-Cmte of Claims: bill for the relief of Andrew H Patterson: recommended its passage.

On Wed, at Roxbury, Mass, a boiler in the kitchen of the house of Mr Saml A Way exploded & scalded Catharine Glennon so severely that she lived but a short time. Catharine Kelley & Mgt Brennahan, being in the kitchen at the time, were both badly scalded. Mrs Way narrowly escaped injury.

Mr John S Weathers, a native of Ky, recently from Missouri, was shot dead in Falls Co, Texas, a few days ago, by a companion while hunting, who mistook him for a deer. He left a widow & a large family.

Died: on Feb 10, after a long & painful illness, Mrs Nancy Hines, aged about 77 years, relict of the late Henry Hines. Her funeral will be this afternoon, at 2 o'clock, from the residence of her son-in-law, Mr G Bitner, on H, between 18th & 19th sts.

Died: on Feb 10, Charles Wendall, infant son of Eliza & the late Chas King. His funeral is this evening, at 2 o'clock, from the residence of his mother, on M st, between 12th & 13th sts.

Orphans Court of Wash Co, D C. In the case of Wilhelmina Letmate, admx of Christian Letmate, deceased: the admx & Court have appointed Mar 3 next for the settlement of said estate, of the assets in hand. –Ed N Roach, Reg/o wils.

TUE FEB 13, 1855
For sale: a sorrel harness & riding Horse, 6 years old, of fine style & movement. He may be seen at the stable of Robt Earl, H st, near 21st st.

Appointments by the Pres, by & with the advice & consent of the Senate.
Augustus C Dodge, of Iowa, to be Envoy Extra & Minister Pleni of the U S to Spain.
Leonidas Martin, of Ala, to be Consul at Mazatlan, in Mexico.
Saml P Collings, of Pa, to be Consul for the Empire of Morocco.
W W Banks, of Va, to be Consul at Aquas Calientas, in Mexico.

Obit-died: on Jan 12, 1855, at Shreveport, La, after a brief illness of [as was supposed by his physicians] yellow fever, John W Burton, son of Alfred Burton, of Beattie's Ford, N C, aged about 36 years. He was a lawyer of ability, & at the time of his death had a good & increasing practice.

Senate: 1-Cmte on Revolutionary Claims: bill for the relief of the heirs & legal reps of Gen Wood, deceased: passed. Same cmte: bill for the relief of the heirs & legal reps of Jos Savage, deceased: passed. Same cmte: adverse reports on the following: of Wm A Graham; of the heirs of Alex'r Harper; of the heirs of Wm Beatty; & of the heirs of Johannes Schultz; & to be discharged from the further consideration of the memorial of the administrator of Curtis Grubb: which was agreed to. 2-Cmte on Public Lands: asking to be discharged from the consideration of the memorial of A S Bender, & that it be referred to the Cmte on Military Affairs. 3-Cmte on Military Affairs: joint resolution for the relief of Joel Henry Dyer: recommended that it pass. 4-Cmte on Patents: adverse report on the memorial of Jas H Stimpson. 5-Cmte on Roads & Canals: adverse report on the memorial of Mary W Perrine, asking payment of whatever amount should appear to be due her late husband as one of the contractors on the Louisville & Portland canal.

Nathl Frost, of Kennebec Co, Maine, has been convicted in the U S District Court on 2 indictments charging him with committing & aiding in the commission of forgery in connexion with attempts to procure bounty land. The court imposed in one case a fine of $300, & in the other a fine of $200, & one day's imprisonment in each case.

WED FEB 14, 1855
Mrs Washing Castle was burnt to death at Albany on Sat by the explosion of a camphene lamp.

Rev Dr Cooke, of Lynn, Mass, gave his people, as an afternoon discourse, on Jan 21, a sermon which was preached on the same day of the same month in 1655, just 200 years before, before the same society, by Rev Thos Cobett, who was then its pastor.

Mrd: on Feb 13, by Rev Mr Hodges, Jas G Sasscer to Miss H M Southoron, all of Wash.

Died: on Tue, Charles William Frailey, elder son of Chas S & Caroline M B Frailey, in his 15th year. His funeral will take place on Thu next at 2 o'clock.

Appointments by the Pres. by & with the advice & consent of the Senate.
Collestors of Customs:
W M Harrison, of Richmond, Va, vice John Lynch, deceased.
H W Moreland, Yorktown, Va, vice P J Barziza, resigned.
A D Banks, Petersburg, Va, vice L Lunsford, resigned.
Jos Ramsey, Plymouth, N C, re-appointed.
T C Porter, New Orleans, vice S W Downs, deceased.
Naval Ofcr: John McClintock, Portsmouth, N H, re-appointed.
Surveyors:
Martin Russell, Troy, N Y, vice E Brownell, resigned.
Wm E Starke, New Orleans, vice T C Porter.
Philip Harvey, Burlington, Iowa, vice A W Carpenter, resigned.
Appraiser: Francis Leech, New Orleans, vice Wm E Starke.
Assist Appraiser: W P Reyburn, New Orleans, vice Francis Leech.

Mr Henry Berry, represented to be a most worthy citizen, on Mon, severely if not dangerously injured by an accident, while at work at the Washington Navy Yard.

THU FEB 15, 1855
Executor's sale of valuable real estate in Alexandria city at auction, Mar 1: desirable lot & modern built dwlg house thereon, on Alfred st, between King & Cameron sts, late the residence of Hugh C Smith, deceased. –Saml J McCormick, auct

Senate: 1-Ptn from A H Mechlin, in behalf of the families of the ofcrs & crew of the U S schnr **Sea Gull**, asking that the same relief may be extended to them as has been granted in similar cases. 2-Ptn from Jacob Cutter, R C Cutter, & other sureties of Chas W Cutter, late navy agent at the Portsmouth navy yard, asking to be released from liabilities on his surety bonds. 3-Ptn from Adam D Steward, late inspector of customs at Michilimackinac, asking to be released from a judgment obtained against him by the U S. 4-Ptn from Henry Volcker, asking to be confirmed in a title to a tract of land in New Mexico. 5-Ptn from John Temple, asking confirmation of a tract of land in the Bastrop grant. 6-Ptn from Edmund Falling, an Eastern Cherokee, asking to be allowed his share & also his wife & children's share of the per capita appropriations for the Cherokee Indians allowed under various acts of Congress.

Cmte on Naval Affairs: asked to be discharged from the consideration of the ptn of memorial of Jacob Cutter, R C Cutter, & the sureties of Chas W Cutter, & that it be referred to the Cmte on the Judiciary. 7-Cmte on the Post Ofc & Post Roads: Memorial of Richd S Coxe, asking compensation for legal services as counsel for the Post Ofc Dept, submitted a report, with a bill for the relief of Coxe. 8-Bill for the relief of G A Magruder, cmder in the U S Navy: referred. 9-Bill for the relief of Capt Jas McIntosh, of the U S Navy: referred. 10-Cmte on Pensions: bill to continue half-pay to Mrs Leuright Browning for a further term of 5 years. 11-Cmte of Claims: bill for the relief of Wm Hagerty: passed. Same cmte: bill for the relief of

Medford Caffey, of Tenn: passed. 12-Cmte on Revolutionary Claims: bill for the relief of Maria Stephenson, widow of Geo Stephenson, deceased. Same cmte: bill for the relief of the heirs & legal reps of Capt John de Treville, deceased. 13- Cmte on Military Affairs: asked to be discharged from the consideration of the bill for the relief of Catharine M Hamer, widow of Gen Thos L Hamer: referred to the Cmte on Pensions: which was agreed to. 14-Ptn from Dr Edmund Du Barry, a surgeon in the navy, asking to be allowed certain arrearages of pay. 15-Cmte on Commerce: bill for the relief of Chas W Morgan, Wm R Rodman, & Edw Merrill, submitted an adverse report on the same. Same cmte: asked to be discharged from the consideration of the ptn of W C Dennis, of Florida, asking an imposition of duty on salt, & that it be referred to the cmte on Finance. Also, memorial of John C McLemore & others, citizens of Calif, asking a port of entry to be opened at the junction of the Gila & Colorado rivers. 16-Cmte on Naval Affairs: bill for the relief of the legal reps of the late Capt Jesse D Elliot. Same cmte: bill for the relief of the families of the ofcrs & crew of the schnr **Seagull**: passed. Same cmte: discharged from the memorials of Mary Portman & Isabella Duffy. Same cmte: asked to be discharged from the consideration of the memorial relating to the claim of the legal reps of Thos P Jones: which was agreed to. 17-Cmte on Military Affairs: adverse report on the memorial of Danl Nippes.

Married, on a cake of floating ice, in the Ohio river, opposite Rising Sun, on Jan 30, by Rev Mr Collard, Rev Jas H Brooking to Miss Sallie Craig, all of Boone Co, Ky.

Brigham Young is building 2 large & beautiful houses, adjoining that which he occupies now in Salt Lake city, to accommodate his increasing family. Brigham Young now rejoices in between 50 & 60 wives, & from 45 to 50 children. Elder Kimball, one of the Mormon apostles, has between 60 & 70 consorts. –Balt American

Alex'r Bailie, a liquor dealer of Pittsburg, of intemperate & eccentric habits, locked himself in his room while crazed with drink, & remained there several days before he was found dead. He was about 60 years of age & at one time a leading merchant of Pittsburg.

Appointments by the Pres, by & with the advice & consent of the Senate.
Thos Welsh, of Ala, Receiver at Montgomery, Ala.
Geo H Ambrose, of Oregon Territory, to be Agent for Indians in Oregon Territory.
Nathan Olney, of Oregon Territory, to be Agent for the Indians in Oregon Territory.
Robt Benguerel, of La, to be Register at Apelousas, La.
Chas H Morrison, of La, to be Receiver at Ouachita, La, vice Peyton G King, resigned.
Robt D Hadden, of Miss, to be Receiver at Columbus, Miss.
Wm L Caldwell, of Ill, to be Receiver at Shawneetown, Ill, vice Saml K Casey, resigned.

Mrd: on Wed, by Rev John C Smith, Mr John A Stownell to Miss Mary V Annis, both of Va.

On Sunday last [says the Barre Patriot] Mrs Mary Farrar, of Petersham, celebrated her 100th birthday by attending meeting at the Unitarian Church. She appeared in good health, rose & stood unsupported during the singing, & remained to join in the communion service. In the same slip was her brother, Capt Joel Brooks, who is in his 97th year. In another part of the house was Mrs Bethiah Covel, who is in her 91st year. The thermometer stood in the morning only 2 degrees above zero, & a strong wind blew from the n w through the day. Several were present who had seen nearly 80 winters, & several others further advanced in life would have joined the congregation had it not been for the extreme severity of the cold. –Boston Transcript

Things in Mexico. Gen Villalva, whom the Mexican papers have reported killed at least half a dozen times, is in the vicinity of Mezcala with a strong detachment, & intercepts all communication between the troops at Chilpantzingo & Santa Anna.

Wash City Ordinance: 1-Act for the relief of Mrs Mary Nevitt: the Collector of Taxes to credit her with $15.50, the amount erroneously assessed on her for opening & paving an alley in square 347. 2-Joint resolution authorizing Geo Deas to enclose a portion of the alley in square 105; provided he shall first pay for said ground $500: this Corp binds itself to give the said Geo Deas a fee simple title in such portion of said alley, whenever the authority to do shall be vested in it by act of Congress.

Chancery sale: by decree of the Circuit Court of Montg Co, Md, in the case of Waters vs Waters & others, the subscriber, as trustee, will offer at public sale, on Feb 21, the real estate of which the late Dr Cyrus Waters died seized, containing about 40 acres, more or less, near the village of Unity, in said county, with a 2 story stone dwlg, barn & stable, meat & carriage house & diary. Immediate possession will be given to the purchaser. –Richd P Jackson, trustee

FRI FEB 16, 1855
Orphans Court of Wash Co, D C. Letters of administration on the personal estate of John Brereton, late of Wash Co, deceased. –Eliza A Brereton, John Hoover, adms

Senate: 1-Cmte on Revolutionary Claims: act for the benefit of the heirs of Philip R Rice, deceased: &, act for the relief of the children & grandchildren of Thos Morris: recommended their passage. 2-Cmte on the Library: bill for the relief of Titian R Peale. 3-Cmte on Private Land Claims: bill for the relief of Robt Graham. 4-Cmte on Public Lands: bill for the relief of Henry H Marsh: who had been before Congress ever since 1838, with the bill passing first one House & then the other without ever receiving the joint action of both: bill was passed.

Mr C H Brainard, of Boston, has just published a most excellent lithographic portrait of Rev Byron Sunderland, of Wash City, which is fully equal to any of the portraits heretofore included in his collection. This picture of Mr Sunderland is drawn by Grozelier, of Boston, from a daguerreotype by Vannerson, of Wash City, & is for sale at the principal bookstores.

Died: on Feb 11, at Wheeling, Va, Jas E Gaither, formerly of Wash, after a brief illness of a few days.

Died: on Feb 7, at the residence of her father, in Fairfax Co, Va, in her 8th year, after a long & painful illness of 3 years, Ellen Arnot Dickens, youngest daughter of Francis A & Mgt H Dickens. Her funeral will take place from the church of the Epiphany today at 12 o'clock.

Died: on Thu, Frederick, son of Thos & Mary Altemus, in his 4th year. His funeral is this afternoon at 2 o'clock.

Bridge Architecture. Mr H Howe, inventor of the new system for constructing bridges, of which the models Uncle Sam tested at the Crystal Palace, N Y, & now exhibited at the Smithsonian Institute, are a part, offers his professional services in Wash City. Is at present at the corner of 4½ st & Missouri ave.

Orphans Court of Wash Co, D C-Feb 3, 1855. In the case of Jennings Pigott, adm of John W Strong, deceased, the adm & Court have appointed Mar 6 next, for the final settlement of said estate, of the assets in hand. –Ed N Roach, Reg/o wills

Circuit Court of Wash Co, D C. Lynch vs Lockery et al. The trustee reports he has sold lot 26 in square 728 to Jas Lynch for $2,030, & he has complied with the terms of sale. –John A Smith, clerk

SAT FEB 17, 1855
Prof Alex Kennedy was found dead in Alton, Ill, a few days since. His death was occasioned by want & exposure from long & constant dissipation. He was a graduate of Dublin Univ, & afterwards the Prof of Belles Lettres in Belfast College, Dublin. An an elocutionist he had very few superiors. But his talents availed him little in this country, such were his habits of dissipation.

Household & kitchen furniture at auction on: Feb 24, by deed of trust dated Aug 21, 1854, from Mary Jacobs to the subscriber, of the land records of Wash Co, D C, in liber J A S No 85, folios 69 to 74. –John L Smith, trustee -Green & Scott, aucts

Teacher wanted: a good Classical, Mathematical, & French scholar. Address Rev Wm N Ward, Lyell's Store post ofc, Va.

Mr John Heslep, acting treasurer of Tuolumne Co, was murdered on the 18th. The murderers then rifled the safe. $15,000 was received the day before by the treasurer. Crane Griffiths, a native of England, lately from Austrailia, was immediately arrested & confessed the next morning. Griffiths was hung upon a tree 10 hours after he committed the crime. What adds to the enormity of his crime is that fact that in coming to Sonora he brought a letter of introduction to the Messrs Heslep from their brother, Judge Heslep, of San Francisco, the consequence of which was that they befriended & assisted him.

Died: on Fri, at the residence of J M Wilson, James Kerr, infant son of Edw J & M A Leyburn, aged 1 year & 2 months. His funeral will today at 11 A M, from 288 G st.

Senate: 1-Bill for the relief of Whitemarsh B Seabrook, Jos Whaley, & others, ofcrs & members of the Edisto Island Co, of S C: passed. 2-Bill for settling the claim of the legal reps of Richd W Meade, deceased: postponed. Also, the bill for the relief of Amos Kendall & John E Kendall; & the bill for the relief of Jos Nock were laid on the table. 3-Rejected: bill to confirm the claims of John Erwin to a certain tract of land in the Bastrop grant; bill for the relief of Mgt A Copley, of the State of La; bill for the relief of Sophia Kirby; & bill for the relief of L E L A Lawson, sole surviving heiress of Gen Eleazur W Ripley, deceased.

Coroner's sale: by writ of fieri facias, issued out of the Circuit Court of PG Co, Md: public sale, at the Court-house door in Upper Marlboro, on Mar 15, all the estate, right, title, interest, property, claim, & demand at law & in equity of Robt *Reyworth & Geo K Bailey, claimants of, in, & to the following property: a tract or part of a tract of land in said county called **Deakins' Hall**, supposed to contain about 210 acres, now in the possession & occupancy of the said Geo K Bailey, & adjoining the lands of Col Jasper M Jackson & Edw Simms, levied on & taken in execution as the property of the said Robt Keyworth & Geo K Bailey, claimants, & will be sold to satisfy a judgment against them in said court in favor of Jas Watson & Jos H Hildeburn. –Jno H Sansbury, coroner [*Copied as written.]

MON FEB 19, 1855
Senate: 1-Ptn from the citizens of Ill, asking that a pension may be allowed to Wm Young, who was wounded in firing a salute in honor of Pres Fillmore on the occasion of his visit to that State. 2-Cmte on Commerce: bill to change the name of the American-built steamer **Fanny Fern** to that of the steamer **Thomas H Stewart**: passed. 2-Cmte on Private Land Claims: bill for the relief of Cephise Piseros, widow of Louis La Branch, of the Parish of St Chas, La. 3-Cmte on Naval Affairs: bill for the relief of Chas G Swett. 4-Cmte on Pensions: adverse report on the bill to pay the heirs of Stephen Morrell, deceased, the amount due their father for a pension. 5-Cmte on Foreign Relations: adverse report on the case of Robt M Hamilton. 6-Cmte on Public Lands: adverse report on the memorial of Jas Harper & Robt W Harper.

7-Cmte on Pensions: adverse report on the ptn of Thos H Bingham.

Died: Feb 13, at his residence, Barnaby, PG Co, Md, Henry A Callis, in his 73rd year.

The death lately of Col Staniford, which was published on Feb 13, was born in Windham, Conn. He joined his regt in the city of Mexico, & accompanied it to the U S at the conclusion of the war.

The vacant panel in the Rotundo of the Capitol has at length been filled with the Historical Picture of De Soto's Discovery of the Mississippi River, painted by Mr Wm H Powell, in compliance with an order of Congress. Mr Powell's model for De Soto's horse was Ab-El-Kader's battle horse, then in the imperial stables at St Cloud. There are now eight historical paintings in the Rotundo of the Capitol:
1-The Landing of Columbus
2-The Discovery of the Mississippi by De Soto.
3-The Baptism of Pocahontas.
4-The Embarcation of the Pilgrims.
5-The Declaration of Independence.
6-The Capitulation at Saratoga.
7-The Capitulation at Yorktown.
8-Washington Resigning his Commission. The first four pictures were painted respectively by Vanderlyn, Powell, Chapman, & Weir. The others were painted by Gen Trumbull.

Mrd: on Feb 13, by Rev F Israel, in Union Chapel, Chas A Perkins to Miss Sarah L, youngest daughter of G L Thompson, all of Wash City.

Mrd: on Feb 15, by Rev Dr Buck, Mr Spencer C Benham, of Canandaigua, N Y, to Miss Sallie E, daughter of Wm G W White, of Wash City.

Died: on Feb 7, after a lingering illness, Susan D, wife of Robt T Bassett. Her funeral will be from the residence of her husband, on East Capitol st, Capitol Hill, at half past 3 o'clock this afternoon.

Died: Feb 13, at his residence, Barnaby, PG Co, Md, Henry A Callis, in his 73rd year.

$10 reward for the return of a Horse & Wagon, supposed to be stolen. Bring to me at the Centre or Northern Markets. –Geo Carll

The Charleston Mercury of Feb 15 announces the death Col Francis Kinloch Huger, in his 83rd year. He was the son of Maj Ben Huger, who was killed before the lines at the siege of Charleston, in the Revolutionary war, & was the father of Col Ben Huger, of the Ordnance, who rendered distinguished services in the war with Mexico. He is known for his daring & almost successful attempt [in connexion with

Dr Eric Bollman, of Phil] to liberate Lafayette from his Austrian prison, 60 years ago. The failure of the enterprise left him in a captivity as hard as that of the hero he had sought to liberate. Upon his return to his native county, during the troubles with France in 1798-99, he held the commission of Capt of Artl until the settlement of that dispute. On the breaking out of the war of 1812, Pres Madison sent him a commission as Col of Artl, & in this capacity he served through the war. He also served the State in both branches of the Legislature. [No death date given-current item.]

The fire at Alexandria, on Fri, occurred in the block of frame bldgs on Union st, opposite the Ferry slip, belonging to Mr Arthur W Taylor, & occupied by Messrs Geo W Harrison & Michl O'Sullivan as grocery stores, which were totally destroyed. Mr Harrison was fully insured. Mr O'Sullivan was not insured, his children had a narrow escape, being taken from the bldg while it was in flames. O'Sullivan has also lost some $500 in bank notes. This calamity is attributed to incendiarism.

TUE FEB 20, 1855
The Jefferson Circuit Court was engaged yesterday in the trial of a combined suit for breach of pomise to marry & slander. The plntf, Miss Sarah Goodman, alleged that she was engaged to be married to Julius Edil, &, pending the engagement, he spoke slanderous words of her, & then said that on account of the truthfulness of the words uttered he would not marry her. Edil made no answer. A jury was sworn to assess the damage. The plntf was a woman of good character. The jury found for plntf in $3,000. It is doubtful whether the judgment will ever be enforced, as Edil has left the place. –Louisville Courier, 14th.

John Licklider, son of Mr Geo Licklider, residing near Shepherdstown, Jefferson Co, Va, shot a few days since, on the farm owned by his father, a grey eagle measuring between the ends of the wings 7 feet 2 inches. So states the Shepherdstown Register.

In an affray yesterday between 2 white men, Henry Webster & Danl Gould, at a little shop kept by Mrs Gibson near the 12th st bridge, the former was severely cut in the abdomen. Gould was arrested & commited to prison by Justice Clarke. Dr Force was prompt to the relief of the wounded man, whose condition is critical.

The public are invited by the Philodemic Society of Gtwn College to attend a celebration of Feb 22, at 3½ o'clock, when an oration will be delivered by a member of the society. –Wm H Gwynn, A Bechnel, R C Combs, Cmte of Invitations

Orphans Court of Wash Co, D C. In the case of Adeline Sergeant, excx of John Sergeant, deceased, the excx & Court have appointed Mar 10 next, for the final settlement of said estate, of assets in hand. –Ed N Roach, Reg/o wills

Senate: 1-Ptn from C E Anderson, late Sec of Legation to France, asking to be allowed additional compensation for the time he acted as charge de affaires at that Court. 2-Ptn from Carrington Wilson, asking the extension of his patent for an improvement in the cooking stove. 3-Ptn from the widow of Truman Clarke, of the war of 1812, asking a pension. 4-Ptn from Jas Robertson, asking indemnity for his arrest & imprisonment by order of the Senate. 5-Ptn from Polly Scott, widow of John W Scott, asking to be allowed the bounty land & pay to which her son was entitled for his military services in Mexico. 6-Cmte of Claims: resolution in favor of Wm Monaghan: passed. 7-Cmte of Claims: settlement of the accounts of the late Gov Burt: passed. 8-Cmte on Pensions: bill for the relief of Mrs J Josephine McClellan: [memorial was recommitted.] 9-Cmte on Indian Affairs: asked to be discharged from the consideration of the ptn of Scott Campbell, interpreter to the Sioux Indians, & that it be referred to the Cmte on Private Land Claims: which was agreed to. 10-Cmte on Revolutionary Claims: adverse report on the memorial of Susannah Hayne Pinckney, daughter of R Shubrick, of the Revolutionary army. Same cmte: adverse reports on the memorials of the heirs of Col Chas Lewis, & of the heirs of Lt Col Uriah Forrest.

Concord, Feb 18. Mr Barton, editor of the Concord Reporter, dropped down dead yesterday from disease of the heart. He had just completed a speech at a political meeting, & was in the act of taking his seat when he fell & expired.

Columbian College, Wash, Feb 19, 1855: the trustees are maturing arrangements to increase the number of the Faculty. If sustained by its friends they will be able, at the opening of the next session, Sept 26, to secure & support the following Faculty, viz: Pres, Rev J G Binney, D D, of Augusta, Ga; Prof of Astronomy & Mathematics, Wm Ruggles, L L D, now at the College; Prof of Rhetoric & Belles Lettres, not yet appointed; Prof of the Latin & Greek Languages, Rev A J Huntington, A M, now at the College; Prof of Chemistry & Natural History, Lewis H Steiner, M D, of Md; Prof & Mathematics & Natural Philosophy, E P Fristoe, A M, of Va; Tutor in the Latin & Greek Languages, L R Gwaltney, A B, now at the College. Persons willing to aid in this object may do so through any of the Trustees residing in Wash, viz:

Col Jas L Edwards, Pres
Dr S C Smoot, Sec
Dr Wm Gunton
Dr L D Gale
Andrew Rothwell
Rev S P Hill
Wm Q Force, Treasurer Columbian College

Prof C C Jewett
Rev G W Samson
Isaac Clarke
Dr Wm V H Brown
Chauncey Bestor
Geo J Abbott

We have read the above & cordially commend the plan it proposes:
John C Smith, Pastor 4th Presbyterian Church
B Sunderland, Pastor 1st Presbyterian Church
Geo D Cummins, Rector of Trinity Church
Jas H Brown, Pastor of Wesley Chapel

Jas A Duncan, Pastor of M E Church South
Jas Read Eckard, Pastor 2nd Presbyterian Chuch
D Evans Reese, Pastor 9th st M P Church

Valuable & extensive Mill property for sale: by deed of trust dated Jun 13, 1847, by Nathl B Butler & Susan M, his wife, of record in the Clerk's ofc of the County Court of Fauquier Co, Va: public auction on the premises, on Mar 15 next: property at Weaversville, in said county, known as the *Weaversville Mills*; located on Cedar Run. —John P Philips, trustee

WED FEB 21, 1855
Senate: 1-Ptn from Castner Hanway, asking to be indemnified for damages sustained in consequence of his arrest & imprisonment under a false charge of high treason against the U S: referred to the Cmte on the Judiciary. 2-Cmte on Revolutionary Claims: bill for the relief of Chas J Davis, adm of Capt John Davis, an ofcr in the war of the Revolution, recommend its passage. 3-Cmte on Foreign Relations: bill for the relief of Geo P Marsh. Same cmte: adverse reports on the memorials of Jas Selkirk & of Wm R Glover. 4-Cmte on Naval Affairs: adverse report on the memorial of Dominic Lynch. 5-Memorial of Jas Thompson & other practical engineers in relation to a test of Miller's steam condenser: referred to the Cmte on Commerce. 6-Bill for the relief of Mrs J Josephine McClellan: to grant a pension to the widow of Brvt Col McClellan, an ofcr who had greatly distinguished himself in the war with Mexico: bill was considered & passed.

Nelson Driggs, a notorious counterfeiter, was arrested on Thu last at Chicago, where he had arrived the previous day. Counterfeit & altered notes to the amount of $30,000 was found on his person & amongst his baggage.

It is reported that Mr R Lockwood sold his painting of "The Last Judgment" to the new Roman Catholic Cathedral in Phil for $12,000, reserving to himself the privilege of engraving it; 4,000 subscribers to which have been received at $10 each.

Robt T Luckett, a prominent citizen of Loudoun Co, Va, fell from his horse on his way home from Aldie, [where he had been performing his duties as a magistrate,] on Feb 16, &, after struggling towards his home for some distance, sank down from exhaustion & exposure, as is supposed, & expired. [Mar 22nd newspaper: Obit-died: Robt T Luckett, of Loudoun Co, Va, suddenly. He was a graduate of the Univ of Va; had frequently represented his county in the Legislature; & was in discharge of his duty as Justice of the Peace at the time of his death. She who mourns him, the stricken partner of his life, the sharer of his joys, mourns all that woman could lose. He is gone! in the meridian of his days.

Dr Blarck, a German physician of Cincinnati, has been held in $1,000 to appear at court on the charge of improperly puncturing an aneurism in the leg, the patient having died under the operation.

Died: on Feb 19, Grace W Mettrigger, aged 11 years. Her funeral will take place from the residence of her uncle, Mr Isaac Bassett, 2nd st, Capitol Hill, this afternoon, at 3½ o'clock.

House of Reps: 1-Ptn & accompanying documents of the heirs of Wm McCoy for compensation for work done on the Nat'l road. 2-Ptn of Andrew P Wentworth & 30 others, citizens of Ross Co, Ohio, praying Congress to establish a post route from Waverley, Pike Co, to Boonsville, Ross Co, Ohio.

Fire last evening, on G, between 6th & 7th sts, destroyed the carpenter shop owned by Mr Henry Lyles, & occupied jointly by him & Mr Thomas, box maker. The carpenter shop of Mr J G Robinson was slightly damaged. The fire was undoubtedly the work of an incendiary.

An English Ofcr frozen to death. The last advices from the Crimea state that Brvt Maj McDonald, 88th Regt, was frozen to death in the trenches before Sebastopol. [Feb 22nd newspaper: Maj Macdonald, of the 89th Regt, was frozen to death on Jan 16. On Jan 17th, 14 men of the 46th were buried, the majority of the deaths being caused by the severity of the weather.]

Died: on Feb 20, Mr Isaac Hall, of the firm of Hall & Brothers, in his 34th year. He was endeared to his family & an extended circle of friends by his generous impulses. His funeral is on Thu morning at 8 o'clock, from the residence of his brother, Barach Hall, on F st, between 6th & 7th sts.

Died: on Feb 8, at his residence in Fayette Co, Penn, Col Thos Boyd, in his 78th year. The deceased was born in Berkeley Co, Va, but has resided nearly 70 years on the farm upon which he died, & served several years in the Legislature of his adopted State. He was favorably known for his political & private integrity, sound judgment, & moral worth.

Wash City Ordinances: 1-Act for the relief of Hall & Brother: the sum of $122.75 be paid to them for a balance due for carpeting the City Hall. 2-Act for the relief of Gales & Seaton: the sum of $646.50 be paid to them for their bill for printing the laws of the Corp.

Wm S Clary has purchased the Wood & Coal Yard lately owned & carried on by A Gladmon, on 5th st, between H & I sts.

Naval Appointments:
Captains: Chas H Bell & Wm Bigelow
Cmders: H H Bell & Wm Smith
Lts: C C Simms, H A F Arnold, T Pattison, J Myers, J Higgins, & R Aulick
Surgeons: R W Jeffrey, F M Potter, S Addison, & W A Nelson.
Assist Surgeons: W G Hay, D B Conrad, J E Sample, W F Hord, & Wyatt M Brown
In the Marine Corps we learn that commissions has also been issued as follows:
Capt, A Garland
1st Lts: T Y Field & G C McCurdy   2nd Lts: A G Dallas & H B Tyler, jr

A Phil paper says: "The most strenuous efforts have been made this week for the pardon of Dr Beale. After a full hearing of the case, Gov Pollock positively refused to grant a pardon." [Apr 3rd newspaper: Phil, Apr 2. In the Supreme Court this morning Chief Justice Lewis gave a decision granting a writ of error in the case of Dr Beale, on the ground that the jury which tried that case, instead of being sworn to render a verdict according to evidence, were sworn to try the guilt or innocence of the dfndnt; & also that the dfndnt, instead of being sentenced to solitary confinement at labor, was sentenced to imprisonment at hard labor.]

Furnished house for rent: the subscriber will rent his house, with the furniture & stable, at 405 13th st, between G & H sts. For sale, a Horse & Carriage.
–Chas Dummer

THU FEB 22, 1854
Senate: 1-Cmte on Commerce: bill for the relief of John R Powers, agent in charge of the property of the U S in Michigan city, Indiana, & of Isaac S Smith, of Buffalo, N Y: reported back with an amendment.

Circuit Court of Wash Co, D C, in Chancery, in the cause wherein Darius Clagett is cmplnt & Keally & other are dfndnts: sale on Mar 15 next, on the premises, all that piece of ground & improvements, a 2 story house, in Wash City, on Lot E in square 408, formerly belonging to Mrs Sarah Spratts, fronting 25 feet 10 inches on 9th st west. By deed of trust dated Sep 13, 1843, of the land records of Wash Co, D C.
–John B Clagett, trustee -Jas C McGuire, auct

Laws of the U S passed at the 2nd Session of the 33rd Congress of the U S A: 1-Act to change the name of the schnr **Henry Plantagenet** to that of the schnr **A G Brown**: an American built schnr now owned by Ebenezer Clark, of Jackson Co, Mississippi. 2-Act to provide compensation for the services of Geo Morell in adjusting titles to land in Michigan, approved Aug 1, 1844, be construed so as to give to Judges Woodbridge & Chipman, named in said act, the compensation therein provided, only from the date of the termination of their appoints as such judges.

Salisbury [*N C] Banner: Mr Maxwell Chambers, of that county, lately deceased, has willed to Davidson College $30,000. He also left $30,000 to the Presbyterian Church at Salisbury. [*Looks like N C.]

Mrd: on Feb 20, at the Church of the Ascension, Miss Mary B McPherson to Mr Chas F Perrie, both of Wash City.

Died: yesterday, at *The Cottage*, the residence of his sister, Miss Ann Carroll, Wm Carroll, in his 72nd year. His funeral is this afternoon at 3 o'clock.

Died: yesterday, Mr Edw S Harris, printer, a native of Md. His funeral is this afternoon, at 3 o'clock, from 500 7th st.

Obit-died: on Feb 21, in Wash City, Maj John G Camp, of Sandusky, Ohio, in his 67th year. He was an ofcr in the war of 1812, & rendered services on the Northern frontier which won for him the confidence & esteem of all who were connected with him. His remains will be taken to Sandusky by the express train of this afternoon.

For rent: the 2nd story of the store-house on the corner of 7th & D sts, over Mr Wm Linton's grocery, lately occupied by T J Magruder, wholesale shoe dealer. Apply to T J Magruder, D st, between 6 & 7th sts, or Saml Fowler, 427 F st, between 6 & 7th.

FRI FEB 23, 1855
Senate: 1-Ptn from Wm A Powell, asking further compensation for executing the painting of the discovery of the Mississippi by De Soto for the vacant panel in the rotundo of the Capitol. The memorialist says that his painting contains over 50 figures all of which were painted from living models, & at an expense of $8,000; that to avail himself of living models & arms & armor belonging to the epoch of De Soto he was compelled to remain in Europe 4 years to complete his work; that he has devoted 4 years of his life, at an average labor of 8 hours a day; &, in consideration of his having received but $2,000 above actual expenses incurred, appeals to Congress for a futher appropriation of $5,000. 2-Ptn from Wm H De Forrest asking compensation for powder destroyed at Punata Arenas during the bombardment of Greytown by Capt Geo N Hollins, of the navy. 3-Ptn from Hannibal Fauk & Eliza S Collier, asking confirmation of their title to a tract of land in the Bastrop grant. 4-Ptn from Emma Du Barry, widow of a surgeon of the U S Navy, asking to be reimbursed for extraordinary expenses incurred by her late husband in Hong Kong in the service of the Gov't. 5-Cmte of Claims: joint resolution for the relief of Hall Neilson, & asked its immediate consideration: but it was objected to.

House of Reps: 1-Ptn of Wm Langfit, sen, of Va, asking remuneration for losses sustained for carrying the U S mail.

The firm of J L Rider & Co is this day dissolved by mutual consent. J L Rider is authorized to receive all debts due said firm, & will pay all claims. He will hereafter conduct the Grocery business on his own account, Pa ave & 20th st.
-Isaac Paul, Chas H Brown, J L Rider

Dissolution by mutual consent of the firm existing between John F Dyer, having purchased the interest of Geo J Thomas in the same. –G J Thomas, John F Dyer

For rent: brick house at corner of 8th st & Ga ave, the next house to the navy-yard gate. Apply next door to Jas Rhodes.

Mr Isaac Edge, pyrotechnist, of Jersey City, invented a new & powerful double-action & chambered rocket for Gov't service; bids fair to rival the famous Congreve or French rocket, whose services are well known in the present European war.

SAT FEB 24. 1855
Circuit Court of PG Co, Md, sitting as a Court of Equity: Feb, 1855. John L Townshend & Jane Townshend, vs John G Townshend, Geo W Townshend, Danl W Townshend, & others. The suit is to procure a decree for the sale of the real estate whereof John Townshend died intestate, for the purpose of distributing the proceeds of said sale among the parties thereto entitled, his heirs & legal reps. John Townshend died in 1846 seized of a real estate supposed to contain about 1,500 acres, & that it has been finally decided on the issues touching the sanity of the said John Townshend & the validity of a paper writing purporting to be his last will & testament; that the said John Townshend died intestate, whereby all his real estate descended to his legal heirs & legal reps; that his heirs & legal reps are as follows: the cmplnt, John L, who is the son of Leonard Townshend, deceased, a brother of said intestate; the dfndnts, John G, Geo W, Danl W, Mgt V Walker, Ann, & Saml Gilbert, are infant children of Geo S Townshend, another son of said Leonard, & who died in 1854, & whose widow Jane, the other cmplnt, is entitled in virtue of her marriage with the said Geo S to a dower interest in said lands, which lands she prays may be sold & that she may receive her interest according to the laws of the State in money; Mary Townshend, Wm T Robinson, Jeremiah Townshend, Wm B Townshend, John F Townshend, Priscilla Townshend, Jeannette Burch, Jane, wife of Henry M Tomlin, & Mary, wife of Townley B Robey, & Tobias G Townshend, all of whom reside in Md, in part the heirs & legal reps of Wm Townshend, a brother of said intestate, & who died since the said intestate; that Saml Townshend, who resides in Phil, & Verlinda, the wife of Jas H Tennella, who resides in the State of Va, & the other & remaining children & reps of the said Wm, who is a deceased brother of said intestate; that Saml Burch, Henry Burch, & Eliz Blacklock, wife of ___ Blacklock, [or their reps, if the said Saml Henry & Eliz, or either of them, are dead,] are entitled to a share in said estate, the said Saml Henry & Eliz being children & only reps of Mrs Eliz Burch, a deceased sister of said intestate, & that they are non-residents; the first name, if now alive, is a resident of Oregon Territory, & the others, Henry Burch

& Eliz Blacklock, when last heard from, were residents of the State of Ky. All the above named persons are made parties to the bill, & it is insisted that it would be to the interest & advantage of all the parties interested that the said land should be sold & the proceeds be distributed among the parties thereto entitled. Absent dfndnts to appear in this Court, in person or by solicitor, on or before the 2nd Monday of Aug next. -Edw W Belt, Clerk of the Circuit Court of PG Co, Md.

Household & kitchen furniture at auction on: Feb 28, at the late residence of Geo Johnson, deceased, at 60 K st, between 24th & 25th sts. -Green & Scott, aucts

The Gardiner case in Chancery. This case, which was before the Cicruit Court since Feb 12, was yesterday brought to a close. The Court is satisfied that the claim set up by Geo A Gardiner for damages, as allowed in the award of the Com'rs, was false & unfounded; that the award was obtained by fraud, & was null & void; & that the money paid out of the Treasury of the U S under such circumstances continued its character as the money & property of the U S, & may be followed into the hands of Messrs Corcoran & Riggs, who are not the true owners of the said fund. The Court made a decree to the effect that the awards were obtained by Geo A Gardiner by means of false swearing, forgery, & fraud, & were therefore null & void; that his estate is indebted to the U S in the sum of $428,750, with interest from May 16, 1851; that Corcoran & Riggs should bring into Court on the 4th Monday of Mar next the stocks & securities in their hands, amounting to $89,000, being part of the funds obtained by Gardiner under said awards, & also an admitted balance in cash of $8,737.46; & that the cause be referred to Walter S Cox, as special auditor, to state an account of said Corcoran & Riggs of dividends collected by them.

Senate: 1-Resolved, that there be paid to the widow of the late Hon Moses Norris, deceased, out of the contingent fund of the Senate, the amount for the funeral expenses of the deceased that was paid to the widow of Hon Wm Upham, late a Senator, for a similar purpose; the the expense of the cmte & ofcrs of the Senate who accompanied the remains to New Hampshire be also paid out of the contingent fund, under the direction of the cmte of arrangement.

House of Reps: 1-Cmte of Claims: bill for the relief of Franklin Chase: committed. Same cmte: bill for the relief of Gad Humphreys: committed. 2-Cmte on Commerce: bill for the relief of Henry Little & Jacob Felch: committed.

Valuable land in Iowa for sale: the s e quarter of section 8, in township 78, north of range 14, in the district of lands subject to sale at Iowa city, Iowa, containing 160 acres. Apply to Pollard Webb, real estate agent, ofc on Pa ave, 7 doors east of the Nat'l Hotel, Wash City.

Mrd: on Feb 22, at the E st Baptist Church, by Rev G W Samson, Mr Peter Colison to Miss Helen P Kersey, both of Wash.

Mrd: on Feb 20, at the Church of the Ascension, by Rev Henry Stanley, Mr Chas F Perrie to Miss Mary B McPherson, all of Wash City.

Died: on Feb 23, at the U S Hotel, in Wash City, Benj Laurent, of Mexico, & late of London, in his 50th year, sincerely regretted by his numerous friends.

Died: on Feb 23, Benj F McCathran, aged 21 years. His funeral is on Sunday at 3 o'clock, from his late residence, 543 E st, between 9th & 10th sts.

Died: on Feb 18, at Brooklyn, N Y, of consumption, Mrs Susannah B Winchester, wife of Jonas Winchester, late of Calif, aged 43 years.

Died: on Feb 22, in Wash City, Ann Eliza, infant daughter of E P & Rebecca W Miller, aged 7 months.

Senate: 1-Memorial from David Holt, a soldier of the war of 1812, asking to be allowed to locate his 30 acre bounty land warrant on a certain tract of land not subject to private entry, with the privilege of entering the residue of said tract by private entry.

House of Reps: 1-Cmte on Patents: bill for the relief of Cyrus H McCormick: committed. 2-Cmte on Public Lands: bill for the relief of Mrs Felch, widow of Rev Cheever Felch, deceased: committed. Same cmte: adverse report on the ptn of Sarah Viney, sister & admx of John Viney. Same cmte: bill for the relief of Mark Bean & Richd H Bean, of Ark: committed. 3-Cmte on the Post Ofc & Post Roads: bill for the relief of Danl Searle & Co for extra servce rendered: committed. Same cmte: settlement of the claims of the late firm of C M Strader & Co: committed. Same cmte: bill for the relief of Robt Jemison & the legal reps of Benj Williamson, with an adverse recommendation: & it was laid on the table. Same cmte: bill for the relief of Uriah P Monroe: committed. 4-Cmte on the Judiciary: bill for the relief of Magdalena Van Ness, widow of Cornelius P Van Ness, deceased: committed. 5-Cmte on Revolutionary Claims: bill for the relief of the legal reps of David Noble, deceased: committed. Same cmte: bill for the relief of Wm Craig: committed. Same cmte: bill for the relief of the heirs of Capt Joshua Chamberlain, deceased: with a favorable recommendation: committed. 6-Cmte on Private Land Claims: bills committed: relief of: Jas Lindsay; of Wm Dempsey; & of the heirs of Jacob Moyer. Same cmte: adverse reports on the ptns of J L Hickman, of David Maynard, & of Edw Sylvester. 7-Cmte on Indian Affairs: bill for the relief of the heirs of Mary Jemison, deceased: committed. Same cmte: adverse report on the ptn of Elisha R Sprague, trustee of Wm B Heart. Same cmte: adverse report on the memorial of the Chief of the Saut de Ste Marie band of Chippewa Indians, & on the ptn of Feliz Argenti. Same cmte: adverse report on the ptn of John Fox & 8 other Tuscarora Indians. 8-Cmte on Naval Affairs: bill for the relief of Jos White & a bill for the relief of Andrew Armstrong: committed. Same cmte: bill for the relief of Otway H

Berryman, with a favorable recommendation: committed. Same cmte: bill for the relief of Harrison Hough: committed. Same cmte: bill for the relief of Capt Thos Ap Catesby Jones, with a favorable recommendation: committed. Same cmte: bill for the relief of Robt Joyner, with the recommendation that it do not pass: laid on the table. 9-Cmte on Foreign Affairs: memorial of Lt M F Maury, of the U S Navy, in behalf of the Memphis Convention, & in favor of the free navigation of the river Amazon, made a report thereon: ordered to be printed. Same cmte: adverse report on the ptns of Thos W Mather & Wm R Glover. 10-Cmte on Revolutionary Pensions: adverse reports on the ptns of Sally Shedd ; of Maj Edw Waller; of Mary Miller, one of the heirs of Elnathan Sears, deceased; on the ptns of Jos Kirk, of Morgan Co, Ohio; of Geo W Samson & Maria S Johnson; of Sally Ketchum; of Susan Scott, widow of Wm Scott; & on the ptn of Smith Crane. Same cmte: bills committed: relief of: Jesse French, of Braintree, Mass; of Mary F B Levely; of Robt H Stevens; of Chas H Pointer; of Danl Nickel; of Mrs Nancy Wetherford, widow of Col Wm Wetherford; of Geo W Whittier, of Newfield, Maine. Pension to Dolly Empson. Bill to enable P M Kent, late pension agent at New Albany, Indiana, to adjust & settle his accounts. Same cmte: adverse reports on the ptns of Lathrop Foster; of Thos Priddy; of Thos W McMahon; of Hezekiah Wingate; of Warren Drake; & of Elisha Beshe; & of Irene G Scarritt, widow of Jeremiah M Scarritt. Same cmte: bill granting a bounty land warrant to Ozias Hart, of Seneca Co, Ohio: committed. 11-Cmte on Patents: adverse reports on the ptns of Alex'r Mitchell; of Jos Nock; of Danl Pettibone; & of Andrew Morse, jr. 12-Cmte on Military Affairs: bill for the relief of Brvt Brig Gen John B Walbach, U S Army; of Jacob Dodson; of Geo W Torrence; of the heirs of the late Col John Hardin; of Mrs Anne W Butler; joint resolutionf or the relief of Jos Aymer: committed. Same cmte: adverse report on the ptn of Chas W Ogden. 13-Cmte of Claims: bill for the relief of Cassius M Clay: committed.

Valuable square or lock of ground for sale in Wash City, being square 624. Title is unquestionable. Inquire of Chas H B Dart, at ofc of Gas Light Co, 8th st & Penn ave, or W B Todd, between 6th & 7th sts.

MON FEB 26, 1855

Senate: 1-Memorial from C Ludwig Richter, asking Congress to make an appropriation for a bronze bust in commemoration of Thos Jefferson, & that he may be employed to execute the same. The memorialist sends a description, which would require an appropriation of $65,000; Congress to furnish the necessary metal, which amounts to 80,000 cwt. 2-Memorial from D O Shattuck, asking a revival of the act of 28th Feb, 1854, supplemental to the act to establish & settle private land claims in the State of Calif.

Mrd: on Feb 20, at the Potomac House, Wash, by Rev Mr Henry, Mr Robt Latham to Miss Susan S Deneal.

Mrd: on Feb 24, at St Dominick's Church, by Rev Mr Clarkson, Jas Donovan, M D, of St Landry's, La, to Miss Mary T Hodgkinson, of Wash City.

Died: on Feb 25, of consumption, Joanna Morarity, in her 22nd year. Her funeral is this afternoon, at 3 o'clock, from the residence of L Richardson, 428 M st, between 13th & 14th sts.

Died: on Feb 24, at his residence, in Gtwn, D C, after a severe illness, in his 66th year, Mr Walter Smoot. His funeral will be from Christ Church, this afternoon, at 4 o'clock.

Died: on Feb 24, after a lingering illness, Mrs Sarah Sinon, relict of the late Thos Sinon, aged 58 years. Her funeral will be this evening, at 4 o'clock, from the residence of her sister, Mrs Hughes, corner of 2nd & G sts.

The undersigned have associated in business under the name of Johnson, Guy & Co, at the old stand of Woodward & Guy, Penn ave, between 10th & 11th sts, a general assortment of hardware, bldg materials, cutlery, stoves, & grates. –Wm J Sibley, R C Johnson, B F Guy

On Tue 2 young gentlemen, students at Emory & Henry College, Saml Meek & ___ Cole, both of this county went into the field to try a double-barrelled pistol. Young Meek fired one barrel, put the muzzle to his mouth to blow the smoke through the tube, when the other barrel exploded. He lingered in great agony for 2 hours, but nothing could be done to save his life. He was about 18 years of age, & an attentive student. –Abingdon [Va] Dem

No 1046: in Chancery, Baker & Givenny, excs of Terrence Looby, vs Chas McGarvey's heirs. The trustees in the above cause report the sale of the real estate of Chas McGarvey on Dec 28 last, John McGarvey was the purchaser of part of lot 1, in square west of square 4, in Wash City, fronting 17 feet on K st & 25 feet on 27th st west, with bldg thereon; & also one undivided moiety, or half part of lot 11 in said square, for the sum of $1,000, & hath complied with the terms of sale. –John A Smith, clerk

TUE FEB 27, 1855
Senate: 1-Cmte on the Judiciary: adverse report on the bill for the relief of Fred'k Griffing. 2-Cmte on Private Land Claims: bill for the relief of Jas P Rowan. Same cmte: bill to confirm Jos Wanderstrand in his title to certain lands. 3-Cmte on Pensions: bill for the relief of Lemuel Wooster. Same cmte: bill for the relief of Mrs Irene G Scarritt.

Dissolution this day of the firm of Moore & Hubbard by mutual consent.
–J W Hubbard, Wm M Moore

Post Ofc Embezzlement in New Orleans. The Grand Jury of the U S District Court at New Orleans has found true bills of indictment against Richd A Lafonte & Richd A Nixon, charged with embezzling money from letters in the post ofc, where they were employed as clerks. Both these young men have forfeited their bonds & left for parts unknown.

Wash City Ordinances: 1-Act for the relief of Wm Thompson: to pay him $166.15, being the amount due for publishing the proceedings laws, etc, of this corporation, of his contract of Nov 18, 1854. 2-Act for the relief of Robt R Pywell: he is hereby authorized to erect a brick stable, fronting on the bldg line of 8th st west, between D & E sts north: it shall not be used for the purpose of stalling or grooming horses.

Died: on Feb 28, at Alexandria, Va, Mrs Julia Acken, in her 65th year, wife of Wm D Acken, of Wash, where she had resided upwards of 50 years.

Died: on Feb 26, Mrs Mary Tanner Darby, relict of the late Wm Darby, & daughter of the late Benj Tanner, of Phil.

Died: on Feb 26, Richard Edward, infant son of Jos E & Martha P Rawlings, aged 57 years. His funeral will be Tue afternoon at 3 o'clock.

Died: on Feb 23, of chronic croup, Ninian Beall, son of Geo W & Eliza J Hopkins, aged 5 years.

Obit-died: Dorothy Wordsworth, the only sister of Wm Wordsworth, the poet, died at Rydal Mount, in Westmoreland, on Jan 25, in her 84th year. She was born on Christmas day, 1771, & from girlhood [though not from childhood] was the constant & chosen associate of her illustrious brother. Wordsworth was as fond of his sister as Chas Lamb was of his sister. Mary Lamb lived single, so did Dorothy Wordsworth.

Died: on Dec 29 last, at Brighton, Miss Sarah Rogers, the only sister of the poet of The Pleasures of Memory, who happily still survives. Miss Rogers had all her brother's taste for art & literature. Her house in Hanover Terrace was elegantly filled with choice examples of art from Giotto to Stothard, brought as much by her own good sense as by her brother's example & assistance. Some of her best pictures she is understood to have left to the Nat'l Gallery.

Mr Powhatan Ellis Shepherd, former of Princess Anne Co, Va, died lately in St Louis from the effects of wounds received in a sham fight in the armory of the Young American Greys, to which he belonged. The musket was loaded with bullets & buckshot, which was not known to the young men. It is supposed that it was loaded during the late election riots in St Louis & placed aside without being used.

The Cleveland Herald states that various robberies of the mails at the Salem post ofc, in Ohio, have been committed by Thos J Walton, a clerk in that ofc, & Jos S Wilson, a son of the postmaster. Both young men have been arrested.

The last of Braddock's defeat. Died: in Williamstown, Mass, Jan 27, Ishmael Titus, colored, of the extraordinary age of 109 or 110 years. He was born a slave in Va, & when Gen Braddock set out on his ill-fated expedition the master of Ishmael was employed by the commissary to transport subsistence stores for the army, & took Ishmael with him.

St Helena: 1815: arrival of Napoleon Bonaparte, Oct 15. 1821: the decease of Napoleon Bonaparte, May 5. 1838-Prince Wm Henry Frederick, a grandson of Wm I, King of Holland, landed at St Helena, the first Prince of the blood of any European nation who ever visited the island.

Household & kitchen furniture for sale: from the estate of the late John D Brown. I offer also the lease of the bldg in which is contained *Appollo Hall*.
-Jas C McGuire, administrator

WED FEB 28. 1855
Senate: 1-Memorial from Isaac Knight, asking the aid & sanction of Congress to enable him to carry out his improvement in lighthouse signals to prevent shipwreck, & save passengers & property in case of shipwreck on the coast. 2-Ptn of H O Claughton, asking to be allowed an amount paid by him for ofc rent while acting in the capacity of commercial agent for the Netherland division of the Island of St Martin, West Indies. 3-Bill for the relief of John M Bowers, agent in charge of the property of the U S at Michigan city, Indiana, & of Isaac S Smith, of Buffalo, N Y: passed.

Henry Addison, was on Monday last re-elected Mayor of Gtwn.

Died: after an illness of 2 days, Harrison Shipley, son of Thos C Donn, in his 14th year. His funeral is on Thu, at 3 o'clock, from the residence of his father on H, between 4th & 5th sts. [No death date given.]

Matthew Simmons, a German employed at the rasp manufacturing establishment of Mr Shelley, in Albany, was drawn over a shaft & dreadfully injured. He was alive when taken down & carried to his house to his poor wife & family. -Albany Argus

Boston, Feb 26. The farm of 800 acres, with the bldgs thereon, known as Danl Webster's homestead, in Franklin, N H, was sold at auction on Thu for $15,000, & Rufus L Tay, of this city, was the purchaser.

The residence in Wash City of Hon Thos H Benton, of Missouri, on C st, between 3rd & 4 ½ sts, was destroyed by fire yesterday, together with nearly all of the furniture, the library, & most of all the manscript papers of Mr Benton. One of his daughter took refuge at Col Fremont's, one of the adjacent dwlgs. There was no insurance. The cause of this conflagration was a defective chimney flue.

Rev M D Conway will be ordained Pastor over the First Unitarian Church in Wash City, this evening, the 28th. The public is invited to attend.

THU MAR 1, 1855
Senate: 1-Ptn from Randolph Clay, for compensation as Minister to Peru from the date of his appointment to the time from which he commenced to receive it. 2-Ptn from citizens of Randolph Co, Ill, asking that Valentine G Wehsheim may have his pension increased. 3-Cmte on the Judiciary: bill for the relief of Jos Ridgeway: recommended its passage. 4-Cmte on Foreign Relations: joint resolution to pay Wm H De Forrest $12,000 for a quantity of powder destroyed at Punta Arenas: a substitue for the original resolution. 5-Cmte on Military Claims: bill for the relief of Geo C McCerren: recommended its passage.

House of Reps: 1-Cmte of the Whole: discharged from the consideration of the ptn of bill for the relief of the heirs of Brig Gen Richd D Mason: when it was read the third time & passed. 2-Cmte on the Judiciary: bill for the relief of R R Ward, J G Halleck, & Jacob Little: committed.

The copartnership of Sweeny, Bestor & Co, is this day dissolved by mutual consent. -H B Sweeny, W C Bestor, J L Dufief, Saml Fowler. Anna R O'Neal, H B Sweeny, excs of T O'Neal.
+
The undersigned have this day formed a Copartnerhsip for the purpose of transacting a Genr'l Exchange, Collection, & Banking Business, under the firm of Sweeny, Rittenhouse & Co. The business, as heretofore conducted under the firm of Sweeny, Bestor & Co, will be continued, without interruption, by Sweeny, Rittenhouse & Co. -H B Sweeny, C E Rittenhouse, J L Dufief, Saml Fowler, W T Herron, Wash City.

Obit-died: on Tue, at his residence in N Y C, aged 46 years, Hon Henry Pierrepont Edwards, Judge of the Supreme Court of the State of N Y. He had been ill for some weeks. He was born in New Haven, & was the 2nd son of Govn'r Edwards, of Conn, & grandson of Rev Jonathan Edwards, the distinguished author of the Treatise on the Will. Judge Edwards passes to the grave justly honored & widely mourned.
–N Y Courier

Pews for sale or rent: in Trinity Church, 3rd st. For terms apply to Mr D W Middleton, Capitol Hill, or to Fred Koones, Reg'r T C at the Navy Agent's Ofc.

Wash Corp: 1-Ptn from Alex'r Borland, agent for the heirs of Jas Moore, asking to be paid certain money due from the sale of lots 15, 18, & 19, in square 216, sold at tax sale Dec 8, 1838: which was referred to the Cmte on Finance. 2-Ptn from Jon Guttenson for the remission of a fine: referred to the Cmte of Claims. Same for Geo W Wren. 3-Cmte of Claims: act for the relief of Mary Sullivan: passed.

$20 reward for servant woman Maria, light compleion, who left the house of the subscriber, on 8th st, Wash, on Feb 27. All persons are cautioned against harboring or buying her. –E W Hansell

FRI MAR 2, 1855
Appointment by the Pres, by & with the advice & consent of the Congress. Gen Winfield Scott, of the Army of the U S, to be Lt Gen by brevet in the same, for eminent services in the late war with Mexico, to take rank as such from Mar 29, 1847, the day on which the U S forces under his command captured Vera Cruz & the Castle of San Juan de Ulua.

Senate: 1-Cmte for the Dist of Columbia: bill for the relief of Wm G Howison: passed. 2-Cmte on Pensions: bill for the relief of Anthony Phelps, of Hardin Co, Ky. Same cmte: bill for the relief of Danl Doland. Same cmte: recommended that the following pass: relief of Wm Brown; of Jas McIntire; of Eliz Foreman; of Isaac Allen, of Turner, Maine; of Wyatt Griffith, of Wash Co, Tenn; & of Chas H Pointer. Same cmte: recommended that they do not pass: relief of Solomon Lafollett; of Thos C Ramsey & Ananias O Richardson & Jas McLaughlin; of Geo M Bentley, of Indiana; & increase of John C Burton's pension. 3-Cmte on Private Land Claims: asked to be discharged from the consideration of the memorial of Alex'r McKee: which was agreed to. 4-Cmte on Pensions: bill for the relief of Chas H Pointer. 5-Bills passed: relief of Thos Underhill, exc of Thos Underhill, deceased; for the benefit of the heirs of Philip R Rice, deceased; & relief of the children & grandchildren of Thos Morris. 6-Adverse report on the act for the relief of the legal reps of Henry Hoffman. 7-Bill for the relief of Sarah Morris, only heir of Robt Mitchell, deceased: passed. 8-Bill for the relief of Anne E Cook: passed. 9-Bill for the relief of Wm G Preston: passed.

U S Agricultural Society met yesterday & elected the following ofcrs:
Pres: Marshall P Wilder, of Mass
Vice Presidents:
John D Lang, Maine
H F French, N H
Fred Holbrook, Vt
B V French, Mass
Jos J Cooke, R I
John T Andrew, Conn

Henry Wager, N Y
Isaac Cornell, N J
Isaac Newton, Pa
C H Holcombe, Del
H G S Key, Md
G W P Custis, Va

Henry K Burgwyn, N C
Jas Hopkinson, S C
D A Reese, Ga
A P Hatch, Ala
A G Brown, Miss
J D B DeBow, La
Gen Whitfield, Kansas
J T Worthington, Ohio
B Gratz, Ky
M P Gentry, Tenn
Jos Orr, Indiana
J A Kinnicutt, Ill
Thos Allen, Mo
Exec Cmte:
John A King, N Y
C B Calvert, Md
A L Elwyn, Pa
J Wentworth, Ill
Sec: Wm S King, Boston, Mass
Treasurer: B B French, Wash, D C

T B Flournoy, Ark
J C Holmes, Mich
Jackson Morton, Fla
T G Rusk, Texas
J W Grimes, Iowa
B C Eastman, Wis
J M Horner, Cal
Jos H Bradley, D C
S M Baird, New Mexico
H H Sibley, Minn
Jos Lane, Oregon
J L Hayes, Utah
Mr Giddings, Nebraska

B Perley Poore, Mass
A Watts, Ohio
John Jones, Del

House of Reps: 1-Joint resolution for the adjustment of the accounts of John D Colmesnil: passed. 2-Bill for the relief of Jesse French, of Braintree, Mass: passed. 3-Bill for the relief of the heirs of Mary Jemison, deceased: passed. 4-Bill to contunue the pension of Francis E Baden: passed. 5-Joint resolution for the relief of Clark Mills: passed. 6-Ptn of Yates Rogers & others for bounty to the owners of the schnr **Scituate**, of Dennis, Mass: presented. 7-Ptn of Gen G G Cushman & others, of Maine, for amendments of the laws for arming & equipping the militia of the U S.

Died: on Feb 28, at Gtwn, Mary, wife of Jas O'Donnoghue. Her funeral will take place this morning at 10 o'clock, from the residence of Mr T O'Donnoghue, 1st st.

Died: on Feb 28, at the Treasury bldg, very suddenly, Mr Saml S Whiting, in his 52nd year. His funeral will take place this morning from the residence of Mr Jos Thompson, on Missouri ave, at 11 o'clock.

Three steamers sunk. The steamer **Dresden** came in contact with a sunken wreck, at widow Merriweather's, a few miles below New Madrid, on Thu. The steamer **James Robb** struck a log near the foot of Devils' Island, above Capt Girardeau, on Sat, which tore away part of her hull. The steamer **H D Bacon** left St Louis for New Orleans on Thu. She struck a log near Widow Beard's Island, which broke her hog chains & some of the timbers in her hull, causing her to leak slightly. No lives lost.

Cincinnati Retreat for the Insane, in charge of Edw Mead, M D. This Institution is open for the reception of patients. Persons wishing to bring their own servants for the comfort of a patient can make a special arrangement to that effect.

SAT MAR 3, 1855
Senate: 1-Act for the relief of Jas Holstein. 2-Resolution from the House of Reps for the relief of Clark Mills: passed. 3-Bill to settle the claim of Alfred G Benson was taken up.

The Boston Traveller gives the particulars concerning the death of Mrs Farley, who died in Lynn, on Tue, from the effects of ether administered for a dental operation. A coroner's inquest revealed the lungs of the deceased were diseased, & her death was probably brought on by the inhalation of ether.

Obit-died: the Hon Wm Dubose died on Sat last at his residence in St Stephen's Parish, S C. For many years he was a member of the State Legislature, both as a Senator & Rep, & was also Lt Govn'r of the State.

Hon Wm Jackson, formerly a Rep in Congress from Mass, died at his residence in Newton, Mass, on Tue last. He was one of the pioneers of railroad enterprises in Mass.

Mrd: on Thu, by Rev John C Smith, Mr John T Edd to Miss Mary E Hamadinger, both of Alexandria, Va.

Died: on Mar 1, in Wash City, Mathew Calbraith, son of Lt Mathew C & Harriet Eliz Perry, aged 8 months.

Died: on Mar 2, Mrs Ann C, wife of W N Ball. Her funeral is this afternoon at 2 o'clock, from the E st Baptist Church.

For sale or rent: that valuable property at the corner of F & 20th sts west, in square 103, well known as the former residence of Mrs Ramsey. Apply to Mr Richd Smith, in Wash, or to the subscriber, on the Heights of Gtwn. –H C Gunnell

Great Bargains. I have just received a splendid assortment of collars, laces, & bonnets, which I will sell at reduced prices. –Ruth A Peaco, 12 Market Space

MON MAR 5, 1855
Senate: 1-Bill for the relief of the legal reps of Wm A Christian: passed. 2-Bill for the relief of the widow of W Irving, deceased: passed. 3-Bill for the relief of Thos C Ramsey & Ananias O Richardson, & Jas McLaughlin: although this bill was reported adversely, Mr Jones gave so glowing a description of the acts of the parties that it was passed in the face of all opposition. 4-Bills passed: relief of-John Dugan; of

Titian R Peale; of Ferdinand Clark; of Jas Hughes; of Jeptha L Heminger; of Joel Henry Dyer; of the heirs of Lt Andrew Finley; of the heirs & legal reps of Capt John De Treville; & of L R Lyon & Dean S Howard, of the State of N Y.

House of Reps: 1-Joint resolution for the relief of Abigail Strafford: passed. 2-Bill for the relief of Franklin Chase: passed.

Appointments by the Pres, by & with the advice & consent of the Congress.
Court of Claims: Judge Gilchrist, of N Y; Judge Isaac Blackford, of Indiana; & Jos H Lumpkin, of Ga. Montgomery Blair, of Wash, Solicitor. Israel D Andrews, of Maine, Consul General for the British North American Provinces, [an ofc recently created.] John Romely Brodhead, of N Y, Consular Agent [or Com'r] for Japan, to reside at Samodi.

Military appointments: For the two Cavalry Regts.
Cols:
Brvt E V Sumner, Lt Col 1st Dragoons
Maj Albert S Johnson, Maj of Pay Dept
Lt Cols:
Brvt Col R E Lee, Capt of Engineers
Brvt Lt Col J E Johnston, Capt Topographical Engineers
Majors:
Brvt Lt Col W J Hardee, Capt 2nd Dragoons
Brvt Lt Col Braxton Bragg, Capt 3rd Artl
Brvt Maj W H Emory, Capt Topographical Engineers
Benj McCulloh, of Texas
For the two Infty Regts:
Cols:
Brvt Col Geo Wright, Lt Col 4th Infty
Brvt Lt Col Ed B Alexander, Maj 8th Infty
Lt Cols:
Brvt Col Chas F Smith, Maj 1st Artl
Brvt Lt Col Silas Casey, Capt 2nd Infty
Majors:
Brvt Lt Col W H T Walker, Capt 6th Infty
Brvt Lt Col Edw J Steptoe, Capt 3rd Artl
Brvt Lt Col E R S Canby, Capt Adj General's Dept
Capt H W Benham, Capt Engineers
The Pres made no nomination, we understand, for the new Brigadiership created by the Army bill.

Stray cow came to the subscriber's premises in Oct last. Owner is to come forward, prove property, pay charges, & take her away. –Fred'k Cox, living on Mrs Britton's farm, near Bladensburg.

Robt Mills, civil engineer & architect, died in Wash City on Mar 3. He was a native of S C, but had been a resident of Wash for 25 years, & had acquired here no little fame as the architect of several of the public edifices, including the Post Ofc Dept, the Treasury Dept, & the Patent Ofc.

Local Matters. Mr Nathan Whitely, of 131 West 18th st, N Y, whose perfumed crystals, or spirit of flowers, are on exhibition at the Metropolitan Mechanics' Institute, died in this city on Sat last after an illness of 3 or 4 days.

TUE MAR 6, 1855

Notice. To John McDowell & Wm McDowell, formerly of the State of Va. The above named are notified that in a suit pending in the Circuit Court of Amelia Co, Va, between Jas McDowell, adm of Peter McDowell, deceased, & others, plntfs, & Wm H Robertson, adm of Eliz S Morgan, deceased, & others, dfndnts, a decree was pronounced at the Oct term, 1854, of the said Court of which the following is an abstract: "And the dfndnts, John McDowell, the elder, & Wm McDowell, the elder, as to whom it is stated in the proceedings that they left this commonwealth more than 7 years ago, & have not since been heard of, not having appeared to claim the amounts to which they are entitled as heirs & distributes of the said decedent, the Court doth adjudge, order, & decree that Thos T Giles, hereby appointed a special com'r for that purpose, do cause a proper abstract of this decree, giving notice of their rights in this cause, to be published once a week for 6 weeks in one of the newspapers published in the city of Richmond, & also, in one of the newspapers published in Wash City." The object of the above mentioned suit was to make partition & distribution of the estate of Eliz N Morgan, late of Amelia Co. The above named John McDowell & Wm McDowell, or those entitled to claim under them, have a right to one-fourth of the estate as the share of each of the said parties, amounting to about $800. If the said parties, or either of them, or any persons showing a right to their shares, or to the share of either of them, will appear to claim such share, the same will be decreed accordingly; otherwise such share as is not claimed will be decreed to the other heirs & distributes of the said decedent in the manner required by law. –Thos T Giles, Spec Comm

Trustee's sale of brick house & lot: by deed of trust from Wm D Akin, dated Aug 11, 1853: recorded in Liber J A S No 66, folios from 147 to 150, of the land records for Wash Co, D C: all that piece of ground being part of lot 17 in square 374, fronting on I st, with a good brick dwlg. –Henry Naylor, trustee -Green & Scott, aucts

Household & kitchen furniture at auction on Mar 8, at the residence of J H Eberbach, on Pa ave, between 21st & 22nd sts. Excellent furniture. -Green & Scott, aucts
+
Auction of choice old wines, liquors, stock & fixtures of a Confectionary Establishment, on Mar 9, at the Confectionary store of J H Eberbach, on Pa ave, between 21st & 22nd sts. -Green & Scott, aucts

Appointments: Robt Ould, of Gtwn, & Wm B Cross, of Wash City, to codify the laws of the Dist of Columbia. David H Burr, Surveyor Genr'l of Utah.

Mediterranean squadron. The U S ship **Saranac** was to leave on Mar 5 for Leghorn, to obtain the body of Capt Wyman, U S navy, which was to be sent home in the ship **Levant**. The sailor who was hung on Jan 19, for the murder of a shipmate on board the **Levant**, acknowledged the justice of his sentence & confessed to the murder of a man in New Orleans some years back.

Breach of Promise. A case of this kind was tried in Orange Co, N Y, last week. Charlotte Wright prosecuted Langford R Brown for breach of promise of marriage, & it appeared that about 3 years ago the dfndnt commenced paying attentions to the plntf, & about 2 years ago asked her in marriage of her parents, whose consent was given. He continued to visit her until Sept last, when he left her & refused to marry her. The jury found a verdict for the plntf of $3,500.

Late English papers report the death on Feb 2 of the venerable Rev G Fletcher, at the age of 108 years. He was born on Feb 2, *1847, at Clarbrouf, in Nottinghamshire. From 6 years of age he had been brought up in the tenets of Wesleyism, & remained a member of that body til his death. He spent 83 years of his life in active pursuits. He was at the battle of Bunker's Hill, & followed Abercrombie into Egypt, where he gained the esteem & respect of his ofcrs. [*Copied as written.]

Jas Wallace aged 14, was killed by his brother, age 12 years old, in the town of Ohio, in this county, on the 17th ult. A quarrel had occurred between the two, growing out of an attempt on the part of the deceased to chastise a twin brother of the younger lad. By some means he obtained a loaded pistol & discharged its contents into the head of the deceased. The mother of the boys was present but unable to prevent the catastrophe.
-Mohawk [N Y] Courier

Henry Parry, Pa ave, between 18th & 19th sts, Wash: Manufacturer of Marble Mantels, Monuments, & Tombs.

Oysters supplied by L Coulter, Annapolis, to Mr Chas Werner, Pa ave, between 6th & 7th sts, his agent.

For sale: a valuable Market Garden & Dairy Farm, on the Potomac river, in Fairfax Co, Va, containing 500 acres. –Catesby Ap R Jones

Farm for sale, containing 181 acres, in PG Co, Md, on the New Cut road, adjoining the farm of Chas S Middleton, late sheriff of said county. –Andrew Payne

Fires: 1-At Fredericksburg, Va, on Tue, 3 houses belonging to J Grots & 2 to Mr Sacrey were destroyed by fire. 2-The mansion of Maj John Goss, in Albemarle Co, Va, was destroyed by fire on Wed last.

Criminal Court-Wash. Grand Jury:

W W Seaton	Robt White	M Shanks
Wm Gunton	Saml Drury	J N Fearson
Leonidas Coyle	Geo Mattingly	J Walsh
B O Tayloe	Abner H Young	B J Semmes
Nich Callan	Saml Pumphrey	D B Johnson
Chas W Pairo	G C Grammer	C R Belt
W F Bayly	H Crittenden	Richd Jones
C L Coltman	W H Edes	

Traverse Jury:

Willard Drake	T A Tolson	J Plowman
C F P Cummin	T Crown	R B Owens
W P Drury	H O Whitmore	J Barnard
E Edmondston	Chas Munroe	S Hermon
A W Denham	T Scrivener	H G Murray
W B Downing	W T Upperman	A P Waugh
Aug Davis	W Dawson	W Stewart
T J Crane	W Flannen	J T Fenwick
Jos Abbott	B F Moxley	J Simmons
R Stoops	P Stevens	
W Wise	A Butler	

Fatal accident. A young man named Edw Long was crushed to death on Fri at the Washington railroad station, the two cars between which he was standing having closed upon him.

Mrd: on Feb 26, in Oswego, N Y, by Rev Mr Kellogg, Mr Fred L Harvey, of Wash City, to Miss Helen M Ford, of the former place.

Mrd: at Waveland, Fauquier Co, Va, by Rev Mr Shield, Col Wm B Gaulden, of Georgia, to Miss Laura G, daughter of Hon Bedford Brown. [No date given-current item.]

Died: on Mar 4, Mrs Sophia Johnson, widow of the late Baker Johnson, of Fred'k Co, Md, & daughter of the late Geo Grundy, of Balt.

Died: on Jan 24 last, in Sacramento, Calif, Clement W Coote, formerly of Wash City, aged 36 years.

Died: on Feb 5, in Wash City, Henry W Gray Thomas, young son of Geo C & Fannie Gray Thomas. His funeral will be from the residence of the parents, 451 N Y ave, on Wed at 12 M.

Foreign items. 1-Jas Montgomery, the poet, who died last year, left an estate which has just been sworn under L9,000. Southey died worth about L7,000 & Wordsworth as much, while Rogers is a millionaire. 2-Ferdinand, Duke of Genoa, who expired at Turin on Feb 6, was the 2nd son of the late King Chas Albert, & only brother of the present Sovereign of Piedmont. He was born Nov 15, 1822, & married, 4 years ago, to the daughter of Prince John, now King of Saxony. The present situation of King Victor Immanuel is one to call forth sympathy. Within a few weeks, & almost in the act of taking part in the European war, he has lost his mother, his wife, & now his brother.

For sale: by decree of the Orphans Court of Wash Co, D C. I shall offer for sale the property at the corner of 10th & E sts, formerly known as the old **Medical College** & lately as the **Masonic Hall**. Apply to Wm Nourse, at Pairo & Nourse's banking-house. –Sarah H Nourse, Guardian

Restaurant & fixtures for sale: as agent for Mr Wm H Campbell, I offer his wines, liquors & entire stock now in the Waverley House Restaurant, at N J & Pa ave, Capitol Hill. I also offer for sale part of his household & kitchen furniture.
–P A Desaules, agent

WED MAR 7, 1855

We have dates from Honolulu to Jan 13. The funeral of the late King, Kamehameha, took place on Jan 10. The procession extended upwards of half a mile, & composed of not less than 5,000 persons. 15,000 of the inhabitants of Oahu & adjacent islands were assembled to witness it. The next day Kamehameha IV, made his first public appearance as King in the large native church.

Edson D Bascom, convicted at New Haven of robbing the mails was sentenced on Sat last on 3 indictments to hard labor in the State prison for 7 years & 3 months.

Died: on Feb 5, Sarah Ann, consort of Nathan Lewis, in her 37th year. Her funeral is this afternoon at 2 o'clock, from her late residence near the Navy Yard.

Stock & fixtures of a Shoe Store at auction: on Mar 10, at the store of Mr H O Noyes, on Pa ave, near 13th st. -Jas C McGuire, auct

For rent: one of those large 4 story houses on G st, No 436, lately occupied by Senator Toombs, of Ga, containing 17 rooms, with gas & gas fixtures complete, bath room, & water in the yard. Inquire of Saml Magee, 411 7th st, between G & H sts.

Farm for sale: intending to change my residence, I offer for sale the Farm on whichI reside, near Allen's Fresh, Chas Co, Md, contains about 400 acres of land. All the bldgs are nearly new & in good order. Possession given as soon as desired.
–Wm D Merrick

THU MAR 8, 1855

Extensive sale of groceries & liquors, by virtue of distrain for house rent due & in arrears: on Mar 10, at the grocery store of Thos Delaney, on La ave, between 6th & 7th sts, all of the goods in the establishment. –R B Hughes, Bailiff
-Green & Scott, aucts

Appointments by the Pres, by & with the advice & consent of the Congress.
John J Gilchrist, of N H, Jos H Lumpkin, of Ga, Isaac Blackford, of Ind, to be Judge of the Court of Claims.
Montgomery Blair, of D C, to be Solicitor for the U S, to represent the Gov't before the Court of Claims.
Robt Ould & Wm B B Cross, both of D C, to revise & codify the laws of said District.
Wm R Woodward, Danl Smith, John S Hollingshead, Chas P Wannall, Zachariah Walker, Saml Drury, & Henry Haw, to be Justices of the Peace for Wash Co, D C.
Josiah Minot, of N H, to be Fifth Auditor of the U S Treasury, vice Stephen Pleasonton, deceased.
Jos L Haywood, of Utah, to be U S marshal for the Territory of Utah, whose term of service has expired.
Eli R Doyle, of Nebraska, to be Marshal of the U S for the Territory of Nebraska, vice Mar W Izard, resigned.
Saml H Treat, jr, to the Judge of the District Court of the U S for the southern district of Ill.
W Joshua Allen, to be District Atty of the U S for the southern district of Ill.
Archimides C Dickson, to be U S Marshal for the southern district of Ill.
Norman Eddy, to the U S Atty for the Territory of Minn, vice John E Warren, removed.
Israel D Andrews, of Maine, to be Consul Gen to reside in the British North American provinces.
John Romeyn Brodhead, of N Y, to be Consul Gen, to reside at Simoda, in Japan.
G C Cushman, of Maine, to be Com'r under the reciprocity treaty between the U S & her Britannic Majesty, concluded Jun 5, 1854.
Chas W Dean, of Ark, to be Superintendent of Inidan affairs for the southern superintendency, vice Thos S Drew, removed.
Henry M Rector, of Ark, to be Surveyor Gen for the district of Ark, vice Geo Milbourne, removed.
David H Burr, of D C, to be Surveyor Gen for the Territory of Utah.
Consuls:
Nathl Bolton, of Ind, at Geneva, Switzerland.

S D Mulloway, of Texas, at Monterey, Mexico, vice Wm R Glover, resigned.
Jas Arrott, of Pa, for the port of Dublin, Ireland, vice Robt L Loughead, deceased.
A V Colvin, of Fla, for port of Demarara, in British Gulana, vice C W Denison, resigned.
Henry W De Puy, of N Y, at Carlsrue, in the Duchy of Baden, in Germany.
N A Haven, of N Y, for St Jago, Cape Verde islands, vice John Z Forney, resigned.

Inspectors of the Customs:
Jesse Thomas, for port of Nashville, Tenn.
John C O Grady, for port of Madisonville, Fla
Edw H Ward, port of Jacksonville, N C.
Felix R Lewis, for port of Jeffersonville, Ind.
John E Johnson, port of Baysport, Fla.
Jas H Durst, for district of Brazos de Santiago, vice Stephen Powers, removed.
Isaac Williams, for port of San Pedro, Calif.

Indian Agents:
Maxwell McCaslin, of Pa, for Osage River agency, vice Ely Moore.
Benj F Robinson, of Kansas Territory, for Delaware Indians.
John Montgomery, of Kansas Territory, for Kansas tribe of Indians.
John W Whitfield, of Kansas Territory, for Upper Kansas Indians.
Edwin A C Hatch, of Minnesota Territory, for the Blackfeet & other neighboring tribes.
Robt Campbell, of Ohio, for the Kickapoo Indians.
Robt C Miller, of Kansas Territory, for the Shawnee & Wyandott Indians.
Thos S Swiss, of Ill, for the Upper Platte agency, vice John W Whitfield.
Jas R Vineyard, of Sacramento City, for Calif.

Registers of Land Ofcs:
Harvey Morgan, at Dixon, Ill, vice Wallace, resigned.
John A Parker, of Va, in Nebraska Territory.
Geo Hyen, of Miss, at Fond-du-lac district, Wisc.
Jas D Jenkins, at Turkey River district, Iowa
Wm H Merritt, at **Fort Dodge** district, Iowa.
S P Yeemans, at Sious River district, Iowa.
R J Hamilton, at Chicago, Ill, vice Long, removed.
Ely Moore, of Kansas Territory, in that Territory.
Lafayette Mosher, at Winchester, Oregon Territory.

Receivers of Public Moneys:
Thos C Shoemaker, for the district of lands subject to sale in Kansas Territory.
Adison R Gilmore, for the district of land subject to sale in Nebraska Territory.
Simeon Mills, for Fond-du-lac district, Wisc.
Madison Post, of Fla, for Tampa, Fla.
Ariel K Eaton, for Turkey River land district, Iowa
V V Antwerp, for **Fort Dodge** land district, Iowa
John B Lash, for Sioux River land district, Iowa
Geo W Lawson, at Winchester, Oregon Territory.

The undersigned, named exc in the last will of Jas Ratrie, deceased, having taken out letters testamentary, will offer for sale, on Apr 10, in front of the premises, the following valuable property in Wash City: part of lot 1 in square 881, fronting 22 feet on 7th st east, with a 2 story brick house. Also, vacant lot 2 in square south of square 999. Property is near the Navy Yard. Apply to H O Clampton, atty at law, Alexandria, Va, or to Messrs Green & Scott. –Thos Redin, exc of Jas Ratrie, deceased. -Green & Scott, aucts

Trustee's sale: by decree of the Circuit Court for PG Co, Md, as Court of Equity: public sale on Mar 29, at the late residence of Oliver B Magruder, deceased, the real estate of which he died seized & possessed, supposed to contain about 700 acres of land: about 4 miles from the village of Bladensburg; has a comfortable frame dwlg nearly new & necessary bldg for farming operations. Will be shown upon application to Mrs Rosanna Magruder, who resides thereon. –N C Stephen, trustee

Wash City Ordinances: 1-Act for the relief of Wm D Acken: the fine of $20 imposed on him in relation to the erection of wooden houses, is remitted provided he pay the costs of prosecution. 2-Act to refund P T & J Ellicott certain money erroneously paid: the sum of $50.01, for taxes paid on lot 4 in square west of square 484.

FRI MAR 9, 1855
Fears are entertained for the safety of the U S ship **Decatur**, as nothing definite has been heard from her since leaving Rio Janeiro. Our latest advices from Valparaiso are to Jan 14, up to which time no tidings of her had reached that port. –N Y Com Adv

Rt Rev Ignatius Aloysius Reynolds, aged 56 years, died on Tue last at Charleston, S C, of which diocese he had been the Catholic Bishop for 11 years. His parents were among the earliest emigrants from Md to Ky. He was educated in Bardstown, but completed his literary & ecclesiastical studies in Balt.

At St Louis, on Feb 28, Deputy Marshal Brand was killed almost instantly by the discharge of a revolving pistol in the hands of Robt McO'Blennis. McO'Blennis was arrested & committed to prison.

On Sunday the residence of Mr Jas Short, near the Navy Yard, in Brooklyn, was discovered to be on fire in the garret. Mr Short had a family of 6 children, 5 of whom slept in the upper part of the house. All of the family escaped except Edw & Jas, aged 12 & 17, who were suffocated by the smoke & consumed with the bldg. John, the eldest boy, was badly burnt about the head, breast, & arms.

At Weldon, N C, on Mar 5, Patrick McGown, mail agent, was attacked by 3 men, two of them named Everett [father & son] & the other Price. McGowan was supposed not to recover. The affray was from a misunderstanding.

A man named Homes, formerly of Albany, but recently of Calif, having arrived at N Y last Sun in the Star of the West, died in the cars of the Hudson River Railroad Co, at Poughkeepsie, on Monday.

Cadets appointed at large for 1855 by the Pres of the U S:
Alex'r J McIntosh, of Ga, son of Capt McIntosh, of the navy.
Wm W McCreery, of Va. Father lost in the **Grampus** & his uncle in the Albany.
John Birdsall, of N Y, Father died in the service.
Wm H Marriott, of Md. Father distinguished in the military service of the country.
Dudley Riley, son of the late Gen Riley.
Pierce M Butler, s/ the late Col Butler, who fell at Churubusco.
Frank Huger, son of Col Huger, U S Army.
Chas S Bowman, son of Capt Bowman.
Robt W Mitchell, of Pa.
Jas P Martin, of Ky.

On Sunday Henry Bender, an aged gentleman, living on the Bristol turnpike, above Frankford, died from the effects of that distressing malady, hydrophobia. Last Oct he was bitten by his own dog, who was rabid, as was also one of his horses, which shortly afterwards died. –Phil Ledger

The trial of Romain, Madder, & Keefer, for the murder of John Dunbar, jr, in Jan last, in *Fort Wayne*, Ind, took place last week, & resulted in a verdict of guilty. [Mar 16th newspaper: John Dunbar, formerly of Ohio, was murdered by Madden, Keefer, & Romine, a few weeks since, at *Fort Wayne*, Ind, to effect the robbery of the deceased, from whom they got less than $100. They were all sentenced last week to death by rope. They are all bad men, who have been guilty of many crimes, & Madden & Keefer have been in the State prison. –Boonsville [Ind] paper]

Mrd: Mar 5, by Rev Smith Pyne, D D, Saml L Gouverneur, jr, of Alleghany Co, Md, to Marian Campbell, daughter of the late Jas Campbell, for many years Surrogate of N Y C.

Died: yesterday, Miss Ann Maria Harrington, a native of Va, but for many years a resident of Wash City. Her funeral will take place tomorrow at half-past 3 o'clock, from her late residence on East Capitol st.

Died: on Mar 7, at the residence of her son, on the Heights of Gtwn, Hannah M, relict of the late Roger Boyce, of Hartford Co, Md.

Died: on Feb 28, at New Orleans, of consumption, Francis T Porter, an assist editor of the Picayune, aged about 38 years.

Died: on Feb 22, at Chicago, Ill, Mrs Jane Ann Fowler, in the season of youth & hope, & happiness. Her remains have been deposited with those of her kindred, at Washington, Conn.

Died: on Feb 28, at New Orleans, La, Dr P Louis Massey, for the last 15 years a well-known & accomplished chemist of that city. To his numerous acquaintances in this District this sad intelligence will be received with melancholy interest.

Died: on Feb 1, at Winchester, Va, Mrs Anne Evelina Tucker, relict of the late Hon Henry St Geo Tucker, of Va, in her 66th year. She was one of the few relics that remain among us as memorials of ancient worth. Her accomplished husband, whose brilliant endowments secured for him the highest political & judicial stations which the State of his nativity could bestow, listened with respect & consideration to her intelligent & pious counsels. She was a model of maternal affection, & ever ready to advance the comfort of her children. She sought & found the mercy of God, & united herself to the Presbyterian church. She died in the presence of her children. Her remains were conveyed to the Kent st Presbyterian church, where a discourse was preached, after which all that was mortal of this lamented lady was deposited by the side of her husband, to await with him the dawn of the resurrection. –S T

Albany, Mar 6. Phelps, under sentence of death for the murder of his wife, escaped from jail this morning by locking the jailer in his cell, but he was recaptured four miles from the city.

Information wanted of John Edgar, born in Cumberland, Eng, left Liverpool in the ship **John Jay**; the last heard of him he resided in Va, since then in New Orleans. Should he see this, & address a letter to John Bateman, N Y, or the British Consul, New Orleans, or, if in Washington, inquire at the ofc of the Nat'l Intelligencer, he will hear of something to his advantage. Any information concerning him will be thankfully received by John Batemen, N Y.

Farm near Washington for sale: the undersigned offers her Farm, in Alexandria Co, Va, 2 miles from Gtwn, D C: contains 70 acres of land, with a neat & modern frame dwlg, & back bldg; stable & corn house. Inquire of Malcolm Douglas, living adjoining, who will show the premises. Title indisputable. –Mrs S Hamilton

SAT MAR 10, 1855
Died: on Mar 8, after a short illness, Owen Connolly, in his 51st year, a native of the county of Leitrim, Ireland. His funeral will take place on Sunday at 3 o'clock, corner of Md ave & 3rd st.

Died: on Fri, Donald Stewart, aged 46 years. His funeral will be on Sunday at 2 o'clock, from his late residence, at the corner of 11th & H sts.

Died: on Fri, at the house of her son-in-law, Richd Lay, Mrs Ann Mattingly, aged 73 years, of a short but very severe illness. Solemn requiem mass will be offered for the repose of her soul at 10 o'clock this morning, in St Patrick's Church, from which her funeral will take place immediately after mass.

Household & kitchen furniture at auction on: Mar 21, at the residence of his Excellency J M Terado, the Peruvian Minister, on Pa ave, between 23rd & 24th sts. -Jas C McGuire, auct

By order of distrain for house rent due to Wm Morrow by Alfred Hunter, we will expose at public sale, on *Feb 13, 1855, at our Auction Store, Wash City, the goods & chattels of Alfred Hunter. -Green & Scott, aucts, for R B Hughes, bailiff [*Copied as written.]

Wilmington Herald: How many people in N C are aware of the fact that, after the Revolutionary war, the State of N C made a grant to Gen Nathl Greene, the great cmder of the army of the South during that war, of 25,000 acres of land? Not many we suppose. The Confederation had no treasury, or but an empty one, in the Revolutionary war. Va gave a large number of shares in certain public works to the great Washington; S C gave to Gen Greene 10,000 guineas, & Ga gave him 5,000 guineas, & N C added 25,000 acres of her most valuable land. Georgia, besides the money, added a beautiful estate in lands, & gave another [adjoining] to his friend Gen Wayne.

John M Holland, a member of the Md State Senate from Worcester Co, died at his residence on Sat last. In politics he was a Democrat.

Fire in St Mary's, Ga, on Mar 3. S Burns' cotton gin manufactory was destroyed. The following comprise the list of the sufferers, viz: J Bashlott, Jos Arnow, P Arnow, J Vocell, [estate of Silvanus D Pacetty,] Saml Burns, Messrs Gibbean & Dufour, John Bessent, & R D Fox.

Boston, Mar 9. At South Gardiner, Maine, on Wed night last, two elderly ladies, sisters of the late Abner Kneeland, were murdered. The house had been ransacked. A vagrant had been arrested on suspicion.

MON MAR 12, 1855
The Barnstable Patriot has an advertisement in which the birthplace & homestead of Jas Otis, the illustrious patriot of Revolutionary memory, is offered for sale. *Marshfield*, the chosen seat of Danl Webster, is to be sold by auction on Mar 14. [Mar 15th newspaper: the sale of *Marshfield* is postponed to Mar 28, in consequence of the inclemency of the weather.]

Household & kitchen furniture at auction on: Mar 15, at the house, 450 H st, lately occupied by Hon Mr Penington. -Green & Scott, aucts

Gen Jail Delivery at Macon, Ga. Saml Scoville, charged with the robbery of the Marine Bank; Luke Nowell, charged with the murder of Peter Curry; & one Raley, charged with negro stealing, escaped from Bibb Co jail on Feb 24. All were confined in cells in the 3rd story of the jail, but managed, by saws, files, & probably skeleton keys, to get down to the first floor and picked a large hole through the wall. The sheriff offered a reward of $500 for their arrest.

The widow of Mr Wm Horn, fireman, who was killed at Newcastle [Delaware] Railroad in Aug last, prosecuted the Phil, Wilmington, & Balt Railroad for damages, & the court ordered an arbitration, which awarded her $5,000.

U S Patent Ofc, Wash, Mar 6, 1855. Ptn of Jas Brett, of Matteawan, N Y, praying for the extension of a patent granted to him on Jul 10, 1841, for an improvement in key-wrenches, for 7 years from the expiration which takes place on Jul 10, 1855. -Chas Mason, Com'r of Patents

Died: on Mar 10, after a short illness, Edmund V Rice, in his 31st year. His funeral will take place on Tue at 3 o'clock, from his late residence on Capitol Hill, corner of 1st & B sts.

Died: on Mar 6, at Charlotte Hall, St Mary's Co, Md, in her 29th year, Mrs Mary A E Bean, wife of Dr H H Bean & daughter of the late Jas Miltimore, formerly of Newburyport, Mass. She was a devoted & pious member of the Episcopal Church.

Wilmington, Mar 10. Three bldgs belong to Mr Gretsche's powder mill establishment were blow up today, instantly killing one of the workmen, John Kane. [Mar 14th newspaper: the two men killed were Wm McDonald & Jas Kane. Richd Fagan, Jas Dunbar, & Danl Bradley were severely injured.]

The business relations existing between Hunt & Donaldson, Dentists, have been dissolved by mutual consent. Dr Hunt will continue the practice of Dentistry at the same place. Dr Donaldson has opened his ofc at 7th & D sts, over the Patriotic Bank. They were associated for more than 5 years. –R Finley Hunt, R B Donaldson

U S Patent Ofc, Wash, Mar 9, 1855. Ptn of Wm S George, of Balt, Md, praying for an extension of a patent granted to him on May 29, 1841, for an improvement in Machines for riving & dressing shingles, for 7 years from the expiration of said patent, which takes place on May 29, 1855. -Chas Mason, Com'r of Patents

TUE MAR 13, 1855

Valuable tracts of land near Wash City at public auction: on Mar 20, at our Auction Rooms, 4 tracts of land, containing about 50 acres each, partly in Montg Co, but principally in Wash Co, D C, opposite the farm of Jos H Bradley, about 4½ miles from Wash. John Parker, living adjoining, will show the property.
-Jas C McGuire, auct

Orphans Court of Wash Co, D C. Letters of administration on the personal estate of Saml S Whiting, late of Wash Co, deceased. –J W Patterson, adm

Orphans Court of Wash Co, D C. Letters testamentary on the personal estate of Eliz A Newman, late of Wash Co, deceased. –E R Larned, Benj F Larned, excs

Geo Catlin, the famous Indian portrait painter, traveler, & champion of the red men, has been heard from on the head-waters of the Amazon, painting the portraits & taking notes of the manners of the uncouth tribes in those regions, lately made so interesting by the reports of Lts Herndon & Gibbon.

Messrs Taylor & Maury have just received from London 8 pictures in water colors by J G Philp, intended for the Exhibition at N Y, but, having arrived in this country too late, are now at their store. The subjects are chiefly Marine, illustrating the iron-bound coast of old England.

Juan Pages, recently convicted of manslaughter at New Orleans, for having killed a man in a duel, has been sentenced to 30 days' imprisonment in the State prison. The Judge said he could sentence him to 20 years or less; but since he had been, during your residence of 20 years, honest & upright in all your relations of life, sentenced him to the 30 days.

Three men, Robt Ramsay, John Landrican, & Jeremiah Curtain, were smothered to death in the flouring mill of Wm Baker, in Seymour West, Canada, a few days since. They were at work on the lower floor, when the floor above gave way, letting down about 3,000 bushels of grain. A horrible death, indeed!

Mrd: on Mar 12, in Wash City, by Rev S P Hill, Mr Albert M Snyder to Miss Mary Ellen Holland.

Died: on Mar 11, Elizabeth Mary, eldest daughter of W G & Sophia Ridgely. Her funeral will be this afternoon at 3½ o'clock, from the residence of her father, Cox's row, 76 First st.

Died: on Mar 11, in Wash, D C, Helen Josepha, daughter of Cornelius & Emma Stribling, aged 16 months & 15 days.

Died: on Mar 12, Mr Michl Brady, a native of county Cavan, Ireland, & for the last 10 years a well known resident of Wash City. His funeral will take place from his late residence on Pa ave, at 6½ o'clock on Wed morning, Mar 14.

Circuit Court of Wash Co, D C-Oct Term, 1854. Lloyd Dorsey vs Jos H Bradley, exc of Eliza G Moreland; Jos Bradley, Cynthia Barry, Jane Barry, Peter O Barry, Arthur Nelson & Malvina his wife, & Virginian Byng. The object of this bill is to procure a decree for the sale of the real estate described in the bill, being: lot 16, & parts of lots 15 & 17, in square 290, in Wash City, & the undivided moiety of the west half of lot 4 in square 460, in said city; which said real estate Eliza G Moreland was seized & possessed of at the time of her decease, & which cmplnt, alleging himself to be a creditor of said deceased, claims to have sold for the payment of debts due by deceased. The bill states the indebtment of Eliza G Moreland to cmplnt upon a balance of account particularly set forth in the bill, for $181.15, with interest thereon, by average, from Sept, 1848. It states the seising & death of said Eliza; that she prior to her decease & after she became seized of said real estate, devised a part thereof, viz: lot 16 in square 290, & an undivided moiety in the west half of lot 4 in square 460, to the said Jos H Bradley, whom she also appointed executor, upon trust to pay certain portions of the rents & profits of said lots to Cynthia Barry, Jane Barry, & Peter O Barry, & certain other portions to the said Malvina Byng, now Malvina Nelson, & Virginia Byng; & upon the happening of certain contingencies to convey said lot 16 to the said Cynthia, Jane, & Peter, or the survivor or survivors of them; & upon the happening of certain contingencies to convey to such children as the said Maloma & Virginia, or either of them, might leave at their decease, or the decease of either, a fee simple estate in said undivided moiety of said part of lot 4 in square 460; & in case of the decease of both Malvina & Virginia Byng, without issue, then to convey the same in fee to Jos Bradley; & by the residuary clause of her will the testatrix devised parts of lots 15 & 17 in square 290, as particularly described in the bill, to Malvina & Virginia Byng. The bill further states the probate of will, the grant of letters testamentary, & the deficiency of personal assets to pay debts & the liability of said real estate for the payment; & that said Arthur Nelson & Malvina his wife & Virginia Byng, reside out of the District of Columbia, & prays publication against said non-residents. Absent dfndnts to appear in thie Court, in person or by solicitor, on or before the 1st Monday of Aug next. –Jas S Morsell, Assist Judge Circuit Court -John A Smith, clerk -Wm M Merrick, cmplt's solicitor

WED MAR 14, 1855
N Y correspondent: Capt Saml C Reid, well known as the cmder of the brig **Gen Armstrong**, is dangerously ill at his residence in this city, & his friends despair of his recovery.

By order of the Orphans Court of Wash Co, D C: sale of saddles & harness at the store lately occupied by J H Thompson, deceased, & all the stock in the store.
–Gustavus Waters, adm -Green & Scott, aucts

Wash Corp: 1-Ptn from Saml Warner, asking permission to erect 2 frame houses near his brick bldg: referred to the delegation from the 6th Ward. 2-Ptn from Mgt Tenant for the remission of a fine: referred to the Cmte of Claims. 3-Act for the relief of Richd A Boarman: referred to the Cmte on Police. 4-Cmte of Claims: asked to be discharged from the consideration of the ptn of T M Brush for the remission of a fine: it was carried in the affirmative. 5-Ptn of J T Denson, Chas Beall, & others, in relation to hog-pens: referred to the Cmte on Police. 6-Cmte of Claims: bill for the relief of Francis Hutchins: passed. Same cmte: adverse report on the ptn of John Fletcher, & asked to be discharged from the consideration of the same: which was agreed to. Same cmte: bill for the relief of Wm Jacobi.

Mrd: on Mar 4, by Rev Stephen P Hill, John W Hays to M A C Ridgway, both of Wash City.

Mrd: on Mar 12, by Rev Stephen P Hill, Albert Martyn Snyder to Mary Ellen Holland, all of Wash City.

Died: on Mar 10, after a short but severe illness, Mrs Sarah Scott, in her 20th year. Her funeral will take place from the residence of her husband, on H st, near 4th, today at 10 o'clock A M.

Died: on Mar 12, Richd Dement, [for more than 40 years a Gov't clerk,] after a brief illness of a few hours, in his 58th year. His funeral is this afternoon, at 4 o'clock, from Trinity Church.

Law passed at the 2nd session of the 33rd Congress: 1-Reimburse John Whitfield, late agent for the Indians on the Upper Platte, the amount expended by him for ransom for Cheyennes, & clothing, & transportation to the States of one white & 10 Mexican prisoners: $170.

THU MAR 15, 1855
Sale of horses, by order of the Orphans Court of Wash Co, D C: on Mar 17, in front of our Auction store, by order of the administrator of C W Stewart, deceased. -Rothwell & Brown, aucts

The following ticket has been nominated for the ensuing election in Va, to take place on the 4th Thu in May next: 1-Thos Stanhope Flournoy, of Halifax Co, for Govn'r. 2-Jas M H Beale, of Mason Co, for Lt Govn'r. 3-John M Patton, of Richmond City, for Atty Genr'l.

An aged man, Jas Baily Faris, was arrested at Phil on Fri on a charge of being a counterfeiter of coins. Upon searching his house various dies & tools were found, & a large quantitiy of bogus Spanish fips, levies, & quarters. He is 74 years old. After an examination, he was committed to jail.

Mrd: on Mar 13, by Rev Dr Pyne, at St John's Church, J M Smith, of Michigan, to R M Smith, of Wash.

Died: on Tue last, Mr Jeremiah Sullivan, in his 60th year, long a respectable & esteemed citizen of Wash. His funeral is today from the residence of Mr Hugh Lockery, on Capitol Hill. [No time given.]

Wash City Ordinances: 1-Act for the relief of Jas T Ferry: to pay a balance due for constructing the sewer on the south side of Pa ave, between 4½ & 6th sts, as authorized by act approved Mar 23, 1854, the sum of $62.57 is appropriated out of the funds of the 4th Ward. 2-Act for the relief of Wm Shorter: to refund Wm Shorter, [colored] the sum of $5, that being the amount of a fine imposed on & paid by him, for an alleged violation, which now appears without just cause.

Concord, N H, Mar 14. 1-Letters from Meredith state that Jas W Dargan, Geo Clark, Nathl Nichols, S M Tuck, & John O M Ladd died from injuries received yesterday at the disastrous accident in the town hall. Many other persons are not expected to survive. Over 100 persons had bones broken. 2-The greater part of the town of Bath, Grafton Co, has been burnt, & at the latest accounts the fire was not subdued. [Mar 16th newspaper:while the vote for Moderator was proceeding in the new townhouse a portion of the floor fell in, & 300 persons were precipitated into the space beneath, which was filled with stones, timber, & rubbish. The cause of the accident was a rotten joist in the center of that part of the floor. John Leavitt, Hiram Plummer, C B Tuttle, & Thos Eastman are dangerously injured. Mr Plummer had his back broken.[

A young lady solicits for herself a situation at the South as Teacher. The Latin, French, & Spanish languages may be taught, also the higher Mathematics & other higher English studies. Instruction can also be given upon the Piano Forte. Address Julia P Hill, Bangor, Maine.

Orphans Court of Wash Co, D C. Letters of administration de bonis non, with the will annexed, on the personal estate of Timothy Winn, late of Wash Co, deceased. -Rebecca Winn, Admx de bonis non, w a

Obit-died: on Sat, at his residence in Watertown, Mass, Mr Jas Brown, one of the senior partners of the eminent publishing house of Little, Brown & Co, of Boston. He had long been afflicted with a painful, incurable disease, from which, however, such a serious result had not been so soon anticipated. He returned from a visit to Washington only a few days previously, & on Fri was not supposed to be in danger. He was born in 1800, & from the humblest origin, by his own exertions, he succeeded in acquiring every thing which is usually supposed in this world to insure happiness. This sudden death will carry its deepest lasting pang into the immediate family of which the deceased was the head.

FRI MAR 16, 1855
Household & kitchen furniture at auction on: Mar 22, at the residence of Mrs Wells, on 1st st, Capitol Hill, near Pa ave: excellent assortment. -Green & Scott, aucts

Trustee's sale of Groceries, Liquors, & Store Fixtures, at auction: on Mar 28, at the grocery store of Francis N Roche, corner of 13th & F sts, by deed of trust dated Feb 22, 1855. –John C C Hamilton, trustee -Green & Scott, aucts

Fatal affray in Alexandria on Sat night, as person were returning from Heller's exhibition, some difficulty occurred between Emory Crump & Jos Bloxham, on King st, which resulted in the interference of Geo W Crump, brother of Emory Crump, who stabbed Bloxham in the back with a dagger, causing his death in about 15 minutes. Bloxham, who was a cripple, had been at the exhibition, & the two Crumps & others made game at him. He retorted with a blow from his crutch on the head of Emory Crump, whereupon Geo Crump stabbed the cripple in the back. Geo Crump is a young man, a carpenter by trade, & has heretofore borne a good character. He was committed to jail.

Henry D Bird, for many years the energetic Pres of the Petersburg & Roanoke Railroad Co, has been arrested on the charge of having embezzled some $25,000 of the company's funds.

Annual commencement of the Medical Dept of Gtwn College, was held last evening. The degree of doctor of medicine was ready by Prof Young, & conferred upon the following gentlemen by Rev Bernard A Maguire, the Pres:

Jos C R Clarke, of Missouri   Chas R Queen, of D C
Jos A Smith, of Md   Johnson V D Middleton, of D C
Louis Saur, of D C   O A Dailey, of Wash
Jas Grey Jewell, of Miss   Michl R Shyne, of Wash
J Edw Willitt, of Md
The annual address was deliverd by Prof J M Snyder.

Jas Y Davis has been elected Capt of the Wash Light Infty, vice E C Carrington, resigned.

A laborer named Cratty, a drinking man, residing in the 7th Ward, committed suicide on Wed by shooting himself, after telling his wife that he intended to do so.

The copartnership under the firm of T Bastianelli & Co, is hereby dissolved by mutual consent. –J Galligan & Son, T Bastianelli

For rent: the dwlg house lately occupied by Cmdor Morris, I & 16th sts. It is in the neighborhood of Pres Square & St John's Church. –Chubb Brothers, Bankers

Mrd: on Thu, by Rev John C Smith, Mr Geo G Coons to Miss Mary Jane Ostrander, both of Va.

Died: on Mar 14, Jos M Peerce, in his 35th year, leaving a widow & 3 small children to mourn their loss. His funeral will take place this morning at 10 o'clock, from St Patrick's Church.

Died: on Mar 14, Richd H Gordon, in his 33rd year. His funeral is this day at 4 o'clock, from the residence of Mr Osborn Mockabee, on M st, between 12th & 13th.

Died: on Mar 14, after an illness of 4 days, Ella, eldest daughter of Andrew & Drucilla Hancock, aged 12 years & 3 months. Her funeral is this day, at 11 o'clock, from the residence of her father, on Pa ave, between 12th & 13th sts.

SAT MAR 17, 1855
Household & kitchen furniture at auction on: Mar 22, at the residence of Chas W Havenner, on C st, between 4½ & 6th sts. –C W Boteler, auct

Appointments & promotions in the Revenue [Marine] Service.
Wm B Whitehead, dropped at the reduction of the service in 1853, reappointed a Capt.
First Lts promoted to be Capts: John Faunce & Chas W Bennett.
Thos S S Chaddock, formerly a 1st Lt, reappointed to same grade.
2nd Lts promoted to be 1st Lts: Wm J Rogers, John M Jones, G R Slicer, A D Stanford, & W M J Godwin.
3rd Lts promoted to be 2nd Lts: Jos Amazeen, J G Reynolds, W B Berryman, D C Constable, John M Nones, Jas E Hainson, & Richd A Morsell.
Appointments to 3rd Lt: Johnston de Lagnel, Jas H Claridge, Constantine A Richardson, Henry C Hunter, Wm E Hudgins, Henry Key, John Quin, Jas F Milligan, R G Auchinloss, R P Noah, Stephen Longfellow, & John H Gladding.
-Star

Dennis Driscoll, aged 60 years, was killed by the cars on the Germantown road, near Phil, yesterday morning. He was intoxicated.

The sale of the Library of the late Edw D Ingraham, of Phil, is to be commenced at the rooms of M Thomas & Sons, 57 & 69 South 4th st, Phil, next Tue morning, & will be continued every day & evening until completed. –North American

Crockery, glassware, & store fixturnes at auction: on Mar 19, at the store of Mrs Davis, on the west side of 7th st, between L & M sts. -Green & Scott, aucts

Mr Wm Lamden, an aged shipwright, of Balt, was on Thu knocked from the staging while at work in the NavyYard, & fell some 18 feet. He was severely injured, but we hope not dangerously.

A Hook & Ladder Co, composed, as we are informed, of respectable young men of the 4th Ward, in Wash City, has just been formed. Its ofcrs are: Pres, John T Suter; 1st Vice Pres, A Sioussa; 2nd Vice Pres, J T Chauncy; Treasurer, R H Payne, Sec, Char E Orme.

Horrid story from Port Gibson, Miss. A member of the church who had been suspended had made application to be reinstated, & all the members consented except Dr Woodward, the pastor. The excommunicated member became indignant & rushed upon Rev Dr Woodward & stabbed him in the heart, in front of the pulpit of the Methodist Church. The reverend martyr expired instantly.

Mrd: on Mar 15, by Rev J G Butler, Edw Otto Freyhold to Agnes E Ch B Von Gluemer, both of Wash City.

Died: on Mar 15, Mr Isaac H Wailes. His funeral is on Sabbath afternoon at half past 2 o'clock, from his late residence, on Capitol Hill.

To Teachers. I wish to dispose of the extensive property known as **Rugby Academy**. The bldgs are new & in excellent repair. They afford accommodations for 300 pupils. Plans may be obtained from the proprietor, on the premises, or from J C G Kennedy. –G F Morison

MON MAR 19, 1854
Household & kitchen furniture at auction on: Mar 21, at the residence of his Excellency J M Tirado, the Peruvian Minister, on Pa ave, between 23rd & 24th sts: his excellent household effects. -Jas C McGuire, auct

Richmond Enquirer: biographical sketch of the late John S Barbour, of Va. John S Barbour was the son of Mordecai Barbour, a soldier of the Revolution & an ofcr at the memorable siege of Yorktown. John S Barbour was born in Culpeper Co on Aug 8, 1790. He was at Wm & Mary College but a single session, 1808-09. He resided for 2 years with his friend & relative, the late Gov Jas Barbour, & studied law under his direction. He enlisted as a private soldier on the breaking out of the war of 1812, & was speedily promoted to aid-de-camp to Gen Madison. In 1823 he was elected to the House of Reps from Fauquier district. He breathed his last with calmness & resignation, surrounded by sorrowing friends & a weeping family, on Fri, Jan 12, at **Fleetwood**, his residence in Culpeper Co. Mr Barbour was united in marriage to Eliza Byrne, of Petersburg, who survives him, a model of matronly virtues & Christian mildness. He leaves 6 children among whom the State has been prompt to recognize some as the inheritors of their father's abilty & talents for usefulness.

Orphans Court of Wash Co, D C. Letters of administration on the personal estate of Owen Connolly, late of Wash Co, deceased. –Eliz Connolly, admx

In Chancery. Levin M Powell & Jeannette C Powell, cmplnts, & Wm A Bradley, Sydney A Bradley, Chas M Thruston, Wm T Thruston, Horatio G Thruston, Jeannette Thruston, Dickerson P Thruston, [John G Lowe their guardian,] Eliza T Thruston, [Geo A Thruston her guardian,] Sarah Thruston, Chas M Thruston, [son of Thos L Thruston,] Hellen K Thruston, Thos W Thruston, [Sarah Thruston his guardian,] Fannie C Thruston, & Jeannette B Thruston, Alfred B Thruston, & Sydney Thruston, [Saml Hanson, jr, their guardian,] dfndnts. The Circuit Court of Wash Co, D C, on Feb 20, passed an interlocutory order in the above cause, referring the same to the subscriber to examine & state the accounts of said Levin M Powell, as trustee of Wm T Thruston; & also to examine into & ascertain whether the family agreement in the bill mentioned hath been executed & performed by the respective parties thereto, & what amounts, if any, the several parties have received by way of advancement, exclusive of the matters referred to in said agreement, during the lifetime of the late Buckner Thruston, deceased; & further to inquire into & ascertain the condition & value of the estate mentioned in said bill, & whether a sale thereof, if made, would be for the benefit & advantage of said Wm T Thruston as well as of the other heirs of said B Thruston, & to report to the Court. I shall commence said investigation & examinations in my ofc, in City Hall, Wash, on Mar 24.
–W Redin, auditor

In Chancery. Abram Barnes, John T Mason, Melchor B Mason, Virginia M Mason, John O Wharton & Eliz his wife, & Thompson Mason, [heirs of John T Mason,] against John Mason, Jas M Mason, Saml Cooper & Sarah Ann his wife, Cecilius C Jamison & Catherine E his wife, Manidier Mason, Murray Mason, Eilbeck Mason, Barlow Mason, & Sidney S Lee & Nannie his wife, & Ann M Mason, [widow & heirs of John Mason.] By an interlocutory decree of the Circuit Court of Wash Co, D C, I am directed to state the account of the trustee, & to ascertain & report the names of the persons to whom the balance of the trust fund is owing & the proportions in which they are entitled to the same. The parties above are notified that on Mar 23, at my ofc, in Gtwn, I shall execute the said order. –W Redin, auditor

N Y, Mar 18. The Coroner's investigation of the Wm Poole tragedy terminated last evening. The verdict charges Louis Baker with the murder of Poole, & Turner, Paudeen, McLaughlin, Hyler, Van Pelt, Lynn, Morrissey, & Jas Min as accessories. [Mar 20th newspaper: the death of Wm Poole was caused by a gunshot wound from a pistol in the hands of Louis Baker, of Stanwix Hall, in Broadway, on Feb 25, 1855. We find that Jas Turner & Patrick McLaughlin, alias Paudeen, were guilty of aiding & abetting in the murder of Mr Poole. We find John Hyler, Cornelius Linn, & Chas Van Pelt guilty as accessories before the fact. We find John Morrissey guilty of an assault with an intent to take the life of Wm Poole, & he was an accessory to the murder by association on the evening preceding the murder. We likewise find Jas

Irvin accessory before the fact. They were not bailable & were committed to prison to await the action of the Grand Jury.] [Mar 21st newspaper: Patrick McLaughlin, alias Pargene, Chas Van Pelt, & Cornelius Linn, alleged accessories to the murder of Bill Poole, had a preliminary examination at N Y on Monday. Pargene said he was a native of N Y, is 38 years of age, & by trade a stone-cutter. Van Pelt said he was a native of N Y & a butcher. Linn said he was a native of N Y, & his trade a jeweller. The prisoners were locked up to await the action of the Grand Jury.]

Died: on Mar 17, Sarah Talburt, relict of the late Alex'r Talburt, of Wash City, in her 63rd year. Her funeral is this afternoon at 3 o'clock, from her late residence on 9th st, near I st.

Died: yesterday, at the residence of his father, near Gtwn, C A Morton, in his 30th year. His funeral will take place from Christ Church, Gtwn, today at 3:30 P M.

Died: on Mar 18, Mr Robt W Clarke, of hemorrhage of the lungs, in his 29th year. His funeral will take place this day at 3 o'clock, from the residence of his brother, Mr Richd W Clarke, on north A st, No 53, Capitol Hill.

Died: on Mar 11, at New Orleans, in her 35th year, Mrs Fanny Smith Bullitt, daughter of the late Benj Smith, of Louisville, Ky, & wife of Alex'r C Bullitt.

Obit-died: on Mar 11, Eliz Mary, eldest daughter of W G & Sophia Ridgely. The grass will be green upon her grave, for the tears & blessings of many friends will hallow it.

TUE MAR 20, 1855
Wm M Chauvenet, Assist Prof of French, died at the Naval Academy, Annapolis, on Mar 15. He was a native of France, but from early manhood a resident of Pa.

Naval: the U S ship **Vandalia**, Jno Pope, Cmder, was in Shanghai Dec 11th, & had a guard of her men on shore for the protection of the settlement. The surveying vessels steamer **John Hancock** & schnr **J Fennimore Cooper** were also at Shanghai at the same date refitting for a cruise to the northward.

Viscount Ponsonby, the veteran statesman & diplomatist died on Thu, at Brighton, at the advanced age of 84 years. The deceased peer was the son of the first Baron Ponsonby, by the 4th daughter of the 3rd Viscount Molesworth. He is succeeded in the barony only by his nephew, Wm, son of the late Hon S Wm Ponsonby, KC B. London paper of Feb 24.

Household & kitchen furniture at auction on: Mar 27, at the residence of Dr J G Jewell, on the south side of I st, between 9th & 10th sts. -Jas C McGuire, auct

Executor's sale of very valuable real estate: on Apr 16, on the premises, the subscriber, as executor of the late Chas B Davis, will sell at public auction the west half of lot 5 in square 377, fronting 32 feet on E st, between 9th & 10th sts: with a 2 story brick dwlg house & back bldg. –Geo A Davis, exc -Jas C McGuire, auct

Trustee's sale of house & lot near the Navy Yard: on May 4, on the premises, by deed of trust dated Mar 26, 1852, & recorded in Liber J A S No 40, folios 319 etc, of the land records for Wash Co, lot 1 in square 926, at the corner of G st south & 9th st east, under a ground rent of $20 per annum, for the period of 99 years, from Sep 18, 1851, with a 2 story frame dwlg with back bldg. –Jno W McKim, Rich H Clarke, trustees -Jas C McGuire, auct

Milwood Academy, Shade Gap, Huntingdon Co, will open on the 1st Mon of May. Principal's address is Easton, Pa, until Apr 1, after which, Shade Gap, Huntingdon Co, Pa. Apply to W H Woods, Principal, or J A Williamson, Gen Land Ofc

Orphans Court of Wash Co, D C. Letters of administration on the personal estate of Robt Mills, last of Wash Co, deceased. –J W Webb, adm

Public sale: by order of the Orphans' Court of PG Co, Md: sale at Nottingham, PG Co, on Mar 30, 38 servants, belonging to the estate of the late Sarah M Worthington; among them are 2 first rate carpenters & a good many young & valuable negro men & women. –C C Magruder, J H Waring, adms of S M Worthington

Mrd: on Mar 8, in Phil, by Rev U G Harris, Jas J Miller, of Wash City, to Mary J, daughter of the late John Crosby.

Died: on Mar 19, at the residence of his grandfather, Thomas Brown, Thomas Brown Hoover, son of Rev John W & Emily S Hoover, aged 1 year & 5 months. His funeral is on Wed at 3:30 o'clock, from the residence of his grandfather, on West st.

WED MAR 21, 1855
Appointments & transfers for the four new regiments.
10th Regt of Infty-Riflemen
Captains:
Brvt Capt Henry F Clarke, of Pa; 1st Lt Sep 8, 1847, 2nd Artl. Brevetted for gallantry in action; distinguished in battles of Monterey, Churubusco, Molino del Rey, & Chepultepec. First commissioned, 1843.
Brvt Capt Franklin Gardner, of Iowa; 1st Lt Sep 13, 1847, 7th Infty. Twice brevetted for gallantry in action; distinguished in battles of Monterey, Cerro Gordo, & Chepultepec. First commissioned, 1843.
Brvt Capt Jas G S Snelling, of Ohio; 1st Lt Jan 22, 1849, 8th Infty. Twice brevetted for gallantry in action; distinguished in battles of Contreras, Churubusco, & Molino del Rey, [where he was wounded.] First commissioned, 1843.

Brvt Capt Barnard E Bee, of S C; 1st Lt Mar 5, 1851, 3rd Infty. Twice brevetted for gallantry in action; distinguished in battles of Cerro Gordo, [where he was wounded,] & Chepultepec. First commissioned, 1845.

1st Lt John C Symmes, of Ohio; 1st Lt, Jul 1, 1853, ordnance. First commissioned, 1847.

Matthew S Pitcher, of N Y, captain 10th Infty, promoted major 11th Infty; served in war with Mexico.

N Seymour Webb, of Conn, capt 9th Infty, brevetted major for gallantry in battle of Chepultepec.

Albert Tracy, of Maine, 1st lt & capt 9th Infty; brevetted capt for gallantry in battle of Chepultepec.

Jesse A Gove, of N H, 1st Lt, 9th Infty, served in war with Mexico.

Jas P Barker, of Delaware; served in Florida war.

1st Lts:

2nd Lt Jos T Tidball, of Ohio, 2nd Lt Mar 21, 1850, 6th Infty; active service on Indian frontier. First commissioned, 1849.

2nd Lt Alfred Cumming, of Ga, 2nd Lt Jul 16, 1850, 7th Infty; active service on Indian frontier. First commissioned, 1849.

2nd Lt Cuvier Grever, of Maine; 2nd Lt Sep 16, 1850, 4th Artl; active service & frontier explorations. First commissioned, 1850.

2nd Lt Louis H Marshall, of Md; 2nd Lt, Mar 5, 1851, 3rd Infty; active service on Indian frontier. First commissioned, 1849.

2nd Lt Henry E Maynadier, of D C; 2nd Lt, Feb 29, 1852, 1st Artl; active service on Indian frontier. First commissioned, 1852.

Henry B Kelly, of Louisiana; 2nd & 1st Lt, 14th Infty in war with Mexico.

Jas Findlay Harrison, of Ohio; 1st Lt & Quartermaster of volunteers in war with Mexico.

Wm Clinton, of Pa; 2nd Lt volunteers in war with Mexico.

John McNab, of Vt; sgt major 2nd Infty in Florida war; sgt major 9th Infty in war with Mexico.

N A M Dudley, of Mass.

2nd Lts:

2nd Lt Peter T Swaine, of N Y; 2nd lt, Dec 31, 1852, 1st Infty. Active service on Indian frontier. First commissioned, 1852.

2nd Lt John H Forney, of Ala; 2nd lt, Oct 24, 1853, 7th Infty. Service on Indian frontier. First commissioned, 1852.

2nd Lt Lyman N Kellogg, of N Y; 2nd lt, Feb 28, 1854, 2nd Infty. Active service on Indian frontier. First commissioned, 1852.

2nd Lt Lawrence A Williams, of D C; 2nd lt, Jun 22, 1854, 4th Infty. Service on Indian frontier. First commissioned, 1852.

2nd Lt Jas Deshler, of Ala; 2nd lt, Jul 1, 1854, 3rd Artl. Service on Indian frontier. First commissioned, 1854.

W H Rossell, of N J.

Alex'r Murray, of Pa.

Malcolm H Nicholls, of Louisiana.
Wm Kearny, of Missouri.
Curtis Dunham, of Kansas
9th Regt of Infty-Riflemen.
Captains:
Brvt Maj Pinkney Lugenbeil, of Ohio; 1st lt, Jun 29, 1846, 5th Infty. Twice brevetted for gallantry in action; distinguished in the battles of Contreras & Churubusco, [where he was wounded,] Milino del Rey, & Chepultepec. First commissioned, 1840.
Brvt Capt Fred'k T Dent, of Missouri; 1st lt, Feb 11, 1847, 5th Infty. Twice brevetted for gallantry in action; distinguished in the battles of Contreras, Churubusco, & Molino del Rey, where he was wounded. First commissioned, 1843.
1st Lt Francis E Patterson, of Pa; 1st lt, Oct 29, 1848, 1st Artl. Private in McCullough's company of Texas Rangers from May 1, to Jul 31, 1847. Appointed 2nd lt 1st Artl Jun 24, 1847.
Brvt Capt Geo E Pickett, of Ill; 1st lt, Jun 28, 1849, 8th Infty. Twice brevetted for gallantry in action; distinguished in the battles of Contreras, Churubusco, Molino del Rey, & Chepultepec. First commissioned, 1846.
1st Lt Chas H Winder, of Md; 1st lt, Apr 5, 1854, 3rd Artl. Soldierly conduct on the wreck of the steamer **San Francisco**. Now on frontier service. First commissioned, 1850.
Dickinson Woodruff, of N J; lt col of the N J btln in the war with Mexico.
Francis L Bowman, of Pa; major of Pa volunteers; distinguished in the action of La Vega in the war with Mexico.
Presley N Guthrie, of Ohio; capt, 11th Infty; brevetted major for gallantry at Contreras & Churubusco, & distinguished & wounded at Milino del Rey.
Jas J Archer, of Md; capt of voltigeurs; brevetted major for gallantry in the battle of Chepultepec.
Crawford Fletcher, of Ark; 1st lt of volunteers in the battle of Monterey; distinguished in the battle of Buena Vista.
1st Lts:
2nd Lt Henry M Black, of Pa; 2nd lt, Aug 20, 1847, 7th Infty. Active service on the Indian frontier. First commissioned, 1847.
2nd Lt John M Fraser, of Miss; 2nd lt, Jun 30, 1850, 2nd Infty. Active service on Indian frontier. First commissioned, 1849.
2nd Lt Thos E English, of Pa; 2nd lt, Jul 31, 1850, 5th Infty. Active service on the Indian frontier. First commissioned, 1849.
2nd Lt Alden Sargent, of Missouri; 2nd lt, Apr 15, 1851, 6th Infty. Active service on the Indian frontier. First commissioned, 1850.
2nd Lt J Van Noast, of N Y; 2nd lt, Aug 22, 1853, 3rd Artl. Soldierly conduct on the wreck of the steamer **San Francisco**. Now on frontier service. First commissioned, 1852.
Lyman Bissell, of Conn; 1st lt & capt 9th Infty in the war with Mexico.

A T Palmer, of Maine; 2nd lt 9th Infty; brevetted 1st lt for gallantry at Contreras & Churubusco, where he was wounded.

Saml R Harrison, of Texas; 2nd lt of volunteers; distinguished at Buena Vista.

Alex'r P Ten Broeck, of N Y; sgt 3rd Infty in the battles of Palo Alto & Resaca de la Palma; then 2nd lt, 10th Infty in the war with Mexico.

Geo W Carr, of Va; 2nd lt voltigeurs. Served in Mexico.

2nd Lts:

2nd Lt Chas R Woods, of Ohio; 2nd lt, Jul 31, 1852, 1st Infty. Active service on Indian frontier. First commissioned, 1852.

2nd Lt Hugh B Fleming, of Pa; 2nd lt, Jun 9, 1853, 6th Infty. Active service on Indian frontier. First commissioned, 1852.

2nd Lt Henry Douglass, of N Y; 2nd lt, Dec 31, 1853, 8th Infty. Service on Indian frontier. First commissioned, 1853.

2nd Lt Wm Myers, of Pa; 2nd lt, Dec 31, 1853, 4th Infty. Active service on Indian frontier. First commissioned, 1852.

2nd Lt Wm A Webb, of Maine; 2nd lt, Dec 31, 1854, 5th Infty. Active service on Indian frontier. First commissioned, 1853.

Israel Miller, of N Y. Served in war with Mexico.

Edmund J Harvey, of Va.

Chas A Reynolds, of Md. Served in war with Mexico.

David B McKibbin, of Pa

2nd Regt of Cavalry.

Capts:

Brvt Maj Earl Van Dorn, of Miss; 1st lt, Mar 3, 1847, 7th Infty. Twice brevetted for gallantry in action; distinguished in battles of Monterey, Cerro Gordo, Contreras, Churubusco, Chepultepec, & city of Mexico, where he was wounded. First commissioned, 1842.

Brvt Capt Edmund K Smith, of Fla; 1st lt, Mar 9, 1851, 7th Infty. Twice brevetted for gallantry in action; distinguished in battles of Palo Alto, Resaca de la Palma, Cerro Gordo, & Contreras. First commissioned, 1845.

Brvt Capt Jas Oakes, of Pa; 1st lt, Jun 30, 1851, 2nd dragoons. Twice brevetted for gallantry in action; distinguished at Medelin & battles of Churubusco & Molino del Rey; wounded in confict with Indians in Texas. First commissioned, 1846.

Brvt Capt J N Palmer, of N Y; 1st lt, Jan 27, 1853, mounted rifles. Twice brevetted for gallantry in action; distinguished in battles of Contreras, Churubusco, & Chepultepec, where he was wounded. First commissioned, 1846.

1st Lt Geo Stoneman, of N Y; 1st lt, Jul 25, 1854, 1st dragoons. Served in Calif campaigns during the war with Mexico, & since in operations against Indians & in frontier explorations. First commissioned, 1846.

Theodore O'Hara, of Ky; capt quartermaster for volunteers, & brevetted major for gallantry in the battles of Contreras & Churubusco.

Wm R Bradfute, of Tenn; lt in 1st Tenn volunteers disbanded, capt 3rd Tenn volunteers, & served to the close of the war with Mexico.

Chas E Travis, of Texas; capt of Texas volunteers now in service against Indians.

Chas J Whiting, of Calif; lt of Artl in the Florida war.
Albert G Brachett, of Indiana; 1st lt of volunteers in war with Mexico.

1st Lts:
2nd Lt N G Evans, of S C; 2nd lt, Sep 30, 1849, 2nd dragoons. Active service on Indian frontier. First commissioned, 1848.
2nd Lt Rich W Johnson, of Ky; 2nd lt, Jun 10, 1850, 1st Infty. Active service on Indian frontier. First commissioned, 1849.
2nd Lt Jos H McArthur, of Missouri; 2nd lt, Aug 12, 1850, 5th Infty. Active service on Indian frontier. First commissioned, 1849.
2nd Lt Chas M Field, of Ky; 2nd lt, Jun 30, 1851, 2nd dragoons. Active service on Indian frontier. First commissioned, 1849.
2nd Lt Kenner Garrard, of Ohio; 2nd lt, Jun 30, 1851, 2nd dragoons. Active service on Indian frontier. First commissioned, 1849.
Alex'r H Cross, of D C; 1st lt voltigeurs; distinguished at battle of Chepultepec.
Wm H Jenifer, of Md; 1st lt 3rd dragoons in war with Mexico.
Wm B Royall, of Missouri; 1st lt volunteers in war with Mexico.
Wm P Chambliss, of Tenn; 2nd lt volunteers in war with Mexico.
Robt Nelson Eagle, of Texas. Served in the war with Mexico, first in foot & afterwards in mounted volunteers.

2nd Lts:
2nd Lt John T Shaaf, of D C; 2nd lt, Jun 9, 1853, 6th Infty. Active service on Indian frontier. First commissioned, 1851.
2nd Lt Geo B Cosby, of Ky; 2nd lt, Sep 16, 1853, mounted rifles. Active service on Indian frontier; distinguished & wounded in combat with Indians in Texas. First commissioned, 1852.
2nd Lt Geo B Anderson, of N C; 2nd lt, Mar 21, 1854, 2nd dragoons. Active service on Indian frontier. First commissioned, 1852.
2nd Lt N B Sweitzer, of Pa; 2nd lt, Jul 25, 1854, 1st dragoons. Service on Indian frontier, 1853.
2nd Lt Wm W Lowe, of Iowa; 2nd lt, Oct 22, 1854, 1st dragoons. Service on Indian frontier. First commissioned, 1852.
Edwin R Merrifield, of Michigan. Served in war with Mexico.
Geo Hartwell, of Wisconsin.
Jos Minter, of Wash Territory. Explorations in Texas & Oregon.
Chas N Phifer, of Mississippi.
Robt C Wood, jr, of Louisiana.

1st Regt of Cavalry.

Capts:
Brvt Maj Robt S Garnett, of Va; capt, Mar 9, 1851, 7th Infty. Twice brevetted for gallantry in action; distinguished in battles of Palo Alto & Resaca de la Palma, Monterey, & Buena Vista. First commissioned, 1841.
Brvt 1st Lt Delos B Sackett, of N Y; 1st lt, Dec 27, 1848, 1st dragoons. Brevetted for gallantry in battles of Palo Alto & Resaca de la Palma. First commissioned, 1845.

Brvt 1st Lt Thos J Wood, of Ky; 1st lt, Jun 30, 1851, 2nd dragoons. Brevetted for gallantry in action; distinguished in battles of Palo Alto, Resaca de la Palma, & Buena Vista. First commissioned, 1845.

Brvt Capt Geo B McClelland, of Pa; 1st lt, Jul 1, 1853, engineers. Twice brevetted for gallantry in action; distinguished in battles of Contreras, Churubusco, Milino del Rey, & Chepultepec. First commissioned, 1846.

1st Lt Saml G Sturgis, of Pa; 1st lt, Jul 15, 1853, 1st dragoons. Served in war with Mexico; distinguished in combat with Indians in New Mexico. First commissioned, 1846.

W W de Saussure, of S C; Capt Palmetto Regt; wounded in battle at Churubusco; distinguished in battle at Belengate.

Wm D Wilkins, of Michigan; 1st lt, 15th Infty; brevetted 1st lt for gallantry in several affairs with guerillas in Mexico.

Wm B Reynolds, of Ill; 2nd lt volunteers; afterwards 2nd lt, 16th Infty in war with Mexico.

Geo T Anderson, of Georgia; 2nd lt Georgia mounted volunteers in war with Mexico.

John T Coffee, of Maine.

1st Lts:

2nd Lt Wm N R Beall, of Ark; 2nd lt, Apr 30, 1849, 5th Infty. Active service on Indian frontier. First commissioned, 1848.

2nd Lt Geo H Stewart, of Md; 2nd lt, Nov 11, 1849, 2nd dragoons. Active service on Indian frontier. First commissioned, 1848.

2nd Lt Jas McIntosh, of Florida; 2nd lt, May 15, 1851, 8th Infty. Service on Indian frontier. First commissioned, 1849.

2nd Lt Eugene A Carr, of N Y; 2nd lt, Jun 30, 1851, mounted rifles. Active service on Indian frontier; distinguished in combat with Indians in Texas. First commissioned, 1851.

2nd Lt David Bell, of Iowa; 2nd lt, Oct 9, 1852, 2nd dragoons. Active service on Indian frontier; distinguished in combat with Indians in New Mexico. First commissioned, 1851.

John M Perkins, of Ala; in Texas Rangers at battle of Buena Vista; afterwards 1st lt, 13th Infty in war with Mexico.

Edw J Dummitt, of Florida, 1st lt, 13th Infty in war with Mexico.

Alfred Iverson, jr, of Georgia; 2nd lt, mounted volunteers in war with Mexico.

Harry Love, of Calif; service against Indians.

Frank Wheaton, of Rhode Island; frontier explorations.

2nd Lts:

2nd Lt David S Stanley, of Ohio; 2nd lt, Sep 6, 1853, 2nd dragoons. Served on Indian frontier. First commissioned, 1852.

2nd Lt Philip Stockton, of N J; 2nd lt, Oct 11, 1853, 8th Infty; served on Indian frontier. First commissioned, 1852.

2nd Lt Thos Hight, of Indiana; 2nd lt, Mar 24, 1854, 2nd dragoons. Served on Indian frontier. First commissioned, 1853.

2nd Lt Benj Allston, of S C; 2nd lt, Oct 22, 1854, 1st dragoons. Served on Indian frontier. First commissioned, 1858.
2nd Lt Jas E B Stuart, of Va; 2nd lt, Oct 31, 1854, mounted rifles. Service on Indian frontier. First commissioned, 1854.
Peter Parkinson, jr, of Wisconsin.
Wm W Kirkland, of N C.
Eugene Crittenden, of Ky.
Wm A B Jones, of Iowa.
H T Clarke, of Rhode Island, late non-commissioned ofcr of dragoons.

We the undersigned have this day assembled to witness the laying of the foundation of the monument which is to make the initial point of the boundary between the U S & Mexico; on the part of the U S by Wm Hensley Emory, & on the part of Mexico by Jose Salazar. Latitude 31 degrees 47/.

W H Emory, U S Com'r
C Radyieninski, Sec
Joel L Ankrim, District Judge
E B Alexander, Lt Col Com'g **Fort Bliss**
Caleb Sherwood, Collector
E K Smith, Commanding Escort

Jose Salazar, Com'r
Jose Sanchez, Prefecto
Antonio Lopedo, Commandante
Gaudaloups Miranda, Vice Consul
Vicente Aguierre, Administrador
Jan 31, 1855

Criminal Court: Wm F Magraw has been convicted of an assault upon Mr W H Hope, one of the editors of the Star, & fined $100.

Wm Umberfield & Mike Murphy, 2 young men lately sentenced for 1 year to the jail in Wash City for an assault, escaped on Monday night, having by some means obtained instruments & removed the iron bars of the window of their cell.

After nealy 20 years service as pastor of a Presbyterian church at Milroy, Pa, this gentleman returned to the home of his kindred in Wash City in 1849, where he established an excellent academy, & conducted it until Jul, 1854, when he departed for Iowa in pursuit of a new home, but immediately found a grave at Salem, in that State. Recently 2 members of the church at Milroy were sent to Salem by the congregation of that church to disinter his remains & carry them to Milroy for permanent sepulchre. This sad duty having been performed, the remains of Mr Nourse now repose in the burial place at Milroy, guarded by a people who loved him well, as did all who ever knew him.

Richd Hosmer, formerly a member of the Mass Legislature, was killed at Templeton last week by his foot being caught in a saw mill & cut completely off above the ancle.

Jas Parks has been found guilty of murder in the 1st degree at Cleveland, Ohio, for killing Wm Beatson.

Died: on Mar 19, Mrs J Leigh Lackey, wife of R J Lackey. Her funeral is today at 2 o'clock, from 13th & E sts.

Died: Mar 20, Ida Virginia Hall, youngest daughter of Baruch & Virginia B Hall, aged 18 months. Her funeral is this morning at 11½ o'clock, from 424 F st, between 6th & 7th sts.

Died: on Mar 17, Evan Jones, of N, of Montgomery, Md.

Notice to the heirs at law of Betsey Black, [colored,] deceased. Balt, Feb 17, 1855. By order of the Orphans' Court for Balt city, passed on the above date, notice is given to all persons interested as heirs at law & distributees of the estate of Betsey Black, [colored,] late of the city of Balt, deceased, to appear at this Court, in person or by solicitor, on or before Jun 1 next, to assert any claims they may have to the distribution of the residue of the said estate. Maria Stewart, admx

Orphans Court of Wash Co, D C. Letters of administration on the personal estate of Henry A F Felson, late of Wash Co, deceased. –Eliz P Felson, admx

Orphans Court of Wash Co, D C. Letters of administration on the personal estate of Michl Brady, late of Wash Co, deceased. –Margaret Brady, admx

THU MAR 22, 1855
Several months ago a young lady, Emma Moore, mysteriously disappeared from her home in Rochester, N Y, & much interest was excited in her fate. Large rewards were offered by the public authorities. Her body has been found under the ice in a mill race, & identified by her jewels & bonnet. She had been missing about 4 months, & appearances indicate that the body had been all the time under water; but the manner & means of her death remain a mystery.

Trustee's sale of valuable improved property at auction: on Apr 12, in front of the premises, by deed of trust from Sandy Elkins & wife, dated Aug 10, 1854, recorded in Liber J A S No 84, folios 191 thru 194, of the land records for Wash Co, D C: sale of part of lot 8 in square 211, containing 5,525 square feet of ground, more or less, with a good new 2 story brick house. –Thos Lewis, trustee -Green & Scott, aucts

U S Patent Ofc, Wash, Mar 21, 1855. Ptn of Chas F Hobe, of N Y, N Y, praying for the extension of a patent granted to him for an improvement in the manner of making the slides of extension tables, for 7 years from the expiration of said patent, which takes place on Jun 22, 1855. –Chas Mason, Com'r of Patents

Conference of the Methodist Episcopal Church, at Balt, closed yesterday. List of appointments for the Potomac District:
Potomac Dist: John Lanahan, P E
Alexandria: W G Eggleston, J N Coombs; Henry C Westwood, Princess st.
Washington: F P Phelps, Foundry; R L Dashiell & G H Day, Wesley Chapel & Capitol Hill; Geo Hildt, M A Turner, sup, McKendree & Fletcher Chapel; Francis H Richey, Ebenezer; Alfred Griffith, W C Steele, J M Hanson, sup, Ryland Chapel & Greenleaf's Point Mission; Fielder Israel W O Lumsden, sup, Union Chapel.
Gtwn: B F Brooke
West Gtwn & Tennally Town: Wm F Speake
Fairfax: David Thomas & Thaddeus B McFalls
Stafford: John W Hoover & Henry Leber
Fredericksburg: Saml Rodgers
St Mary's: Noah Schlosser, one to be supplied, J Bunting, sup
Charles: Marble L Hawley & J Henry Wolff
Bladensburg: Thos H Busey & Jas N Keyes
Woodville: Wm A McKee
Rockville: John S Deale & R R S Hough, Basil Barry, sup
Thos McGee, Asbury & Mount Zion [colored,] Washington.
Jesse T Peck Editor of Tracts & Corresponding Sec of the Tract Society of the Methodist Episcopal Church, member of the Foundry Quarterly Conference.
The Presiding Elders in several districts are as follows:
Balt Dist: Wm Hamilton
North Balt Dist: Henry Slicer
Lewisburg Dist: Mayberry Goheen
Rockingham Dist: Sam V Blake
Winchester Dist: Wm Hirst
Fred'k Dist: Thos H W Monroe
Cumberland Dist: John A Collins
Bellefonte Dist: John Poisal
Northumberland Dist: T R Sargent
Carlisle Dist: A A Reese

Mr Robt Heller gives a varied entertainment this evening at Carusi's Saloon for the purpose of presenting himself before our community as a pianist of distinction.

The Criminal Court yesterday adjourned in expression of its sympathy with P Barton Key, the Dist Atty, the sudden & unexpected death of whose lady on the preceding evening has filled this community with sorrow.
+
Died: on Mar 20, in Wash City, Ellen, wife of Philip Barton Key. Her funeral is today at 12 o'clock M, from the residence of her father, Jas Swan, Franklin st.

Died: on Mar 21, of croup, Jos Denis O'Neale, aged 2 years & 7 days, the youngest child of the late Timothy O'Neale, of Gtwn, D C. His funeral is today at 4½ o'clock P M, from the residence of his mother.

Died: on Mar 19, in Balt, Mary Cecilia, daughter of the late Chas R Ramsay, & grand-daughter of the late Col Henry Ashton, of Wash City.

Died: on Mar 7, in Livingston, Ala, after a short illness, Jas Harvey Thompson, late sheriff of Sumter Co, in about his 35th year of his life. He was a native of Mount Sterling, Ky, & was originally a printer; but, like many others of the craft, he abandoned it in early life for more profitable pursuits. A truer friend could not be found. -D

FRI MAR 23, 1855
Explosion in a bldg of the firework factory of G A Lilliendahl, st Greenville, Bergen Point, N Y, on Wed, took the life of Henry Kleiber, a boy, who was killed by the falling timbers. Lewis Komer was so badly hurt that he died soon after the accident. [Apr 4th newspaper: also died: Emil Brehm, Jacob Nicolay, Fred'k Schmidt, Ferdinand Bauer, & Chas Kleine. Wm Hitten is not expected to live, & the lad Henry Jopman is not expected to recover.]

Five white men, 2 white boys, & 30 colored men were killed by the explosion in the Midlothian coal pits, in Chesterfield Co, Va, on Monday last. The white sufferers are: Saml Gouldin, manager of hands, John Lester, John Evans, Jos Howe, & the 2 boys, Jonathan Jewett & Wm Wright.

Household & kitchen furniture at auction on: Mar 29, at the residence of Prof C C Jewett, corner of 15th & H sts. -Jas C McGuire, auct

Trustee's sale: by deed of trust from C H Winder & wife to the subscriber, & by direction of Wm Hook, the holder of one of the notes secured by such deed: sale on Apr 16 next, of lot 4 in square 168, of Davidson's subdivision of the said square, in Wash City. –Otho Z Muncaster, trustee -Green & Scott, aucts

Rev John F Cook, a man of color, & the founder & pastor of the 15th st Presbyterian Church, died in Wash City yesterday. His walk & conversation were such as to command general respect of white & black.

Soda fountain for sale: subscriber expecting to remove from his present place of business on Apr 1 for the summer months, for the purpose of erecting a new store. -Z D Gilman

Died: on Mar 22, in Wash City, at the residence of Silas L Loomis, Mrs Emma L, wife of J E Marsh, of Roxbury, Mass, aged 27 years, 7 months & 10 days.

The undersigned, having become associated as Bounty Land Agents, under the firm of Polk & Davidge, offer their services to all persons entitled to land under the act of Congress passed on Mar 3,1 855, & other laws of the U S; for the preparation of papers & procuration of land certificates at Wash. –Jas Polk, Francis H Davidge

Died: on Mar 22, Mrs Catherine Stricklin, in her 68th year, a native of PG Co, Md, but for the last 30 years a resident of Wash City.

Died: on Tue last, in Gtwn, John Adams, in his 39th year. His funeral is today at 3 o'clock, from his late residence on 2nd st.

Died: on Mar 22, R H Jewelle, in his 26th year. His funeral will take place at the residence of Mrs E T Duvall, on Sat, at 10 o'clock.

Died: on Mar 20, at Granville, near Warrenton, Va, Mrs Eliz Winter, wife of Danl Payne, in her 72nd year. She was perfectly just in the unwearied performance of every duty as wife, mother, mistress, & neighbor. An extended circle of relatives & friends lament her death. -M

SAT MAR 24, 1855
Trustee's sale: by deed of trust from Geo Eignbrodt & wife, dated Sep 25, 1854: public auction on Apr 7, on the premises, of lot 1 in square 76, in Wash, with 2 new two-story frame tenements. –Walter S Cox, trustee -Green & Scott, aucts

Household & kitchen furniture at auction on: Mar 30, at the residence of J L Davis, at the Cottage at north N & 13th sts. -Green & Scott, aucts

Local Item: on Thu a young son of Mr Barton Hackney, of the First Ward, was accidentally shot by one of his companions while gunning for skylark, & that he on that night died of the injury received.

Mrd: on Mar 20, at Warrenton, Fauquier Co, Va, by Rev J W Tongue, Geo H C Neal, of Wash City, to Ann Amelia, eldest daughter of J R Tongue, of the former place.

Died: yesterday, Mrs Agnes Hamil, daughter of the late Chas Bell, in her 65th year. Her funeral will take place from the residence of her son-in-law, Mr I F Mudd, on D st, between 7th & 8th, tomorrow at 3 o'clock.

Died: on Mar 23, after a protracted illness, Mrs Annie Cavanaugh, in her 21st year. Her funeral will take place from the residence of her father, Geo McNaughton, on 6th, between G & H sts, on Mar 25, at half past two o'clock.

Died: on Mar 23, Marrion W Lord, daughter of John B & Sarah Lord, aged 3 years, 11 months & 20 days. Her funeral will be from the residence of her parents, 4th & G sts, today, at 3 o'clock P M.

Died: on Mar 6, in Brooklyn, Long Island, Cynthia Berry, about 14 months old, daughter of Jos L & Melinda Williams. This little stranger sleeps, not alone, in **Greenwood**. She lies beside a senior sister, who went some years before her. Only a few weeks since she was preceed by 2 senior sisters, who repose together in the **Congressional Cemetery** here. Thus 4 young spirits, after brief joy in time, translated to one & the same angelic home.

Obit-died: on Feb 20 last, on board the U S ship **Falmouth**, of bilious cholic, Passed Midshipman Thos Waterman Brodhead, only child of Hon John M Brodhead, of Wash City, 2nd Comptroller of the Treasury, & grandson of the late Hon John Brodhead, of N H, aged 27 years. The **Falmouth** arrived at Port au Prince on the 22nd instant, & the remains of Passed Midshipman Brodhead, who was acting master of the ship, were entombed in the ***Protestant cemetery*** at that place, with military honors, on the 23rd. Mr Brodhead was appointed a midshipman in 1841, & entered at once on active duty. He spent a portion of the last summer at the home of his father in this city as an invalid, his disease having been contracted while performing his duty in the public service. When ordered to the **Falmouth** his health was by no means restored, but, actuated by that energy of character & detemination to do all his duty, he made no complaint, but, leaving his father, mother, & wife, he went forth to his duty never again to return. He told one of the officers that he had a dear brother in Heaven to receive him. The brother alluded to was Midshipman Alfred W Brodhead. These 2 promising young ofcrs were the only children of their parents, who are now left childless. –F [Mar 26th newspaper: The U S sloop-of-war **Falmouth** cast anchor in the harbor of Port au Prince on Feb 22, & shorly after noon of that day lost Acting Master Thos W Brodhead, of N H. His funeral took place on the 23rd. An armed detachment & 30 marines rendered military honors to the deceased, whose hearse was also followed by a number of the ofcrs of the **Falmouth**.]

The undersigned, R Johnson, residing in Balt, Md, & W S Cox, residing in Gtwn, D C, have associated themselves for the purpose of practicing in the Court of Claims at Wash. –Reverdy Johnson, Monument Square, Balt; Walter S Cox, Gtwn, D C.

U S Patent Ofc, Wash, Mar 22, 1855. Ptn of Chas W Copeland, of N Y, N Y, praying for the extension of a patent granted to him for an improvement in the manner of arranging the low-pressure steam engine so as to adapt its parts to be used by vessels for ocean service, for 7 years from the expiration of said patent, which takes place on Jun 11, 1855. –Chas Mason, Com'r of Patents

N Y, Mar 23. Wm Kissane, the notorious forger, has been sentenced to 2½ years in Sing Sing.

MON MAR 26, 1855
Hon Henry Wilson, Senator from Mass, was attacked with apoplexy on Fri last, whilst engaged in delivering an anti-slavery lecture at the Tremont Temple.

Brook Farm, in Roxbury, Mass, was sold by the great real estate auctioneer, to Arnold W Taylor, with 180 acres of fine land & its expensive bldgs, at $80 an acre, or about $14,400 for the whole. The estate cost the city of Roxbury $30,000. Brook Farm was the headquarters of experimental socialist, who attempted to form an institution in the very heart of New England. The philosophers & philanthropists who were so weak as to suppose that any branch of French Socialism could florish in New England, were part true men & good men, but were all a little cracked in the upper story, & found their farm could not sustain their institution, & the concern was sold out to the city of Roxury for an almhouse. -Boston Courier

Naval: Lt Henry J Hartsteine, U S Navy, has been ordered to the command of the Gov't's expedition to the Arctic Seas, authorized by Congress at its last session. It will fit out at the N Y Navy Yard, & probably sail about June 1st.

Fatal accident in the cars near Tiffin, Ohio, Monday of last week. John Esch dropped some money, & stooping to pick it up, one of Allen's self-cocking pistols fell from a side pocket, & the hammer, striking the edge of the seat, discharged the pistol & killed him instantly. The ball entered his heart.

On Thus last, as the omnibus coaches from the railroad depot were near Alexandria, the driver of Whaley's line, named Francis Weedon, aged about 19 years, accidentally let the reins slip, & in his effort to recover them a sudden jolt of the coach threw him to the ground & his neck was broken by the fall.

Died: on Mar 24, at the residence of Gen Eaton, Margaret Rosa, widow of the late Lt John B Randolph, U S Navy. Her funeral is today at 4 p m.

Died: on Mar 15, at the residence of his father-in-law, on West river, Md, Jos Henry Collins, eldest son of Rev Jno A Collins, of the M E Church.

Died: on Mar 17, in Balt, Md, Eliza A, consort of Jas H Hogg, & the daughter of Mr Wm A Davey, of Wash, in her 30th year.

Died: on Mar 21, in N Y, after a protracted illness, at the age of 37, Madame Evelina De La Forest, wife of Chas A L De La Forest, Consul of France at Boston.

Died: on Mar 4, on board the U S mail steamer **Uncle Sam**, on the passage from San Francisco to Panama, Geo F Lindsay, jr, aged 24 years, son of Capt G F Lindsay, U S Marine Corps.

Died: on Mar 2, Miss Ellen Norris, in her 80th year. She was the daughter of Dr Wm Norris, of White Chapel, Lancaster, Pa, who settled the plantation [more than 100 years ago] on which she resided at her death. Of this family there were 8 daughters & 4 sons, the average of whose ages was beyond 80 years, of whom Mrs Craig & Mrs Johnson survive as a connecting link between the present & the memory of the past. The old homestead on the mountain, so long the seat of kind hospitality, is now vacant. Cousin Ellen, its last occupant, has left it to join the circle of those gone before her, to share with them the reward of a well spent life.
--Warrenton [Va] Flag, 17th.

N Y, Mar 25. The Consul of the Netherlands at this port, Mr Zimmerman, died yesterday morning.

TUE MAR 27, 1855
2nd Lt Geo W Campbell, of the U S Marine Corps, died at Norfolk a day or two since, on board the frig **Columbia**. He was among those down with the fever on the arrival of the **Columbia** from the West Indies.

The mansion house of ***Marshfield***, the residence of the late Danl Webster, & some acres of the homestead surrounding it, are not included in the sale of the proerty to take place on Mar 28.

Household & kitchen furniture at auction on: Apr 2, at the residence of J W Simonton, on 6th st, between D & E sts: excellent furniture. -Green & Scott, aucts

Household & kitchen furniture at auction on: Apr 2, at the residence of Mr W C Butler, 202 Pa ave, corner of 15th st: excellent assortment. -Green & Scott, aucts

A letter in the Providence [R I] Journal, dated at South Kingston, says that there are now living in the southern part of R I, all in good health, 10 persons, the children of the same parents, & the only children they ever had, whose united ages amount to 711, in the following order: 81, 80, 77, 75, 73, 70, 68, 66, 63, & 58. Their name is Tucker, & they belong to one of the most numerous families in our State. For a great many years the family occupied a tract of land in the western part of south Kingstown, know as Tucker town. The second son of Joshua Tucker, now 80 years old, afflicted with rheumatism, goes to the sea with his pole & stands for 3 or 4 hours together to his waist in the breakers sam-humming, or gand-humming, whichever is the right term for that method of fishing for bass.

Wm Jennens, of England, died there in 1798, at 97 years of age, & left an estate worth four millions of pounds sterling, equal to about twenty millions of dollars; of which the real estate, all that is now to be traced, Acton in Suffolk Co, England, was valued in 1726, [the date of his will, in which he left his whole estate to his mother, who died in 1762] at L12,700 sterling; but is now much more valuable. The Herald's ofc, London, has lately furnished the following pedigree of Wm Jennens: Wm Jennens, of Birmingham, died in 1608. He & John [ne'Elyotte] his wife were parents to John Jennens, of Birmingham, who died 1653. The latter was the father of Humphrey Jennens, of Tedington Hall, in Warwick Co, who died in 1690. Humphrey Jennens & Mary [ne'Milward] his wife were parents of Robt Jennens, who died 1726. Robt Jennens, of Acton Pl, county Suffolk, of Bedford Row, & his wife Ann, only daughter of & heir of Carew Guydot, who died 1762, were the parents of Wm Jennens, of Bedford Row aforesaid, of Grosvenor Square, county of Middlesex, of Acton Place aforesaid, esquire, only son; baptized at St Giles, in the Fields, county Middlesex, Sep 4, 1701; died Jun 19, 1798, & was buried at Acton aforesaid 29th same month. Will dated May 3, 1726, administration [with will annexed] granted Jul 56, 1798, to Wm Ligon, & Mary, Viscountess Dowager of Andover, the cousins german & next of kin of the said deceased. Administration de bonis non, etc, Nov 21, 1817, to Catherine, countess of beauchamp, widow, the relict & sole executrix of Wm, [Lygon,] Earl of Beauchamp, deceased. After the reference to Wm Jennens, as above, the "only son," the pedigree only adds: "Other issue from whom the next of kin descended. Note-The present Earl of Howe is now in possession of Acton Place, as the heirs at law of Wm Jennens." The omission in his pedigree of his sister, or sisters, or the chain of relationship by which Lords Beauchamp & Howe obtained the property left by Wm Jennens, as next of kin, is worthy of remark. It will be also observed that Mgt Corbin was married to Wm Lygon, ancestor to Lord Beauchamp, in 1688, 38 years before Wm Jennens made his will, which remained unchanged in a single particular till he died, 1798, or 72 years after it was written. But the link of connexion between the Corbins of Va, & Wm Jennens is also omitted in his pedigree & that of the former. The Corbins originated in Warsickshire, England. It appears that the Corbin descent has been traced lineally about 500 years to Thos Corbin, of Hall End, in the county of Warwick, born in Apr, 1624, married to a daughter of Gawen Grosvenor, of the family of the present Marquis of Westminister. Their 3rd son, Henry Corbin, went to Va in 1650 or earlier, & in 1675 died there. He left the following children: Thos, who died without children; Gawen, married to Jane, the daughter of & heir of John Lane, of York River; Mrs Richd Lee, grandmother of the distinguished Richd Henry Lee; Mrs Wm Lightfoot; Mrs Thos Griffin; Mrs Wm Tayloe, grandmother of the 1st Col John Tayloe, of **Mount Airy**; & Mrs Edmund Jennings. [Edmund Jennings was Pres of the King's Council in Va, succeeded by Robt Carter.] Edmund Jennings, of the Province of Md, its Atty Gen, is supposed to have been the son of Pres Jennings. Gawen Corbin, survivor & heir of Thos Corbin, was father to Richd Corbin, of Lanesville. Gawen Corbin, of Buchingham House, married a daughter of Wm Basset, & left 4 daughters: Mrs Jenny Bushrod, Mrs Joana Tucker, Mrs Alice

Needles, & Mrs Allerton, & a son, [Gawen,] who married Hannah Lee, sister of Richd Henry Lee. Gawen Corbin, of Buckingham, was the eldest son of Richd Corbin, of Laneville, Pres of the King's Council, who married Betty, daughter of Col John Tayloe. Their other sons were John Tayloe Corbin, of Laneville, Richd, Thos, & Francis, of the Reeds, the father of F P Corbin, now at Paris. Richd Corbin, of Laneville, was father to the wife of Carter Braxton, the signer of the Declaration of Independence. From Henry Corbin the family tree seems to have branched luxuriantly, bearing prolific fruit. The Corbin descendants are legion. The first of the name of Corbin, Tayloe, Lee, & Washington, as known in Va, came there almost simultaneously from England, about the time it was expected that Cromwell would assume the Crown. Col Richd Lee, of Stratford Langton, in the county of Essex, England, was a burgess of Va in 1647. John Washington, great grandfather of the Father of his Country, emigrated from the north of England to Va about 1657, & settled in Westmoreland Co. These facts, as stated, are derived from authentic sources, especially the pedigrees, as far as they go, from the Herald's College. An American agent for claims wrote from London the last autumn that he would not touch the Jennings claim, had been cautioned about it; that a deeper froud was never practiced or planned than this claim by indigent knaves who practice law in England; they stimulate inquiry & excite false hopes by newspaper publications & letters, lucri causa. Such was probably the origin of the claim for the Corbins of Va, by one using a nom de plume. There seems to be no further cause for controversy or discussion of the subject. -T

Mrd: on Sabbath evening, by Rev John C Smith, Mr David F Glover to Miss Rebecca Jane Hill, all of Wash City.

Mrd: on Thu, by Rev S A H Marks, Mr Raymond Skidmore to Miss Mary A Caulk, all of Wash City.

Died: on Dec 27 last, on board the U S ship **Independence**, two days out from Rio Janeiro, Passed Midshipman Washington Totten, U S Navy.

Died: on Monday, Mary Eliz, wife of Thos A King, in her 22nd year. Her funeral is on Wed at 3 o'clock.

Wash City Ordinances: 1-Act for the relief of Michl McDermott: the sum of $56.12½ cents to be paid to him for repairs of hose reels for the Columbia Fire Co. 2-Act for the relief of Mrs Euridice F Simms, excx of Elexius Simms, deceased: to pay her the sum of $17.50, being the amount paid for the unexpired license of said deceased.

WED MAR 28, 1855

A Washington prima donna in Italy. Miss Juliana May, of this city, had her debut in an Italian theatre. On Feb 17th she had a triumphant success at Verona in Verdi's trying opera of Rigoleto.

Wash Corp: 1-Ptn from Amelia Baltimore for the remission of a fine: referred to the Cmte of Claims. 2-Cmte on Finance: act for the relief of Rebecca K Billing: passed. 3-Ptn of Jas Barnes for the remission of a fine: referred to the Cmte of Claims. 4-Cmte of Claims: act for the relief of Mgt Tilghman: passed. 5-Ptn of Wm S Venable & others, asking that the curbstones be set & the footway paved on the west side of squares 905 & 906: referred to the Cmte on Improvements. 6-Cmte of Claims: adverse report on the bill for the relief of John Guterson: asked to be discharged from its futher consideration: which was agreed to.

Orphans Court of Wash Co, D C. Letters testamentary on the personal estate of Alex'r Talburt, late of Wash Co, deceased. –Thos W Howard, exc

$25 will be paid for recovery of a double-barreled gun, stolen from my rooms, 49 La ave, last week. The gun was made by Jamieson, of London. –John A Linton

Miss Fanny Morant made her first appearance before a Washington audience on Monday, at the People's Theatre, & surpassed the expectations of all who had formed an opinion of her powers from the notices of the press elsewhere. She personated the character of Julia with fine effect. With a fine contralto voice & much skill on the piano, harp, & guitar, she cannot fail to please.

Villa for sale. The subscriber offers at private sale the Villa in which she at present resides, with 8 acres of land, at **Ellaville**, on the Wash & Balt turnpike road; within 5 minutes' walk of Bladensburg depot on the railroad. Apply to the subscriber, living on the premises. –Mary S Vass

On Fri night week the dwlg of Mr Keller, of Rye Township, Perry Co, Pa, was destroyed by fire & his 3 children perished in the flames. The fire was not discovered until the roof had fallen in, preventing the escape of the children.

Died: on Mar 27, in Wash City, Mrs Eliz Thomson, relict of the late Wm Thomson, of Gtwn. Her funeral is on Thu at 3 o'clock, from her late residence, 9th & H sts.

Trustees of Public Schools will meet at City Hall on Mar 31, at 3 o'clock. By direction of the Board of Trustees, Geo J Abbot, sec.

Jos Huggins, Jeweller & Silversmith, is about to close his store, & offer his entire stock at great bargains. He is determined to sell very low for cash only.

The copartnership existing between Otto Wix & John Duval, in the Blacksmithing business, is this day dissolved by mutual consent. John Duval will settle the business of the late firm; Otto Wix will continue the Blacksmithing business, at his shop, on 7th st, between H & I sts.

THU MAR 29, 1855
Household & kitchen furniture at auction: by order of the Orphans Court of Wash Co, D C: on Apr 3, at the residence of the late Wm H Page, on 5th st, between E & F sts. –R C Page, adm -Jas C McGuire, auct

Household & kitchen furniture at auction: Apr 2, at the late residence of Isaac H Wailes, deceased, on North B, between North Capitol st & 1st st. -Green & Scott, aucts

Proposals for bldg Lighthouse on *Sevenfoot Knoll*, mouth of Patalsco river, Md, will be received until Apr 30 next. Treasury Dept, Ofc Lighthouse Board, Wash, D C, Mar 27, 1855. –Edmd L F Hardcastle, Engineer, Sec

Hon Thos Fitzgerald, formerly U S Senator from Michigan, died on Sunday last.

The frame dwlg of Mr Jos Cross, corner of Va ave & 3rd st, Island, was destroyed by fire on Tue night. It was insured for $500, but was worth about $900. His furniture was insured for $175, which will cover his loss in that particular. The most melancholy incident, however, in this affair was that his invalid nephew, a young man, has been affected seriously, perhaps fatally, by the excitement & exposure to which he was subjected.

Orphans Court of Wash Co, D C. Letters of administration on the personal estate of Isaac H Wailes, late of Wash Co, deceased. –Martha Wailes, admx

Mrd: on Mar 22, at the Potomac House, Wash, by Rev J M Henry, Mr Cader W Dozier to Miss Emily Suit.

Died: on Mar 27, Francis B Lord, son of John B & Sarah Lord, aged 20 months. His funeral will be today at 3 o'clock P M.

Died: on Mar 28, John, only son of John & Eliz Robinson, aged 14 months. His funeral is this evening at 3 o'clock P M from his father's residence, opposite Odd Fellows' Hall, Navy Yard.

The Principal of the Academy at Charlestown, Jefferson Co, Va, resigned his charge, & the Trustees desire to employ a successor. Communicate with the undersigned or N S White, Sec of the Board. –Andrew Hunter, Pres Board of Trustees

Boston, Mar 28. An investigation of the accounts of the Merchants' Bank, caused by the suicide of Thos W Hooper, [as announced yesterday,] the paying teller, discloses no deficiencies in his relations with that bank. He had used, however, $50,000 of the bank's money, which he had made good at the expense of the Atlantic & Grocers' Banks by certifying to two checks, drawn by A S Peabody, which on his certificate were cashed, & the money drawn from those two banks was used to make up his deficit in the Merchants' bank.

Franklin H Sage has opened an extensive Book & Job Printing Ofc, Columbia Pl, corner of 7th st & Louisiana ave.

The undersigned inform that they have succeeded Messrs Dickson & King in the Lumber business, having purchased their entire stock & made large additions therto. -E Pickrell & Co, Water st, Gtwn

Circuit Court of Wash Co, D C-in Chancery. Jas Adams, cmplnt, vs Richd Patton, dfndnt. W Redin, trustee, reported that Thos Goodall became the purchaser of lot H of the subdivision of lots 1 & 30, in square 693, in Wash City, with improvements thereon, for $900; & he had complied with the terms of sale. –Jno A Smith, clerk

FRI MAR 30, 1855
St Petersburgh, 2nd, 6 o'clock, morning. The Emperor Nicholas has received with perfect calmness the communication made by Dr Mandt that there was reason to fear paralysis of the lungs, & only asked, "when shall I be paralyzed?" The physicians cound not give any precise reply. The Emperor then spoke to Dr Carell in Russian & said, "when will suffocation come on?" His Majesty has received the sacrament, bid adieu to his wife & his children, blessed each of them separately, & also his grandchildren, with much calmness & presence of mind, & in a firm voice. The Empress does not allow herself to be overcome by her feelings, & shows herself resigned. –Count Munster. [On Mar 2, at 4 o'clock in the morning, the Emperor received the sacraments, & died at ten minutes past noon. He had been sick for 12 days.] Prince Alexander, who is now Emperor under the name of Alexander II, was born on Apr 29, 1818; he is in his 37th year. He married Apr 2, 1841, the daughter of the late Duke Louis, of Hesse. Three sons & 2 daughters have been born of this marriage. The new sovereign of Russia was initiated at an early age into the affairs of the Empire by the Emperor, his father; he was present at all the Cabinet Councils.
+
The late Czar married Jul 13, 1817, a Prussian princess, Fredericka Louisa Charlotte Wilhelmina, daughter of Fred'k Wm III, King of Prussia. On her marriage she changed her name to Alexandra Foedorovna. By her the Emperor had 6 children: Alexander, born Apr 29, 1818; Mary, born Aug 18, 1819; Olga, born Sep 11, 1822; Constantine, born Sep 21, 1827; Nicholas, born Aug 8, 1831; & Michl, born Oct 25, 1832. The Emperor also leaves two sisters: Mary Paulowna, Grand Duchess Dowager of Saxe Weimar, & Anne Paulowna, widow of the late King of Holland.

+
The family of the late Czar. The Emperor Nicholas leaves the following numerous family: His wife, the Empress Alexandra Fedorowna, [formerly called Frederica-Louisa-Charlotte-Wilhelmina,] daughter of the late Frederic Wm III, King of Prussia; was born Jul 13, 1798, & is in very weak health. Issue of this marriage are: First. Alex'r Nicolaivitch Cesarovitch, the present Emperor; born Apr 29, 1813; married Apr 28, 1841, Maria Alexandrovina, the present Empress, [formerly Maximilienne-Wilhelmina-Augusta-Sophia-Maria,] born May 8, 1824, daughter of the late Louis II, Grand Duke of Hesse. Issue of this marriage: Nicholas Alexandrovitch, the present Crown Prince, born Sep 20, 1843; Wladimir Alexandrovitch, born Apr 22, 1847; Alexis Alexandrovitch, born Jan 14, 1850.
Second: Maria Nicolaievna, born Aug 8, 1819; married Jul 14, 1839, to Maximilian, Duke of Leuchtenberg, Prince of Eichtedt; became widow Nov 1, 1852.
Third: Olga Nicolaievna, born Sep 11,1822; married to Charles, Prince Royal of Wurtemburg, Jul 13, 1846.
Fourth: Constantine Nicolaivitch, born Sep 21, 1827; married Sep 11, 1848, to Alexandra Josefovna, daughter of Joseph, Duke of Saxe-Altenburg; was born Jul 20, 1830; issue, a son & a daughter.
Fifth: Nicolas Nicolaivitch, born Aug 8, 1831.
Sixth: Michl Nicolaivitch, born Oct 25, 1832.
The late Czar also leaves two sisters: Maria Paulovna, Dowager Grand Duchess of Saxe-Weimar, & Anna Paulovna, widow of Wm II, King of Holland. Also, a sister-in-law-Helena Paulovna, widow of the Grand Duke Michael, & daughter of the late Prince Paul, of Wurtemburg. This lady's daughter, the Grand Duchess Catherine Michaelovna, is married to the Duke George of Mecklenburg-Strelitz.
+
[Apr 6th newspaper: On Jan 27 [Feb 8, N S,] Emperor Nicholas was taken ill with influenza, but continued to occupy himself as usual with the affairs of State. After the inspection of the soldiers, on Feb 9, [21st ns] he went to see the Grand Duchess Helen Pavlovna, widow of his late brother, the Grand Duke Michael, & from her palace to the Minister of War, who was then unwell. On the 11th he was obliged to take to his bed, & dangerous symptoms began to manifest themselves with incredible rapidity. On Fri, Feb 18, [Mar 3,] the sovereign who, for nearly 30 years, embellished the throne of Russia, was no more.]

Hon Wm S Archer died suddenly at his residence in Amelia Co, on Wed, having retired the previous evening in his usual health.

Despatch from Concord, N H, conveys the painful intelligence of the death of Mrs Eliz A McNiel, widow of the late Gen John McNiel, & sister of the President of the U S, aged 68 years. -Union

The Fred'k [Md] Examiner records the death of Mrs Eliz Hammond, of New Market district, aged 96 years, Mrs Mgt Keefer, of Fred'k, aged 96, & Mrs Nelson, wife of Gen Roger Nelson, of Revolutionary memory, & mother of Judge Nelson, aged 84. [No death dates given-current item.]

Shocking affair in the billiard saloon of the St Chas hotel at New Orleans on Mar 20. John Duffy, a large owner of hacks, was tried about 4 years ago for the murder of Dr Weymouth, & Wm C Harrison, a steamboat pilot & a young man much respected, was the principal witness against him. On Mar 20th they met in Gravier st, & another altercation ensued. Harrison drew a pistol, & Duffy fled into the billiard saloon pursued by Harrison, who fired 6 shots at him, one penetrated the heart, & he fell dead. Another shot took effect on Dr Parsons, who was seated in a chair at one side of the billiard room, & he lived long enough to run outside where he died. Dr Parsons was a young man who had graduated a day or two previous, & had been married only a few months. Harrison immediately surrendered himself.

Circuit Court of Wash Co, D C, in Equity. Jas F & Mary F Ritter vs Wm H & H G Ritter. The trustees reported that they have sold parts of lots 40 & 80, in Old Gtwn, to Wm H & H G Ritter for $4,485, & part of lot 80 in Old Gtwn, to Jas F Gross for $1,425, & that they have complied with the terms. –Jno A Smith, clerk

For sale: 60 acres of land, with a new & comfortable house, lying close to the Canal, half-way between Wash & Alexandria. Apply to Maj G Tochman, at *Summer Hill*, Alexandria Co, Va, 3 miles from Wash, D C.

The House Carpenters' Society of Wash has determined upon demanding the following rates of wages, viz: from Mar 1st to Dec 1st, $2, & for the other 3 months 1.75 a day. The ofcrs of this Society are as follows: Pres, Henry Trine; Vice Pres, Geo Sweney; Recoding Scribe, J F C Offut; Financial Cmte, Ephraim Richmond, J H Johnson, & T Moore.

Mrd: on Mar 29, by Rev E P Phelps, Mr F J Waters to Miss Emily A Nalley, all of Wash City.

Died: on Mar 28, George Wm Rodgers, youngest son of Robt & Eliz Nash, aged 5 months.

Obit-died: on Mar 24, Mrs Mgt R Randolph, widow of the late Lt John B Randolph, of the U S Navy. She died after a few days' illness, leaving 5 little children. She was an extraordinary woman. She had many warm friends, & deserved them all. She was an affectionate daughter & a watchful & devoted mother.

N Y, Mar 29. Hon Thos M Woodruff, ex-member of Congress from this city, died last evening of paralysis.

N Y, Mar 29. Capt Moody & crew of the ship **Fanny Giffney** arrived at this port today from St Thomas, & report the total loss of their vessel at sea on Mar 5. They left Liverpool on Jan 30 with a cargo of salt for New Orleans, & when about 20 miles from St Thomas had to abandon her. She sunk in an hour afterwards. She was valued at $40,000.

SAT MAR 31, 1855
Household & kitchen furniture at auction on: Apr 5, at the residence of C L Lombard, on H, between 4th & 5th sts, No 607. -Green & Scott, aucts

Col Benton reached St Louis on Mar 25 with the remains of his wife. The interment took place the next day. [Apr 3rd newspaper: The body was taken from the steamer to the residence of Col Joshua B Brant. At 10 o'clock, Mar 26, the Second Presbyterian Church, 5th & Walnut sts, was filled with friends of Col Benton, drawn together to pay the last tribute of respect to the memory of his deceased wife. The pall-bearers were: Mr John Brady Smith, Andrew Elliot, Mr Kenneth McKenzie, Col Duncan A Stewart, Mr Edw Walsh, Mr Thos Watson, Col Robt Campbell, & Judge Montgomery Blair. Col Benton was accompanied by his daughter, Miss Susan Benton, & two nieces, Miss Mary Benton, of Texas, & Mrs Col Brant, of this city. Mrs Benton was born in Rockbridge, Va, Jul 8, 1794. Her maiden name was Eliz McDowell. Her grandfather was an English gentleman named Jas McDowell, who resided on lands in Va granted members of the family by the English Gov't. Her father was also named Jas McDowell. Eliz was the youngest of 3 children, two of the three being daughters. The son, James, was afterwards Govn'r of Va, & also a member of Congress. On Mar 20, 1821, Miss McDowell was married to Col Benton, in Rockbridge, & subsequently came on with her husband to Missouri. Most of her time was passed at Wash, Col Benton's Senatorial duties requiring him to be in that city more than elsewhere. Mrs Benton was a Presbyterian in religious belief. She gave birth to 6 children, 4 of whom are still living. They are Eliza, now Mrs Wm Carey Jones, of Wash; Jessie Ann, now Mrs Col Fremont; Sarah, now Mrs Richd Taylor Jacob, of Louisville, Ky; Susan, unmarried; Randolph, deceased; & Jas McDowell, also deceased. Some years since Mrs Benton became afflicted with a paralysis, which increased until about a year before her death, when it had completely prostrated her vocal organs, & she was unable to utter a sound. She depended upon a simple pantomime in expressing her wants. She gradually sunk under her disease until in Sept last, when she departed this life. **Error! Bookmark not defined.**-St Lous papers of Mar 27th.]

Orphans Court of Wash Co, D C. Letters of administration on the personal estate of Ricard Ayton, late of Wash Co, deceased. –Mary A Ayton, admx Persons having accounts against the estate of the said *Richard Ayton, deceased, will please present them to Chas S Wallach, my atty. –Mary A Ayton, admx

Died: on Mar 29, at Rockville, Md, the residence of her son, Rev Thos Sewall, Mary Choate, aged 66 years, widow of the late Dr Thos Sewall, of Wash City. During her illness her mind was clear & her faith undoubting. Her last words were, "Come, Lord Jesus, come quickly."

Mrd: on Mar 29, by Rev B F Bittinger, Benj Miller, of Winchester, Va, to Miss Martha, 4th daughter of Jos Libbey, of Gtwn, D C.

MON APR 2, 1855
Splendid Chinese & Japanese household & kitchen furniture at auction on: Apr 9, at the residence of Lt Balch, of the U S Navy, in the Six Bldgs, Pa ave, between 21st & 22nd sts: a very superior assortment. -Green & Scott, aucts

Obit-died: on the 25th ult, at Middlebury, Vt, Saml S Phelps, of introcession of rheumatism, was born at Litchfield, Conn, May 13, 1793. He graduated at Yale College in 1811, & studied at the Litchfield Law School, & in the spring of 1812 he removed to Middlebury, continuing his professional studies in the ofc of Hon Horatio Seymour. He served in the war of 1812, in the ranks, at Burlington & Plattsburg, & was appointed paymaster in the service of Pres Madison. He was chosen Judge of the Supreme Court of Vt in 1831, & was continued by re-elections until 1838. In 1838 he was elected a U S Senator for 6 years, was re-elected for the term ending Mar 4, 1851, & in Jan, 1853, he was appointed by Gov Fairbanks to fill the vacancy occasioned by the death of Senator Upham. -Boston Courier

Col Thos Fitzgerald died at his residence in Niles on Mar 25. He had a few days previously submitted to a surgical operation, but beyond this we are unadvised of his illness. -Detroit Press

Chief Justice Jas Booth, of Delaware, a man highly esteemed for his talents & virtues, died at Newcastle on Mar 29.

Mr Wells J Hawks, one of the Democratic nominees of Jefferson Co, Va, for a seat in the Legislature, respectfully declines the proffered honor. He is said to be one of the most successful carriage-makers in Va, & has no idea of taking a ride in so rough a concern as the political wagon.

Thos Delany, who of late kept a store on Louisiana ave, between 6th & 7th sts, in Wash City, was some days since taken to Balt on a requisition from the Govn'r of Md, charged with obtaining goods in that city under false pretences. He awaits his trial in the Balt jail.

Mr John Wallace, formerly of Wash City, committed suicide at his residence in Montg Co, Md, on Thu evening last, by hanging himself.

Mrd: on Mar 28, by Rev B Sunderland, Mr Wm T Griffith to Miss Mgt Tweedy, all of Wash City.

Died: on Mar 4, in Washington, Georgia, at the residence of her father, Hon Robt Toombs, U S Senate, Louisa, wife of Felix Alexander, aged 22 years.

Died: on Mar 17, in Green Co, Ala, at *Morven*, the residence of her husband, Mrs Mary Virginia Lightfoot, wife of Dr Philip L Lightfoot, in her 37th year. As a mother she was all that the endearing epithet implies.

TUE APR 3, 1855

Among the deaths of the week may be mentioned those of Don Carlos, [Count de Molina,] father to the present Pretender to the Crown of Spain; the Count de Montemolin, Don Carlos, died at Trieste a few days ago, aged 67. Baron Chas De Rothschild died lately at Naples.

Died: on Feb 24, at Stockholm, in her 31st year, Mr Carolina Schroeder, wife of Hon Francis Schroeder, American Minister to Sweden.

Dr Wm M Awl, of Dayton, Ohio, former Superintendent of the Ohio Lunatic Asylum, has returned to Columbus, Ohio, & will resume the practice of his profession.

Mr J J Proctor, of Alexandria, who was known in Wash City as a clerk upon the late census, died suddenly at the former city on Sunday night of a disease of the heart.

Mrd: on Mar 27, at Northampton, Mass, by Rev Wm Allen, D D, Rev Chas Hammond, Principal of Lawrence Academy, Groton, Mass, to Miss Addie Suhm Allen, daughter of the officiating clergyman.

Died: on Apr 2, in Wash City, Mrs Ann McGowan, relict of Bernard McGowan, in her 79th year, a native of Dublin, but for the last 50 years a resident of Wash City. Her family mourns her loss. Her funeral will take place from the residence of her daughter, Mrs Laporte, 11th st, on Wed, at 4 o'clock.

N Y, Apr 2. Mrs Cass, wife of the U S Minister at Rome, died suddenly in that city on Mar 3.

Trustee's sale of household & kitchen furniture, at auction, on Apr 11: by deed of trust dated Dec 22, 1853, recorded in Liber J A S, No 69, folios 123 thru 127, of the land records for Wash Co, D C: sale at the residence of Col L L Taylor, on D st, between 2nd & 3rd sts. –Wm H Ward, trustee -Green & Scott, aucts

Trustee's sale of house & lot at auction: on Apr 23, by a decree of the Orphans Court of Wash Co, D C; confirmed by a decree of the Circuit Court of Wash Co, D C, rendered at its Mar term, 1855, in the case of Andrew J Roche, the following property in Wash, D C, viz: part of lot 5 in square 585, with a frame house, now occupied by said Andrew J Roche. –Edw C Carrington, trustee -Green & Scott, aucts

Trustees' sale of very valuable real estate: on Apr 25, by deed of trust dated Jun 25, 1852, recorded in Liber J A S No 43, folios 234 thru 238, of the land records for Wash Co, D C: public auction in front of the premises: lots 9 & 10 in the subdivision made by the heirs of John Davidson, in square 220, Wash City. –John A Linton, Wm H Ward, trustees -Green & Scott, aucts

Household & kitchen furniture at auction on: Apr 5, at the residence of Mrs Spriggs, on C st, between 3rd & 4½ sts. -Green & Scott, aucts

WED APR 4, 1855
Trustee's sale of house & lot at auction: on May 4, by deed of trust from Thos Ryne & wife, dated Feb 25, 1854, recorded in Liber J A S No 80, folios 213 thru 217, of the land records for Wash Co, D C, all that piece of ground known as part of lot 4 in square 630, in Wash City, with a 2 story dwlg house. –Geo F Kidwell, trustee -Green & Scott, aucts

We have stated before that the ship **James Cheston**, of Balt, [having been abandoned by her ofcrs & crew,] had fallen in with at sea by the British ship **Marathon**, & that the capt of the **Marathon** placed on the abandoned vessel the mate & 6 of his own crew, who succeeded in getting her into Liverpool. The **James Cheston** is a new ship, of about 1,100 tons burden, & was owned by Messrs James Cheston & Son & Hugh Jenkins & Co. She cleared from Balt on Jan 31, 1855, with a valuable cargo of flour, pork & beef, & was insured in Balt, N Y, & Europe to the amount of $300,000. The Balt papers state that there is something strange about the abandonment of this vessel. The fears of the owners are, in view of the well known seamanship & character of Capt White, that this fine vessel has been the scene of a terrible outrage. The crew, & not the captain & ofcrs, are announced as having been picked up at sea by the brig **Two Friends**, which has not yet arrived. [Apr 16th newspaper: the mystery involving the abandonment of the ship **James Cheston**, of Balt, has not diminished. Capt White reiterates the opinion that the abandonment of the vessel was absolutely necessary to save the lives of those on board. Mr Chason, the first mate, states that the log-book published by the captain is wholly incorrect, & not taken from his account as written down day by day. Mr John E S Packsood, the 2nd mate, also denies the truth of the capt's statement, & says he was offered a bribe to sign his protest, which he declined. Each of the ofcrs named have been arrested & held to bail on the charge of barratry.]

Mrd: on Mar 27, A Stollenwerck to Helen, daughter of Capt Chas Whelan, all of Greensboro, Ala.

Died: on Mar 30, in Wash City, Edwin Sylvester, son of M A Eliz & Jas J Kane, aged 1 month & 14 days.

Died: in Washington, of pneumonia, after a short illness, Miss Louisa Baltzer. Her funeral will be from her late residence on Bridge st, in Gtwn, on Thu at 4 o'clock. [No death date given.]

Circuit Court. Judges Morsell & Dunlop. The Court came in this morning for jury trials. The following are the traverse jurors for this term:

Chas F Wood	Mathias Valentine	Patrick McKenna
Jas A Kennedy	John Davis	David Davis
Geo Crandall	John S Devlin	Wm Donnahoo
J B Holmead	Jas Espey	Jacob Havsham
Peter Hepburn	Robt A Griffin	Francis J Murphy
John Waters	Geo Bray	Jas A Brown
H L Chapin	Jas W Watson	Wm Miles
David Fowble	John Scrivner	Jas Fullalove
Geo M Sothoron	Geo McLelland	Albert P Waugh
Thos Marshall	Edmund F Brown	Michl Quigley

Mr & Mrs Botta [late Miss Anne C Lynch] are now at Willard's. Mr Botta is a relative of Botta, the historian.

Lynchburg, Apr 2. On Sat night last, in Wytheville, Va, a man named Jas A Graham walked into the Wytheville hotel, drew a revolver, & in a deliberate manner fired upon Messrs W H Spiller, C Trigg, & Mr Terry, each load wounding the three slightly. Mr Spiller [an old & crippled gentlemen] managed to get out of the house, & being unable to proceed further, lay down upon the pavement. Graham saw him & stepped up & shot him through the head, killing him instantly. He then shot Mr Cox, an employe of the hotel, who is said to be in critical condition. Mr Spiller was a respectable & wealthy citizen. The murderer has thus far eluded arrest. [Apr 9th newspaper: the family of the deceased have offered $1,000 for the apprehension of Graham. He is a man of large frame, about 6 feet two or three inches high, with black hair, short, sandy colored moustache, a good set of teeth, with a laughing but not a pleasant countenence when in conversation.]

Orphans Court of Wash Co, D C. Letters of administration on the personal estate of Richard Dement, late of Wash Co, deceased. –Jane H Dement, admx

THU APR 5, 1855

Bonapartes removed from Italy. The children of Chas Bonaparte, Prince of Canino, who were bereaved of their estimable mother, [the daughter & last surviving child of Jos Bonaparte,] in Rome, a short time since, have been ordered to Paris by the Emperor. A marshal of France has been appointed their guardian & tutor, as the father is not permitted to have the sole charge of them. The Bonapartes have, therefore, all been removed from Italy. It is whispered that the Murat branch cherish hopes of being ultimately restored to Naples.

The late foreign papers announce the death at Triesta on Mar 10th, of Don Carlos, of Spain, who for many years made a prominent figure in the political discussions of Spain, but who for some years past has been almost lost sight of. He was the brother to King Ferdinand VII & uncle of the present Queen Isabella, & was born Mar 28, 1788. On the death of King Ferdinand in 1833, Queen Isabella being only 3 years of age, he disputed her right of succession, & in consequence the country was involved in civil war for 6 years. He was at length driven from the kingdom, &, retiring to France, he was placed under surveillance by the Gov't of Louis Phillippe, & confined for some years to the city of Burgos. Before leaving Spain he married as his second wife the Princess of Beira, of Portugal, the widow of Don Pedro. By his first marriage he had 2 sons, to the eldest of whom, Don Carlos, Count of Montemolin, he ceded in 1845 his claim to the Spanish throne.

Household & kitchen furniture at auction on: Apr 9, at the residence of the late Richd Dement, on 2nd st, between B & C sts. –John Marbury, adm -Jas C McGuire, auct

For sale, the house & grounds recently the residence of the late Col Staniford, U S A, deceased, immediately on the banks of the Choptank river, adjoining the town of Cambridge, Eastern Shore of Md. The house has 3 stories, with an observatory, built of brick & stuccoed. The house is comparatively new. Apply to Mrs Staniford, on the premises; to Capt S W Lecompte, U S N, at Cambridge; or the subscriber, at **Fort Monroe**, Old Point Comfort, Va. –N S Jarvis, exc

Mrd: on Mar 15, at St John's Church, Hagerstown, Md, by Rev Walter Ayrault, John H Gassaway, of Montg Co, Md, to Kate A, only daughter of Alex Armstrong, of that place.

Mrd: on Mar 31, at N Y, by Rev Henry B Smith, Vincenzo Botta, late member of the Nat'l Parliament & Prof of Philosophy in the College of Sardinia, to Anne Charlotte Lynch, of N Y.

Mrd: on Apr 3, by Rev E P Phelps, Mr Robt Downing to Miss Malinda, daughter of Thos Foster, late of Winchester, Va.

Circuit Court of Wash Co, D C-in Chancery. Saml Hamilton & Ann M Hamilton his wife, Robt Wright, Eliz B Wright, Hannah L G Wright, & John E Caldwell, cmplnts, vs Wm B Randolph, John L Bartlett & Ann Bartlett his wife, Morris D Smith, Jas Smith, Elias C Smith, Ann Smith, Susan Smith, Hannah O Caldwell, Elias B C Wright, Anna M C Wright, Robt M Wright, John E Wright, Saml H Wright, & Marion D Wright, dfndnts. The object of this bill is to procure a decree for the partition, among such of the cmplnts & dfndnts as may be entitled to share in the same, of certain lots of ground in the cities of Wash & Gtwn which belonged to Elias B Caldwell, deceased, late of said District, & were by him conveyed to Jas B Caldwell, Matthew St Clair Clarke, & Wm B Randolph, & the survivors of them, for the benefit of the said Elias B Caldwells' wife & children; or in case it should be the opinion of the Court that said lots of ground are not susceptible of specific division, then for a sale thereof & distribution of the proceeds as aforesaid. The bill states that the said Elias B Caldwell did, on May 23, 1825, by his deed of indenture of that date, duly recorded, convey to Jas B Caldwell, Matthew St Clair Clarke, & Wm B Randolph, & their survivors, lots 83, 94, 95, 97, 98, & 99, in the western most addition to Gtwn, D C, & lots 3 thru 8 in square 128, & lot 2 in square 631, lot 14 in square 1,023, lots 8 & 9 in square 569, lots 3 & 4 in square 767, lots 1, 2, south part of 3, & south part of 6 in square 769, in Wash City, D C; also, certain goods, chattels, & effects, in trust for payment of debts & for the support of the wife & children of said Caldwell until the youngest child should arrive at full age, then for division among the said wife & children, with power to make advances to the children as they should arrive at age or marry. That said Caldwell hath since departed this life, leaving a widow, Ann, now residing in the State of Ill, & since said Caldwell's death intermarried with John L Bartlett, now residing in the State of Pa, & 8 children to wit, Ann Maria, wife of Saml Hamilton, John E Caldwell, Harriet J Caldwell, since married to Robt Wright & subsequently deceased, leaving children Eliz B Wright & Hannah L G Wright, now of full age, Elias B C Wright, Ann M C Wright, Robt M Wright, John E Wright, Saml H Wright, & Marion D Wright, infants under the age of 21 years; Jas B Caldwell, Elias B Caldwell, & Susan L Caldwell, all deceased intestate & without issue; Mary C Caldwell, who married Morris D Smith & afterwards died, leaving children Jas Smith, Elias B Smith, Ann Smith, & Susan Smith, infants under the age of 21 years, residing with their father, Morris D Smith, in the State of Ill; & Hannah O Caldwell, residing in said District. That Wm B Randolph is now the sole surviving trustee; that the events upon which final division of said estates was in said deed ordered to be made have occurred, to wit, the payment of debts & the arrival at the full age of 21 years of the youngest of the children, & that no final report nor division as aforesaid has ever been made; that the interests of all the parties call for such report & final division of all of said estates now remaining in the possession of the said surviving trustee. The bill prays an order of publication against the non-resident dfndnts & commissions for taking the answers of said infants. Non-resident dfndnts to appear in this court, on or before the 3rd Monday in Oct next. –Jno A Smith, clerk -R H Clarke, solicitor

Died: on Apr 2, at his residence, **Clover Hill**, in Calvert Co, Md, Richd Becket, a most estimable gentleman in every relation of life, whose death is deeply lamented by a large circle of relatives & friends.

Died: yesterday, in Norfolk, Va, after a long & painful illness, Mrs C R Murphey, wife of Lt P M Murphey, U S Navy, in her 34th year, leaving her bereaved family & a large circle of friends.

Wash City Ordinance: 1-Act for the relief of M M White: the fine imposed for removing 2 loads of sand from Mass ave, is remitted, provided said White pay the cost of prosecution.

FRI APR 6, 1855
The cmte appointed to examine the applicants for teachers' places reported the following who satisfactorily answered 34 questions propounded:

Mary A Mirick	Frances E Hoover	Eliz Ellen Ashdown
Ellen E Janney	Eliza T Ward	Richd A Adams
A V Bates	Ellen L Hawkins	Henry Henshaw
Marcia J Baker	Lucy Ellen Moore	Minnie Turpin
Laura R Hilton	Mary A Brush	Annie V Shaw

Miss Eliza T Ward was elected teacher of the new school, Primary No 5, in the Northern Liberties. Mr Augustus Edson elected assistant in the 2nd District School.

Aaron Rogers, who was supposed to be the only survivor of the guard who was on duty at the time that Andre was executed, died at his residence at Newbury, Mass, on Sat last. Judt 2 weeks previous Mr Rogers fell & fractured a bone, which confined him to his bed, & it was this confinement that immediately caused his death.

Mrd: on Apr 5, by Rev Geo Hilde, Mr Richd Lizear to Miss Martha A Cross, both of Montg Co, Md.

SAT APR 7, 1855
Hon Josiah Minot, recently appointed to be Fifth Auditor of the Treasury Dept, vice Stephen Pleasanton, deceased, has entered upon the duties of his office.

The crew of the U S frig **Columbia** will be discharged under the recent act of Congress, attaching the deserving men permanently to the service, with 3 months' leave of absence & full sea-pay, when they report for duty on board of any of the receiving ships. The Honorable discharges' will be granted, in the discretion of the captain, for fidelity, obedience, & capacity.

Household & kitchen furniture at auction on: Apr 11, at the residence of the late Dr Wotherspoon, 493 17th st, between H & I sts. –R H Coolidge, for the admx –Green & Scott, aucts

Household & kitchen furniture at auction: by deed of trust from Ezra Lease dated Mar 28, 1855, at the Auction Store. –L R Holmead, trustee -Green & Scott, aucts

Mrd: on Thu, in the Fourth Presbyterian Church, by Rev John C Smith, Mr John T S Nicholson to Miss Mary E Harvey, all of Wash City.

On Apr 2nd, a man about 50 years of age, named Burnetson, a mechanic from Balt, came to his death at the steam saw-mill of John H Key, in Chaptico district. He was regularly employed at the mill, & one of the rotary saws accidentally burst, the pieces being scattered in every direction. One of the fragments struck the man on the tope of the head with such force as not only to cleave his skull, but also to cut through his neck, neck-bone, & down into the breast, that portion of his body from the top of his head to the breast being completely divided. His death of course followed instantly. –Leonardtown [Md] Beacon

Runaway committed to the jail of Wash Co, a negro boy who calls himself Abraham Sprigg, about 21 or 22 years of age; says he is free & served his time with Dr Shipley, near Newmarket, in Fred'k Co, Md. Owner is to come forth, prove his property, pay charges, & take him away, else he will be discharged agreeably to law. -W Logan, Sheriff

Hugh B Sweeny, Treasurer, against John J Joyce, excutor, & Francis M & Mary G Dowling, heirs of Wm Dowling. By order of the Circuit Court of Wash Co, D C, I am directed to state an account of the personal estate of said Wm Dowling, of the debts owing by him at the time of his death, & the value of his real estate. Meeting at my ofc in City Hall, Wash, Apr 19, at 11 o'clock. –W Redin, auditor

MON APR 9, 1855
Great sale of superior cabinet furniture & house furnishing goods, by order of the Orphans Court of Wash Co, D C. Sale on Apr 17, at the extensive Warerooms of the late John D Brown, known as the Apollo Hall bldg. -Jas C McGuire, auct

Died: on Apr 7, in Wash City, Jane Josephine McClellan, relict of the late Lt Col John McClellan, U S Army, & daughter of the late Saml P Walker. Her funeral is this afternoon at 4 o'clock from her mother's residence.

Died: on Mar 31, at Newport, Rhode Island, Mrs A A Brownell, wife of Capt Thos Brownell, U S navy, aged 60 years.

Died: on Mar 27, at Brooklyn, N Y, of cardiac pleurisy, after a most painful illness of 7 days, aged 6 years & 9 months, Mary Stanley, beloved child of J Stoll & Marianna Cronise, late of Washington.

On Tue last at New River, in Onslow Co, a gentleman attached to the U S Coast Survey, F A Lueber, was severely injured by the accidental discharge of a gun. A negro was handling it when it sent off, sending one shot entirely through the hand of the negro, & wounding Mr Lueber in the face & on the head. Medical attendance was at once procured. –Wilmington [N C] Herald

For rent: the house for many years occupied by the late Hon Danl Webster, & since his death by Hon Mr Preston, of Ky: on D st & La ave, between 5th & 6th sts. Apply to the subscriber at his residence, 432, in the same square & street. –Johnson Hellen

TUE APR 10, 1855

Capt A A Soria, commanding a volunteer artillery company at New Orleans, died there on Apr 2, from injuries received a few days previously by the premature discharge of a cannon when he was firing a salute in honor of a political victory.

Jorace H Hazard, eldest son of A G Hazard, of Enfield, Ct, while proving powder near the Hazard ____, had both eyes put entirely out. He died the same night.

Wm Wigston, a native of England, 64 years of age, died yesterday at 176 Mercer st, dangerously ill from the effects of extreme intoxication. He was well known to men of science. –N Y Courier

Chauncey P Holcomb, a well know farmer of Delaware, died at Newcastle on Thu.

Persons were taken from under the glass house ruins dead. It was recently blown down at Progress, N J. Killed were: John Killen, 24; Isaac Hintzelman, 19; John Sloan, 16; Julius Gennelli, 12; John Gardner, 12; Bishop R Palmer, 16.

Died: on Apr 9, Mrs M Patterson, in her 69th year. Her remains will be conveyed to their last resting place this afternoon, at 4 o'clock, from the residence of her son, J C McKelden, 416 F st.

Died: at his residence, Culpeper Court-house, Va, after a protracted & painful illness, in his 63rd year, Francis J Thompson. He was a native of Hanover Co, Va, but for more than 40 years a resident of Culpeper. For most of that time he has been engaged in active business as a merchant, & for many years as magistrate of the county. He leaves a small family, who have the sympathy of an extensive circle of attached friends. –P [No death date given-current item.]

WED APR 11, 1855

Household & kitchen furniture at auction on: Apr 16, at the quarters of Lt J C Cash, inside the Wash Navy Yard. -Jas C McGuire, auct

The U S sloop-of-war **St Louis** sailed from Spezzia [Sardinia] on Mar 15 for the U S; the ofcrs & crew in fine health. The vessel is ordered to Phil for repairs & the discharge of her crew. She left Norfolk on Aug 22, 1852, & has been in active service in the Mediterranean ever since, visiting Constantinople & other prominent ports. The following is a list of her ofcrs: Cmder, Duncan N Ingraham, of S C; Lts: Alex'r Gibson, Va; Enoch G Parrott, N H; & John S Taylor, Va; Surgeon, J Dickinson Miller, N Y; Assist, Wm F Carrington, Va; Lt of Marines, Israel Green, Wisc; Purser, Ben F Gallaher, Va; Passed Midshipmen: Ralph Chandler, N Y; Chas B Smith, Missouri; Bancrift Gherardi, Mass; Danl L Braine, Texas; Master, Wm D Austin, Mass; Gunner, Moses A Lane, Calif; Boatswain, Alfred Hingerty, Va; Carpenter, Asa Poinsett, Delaware; Sailmaker, B B Burchsted, Mass.

Household & kitchen furniture at auction on: Apr 19, at the residence of the late Thos Ritchie, on Pres' square. -Green & Scott, aucts

In Equity. Armand Jardine against Henry Naylor, Jas C McGuire, Thos Berry, W S Cox, Wm Emmert, Honorine Jardine, Albertine Favier, Louisa Favier, Miriam Favier, Agricola Favier, Malvina Favier, & Theresa Favier. The Circuit Court of Wash Co, D C having an account to be taken of the debts due by the late Agricola Favier, of the amount of his personal estate, & how the same had been administered; of the value of his real estate, & whether it will be necessary to sell the same, or any part thereof, for payment of his debts. Meeting on Apr 21 at my ofc in City Hall, Wash. —W Redin, auditor

Mrd: on Apr 3, in Eutaw, Ala, by Rev John Rice Bowman, Duff C Green, U S Army, to Miss Rebecca J Pickens, youngest daughter of the late Col Jos Pickens.

Died: on Apr 9, after an illness of about a week, Mary, sister of the late John McLeod, formerly of the Central Academy, a native of the county Derry, Ireland, but for the last 21 years a resident of Wash City. Her funeral will take place this Wed, from the residence of Mr Kelly, M st, between 14th & 15th sts, when & where her friends & those of her late brother are invited to attend. [No time given.]

THU APR 12, 1855
Household & kitchen furniture at auction on: Apr 16, at the residence of Ralph Haskins, corner of I & 19th sts. —C W Boteler, auct

Official, Dept of State, Wash, Apr 10, 1855. Information received from David R Diffenderffer, U S Consul at Paso del Norte, Mexico, of the death in that city, on Dec 16, last, of Josephus Blanchard, lately in the employ of the U S Boundary Commission. The proceeds of his effects, amount to $30.23, will be sent by Mr Diffenderffer to the Treasury Dept, to be holden in trust for the legal claimants.

Wilmington [N C] Herald of Apr 9. The Havana News: Don Francisco Estrampes has been garroted, under a conviction of treason. Thus was sacrificed American life in the person of a young man of excellent character & noble impulses. The trial to which he was subjected was a mockery; he was tried for an offence committed before martial law had been proclaimed by the Capt-General. Don Francisco Estrampes was born in 1830 at Vuelta Abajo, in the parish of San Cristobal. His father, Don Adolf Estrampes, was a native of the Lower Pyrenees, in France, & received his education in the city of Pau, the ancient capital of the kings of Navaree. He emigrated to our island at an early day, & married a beautiful & talented daughter of Cuba, the mother of Don Francisco. Both the parents of Estrampes died many years ago, leaving their two sons, Don Luis & Don Francisco, in Vuelta, just verging upon man's estate. They supported themselves very honorable by teaching the French language. Estrampes was surprised at Baracoa, with a vessel loaded with arms & ammunition, which he had brought for the purpose of drenching in blood the beautiful plains of his native country, is known to every body here. The Prensa then goes on to mourn over his remains & sympathize with his honorable brother, good but unfortunate sister, & other respectable relations for their loss & denounces the money-changing misers & charlatans who remained safely in the U S [one named Junta] while they induced Estrampes to this rash venture.

I offer at private sale the farm on which I reside, near Beltsville, Md: house is nearly new. Call & see. –Thos T Hunter.

Orphans Court of Wash Co, D C. Letters of administration on the personal estate of Wm J Langfitt, late of Wash Co, deceased. –M A Langfitt, admx

Died: on Apr 10, after a short but painful illness, Jos Thaw, jr, in his 37th year. His funeral is this evening at 4 o'clock, from the residence of his mother, 434 I st.

Died: on Apr 10, in Gtwn, Miss Mgt Parsons, daughter of Wm Parsons. Her funeral will be this afternoon at 3 o'clock, from the Methodist Episcopal Church.

Valuable real estate at public sale: on May 3, all the real estate of which Thos Fisher, late of Montg Co, died seized, [except lot 2 & 4] lying & being on River road, about 1½ miles below the mouth of Watt's Branch, & on the Chesapeake & Ohio Canal, contains in the whole about 300 acres of land. Lot 1 contains 118 acres; lot 3 contains 159¾ acres, on which the widow's dower is laid; lot 5 contains 78 acres, adjoins the lands of the late A F Fisher, now occupied by Mrs A M Fisher. The improvements are a small dwlg house & stable. Lot 6 contains 94½ acres of land & lies adjoining the Mill of Mr Gamble. Purchasers are referred to the subscribers, or to the family of Mrs A C Fisher, who resides on the property. –Wm H Offutt, Saml Hardesty, Wm O Chappell

Special meeting of the Managers of the Union Benevolent Society will be held on Apr 13. By order of the Board. –Emma E Gurley, sec

Dr Wm P Young offers his professional services to the citizens of Wash. Ofc & residence 312 north 9th st, between L & M sts.

Rappahannock Farm for sale: by decree of the Circuit Court of Westmoreland Co, Va, the undersigned, appointed com'r, will on Jun 20th, offer at public sale, the estate called **Liberty**, the residence of the late Dr P C Robb, deceased, in said county: contains about 1,000 acres of land; with a large & commodious brick dwlg, with all necessary out-bldgs, in good repair. The improvements are calculated to be worth between $8,000 & $9,000. Address the undersigned, at Comorn P O, King Geo Co, Va. Mr Jas Robb, who resides on the farm, will take pleasure in showing it to any persons desirous to purchase. –John P Robb, com'r

Property for sale: the Farm on which the Columbia Trotting Course is at present: contains 104 acres; will be sold in 3 lots each containing 30 acres; on one lot is a large Boarding House; another lot of 30 acres has a Log House; another has a Cottage on it. The farm is bounded on the north by Lt B W Hunter's summer farm. Persons wishing to see the property will please call on the subscriber at the Cottage, & can inquire respecting it of Dr Gunton & Jas Adams, Bank of Wash; David A Hall, C st; Wm D Nutt, Treasury Dept; Mr Hardin, Navy Dept, Wash; or of T M McCormick & Co & T T Hill, Atty, Alexandria. –Wm Jenks, Alexandria Co, Va

FRI APR 13, 1855
Books & prints at auction: on Apr 14, in front of our Auction Store, 6th & Pa ave, by order of R B Hughes, bailiff. Also a lot of furniture & teas. Terms cash. -Green & Scott, aucts

The Marlboro Gazette says that the trial of Henry & Christian Glantz, of D C, charged with shooting Mr E W Duvall, of Bladensburg, in Sept last, has just been concluded. Christian was first tried & acquitted. The jury had not returned a verdict in the case of Henry, who discharged the gun.

The Richmond Despatch has a telegraphic report from Farmville, stating that on Mar 10, the store-house of Messrs Most & White, near Buckingham court-house, was destroyed by fire, & that 2 young men, named Dean & Chenault, perished in the fire.

Lord Erskine died on Mar 19, in Sussex, England. He was the son of the great Lord Erskine, & married, first, in 1800, Miss Cadwallader, of Phil, who died in 1843; secondly, in the same year, Miss Travis, cousin of his first wife. The deceased Peer began his diplomatic career as Minister to the U S at the beginning of the present century, & he only retired from the post of Minister at Munich in 1843. His eldest son, Thos Americus, now third Baron Erskine, is the successor to the title.

Race across the Atlantic. The new ship **Alert**, Capt Smith, & the ship **King Lear**, Capt Eldridge, both sailed from this port Feb 17th, & both arrived at London on Mar 15. The ship **Beacon Light**, Capt Simonson, also sailed hence Feb 23, & arrived at London Mar 16. The ship **Great Republic**, Capt Limeburner, sailed fom N Y Feb 24, & arrived at London Mar 16, having made the shortest passage of the whole. The ship **Donald McKay**, Capt Warner, sailed from this port Feb 21, anchored below Liverpool on Mar 11, & arrived in port Mar 12. The following are her daily runs from Boston to the Irish coast: 210, 235, 200, 147, 70, 130, 421, 199, 175, 255, 182, & 299 miles. Her great run of 421 miles was ascertained by observation, & not dead reckoning. The ship **James Baines** made the passage from this port to Liverpool in 12 days & 8 hours; this is the quickest on record by a sailing vessel. –Boston Atlas

Mrd: on Apr 10, at Millwood, Powhatan Co, Va, by Rev Mr Fisher, Z Wilson Pickrell, of Petersburg, Va, to Matilda, daughter of the late Dr David McCaw, of the former place.

Mrd: on Apr 10, at Trinity Church, by Rev Mr Cummings, Mr John H Davis to Miss Susan E Kidwell, both of Wash City.

Died: on Wed, of pneumonia, Chas S Turner, in his 22 year. His funeral will be this afternoon at 4 o'clock, from the residence of Robt W Smoot, Bridge st, Gtwn.

Wash City Ordinance: 1-Act for the relief of G W Uttermuhle: the sum of $9.94 be refunded to him, this amount was for an over collection for gas light tax on lot 8 in square 452, for the year 1854, the error caused by the Com'r of the 3rd Ward. 2-Act to pay Hanson Brown $30 for work done in the 5th Ward. 3-Act for the relief of G Vanderwerken: the sume of $512 be paid to him for the breaking down of the bridge over Rock Creek, at the termination of K st.

Preparations continue to be made at Constantinople for the reception of Napoleon. In the mean time he & the Empress will visit Queen Victoria on the 16th.

SAT APR 14, 1855 PAGING
Parlor Grand Pianos for sale; second-hand pianos taken in part payment. New Music constantly received. –Richd David, Pa ave

Rev Dr Scudder died in Jan last at Wynberg, near Cape Town, Africa, of apoplexy. He had been 35 years a missionary of the American Board in India. Of his large family of 9 children, 3 sons & 1 daughter are now missionaries in India, 2 sons are under appointment to go out as missionaries, & one son & daughter are in course of training for the game field of usefulness. Mrs Scudder, who was a true helpmate to her husband, was the sister of Rev Dr Waterbury, of Boston. She died several years since.

Thos B Turner, House, Sign, & Ornamental Painter & Glazer: shop on La ave.

A lot of fine mules for sale, & some fine young horses, on terms to suit the times by Jas H Shrives, 7th st.

Died: on Apr 12, Mrs Ann Ward, consort of the late Wm Ward, in her 60th year. Her funeral will take place today, at 2 o'clock, from her late residence, M & 7th sts.

Died: at Oldtown, Alleghany Co, Md, where he had been a practitioner of medicine for many years, Dr John W Mountz, son of John Mountz, of Gtwn, D C. [No death date given-current item.]

Obit-died: on Mar 18, Mary Eliza Wilkinson Graham, in her 24th year, wife of Gen Geo Mason Graham, now of Rapide Parish, La, but formerly of Wash City. To her husband, who was devotedly attached to her, & to her young family, who by this dispensation have been bereaved of a fond, devoted mother, the loss will be irreparable.

MON APR 16, 1855
Household & kitchen furniture & oil paintings at auction on: Apr 25, at the residence of Col B S Roberts, U S A, on the Heights of Gtwn. -Jas C McGuire, auct
+
For sale at public auction: the beautiful **Cottage** belonging to Col B S Roberts, U S Army, on the Heights of Gtwn, corner of 8th & High sts: with nearly 3 acres of land attached. Many handsome residences surround this property. Title indisputable. -Jas C McGuire, auct

Chancery sale: by decree of the Circuit Court of Wash Co, D C, made in the case of Offutt & Co vs Davis' administrator & heirs, No 1,045 equity dated Nov 16, 1854, I will offer at public auction, on May 8 next, on the premises, part of lot 43 in Old Gtwn, said part being distant from Market Space about 33 feet each, fronting 24 feet on the south side of Bridge st, with a 3 story brick house. Also, on the same day: lot 18 in square 38, L & 23rd sts, Wash City. –Walter S Cox, trustee
-Edw S Wright, auct, Gtwn.

House for rent. The subscriber offers for rent, from May 1 next, the house he now occupies on 4½ st, a few door south of the City Hall. Apply on the premises, No 6, 4½ st. -Thos Blagden.

Died: on Apr 14, after a long & painful illness, Sophia Little, relict of the late Israel Little, in her 69th year. Her funeral will be on Monday at 3 o'clock, from the residence of her son, near the Navy Yard.

Died: on Apr 9, at Morristown, N J, after a long sickness, borne with Christian resignation, Mrs Mary A Vail, wife of Hon Geo Vail, M C.

I O O F. The Grand Lodge of Va held its annual sesseion last week in Richmond. On Wed last the following ofcrs were elected to serve the ensuing year:
W H Cook, of Carroll Co, G Master
Nicholas R Trout, of Staunton, D G Master
John R Jackson, of Warren, G Warden
M Segars, of Richmond, G Sec
G W Toler, of Richmond, G Treasurer
W L Hyland, of Marshall, G Chaplain
John C Wade, of Montg, G Marshal
A Grant, of Richmond, G Guardian
A F Santos, of Norfolk, G Conductor
J W Childress, of Richmond, G Herald
J H Robinson, of Lynchburg, G Rep to the Grand lodge of the U S.

Boston, Apr 15. The ship **Wm Layton** was lost at sea on Feb 27, & the stewardess & 2 of the crew drowned. The capt & remainder of the crew were taken off & have arrived here.

Chas J M Gwinn, Atty at Law, Balt, Md, will attend to cases referred to or originating in the Court of Claims in Wash, D C. Communicate with him by letter to Balt, or to Col Jas G Berret, Postmaster, Wash, D C.

TUE APR 17, 1855
Valuable real estate at auction: by decree of the Circuit Court of Wash Co, D C, public sale on May 8 next, in front of the premises, the following real estate in Gtwn, of which Wm Nelson, late of Fairfax Co, Va, died seized, viz: 1-Part of lot 43, on the east side of Market Space, & next south of & adjoining to the store-house of Mr Saml Cropley, fronting 15½ feet on Market Space, with a 3 story brick bldg. 2-The whole of lot 16, lying between Bridge st & Prospect st, fronting 66 feet on each st. It is proposed to sell this lot in 5 parcels, as follows: the eastern part fronting 37 feet on Bridge st; with a 3 story brick house. The west part of said lot, fronting 29 feet on Bridge st, with an old frame bldg thereon. Part of lot 16 which fronts on Prospect st, in 3 separate lots, each will front 22 feet on said st. They are vacant. Sale to commence at lot 43. –John Marbury, trustee -Edw S Wright, auct

Orphans Court of Wash Co, D C. Letters testamentary on the personal estate of Wm Wormley, late of Wash Co, deceased. –Louisa Wormley, excx

Orphans Court of Wash Co, D C. Letters testamentary on the personal estate of John Shea, late of Wash Co, deceased. –Mary Shea, excx

Obit-died: on Mar 30, at Savanah, Margaret Hamilton, the wife of Thos Lynch, of S C, in her 32nd year. The relentless destroyer came to her in the shape of a wasting & inexorable disease, forbidding all hope to her loving friends. She was a native of Va, & the daughter of the late Col John Heath, of Black Heath. She leaves a most devoted husband & children to mourn her loss.

Wash City Ordinances: 1-Act for the relief of Chas Stewart: the sum of $460.20 be paid to him for grading N H ave, between I & L sts north. 2-Act for the relief of Mgt Tilghman: the sum of $8 be paid to her for the hire of a huckster's stand, of which she has been deprived by the clerk of the market in the Northern Liberties.

Died: on Apr 15, of pneumonia, Mr John F Ball, a gentleman competent & faithful in the execution of all his trusts. It is with painful emotions that his associates in the Patent Ofc have heard of his decease. His funeral will take place this day at 10 o'clock, at his residence on Md ave, between 8th & 9th sts.

U S Patent Ofc, Wash, Apr 16, 1855. Ptn of Geo Page, of Wash, D C, praying for the extension of a patent granted to him on Jul 16, 1841, for an improvement in portable circular saw mills, for 7 years from the expiration of said patent, which takes place on Jul 16, 1855. –S T Shugert, Acting Com'r of Patents.

WED APR 18, 1855
In Emanuel, Ga, on Apr 2, Matthew & Saml Williamson & others went to Mr L Wilkies, where there was a party of men, & called to them to come out. Mr J Moseley went out to them, when he was knocked down with a gun, having his jawbone broken, & as his brother Ryler Moseley stooped down to pick him up he was stabbed through & died instantly. Both parties then began to fire, in which Matthew Williamson was killed & Saml Williamson wounded; he has since died. None of either party has as yet been arrested.

The Wabash [Ind] Gaz contains an account of the discovery of the bodies of a family of 7 persons near that place, of the name of French, who had been brutally murdered. It appears the family consisted of French, his wife, & 5 children. They were very poor, & lived in a cabin, & in Sept last another family, of the name of Hubbard, went to live with them. During Oct a neighbor proceeded to the cabin to see French, & was told by the Hubbards that the family had moved away, & they had purchased all their corn, garden produce, & furniture, valued at not more than $50. No suspicion of foul play was aroused until recently, when the Hubbards were arrested on suspicion of murdering a man named Boyles. The house was then searched & a portion of the ground floor dug up, which resulted in finding the dead bodies of the entire French family. The Hubbards are all in jail.

A Lady, qualified to teach the English branches & French, desires a situation as teacher or governess. Best references given & required. Address Martha Yates, Martinsburg, Va.

Chas Frankenberger & Co: at the old stand on G & 7th sts: choice lot of Wines, Liquores, & Cigars of the best brands. Oysters served up in every style & furnished to families

Drury M Gray, in Jun last, murdered a young man by the name of Chance, son of Jas Chance, Sheriff of Marion Co, Ill. He was indicted, & being a good deal depressed in mind he hung himself on Fri last to the grating of his cell until quite dead. He had unraveled the woolen stockings which he wore, & constructed a rope sufficient to hang himself.

Mrd: on Apr 17, at Annapolis, Md, by Rev Mr Nelson, Dr Chas McCormich, U S Army, to Mrs Ann Wells, daughter of the late Richd Iglehart, of Howard Co, Md.

Mrd: on Apr 17, at Wesley Chapel, by Rev R L Dashiell, Mr Saml C Middleton, formerly of Woodford Co, Ky, to Miss Mary E Brickhead, of Wash City.

Died: on Apr 5, at Buffalo, Mrs Eliza W, wife of Hon W A Moseley, highly esteemed & deeply lamented by a large circle of friends.

Medical Society of D C: appointed delegates to the next annual meeting of the Nat'l Medical Association:

H Lindsley, M D
J C Hall, M C
F Howard, M D
C Boyle, M C
G M Dove, M D

G Tyler, M D
Jno C Riley, M D
A I Semmes, M D
A Holmead, M D, Rec Sec

Phil, Apr 17. The boiler connected with the cotton mill of C Spencer, at Germantown exploded this morning: T Teltzer, the engineer, was killed.

THU APR 19, 1855

Household & kitchen furniture at auction on: Apr 24, at the residence of E Lallouette, on south side of Pa ave, between 19th & 20th sts, all his furniture & housekeeping effects. -Jas C McGuire, auct

Trustee's sale of valuable house & lot: by deed of trust from Wm F Austin & wife, dated Jan 6, 1854, recorded in Liber J A S No 70, folios 336 thru 340: public auction on Apr 26, on the premises, on First st east, between N & O sts south, part of lot 5 in square south of square 744, fronting on First st, with 2 story frame dwlg house. -Chas S Wallach, trustee -Jas C McGuire, auct

Fitzhugh Carter, a citizen of Fredericksburg, Va, worth $500,000, died last week.

A man named Currier was lately tarred & feathered at Central Plains, Va, because a jury acquitted him on a charge of murder & subsequently of stealing.

John H Jones, charged with having murdered H McCardle, in Iowa, 14 years ago, has just been arrested. [Apr 20th newspaper: The difficulty originated between them over a claim, the land in that vicinity at the time being unentered. McCardle was with his son gathering corn, at the time, when Jones shot the father. The murderer was living in Lockland, Ohio, when the ofcrs arrested him. –St Louis Intelligencer]

Jas A Graham, charged with the murder of Wm H Spiller, at Wytheville, Va, has been committed for trial. It is said his counsel will defend him on the plea of insanity.

Mrd: on Apr 17, in Gtwn, D C, by Rev Bernard A Maguire, Pres of Gtwn College, Mr D A O'Byrne, of Savannah, Ga, to Josephine, daughter of Bennett Clements.

Mrd: on Apr 17, in St Alban's Church, D C, by Rev W L Childs, Thos A Brooke to Mary Kervand Davis, both of the District of Columbia.

Died: on Apr 17, John Duncan, son of John L & Ellen W Hazzard, aged 8 months & 9 days. His funeral is this afternoon, at 3 o'clock, from his parents' residence, Va ave, between 11th & 12th sts.

FRI APR 20, 1855
Capt Thos J Lee, of the U S Topographical Engineers, has resigned, to take effect on Apr 30, 1855. –Star

Four vessels arreived at N Y on Wed with alien steerage passengers: the ship **James Foster**, from Liverpool, with 750; the ship **West Point**, from Liverpool, with 430; the ship **Francis A Palmer**, from Havre, with 415; & the ship **Devonshire**, from London, with 136.

Household & kitchen furniture at auction on: Apr 23, at the residence of Mrs M Bevans, corner of 13th & D sts. -Jas C McGuire, auct

Desirable private residence at auction: by authority vested in me by the last will & testament of Emily Corcoran, deceased: public auction on Mar 2, of the lot & dwlg house, late the residence of the deceased, on West st, between Congress & Wash st, Gtwn, one of the most desirable parts of the town for a private residence. The house contains 14 rooms in all. –H C Matthews, exc of Emily Corcoran, deceased.

Local Matters. Meeting of the Metropolitan Mechanics' Institute: on Wed: the following elections were made: Pres, Jos Henry; 1st V P, Francis Mohun; 2nd V P, Chas F Wood; 3rd V P, Jos Bryan; 4th V P, Wm B Todd; Corr Sec, Thos Rich; Rec Sec, Peter M Pearson; Financial Sec, Henry Janney; Treas, Wm F Bayly, Librarian, Hollis Amidon; Dirs: Phineal J Steer, Thos Creaser, Valentine Harbaugh, Chas Edmonston, Wm H Ward, A Baldwin, Saml Lewis, Jas O'Neil, & Thos Berry.

Dr H C Sims offers his professional services to the public. Ofc n w corner of 4½ st & Pa ave. Residence 390 C st, between 3rd & 4½ st.

Died: on Thu, John Agg, in his 75th year. His funeral will be from his late residence, this day, at 4 o'clock.

U S Patent Ofc, Wash, Apr 19, 1855. Ptn of Alonzo Wheeler & A F Wheeler, excs of Wm E Wheeler, deceased, of the State of N Y, praying for the extension of a patent granted to Alonzo & Wm E Wheeler on Jul 8, 1841, for an improvement in endless chain horse powers for driving machinery, for 7 years from the expiration of said patent, which takes place on Jul 8, 1855. –S T Shugert, Acting Com'r of Patents.

SAT APR 21, 1855
Household & kitchen furniture at auction on: May 2, at the residence of Henry Baldwin, corner of 12th & H sts, by deed of trust from said Baldwin, dated Feb 27, 1855, duly recorded in one of the land records of Wash Co, D C. –C W Bennett, trustee -Green & Scott, aucts

Household & kitchen furniture at auction on: Apr 25, at the residence of Mr Ross Brown, corner of 6th & I sts. -Green & Scott, aucts

Mrd: on Apr 15, by Rev F Israel, Thos Johnson to Miss Jane C Rose, all of Wash City.

Mrd: on Apr 17, by Rev F Israel, Silas S Brady to Miss Mgt King, all of Wash City.

Mrd: on Apr 3, at **Fort Gibson**, Cherokee Nation, by Rev P Reilly, Capt Henry Little, U S Army, to Miss Martha C, daughter of Lt Col P Morrison, U S Army.

Mrd: on Apr 19, at Foundry Parsonage, by Rev E P Phelps, Mr Wm S Laurenson to Mrs Eliz A Stone, all of Wash City.

Died: on Apr 20, Mrs Mgt P Fauntleroy, wife of the late Dangerfield Fauntleroy, Purser of the U S Navy. Her remains will be taken to Alexandria this afternoon, at 2 o'clock, for interment.

Died: on Apr 20, Jos T Walker, of inflammation of the bowels. His funeral will take place from his late residence, 46 Missouri ave, Sunday, at 5 o'clock.

Circuit Court of Wash Co, D C-in Equity. John B Kibby & John S Whitwell against Eliz F Marceron & Jos B Marceron & others. W Redin, trustee, reported that on Dec 8, 1854, he sold part of square 690, in Wash City, with dwlg house, to John B Kibby, for $1,250, & that he hath complied with the terms of sale. –John A Smith, clerk

In Equity. Jos E Law, cmplnt, against Jas Adams, exc of Thos Law, Henry May, adm of Edmund & Thos Law, Lloyd N Rogers, Edmund L Rogers, & Eleanor A Rogers, & others, dfndnts. Re-form & re-state the accounts of the trustee & to report the sums due to the respective parties. Notice is given to the parties above named, & to any persons who may have claims against the estate of the late Thos Law, that on Apr 28, at my ofc, in City Hall, I shall commence the excution of the said order. -W Redin, auditor

Promotions in the Navy:
Chas H McBlair to be cmder, vice Gerry, lost in sloop-of-war **Albany**.
Edw Brinley to be a lt, vice A Lewis, deceased.
Edw Simpson to be a lt, vice McBlair, promoted.
Wm G Temple to be a lt, vice W W Bleecker, lost in the **Albany**.
Geo P Welsh to be a lt, vice M Hunt, lost in the **Albany**.
Saml P Carter to be a lt, vice John Q Adams, lost in the **Albany**.
Wm Nelson to be a lt, vice Henry Rodgers, lost in the **Albany**.
J H Wright to be a surgeon, vice S A McCreery, lost in the **Albany**.
[All to date from Apr 18, 1855.]
Passed Midshipmen W H Wilcox, John T Barraud, Thos Roney, John H Upshur, John Van N Philip, Saml R Franklin, & Francis G Clarke to be masters in the line of promotion. During the absence of Sec Dobbin, the Pres has authorized Chas W Welsh, Chief Clerk of the Navy Dept, to officiate as Acting Sec of the Navy.

MON APR 23, 1855
Robt Swift was hung at Elkton, Md, on Fri last for the murder of Jeremiah Kilhour.

Household & kitchen furniture at auction on: Apr 30, at the residence of Mrs J D Brown, Pa ave, between 14th & 15th sts. -Jas C McGuire, auct

Mrs Rebecca Adams has taken the large & elegant house, 452 13th st, between E & F sts, owned by Gov Toucey, which she has fitted up for the accommodation of those desiring furnished apts either as bedrooms or parlors.

Mrd: in N Y C, Rev J N Steiner to Miss Ann Wendell Evans, daughter of the late Hon Richd Evans, Judge of the Superior Court of N H. They embarked on Apr 3 for Europe. [No date given-current item.]

Naval Board for the examination of assist surgeons in the navy, having concluded its duties, has been dissolved, & the following is the result:
Assist Surg Thos B Steele to rank next below Passed Assist Surgeon Edw R Squibb.
Assist Surg A Nelson Beell next below Passed Assist Surgeon John Ward.
Assist Surg Chas Martin next above Passed Assist Surgeon F M Gunnell.
Assist Surg Chas H Williamson next below Passed Assist Surgeon S Allen Engles.
Assist Surg Edw Shippen next after C H Williamson.
The candidates for admission who passed a satisfactory examination are as follows, arranged according to merit:
1-Albert S Gihon, Pa
2-John S Ketchen, Pa
3-John Vansant, Va
4-Jas Laws, Pa
5-Edwin R Denby, Va
6-Wm Johnson, Dela
7-Francis L Galt, Va
8-Stewart Kennedy, Pa
9-Wm M Page, Va
10-A Clarkson Smith, Pa

Obit-died: Mrs Hamlin, yesterday afternoon, after a lingering illness of many months. She was the eldest daughter of Judge Emery, of Oxford Co. She married & removed with her husband, Hon Hannibal Hamlin, to Hampden, where they have ever since resided. She proved herself an excellent woman, an affectionate wife, & a kind mother. –Bangor [Maine] Mercury

N Y, Apr 22. The steamer **Nashville**, chartered by the Collins Co in place of the steamer **Pacific**, arrived at noon today. She brings Liverpool & London papers of Apr 7. The second day out from N Y, on her outward passage, Mrs Rose Riley, one of the passengers, suddenly disappeared, & is supposed to have thrown herself overboard.

Detroit, Apr 20. The propeller **Oregon**, of Cleveland, exploded her boiler this morning & 10 men were killed, amongst them W S Chapman, the 1st engineer of the boat; Thos Donnelly, the 2nd engineer; Edw McBride & Wm Reed. Capt Stewart had one of his legs broken.

TUE APR 24, 1855
Three young men, John Blous, Geo King, & Wm Bryan, were convicted of murder, at Cayuga, Canada, on Fri, & sentenced to be executed on May 18. They belonged to the Townsend gang of robbers.

Wm B Clarke, of Md, some years ago a Whig candidate for Govn'r of the State, in opposition to Gov Lowe, & late a State Senator, died in Balt on Sat week.

For sale: about 50 acres of land fronting on the public road: 4 miles from Wash. Apply to the subscriber near Tenallytown, D C. –Chas R Belt

Died: on Apr 22, in her 63rd year, Mrs Martha Ann Sanderson, relict of the late Wm Sanderson, leaving a numerous family to mourn her sudden demise. Her funeral will be from the family residence, south of the Eastern Branch Bridge, today at 3 o'clock.

Died: on Apr 19, Edwin, the son of Thos C & Mgt Wilson, after a painful illness of 6 days, in his 17th year.

U S Patent Ofc, Wash, Apr 23, 1855. Ptn of Hiram Dillaway, of Sandwich, Mass, praying for the extension of a patent granted to him on Aug 21, 1841, for an improvement in the construction of moulds for pressing glass, for 7 years from the expiration of said patent, which takes place on Aug 21, 1855.
–S T Shugert, Acting Com'r of Patents.

WED APR 25, 1855
Household & kitchen furniture at auction on: May 1, at the residence of Hon M Macdonald, north side of G st, near 15th st. -Jas C McGuire, auct

Household & kitchen furniture at auction: Apr 28, at the late residence of Mrs J E W Thompson, deceased, on E st, between 12th & 13th sts. –Wall, Barnard & Co, aucts

A private letter from Ceylon mentions the death by cholera of Rev Danl Poor, the venerable Missionary of the American Board. Cholera was raging with great fatality in Ceyton.

N Y, Apr 22, 1855. The U S steam frig **Mississippi** arrived in this port today, 29 days & a few hours from Rio de Janeiro. The **Mississippi** is one of the vessels which composed the Japan squadron under the command of Cmdor M C Perry. List of her ofcrs: S S Lee, Cmder; Edmund Lanier, J M B Clitz, S Nicholson, & W A Webb, Lts; John Kell, Acting Lt; D S Green, Surgeon; Wm Speiden, Purser; John H March, Acting Master; L J Williams, Passed Assist Surgeon; Geo Jones, Chaplain; R Tarsill, Capt of Marines; W F Jones, Jeff Maury, & K R Breese, Passed Midshipmen; S Carn Mish, Midshipmen; Amos Colson, Boatswain; John R Caulk, Gunner; Henry M Lowry, Carpenter; Jacob Stephens, Sailmaker; Jesse Gay, Chief Engineer; Robt Danby & Wm Holland, 1st Assist Engineer; Geo T W Logan, W Henry Rutherford, & G W Alexander, 2nd do; Ed D Robie & John Drum Mercer, 3rd do; Oliver H Perry, Cmdor's Sec; A L C Portman, Cmdor's Clerk; J W Spalding, Cmder's Clerk; W Speiden, jr, Purser's Clerk; Wilhelm Heine, Acting Master's Mate. Passengers: John E Johnson, Passed Midshipman; H G Thomas, Carpenter.

Mr John T Ball, of the Patent Ofc, died about 12 days ago of pneumonia, & on Monday night of this week his brother, Mr Henry W Ball, Surveyor of Wash City, died of the same disease. They were amiable & worthy gentlemen.

Died: on Apr 21, at **Northampton**, his residence, in PG Co, Md, Hon Saml Sprigg, aged 73 years, formerly Govn'r of Md; his native State.

Died: yesterday, after a short illness, Mrs Eliz Walker, aged 79 years, formerly of Gtwn. Her funeral will take place from the residence of her daughter, Mrs Gaither, on 6th st, between G & H sts, on Thu morning, at 10 o'clock.

Woonsocket Patriot: published in the Boston Journal a few weeks since of a family of 6 ladies in Duxbury whose united ages were 470 years, says that in the town of West Hartford, Conn, there is a family of Seldens, comprising 8 brothers & 2 sisters, whose united ages are about 800 years-the youngest being 70 & the oldest nearly 90. A few years ago the members of the family met together at the homestead, & sang the good old tunes which their father & mother sang 90 years ago.

For rent: a large 3 story brick house, with stable & all necessary out-bldgs, on 4½ st south, on *Greenleaf's Point*. –Mary Wheat, 4½ st, *Greenleaf's Point*.

THU APR 26, 1855
Dr Barth, the African traveler, who was reported last summer to have died, still lives, as appears by this letter from Col Herman, the British Consul at Tripoli, Mar 13: You will, I am confident, be delighted to hear that the rumor of Dr Barth's death was unfounded. A letter from him, dated Nov 15 last, reached me yesterday.

The remains of the late Mr Jas B Clarke, of Wash City, were found in the canal yesterday. He had not been seen since Sat last, on which day he probably fell in & was drowned. He was about 43 years of age; & formerly of the dry-goods firm of Clarke & Brisco. He was unmarried, a man of kind & gentle nature.

Mr J C McGuire sold at auction yesterday, the central lot of Mr Jenks' farm, between Alexandria, & Wash, & occupied by the Columbia Race Course. The farm was divided into 4 lots, 3 of 30 acres each & one of 14 acres, which was reserved by Mr Jenks. Mr S P Corbitt bought the center lot, at $107 per acre, & intends to occupy it himself as a permanent residence. Lot 1 was sold for $77.50 per acre. Lot 3, with a very large farm house, was also put up, & $165 per acre bid, but the proprietor, desiring $180, withdrew both this & lot 1 from sale. -Organ

Mrd: on Tue, by Rev John C Smith, Mr John Poor to Miss Rebecca Campbell, all of Wash City.

Died: on Apr 24, of pulmonary consumption, Richd L Smallwood, in his 37th year. His funeral will take place from Wesley Chapel this afternoon, at 3½ o'clock.

Died: on Monday last, at Draneville, Virginia, after a lingering illness, Mrs Ann M Farr, youngest daughter of the late Col Baldwin Dade, in about her 57th year.

Members of the Young Men's Christian Association are requested to attend the funeral of our late brother, R L Smallwood, who was for 2 years a member of the Board of Managers, from Wesley Chapel to *Glenwood Cemetery*, this afternoon, at 3½ o'clock. –W Chauncy Langdon, Chairman Com on the Sick.

U S Patent Ofc, Wash, Apr 24, 1855. Ptn of Lewis G Sturdevant, of Alabama, praying for the extension of a patent granted to him on Jul 23, 1841, for an improvement in the manner of constructing gins for ginning cotton, for 7 years from the expiration of said patent, which takes place on Jul 23, 1855.
–S T Shugert, Acting Com'r of Patents.

Public sale of valuable negroes: by decree of the Circuit Court of PG Co, Md, sitting as Court of Equity, in a cause wherein Eliza Berry, by Richd H Marshall, is cmplnt, & Robt W Brooke & Wm E Berry & others are dfndnts, passed on Apr 13, 1855, the undersigned will expose at public sale, at R H Locker's store, in *Long Old Fields*, on May 17, some 12 or 15 negroes, of both sexes, the property of the trust estate of the late Elisha Berry. –C C Magruder, D C Digges, trustees

FRI APR 27, 1855
Wanted, for a term of years, a genteel residence, containing not less than 5 chambers. A 2 story house with back bldg will be preferred. Address, through the City Post Ofc, F G Fanning.

Administrator's sale of frame house on the Canal, near 7th st Bridge. By order of the Orphans Court of Wash Co, D C, on May 1, on the premises, a 1 story frame house on Corporation lot on 7th st, with back shed, formerly occupied by Richd Ayton.
–C W Boteler, auct -Chas S Wallach, atty

On Monday last a shocking accident on the Canandaigua & Niagara Falls road, in the village of Canandaigua, N Y. As 3 gentlemen were standing together on the track a freight train came in, which caused them to step aside, without observing that a locomotive was backing down towards them on the other track. They were all struck down by the engine. Mr Nathan N Hall was instantly kill; David Pillsbury was so severely injured as to endanger his life; & Mr Nelson was scalped entirely, so as to render his recovery doubtful.

Augusta Tollver, age 4 years, living in N Y, died on Apr 9 from the effects of doses of tartar emetic, served by a druggist in mistake for pulvis antimonialis. The young man who served the medicine has absconded.

Mrd: on Apr 26, in the First Presbyterian Church, by Rev Byron Sunderland, Mr A W Russell, of Rockville, Md, to Miss Julia, daughter of Wm H Campbell, of Wash City.

Died: on Apr 25, May, second daughter of Wm J & Martha Parham, aged 2 years & 9 months. Her funeral is this afternoon at 3 o'clock.

Store in Gtwn for rent, situated on Bridge st, No 120, next door to the Bank of Commerce, & at present occupied by Mr M L Williams. Inquire of T A Lazenby, Bridge st.

SAT APR 28, 1855
Trustee's sale of valuable bldg lot: by decree of the Circuit Court of Wash Co, D C, made in the cause wherein Jas W Strange, Jos C Hushe & Mgt Hushe his wife, late Mgt Strange, are cmplnts, & Mgt Strange, Robt Strange, & French Strange are dfndnts: public auction on May 19 next: lot 7 in square 127, with all & singular appurtenances thereunto belonging. Also, on the same day, on the premises, in Wash City, lot 8 in square 702, with appurtenances thereunto belonging.
-W B Webb, trustee -Jas C McGuire, auct

Mrd: on Apr 26, at Foundry Parsonage, by Rev E P Phelps, Mr Jacob H Clapdore to Miss Ann V Taylor, both of Alexandria, Va.

Mrd: on Apr 26, Ellen M, daughter of Prof N R Smith, of Balt, to D E A, son of Capt J B Montgomery, U S Army.

Mrd: on Apr 24, by Rev S B Southerland, John R Johnston, of Va, to Miss Marcia Ann, daughter of Jeremiah Orme, of Gtwn, D C.

The Anniversary of the Landing at Jamestown will be celebrated in Wash City on May 13. The Jamestown Association have chosen Richd Fendall, their Pres, in place of Thos Ritchie, deceased.

The U S brig **Dolphin** is about to sail from Norfolk to join the African coast squadron. List of her ofcrs: Lt Com E R Thompson; Lts, J M Wainwright & Geo M Ransom; Purser, Geo R Griswold; Acting Master, N H Vanzandt; Passed Assist Surgeon, Edw Shippen; Passed Midshipmen, O F Johnson & Austin Pendergrast. The U S sloop **St Louis**, Capt Ingraham, was at Gibraltar on Apr 1 & was to sail the next day for the U S.

A few days ago the town of Blackville, Monongalia Co, Va, was visited by a destructive fire. It appears that 35 homes were consumed, involving: Wm Lantz lost $6,000; Thos Brock, $6,000; Thos F Brock, $2,000; Fletcher Brock, $2,000; A B Pratt, $2,500; W S Fletcher, $1,000; Widow Fletcher, $300; Geo Burke, $500; & Dr J M Lazzele, $150.

For rent, a good brick shop, for a blacksmith, in square 454, near the Patent Ofc. Apply to J C Lewis, 492 7th st, between D & E sts.

Red Sulphur Springs for sale: by decree of the Circuit Court of Monroe Co, rendered at Oct term, 1854, in the case of Oliver Beirne, plntf, against Andrew Beirne & others, dfndnts, the Com'rs appointed for that purpose, will, on Aug 23, 1855, sell the **Red Sulphur Springs**, with all the lands privileges, & appurtenances thereto belonging. The land consists of 1,348 acres by survey; improvements, all made since 1833, cost about $70,000; accommodates 250 visitors.
–Saml Price & A A Chapman, Com'rs

MON APR 30, 1855
Chancery sale of valuable property: by decree of the Circuit Court of Wash Co, D C, in a cause wherein Iardella & others are cmplnts & Bulger & others are dfndnts: sale of lot 13 in square 517, with a good 2 story-frame house: situated on north H st, between 4th & 5th sts. –John F Ennis, trustee -Green & Scott, aucts

The remains of the late Mrs McNeill, sister of the Pres of the U S, arrived in Wash City from N H. The funeral took place from the residence of her son-in-law, Capt Benham, U S Army, at 11 o'clock this morning. Her remains now repose by the side of her distinguished husband, Gen John McNeill, in the **Congressional burying-ground**. –Union of Sunday

The Ripley Circuit Court last week sentenced Mr Muir to the penitentiary for 2 years for forging a note of $20. Mr Muir is probably the richest man in Ripley Co, Indiana. It is supposed his property is worth near $100,000. –Indiana Sentinel

Wm Thompson has been re-appointed by the Pres a Justice of the Peace for the District of Columbia; the appointment to take effect from Apr 1.

Medical Association of the Dist of Col meeting at the City Hospital on Tue next, at 12 o'clock. –W J C Duhamel, M D, acting sec

Equity-No 1,046. Thos Baker & Bernard Givenny, excs of Terrence Looby, against John McGarvey & Jos McGarvey, heirs of Chas McGarvey, dfndnts. By order of the Circuit Court of Wash Co, D C I am directed to state the trustee's account; the debts due from Chas McGarvey; & the parties entitled to distribution & their shares. The above named to appear on May 16, at my ofc-City Hall, Wash, -W Redin, auditor

Sale of a very large & valuable Law & Miscellaneous Library, in Balt, of about 7,000 volumes: of the late Judge Purviance, of Balt. Contains some rare books, such as works of St Jerome, published in 1516; Park's Laws of Maryland, 1727, [the <u>first book published</u> in Maryland;] a Dictionary in 7 languages, printed in 1570. Catalogues will be sent free of expense by writing by mail to Robt Purviance, jr, administrator of John Purviance, South Gay st, Balt, or to E Beatty Graff, Atty at Law, under Barnum's, Fayette st, Balt.

Contributors to the Fund for the Erection of a Monument to the late Stewart Holland, of the ill-fated steamer **Arctic**, are to meet at the counting room of the Union Ofc on Mon next, at 5 o'clock, for the purpose of selecting a cmte to take charge of the fund.

TUE MAY 1, 1855

Chancery sale: by decree of the Circuit Court of Wash Co, D C, made in the cause of Wm Bird et al vs Horatio Maryman, exc of Zachariah Hazel et al, No 886, Chancery: public auction on Mar 22, of part of lot 3 & 4 in square 784, fronting on Md ave. Also for sale lots 14 & 15 in square 867 on North B st. –Walter S Cox, trustee –Green & Scott, aucts

The stern-wheel steamer **Wm Knox**, Capt Yard, from Ironton & Cincinnati, with a full cargo & 150 passengers, chiefly emigrants for St Louis, was totally destroyed by fire on Sunday, in the Ohio river, at Flint Island. The passengers were compelled to jump into the river & swim ashore, the distance but a few feet, but the stage-plank was too short to reach. –Louisville Courier

G W Kendall, the Postmaster of this city, was arrested on Apr 24, by one of the deputies of the U S Marshal, on a warrant from U S Com'r Lusher, which had been issued by that functionary upon an affidavit being made before him by Mr Blair, one of the Government's secret mail agents. In this affidavit Mr Kendall is charged with having feloniously disposed of a letter containing $600 which was directed to Messrs Wills, Rollins & Co, of this city. Hon John Slidell, U S Senator, appeared as security for the accused. -New Orleans Bee, 24th.

By a resolution of Congress, approved Jan 24, 1854, provision was made to present to Maj Gen John E Wool a token of the appreciation of his country of the services rendered by him in the battle of Buena Vista, in which he so signally distinguished himself. The work of the manufacturing the present was given to Mr Saml Jackson, of Balt, & is completed. The upper part is a spread eagle, on the breast of which is a shield bearing the words "Buena Vista, February 22 and 23, 1847." The sword was made after a design from Lt Benton & cost $1,500. -Balt American

This morning Mr Josiah F Polk, of Wash City, was removed from this third class [$1,000 per annum] clerkship in the ofc of the Second Auditor of the Treasury. -Star

Wash City Ordinances: 1-Act for the relief of Mary Sullivan: the fine imposed upon her for an alleged violation of the law against selling intoxicating liquor without a license is remitted: provided she pay the costs of prosecution. 2-Act for the relief of Jas Watson: fine is remitted provided he pay the costs thereof. 3-Act for the relief of Jacob Kleiber: to be paid $50 for extra services rendered as messenger to the Mayor & Register's ofc since Aug 15 last. 4-Act for the relief of Francis Hutchins: to refund to him $7, the amount paid by him Dec 27, 1854, on an improvement on a part of lot 1 in square 515, assessed to John S Boss, said improvement belonging to said Hutchins, & untenantable until after Jan 1, 1854.

Died: on Apr 30, Mrs Eliz J Wimer, aged 28 years, wife of Jas Wimer, of consumption, which she bore with Christian grace & fortitude. Her funeral will take place today at 4 o'clock, from her late residence on 6th st, near Louisiana ave.

Syracuse, Apr 30. Last night the train from Rochester ran over a horse, which threw the hind car down an embankment of 20 feet, instantly killing M O Wilder, a lawyer of Canandaiga, & badly injuring S H Ingersoll & Clinton Crainard, of N Y; Wm Hall & Z Turmen, of Skaneatles; Chas Iseuring & Jos Lieb, of Syracuse; M Becker, of Rochester, & the brakeman.

WED MAY 2, 1855
Hon A C Dodge, our new Minister to Spain, left Wash City yesterday for N Y, accompanied by Mrs E W Pendleton, of Wash City, Mrs Dr Linn, of Missouri, widow of the late Senator Linn, & daughter. -Globe

The "Organ" of last evening publishes the following as a complete list of the new Cadets appointed to West Point for the present year:

Abbot, Jacob: Miss
Allen, W H: Penn
Andrews, John N: Del
Ashe, John G: N C
Bacon, John: Tenn
Bates, Geo W: Mo
Beck, Wm B: Penn
Berill, John M: Ky
Birdsall, John: At large
Bonesteel, Jacob P: Wis
Bowen, Nicholas: N Y
Bowman, C S: At large
Burloch, Fred F: Conn
Butler, P M: At large
Chamberlain, W W: N Y
Cushing, S F: R I
Dean, John: Penn
Edson, Theodore: Mass
Edwards, N M: Ky
Embrich, Fred: Penn
Gibs, Wm G: S C
Gilmer, John C: N C
Glens, Robt H: Va
Griffing, Geo J: N Y
Hall, Robt H: Ill
Hazlett, Chas E: Ohio
Hollister, Geo L: N Y
Hook, jr, Cornelius: Ill
Hopkins, Edw: N Y
Huger, F: At large
Johnson, R Z: Ohio
Jones, W G: Ohio
Jordon, Wm H: Ohio
Kellogg, Josiah H: Penn

Kent, Francis S: Penn
Knox, Gilbert L: Ohio
Laramee, W H: Nebras
Livingston, C E: Penn
Lewis, Martin: Ohio
Lynn, Saml D: Ind
Lyon, Chas D, Mich
Maitland, John A: Penn
Marbury, Horatio: Penn
Marriott, W H: At large
Marsh, S J: Mass
Marion, W A: Ark
Martin, Jas P: At large
Matterson, M: N Y
Mills, Anson: Ind
Mishler, L: Penn
Mitchell, R W: At large
Myers, G R: N Y
McCreery, jr, Wm H: At large
McFarland, W: N Y
McGowan, J A: Cal
McIntosh, A J D: At large
McIntyre, H C: La
McNally, Robt: N Y
Norris, Jas B: N H
Parker, Jas: N C
Parker, H C: La
Pennington, A _ M: N J
Porter, Horatio: Penn

Porter, Jos P: Mo
Potter, Carroll H: R I
Powell, Albert M: Md
Ransour, S D: N C
Ranal, A M: N Y
Ricketts, Wm W: Penn
Riley, E B D: At large
Ritnour, O P: Ill
Robinson, Jas A: Ca;
Rugg, Dewitt C: Ind
Scott, Abel S: Va
Shoemaker, E W: N M
Sloan, jr, B F: S C
Small, R S: Penn
Smith, Alfred T: Ill
Sweet, John J: Ill
Taber, Jas M: Miss
Talbot, Lycurgus: Kans
Taylor, Richd: Fa
Tardy, jr, J A: N Y
Thomas, Winfield S: Ga
Vanderbilt, G W: N Y
Warner, Jas M: Va
Williams, Ridon: Ohio
Wilson, John M: Wash
Whitmore, J M: Mass
Wesley, Merritt: Ill

Orphans Court of Wash Co, D C. Letters of administration on the personal estate of Eliz Thompson, late of Wash Co, deceased. –Louisa Thomson, admx

Jos Roberts, Jas Williams, W W Drake, & Geo Franz, seamen on board the Balt ship **James Cheston** at the time she was abandoned at sea, & who, after being taken aboard the ship **Two Friends**, were transferred at Galveston, Texas, where they had an examination before A Hughes, the U S Com'r. Their evidence contains little that is new.

Naval Court Martial commenced on Sat on board the receiving-ship **North Caro**lina, at the Brooklyn navy-yard, for the trial of charges preferred by Lt Webb against Passed Midshipman Murray, & counter-charges by Murray against Webb. Both ofcrs were recently attached to the steam-ship **Mississippi**, of the Japan squadron. Many of the late ofcrs of the ship are detained as witnesses.

Elkton, Cecil Co, Md, Apr 27, 1855. Gen Fenwick Williams who was the subject of an extraction from the London Times copied into the Mirror, is a native of the small town of Annapolis, Nova Scotia, where he was born about 1800. At age 13 he embarked for England, where he prosecuted his studies as a cadet at Woolwich until 1823. In 1825 he obtained a commission as 2nd Lt in the Royal Artl, & was soon sent to the Island of Ceylon, where he was for 10 years superintending the construction of roads, bridges, & fortifications, which were all made by the Military. In 1850 he received from the Sultan a commission as Lt Col, & in the same year was promoted to a majority in the British army. In 1854 he made a short visit to his relatives in American, [not in N Y, for there he had none,] & among them to my wife, his niece. During this visit he was gazetted in England "Knight Companion of the Bath." Gen Williams is now stationed at Karz & Erzeroom, having under his command 20,000 Turks, & awaiting orders to proceed to active operations in the province of Georgia. Gen Williams was never on the Island of St Kitts, was not a relative of Sir Chas Maxwell, & was never in the U S except for a few weeks in 1824 & for a few days in 1854. –Edwin Arnold

Wash Corp: 1-Cmte of Claims: asked to be discharged from the consideration of the ptn of the legal reps of Richd Holmes, deceased: discharged accordingly. Same cmte: Act for the relief of Isaac Ten Eyck: passed. 3-Ptn of J Keating, W W Seaton, & others, for the improvement of North Capitol st near N Y ave: referred to the Cmte on Improvements. 4-Ptn of Mgt Magle, praying the remission of a fine for selling liquors in a less quantity than a pint: referred to the Cmte of Claims. 5-Cmte of Claims: asked to be discharged from the consideration of the ptns of Saml Sylvester, F Gibson, & Amelia Baltimore: discharged accordingly. Same cmte: act for the relief of Jacob F King: & act for the relief of Wm Rupp: laid over for further consieration. Same cmte: bill for the relief of Henry Sceitz: rejected.

The Wash Light Infty, Capt Jas Y Davis, encamped on the Wash Monument grounds yesterday. They were escorted by the Pres' Mounted Guard, Capt Peck. The Nat'l Guards, under command of Capt Tait, had a parade for target practice. These companies elicited general commendation for their good discipline & military bearing.

Private letters from Munich, in Bavaria, state that the bronze statues of Patrick Henry & Ludwig Van Beethoven are ready for shipment to America. The former is the size of life & is intended for the monument to Washington at Richmond, Va; which monument is to consist of a group of 6 statues surrounding the pedestal of the statue of Washington himself.

$150 reward for runaway negro man Hezekiah Tabbs, about 40 years of age.
-Jas Thomas, Post Ofc, Chapitco, St Mary's Co, Md.

Mrd: on Apr 19, in Norfolk, Va, at Mrs Chandler's, by Rev Mr Minnegerode, Jno Wythe Parks to Miss Victoria W Marchant, all of that city.

Mrd: on Apr 27, at the Capitol Hill Parsonage, by Rev Gideon H Day, Chas J Ihrie to Miss Mgt R Marshall, all of Wash City.

Mrd: on May 1, at Wyoming, PG Co, Md, by Rev Dr Marbury, Calhoun Benham, of San Francisco, Calif, to Bettie, daughter of the late Wm L Marbury, of PG Co, Md.

Died: on May 1, Lizzie Beall, infant daughter of J R & Caroline McAlister, aged 6 months. Her funeral will take place this evening at 4 o'clock.

Died: Apr 26, in the city of Balt, Marie Clapier, aged 23 years, wife of Campbell Morfit, of the above place, & daughter of Henry & Caroline C Chancellor, of Germantown, Pa.

Died: on May 1, Mrs Jane Isabella, wife of the late Dr John T Swann, of Va. Her funeral will be from the residence of Mrs Seldon, 348 N Y ave, near 10th st, this afternoon at 4½ o'clock. Her remains will be taken to **Glenwood Cemetery**.

Phil, May 1. Wm Maughan, aged 70 years, one of the oldest pressmen in this city, was instantly killed this morning at the printing establishment of Messrs Stavely & McCalla. His body was caught in the machinery of one of the steam presses & awfully mangled, causing instant death. He had been employed there for more than 20 years, & was known among the craft as a sober, honest, & industrious man.

Fashionable Millinery: Pa ave, next to 10th st. –Geo F Allen

Orphans Court of Wash Co, D C. Letters of administration on the personal estate of Thos Gunton, late of Wash Co, deceased. –Wm Gunton, adm

Chancery sale of valuable improved & unimproved real estate: by decree of the Circuit Court of Wash Co, D C made in the cause wherein John A Fraser is cmplnt, & John Walker, Ellen S Fraser, & others, heirs at law of Simon Fraser, deceased, are dfndnts, No 899 in Chancery: public auction of lots 1 thru 24 in square 412, fronting on 8th & 9th sts, between E & F sts, with a 3½ story brick dwlg house on lot 8, & a 2 story brick dwlg house on each of lots 18 & 19; lot 4 in square 388, fronting on F st, with a 2½ story frame dwlg house; part of lot 3 in square 730, fronting on Pa ave; part of square 472, fronting on Water st, with the valuable Wharf thereto attached & belonging, extending to the channel of the Potomac river, & now occupied by Geo Page & used as a steamboat wharf. The sales will be on May 24th & 25th, & 29th.
–Chas S Wallach, Edw Swann, trustees -Jas C McGuire, auct

Orphans Court of Wash Co, D C, May 1, 1855. In the case of Mich Lauxman, adm of Martin Lauxman, deceased, the administrator & Court have appointed May 29 for the final settlement of the estate, of the assets in hand. —Ed N Roach, Reg of Wills

THU MAY 3, 1855
Lt Wm C Chaplin, of the U S Navy, died at the Chelsea naval hospital [Boston] on Sunday. He was a native of Pa, & entered the navy in 1826. He was stationed at Boston for the enlistment of seamen.

A breach of promise case was recently tried at Lyons, Wayne Co, N Y. The plntf Nancy C Servoss & the dfndnt Willis Kelly. A verdict was given by the jury in favor of the plntf for $3,500.

The Catholic Provincial Council, to assemble in Balt on May 6, will be composed of the following Prelates: Rev Francis Patrick Kendrick, D D, of Balt, Md; Rt Rev Richd Vincent Whelan, D C, of Wheeling, Va; Rt Rev Jas M Young, D D, of Erie, Penn; Rt Rev Michl O'Connor, D C, of Petersburg, Penn; Rt Rev John McGill, D D, of Richmond, Va; Rt Rev John M Neumann, D C, of Phil, Pa. -Sun

Public auction at the tavern of Saml Lumin, in Cumberland, on May 25: 300 acres of land, on Buffalo creek, 4 miles west of Selbysport. A valuable Mineral Spring has been analyzed by Dr David Stewart, of Balt. This land lies between the Balt & Ohio Railroad & the Pittsburgh & Connellsville Railroad, about 16 miles from each & 9 miles south of the Nat'l Road. I may be found at Mr Stephen Riley's, near the premises, & near the ***Blooming Rose*** property. Or address Ralph Thayer, postmaster at that place.

Mrd: on May 1, at Wesley Chapel Parsonage, by Rev R L Dashiell, Mr Richd H Brown to Miss Nancy Keys, of Laurel, Md.

Mrd: on May 1, by Rev Mr Phelps, Wm H Greene, of Brooklyn, N Y, to Miss Hattie A Lovejoy, of Wash City.

Mrd: on May 1, by Rev F Israel, Geo O Streaks, formerly of Jefferson Co, Va, to Eliz R Fowler, of Wash.

Mrd: on Apr 25, at the residence of Mr John A Spillman, Warrenton, Va, by Rev Dr Wm Wicks, Mr Wm P Hilleary, late of Marysville, Calif, to Miss Harriette A McIlhany, of the former place.

Died: on Apr 28, after a long & painful illness, Mr Josias Clements, aged 50 years, leaving a wife & 6 children to mounr his loss.

Died: on May 1, at the residence of her daughter, 574 N J ave, in the full reliance of a blissful immortality, Mrs Patience Gordon Minchin, a native of Phil, & for more than 50 years a highly esteemed & respected resident of Wash City.

Died: on Apr 25, in Gtwn, Edward Marion, infant son of Geo W & Mary Ann Varnell. Thus in one short week has the mother been called from her last of earth to embrace the sainted infant that had passed to heavenly bliss.
+
Died: on May 2, in Gtwn, of bilious congestion, Mrs Mary Ann, consort of Mr Geo W Varnell, in her 41st year, leaving a large family of interesting children, a doating husband, & numerous friends to mourn with them this bereavement. Her funeral is today at 3½ P M, from the late residence on market, near Bridge st.

Died: on May 2, in Alexandria, Va, Mrs Mgt Rock, relict of Richd Rock, in her 67th year. Her funeral is today at 4 o'clock P M, from her late residence in Alexandria.

Died: on Apr 30, at **Fort Plain**, Montg Co, N Y, Jos F Moffett, of Wash, D C, age 32 years.

FRI MAY 4, 1855
Calif: in a dispute at the U S Hotel, at Monterey, Jeremiah McMahon & Dr Sandford shot each other with revolvers, resulting in the immediate deaths of both. The quarrel arose from a law suit. McMahon was from Phil & Dr Sandford from N Y.

Advices from Utah to Mar 1: 1-Col Steptoe's appointment to succeed Brigham Young as Govn'r caused great discontent, & ptns were circulated praying the reappointment of Young. 2-Dr Garland Hart, the Indian agent of Utah, had arrived at Salt Lake City & entered on his duties. 3-Walker, the famous Utah chief, died near Fillmore city on Jan 29.

Mr Wm B May, of Roxbury, Mass, accompanied the famous nunnery cmte on their visit to Rosbury, stating that he had a particular reason for wishing to see the inside of a convent, because he had a sister in a convent in Emmittsburg, Md, whom he believed he should not be allowed to see if he should attempt to, & whom he had reason to believe was detained as a nun against her will. The Boston Daily Advertiser makes the following statement, putting a different face upon the matter: "Within a few days past this gentlemen has visited Emmittsburg, where he found that he was admitted freely to the presence of his sister, & allowed unrestrained conversation with her. She had no wish to leave the establishment." Even if the rules of the convents here were as stringent as is pretended, they could not stand against the process of the regular courts of law.

Wm Franklin Carr has been sentenced to be hung on May 25 for the murder of his own father, in Holmes Co, Mo, on Sep 17 last.

Mrs Betsey Leonard, widow of the Late Capt John Leoanrd, of Keene, N H, is just 100 years old, & is expected to take a trip to Boston next week to visit some friends. Her husband was one of the "minute men" & fought at Bunker Hill. Mrs Leonard was married to her late husband in 1775. –Boston Herald

The Balt Sun gives a list of the oldest Postmasters in the U S, at the head of which stands the name of John Bickel, of Jonestown, Lebanon Co, Pa. He speaks of his appointment as follows: My father's name was John Bickel, & I was commissioned John Bickel, jr. My father was in the Revolutionary war, & lived to be 89 years old. He died about 9 years ago. I was appointed Postmaster under Jefferson's administration, by Gideon Granger, on Sep 23, 1802, so that I have held the ofc 53 years next Sept. I am now 82 years old, & do all my business myself.

Mrd: on May 1, in PG Co, by Rev J Scrivener, Mr Horace E Nichols, of Fairfax Co, Va, to Miss Charlotte Martin, of PG Co, Md.

Mrd: on May 1, at E st Baptist Church, by Rev G W Samson, B T Swart, of Fauquier Co, Va, to Sallie A, daughter of Jos Bryan, of Wash City.

Died: on May 3, in her 40th year, Mary A, consort of Edmund J Ellis. Her funeral is today at 2 o'clock P M, from her residence on 8th st, between G & H sts.

Balt, May 3. Mr Powell, who was under trial in the U S District Court charged with purloining money from letters in the Balt post ofc, was today acquitted. Hon Reverdy Johnson & Z Collins Lee were counsel for the accused, both of whom made powerful efforts in his behalf. Mr Lee was peculiarly happy & eloquent.

Circuit Court of Wash Co, D C-in Equity. Jas Lynch vs Hugh Lockery et al. Trustee reported he sold a leasehold for 99 years in part of lot 17 in square 729 to Hugh Lockery for $1,875, & he has complied with the terms of sale. –Jno A Smith, clerk

SAT MAY 5, 1855
Hay! Just received per schnr **J Holmes**, & now landing at Page's wharf, foot of 7th st, a prima article of Timothy Hay. Apply to Mattingly Brothers, on the wharf.

Teacher wanted: the trustees of the Female Academy of Somerset Co, wish to employ a lady who has had experience in teaching as Principal of the school. Salary will be $450 per anum. Address the cmte at Princess Anne, Somerset Co, Md.
–Saml W Jones, Matthias Roberts

For sale: a fine bob-tail Bay Horse. Works well in single or double harness, & rides well under saddle. Can be seen at my Livery Stable, High st, Gtwn, D C.
–Jas F Essex

For sale: the valuable estate in Albemarle known as **Farmington**: the property of the late Gen Bernard Peyton, lying in said county, on the waters of Ivy Creek, 4 miles above Charlottesville, adjoining the lands of Messrs Wm Garth, John T Randolph, & others, containing, by recent survey, 881 acres. The dwlg is of brick, spacious, renovated & improved within the past 2 years. –T J Peyton, Richmond, Va

MON MAY 7, 1855

The following are the present Ofcrs & Managers of the Wash Nat'l Monument Society, all of whom, except the Pres & 2nd Vice Pres, were elected on Feb 22 last:

Franklin Pierce, Pres of the U S & ex-officio Pres
Vespasian Ellis, 1st Vice Pres
John T Towers, Mayor of Wash & ex-officio 2nd Vice Pres
Geo H Plant, 3rd Vice Pres
John M McCalla, Treas
Chas C Tucker, Sec

Managers:

Henry Addison	Thos D Sandy	Jos Libby, sr
Chas R Belt	Jos H Bradley	Thos A Brooke
French S Evans	Saml C Busey	John N Craig
Chas W Davis	Jas Gordon	
Saml E Douglas	Robt T Knight	

On Thu 3 of the Cincinnati police arrived in N Y having in custody Lorenzo Chapin, Amasa Chapin, & Benj Erie, who, with Benj W Kimball & others arrested, stand indicted for fraudulently obtaining $4,509 from the Atlantic Mutual Ins Co, being the amount of insurance upon good which they alleged to have had on board the steamboat **Martha Washington**, which was burnt some years ago on the Mississippi river. The accused were taken before Justice Connolly & committed to prison to await trial.

Four U S sailors, Richd Biddle, Saml Kays, David Hazard, & John McNenny, had made application, throught their counsel, Chas L Jones, to be brought severally before the Circuit Court on a writ of habeas corpus. The first 2 were tried some months ago by a court-martial at theNorfolk navy yard, & the last two were tried by a court-martial at N Y, by order of the Sec of the Navy, & convicted of the offences charged, & sentenced to service at hard labor in the penitentiary of this District. Not having been convicted of any offence punishable with imprisonment at hard labor, they pray writs of habeas corpus may issue to bring them before the court; & if it shall be found that their confinement is illegal & contrary to law, they may be discharged. This morning the 4 sailors were brought into the Circuit Court by the Warden of the penitentiary. Chas Lee Jones argued in their behalf, & was replied to by P B Key, for the U S. The prisoners were remanded, the Court reserving its decision in this case, which will probably be pronounced next week. -Star

Appointments: 1-Robt M McAram to be Lt in the navy. 2-Wm D Whiting to be master in the navy. 3-Arthur S Nevitt to be postmaster at New Orleans, vice R W Adams, declined.

For sale: a thorough-bred Canadian Stallion, 7 years old, kind & sound, & a fine driver in single harness. Can be seen at John R Sutton's, Franklin Stable, 8th & D st.

Mrd: on May 2, by Rev Mason Noble, Wm M McCauley to Miss Virginia Guiton.

Circuit Court of Wash Co, D C. Ptn of Jonathan Seaver, Geo Shoemaker & others. The Surveyor of this county having made his return to the order of this Court, passed on Nov 28 last, to lay out a private road or way from the Quaker burying ground to the county road in this county, & having laid out the same across the land of the heirs of John Q Adams, it is this 2nd day of May, 1855, ordered by the Court that the said report & return of the said Surveyor be confirmed. –Jno A Smith, clerk

Orphans Court of Wash Co, D C. Letters testamentary on the personal estate of John Agg, late of Wash Co, deceased. –E J Middleton, exc

TUE MAY 8, 1855
A London journalist, announcing the death of Mr Jas Brown, of Boston, ["the partner of the house of Messrs Little, Brown & Co,"] says that thereby literature has lost a very useful friend & the publishing interest of Great Britain a backbone of support. His orders in England have varied from L20,000 to L50,000, during the 3 months of the year he was in London.

Mr J Silk Buckingham has begun to publish his autobiography in England. The two first volumes, though extending to upward of 800 pages, only bring the narrative down to 1815, leaving the incidents of the subsequent 40 years, & as much longer as Mr Buckingham may live, to be recorded.

Court of Claims: the undersigned has opened a Law Ofc at the corner of 14th & F sts, in the rear of Willard's Hotel. –John S Tyson

Mrd: on May 7, by Rev John E Bates, of Indiana, Albin Schoeph, late of Hungary, to Miss Julia B, daughter of the late Rev Wm Kesley, of Wash City.

Died: on May 7, Elizabeth, infant daughter of Jas & Eliz J Wimer, aged 9 months. Her funeral is this afternoon at 4 o'clock.

Six cent reward: ran away from the subscriber on May 2, 1855, Jas McNamee, an indentured apprentice to the Coachsmithing. Reward will be paid on delivery in Wash, D C. All persons are forewarned against harboring or employing said apprentice. –M McDermott

Valuable Rappanannock & Fauquier land for sale: having determined to remove to the West, the subscriber offers his farm for sale: contains between 700 & 800 acres, on the Rappahannock river, 8 miles from the Manassas Gap Railroad; with a large new fire-proof brick dwlg, with all suitable out-houses, in good repair. Address the subscriber at **Fleet Hill**, Rappahannock Co, Va. –Saml Chancellor

WED MAY 9, 1955
Trustee's sale of valuable real estate: by decree of the Circuit Court of Wash Co, D C, passed in a cause wherein H B Sweeny, treasurer, & others are cmplnts & Dowling's heirs & others are dfndnts: sale on Jun 4 next of lots 10 & 11 in square 566, on north F st, between 2nd & 3rd sts, & there is upon each lot a 2 story brick house & basement. –John F Ennis, trustee

Judicial appointments in Delaware. 1-Hon Saml M Harringon, L L D, appointed Chief Justice of the State of Delaware, vice Chief Justice Booth, deceased. 2-Hon John W Houston appointed Associate Judge of the Superior Court of that State, vice Judge Harrington. 3-Geo P Fisher appointed Atty Genr'l of the State of Delaware. –Phil American

The following Magistrates of D C have been appointed to constitute the Levy Court of Wash Co, under acts of Congress:
West of Rock Creek: Joshua Pierce, Hamilton Loughborough.
East of Rock Creek: Henry Haw, Zachariah Walker.
City of Gtwn: Robt White, Lewis Carbery, & Jos N Fearson.
City of Wash: Saml Drury, Geo W Riggs, Jas A Kennedy, & Geo McNeir.

Mr Hammond Howe, inventor of Howe's Horizontal Arched Truss Bridge, who recently sojourned for a brief season in Wash City while transacting business with the Patent Ofc, died at Wheeling, on his way toward his home in Cincinnati, of congestion of the lungs. He was 58 years of age.

Died: on May 6, after a long & painful illness, which he bore with the patience & fortitude of a true Christian, Wm W S Kerr, aged 28 years.
+
The remains of the late Mr W W S Kerr were yesterday followed to the grave by the Light Infty Corps, Wash Lodge of Odd Fellows, & many mourning friends, accompanied by a band of music.

Died: on May 7, in Wash City, at the residence of her son, C F Lowrey, after a lingering illness, Mrs Mary Ehney, late of Charleston, S C, in her 62nd year. Her friends & those of Mr C F Lowery are invited to attend her funeral this afternoon, at 4 o'clock, from 318 6th st, near N Y ave.

Orphans Court of Wash Co, D C. Letters of administration on the personal estate of Jos T Walker, late of Wash Co, deceased. –David Walker, adm

Buffalo, May 8. Advices received from *Fort Leavenworth* of the murder of Malcolm Clark by Lawyer McCrea, on account of election difficulty. McCrea jumped into the river after committing the fatal deed to escape, but was overtaken & conveyed to the guard-house. It is rumored that McCrea has been lynched & his house burnt.

Boston, May 8. The ship **Living Age**, reported lost in the China Seas, is the American vessel of that name, bound from Shanghai to N Y with a cargo of teas valued at $400,000. She was heavily insured in Boston & N Y.

Llangolen for sale: the farm, formerly the residence of Hon Cuthbert Powell, deceased: containing 792 acres, in Loudoun Co, at the foot of the Blue Ridge Mountain, within 3 miles of Uppervile, Fauquier Co; improvement consist of a stuccoed brick dwlg house, of modern style, overseer's house, carriage house, ice house, barn, negro quarters, & other bldgs. Price $40,000: $5,000 at the time of possession; one third of the whole amount at the expiration of 12 months thereafter, & the remaining two-thirds on Jan 1, 1863. Interest on the deferred payments to be paid annually, & all to be well secured. Address J G Gray, M D, near Upperville, Fauquier Co, Va.

THU MAY 10, 1855
Capt Button, of barque **Clara Winsor**, arrived at N Y from Port au Prince, reports that on Mar 19 he saw a wreck, with 2 men standing on the bow waving their hats; hove to & got out a boat & succeeded in taking them off. The wreck proved to be the schnr **John Clark**, Capt McRay, hence for Jacmel. The men stated that they were all that was left out of 7 men that sailed in the above schnr from N Y on Mar 3, bound for Jacmel; that on Mar 7 a squall struck the schnr & the vessel filled with water. The two saved are Robt McRay [capt's son] & Chas Lovell.

Edw J Roye, one of the candidates for Pres of Liberia, was some 10 years since a barber in Terre Haute, Indiana, from which place he emigrated to Liberia. He is now editing & publishing a paper. He is, we believe, a pure African, certainly a black man. Stephen A Benson, the other candidate, is of unmixed African descent, went with his parents to Liberia when a mere child, before the time of Gov Ashmun's arrival in 1822, was taken captive by the natives in the war of Dec of that year, & was finally restored to his home after an absence of several months. He is the principal merchant at Bassa Cove & has filled the ofc of judge & is now the Vice Pres of Liberia. –Colonization Herald

Dress-making: Miss E E McDonald, successor to Mrs Ann H Clark, will open her summer Millinery on May 12, at her well known establishment, 71 Bridge st, 3 doors east of the Post Ofc, Gtwn.

This morning, Wm B Sloan, standing near the corner of Lake & Clark sts, engaged in the purchase of some trees there exposed for sale, a heavy iron insulator, weighing several pounds, fell from a telegraph pole above his head, striking & fracturing the fore part of his skull. His condition is critical. –Chicago Journal of May 6

Miss Anna J Oliver, late of Phil, has taken the front parlor upstairs over Miss E E McDonald's millinery establishment, to conduct the Dress making in all its different branches.

Farm for sale: contains 175 acres, in PG Co, about 10 miles from Wash City; with a very comfortable frame dwlg upon it. Possession given immediately. Inquire of Henry N Lansdale, in person or through the post ofc.

Orphans Court of Wash Co, D C. Letters of administration on the personal estate of Jos M Peerce, late of Wash Co, deceased. –Eliz C Peerce, admx

N Y, May 9. Johnson P Lee, auctioneer of N Y C, whilst getting out of the Hudson River railroad cars this morning, was struck by the hind car & so seriously injured that he died in a few minutes.

Thos F Bowie & Albert Stuart, Attys & Councellors at Law: have associated themselves for the purpose of practicing their profession before the Court of Claims, recently established by act of Congress at Wash City. Address Gen Thos F Bowie, at Upper Marlboro, Md, or Albert Stuart, at Alexandria, Va.

FRI MAY 11, 1855

Hon Walter T Colquitt, formerly a Rep & more recently a Senator in Congress from the State of Georgia, died at Macon on May 7.

Ex-Govn'r Seabury Ford, of Ohio, died at his residence at Benton, Ohio, on May 9.

The U S brig-of-war **Dolphin** sailed from Norfolk on Wed for the coast of Africa. List of her ofcrs: Lt Comm Edw R Thomson, Lts: J M Wainwright & Geo M Ranson, Passed Assist Surgeon Edw Shippen, Purser Geo R Griswold, Acting Master N H Vanzandt, Passed Midshipmen: O F Johnson & Austin Pendergrast.

Farm for sale: about 100 acres in Fairfax Co, Va, 3½ miles above Gtwn, with a new frame dwlg house, with necessary outbldgs. Inquire of J F Brown, War Dept.

At the Norfolk Navy Yard on Sat, Lewis Armstrong, about 14 years of age, son of Capt Wm M Armstrong, U S Navy, was walking across the staging of one of the ships there, missed his footing, & fell 30 feet to the ground. He was not discovered for 2 hours when some carpenters heard his groans. His recovery is considered extremely doubtful.

Capt Jas Munroe, of the 6th Infty U S Army, has resigned, to take effect from May 9.

Administrator's sale of valuable stallion: by order of the Orphans Court of Wash Co, D C: the horse called Moscow, belonging to the estate of the late Chas W Stuart. Public sale on May 17 in front of the auction store. –Chas B Wallach, adm –Jas C McGuire, auct

Desirable bldg lot at auction: on Jun 12, on the premises, by deed of trust from Basil Lancaster, dated Sep 22, 1848, recorded in Liber J A S No 1, folios 380, of the land records for Wash Co: lot 28 in square 197, fronting on 15th st. –Jas H Collins, trustee –Jas C McGuire, auct

Died: on May 9, suddenly, at the residence of his son-in-law, Mr Thos H Osbourn, PG Co, Md, Mr S E Scott, formerly a merchant of Gtwn, D C, aged 54 years.

The "Organ" of yesterday says: during the progress of the trial of L Mackall vs the Corp of Gtwn, in the Circuit Court on Tue, Mr John Mountz, the Clerk of the Corp, was called as a witness, & upon inquiry he stated he had been Clerk of that Corp for 64 years, ever since 1791. His intellect & memory are very clear. He is also Clerk of the Levy Court of D C.

Nominations for Wash City Ofcrs: [All nominees of the Anti-Know-Nothings.]
Mr Robt J Roche for City Collector
Mr Wm J McCormick for City Register
Mr S T Abert for City Surveyor
For Alderman:
Wm B Magruder	DR A Y P Garnett	J C Fitzpatrick
Thos Miller	Jacob Gideon	Dearborn Johnson

For Common Council:
Chas Abert	Thos B Entwistle	T E Hutchinson
E H Fuller	Erastus M Chapin	W H Thompson
John H Eaton	Richd H Laskey	J W Meade
Wm Orme	Jas A Kennedy	Saml Pumphrey
F Jefferson	Dr Noble Young	Henry A Clarke
Thos J Fisher	J L Clubb	Saml Taylor

For rent: several very pleasant apts, furnished or unfurnished: near the State Dept. Apply at 442 15th st, & N Y ave, over Dr Nairn's drug store, or at 216 Pa ave, adjoining Willard's Hotel.

Wash Corp: 1-Ptn of Mrs Ann Best, praying the remission of a fine: referred to the Cmte of Claims. 2-Cmte of Claims: asked to be discharged from the consideration of the ptns of Mary Ann Phillips & John Joy: which was agreed to. Same cmte: bill for the relief of Wm B Cheever: laid over.

For rent: commodious 2 story brick dwlg on the corner of B & 8th sts, adjoining the residence of Col Seaton, lately occupied by Col Fitz Henry Warren. Fixtures for gas have been recently introduced in the bldg. Possession given about May 15. Apply to the subscriber on 8th st, between E & F sts. –John F Boone

Wash Musical Convention: on Tues morning: following ticket unanimously elected: Pres: T J Magruder, of Wash. Vice Presidents: John Swentzel, J W Alby, & Chas W Logan, of Balt; Wm T Webb & W H Murphy, of Norfolk, Va; F A Tucker, of Wash. Secs: F Glenroy, of Wash; R B Logan, of Balt. Treas: Thos McGill, of Wash.

Cincinnati, May 9. G H Godey & Eliz Williams were arrested here today for counterfeiting $25,000 spurious bills on the Farmers' Bank of Charleston, S C. The notes were found in the possession of the accused.

Desirable country seat for sale: about 30 acres with a very superior Brick bldg: good stone kitchen, & necessary out-bldgs: in Loudoun Co, Va, about 40 miles from Alexandria, Va: commanding view of the Blue Ridge Mountain. Apply to Amos Denham, 294 First Ward, Wash, D C.

SAT MAY 12, 1855

Household & kitchen furniture at auction on: May 16, at the residence of Mr S C Wroe, on C, between 2nd & 3rd sts, near the Trinity Church. -Green & Scott, aucts

Trustee's sale of valuable improved property in Jackson alley at auction: on Jun 11 next, by deed of trust from Jos Davis & Geo W Garnett to the subscriber, dated Apr 5, 1854, recorded in Liber J A S 77, folios 133 thru 136, of the land records for Wash Co, D C: part of lot 41 in square 10, near the lot on which John T Catlet resides & adjoining the premises on which Mrs Foy resides, with a large 3 story brick bldg & brick wall enclosing the entire lot. –Benj Charlton, trustee -Green & Scott, aucts

New & excellent top buggy at auction: on Sat, in front of the Auction rooms, by order of the Orphans Court of Wash Co, D C. Buggy belonging to the estate of the late J D Brown. -Jas C McGuire, auct

U S Patent Ofc, Wash, D C: May 10, 1855. Ptn of Saml Slocum, of Smithfield, R I, praying for the extension of a patent granted to him on Sep 30, 1841, for an improvement in machines for sticking pins into paper, for 7 years from the expiration of said patent, which takes place on Sep 30, 1855. –Chas Mason, Com'r of Patents

Stray cow came to my premises about 4 months ago. Owner is to prove property, pay charges, & take her away in the course of 2 weeks, or she will be disposed of according to law. –Jos Frey, 11th st, near Coleman's brick kiln.

Potatoes for sale: Maine Mercer Potatoes. –N B Hartley, 111 Water st, Gtwn.

Mrd: on May 10, by Rev W C Steel, Mr Thos C Mockabee to Miss Mary E Jones, both of Wash City.

Mrd: on May 8, by Rev Mr Hodges, Mr John E Lacy to Miss Jane R Lynch, of Chas Co, Md.

Landing of the Pilgrims of Md: the Cmte of Arrangements of the Young Catholic's Friend Society, of Gtwn, D C, having chartered the safe & commodious well known steamer **Powhatan**, Capt Mitchell, announce to the public that the steamer will leave Gtwn on May 14, at 1 P M, & Alexandria 1½ O'clock, touching at different landings on the Potomac for passengers going & returning; staying 2 nights at Piney Point. Tickets for the round trip, including everything: $5.00. This is in celebration of the Landing of the Pilgrims. Apply to Geo Mattingly, at the Steamboat Wharf, Wash; & John A Roach, Union st, Alexandria, Va. –B J Semmes, John L Kidwell, John J Bogue, Francis Harper, Andrew Goddard

Farm for sale: subscriber offers his valuable farm called ***Oakland***, in Chas Co, Md, convenient to Benedict, my shipping place, 1 mile from churches, & the same distance from the Misses Martin's flourishing Female Academy. The dwlg is a 2 story brick, in a beautiful oaked grove; kitchen & overseer's house, meat house, ice-house, corn-house, granary, carriage house, stables & barns: 1,000 acres more or less. –Alfred W Gardiner

MON MAY 14, 1855
The steamer **Keystone State**, at Phil, from Savannah, reports that on Fri last, in Delaware Bay, she was run into by the schnr **Adrian**, bound for Fall river. The **Adrian** sunk in 15 minutes. Three of the crew were saved; but Geo B Mallett, the captain, & Prince A Lovell, the cook, were lost. Off Bombay Hook, at 2 o'clock on Sat, the steamer was again run into by the schnr **Little Tour**. The schnr filled & went down in 10 minutes, but all hands were saved.

An autographed letter of Geo Washington was recently sold at auction in London for fifty pounds sterling.

On May 4, Willis Hester, aged about 41, was executed at Pittsborough, N C. He was a native of Orange Co, where he committed the last crime for which he suffered. His case was removed to Chatham for trial, & there he was executed.

On May 2, at Memphis, Tenn, a young man, in a spirit of levity, said to Mrs Green Warmley, a respectable lady in delicate health, that her husband had been seriously injured by a dray running over him. The shock caused her to faint, & in a short time she was a corpse.

Orphans Court of Wash Co, D C. Letters of administration on the personal estate of Mary Ebney, late of Wash Co, deceased. –C F Lowrey, adm

Died: on May 13, Thomas, infant son of John P & Eliza J Faherty, aged 7 months. His funeral is this afternoon at 2 o'clock, from his father's residence, 5th & G sts.

Farm in D C for sale: the subscriber offers the valuable farm upon which he resides, 4 miles from Wash City, fronting on Rock Creek Church road: contains 100 acres; with a good dwlg house on the premises. Apply to A Bielaski, on the ground, or at 26 General Land Ofc.

Having this day, Mar 13, 1855, sold my entire stock of Fancy Goods, good will, & fixtures in store, 18 Pa ave, I do most respectfully beg leave to call the particular attention to my friends & customers to the immediate settlement of their accounts, either by cash or notes at short date. –Prathby J Stevens

TUE MAY 15, 1855
Appointments in the Patent Ofc: Wm Chauncy Langdon, of Ky, an Assist Examiner, has been promoted to be Chief Examiner of Patents, at $2,500. Thos H Dodge, of N H; Wm Read, of Dela; Isaac D Toll, of Mich; & Amos T Jenckes, of R I, to be Assist Engineers, at $1,800.

E Warren Moise, the U S Atty for the Eastern district of Louisiana, on May 5, announced to the Circuit Court at New Orleans that he had resigned his ofc. The resignation is understood to be because of the selection by the Gov't of Hon Isaac E Morse to prosecute the charge of mail robbery against W G Kendall, the late Postmaster of New Orleans. [May 24th newspaper: W G Kendall has again been arrested on a similar charge & we understand, will be examined next week. New Orleans Bulletin of May 17.]

Saml H Huntington, of Conn, was yesterday appointed Clerk of the Court of Claims.

Rev Dr Barry, Roman Catholic Vicar Genr'l of Savannah, Ga, has been appointed Bishop of that diocese, vice Bishop Reynolds, deceased. Confirmation by the Pope is required.

The late Wm Maginn, L L D, of the Univ of Dublin, flourished for many years as the Sir Morgan O'Doherty of the Scottish magazines & other periodicals. Long before his death he obtained the title of the Modern Rabelais.

Wash City Items. 1-Miss H N Henshaw has been promoted to a teachership in the 3rd District Public School of Wash in the place of Mrs J Wall, a meritorious teacher, who has resigned, & Miss Eliz Ellen Ashdown, a graduate of one of our public schools, has been elected assist teacher in Primary No 2. 2-Mr Wm J Williams has contracted to build the new Western Market House for $9,125, upon the plan of Messrs Baldwin & Nenning, architects.

We learn from the Panama Star that Mr J E Baker, proprietor of the Verandah Hotel; Mr Robt K Carter, purser of the Pacific Steam Navigation Co; Dr Watson, an American physician, for some time resident in Tabago; a German physician, name unknown, & another German gentleman, were all drowned in Tabago Bay on Apr 25 by the upsetting of a sailboat.

The little daughter of Mr Collins, a laboring man residing on G st, died on Sunday from the effects of being burnt by her clothes accidentally taking fire on Fri. She was 10 years old.

Mr J F Polk is to lecture at Temperance Hall this evening on the early history of Maryland.

Died: on May 14, after a short but painful illness, Benj Ellin, a native of Sneath, Yorkshire, England, & for the last 15 years a resident of Wash City. His funeral will take place this afternoon, at 3 o'clock, from his late residence, Q & 16th sts.

Phil, May 14. The Jury in the case of Jas G Barnard, charged in the U S Circuit Court with engaging in the slave trade & piracy in the brig **Grey Eagle**, have returned a verdict of not guilty.

Rochester, May 12. Martin Eastwood, found guilty last night of the murder of Edw Brereton, was today sentenced to be hung on Jun 29; since which Lewis Lerock, implicated in the same murder, has made a confession, & has been sentenced to 8 years in the State prison. [May 17th newspaper: Martin Eastwood, a young man, said he did not intend to kill Brereton, but he was under the influence of intoxicating drinks, & the excitement by his striking me with a stone, I did not know what I was about.]

Desirable Pew for sale in Trinity Church. Apply to Pollard Webb, ofc on Pa ave, 7 doors east of Nat'l Hotel.

Mr S B Wright, of Burlington, Iowa, was robbed of $1,000 in money & $2,000 in drafts, on board a steamboat, while on his way to St Louis, Mo, & a Mr Nutt also lost $50 in money & a breastpin.

WED MAY 16, 1855
The Executive Cmte, on behalf of the First Regt Third Brigade of the Militia of D C, will hold their first Grand Ball at the Nat'l Theatre on May 21, 1855. Prof Munder has volunteered his services as Floor Manager. Tickets can be procured at Flint's Hotel; Wm F Bayly's Stationery Store; M A Stevens' Fancy Store; Wilson & Hayward's Union Hall; & of any of the Exec Cmte. Cmte of Reception:

Col Hickey
Col Riley
Maj Keyworth
Adj Bacon
Surgeon Morgan
Quartermaster McCollum
Qr Mas Sgt King
Capt Davis
Capt Towers
Capt Bright

Capt Tait
Capt Key
Capt Peck
Capt Schwarzman
Capt Devers
Lt Com Mulloy
Capt Sheckell
Capt Jamison
Capt Reese

Managers on the part on the Military:
Wash Light Infty: Serg Jas E Powers; Henry Warner; Chas E Nelson
Nat'l Greys: Serg Eagan; Corp Maguire; Jno Bradley
Boone Rifles: Pioneer Robinson; Serg Buckingham; Henry Green
Nat'l Guards: Ensign Lloyd; Serg Bishop; Priv Johnson
Montgomery Guards: Serg McEniry; Sec O'Sullivan; Priv O'Leary
Pres' Mounted Guard: Serg Hayward; Sam Owens; John T Evans
German Yeagers: Serg Ruppell; Conrad Finkman; Julius Viedt
American Riflemen: Serg Gibson; Corp Champion; John Y Donn
Wash Highlanders: Serg Campbell; Jas Harrover; Andrew Bain
Scot Guards: Serg Keyworth, Geo McKean; Chas Masi
Union Guards: Qr Mas Donelly; Serg Harrison; Priv O'Callahan
Marion Rifles: Serg Foxwell; Henry Keefer; Serg Galt

Managers on the part of the Citizens:
Geo Washington Parke Custis
Hon J T Towers
Walter Lenox
Peter Force
Silas H Hill
W W Corcoran
B B French

G Parker
J H Eaton
W H Winter
A Provost
J F Coyle
R Wallach
Chas Maury

S Redfern	W F Bayly
R Smith	M Brown
W T Dove	Dr W B Magruder
John Ennis	S P Franklin
J P Pepper	Vespasian Ellis
S C Barney	R Coyle
G S Gideon	W H Thomas
H Cameron	H Taylor
C S Wallach	J D Hoover
H Sweeney	Arch Campbell
E S Pendleton	Jas Adams
Franck Taylor	Thos Parsens
Edw Owen	E C Morgan
Chas Kloman	J A Linton
Francis Mohun	Jos Gales
E Doyle	Andrew Hancock
Wm Dougherty	H S Polkinhorn
A N Clements	A Dickins
G Ennis	J H Kirkwood
C Dunnington	A T Kickhoffer
John L Wirt	A S H White
R J Roche	S Lewis
J L Henshaw	G A Jillard
J W Forney	J J Joyce
T Carbery	P A Hoe
Jas G Berret	E Wheeler
C Hill	J C McGuire
C Wheeler	W J McCormick
Dr Maynard	R Stuart
T S Donoghue	Jas Clarke
B F Middleton	J C Fitzpatrick
E F Bell	J H McBlair
B J Semmes	W E Spalding
C B Calvert	Alex Lee
H A Willard	Thos Berry

Exec Cmte:

Lt Clarke, Infty	Lt Simms, Amer Rifles
Lt Shekell, Nat Greys	Lt Wallingsford, S Guard
Lt Sanderson, B Rifles	Lt Flint, Pres M Guard
Lt Riley, Mount Guards	Lt Rowe, Marion Rifles
Lt Debile, Ger Yeagers	Lt Briggs, Union Guards

Capt Reese, Highlanders
Capt J Y Davis, of the Light Infty, Treasurer

Wash Corp: election of Comr's of Election for the several Wards:

Jas Carroll	Eleazer Brown	J H Boss
Jas M Dorsett	J H G McCutchen	Wm P Ferguson
J W Delaway	Chas C Martin	Jas A Brown
John M Donn	Jackson Pumphrey	Edmund Barry
Wm P Shedd	Edw S Allen	Saml S Briggs
Joshiah Melvin	Thos C Donn	Nimrod Garrettson
Saml Grubb	J P McKean	Henry N Ober

A German, Peter Ritz Gatcher, aged 51, & Wm Jones, 23, from the Isle-of-Man, stepped from the emigrant train on Friday at this depot, when stopped on a bridge to take on wood & water, & they fell 60 feet & were killed instantly. –Ashtabula [Ohio] Telegraph, May 12.

Mrd: on May 14, at Balt, by Rev Dr Backus, Nathl Pope Causin, of Wash, to Eliza Mactier, daughter of Mr Danl Warfield, of Balt.

Died: on May 14, Saml Whitall, in his 81st year. His funeral will take place this afternoon, at 4½ o'clock, from his late residence, **Belle Vue**, Gtwn Heights, Gtwn.

Died: on May 15, at **Mount Henry**, near Wash City, in his 73rd year, Henry Young Naylor. His funeral will be this afternoon at 4½ o'clock, from the residence of his brother, Col Henry Naylor, a short distance across the Eastern Branch bridge.

Orphans Court of Wash Co, D C. In the case of Jas F Haliday, administrator of Christopher R Byrne, deceased, the administrator & Court have appointed Jun 5 next, for the final settlement of said estate, of the assets in the hands of the administrator. –Ed N Roach, Reg/o wills

THU MAY 17, 1855

Capt Henry Coffee, 1st Artl, Assist Professor of Ethics at the U S Military Academy, having accepted the appointment of Professor of English Literature at the Univ of Pa, vice Prof Henry Reed, lost in the Arctic, has tendered the resignation of his commission in the U S Army.

Treaty was made & concluded at Calapooia Creek, Douglas Co, Oregon Territory, on Nov 29, 1854, by Joel Palmer, Superintendent of Indian Affairs, on the part of the U S, & the chiefs & heads of the confederated bands of the Umpqua tribe of Indians & of the Calapooias residing in Umpqua Valley.

Jas C McGuire, auct, on Tue sold the lot on the n e corner of D & 7th sts, fronting 25 feet on 7th st & 54 feet on D st, for $8,050 to Mr W B Kibbey; & Messrs Green & Scott, on the same day, sold lot 25 in square 728, fronting on North A st 24 feet, between 1st & 2nd sts east, for 22½ cents per foot. This lot is about 127 feet deept.

An old colored man, known as Uncle Phil, in the service of & we believe belonging to Mr Isaac Skaggs, who resides 2 miles beyond Bladensburg, was yesterday fatally injured by the train of passenger cars. He was driving a pair of oxen before a cart, immediately in front of Mr Skaggs' residence, & being deaf, did not know the train was approaching. His injuries were severe & he was brought to the Infirmary in Wash City. He remained unconscious & died last evening.

John S Meehan returns his heartfelt thanks to the members of the Columbia Fire Co, & his fellow citizens, for saved his dwlg house from injury, when his stable was destroyed by fire yesterday morning.

For rent: brick house on the corner of Mass ave & 10th sts. Apply to Geo T Langley, on L st, between 9th & 10th sts.

Lucinda C Nevers, of **Long Meadow**, Mass, recovered $5,249.31 of Saml C Booth for injuries sustained by the bite of dfndnt's dog, at the present session of the Supreme Court at Springfield, Mass.

Affray at Norfolk, Va, on Sunday, in the bar-room of Mr Harrison, between 2 boatmen from Staten Island, John Decker & Wm A Gosline, & John Murphy, of Norfolk. Murphy was waylaid on his return home & murdered in cold blood. The murderers were arrested & are now in jail.

N Y, May 15. The barque **Grapeshot** returned to this port this afternoon from the Canary Islands, with Baker, the alleged murderer of Wm Poole. The **Grapeshot** arrived off Palmos in 17 days from this port, & laid in & off till the ship **Isabella Jewett** hove in sight, when she boarded her & captured the fugitive.

Refrigerators for sale: Geo W Wight, La ave, opposite Bank of Wash.

Notice of the Removal of the Land Ofc from Clinton to Warsaw, in the State of Missouri. Given under my hand at Wash City May 15, 1855. –John Wilson, Com'r of the Gen Land Ofc.

FRI MAY 18, 1855
From Cuba: The prisoner J H Felix is kept still here, & hopes are entertained by his friends that he will be given up to the U S. If demand had been made for him in due form no doubt he would have been released long since.

Obit-died: the Columbia papers record the death of D J McCord, in that place, after a brief illness. He at one time was the State Reporter, a Trustee of the S C College, a member of the Legislature, & Pres of the Branch Bank of the State in Columbia. -Charleston News [No death date given-current item.]

Mrs Geo Clinton, who died in N Y on May 12, was the youngest daughter of Walter Franklin, who, at the middle of the last century, was the wealthiest merchant in N Y C. She was born in the old mansion house in Cherry st, now known as Franklin square, which was afterwards occupied by Gen Washington. She inherited it from her father & lived in it up to the time of her death. She was married to Geo Clinton, a brother of Gov De Witt Clinton; & in the same house, a short time after, De Witt Clinton himself was married to her sister, & on the same evening citizen Genet was married to another sister, a daughter of her mother by a second marriage. During her long life Mrs Clinton was respected & beloved by numerous friends. –Albany Journal

On Wed afternoon Mr Richd Rawlings, bricklayer, who resides in the 1st Ward, was badly bruised by falling from a height of about 20 feet. He is in much pain, but his life is not considered in danger.

Davis Reed, of Gtwn, was drowned on Wed last. A party of some 30 gentlemen, who had been invited to visit by the proprietor, were returning him in the steamboat Salem, when, as the vessel was passing the Observatory, a railing against which Mr Reed was leaning suddenly gave way, & he fell into the river. The night was dark & all efforts to rescue him were in vain. He was the only son of Robt Reed, the venerable Pres of the Farmers' & Mechanics' Bank, & was not only the pride & idol of his parents, but was universally respected & beloved. He was on the eve of being married to a lady of Rockville. The sad calamity seems to be deeply felt by the whole community.

Gen John H Eaton declines to be a candidate for a seat in the City Councils.

Successful bidders for the Washington Aqueduct were Mr H N Decker, of Albany, N Y, & Mr Felix Duffin, late of Ohio. Mr Decker's contract will amount to about $35,000, & Mr Duffin's to $87,000. -Union

Hamilton Loughborough, son of the late Nathan Loughborough, & not Nathan Loughborough, was inadvertently announced in our papers, was elected a member of the Board to consider the report of the codifiers for the district under the late act of Congress. He was elected by the unanimous vote of the Levy court of Wash Co, D C.

Runaways committed to the jail of Wash Co, Md: 2 negro men, Abraham Stoops, about 22 or 23; & Henry Hutchison. Both state they were recently discharged from the Md penitentiary. Owners of the above negroes are to come forth, prove their property, & take them away, else they will be discharged agreeably to law.
-Wm Logan, Sheriff

House to let: commodious brick house, with all modern improvements, on D st, between 2nd & 4th sts. Immediate possession will be given. Inquire of O Whittlesey, 21 Indiana ave.

Mrd: on May 15, by Rev Mr Hodges, John W Granger to Miss Eliz Padget, all of Wash.

Mrd: on May 15, by Rev J R Eckard, Benj S Howard, late of Beaufort District, S C, to Jane A, daughter of Henry R Schoolcraft, of Wash City.

Mrd: on May 15, by Rev John B Byrne, John Clemson, jr, of Md, to Miss Louisa, 2nd daughter of Maj Osborne Cross, U S Army.

Mrd: on May 15, by Rev Gideon H Day, Mr Richd P Mitchell to Miss Mary E Wilson, all of Bladensburg, Md.

Mrd: on May 17, at the Wesley Chapel Parsonage, by Rev R L Dashiell, Mr Thos M Weems to Mrs Mary E Franklin, both of Anne Arundel Co, Md.

Died: on May 17, Sarah Ann, daughter of Saml J Johnston, aged 15 years. Her funeral will be this afternoon at 2 o'clock, from her father's residence, 323 North B st.

Died: on May 15, at **Mount Henry**, near Wash City, in his 73rd year, Wm Young Naylor.

Died: on May 16, in Balt, Md, Saml Caughy, aged 53 years.

Died: on May 16, J D Read, in his 31st year. His funeral will be from the residence of his father, on Gay st, Gtwn, this afternoon at 5 o'clock.
+
Masonic: Members of the Potomac Lodge No 5, Gtwn D C, are to meet this day to attend the funeral of brother J D Reed. –M Adler, sec
+
[May 19th newspaper: the body of the late Mr Reed of Gtwn, was found very near where he was drowned.]

Information wanted of Jas Totten, of Phil, but a resident of Wash for the last 4 or 5 years, prior to fall of 1854, when he left for New Orleans, since which his friends can get no tidings of him. Any person knowing his whereabouts will confer a favor on his family by addressing Thos Totten, Fiddler st, No 20, Kensington, Phil.

SAT MAY 19, 1855

The late Mr Jas Johnson, who died in Boston week before last, was a native of Andover & unmarried. The Andover Advertiser states that he has left an estate of $500,000 or more. This large amount is to be divided equally between his brothers & sisters. The two brothers & one of the sisters reside in North Andover. The wife of Rev Asa Cummings, of Portland, Me, editor of the Christian Mirror, & the widow of the late Dr Dale, of Gloucester, are the other 2 heirs to this property. The portion of each will probably exceed $100,000. The part of the property which falls to the lot of the editor of the Christian Mirror will be bestowed upon a liberal & honest man. -Salem Gaz

Wagon & Tavern Stand, Gtwn, D C: for sale at public auction, on Jun 8 next, by a decree of the Circuit Court of Wash Co, D C: the whole of lot 16, in the original plan of Gtwn, D C, with the improvements thereon, part of the estate of the late deceased Wm Nelson. This lot lies near the market-house, between Bridge st & Prospect st, & fronts 66 feet on each st. –John Marbury, trustee -Ed S Wright, auct

On Tue last John O Day was drowned in the Potomac, having accidentally fallen from a boat between the White House & **Fort Washington**.

The Tent of Washington. There were 2 tents, or rather marques, attached to the baggage of the Cmder-in Chief during the Revolutionary war. The larger, that can dine about 40 persons, formed the banqueting hall for the grand banquet given by Washington to the ofcrs of the 3 armies immediately after the surrender of Yorktown, when the victor made the feast & the vanquished were his guests. The smaller or sleeping tent has a history of touching & peculiar interest attached to it, as related by Col John Nicholas, of Va, an ofcr of the life guard. He said, although the headquarters were generally in a house, yet we always pitched the smaller tent in the yard, or immediately adjacent to the quarters, & to this tent the chief was in the constant habit of retiring to write his despatches. His orders to the ofcr of the guard were: Let me not be disturbed; when I have completed my dispatches I will come out myself. Let the expresses be mounted & in waiting. Often would a courier arrive, bloody with spurring & shouting dispatches from Gen __ to the Cmder-in-Chief. Often the travel soiled courier would have time to breathe a little after a desperate ride, till, parting the door-folds of the tent, would appear the man of mightly labors, the despatches ready sealed in his hand. The tents were originally made in Phil in Aug, 1775, under the direction of Capt Moulder, of the Revolution. They were first pitched on the heights of Cambridge, in 1775, & are now preserved in the portmanteaus in which they were carried during the whole of the war of independence. We learn that it is the intention of Mr Custis to bequeath these venerated relics of the Revolution & of Washington to the American army, to be preserved among the military archives of the nation at the seat of government; till which time they will be preserved where they have been for half a century, at **Arlington House.**

In the search for the body of Mr Reed, they also found the body of Mr Henderson, of PG Co, Md, who had left his little son in charge of of his wagon at Gtwn on Tue last, & had not been heard of afterwards.

Habeas Corpus cases. 1-Wm Wells, who, being sentenced to death for the crime of murder, was, through the clemency of Pres Fillmore, saved from that awful penalty, &, with his own assent, condemned to the penitentiary for life as an alternative. The absence of power in the Pres to impose other penalty than that in terms prescribed by the statues formed the ground of petition, which was argued by Mr Chas Lee Jones for the petititoner, & by Mr P B Key, for the U S. Decision: the Pres has the right as a sequence to use the penitentiary for the purpose. The culprit was accordingly remanded to prison. 2-The other case was of 4 U S sailors who, by virtue of the sentence of a court-marital in N Y, & one in Norfolk, were brought to the penitentiary of this District. They contended through their counsel, Mr C L Jones, that their confinement was illegal, they not having, as they state, been convicted of any offence punishable with imprisonment at hard labor under the laws of the U S or D C. Judge Dunlop pronounced the decision of the Court. He referred to the petition of Richd Biddle, who is appeared was enlisted in the naval service as a sailor in Oct, 1852, for the period of 3 years. He was tried by a general court-martial at Norfolk for mutinous conduct & language on Feb 23, 1854, convicted, & sentenced to 10 years' imprisonment at labor in the District penitentiary. Same was approved by the Pres of the U S. The jurisdiction of the court-martial had not been denied, but it was insisted that it exceeded it's authority by passing the sentence. The Circuit Court could not look beyond the record, & decided that Richd Biddle should be remanded; & that the same principal be applied to the other 3 cases. After the judgment had been pronounced Mr C L Jones, the counsel of the sailors, entered a suit of damages against the U S Marshal for the false imprisonment of his clients, & the case will be carried on appeal to the Supreme Court of the U S.

Napoleon, Emperor of the French, had a narrow escape from assassination of Apr 28, while on his way to join the Empress in her usual ride in the Champes Elysees. The Emperor, with 2 ofcrs of his household, when near the Barrier de l'Etoile, was approached by a well-dressed man, with an action indicating a desire to present a petition. He advanced within 5 or 6 paces of the Emperor, who had not observed him, when he was discovered by a policemen. As the policeman was proceeding towards him a cab was rapidly driven between them; & in the interval the individual had drawn a double-barrelled pistol, and aiming at the Emperor, discharged both barrels, but without effect. He was immediately seized by the police, but not until he had drawn another pistol & made an attempt to shoot again. One of the balls grazed the Emperor's hat. This would-be assassin is an Italian, named Pianozi, & was formerly in Garibaldi's army. He is in close confinement & will be tried about the middle of May. [May 31st newspaper: Pianozi has been executed. He refused to make any developments, & was exclaiming "Vive la Republique" as the knife fell.]

By order of distrain for rent due to Wm A Bradley by Elias Ellicott, I will expose at Public Sale for cash, on the premises, at the Iron Foundry in Gtwn, D C, on May 25, the goods & chattels of said Elias Ellicott. –H R Maryman, constable

+

Wash, May 18, 1855. This is to inform the readers of the above that the distraint for Rent is in direct violation of an injunction granted by the Court, & is totally illegal, as will be shown. The arbitrator's award brings W A Bradley largely in my debt. –Elias Ellicott

Mrd: on May 15, by Rev Dr Balch, of Balt, Dr Stephen F Balch, of Iowa, to Miss Matilda Boteler, daughter of Hezekiah Boteler, of Pleasant Valley, Wash Co, Md.

Mrd: on May 17, by Rev Mr Hodges, Thos P White to Mary A Collins, all of Wash City.

Mrd: on May 17, at Balt, by Rev Mr Coxe, Capt Innis N Palmer, U S Army, to Kate, daughter of Capt Llewellyn Jones, U S Army.

Died: at his residence, **Woodlawn**, PG Co, Md, Henry Tolson, in his 60th year. His funeral will be on May 20, at 10 o'clock, at St Barnabas Church. [No death date given.]

Albany, May 18. Hon John C Spencer, formerly Atty Gen & Sec of the Treasury, & one of the most eminent lawyers of the country, died last evening in this city.

Appropriations made during the 2nd session of the 33rd Congress:
1-Sec of the Treas to pay to Jas Keenan, consul at Hong Kong, in China, the sum expended by him for the relief of American citizens shipwrecked in Chinese waters in Aug last: $581.58.
2-Re-imburse Cmdor M C Perry, U S Navy, the extraordinary expenses incurred by him on his recent mission to Japan, & as consideration for his eminent public service in effecting a treaty of amity & commerce with that power: $20,000.
3-To pay Robt C Schenck, of Ohio, for his full compensation while employed as envoy extraordinary & minister plenipotentiary of the U S on special mission to the oriental republic of Uruguay, in 1852: $9,000.
4-Sec of State to re-imburse Edw Riddle such sums as shall be satisfactorily shown to have been expended by him, or which said Riddle may have obligated himself to pay, on account of his official position at the Industrial Exhibition at London, England: $26,000.
5-Act for the relief of Frederic Vincent, adm of Jas le Caze, survivor of Le Caze & Mallet. For advances made to the gov't of the U S in the year 1783: $4,896.82.
6-Joint resolution for the relief of Geo W McCerren: for food taken out of his possession, in 1847, by order of the commanding ofcr of the U S army in command at Brazos St Jago, & used in the construction of **Fort Harney**: indefinite.

7-Joint resolution for the relief of Jas Hughes: for clothing he furnished a company of volunteers, engaged in the Seminole war, commanded first by Capt Alex'r B Bradford, & afterwards by Capt Jesse McMahon: indefinite.

8-Joint resolution for relief of Joel Henry Dyer: for his services as judge advocate in the regt in the Seminole war commanded by Col Alex'r B Bradford, less the amount which he has been paid for his services as a private in said company: $820.43.

9-Relief of Zachariah Lawrence, of Ohio: for his portion of the prize money for the capturing & taking into the port of Passamaquoddy in 1813, the British sloop **Venture**: $2,645.40.

10-By the act for the relief of Mrs Helen Mackay, admx of Lt Col Aeneas Mackay, late a deputy quartermaster in the U S Army. For the amount of the receipt of Capt Wm D McKissack, dated May 1, 1847, as well as the receipt of the said Capt Wm D McKissack for a similar amount, dated Aug 14, 1847: $50,000.

11-Act for the relief of John R Bowes, agent in charge of the property of the U S at Michigan City, Indiana, & of Isaac S Smith, of Buffalo, N Y. For all the claims of Bowes: $470.33. For the claims of Isaac S Smith: $453.32.

12-Relief of the heirs & legal reps of Jos Savage, deceased: for 5 years full pay of a surgeons' mate in the continental line of the army of the Revolution, being the full amount of the sum due to the said Jos Savage, deceased, for commutation of half-pay as surgeon's mate in the Va continental line of the Revolutionary army: indefinite.

13-Relief of Danl Searle & Co, for extra services rendered the Post Ofc Dept of the U S during their contract, made in 1835, for carrying the mail, from Jersey City to Oswego, N Y: indefinite.

14-Relief of Chas W Carroll: for compensation & damages for injuries sustained by him by reason of his wrongful arrest & imprisonment as a deserter from the army of the U S: $5,000.

15-Relief of Henry S Sanford: the difference between the salary received by him as sec of legation at Paris, from May 14, 1853, to Jan 22, 1854, & a salary of a charge d'affaires for the same period, with the usual out-fit of a charge d'affaires: $6,223.82 For necessary clerk hire paid by him while at Paris, the further sum: $1,179.63

16-Relief of the children & grandchildren of Thos Morris: the full amount of half-pay for 7 years, due Morris as captain of artl in the Ga line on the continental establishment in the Revolutionary war, & who died in the service of the U S during said war: indefinite.

17-Benefit of the heirs of Philip R Rice, deceased: for the loss of a vessel in the service of the U S during the war of the Revolution: $3,450.

18-Relief of Wm G Howison: for all services as a member of the Auxiliary Guard of Wash City: $167.

19-Relief of Wm G Preston: to re-imburse him for subsisting his command, & foraging the horses of his company, from Ozark to Wash, Hempstead Co, Ark, during the war with Mexico: $375.25.

20-Relief of Sarah Morris, only heir of Robt Mitchell, deceased: for services as one of the captors of the Algerine vessels taken by the American squadron under the command of Cmdor Decatur: $123.73.

21-Relief of Geo W Torrence: for his gallant services at the Nat'l Bridge, Mexico, on Sep 9, 1847, & for extraordinary expenses incurred by him in consequence of wounds he received in the U S service: $1,574.
22-Relief of Andrew H Patterson: for mail bags manufactured by him with the Post Ofc Dept entered into on May 23, 1840: $6,802.
23-Relief of Stephen Lutz, of N Y: amount paid for 31 cases, containing machinery & apparatus for the light, or lantern of a light-house, imported into the port of N Y, in the U S, & which were, through mistake, sold by public sale, by order of the collector of the port of NY: indefinite.
24-Relief of the heirs of Lt Andrew Finley: one year's extra pay as a lt in the Pa line in the continental establishment of the war of the Revolution, as promised in the resolves of Congress: indefinite.
25-Relief of Ferdinand Clark: for duties imposed by act of Jun 30, 1834, on the Spanish brig **Conde de Villanueva**, Capt Carlos de Agao, & paid to the Collector of the port of Charleston, S C, previous to the clearance of said vessel, on Sep 11, 1835: indefinite.
26-Relief of Thos S Johnson, of the Territory of New Mexico: for 32 wagons, the propery of Johnson, taken by the ofcrs of the U S army, & appropriated to necessary public use: $4,800.
27-Relief of Titian R Peale: for losses he sustained of his private property when wrecked in the U S ship **Peacock**, at the mouth of the Columbia river: $1,782.20.
29-Relief of the heirs of Thos Parke, deceased: for the value of certain sails & rigging sold by said Parke to Capt Harding, as agent of the U S, during the Revolutionary war: $800.
30-Relief of Franklin Chase: for a share of the proceeds of the sale of the schnr **Oregon** & cargo, seized in Apr, 1848, under the Pres' regulation of Mar 1, 1847, at the port of Tampico, during the war with Mexico: indefinite.
31-Relief of Madalena Van Ness, widow of Cornelius P Van Ness, deceased: for services rendered by said Van Ness, in the seizure of goods imported into the district of Vt, in violation of the laws of the U S during the years 1813 & 1814, while he was collector of the customs for said district, for which service he did not receive the award provided by law in such cases: $9,000.
32-Relief of L R Lyon & Dean S Howard, of the State of N Y: for the balance due them for constructing a dredging machine at Whitehall, N Y, under contract entered into on Nov 2, 1836: & a dredging machine to be delivered at Monroe, Mich, by contract entered on Oct 15, 1836: $8,617.81.
33-To pay Norman R Haskell, of Mich, in full of charges as custodian of public property: $350.56.
34-To enable the Sec of State to cause the accounts of Jos Eve, deceased, late charge d'affaires of the U S to the late republic of Texas, to be audited & adjusted by the propery accounting ofcrs of the govn't & that the amount found due thereon be paid to Betsey W Eve, widow of said Jos Eve: indefinite.

35-To enable the Pres of the U S to contract with Hiram Powers for some work of art executed, or to be executed, by him, & suitable for the ornament of the Capitol: $25,000.

36-To enable the Cmte on the Library to pay to Wm H Powell, in full for the picture painted by him for the U S, in addition to the sums heretofore appropriated by law: $2,000.

37-To settle & pay the account of C W Hinman, 3rd assist librarian, from Jul 1, 1854, at the rate of $1,500 per annum: $1,500.

38-To pay the balance directed to be paid Jas F Miller & Pyne-y-oh-te-mah, or either of them, by the Senate amendment to the treaty with the Miami Indians, made in Aug, 1854: $765.

39-Relief of Jacob McLellan: for part of the penalty imposed upon the ship **George Turner**, & paid by McLellan, in Dec, 1851, for an alleged violation of the U S laws restricting the number of passengers in merchant vessels: $450.

40-Relief of Jas S Graham & Walter H Finnall: for the loss sustained by them, by reason of the abandonment by the Postmaster Gen of 2 contracts made by that ofcr with them of the transportation of the mail from Wash to Fredericksburg, & from Fredericksburg to Richmond, which contract was dated Dec 3, 1847: $3,000.

41-Relief of Brig Gen John E Wool: for double rations, from Jul 21, 1821, to May 3, 1833, being the same as have been allowed by the War Dept to other ofcrs of the staff: indefinite.

42-Relief of Purser Francis B Stockton: for the amount of loss sustained by him by reason of making his deposites of public money in the Phoenix Bank, Charlestown, Mass: $67.57.

43-Relief of Thos B Parsons: for disability received while in the naval service of the U S, in successful effort to save the lives of 7 persons, the sum of $3 per month from Sep 1, 1808, to Jun 1, 1835, the same being the difference between the rate of pension of a seaman & that of a coxswain, which grade he filled at the time of the injury: $963.00

44-Relief of Thos Butler: for extra work performed & materials furnished in the construction of a light-house on Execution Rocks, in Long Island sound, by order of the engineer in charge, on Aug 4, 1847: $2,922.

45-Relief of Chas J Porcher, acting purser of the sloop-of-war **Falmouth**: for his services while in the Pacific ocean, from the date of the death of Purser Wm B Hartwell until the appointment of John Y Mason, jr, in his stead, to wit, from Jul 12, 1849, to May 14, 1850, deducting therefrom the amount paid to Porcher for the same period as cmder's clerk: indefinite.

46-Relief of Wm Duer: for necessary expenses incurred while consul of the U S at the port of Valparaiso, Chili, during 1852, in support & defence of Wm N Stuart, an American citizen, arrested & arraigned before the courts of Chili upon a charge of murder, & for the transportation of said Stuart to the U S after his release, together with an equitable advance upon the amount thus ascertained, for the use of the money during the interval: indefinite.

47-Relief of Susan Coody & others: for property destroyed near **Fort Gibson**, by U S soldiers, on May 12, 1845, in the proportion & sums respectively due them according to the report of the Cmte on Indian affairs of the Senate, of date Jan 24, 1850: $1,992.62.

48-Relief of the legal reps of Jas Erwin, of Ark, & others: for the actual loss sustained in consequence of a contract he made with the U S in Sept, 1834, to supply provisions & transportation for the use of the Creek Indians expected to emigrate from the eastern to the western side of the Mississippi river, but who did not emigrate: indefinite. For the actual losses sustained in consquence of a contract made by said Erwin & Danl Greathouse, in his life-time, & the U S, in Dec, 1835, to supply provisions & transportation for the use of the Seminole Indians expected to emigrate from the eastern to the western side of the Mississippi river, but who failed to emigrate: indefinite.

49-Relief of the reps of Thos D Anderson, deceased, late consul of the U S at Tripoli: for contingent expenditures of said consulate from Dec 31, 1821, up to the period when he ceased acting as such consul; & in full for all claims for such expenditures & other demands arising out of said consulate after said Dec 31, 1821, to allow them at the rate of $750 per annum during the said period: indefinite.

50-Relief of the adm of Thos Wishart: for 5 years' full pay of a lt of infty in the continental line of the U S army in the war of the Revolution: indefinite.

51-Act for indemnifying Moses D Hogan for cattle destroyed by the Indians in 1842: by a band of Indians supposed to be a portion of the Sioux, while Hogan was conveying said cattle to a post of the U S, at or near **Fort Snelling**, in pursuance of a contract entered into by Amos J Bruce, sub-agent on the part of the U S for the Sioux Indians: $500.

52-Relief of the legal reps of Col John H Stone: for the half-pay of a colonel in the continental line of the U S army; the said half-pay to commence on Aug 1, 1779, & to terminate on Oct 5, 1804, the day of his death; the same being then due & unpaid to the said Col John H Stone, in virtue of resolution of Congress of Aug 26, 1776: indefinite.

53-Relief of the children & heirs of Maj Gen Baron DeKalb: for claims for services & sacrifices in the war of the Revolution: $66,099.76.

54-Relief of Silvester Humphrey & the heirs of Alex'r Humphrey, deceased: for rebldg the wharf at Staten island after it had been destroyed by the storm of Sep 3, 1821: $2,500.

55-Relief of the adms of Oliver Lee, deceased: for the amount of a judgment recovered by said Oliver Lee against Pierre A Barker, formerly collector of the port of Buffalo Creek, in the circuit court of the U S for the northern district of N Y, in the 2nd circuit, & which was docketed on Aug 30, 1844: $580.32

56-Relief of Saml A Belden & Co: for the duties paid by Saml A Belden & Co to the ofcrs of the U S charged with their collection, in Matamoros, in the republic of Mexico, whilst that city was in the military possession of the U S, upon merchandise, except tobacco, imported by them into Matamoros during that period, which after the restoration of peace between the two countries, they were deprived of, either in the form in which imported, or in the proceeds of sales, by illegal seizure, confiscation, sequestration, or their forced abandonment of the same by the judicial authorities of the Mexican gov't: indefinite.

57-Relief of E J McLane: for his services & expenses as inspector of the customs in the collection district of Brazos de St Jago, Texas, while seizing & detaining horses & mules smuggled into the U S from Mexico: $1,692.45.

58-Relief of Polly Carver, widow & excx of Nathan Carver, deceased: for the payment & full satisfaction of the claims against the gov't of the said Polly Carver, as widow & excx of the said Nathan Carver, deceased: $334.79.

59-Relief of Lincoln Bates: for the damages sustained by him as a night watchman in the public stores at N Y, in Jul, 1849, in suppressing a fire therein, being the amount of his account, as now on file in the Treasury Dept: $55.

60-Relief of Eleanor Hoople of the province of Canada: for care, services, & attention rendered by herself & husband, in 1814, to David Holden, an American soldier: $300.

61-Relief of the legal reps of John Putnam: for his services & money paid for the U S at the port of Genesee, N Y: $795.78.

62-Relief of Gilbert C Russell: for full satisfaction of all balance of claims & demands of every description in his favor against the U S govn't, growing out of, or in any manner connected with, the construction of the fort at Mobile Point, Ala: $20,000.

63-Relief of the heirs of Larkin Smith: for 5 years' full pay of a captain of cavalry, the same being due the said Larkin Smith for services as a captain of cavalry in the U S army in the war of the Revolution: indefinite.

64-Relief of the widow & children of Ezra Chapman, deceased: for 7 years' half-pay of Ezra Chapman, the father of the aforesaid Ezra Chapman, deceased, who was an ensign in the army of the Revolution, & died in the service of the U S, on Sep 1, 1778, & which sum of money was due to the said Ezra Chapman, deceased, on account of the services of his said father, by the provisions of the resolution of Congress passed Aug 24, 1780: $840.

65-Relief of Medford Caffey, of the State of Tenn: for full compensation for his horse & equipage lost in the Seminole campaign of 1818: $106.

66-Relief of Wm Hagerty: for full payment of his claim for grading the street around the Capitol enclosure: $964.80.

67-Relief of Don B Juan Domercq, a Spanish subject: for a quantity of tobacco belonging to him, & taken & used for purposes of defence, by order of Col Childs, at the siege of Puebla, in Mexico, in 1847, & to allow & pay said Domercq for so much of said tobacco, not exceeding in quantity 721 bales, & at a price not exceeding $24 the bale, as shall be proved, to the satisfaction of said Sec, to have been destroyed or lost in consequence of said tobacco having been taken & used as aforesaid: $17,304. For the injury done to 823 bales of tobacco returned to him after being used in barricading the street of Puebla: $823.

MON MAY 21, 1855

Household & kitchen furniture at auction on: May 23, at the residence of Mr Ball, 424 14th st, between H & I sts. –Green & Scott, aucts

Paper hangings, easy chairs, & lounges, at auction: on May 24, at the store of Mr Geo Burheene, on 7th st, opposite the Patent Ofc. –Green & Scott, aucts

Chas Cummer will rent his house, with the furniture & the stable, to a careful & punctual tenant, 405 13th st, between G & H sts. For sale: a horse & carriage.

Trustee's sale of valuable improved property on 7th st: on Jun 25, by deed of trust from Jas A Wise & wife, dated May 9, 1854: public auction of lot 12 in square 429, with a 3 story brick dwlg house. –Nich Callan, trustee -Jas C McGuire, auct

Terrible earthquake in Japan. The island of Niphon, in which Simoda is situated, was visited on Dec 23 by a severe earthquake, which was most disastrous in its effects. The city of Ohosaca, one of the largest in the empire, was completely laid waste. Jeddo itself suffered considerably.

Lewis H Stone, whose trial has been going on for several days past at Rochester, was on Friday found guilty of mail robbery, & sentenced by Judge Hall to 10 years' imprisonment. Gates, his accomplice, subsequently pleaded guilty. These robberies were perpetrated during the months of Sep & Oct last, at Elmira.

Serious affray in Tenn, on May 1. Despatch from Sommerville convey that Orlando Brown & Wm Burton, both citizens of Sommerville, met on the street, exchanged a few words, & the latter shot the former through the thigh, & then stabbed him with a knife. The wounds are considered dangerous. Both are young men of the highest respectablilty. Brown is brother-in-law to Col Meredith P Gentry, & Burton is the son of the clerk of the circuit court of Fayette Co.

Jackson Standard: a few days since 9 men got into a canoe at Westfalls Mill, Vinton Co, Ohio, to cross the creek. Suddenly the little vessel filled with water. Dennison McGinnis & W Napper, were drowned, & M Dordan so severely strangled that he died a day or two afterward with congestion of the brain. The others escaped with great difficulty. –Chillicothe Metropolis

Thos S McCay appointed U S District Atty for the Eastern District of Louisiana, vice E Warren Moise, resigned.

Arthur S Nevitt, recently appointed Postmaster at New Orleans, vice W G Kendall, entered upon the duties of his ofc on May 15.

E G Atkinson, son of the late Gen Atkinson, U S Army, has received the appointment of Sutler at **Fort St Pierre**.

Telegraphic dispatch was received in this city on Sat briefly announcing the death of Gen Chas Gratiot, formerly Chief of the U S Engineer Corps. –Union

Hon Elisha Whittlesey, 1st Comptroller of the Treasury, left Wash City on Fri last for his residence in Ohio, in consequence of the sudden & dangerous illness of his wife.

Died: on May 3, at his residence, near Columbus, Miss, Dr Francis Lightfoot Lee, formerly of Va. He was a son of the late Ludwell Lee, of Loudoun Co, Va, & a grandson of Richd Henry Lee. He early in life removed to S C, & from thence to Miss, where he has resided for many years, &, giving up his profession became a cotton planter.

Miss Jane Shanks, 100 Bridge st, Gtwn, is prepared to accommodate boarders, both transient & permanent, or she will rent her house, furnished or unfurnished, on moderate terms. The furniture is new: fine garden & fruit trees attached.

Notice. The residuary legatees under the will of Mrs Cornelia Lansdale, late of Anne Arundel Co, Md, deceased, are to apply for their respective proportions of said estate. Address Benj E Gantt, Reg/o Wills, Annapolis, Md. –Jas Cheston, surviving exc of Mrs Cornelia Lansdale, deceased.

Real estate at private sale: one frame dwlg house & lot on O st, between 6th & 7th sts, containing 6 good rooms, nearly new. Inquire of Francis Wheatley, lumber dealer, 37 Water st, Gtwn.

Brevoort House, on 5th ave, contains apartments for families or single gentlemen superior to any other hotel in the country. The patronage of the public is respectfully solicited. –Albert Clark, proprietor, N Y.

TUE MAY 22, 1855
Sale of fine northern carriage, horses, harness, buggy, & milch cows: on May 24, in front of the residence of Capt H L Shields, on Franklin Square. -Jas C McGuire, auct

Two little boys, John Henrity & Frank McCann, aged 5 & 6 years respectively, were killed by the fall of a sandbank upon them at Alexandria on Thu last. Though sought by their parents & friends, their fate was unknown until Sat evening.

Rev Mathew G Hamilton, of the Balt Annual Conference of the M E Church, & known in Wash City as a clerk in the service of the Gov't, died in Balt on Sat last, in his 46th year. He was a native of Loudoun Co, Va.

Two children killed by lightning during a heavy storm at South Bend, Ind, on Tue of last week, in the house of Mr Leonard Hain. Wm Hain, aged 13, & Chas, aged 7, were both instantly killed. Lutheria, 8, was severely injured, but it is hoped she will recover. Mr Hain's niece was stunned. Mr Hain was stunned & blinded.

Cincinnati, May 21. Mr Elijah Williams, a rich planter of Barnwell, S C, arrived here today with 8 negroes, his object being to manumit & settle them in Ohio; but just as he stepped from the steamboat into a carriage he fell dead. The negroes having been brought here voluntarily, they are of course free under the State laws. Mr Williams had previously willed them the whole of his estate.

The subscriber offers for sale that valuable property on the corner of 4½ & C sts, opposite to the residences of G C Grammer & Geo Parker, & the new Metropolitan Church. The house contains 13 rooms, besides an attic. Apply to Z D Gilman, druggist, 528 7th st.

In Equity-No 1084. Jos Bryan & Octavia his wife, Jas Towles & Kitty Ann his wife, & Nathan Edmonston, against Wyatt S Berry & Mary Eliz his wife, Kate Moore, & Silas Moore. By an order of the Circuit Court of Wash Co, D C, I am directed to report whether the real estate in Wash City left by the late Brooke Edmonston be susceptible of specific partition, &, if not, whether it will be to the advantage of Silas Moore, the minor dfndnt, & the other parties, that the same should be sold for the purpose of division. The parties above named, & Jas M Carlisle, the guardian ad litem of said Silas Moore, are to attend at my ofc, in the City Hall, Wash, on May 29, in relation to the matters of inquiry in said order. –W Redin, auditor

In Chancery: Circuit Court of Wash Co, D C. Stephen Whitney, John Haggerty, Geo Griswold, Thos E Davis, Nathl Richards, Russell Dart, & Horace L Sill, cmplnts, & Anthony Dey, Wm H Sumner, & Geo Curtis, dfndnts. The above cause, which involves the distribution of the $50,000 awarded under the treaty of Guadaloupe Hidalgo to the dfndnts, trustees of the Galveston Bay & Texas Land Co, the said Court, on May 18, passed the following order: It appearing to the Court that 607 shares of the stock in said Company are not represented in this cause, it is ordered that the cause be again referred to the Auditor to ascertain who are the owners of said shares. –W Redin, auditor

U S Patent Ofc, Wash, D C: ptn of Emily C Pullman, admx of the eatate of Lewis Pullman, deceased, late of Albion, N Y, praying for the extension of a patent granted the said Lewis Pullman on Aug 21, 1841, for an improvement in machines for removing bldgs, for 7 years from the expiration of said patent, which takes place on Aug 21, 1855. –Chas Mason, Com'r of Patents

Died: on May 19, after a brief but painful illness, Mrs Eliz Knowles, in her 32nd year, wife of Thos Knowles, of Gtwn, D C, leaving a husband, 2 small children, & a large number of friends & relations to mourn her untimely loss.

WED MAY 23, 1855
Two boatmen named Linderman, brothers, belong to Catasaqua, were found dead at Mauch Chunk, Pa, on Sun, in the cabin of their boat lying at the wharf. They had been suffocated from coal gas, having closed the cabin & lighted a fire before going to sleep.

Dr Chas H Browne recovered compensation for personal injuries sustained by the railroad accident at Norwalk in May of 1853, before the Supreme Court, at Ipswich, Mass, for $16,000. He & his wife were rescued from the water into which they were plunged, by some men in a boat. Dr Browne received injuries & continued feeble for many months, & at last his heart became affected in consequence of the injury.

Dr C Sharpe & Jas Sharpe, for the alleged murder of their brother, John Sharpe, have been convicted of manslaughter at Charlotte, S C, & sentenced to be imprisoned 12 months & branded with the letter M on the thumb & palm of their left hands.

The charge of embezzlement of the funds of the Petersburg [Va] Railroad Co preferred against Henry D Bird, the late president of the road, has been disposed of by the grand jury at Petersburg ignoring the bill.

Mr Saml Treass has been appointed superintendent of the carpenters' work on the Post Ofc extension bldgs.

Obit-died: on May 3, of Asiatic cholera, on board a steamer near Lake Pepin, on the Upper Mississippi, Dr John B Lewis, of Charlottesville, Va, in his 45th year. He was well known throughout a greater portion of the States of Va, [the land of his nativity] & S C. Born of ancestry whose history is so intimately associated with that of his native State during the stirring times of the Revolution, he inherited in an eminent degree the many noble qualities which gave character to their deeds in those days. A physician by profession, he was deeply skilled in the science of medicine, & remarkably successful as a practitioner. He leaves a bereaved family & friends to mourn his loss.

Teacher wanted: the Trustees of Primary School No 3, Bladensburg district, PG Co, Md, wish to employ a teacher competent to teach arithmatic, mathematics, geography, & grammar, & the usual English branches. A gentleman of good moral character, who will discharge of the duties of the school faithfully, will receive a salary of $350, paid half yearly. Address the undersigned at Buena Vista post ofc. Clement T Hilleary, Henry Phillips, Horatio Beale.

Circuit Court of Wash Co, D C-in Chancery. David English & Otho Z Muncaster, vs Jas C Turner & Jane M his wife, Columbus McLeod, & Thos Williamson & others. The bill states that the cmplnts, at the Mar term, 1847 of the Circuit Court of Wash Co, D C, recovered a judgment against one Enoch Ridgway for $171.54, with interest from Jul 24, 1845, & $11.19 costs of suit; that an execution was issued on said judgment, which execution was returned to the Oct term of said Court Nolla Bona, & which said judgment is still unsatisfied; that the said Enoch Ridgway has no property upon which an execution can be levied; but, as the owner of certain property in Wash City, to wit, part of lot 20 in square 374, subdivided, which he has conveyed away for the purpose of delaying hindering & defeating said cmplnts in the recovery of their said debt; that the said Enoch Ridgway did, among others, by deed dated Nov 6, 1845, convey the said property to one John McLeod & his heirs, in trust to secure a certain debt therein mentioned as due to said Thos Williamson; that said John McLeod hath since departed this life, leaving the said Jane M Turner, Columbus McLeod, & others named in the said bill his heirs at law; that the said debt in said deed mentioned was not real, &, if so, & has been wholly or for the most part paid; that no sale of the said property has been made under said deed, but has ever since & still is in the possession of said Enoch Ridgway, & the rents thereof received by him; that cmplnts have a right to & offer to redeem the said Thos Williamson of any amount that may be due him of said debt; & the object of the said bill is to obtain a sale of the said premises, under the order of the Court, & out of the proceeds thereof to pay first whatever of the said debt may be due & all incumbrances prior to said cmplnts, & afterwards to pay the same cmplnts' debt; & it appearing to the Court that the said Jas C Turner & Jane M Turner, his wife, Columbus McLeod, & Thos Williamson do not reside in this District, but beyond the limits of the same. The non-resident dfndnts are to appear in this Court on or before the first Monday in Oct next. –Jno A Smith, clerk

Died: on May 22, of scarlet fever, Robert B, son of S J & the late Mgt D Little, aged 3 years & 4 months. His funeral is this afternoon at 3 o'clock, from the residence of his father, near the Navy Yard.

Orphans Court of Wash Co, D C. In the case of Israel Wayson, adm of Peter Little jr, deceased: the adm & Court have appointed Jun 12 next, for the final settlement & distribution of the personal estate of said deceased, of the assets in hand. –Ed N Roach, Reg/o wills

Orphans Court of Wash Co, D C. In the case of Saml W Magruder, exc of Sarah A Williams, deceased, the exc & Court have appointed Jun 12th next, for the final settlement & distribution of the personal estate of said deceased, of the assets in hand. -Ed N Roach, Reg/o wills

THU MAY 24, 1855

Appointments by the Pres: 1-G Eustis Hubbard, of Mass, to be commercial agent at Cape Haytien, Hayti, vice John L Wilson, resigned. 2-Thos Sprague, of Calif, to be commercial agent for ports of Cape St Lucas, La Paz, & San Jose, in Lower Calif.

Local Item: a fire broke out on Tue in the brick bldg owned by Mr R Adams, corner of 11th & B sts, & spread to a smaller one owned by Alfred Lee, consuming them. The first was occupied on the ground story by Mr Pettibone as a grain & feed store, & the remainder by Mr Driver, who is a turner, & who lost all his lathes & tools. The store occupied by Mr J D Free as a carpenter's shop burnt along with his tools. Another owned & occupied by Alfred Lee, hay & grain dealer, was full of hay at the time of the conflagration. None of the property was insured.

The First District Court at New Orleans was crowded on May 16 to witness the trial of Patrick Ryan, on the charge of kidnapping a young lady, Miss Honora A Wood, a distant relative, on Apr 17, 1854. He fell violently in love with her & sought her hand in marriage but she positively refused. Miss Wood, a teacher, was returning home from school when Ryan seized her & walked her on board the steamer that was ready to leave. Once on board she communicated her situation to the captain, who took her under his protection to Mobile. On arriving the police repaired to the Lake & arrested Ryan, charging him with kidnapping. A brother of Miss Wood was witness for his sister. Ryan was found guilty, with a recommendation to the mercy of the court. –New Orleans Bulletin

Chancery sale: by decree of the Circuit Court of Wash Co, D C, made in the cause of Arman Jardin et al, vs A Favier's heirs & administrator, dated May 13, 1855: public auction on Jun 15, of lots 1, 2, & 13, in square 119: lots will be sub-divided: parts of

Two men burnt to death on Sat, in a bldg on Franklin st, in Hamtramck. They were in the attic & unable to get out. Their names were J W Burrell & Levi Patrick, both from Maine. –Detroit Daily Advertiser

Valuable farm for sale: **Castle Haven**, containing 517 acres, in Dorchester Co, Md, on the great Choptank river. Improvements are good, consisting of a large & commodious dwlg-house, built of brick, with kitchen & necessary out-bldgs. Apply to the undersigned at Cambridge, Md, or to Jas L Bartol, Spurrier's Court, Balt. -Jas Bujac

Mrd: on May 22, by Rev P D Gurley, D D, Dr Thos J Cathcart to Miss Annie R, daughter of John D Barclay, all of Wash City.

Mrd: on May 22, at Wesley Chapel, by Rev R L Dashiell, Jos H Daniel to Miss Mary L Wheeler, both of Wash City.

Mrd: on May 22, by Rev E P Phelps, Mr Wm Benton, of Loudoun Co, Va, to Miss Catherine W Cocke, of Fauquier Co, Va.

Mrd: on May 23, by Rev E P Phelps, Mr Steward D Downs to Miss Mary E, daughter of Jos Huggins, of Wash City.

Wash City Ordinance: 1-Act granting permission to Levi Pumphrey to erect a livery stable on the bldg line of C st north, between 4½ & 6th sts. The front part of the stable, for 15 feet from the bldg line, shall not be used for the purpose of stabling or grooming horses. 2-Relief of Danl McGuiny: the sum of $800 in full for any claim upon this Corp for injuries & losses sustained by him caused by the falling of the bridge over Rock Creek, at the termination of K st, in May 1854.

FRI MAY 25, 1855

Mr J C McGuire sold at auction on Tue lot 22 in square 254, on F st, between 13th & 14th sts, to Com Smith for 78½ cents per square foot; also, lot 16 in square 102, on H st, between 20th & 21st sts, to W T Herron for 25 cents. Messrs Green & Scott recently sold lot 8 in square 427, fronting on Northern Liberty market space, between 7th & 8th sts, 31 feet, & 100 feet deep, to Wm Parker, for $1 per foot; 6 bldg lots on the corner of south C & 9th sts east, for 2¾, 3, & 4 cents per foot; a lot on H st, between north Capitol & 1st sts east, with a frame house upon it, for $395 cash, to John Cudman; several lots at the corner of Md ave & B st at 9 cents per square foot; & the lot at the corner of 3rd st east & Md ave for $500, dimensions not known.

Large & commodious brick house & lot on Capitol Hill at auction: on Jun 1, on the premises, the well built 3 story brick house formerly occupied by Hon Judge Cranch, on Delaware ave, at B st. -Green & Scott, aucts

A telegraphic dispatch announces the death, in the far West, of Maj Dusenbury, of the U S army. He married a lady in Anne Arundel Co, & was well known & highly respected in Balt, having filled the post of quartermaster here for many years. -Balt Patriot

Since his expulsion by the House of Reps of Mass, Mr Jos Hiss has been endeavoring to obtain a judicial decision as to the right of the House to expel him. His wish has been gratified. The Judge delivered his decision on Wed, that the House had the inherent right in itself to expel Mr Hiss, & that, having used that power, Mr Hiss could not claim any privilege of exemption. He was, therefore, remanded to the custody of the jailor.

Mrd: May 23, by Rev Mason Noble, Mr Alex'r Brown to Miss Eliz Sayers, both of Greenock, Scotland.

We have this day formed a copartnership under the firm of Neal & Havenner, for the sale of Wine, Liquors & Cigars, at wholesale & retail, at 562 7th st, opposite the Centre Market. –J T Neal, C W Havenner

SAT MAY 26, 1855
Appointments: 1-Brvt Maj John Sedgwick, captain 2nd artl, to be major of cavalry, vice McCullough, declined. [Appointed from the Military Academy Jul 1, 1837. Served with his regt [2nd artl] in Florida war & throughout the Mexican war. Brevetted a captain for his gallantry at Churubusco Aug 20, 1847; distinguished in the battle of Molino del Rey; & brevetted major for gallantry at Chepultepec. Succeeded to the command of Duncan's light battery on the appointment of the latter to the ofc of Inspector Gen.]
2-Brvt Maj Geo H Thomas, captain 3rd artl, to be major of cavalry, vice Bragg, declined. [Appointed from Military Academy Jul, 1840, to 3rd artl. Served in Florida war, & there brevetted 1st lt for gallant conduct. Served on Gen Taylor's line throughout the war with Mexico, receiving the brevet of captain for gallantry at Monterey, & of major for the battle of Buena Vista, where he served with a light battery. Afterwards instructor of artl & cavalry at the Military Academy. At present serving at **Fort Yuma**, at the mouth of the Gila river, Calif.]
3-Brvt Maj Robt S Garnett, captain 1st cavalry, to be major 9th infty, vice Benham, declined. [Appointed from Military Academy. Brevet of 2nd lt of artl Jul, 1841. Distinguished in battles of Palo Alto & Resaca de la Palma, May, 1846. Aid-de-camp to Gen Taylor, Jun, 1846. Brevet captain for gallant & meritorious conduct in the attack & capture of Monterey, Sep, 1846. Brevet major for gallant & meritorious conduct in the battle of Buena Vista, Feb, 1847. Capt 7th infty, Mar, 1851.]

M A Tyson & sisters take this method of informing their patrons & the public that their school will be continued as usual in Wash City for day scholars exclusively, & will re-open on Sep 15 next. Apply at the institution on F st, between 12th & 13th sts.

Obit-died: on Wed night last, at his residence near Annapolis, Com Henry E Ballard, age over 70 years. Recently he recovered from a severe attack of pneumonia, but suffered a relapse, which caused his death. He was a native of Md, & entered the service on Apr 2, 1804, over 51 years ago. He received the commission which he held at the time of his death on May 3, 1825, & served 18 years & 8 months at sea & 15 years & 8 months on shore duty. He has not been at sea since 1839. As an ofcr he stook high in the estimation of all connected with our gallant navy, & was universally esteemed as a man & a citizen. -Sun

The Protestant Episcopal Church of St Albans, Rev Wentworth Childs pastor, was yesterday consecrated by Rt Rev Bishop Whittingham. It is about 2 miles from Gtwn, on the Rockville turnpike. Rev Smith Pyne, of St John's Church, Wash, preached the sermon on the occasion.

Gen Chas Gratiot died yesterday, suddenly, after a short illness, at the residence of his son-in-law, Mr Chal P Chouteau, in Wash City, in his 68th year. He entered the Military Academy at West Point in 1804; remained in the army until 1836 or 1837. He served his country with great distinction in the last war with England, & rose from the rank of lt to a brevet brig general, & at the time he left the army was at the head of the engineer corps. A few weeks since he returned with his wife to his native city with a view of making it his home. Thu, after an absence of half a century, he had barely time to inquire for the friends & acquaintances of his youth, & see the few who yet survived, when he is called to depart from among us. Gen Gratiot received a fine education at the Military Academy & was a man of excellent attainments & polished manners. –St Louis Republican of May 19.

Mrs Bibb, wife of Hon Judge Bibb, & another lady, were somewhat injured by cuts & bruises, in an accident to an omnibus in which they were riding to Gtwn on Thu.

Mrd: on May 22, at Cincinnati, Ohio, by Rev Dr Fisher, Maskell E Curwen to Mary T Wright, daughter of Nathl Wright, all of Cincinnati.

Wash City Ordinances: 1-Act for the relief of Geo Hercus: that $8.33 be refunded to him for the unexpired period of his license, said Hercus having closed his business on Jun 1, 1854. 2-Act for the relief of the heirs of Jas Moore: Mayor is to pay to Alex'r Borland, of Wash City, the agent of the heirs of Jas Moore, any surplus which may remain due to lots 15, 18, & 19, in square 216, after deducting taxes due & expenses of sale out of the proceeds of their sale for taxes made on Dec 8, 1838: provided, the agent shall give him satisfactory bond to indemnify the Corp against any loss.

MON MAY 28, 1855
Candy jars, candies, scales & weights, glass case, counters, oyster bar, ice-cream freezers: at auction, on May 30, at the store lately occupied by Fred'k Rupp, on Pa ave, 2nd door west of 3rd st. -Green & Scott, aucts

Charlestown Navy Yard. Thus, Jun 14, has been assigned as the time for launching the new steamer **Merrimac**, now nearly constructed at the Charlestown Navy Yard, Charlestown, provided the orders are not countermanded or some unforeseen mishap does not take place. The sloop of war **Saratoga** lies at the upper wharf, with yards across, waiting further orders.

The resignation of Brvt Capt Henry Coppee, 1st Lt in the 1st artl, has been accepted by the Pres of the U S, to take effect Jun 30, 1855.

Extensive assortment of new & second-hand furniture at auction: on May 31, at Store 395 Pa ave, between 4½ & 6th sts, the entire stock in trade of J R McGregor, who is about to change business. -Jas C McGuire, auct

The late affray in Kansas, from the Detroit Advertiser. We are permitted to publish the following private letter from C McCrea, the man who shot Malcolm Clark a few weeks since at **Fort Leavenworth**, K T. **Fort Leavenworth** Guard House, Kansas, May 8, 1855. Dear Father: Before this note shall have come to hand you doubtless will have heard of my misfortune by the papers, though I fear not exactly according to fact. The question of slavery here has come to such a pitch of excitement that we are on the eve of a civil war, & it has been my misfortune to strike the first fatal blow at a meeting relative to claims, which took a strong party turn, as every thing in this devoted Territory does. I was heard by the bully & leader of the opposite party to call some of the proceedings a fraud, [i e deciding a vote against two-thirds.] He rushed at me with a piece of two-by-four scantling. I fled from him till he struck me, then I shot him through the body. He died in about 10 or 20 minutes. I was also shot at as I received Clark's blow, but not wounded; was afterwards shot & slightly wounded. Our party was as great on the ground as the pro-slavery, or we should have had some more work to do. I expect to get out on small bail soon. Your affectionate son, C McCrea. [Jun 26th newspaper: McCrea publishes a statement of the affair, which, if true, shows that the killing was purely in self defence. He charges that a conspiracy had been organized against him, & he was struck 3 times with a club, & Clark's gang rushed on to kill him when he fired. -Sun]

Trustee's sale, by deed of trust, dated Apr 6, 1854, recorded in the land records of Wash Co, D C, in Liber J A S 74, folios 278: public auction on Jun 15, on the premises, of part of lot 1 in square 630, fronting on D st north 160 feet, & on north Capitol st 167 feet, being the whole of said lot 1, except a part taken from the extreme north end thereof, 35 feet & 10½ inches on north Capitol st by 120 feet in depth, the said part hereby advertised for sale containing about 26,720 square feet. The property is situated near the Railroad depot. The title is believed to be unquestionable. –Saml Chilton, trustee -Jas C McGuire, auct

Obit-died: Hon Wm S Holabird, at his residence in Winsted, Conn, on May 22. He was a prominent lawyer of Litchfield Co, was U S Atty for the District of Conn from 1833 to 1840, & Lt Govn'r of the State in 1842-'3.

A dispatch from Nashville announces the sudden death in that city of Rev Dr Lindsley, a distinguished minister who was in attendance upon the Presbyterian Genr'l Assembly from New Albany, Indiana. [No death date given-current item.]

Mrs Dillon, of St Albany, Vt, was recently found guilty of 25 offences against the liquor law, & fined $20 for each offence, making in all $500 & costs. She was also sentenced to 4 months' additional imprisonment, making 9 months in all. Mrs Dillon appealed.

The N Y Express says: Ellen Ann, only daughter of Saml Osgood, aged 15, & Virginia, daughter of E G Burling, were drowned while bathing at Eastchester on Saturday.

Local Matters: It has been reported that throughout this city that Hon Henry A Wise, who had just been elected Govn'r of the State of Va, was on Sat evening to be greeted with a serenade by his political friends in this community, & that he would address them from the portico of Browns' Hotel. When he began to speak his voice was literally drowned by interruptions, & finding he could not be heard, he & his friends left their opponents in possession of the ground.

Dept of State, Wash, May 25, 1855. Information has been received at this Dept from Thos W Ward, the U S Consul at Panama, of the death of Mrs Jas Cummins, a passenger from San Francisco by the steamer **Golden Age**, a few hours after the arrival of that vessel at Panama, on May 2. Further information can be obtained by addressing this Dept.

Health report: ofc of the Board of Health: interments during the month ending Apr 30, 1855: 72. By order of the Board, H P Howard, M D, President.

On Thu an election for ofcrs of the Philharmonic Society was held, resulting as follows: Pres, J L Clubb; 1st V Pres, J C Foertsch; 2nd V Pres, F Glenroy; Rec Sec, W Parkhurst; Corr Sec, J F I McClery; Treas, H Pugh; Librarian, E Jones, Board of Dirs, J A Stewart, H O Noyes, S V Noyes, J B Dawson, G L Sheriff, & __ McQuade.

Mrd: May 24, by Rev W C Steel, Mr Geo Posey to Mrs Sarah Pullin, both of Wash.

Orphans Court of Wash Co, D C. In the case of Louisa A Wotherspoon, admx of Alex'r S Wotherspoon, deceased, the admx & Court have appointed Jun 18 next for the final settlement & distribution of the personal estate of said deceased, of the assets in hand. –Ed N Roach, Reg/o wills

Balt, May 26. Most destructive fire broke out in the extensive drygoods jobbing house of Messrs Slingloff, Stevens & Co, at the corner of Balt & Howard sts. Flames spread rapidly, destroying the adjoining stores, occupied by Messrs Bennett, Magee & Baum, Dailey & Massey, Norris, Caldwell & Co, Mr T S Bentz, Mr R Torrence, Mr J Casper, & others.

Wilkesbarre, Pa, May 26. Fire here this morning destroyed the stores of Messrs Norgan, Frederick & Wilson, Wm Loomis, J Lewis, & the law ofcs of G B Nicholson; also, the Bedford Hotel, kept by S H Peterbaugh, & the dwlgs of Messrs Lord, Butler, Dr Boyd, & others. Most of the property is insured, except Dr Boyd's.

Will be ready on Jul 1, a new American book, beautiful & affecting. The Old Farm House, by Mrs Caroline H Butler Laing. Illustrated with beautiful engravings by Van Ingen, from original designs by White. 1 Vol, 12mo, Extra Red & Blue Muslin, Gilt, $1.25. –Chas H Davis, Publisher, Phil.

Oak Hill Cemetery, Gtwn. The proprietors of lots in the above Cemetery who are members of the Corporation are required by the charter of the company to hold a general meeting in the Cemetery on the first Monday of Jun in every year, to elect four persons from among their number to manage the affairs of the company for one year, or until others are chosen in their place. The lot holders are respectfully invited to meet in the Chapel within the Cemetery enclosure at 5 o'clock P M on Monday, the 4th day of June next, for the purpose aforesaid. –Jno Marbury, Pres O H Cemetery Co.

TUE MAY 29, 1855

Hon John Slidell, accompanied by his wife & family, arrived at their residence in Wash City yesterday. They left New Orleans on May 20. Cmdor Perry, of the U S Navy, also arrived in this city yesterday.

Announcement that Saml C Gage had been nominated for Govn'r of Maine by the Know-Nothings in a State Convention is a silly hoax. No Convention has been held.

Meeting of the Medical Alumni Association of Gtwn College, D C, held on May 22, the following ofcrs were chosen for the ensuing year, viz:

Dr S J Radcliff, Pres Dr O A Daily, Cor Sec
Dr W Evans, 1st V Pres Dr T C McIntire, Treas
Dr J Hall Moore, 2nd V Pres Dr Jos A Smith, Librarian
Dr J V D Middleton, Rec Sec

Jos Williams has been convicted of the murder of his father in Person Co, N C, & sentenced to be hanged. Twelve months ago the case was removed to Caswell Co. The murdered man, Frank Williams, had considerable property, & for years he & his son had lived unhappily together, the only white persons on the plantation. The prisoner complained that his father would aid other people & would not aid his children; that the property came by his mother & that he meant to have his part.

Two sons of Rev Jas Walton, Eddie & John, 12 & 14 years old, were drowned in the Big Black river, near Bowle's Ferry, Miss, on May 3. They ventured out too far.

Boston, May 26. Before the Supreme Court today in Cambridge Saml Hillard, on trial for the murder of Jas L Warren, was allowed to enter a plea of guilty of manslaughter, & then sentenced to the State prison for 5 years. John L Chapman, convicted of the murder of Cozzens, was sentenced to the State prison for 1 year, & afterwards to be hung, on such a day as the Govn'r may appoint.

Local Items: Wash City was excited by the sound of martial music, the measured tread of the solidery, & all the pomp of war. With the exception of the Light Infty, commanded by Capt Jas Y Davis, which has performed much service of late, the entire Regt of Volunteers was in line, consisting of the following companies:

Pres' Mount Guard: Capt Peck
Nat'l Guards: Capt Tait
Highlanders: Capt Reese
American Rifles, Lt Simms
Montg Guards: Capt Key
German Yeagers: Capt Schwartzman
Boone Rigles: Capt Bright

Nat'l Greys: Capt Lem Towers
Union Guards: Capt Mulloy
Marion Rifles: Capt Sheckell
Scott Guards: Capt Jamieson
Union Infty, [boys company:] Capt Lasselle

Notice is given that the Mayor of Wash City has received application for a deed to be given to the subscriber for lot 32 in square B, by virtue of a bond of conveyance executed by the Comrs of Low Grounds, dated Aug 24, 1824, to Wm Jones, who, at public sale made by said com'rs on said day, was the purchaser of said lot, which said lot, by subsequent assignments & conveyances, duly recorded in the clerk's ofc, has become the property of the undersigned, & the said bond properly belongs to him, but has been lost or mislaid so that it cannot be found. This is therefore to give notice that the Mayor's ofc on or before Jun 25, 1855, will grant a deed for said lot to the subscriber. –Mathew G Emery
+
Same for lot 14 in reservation 11, regarding conveyance executed by the Comr's of Low Grounds, dated Jul 8, 1822, to Saml Miller: said certificate lost or mislaid so that it cannot be found. Mayor to grant a deed for said lot. –Wm B Todd

Mrd: on May 28, by Rev F Israel, Jas T Truman to Mrs Rhoda Ann Havener, both of Loudoun Co, Va.

WED MAY 30, 1855
Havana, May 22, 1855. The U S frig **Constitution** arrived here on May 16, Cmder John Rudd, & wearing the broad pennant of Cmdor Mayo, of the African coast squadron-Lts, G F Hazard, B M Dove, Saml Larkin, Wm R Gardner, C R P Rogers, & A G Clary; Fleet Surgeon, M G Delancy; Purser, J H Watmough; Brvt Maj Marine Corps, N S Waldron; Passed Assist Surgeon, J L Burtt; Assist Surgeon, J C Coleman; Acting Master, Colleville Terrett; Cmdor's sec, Llewellyn Boyle; Cmdor's clerk, Edw Cobb; Capt's clerk, Wm L Swayze; Midshipmen, Wm L Bradford, Wm H Dana, & Aeneas Armstrong; acting boatswain, E Chamberlain; gunner, S Lewis; carpenter, Lewis Holmes; sailmaker, Wm Bennett; boatswain [supernumerary appointed for meritorious conduct in efforts to save life] & acting master's mate, W S Howard. In a cruise of 2½ years but 2 men were lost out of 500, which is much in favor of the ofcrs & their management & influence. The steamer **San Jacinto** arrived on May 19. Cmdor Mayo transported a few men to meet the wants of that steamer, & left on May 21 to call at Key West, & thence for Portsmouth.

Portland Advertiser: on May 23, as a heavily loaded four horse team, driven by Mr Alex'r Fassett, was crossing the Madison Bridge, across the Kennebec river, on its way from Morridgewock to Anson, the bridge gave way, & the team, driver, & 2 of the horses fell 60 feet into the stream. Mr Fasset was drowned.

Discouraging accounts have been received at the Navy Dept concerning the safety of the U S brig **Porpoise**, which was last heard of on Sep 21, we publish below a list of her ofcrs & crew: Muster-roll of the U S brig **Porpoise**:
Commanding: Wm King Bridge, acting lt. Ofcrs: Wm Riley, acting lt; Sylvanus J Bliss, acting lt; Wm Van Wyck, acting lt; Geo F B Baber, acting master; Jas H Stuart, assist surgeon; Saml J Potts, capt's clerk.
Crew: H Wentworth Greene, purser's steward; Jas S Goodwin, yeoman; John Allison, boatswain's mate; Henry Williams, boatswain's mate; John Fanning, 2nd gunner; Alva Waldo, carpenter's mate; Martin Ravens, sailmaker's mate; Jas Stump, ship's cook; Melvin Martin, capt of the hold; Albert Meteer, armorer; Thos Hill, ship's cpl; Manuel Nabrega, wardroom steward; Wm H White, quartermaster; Wm Graham, quartermaster; Lewis Johnson, quartermaster; David Boorland, capt forecastle; Geo Swan, capt forecastle; Jas Livingston, capt top; Wm Law, capt top; John O'Brien, capt of guard; Antonio Denniz, cooper; John B Higham, hospital steward; Awong, capt's cook; Jos Edwards, ward-room cook.
Seamen: Michl O'Hallaron, Adam McNab, Wm Ray, Robt Wilson, John Reed, Wm Winchester, Robt A Middleton, Edw D Myers, Thos Bourne, Chas L Edders, John Sylva, John W Thomas, Francis Newton, John Montague.
Ordinary Seamen: Chas Nessler, John F Saker, John Munroe, Wm Hunt, Joachim Soza, John Freely.
Landsmen: Arthur Seymour, Wm Queen, Wm Lewis.
First Class Boys: Danl Ross, Robt Williams, Antonio Rodrigues, Manuel Gomez, August Avelyn, John Praeda, Pedro Joseph, Thos Breslyn.

A Sad Case. The eyesight of Lord Chas Wellesley is irretrievably lost. He is brother & heir presumptive of the Duke of Wellington.

Two well-known faces in London society have died: Sir Robt Harry Inglis & the widow of Sir Huphrey Davy. Few saw Lady Davy without thinking of by-gone times, when [as Mrs Apreece] she was the center of a circle of fashion, the lively lady who won the heart of Sir Humphrey Davy, whom she married 40 years ago, & six & twenty years have passed by since Sir Humphrey died & Lady Davy was seen in widow's weeds. The dinners of Sir Robt in Bedford square & the at homes in Park st of Lady Davy will long be remembered. –Illustrated London News.

Sir Geo Head died on May 2 in his 74th year. He had been employed in Canada, Nova Scotia, & Ireland. He gained repute in literature by his "Forest Scenes in the Wilds of North America," & his home "Tour in the Manufacturing District of England." At the period of his death he was Deputy Knight Marshal to the Queen.

For rent: that commodious brick dwlg, 618, recently occupied by Col W B Randoph, on Md ave, between 12th & 13th sts. Apply to E Pickrell & Co, Water st, Gtwn.

Mrd: on May 28, at the Capitol Hill Parsonage, by Rev Gideon H Day, Mr Henry C Ellis to Miss Mary McIntosh, all of Wash City.

THU MAY 31, 1855
Lots in square 144 for sale at public auction: by authority of a deed of trust executed by C H Van Patten on Jan 1, 1848, recorded in Liber W B 140, pages 205 thru 209: sale of lots 10 thru 16 in said square, fronting on E st north & 18th st west. By order of the trustee. -Jas C McGuire, auct

Wash Corp: 1-Ptn of Henry Olive, praying for the remission of a fine: referred to the Cmte of Claims. 2-Cmte of Claims: asked to be discharged from the consideration of the ptn of Lawrence Malone: laid on the table. 3-Act for the relief of Mrs R K Billing: decided in the affirmative.

Hiram King, No 393, will have 2 large rooms on C st between 3rd & 4½ sts, for rent, on Jun 1.

Died: on May 29, Estele Condict, youngest daughter of David H & S Augustine Burr, aged 8 years.

Public attention is called to the sale of the valuable property at the corner of north E & 10th sts west, known as the old *Medical College*, to take place on the premises, on Jun 1. -Jas C McGuire, auct

FRI JUN 1, 1855
Eruption of *Mount Vesuvius*. The best account can be found in the London Daily News: Naples, May 10, 1855. The lava has now advanced 10 miles from its source, & is now doing terrible damage. On May 7 the crater, at the very summit, fired, as it were, two heavy cannonades, & after sending forth lightning, flames, & stone broke up altogether. Lava pours forth & runs on the side of the Cavello as far as the Minatore; here 4 other craters have formed which throw up bitumen. The danger is very great. The expectation is that the lava, should the eruption continue, will flow down to the Ponte Maddaloni & into the sea.

At Rochester, N Y, on Monday last, Mr Fillmore G Hutchinson, a member of a company engaged in firing a salute in honor of the late policical victory in Va, was sadly mutilated by the premature discharge of a gun, owing to neglect in swabbing it. He is a steady & industrious young man, & it is supposed that his life will be saved.

Mary Ann Wilkinson, 18 years old, residing with her parents at Saratoga Springs, was poisoned by taking a dose of acid by mistake for a preparation for a cold. She had dressed herself to attend church, but the dose quickly killed her.

Dr Eldridge, of Leroy, Ill, druggist, took a large dose of strychnine instead of morphine recently, causing his death in a few moments.

Wm George, of North Chelmsford, a student at Norwich, [Vt] Military Academy, accidentally shot himself in the former place, on May 23, while firing at a target.

A man named Fitzpatrick died yesterday in the Infirmary of Wash City in consequence of injuries inflicted upon him on Sat last by a colored man named Geo Raglan. Raglan had just come out of prison, where he had been confined during 2 or 3 months because of his violent, vindictive, & unreasonable conduct in assailing unoffending persons.

Horatio Appleby, employed in the blacksmith shop at the Capitol works, was on Wed severely but not dangerously injured by a blow on the head from a lever connected with the machinery which had gone wrong.

At Alexandria Geo W Crump has been found guilty of murder in the 2nd degree in causing the death of Jos Bloxham, & condemned to the penitentiary for 12 years.

Mrd: on May 29, by Rev Mr Hodges, Francis W Casey, of Balt, to Miss Mgt V Gibbs, of Wash.

Mrd: on Thu, by Rev John C Smith, Jas Mitchell, jr, of Wilmington, N C, to Miss Jane Adeline Gates, of Wash City.

Died: on May 22, in the city of Jackson, Miss, after a brief illness, in her 30th year, Mrs Amanda T Corley Terrett, a native of that State, & the wife of Wm H Terrett, formerly of Fairfax Co, Va.

SAT JUN 2, 1855
The propeller **Arctic** & the barque **Release**, forming the expedition to go in search of Dr Kane & his companions, who sailed in 1852 for the purpose of obtaining information of the fate of Sir John Franklin & his companions, departed from the Brooklyn navy yard, N Y, for the Arctic seas on Thu. They will anchor at Sandy Hook, & remain a few days to afford time for adjusting their compasses & make other preparations. Ofcrs of the barque **Release**: Henry J Harsteine, Lt Commandant; Wm L Lovell, Acting Master; Jos P Fyffe, Passed Midshipman; Elisha K Kane, Assist Surgeon; Van Rennselaer Hall, Boatswain. Ofcrs of the propeller **Arctic**: Chas C Simms, Lt Commandant; Watson Smith, Acting Master; Harman Newell, Engineer; Saml Whiting, Acting Boatswain. –N Y Courier

Official, Dept of State, Wash, May 31, 1855. Information received from the Legation of the U S at Honolulu of the decease, in the Sandwich Islands, of Jas Hassell, who is supposed to have been a native of Boston, Mass, & whose estate leaves a considerable sum of money in the hands of the public administrator. Documents substantiating the claims of the legal reps of the aforesaid Hassell may be transmitted to this Dept.

Mrd: on May 31, in the F st Presbyterian Church, by Rev P D Gurley, D D, Mr Bushrod M Reed to Miss Ann L Wilson, both of Wash.

Mrd: on May 31, by Rev W C Steel, John Wesley Rogers to Miss Jane Eliz Farnum, both of Wash City.

Mrd: on May 29, by Rev Mr Duncan, Mr Jas F N Davis to Miss Martha E Sewell, all of Wash City.

Died: on Jun 1, Mrs Martha E, in her 18th year, wife of Mr Jas N W Davis. Her funeral is this evening at 4 o'clock, from the residence of her parents, on 8th st, between I & K sts.

Obit-died: on May 15, at Key West, Fla, Mrs Ellen Mallory, in her 64th year. Mrs Mallory was born in Ireland; came with her uncle to America while still a young girl; soon after married Mr Mallory, of Conn; settled at Key West in 1822. Her husband died in 1825, leaving her living far removed from any of her relatives, with 2 young children, & but little means of support. By her industry & economy she supported herself & educated her son, the present Senator from Fla, in the schools of the north. She literally fed the poor & clothed the naked. She died full of Christian faith & hope, & in full communion with the church. –W M -Key West, May 24, 1855.

Monsieur Godard, the celebrated aeronaut, died suddenly at New Orleans on May 26. He was alive & well the preceding evening.

Boston, Jun 1. The steam mill of Wm Dickinson, Sutten's grist mills, Waite, Chalsey & Co's iron works, Guilding, Gregory & Co's planning miller, & several other bldgs at Worcester, Mass, were destroyed by fire last night. Loss: $60,000.

U S Court of Claims, Bounty Land & Genr'l Agency at Wash. Saml Yorke Atlee, Atty at Law, & for many years attached to the Treasury Dept of Wash, offers his services to his friends & the public generally in the prosecution of claims before the new Court of Claims, Congress, or any of the Depts.

MON JUN 4, 1855
West Point Military Academy: annual examination: Meeting of the Board of Visiters: the Graduating Class: Exercises of the Day. West Point, Cozzens' Hotel, Jun 1. The present Board consists of 14 members, the Pres having failed to supply the vacancies caused by the resignation of 2 of the nominees. They are:

Hon Amos Wiswel, Maine	Col Jas W Armstrong, Ga
Hon Isaac Davis, Mass	Maj Jas G L Huey, Ala
Rev G Coit, Conn	Hon J F Cushman, Miss
Rev Francis Vinton, D D, N Y	Chas Negus, Iowa
Col H Shubart, Pa	Col Hans Crocker, Wisc
A B Hanson, Md	Dr Jas Jones, La
S H Lee, N C	Prof W W Mather, Ohio

The following gentlemen compose the graduating class this year:

Cyrus B Comstock, Mass	John R Church, Ga
Cornelius Van Camp, Pa	Lewiss Merrill, Pa
Godfrey Weltzel, Ohio	Wm R Hazen, Ohio
Junius B Wheeler, N C	Chas W Thomas, at large
Ebeneze Gay, N H	Alfred T A Torbert, Dela
Geo H Elliot, Mass	Edw L Hartz, Pa
Saml Brock, jr, Mass	Geo D Ruggles, N Y
Michl P Small, Pa	Clarence E Bennett, N Y
John V D DuBois, N Y	Wm W Averell, N Y
Francis A Sloup, Ind	Jas Hill, at large
John W Turner, Ill	Tim'y M Bryan, jr, Pa
Alex'r S Webb N Y	Jesse K Allen, Ill
Danl McM Gregg, Pa	Wm R Pease, N Y
Jas Wheeler, jr, N Y	Henry M Lazell, Mass
Fred'k L Childs, at large	Henry W Freedley, Pa
Francis R T Nichols, La	Robt C Hill, N C
Albert N Colburn, Vt	Geo McG Dick, Pa

The following ofcrs have been appointed to constitute the Board for the selection of the Reserved List of navy ofcrs: Capts: Wm B Shubrick, M C Perry, C S McCauley, C K Stribling, A Bigelow. Cmders: G J Pendergrast, Franklin Buchanan, S F Du Pont, Saml Barron, Andrew H Foote. Lts: J S Missroon, R L Page, S W Gordon, W L Maury, Jas S Biddle

The newspaper reports that Thos Thumb, the celebrated little great man, was married, at Webster, on Thu last, to Miss Vinton, of Bridgeport, Conn. [Jun 11th newspaper: the N Y Evening Post has been authorized to say that there is no truth in the story of Tom's marriage.]

Dept of State, Wash, Jun 1, 1855. Information has been received from Robt C Murphy, the U S Consul at Shanghai, of the death of Saml Holtz & And Anderson, both citizens of the U S. –Jun 4 [No other information.]

New Orleans Delta of May 27. On May 26 Salvador Vidsea, a well-known citizen belonging to the Portuguese Society was taken ill & willed a large portion of his property to B Paradeda, a dear friend of his. Being about to die he sent for the latter, who entering his sick room, was suddenly attacked with cholera, & had to be conveyed home. Both died about the same time, & were buried together yesterday by the Portuguese Society, who attended the funeral in a body. The friends are not parted in death.

Three men to be hung: our First District Court has at last found a jury who are not afraid to assume the responsibility. Consigned to the gallows are 3 murderers: Dan Callaghan, the leader in the Corudroy alley tragedy; John Shields, who murdered Hoey; & Patrick Kennedy, who in cold blood took the life of Jas Cruise. All will have to suffer death for their crimes. New Orleans Delta, 27th.

The U S ship **Lexington** was sold at auction at the Brooklyn Navy Yard on Friday for $4,850.

The Artillery Company, to be attached to our regt of volunteers, has been formed, & the following ofcrs elected: Capt, Chas C Mills; 1st Lt, Jackson Pumphrey; 2nd Lt, John T Crampsey; & 3rd Lt, Saml C Espey.

Furniture for sale & house to rent. House is new. Apply to J T Stephens, 505 7th st.

Mrd: on May 31, at McKendree Chapel Parsonage, by Rev Geo Hildt, John E Lewis, of Wash City, to Miss L Alice Fisher, of Montg Co, Md.

Mrd: on Jun 2, in Balt, at the First Presbyterian Church, by Rev Dr Backus, Henrietta, eldest daughter of E Lee, of Balt, to Dr John W Palmer, of N Y.

Mrd: on May 31, at Trinity Church, Richmond, Va, Thaddeus S Sturgis, to Mary Ann Stockett, daughter of Rev C A Davis, pastor of the Church.

Phil, Jun 3. Thos Bailey Russum committed suicide in N Y last night. He formerly kept a tailor's shop in this city, & was some years ago appointed Collector of San Francisco.

TUE JUN 5, 1855
Examination at the Naval Academy commenced on Friday at the U S Naval Academy. The following ofcrs were present: Capts John Thos Newton, John B Montgomery, Joshua R Sands; Cmders Jos B Hull, Chas H Davis.

Trustee's sale of valuable house on the corner of F st south & 3rd st west. By deed of trust from John F Tolson & wife: public sale on Jun 28, on the premises, parts of lots 24 & 25 in square 539, fronting on F st south, with a well built 2 story frame house, with brick bakery attached. –Chas S Wallach, trustee -Jas C McGuire, auct

Potomac Pavilion: **Piney Point**, St Mary's Co, Md: desirable place for Health & Sea Bathing will open for visitors on Jun 15, with nothing left undone that will promote the comfort of its guests. –W W Dix, proprietor

$5 reward for return of a bay horse mule that strayed from the premises of Jos Ehrmaunhout's hotel, Gtwn, on Jun 2. –Robt H Boteler

Valuable real estate at public sale. By virtue of an order of Montgomery Co Court, made in the case of the ptn of John Offutt & others to divide the real estate of which Andrew Offutt, late of said county, died seized, the subscribers will sell at Public Auction, on the premises, on Jun 22, all the real estate of said deceased, not heretofore sold, viz: Lot 1, being the farm on which said Offutt lived at the time of his death, containing 408 acres of land, 209½ of which are assigned the widow as her dower.
But an arrangement has been since made by which it can now be sold free of dower. This farm will be sold entire, or divided to suit purchasers. It lies on the public road leading from Gtwn to the mouth of Monocacy, about 22 miles from the former & 10 from the latter, 2½ miles from Darnestown. It lies equidistant between a Baptist & Methodist meeting-house, about 1 mile from each. The house is a large brick mansion, 4 rooms on the lower floor & 4 on the second; an excellent cellar, divided into 3 rooms; a brick dairy, barn, stable, corn & tobacco houses. We will also offer for sale, at the same place, a house & lot in the forks of the roads at Dawsonville, a good stand for a store or a mechanic. Likewise, a small island, called **Cow Island**, in the Potomac river, about 2 miles below the Great falls, containing 6¼ acres.
-Richd Gott, Wm A Chappell, John H Gassaway, Elbert Perry, Nathl Clagett

Real Estate at public vendue. By decree of Montg Co Court, sitting as a Court of Equity, in the case of Walter Magruder & others, vs John Brewer, admof Erasmus Perry & others, the subscriber, as trustee, will expose to public sale, on Jun 20, the following real estate lying in said county, to wit: a farm adjoining Dr Duvall's mill farm, contiguous to the lands of Messrs Robt Y Brent, Geo Knowles, & others, within 10 miles of Gtwn; improvements are a frame dwlg house with 8 rooms & a good cellar, with kitchen attached to the dwlg; also a dairy, negro quarters, 2 large frame barns, corn-house shedded, blacksmith shop, & stables: contains 194¾ acres of land, more or less. –John Brewer, trustee

The ceremony of Confirmation was administered by the Catholic Archbishop Kenrick, of Balt, on Sunday, at Gtwn, to 32 persons at the College & 22 at the Convent; & in the afternoon, at Alexandria, to 152 persons.

Mrd: on May 30, in Chas Co, Md, by Rev Jno M Todd, Dr Ashton Miles, of the U S Navy, to Miss Mary Jane Stuart, both of the city of Balt.

Mrd: on May 31, by Rev Mr Keefe, Francis A McGee, of Wash, D C, to Miss Virginia F Robinson, eldest daughter of Dr E C Robinson, of Norfolk City, Va.

For sale: the subscriber intending to remove to the country, will sell at private sale her house & lot in Rockville, Md. The house is a 2 story brick, with a fine cellar & garret, & contains 8 rooms: contains over 1 acre of land. Apply to the subscriber, at Rockville, Md. –Ursula Willcoxen

WED JUN 6, 1855
Appointments by the Pres: 1-Buckingham Smith, of Florida, Sec of Legation at Madrid, vice Horatio J Perry, recalled. 2-John B Blake, Com'r of Public Bldgs, vice B B French, resigned.

Choice collection of rare & valuable oil paintings at public auction: on Jun 12, at the Saloon over Farnhan's Bookstore, 11th & Pa ave, paintings selected with great care by H N Barlow, from various galleries on the Continent. Amongst them will be found specimens of Domenichino, Velasquez, Sir Godfrey Kneller, A Van Willies, Jno Wilson Gainsboro', Murilla, Vernet, Poussin, Shayer, jr, & others.
-Jas C McGuire, auct

The new Washington City Councils:
Aldermen:
Wm B Magruder
Thos Miller
John Tretler
Matthew G Emery
Common Council:
Chas Abert
John B Turton
Edw H Fuller
Thos J Fisher
Wm Orme
Ferdinand Jefferson
J T Walker
Jas Towles
J H G McCutcheon
John Ball
Alex'r McD Davis
Assessors:
Wm H Clampett
Wm Douglass

Saml C Busey
Robt Clark
John L Smith

J T Clements
Amon Baldwin
J H Peters
John Bohlayer
Geo R Ruff
John Bayne
Josiah Venable
Thos E Lloyd
Saml Y AtLee
Jackson Pumphrey

Israel Wayson
-John T Towers, Mayor

Parks, the murderer, who made an attempt to take his own life a few days ago, was executed at Cleveland on Friday.

Another victim for the Gallows. Patrick Kennedy was on trial in the First District Court on Sat, May 26, for the murder of Jas Cruise, on Feb 11 last, at a grogshop at Poet & Greatmen st, & convicted without any qualification. He makes the 5th person awaiting the gallows now in the parish prison. —New Orleans Com Bulletin

Died: on May 17, at his residence in PG Co, of apoplexy, Henry Tolson, in his 62nd year. Candid, straightforward, & noble-minded, he was yet tender-hearted & affectionate. The deceased leaves a widow, a large family of children, & a great many friends to mourn his loss.

Died: on Jun 5, Mary Kate, 2nd daughter of Jas & Catharine J Sutton, aged 5 months & 23 days. Her funeral will be from the residence of her parents, 459 10th st, this afternoon at 3 o'clock.

Mr Herman F D Huntemuller, a worthy young merchant of Balt, met with his death on Sat morning, at his country seat on Liberty road. When he was coming down stairs & had a loaded pistol in his pantaloons pocket, when by some accident it exploded, the ball entering his thigh, tearing away the flesh, & severing the femoral artery. His family found him in a dying condition from the great loss of blood, & in less than 10 minutes he was a corpse. He was but 22 years of age, & was married but 6 weeks since, being surrounded by all that could make life happy. -American

The Pawtucket Gaz says that on May 29 a little daughter of Mr Jas C Aldrich, of Pawtucket, was found lying upon her bed inhaling the odor of a bottle of chloroform liniment which had been left within her reach. It was taken from her & she was found half an hour afterwards dead.

THU JUN 7, 1855
Trustee's sale: by deed of trust from Messrs Garrett & Davis, dated Aug 17, 1854, to the subscriber, & by the direction of Henry Sothoron, the party secured by such deed: public auction on Jul 16 of part of lot 26 in Rothwell & Naylor's subdivision of square 425, in Wash City, on 7th st, between L & M sts, with an excellent dwlg house & other improvements thereon. –W Redin, trustee -Green & Scott, aucts

Kingston [Canada] Whig. Five men drowned on May 31, belonging to Amherst Island, opposite Bath, about 18 miles from Kingston, when their boat upset about 1 mile from shore. Drowned were J Turner, J Deuno, J Smith, & T Huff & his brother. A Deuno was saved.

South Carolina Historical Society meeting on Sat last: the following ofcrs elected for the ensuing year.
Jas L Pettigru, Pres
Dr Jas Moultrie, 1st V Pres
Wm Gilmore Simms, 2nd V Pres
Wm Jas Rivers, Corr Sec
Fred'k A Porcher, Rec Sec
Dr A B Williman, Treasurer
Curators: Dr J E Holbrook, Isaac W Hayne, O Hammond, Geo S Bryan, B R Carroll, Dr S H Dickson, & Dr L A Frampton.

From an old diary of the distinguished Andrew Ellicott, his grandson J C G Kennedy, of Wash City, has copied extracts, giving an account of Capt Lynch, of Va, who appears to have been the man who introduced & gave a name to the wild justice known in our country as Lynch Law. Capt Lynch was the author of the lynch laws so well known & frequently carried into effect some years ago in the Southern States, in violation of every principle of justice & jurisprudence. Mr Lynch resided in Pittsylvania, Va, when he commenced legislator & carried his system into effect. This self-created judicial tribunal was first organized in the State of Va about 1776, from whence it extended southward. Mr Lay, his neighbor, was one of the members of the organization. Since leaving Va he has resided on the Olenoy, one of the branches of the Saludy. The Olenoy appears to be one of the principal seats of a disorder known in that country by the name of the milk sick, which is supposed to proceed from some vegetables eaten by cows.

Chesapeake & Ohio Canal Company met on Jun 4 for the election of Pres & Directors for the ensuing year. Of the 5 Com'rs of the Board of Public Works of Md 4 were present: Messrs Chas R Stewart, Saml Chamberlain, M N Falls, & Joshua R Nelson. Messrs Stewart & Chamberlain nominated the following ticket for Pres & Directors: for Pres, Saml Hambleton, of Talbot Co, Md. For Directors: Saml P Smith, of Alleghany Co; John G Stone, of Washington Co; Alex'r B Hanson, of Fred'k Co; Richd I Bowie, of Montg Co; Jas A Magruder, of Gtwn, D C; & Geo H Smoot, of Alexandria, Va. Messrs Falls & Nelson nominated the following ticket: for Pres, Wm D Merrick, of Chas Co, Md; & for Directors, Chas M Thruston, of Alleghany; Geo Schley, of Washington Co; Wm J Ross, of Fred'k Co; Coleman Yellott, of Balt City; Thos F Bowie, of PG Co; & Wm W Seaton, of Wash, D C. The voting was equally divided, no choice was made; the proceedings were referred to the Hon Dennis Claude, Treasurer of the State of Md. Mr Claude has decided in favor of the ticket nominated by Messrs Stewart & Chamberlain.

The Library of the late Judge Purviance, of Balt, will soon be disposed of at public sale, & is one of the largest collections in the Union.

Obit-died: on May 21 last, at Key West, Agnes Wirt, 3rd daughter of Hon Thos Randall, of Tallahassee, Fla. The disease, consumption, which terminated her mortal existence was protracted & at times painful, yet she evinced always perfect submission in her affliction.

Second list of the ofcrs on the barque **Release**: H J Hartstein, Lt Commanding; Wm S Lovell, Acting Master; Jos P Fyffe, Passed Midshipman; Jas Laws, Assist Surgeon; Chas Lever, Capt's Clerk; V R Hall, Boatswain; John Blinn, Boatswain's Mate; Wm Smith, Boatswain's Mate; Benj Moore, Sailmaker; Chas Williams, Carpenter's Mate; Wm Henry, cook; John Haley, Andrew Larson, Wm Carey, David Batay, Geo Davys, John Smith, Wm Phinney, Chas Johnson, Thos Ford, Lewis Lawrence, Francis Taylor, Byron Potter, Thos Franklin, seamen. Ofcrs of the propellar **Arctic**: C C Simms, Lt Commanding; Watson Smith, Acting Master; John K Kane, Assist Surgeon; Harman Newell, Engineer; Wm Richardson, Acting Carpenter; Saml Whiting, Acting Boatswain; Robt Bruce, Boatswain's Mate. Jno Van Dyke, Steward; Wm Johnson, Assist Engineer; Wm Groves, John Thompson, Abraham Haskell, Walter Wilkinson, Geo Bidwold, Jas Bottsford, Geo Price, John Brown, Jos Brown, Richd Hartley, Geo Tyler, John Fox, John Gilbert, seamen. Three of the above individuals were with Lt De Haven in his expedition in search of Sir John Franklin, vix: Wm S Lovell & John Blinn, of the **Release**, & Robt Bruce, of the **Arctic**.

New Orleans paper: Mr D P Blair, mail agent, was arrested in that city on May 27 by the U S Marshal, in virtue of a warrant issued on the affidavit of J J McCormack, charging him with opening letters in the post ofc contrary to the laws of the U S. [Jun 13th newspaper: the grand jury of the U S Court at New Orleans have ignored the bills against D P Blair & Geo Whitman, post ofc agents, for opening a letter with a design to obstruct correspondence.]

Fauquier White Sulphur Springs, Va: will be opened on Jun 15. –Alex'r Baker, late of Washington.

Edw M Linthicum, Chas A Buckey, & John Marberry, jr, cmplnts, vs Nicholas Gassaway, Geo Peter, jr, & Levinia Peter his wife, Alex'r Darnes & Mary Darnes his wife, John H Gassaway, Jane A Gassaway, Wm A Gassaway, & Laura Gassaway, dfndnts. In the Circuit Court of Wash Co, D C, sitting in Chancery-Bill of revivor. The bill states that the cmplnts filed their bill of complaint in said Court on Dec 6, 1852, against Hanson Gassaway, as therein stated; that they associated as partners in trade on Jul 1, 1845, & carried on business as hardware merchants; that the cmplnt, Edw M Linthicum, had before that day carried on the same business on his separate account; that the said Edward, for a long time prior to the formation of the said partnership, & your orators afterwards sold to the said Hanson Gassaway large quantities of hardware & other merchandise on credit, to be by him retailed for his own profit; that in order to secure to the said Edward any balance of debt that might, be owing to him & the cmplnts, any debts whatsoever that might be owing to them by the said Hanson, whatsoever that might be owing to them by the said Hanson, growing out of their dealings, the said Hanson Gassaway caused lots 7 & 8 in Davidson's division of square 367; lot I & K in Wilson & Callan's division of the same square; lot 6 in square 2, & lot 2 in square 72, all in Wash City, D C, to be conveyed to the said Edw M Linthicum & his heirs by deeds absolute & indefensible on their face, but with the understanding that the said Edw M Linthicum & his heirs should hold the same, after satisfying all debts due to himself & to the cmplnts, for the use of said Hanson Gassaway, his heirs & assigns. Edw M Linthicum stated in the bill of cmplnt that there is owing from the said Hanson Gassaway to him & chargeable on the said lots the sum of $21; & the cmplnts charge that there is due to them from the said Hanson Gassaway & chargeable on the said property the sum of $1,282.03, & the cmplnts pray that the said property may be sold under a decree of the said Court, & that the said debts may be paid. The cmplnts in their bill of revivor state that the said Hanson Gassaway hath died intestate & without issue, whereby their said suit has abated, & that the said Nicolas Gassaway, Lavinia Peter, the wife of Geo Peter, jr, Mary Darnes, the wife of Alex'r Darnes, John H Gassaway, Jane A Gassaway, Wm A Gassaway, & Laura Gassaway are his heirs at law. They state that the said Hanson Gassaway, although summoned, did not appear in the said suit & answer the said bill. The object of the cmplnts is to have their said suit revived & put in the same plight against the said named heirs at law of the said Hanson as the same was against him at his death, & that he may have the same relief against them as is prayed against said Hanson in the said original bill of cmplnt. And forasmuch as it appears to the Court that the said Nicholas Gassaway, Geo Peter, jr, & Lavinia his wife, Alex'r Darnes & Mary his wife, John H Gassaway, Jane A Gassaway, Wm A Gassaway, & Laura Gassaway do not reside within the Dist of Col & are not to be found therein: It is by the Court ordered that they appear in the Court, on or before the 4th Monday in Oct next. –John A Smith, clerk

Local: fire yesterday on the south side of Pa ave, near 13th st, destroyed a house owned by Mr W H Prentiss & occupied by Mr King, cabinetmaker, & Messrs Shutter & Kohlert, painters; a house owned by Mr G C Grammer & occupied by Mrs Balcher; & Appollo Hall, owned by Mr Wm Morrow & occupied with goods belonging to the estate of the late Mr J D Brown, furniture dealer, & by a barber, also. A negro boy, arrested yesterday for stealing from the burning bldg, was proven to have bought matches on the day before. The loss is estimated at from $8,000 to $10,000. Mr Prentiss & Mr Morrow were each insured to the amount of $600.

Mrd: on Jun 5, in Foundry Church, by Rev E P Phelps, Mr John W Groves to Miss Mgt Ann Waters, both of Prince Wm Co, Va.

Died: on Jun 6, after a lingering illness, Mary, wife of Lt John A Dahlgreen, U S Navy. Her funeral is this afternoon at 5 o'clock.

FRI JUN 8, 1855
Mrs Whittlesey, wife of Hon Elisha Whittlesey, received a paralytic shock at the family residence in Canfield last Thu. Her husband reached home from Wash on Sat. Her numerous family of children in like manner were summoned, to witness the departing of their parent. At last accounts no hopes were entertained of her recovery. -Ohio paper

From Calif: 1-Cornelius Mason, a butcher in San Francisco, was shot dead on May 13 by Wm Wilson, when the latter was negligently handling a loaded pistol. No blame, save that of gross carelessness, was ascribed to Wilson. 2-Wm Franklin was drowned in Stanislaus river, at the ferry, on May 4, while attempting to place a plank in the water for the purpose of throwng more water into his sluices. He by some means fell ito the water & was swept down the rapids. 3-Wm J B Todd, formerly of N Y, committed suicide at Sonora by blowing off the top of his head with a pistol. 4-John Reed, a compositor in the ofc of the Sacramento Journal, committed suicide in that city by taking strychnine. A mania for gambling appears to have led to the commission of the deed. 5-The Mountain Messenger, published at Gibsonville, furnishes the following: He had given himself 2 names, Patrick M Guffin & Patrick Carline. He was with another whose name was not learned, who reached the hill & gave the alarm. The miners turned out, &, after a great deal of labor, succeeded in finding him barely alive. A cmte was appointed by a public meeting to take care of him. He lived 3 days. His age was about 30 years, a plasterer by trade, & a native of Boston. His effects were placed in the hands of a cmte. Upon his person was found a cross & other Catholic insignia.

Oregon papers: trial of Burris for the murder of his wife & 4 children. One witness testified that when she arrived at the burning house he was staggering, crazy & drunk. He said his wife & children were all burnt & he said he did it. I never heard from his wife or any one else that there was any jealousy or any difficulty in the family. The jury returned the prisoner not guilty by reason of derangement of mind. He was remanded to jail, & had steadily refused food & drink for the last 10 days.

Runaway was committed to the jail of Wash Co, on May 22, a negro man who calls himself Jas Reed; about 26 years of age; says he is a free man, & served some time as a waiter in a hotel in Balt kept by Talbot C Etchitson. Owner is to prove property, pay charges, & take him away. –Wm Logan, sheriff

Departure of troops for the Indian country. A btln, consisting of 4 companies of the 2nd regt of U S Infty, under the command of Brvt Brig Gen E A Hitchcock, Col 2nd Infty, left Carlisle barracks, Pa, on Sat. The btln is composed of company A, Capt C S Levell, 1st Lt Caleb Smith, & 1st Lt Jas Curtass; Co D, Capt W M Gardner, 2nd Lt J D O'Connell; company G, Brvt Maj H W Wessells, Capt commanding, & 2nd L S T Sheppard, 2nd Dragoons, [temporarily attached;] company I, Capt Delozier Davidson, 1st Lt T W Sweeny. 1st Lt Geo H Paige, regimental quartermaster & acting adjutant, & Assist Surgeon D T Magruder, form the staff of the command. The btln numbers about 350 rank & file, & both ofcrs & men are in excellent health, &, from their high state of discipline, will be very efficient against the Indians of Nebraska. They are bound for **Fort Pierre**, on the Upper Missouri, but will stop at **Fort Leavenworth** to await a rise in the river. The post to be established at **Fort Pierre** will be about 800 miles above **Fort Leavenworth** & in the heart of the Sioux country.

The Boston Journal states that a beautiful little girl, 14 months old, daughter of Hon Albert Adlen, of East Cambridge, had been put to bed for her usual afternoon nap, & about an hour later her mother went into the room & found the little one was suspended behind the bed, with the back of her head against the wall & her chin resting on the mattress. She was immediately taken up & a surgeon called, who said she had probably been dead for an hour.

A party for Iowa, consisting of a man & 4 sisters, left <u>Cumberland, Md</u>, for that place several weeks since. They proceeded down the Ohio, but going up the Mississippi were all swept off by the cholera. [Names not given.]

A lot of ground, 20 by 91 feet, on 9th st, above I, has been sold at fifty cents a square foot. Messrs Green & Scott, aucts; Mr Isaac Hackett, purchaser.

Valuable estate in PG Co, Md, the subscriber, intending a change of residence, offers at private sale his private residence, *Italian Hill*, containing 100 acres of land, within 2 miles of Alexandria. The dwlg house is a commodious Italian cottage, built within the last 4 years; other farm bldgs are all new & complete. Terms liberal. Address G M F, or Thos Grimes, Mount Welby Post Ofc. –Gustavus M Finotti, PG Co, Md.

Mrd: on Jun 6, at St Matthew's Church, by Rev Mr Boyle, Dr Franklin Waters to Mrs Mary A Brooke, both of Montgmery Co, Md.

Meeting of the managers of the Union Benevolent Society on Jun 8, at their rooms on 7th st, between D & E. –Emma E Gurley, sec

Alex Rutherford returns his unfeigned thanks to his fellow citizens for their efforts to save his property from destruction by fire on Jun 6, especially the members of the Perserverance Fire Co.

SAT JUN 9, 1855
Country seat for rent or sale: the place adjoining & east of Kalorama, just without the limits of Wash City, containing about 15 acres of land, with commodious brick dwlg & out-houses. Apply to C W Pairo, exc, opposite the Treasury.

Furnished house or rooms for rent: on nw corner of 13th & F sts, a very healthy location & good water. Apply at the store on the premises to John J Joyce.

Mrs M C Greer, 569 Pa ave, announces that she has several large & well furnished rooms, which she will let either with or without board. Reasonable terms to persons finding their own furniture.

Mrd: on May 31, at the Wesley Chapel Parsonage, by Rev R L Dashiell, Mr Jas Borroughs to Miss Catharine Beard, both of Montg Co, Md.

Mrd: on Jun 7, in Wash City, by Rev Byron Sunderland, Hon Wm C McCauslin, of Steubenville, Ohio, to Miss Martha R Browning, of Wash City.

Died: on Jun 8, Mrs Mgt E Mockbee, consort of Richd Mockbee, [formerly of Wash, but more recently of St Louis, Missouri,] in her 36th year. Her funeral will be from Rev Mr Carother's church, 5th & I sts, at 3 o'clock this afternoon.

Died: on Jun 8, after a lingering illness, Wm Dant, aged 64 years. His funeral will be tomorrow, Sunday, at 4 o'clock, from his late residence, 452 D st.

$100 reward for black man, about 21 years of age, calls himself John Ambrose Stuart. $100 is taken this side of the Eastern Branch Bridge or in Va or any other State, or I will give $50 reward if taken in PG, St Mary's, Calvert, or Chas Counties. -W A Mudd

Dr Nathan Smith Lincoln has removed to 276 Pa ave, 2nd door from the Kirkwood House. Having been for several years the assist of Prof Nathan R Smith at Balt, Dr Lincoln will continue to give special attention to surgery & the diseases of the eye.

MON JUN 11, 1855
The following ofcrs have been ordered to report on Jun 25 for duty on the U S ship **Potomac**, the flag-ship of the home squadron, Cmdor Hiram Paulding: Cmder, Levin M Powell; Cmder Jas L Lardner, Capt of the Fleet & Ordnance Ofce; Lts, Melancton Smith, Wm L Herndon, L B Avery, Maxwell Woodhull, [flag,] D McN Fairfax, Edw Brinley; Master, Geo C Morgan; Purser, H M Hieskell; Chaplain, Thos R Lambert; Boatswain, Amos Colson; Gunner, Wm H Hamilton; Carpenter, J G Thomas; Sailmaker, Jas Ferguson.

Appointment by the Pres: Wm T Thruston, of Rhode Island, to be Commerical agent at the island St Christopher, West Indies.

Fairmount Virginian. A youth, only 16 years old, son of Mr T J Clagett, of Fairmount, Marion Co, Va, lost his life on Friday of last week while attempting to save the life of his father, who was placed in a perilous situation by losing control of a boat while crossing Valley river. The son, knowing his father could not swim, & being an excellent swimmer himself, plunged into the swollen stream to save his father, but his father reached the shore in the boat, while his son sunk only to rise a corpse.

Cincinnati papers: on Wed the tunnel of the Cincinnati & Dayton railroad fell when 11 men were employed in the tunnel. Jas Coleman was dangerously injured. Five were dead: Jas Pierce, Dennis Drynan, John Collins, Patrick Hagerty, & Philip Devire, a single man of 35.

We learn from the Cincinnati Gaz that on Thu last the District Court allowed the writ of error in the case of the State of Ohio vs Wm H Arrison, who was some time ago convicted of murder for having killed a man & his wife in Cincinnati by means of an infernal machine. Judge Flinn erred in his charge to the jury by saying to them, "If you find the defendent guilty you must find him guilty of murder in the 1st degree." It was not stated that they might convict of manslaughter, & no discretion was left them in regard to any other grade of the crime. The case may come to be entirely out of the jurisdiction of any tribunal.

Capt John Reese, of the Washington Highlanders, has resigned.

For sale: a good family horse & carriage. Inquire at the stables of Mr Robt Earl, in the First Ward.

Wash Co, D C. I certify that Mr Amos Davis, of said county, brought before me, as an estray trespassing on the enclosures of Mrs Eliz Wood, a dark iron gray fill. –C H Wiltberger, J P. Owner is to prove his property, pay charges, & take her away from the farm of Mrs E Wood, on the road leading from Wash City to **Glenwood Cemetery**, about half a mile north of it.

Mrd: on Jun 23, at Ryland Parsonage, by Rev W C Steel, Mr Thos Moore to Miss Jane Knot, both of Wash City.

Mrd: on Jun 7, in Gtwn, by Rev W C Steel, John N Torreyson, of Loudoun Co, Va, to Miss Eliza J Gordon, adopted daughter of Danl S Gordon, of Gtwn.

Mrd: on Jun 7, in Gtwn, by Rev Henry Slicer, John W England, of N Y, to Mary Ellen, daughter of Judson Mitchell.

Died: on Jun 4, at Canfield, Ohio, Mrs Polly Whittlesey, wife of the Hon Elisha Whittlesey, in her 69th year. Within a few months of half a century she has walked by the side of her faithful & devoted husband, & has left an unbroken family of children & numerous grandchildren, whose affection for her was only equaled by her ceaseless interest in their happiness. Though suffering from paralysis, which affected all one side, yet the mind remained unclouded, though the power of speech was withheld. Her family & friends were able to communicate with her in some degree. She was a humble & sincere Christian for many years.

Wash City Ordinances: 1-Act for the relief of Rebecca K Billing: excx of the late W W Billing, to pay her $267, in full for extra services rendered by her late husband while he was one of the collectors of Wash City taxes. 2-Act for the relief of Wm Linton: to pay him $40, being the excess of license paid by Linton to this Corp.

Virginia Female Institute, Staunton, Va. Rt Rev Wm Meade, D D, Pres of the Directory; Rt Rev John Johns, D D, V Pres of the Directory; Rev R H Phillips, Principal; Rev J C Wheat, Vice Principal. Mr & Mrs H W Sheffey, Heads of the Family. The next session will commence on Sep 12. References:
Rt Rev N H Cobbs, Montg, Ala   Levin Luckett, M D, Alexandria, Va
Hon T Reavis, Gainesville, Ala   E H Martin, Opelousas, La
Hon A H H Stuart, Staunton, Va
Profs Bledsoe, Minor, & Maupin, Univ of Va
Col F H Smith Military Institute, Lexington, Va

Died: on May 22, at his residence in Culpeper Co, Va, Col John Thom, after long confinement from the infirmities of age. His father was in the rebel army of Chas Edw Stuart [the Pretender] at the battle of Culloden, immediately after which he emigrated to Va & settled in Westmoreland Co, where the subject of this notice was born, between the years 1770 & 1771. The first years of his manhood were devoted to the education of a large family of orphan brothers. He served with credit to himself as cmder of the company from his adopted county in the war with Great Britain of 1812-15, & from the exposure & hardship he incurred at Camp Holly, near Richmond, he never entirely recovered. He represented his district in the Senate of Va for several consecutive terms, at a period when such a position was something more than a mere shadow of compliment. He leaves a large family of children & numerous friends & connexions throughout the country to mourn his loss.

TUE JUN 12, 1855
A shocking affair occurred near Owensville, Ind, on Wed, which resulted in the burning to death of Dr Morgan, of that place. He retired to bed, drunk as usual, while his wife & family were working in a corn-field near by. They discovered the house a mass of flame & saw Morgan fall through the 2nd floor, unable to save himself. Thus perished a men who at one time stood high in the confidence of the community where he resided. –Mount Carmel Register

When Mr Albert Morgan kept the Pavilion at Goucester several years ago one of his guests was an Englishman named Erskine. He was attacked with the smallpox, & while all other attendants deserted him, Mr Morgan ministered faithfully to his wants till he recovered. A day a two ago the British Consul communicated to Mr Morgan that Mr Erskine had deceased & left him by will the sum of $125,000. –Boston Post [Jun 15th newspaper: There is no truth in the statement that Mr Albert Morgan, of Boston, has been left a large fortune by a member of the Erskine family in England.]

Mrd: on Jun 4, at St Matthew's Church, M G de Boilleau, Charge d'Affaires to France, to Miss Susan Benton, youngest daughter of Hon Thos H Benton, of Missouri.

Mrd: on Jun 5, by Rev Dr A G Fairchild, at the house of M Gay, in Morgantown, Va, Hon Wm G Brown to Margaret P, daughter of Mr Gay.

Died: on Jun 6, in N Y C, Mrs Rachel Lenox, wife of Walter Lenox, of Wash City.

Died: on Jun 10, Henry C, infant son of Edw & Mary A Waite, aged 11 months.

Died: on Jun 5, at Pittsburgh, Mrs Wm Croghan Denny, daughter of Maj Denny, U S Army.

Wash City Ordinances: 1-Act refunding to B F Stewart $50, the amount of an unexpired license for keeping billiard tables. 2-Act to refund to Norman B Smith $6.20, the amount paid on lots 2 & 3 in square 243, for the years 1851 & 1852, & which taxes had previously been paid by Wm Ruggles, jr. 3-Act for the relief of Jonas P Keller: to pay him $2.62½, overpayment of taxes on part of lot 1 in square 254. 4-Act for the relief of Ann Best: the fine imposed upon her for harboring a dog without license is remitted: provided she pay the costs thereon. 5-Act for the relief of F S Myer: to be paid $24 for services rendered as police magistrate, between Jan 20 & Mar 11, 1855. 6-Joint resolution authorizing the payment of the balance of the salary of the Surveyor, [late Henry W Ball,] to his widow, from the date of his death to May 31, 1855, inclusive. 7-Joint resolution in relation to the reward offered by the late Mayor for the arrest of incendiaries, 1853. Person or persons entitled to said reward for the arrest of Jack Shepherd & John F West.

WED JUN 13, 1855
The Catholic Bishops in the U S of American birth: Bishops John Fitzpatrick, of Boston, Mass; D W Bacon, of Portland, Maine; John Timan, of Buffalo, N Y; John McCloskey, of Albany, N Y; Jas R Bayley, of Newark, N Y; Jas M Young, of Erie, Pa; Richd V Wheelan, of Wheeling, Va; John McGill, of Richmond, Va; Richd P Miles, of Nashville, Tenn; M J Spaulding, of Louisville, Ky; & Geo Carroll, of Covington, Ky.

Columbian College, D C, will open the ensuing session on the last Wed in Sept. Faculty: Rev J G Binney, D D, Pres & Prof; Wm Ruggles, L L D, Prof; Rev A J Huntington, A M, Prof; Chas C Jewett, A M, Prof; Lewis H Steiner, A M, M D, Prof; E T Fristoe, A M, Prof; Wm E Jillson, A M, Prof; R C Fox, A B, Tutor.

The Detroit Daily Advertiser announces the death of Hon Andrew Parsons, formerly Govn'r of Michigan. He died at his residence at Corunna on Wed. His disease was consumption.

$10 for two horses that were stolen or strayed from the premises of the subscriber, 210 N Y ave, near Seaton's garden, on Jun 3. –Edw Towers, 210 N Y ave.

War Dept: Hon Jefferson Davis Sec of War.
Commanding Gen's Ofc: Lt Gen Scott, of N Y.
Adj Gen's Ofc: Col Saml Cooper, Adj Gen; Assistants: Lt Col W G Freeman, Maj Geo Deas, & Capt Seth Williams; Judge Advocate, Maj John F Lee; 9 clerks & 1 messenger.
Quartermaster Gen's Ofc: Gen Thos S Jesup, quartermaster gen; Chas Thomas, assist quartermaster gen; Capt M M Clark, district quartermaster; Maj H C Wayne, in charge of clothing branch; 11 clerks & 1 messenger.
Paymaster Gen's Ofc: Col B F Larned, paymaster gen; Maj St Clair Denny, district paymaster; 8 clerks & 1 messenger.
Commissary Gen's Ofc: Gen Geo Gibson, commissary gen; assist, Capt A E Shiras; 6 clerks & 1 messenger.
Surgeon Gen's Ofc: Gen Thos Lawson, surgeon gen; assistants, Dr R C Wood & Dr Richd H Coolidge; 3 clerks.
Engineer Ofc: Gen Jos G Totten, chief engineer; assist, Lt John D Kurtz; 5 clerks & 1 messenger.
Topographical Bureau: Col J J Abert, colonel of the corps; assist, Lt M L Smith; 4 clerks & 1 messenger.
Ordnance Bureau: Col H R Craig, colonel of ordnance; assist, Capt Wm Maynadier; 8 clerks & 1 messenger.

Alexandria Gaz: the remains of the late gallant & lamented Gen Childs, U S Army brought on from Tampa, Fla, where he died, arrived here on Sunday & were buried yesterday in the cemetery at this place, without parade, but amidst the tears & regrets of many of his relations, connexions, & friends, who cherish his memory.

Two little boys, one 5 & the other 7 years of age, sons of Mr Benj Dexter & Mr Chas Kempton, of New Bedford, left their homes on Friday & were found on Saturday asleep near the road side in the eastern part of Fairhaven. They were searched for during the night. The boys had become bewildered & lost their way.

Rev Mason Noble, a chaplain in the U S Navy, has been ordered to sea in the frig **Congress,** soon to sail. During the 2 years he has been stationed at the navy yard in Wash City he has found opportunity to build a fine church edifice & to bring together an excellent congregation in the 7th or Island Ward.

Official, Dept of State. Wash, Jun 11, 1855. The following card is published at the suggestion of the Minister Resident of the U S at Berne, Switzerland:
Card-Jos Block, of Switzerland. Information is wanted of this young man, lately a sailor on board the ship **Moses Taylor,** Capt French; supposed to have left that ship in New Orleans about Mar, 1855. He will receive a letter containing news of importance on application to the Swiss Consul at Wash.

Mrs Robinson to be hung. The Supreme Court on Sat gave a decision in the application made for a new trial in the case of Henrietta Robinson, the "veiled murderess", affirming the proceedings of the Court of Oyer & Terminer, before whom she was tried & convicted, & directing that she be sentenced & the law executed. -Albany Argus

At the session of the Court of Common Pleas at Newburyport, Mass, last Wed, W B Fairfield, alias Bowers, having been convicted on a charge of adultery, was sentenced to 12 days' solitary confinement & 3 years in the State prison. This is the extent of the law.

Another fatal accident from camphene: some 10 days since Frank Brown, who resided on the York road, about 1 mile beyond the Balt City limits, while lighting a pipe the fire communicated to a bottle of oil which exploded, burning him horribly. He lingered in the most intense agony up to Sat last, when death relieved him from his earthly sufferings. –Balt Sun

Robt Dickey, charged with the murder of Henry Clay St Clair, in Fairfax Co, Va, on Dec 30 last, was tried in the circuit court of that county last week & found guilty of murder in the 2nd degree. The term of his imprisonment in the penitentiary was affixed at 18 years.

Died: on Jun 10, in Wash City, Mrs Sarah W Walsh, consort of J Carra Walsh, & daughter of the late Capt McCall, of the U S Navy.

Died: on Jun 12, Charles William, infant son of Richd & Sarah Ann White, one month old. His funeral is at 5 o'clock P M this day, from 4th & I sts.

For rent: the store now occupied by Jos Huggins, 214 Pa ave. –E Owen & Son

For rent: the dwlg lately occupied by Senator Seward, F, between 6th & 7th sts. Apply at the ofcs of J C Lewis, 7th st.

THU JUN 14, 1855
The new noble ship **Merrimack**, will be first launched of the steam frigates ordered to be added to the Navy by the act of Congress of 1854. She will be launched this day, Jun 14, from the navy yard at Charlestown, Mass. The editor of the Boston Post, through the kindness of Cmdor Gregory, & with the permission of E K Delano, the naval constructor for that district, has been permitted to examine her. She was designed by John Lenthall, Chief of the Bureau of Construction, Equipment, & Repairs, & the design has been faithfully carried out by Mr Delano & by Mr Melvin Simmons, the master carpenter of the yard.

A detachment of 240 U S troops, from Govnr's Island, N Y, went up Lake Erie on Fri, on board the steamer **Plymouth Rock**, on their way to St Louis. The detachment was under the command of Maj Garnett.

J M Palmer, Deputy Marshal at Canandaigua, last week arrested Mrs Dianthe Phelps at Columbus, near Harrisburgh, Pa, on a warrant issued against her by the U S Com'r Boyce, in this city, in which she is charged with being an accomplice in the robbery of U S mail bags at Elmira in Nov last. In default of $2,000 bail, she was committed to the Ontario Co jail for indictment at the June term of the U S Circuit Court, to be held at Canandaigua on Jun 19. –Utica Gaz

Trustee's sale of valuable property on 6th st: by a decree of the Circuit Court of Wash Co, D C, sitting in Chancery, passed May 8, 1855, in a cause wherein Aaron O Dayton is cmplnt & Jas P McElfresh & Jas A Watson dfndnts, the undersigned will sell at auction, on Jul 10, the following property: lot 18 in square 453, with bldgs & improvements thereon. –W B Webb, trustee -Jas C McGuire, auct

Runaway was committed to the jail of Wash Co on Jun 4, a negro man Edw J Brown, sometimes Sad Nelson Brown, about 36 years of age; says he is a free man from Charlestown, Va, & had his home with John W Gardner. Owner is to come forward, prove his property, pay charges, & take him away, else he will be discharged agreeably to law. –Wm Logan, sheriff

Yesterday a frame dwlg-house, on G st, near 5th, belonging to Lt B Hunter, U S Navy, & worth some twelve or fourteen hundred dollars, was consumed by fire. The fire injured the adjacent brick houses belonging to Mr Wm G Deale, who was insured. Mr Jas Harrover lost a finger by an accident while working at this fire. The spirit of incendiarism is again in our midst.

The statue of Judge Story, by his son, Wm W Story, has now been in the Boston Athenaeum for a week, & is considered by all who knew the Judge to be a most successful work. It is larger than life size, clothed in the judicial gown of the Judges. It will ultimately be placed in the new chapel at Mount Auburn.

Judge Roosevelt made an important decision in the divorce case of Mrs Curtiss against Dr Jos T Curtiss before the Circuit Court in N Y on Thu last. It was shown that Dr C had obtained a divorce in Indiana, since when he has married & lived with another lady, for which Mrs Curtiss brings an action for a divorce. Judge Roosevelt held, for the purposes of this suit, that a decree of divorce obtained in Indiana against a party not residing there, but living in this State, is not valid or binding here. Judgment in the above case is reserved.

Mrd: on Jun 9, at **Rosedale**, D C, by Rev B Maguire, Pres Gtwn College, Angel De Yturbide, Sec of the Mexican Legation, to Alice, daughter of the late John Green.

Died: yesterday, at her residence in Wash City, in her 84th year, Mrs Ann Tayloe, relict of the late Col John Tayloe, of **Mount Airy**. She was one of the very limited number of the earliest inhabitants of Wash, of which she has been a resident near 54 years. To her own family, by whom she was revered, her loss is irreparable. Her remains will be taken to the family vault in Va.

Orphans Court of Wash Co, D C. In the case of Thos F Semmes, adm of Jos L C Hardy, deceased: the adm & Court have appointed Jul 3 next for the settlement of said estate, & distribution of the assets in hand. –Ed N Roach, Reg/o wills

Retraction: the St Paul Times announced the death of Dr Day, of cholera, in that city, some days since. The paper of May 17th: We retract, we apologize, we blush, we beg pardon, & for ourselves, but for shame of rumor. Dr Day says that is isn't so; that rumor lies; that he isn't dead; that he can prove it.

FRI JUN 15, 1855
For rent: 2 story brick house, with back bldg, on 2nd st, Gtwn, adjoining the residence of Mrs Bodisco. Apply at the ofc of Brooke B Williams.

Foreign Items. 1-Lord Strangford, formerly Minister to Brazil & other Courts, died on May 29 at an advanced age. 2-Lord Chas Manners is also dead, aged 74 yers.

Mrd: on Jun 14, at St Johns' Church, Gtwn, by Rev N P Tillinghast, J W Hester, of Va, to Miss Eliza R, daughter of Thos B Addison, of the former place.

Mrd: on Jun 12, by Rev Mr Israel, A Graham Worden, of Michigan, to Jeannie Ogden, daughter of Col Wm Ogden Niles, of Wash City.

Valuable improved property near the Navy Yard at auction: on Jun 21, part of lot 3 & all of lot 4 in square 881, it being the property belonging to Mr Saml T Little, on south L, between 6th & 7th sts. On lot 3 is a good brickdwlg house. Lot 4 has a front on L st of 50 feet. Title indisputable. -Green & Scott, aucts

The Board of Naval Examiners is still in session at Annapolis, Md. The following midshipmen have passed a satisfactory examination before the Board, & now take rank as passed midshipmen: of the class of 1848: J S Skerrett, E T Spedden, E K Owen, W T Glassell, J R Stillwell, D G Livingston. Of the Class of 1849: B B Loyall, C H Cushman, G F Stanton, W H Cheever, H A Adams, B B Taylor, W H Ward, J W Dunnington, H M Garland, Jesse Taylor, jr, J G Maxwell, Henry Erben, F E Shepperd, T P Pelot, E P McCrea.

New Catholic Bookstore, 9th st, between D & E, no 468. –W F Keefer

Orphans Court of Wash Co, D C. Letters of administration on the personal estate of Wm Bird, late of Wash Co, deceased. —Wm Bird, Eburn Bird, adms

Chancery sale of valuable improved real estate & market garden. By decree of the Circuit Court of Wash Co, D C, made in the case wherein Mary Hoffman, admx & heir-at-law of Thos Moore, deceased, is cmplnt, & Hannah Moore, & Jas Moore & Laura Ann Moore his wife, heirs-at-kaw of said Thos Moore, deceased, are dfndnts, No 1,067 in chancery: public auction on Jul 10, 1855, on the premises, the whole of square 303, in Wash City, fronting 310 feet on each of 11th & 12th sts west, & 202 feet 2 inches on each of V & W sts north, containing about 62, 672 square feet of ground, with bldgs & improvements-a 2 story brick dwlg house & frame stable. -Chas S Wallach, trustee -Jas C McGuire, auct

SAT JUN 16, 1855
$200 reward for runaway negro man belonging to Wm C Fowler, of Calvert Co, Md, named Henry Ross, age 35 years, who escaped from Upper Marlboro Jail, PG Co, Md, on May 25, 1855. He has a family residing in Chestnut Alley, Balt.
—Wm C Fowler, Dunkirk, Calvert, Md, Jun 11, 1855.

A little son of Mr C M Keys, of Wash City, had his collar bone broken at a picnic in Arlington on Thu afternoon.

Mrd: on Jun 6, at Rockville, by Rev Mr Russell, E Barret Prettyman to Lydia F, daughter of Capt Z F Johnston, U S Navy.

M'lle W De Boye's Concert of Classical Musical will positively take place on Jun 22, at Carusi's Saloon, having to be unavoidably postponed by the impossibility of Prof Ahrend's attendance on Jun 18. Tickets 50 cents, to be had at all the principal hotels, music & bookstores.

MON JUN 18, 1855
Trustee's sale of valuable improved & unimproved real estate. In pursuance of a decree of the Circuit Court of Wash Co, D C, passed in a cause wherein Levin M Powell & Jeannette C Powell are cmplnts, & Wm A Bradley, Sydney A Bradley, Chas M Thruston, Wm T Thruston, Horatio Gates, Eliza, Jeannette, & Dickerson Phillips Thruston; Sarah Thruston, Chas M, Helen K, & Thos W Thruston; Fannie C Thruston, Jeannette B, Alfred B, & Sydney Thruston are dfndnts, the undersigned trustees, appointed under said decree, will sell at public auction, on the premises, on Jul 12 next, the whole of square 528. On Jul 13: original lots 6 thru 8 in square 690; a portion improved by good substantial houses, the rest unimproved. On Jul 16, lot 18 & part of lot 19, in square 690, improved by a well built 3 story brick house, back bldg, & stable. —W B Webb, Jos H Bradley, jr, trustees -J C McGuire, auct

Mrd: on Jun 12, at *Mount Airy*, Va, by Rev Dr Coffin, Dr J M Snyder, of Gtwn, D C, to Sophia C, daughter of Wm H Tayloe.

The Montpelier Farmer says that, on the occasion of the late dangerous illness of the widow of Hon Saml Prentiss, formerly U S Senator, nine sons, eight of them lawyers, & the ninth clerk of the U S District Court of which his father was judge, assembled at the paternal mansion in *Montpelier*.

On Thu at Sharp's Rifle Factory, in Hartford, Mr Willis North, one of the workmen, was clipping off shavings from a bar of steel, when a shaving struck him, producing but little feeling of injury. In a few minutes he showed signs of a serious injury & shortly expired. The small bit of steel must have entered his heart.

<u>Annual examination of Public Schools, Wash:</u>
Teachers:

Miss M G Wells	Miss H R Baker	Mrs Ogden
Miss E Parsons	Mrs E Myers	Mrs Rodier
Miss J F Acton	Mrs E Clark	Mr Goldsmith
Mrs S E Coale	Mrs Skidmore	Mr Edson
Miss C McCarthy	Miss C Campbell	Mr J Thompson
Miss F Elvans	Mis E Billings	Mr J Fill
Miss A K Lowe	Miss J Moss	Mr T M Wilson
Miss L H Randolph	Miss M A Lee	Mr S Kelly
Miss E Ashdown	Miss H U Henshaw	Miss Milburn
Miss J Thompson	Miss A Adams	Miss Martin
Miss F Henshaw	Mrs S J Thompson	Mrs Randolph
Mrs M Freeman	Mr H M McCathran	Miss Middleton

Glenwood Cemetery, ofc 292 Pa ave, corner of 10th st, over the Savings Bank. This Cemetery is laid out on the plan of the celebrated Greenwood, of N Y, & situated on the high ground distant one & a quarter mile north of the Capitol, North Capitol st leading directly to the gateway. This Company have received a charter from Congress, appropriating their ground forever to burial purpose, making a fee title to the purchaser, & prohibiting all encroachments from legislation or otherwise, which is of vast importance to those who wish their dead to repose where they have placed them, for it has become a custom in all cities, when the burial ground has become valuable for other purposes, to sell it & throw the dead promiscuously into one large pit, & legal measures cannot prevent it, as no titles are given to the ground. N B. Pamphlets, with a map, the charter & bye-laws, & all other information, can be obtained at the office; also, all orders for interments left with Mr James Harvey, No 410 7th st, or any other undertaker, will be promptly attended to. Office open from 10 to 12 A M.

Gtwn: for sale-three story brick house on Bridge st, Gtwn, next adjoining the Drug Store of R S T Cissel. –Jno Marbury

Wm D Bammistle, of Adrian city, Mich, ascended in a balloon from that place, on Jun 8, at 10½ in the morning, & descended in Clarion Co, in Pa, at 2½ in the afternoon, making the computed distance of 350 miles in the extraordinary short time of 4 hours. –Phil Ledger

Franklin, son of Richd Curtis, of Bath, was drowned on Tue; & George, son of David Bryant, was drowned on Jun 6 at Five Islands, on the Penobscot river. –Boston Jour of Fri.

For rent: convenient 4 story & basement dwlg-house, No 482 12th st, between E & F sts, recently built, having been papers & painted within a few weeks past. Neighborhood & location the best & most healthy. Rent moderate, & possession given immediately. Apply to Jas J Miller, 7th st & La ave.

TUE JUN 19, 1855
Closing sale of Dry Goods this day, at the store lately occupied by Hall & Brother, 7th st: silks, wool, lawns, lace, muslins, silk gloves, & tassels. -Jas C McGuire, auct

In a Circuit Court for Lewis Co, Ky, a suit of slander-Miss Eliza Barkley vs Wm Giddings-was tried, & a verdict rendered for $10,000 damages. Giddings had paid his addresses to Miss Barkley, & had been rejected previous to making the slanderous charges which the jury has so signally punished in damages.

Mrs C Ruoff, Milliner, lately from N Y, has taken rooms at 16 East Capitol st, where she intends to keep on hand a splendid assortment of the latest Spring styles.

Ice Cream of the best quality delivered to families, parties & fairs, at 37½ cents per quart, in fancy moulds or plain freezers. –M T Martinet, 10th st, between D & E sts.

Died: on Jun 18, Peter Parker, aged 19 months, son of Prof Chas G Page. His funeral will be tomorrow at 5 o'clock P M, at his residence.

The Cedars for rent: beautiful residence on the Heights of Gtwn. For terms apply to F A Lazenby, Bridge st, or to the subscriber at Bellevue, 2½ miles above Gtwn. –W D C Murdock

WED JUN 20, 1855
Household & kitchen furniture, & family carriage at auction on: Jun 27, at the official residence of Cmdor Paulding, Wash Navy Yard. -Jas C McGuire, auct

Great surgical operation. The wife of Mr Jos Richardson, of Boone Co, Ky, who was brought to this side of the Ohio river, in Delhi township, for surgical relief, was operated on May 22 & had a tumor weighing more than 40 pounds, growing for 2 years, cut from the interior of her abdomen. This terrible operation was performed by Dr Litzenberry, in this county, assisted by his partner, Dr Leonard, & Drs Lindsey & Gaines, of Delhi township. Dr Dodge, of this city, administered ether with his usual efficiency. Mrs Richardson is now, [15th days after the operation] improving rapidly, & feels well enough to sit up. –Cincinnati Commercial, 6th.

Wm Franklin Carr, convicted of the murder of his father in Holmesville, Miss, was executed on Jun 6. He admitted having committed the deed, but said he thought the gun with which he fired at his father was empty.

Criminal Court-Wash: list of Grand & Petit Jurors:

Grand Jurors:
Wm Gunton	Jos Bryan	Zadock W McKnew
Jeremiah Orme	John H King	Henry Haw
Jas L Edwards	Joshua Pierce	Geo A Bohrer
Wm B Magruder	Jas A Kennedy	Richd Jones
H Loughborough	Augustus E Perry	Geo McNeir
Zachariah Walker	Wm T Dove	Zadock D Gilman
W M Morrison	Francis Mohun	Wm H Tenny
Chas L Coltman	John L Kidwell	

Petit Jurors:
Jas B Holmead	Thos Taylor	Jacob Barker
David W Oyster	John Cruikshanks	H W McPherson, jr
Walter Stewart	David Shoemaker	Saml C Espey
Stephen Harmon	H O Whitmore	Jacob Harshman
Richd Harrison	A W Divine	Geo Harvey
Francis H Elwell	G S Noyes	Theodore Meade
Wm P Doury	David Davis	Isaac A Montrose
Peter Brenner	Thos Towner	Jas Barnard
Jos Lyons	Geo McNaughton	Jeremiah Smith
Jas Lynch	Thos J Crane	Jesse Lipscomb

A German, missing since Jun 11th from Gtwn, was on Sunday found dead in the canal at the Great Falls, & with marks of violence upon his person. [No name given.]

For sale: desirable residence on F st between 13tth & 14th sts. Apply to Richd Burgess, 249 F st.

Orphans Court of Wash Co, D C. Letters of administration on the personal estate of Fred'k Hager, late of Wash Co, deceased. –Theresa Hager, admx

Soldiers-1812. Soldiers of the war of 1812 met at City Hall on Jun 18, & reported the form of a Constitution for the gov't of the Associated Soldiers of the War of 1812 for the District of Columbia, as also the names recommended for ofcrs of the Association for the ensuing year, which were unanimously adopted. They are: Col Wm W Seaton, Pres; Col John S Williams, 1st V Pres; Col Wm Doughty, 2nd V Pres; John Underwood, Sec; Jas McClery, Treas; Dr Peregrine Warfield, Surgeon. Exec Cmte: Gen Roger C Weightman, Richd Burgess, & Wm G Ridgely.

Miss Brooke's English & French Boarding & Day School, 138 Pa ave. Miss Brooke, from Phil, having taken the house at the corner of 19th & Pa ave, in the block known as the Seven Bldgs, will open on Sep 10, 1855. She acquired experience at St Mary's Hall, Burlington, N J, & the Espicopal Female Institute, Phil. Reference: My good friend, Miss Brooke, is a most estimable lady, of great intelligence, whose qualifications as a teacher entitle her to high consideration. –Alonzo Potter

In Chancery. Chas A Davis, Geo A Davis, & Alex'r McD Davis vs Nathan Fales, Wm Fales, Nathan Fales, jr, Henry Fales, Mary V Fales, Maria Stewart & Wm Stewart, Nathl B Keene, Mary D Keene, Alex'r McD Keene, Maria S Keene, Geo L Keene, John H Keene, & Charlotte K Keene. The bill is to procure a decree for the sale of a certain real estate, in Wash City, of which Chas B Davis died seized. Davis died about the year 1839, first having duly made & published his last will & testament, whereby he devised his said real estate, which is particularly described in the bill, to his wife, Eliz Davis, during her single life, & after her death the same to be divided equally between his children, Chas A Davis, Geo A Davis, Alex'r McD Davis, & Susan Elenor Keene, & his step-daughter, Eliz Fales; that the said Susan E Keene hath departed this life intestate, leaving surviving her her husband, Nathl B Keene, & Mary D Keene, Alex'r McD Keene, Maria S Keene, Geo T Keene, John H Keene, & Charlotte K Keene, her children & heirs-at-law; that the said Eliz Fales has also departed this life intestate, leaving surviving her her husband, Nathan Fales, & Wm Fales, Nathl Fales, jr, Henry Fales, Mary V Fales, & Maria Stewart, her children & heirs-at-law; that the said Chas A Davis & Geo A Davis are the surviving excs named in said will; that said will hath been proven & letters testamentary therein obtained by said Geo A Davis; that said Geo A Davis & Chas A Davis were authorized by said will to make an equal division of said real estate between the devisees named in said will; but that the said real estate is not susceptible of such equal division, & that it will be for the interest & advantage of the dfndnts, as well as of the cmplnts, to sell the same & divide the proceeds thereof between the parties in proportion to their respective interests; & that the said Nathl B Keene, Wm Fales, Nathan Fales, jr, & Henry Fales reside out of D C, & beyond the jurisdiction of this Court. Absent dfndnts to appear in this Court, in person or by solicitor, on or before the 4th Monday of Oct next. –Jno A Smith, clerk

Mrd: on Jun 18, by Rev J G Butler, Geo Gideon Larner to Miss Emma V Mulloy, both of Wash City.

Died: on Jun 18, Miss Sarah V, daughter of the late Edgar Patterson. Her funeral will take place from the residence of her mother on West st, Gtwn, this afternoon at 5 o'clock.

Died: on Jun 19, at the residence of her son-in-law, Geo W Riggs, jr, in Wash City, Mrs M C Shedden, relict of the late Thos Shedden, in her 75th year. Her funeral services are this afternoon, at 3½ o'clock P M, in St Matthew's Church.

THU JUN 21, 1855
Naval: the U S practice ship **Preble**, will sail from Annapolis on Jun 27 on a short cruise. List of her ofcrs: Jos F Green, lt commanding; Robt H Wyman, lt; B F Gallaher, purser; John Ward, passed assist surgeon; Wm H Parker, master; Saml R Franklin, master; Wm K Mayo, acting master; W McGunnegle, passed midshipman.

For rent: 2 story brick house now occupied by J W Brown, on F st, between 14th & 15th sts. This house stands back from the street, & has fine shade trees in front. -Tho Carbery

Valuable servants for sale: by order of the Orphans Court: sale in the town of Upper Marlborough, on Jul 11. –J H Waring, C C Magruder, adms of S M Worthington.

Edw Hogan, 8 years of age, who lived with his parents in James st, N Y, died on Sunday of compression of the brain, produced by a fall. On the day previous he, with other children, were in a brewery, when John Farmer, one of the hands, gave him a pint of beer, which he drank & soon became intoxicated. He went into the yard of a public school to pay, when he fell backward, striking his head. The injury he sustained proved fatal.

Mrd: on Jun 19, in Gtwn, D C, by Rev Dr Norwood, F W Hanewinckel, of Richmond, Va, to Roberta C, daughter of Wm S Nicholls, of the former place.

Died: on Jun 20, Florence, youngest daughter of Geo & A S Parker, aged 3 months & 6 days. Her funeral is this afternoon, at 4½ o'clock, from the residence of her father, corner of 4½ & C sts.

$10 reward for 4 cows that strayed on Monday last. Reward will be paid for their delivery at my house, or in proportion for any one or more of them.
–Chas Dyson, corner of north D & 2nd sts.

FRI JUN 22, 1855
Household & kitchen furniture at auction on: Jun 27, at the residence of Mr Saml I Little, on L, between 6th & 7th sts. -Green & Scott, aucts

Board of Naval Ofcrs appointed by the Pres to carry into effect the act of Congress "to promote the efficiency of the navy" met in Wash City on Wed last for the discharge of the duty assigned to them. Ofcrs who compose the Board:
Capts: Wm B Shubrick, Matthew C Perry, Chas S McCauley, C K Stribling, Abraham Bigelow.
Cmders: G J Pendergrast, Franklin Buchanan, Saml F Du Pont, Saml Barron, Andrew H Foote.
Lts: John S Missroon, Richd L Page, Sylvanus W Gorden, Wm L Maury, Jas S Biddle. Cmdor Shubrick, as senior ofcr, presides over the Board.

Hon Kenneth Rayner, of N C, Albert Pike, of Ark, Jacob Broom, of Pa, & John Cunningham, of S C, are stopping at the Nat'l Hotel.

Jas H Burton, late master armorer in the Nat'l Armory at Harper's Ferry, Va, but for some months past a resident of this city, has received from the British Gov't the appointment of engineer of the British Nat'l Armory at Enfield, near London. Although that armory is under the command of Capt Dixon, of the Royal Artl, Mr Burton will have the entire direction of the manufacturing operations of the establishment. –Springfield [Mass] Republican

Obit-died: on Jun 17, at his residence on the Cattaraugus Reservation, Henry Two-Guns, [Ha ja-on-gueh,] head chief of the Seneca Nation of Indians, aged 75 years. He was a step-son of the famour orator Red-Jacket & was born within the limits of the now city of Buffalo. He was engaged in the war of 1812, espousing the cause of his great father, the President; participated in the battles of Bridgewater & Chippewa; & for a long series of years exercised a controlling influence over his nation. A bright star had fallen, & gloom & darkness brood in its place! N T Strong, Seneca Chief

I offer for sale my farm *Norwood*, on Morattico creek, near the Rappahannock river, Lancaster Co, Va: contains 538½ acres: excellent dwlg house & all convenient out-houses. Apply to me, near Mill View P O, Fauquier Co, Va. –John B Downman

Partnership dissolved by mutual consent on Jun 18. The Furniture business will be continued by A Rothwell, at the Store on 7th st. –A Rothwell, T B Brown

For sale, a valuable negro woman, aged 33, with or without 2 children, aged 6 & 8 years, for whom the owner has no use. For terms apply to R J Bowie, of Rockville, or W H Chichester, Brookeville, Montg Co, Md.

Andrew J Berry & his wife were killed by lightning at Multona Springs, Miss, May 30th.

Gertrude Elmsbury, a German girl, aged 22, lost her life in N Y on Fri by the bursting of a camphene lamp.

Two drunken men, John McNally & John McMullen, were run over & killed by the Harlem cars in N Y C on Sat.

Mrd: on Jun 20, at the Wesley Chapel parsonage, by Rev R L Dashiell, Wm G Deale to Emeline, daughter of Jas B Phillips, all of Wash City.

Mrd: on Jun 21, at St John's Church, in Wash City, by Rev Smith Pyne, Cmdor Breese, U S Navy, to Emma, daughter of the late Thos Lovett, of N Y.

SAT JUN 23, 1855

Circuit Court of PG Co, as Court of Equity, Jun term, 1855. Jesse L Heiskell et al vs Susan A M Heiskell. On Sep 23, 1852, Thos Ellis & Chas Ellis, of the city of Richmond, Va, filed their petition in this cause, representing that they recovered a judgment in the county court for Albemarle, Va, against Jesse L Heiskell, the cmplnt in said cause, on Oct 29, 1850, for $938.05, part thereof, from Oct 16, 1847, & on $38, the residue thereof, from Jun 14, 1847; also, $5.96 cost; that the said Jesse L Heiskell does not reside in the State of Md, & that he has no property whatsoever out of which they can make their debt, except his interest in the proceeds of sales of the real estate of his deceased father, Alex'r H C Heiskell, sold under the decree passed in this cause; that they have instituted proceedings at law by way of attachment against the goods, chattels, rights, & credit of the said Jesse L Heiskell, & caused the same to be laid upon the proceed of sale of said real estate in the hands of C C Magruder, trustee, & praying that the interest portion of said trust fund to which the said Jesse L Heiskell is entitled, or so much thereof as may be necessary, be appropriated by an order of this Court to the payment of said debt, interest & cost; & as Jesse L Heiskell is a non-resident, an order of publication against him be passed; & he is to appear in this Court, in person or by solicitor, on or before the first Mon of Nov next. -Peter W Crain -Edw W Belt, clerk of the Court for PG Co, Md.

The Laurel cotton factory, on the Patuxent river, in PG Co, was totally destroyed by fire on Wed. The grist-mill, store, & other bldgs near by were preserved. By this calamity 260 operators are thrown out of employment. The factory belonged to the Patuxent Co, of which W H Keighler, of Balt, is Pres.

On Sat Jos Wyckoff, a son of Saml Syckoff, of Six-Mile Run, was mowing with one of the regular mowing & reaping machines on his farm. He stopped to oil the machine, & in getting on he slipped & fell just behind the cutting bar. His left arm was thrown in front of the knife & was instantly severed above his wrist. Dr McKissack, of Millstone, in the present of Drs Schenck & Mosher, very successfully amputated the arm, & the patient was doing well. —Somerset [N J] Whig

Mrd: on Jun 20, at Trinity Church, by Rev Geo Cummins, Shelby Clarke to Lizzie A, daughter of Thos Woodward, of Gtwn, D C.

From the North China Herald of Apr 7. The number of sailors recently run away from merchant vessels in the harbor induced the Consul of the U S of America, Robt C Murphy, to request a suitable force from Capt McCluney, of the U S war-steamer **Powhatan**, & sent them, under charge of Mr Whiting, with a warrant countersigned by the British Consul, to Woosung, on Sat last, in order to bring back as many of the sailors of America & Great Britain as could be discovered in the places of concealment they resort to at that village. On Sun Mr Boatswain Whiting, [a very trustworthy ofcr, who, for his good conduct, has frequently enacted the duties of a lt upon an emergency] went with his men to a house known to be frequented by runaway sailors & demanded admittance. This was refused, & Mr Whiting ordered an entrance to be forced with the butt end of the musket. The gun went right through the door, &, catching the trigger, fired off the musket, & the ball struck Whiting under his belt & killed him instantly. The men brought back the body of their ofcr to Shanghai, & on Mon was interred at the cemetery with all naval honors. The U S Consul, Mr Murphy, Capt McCluney, his ofcrs & men, attended to do honor to the melancholy ceremony, & the fine band of the Powhatan performed. Rev C Keith, of the Protestant Church, U S Army, performed the service.

Died: on Jun 20, Willie, infant son of Thos & Mary McGill.

Died: on Jun 9, at sea, William, youngest son of Wm M & Mary M Boyce, of Gtwn, D C.

Circuit Court of PG Co, Md, sitting in Equity: Jun Term, 1855. John F M Lowe vs Sophia A Lowe & others. The object of this suit is to procure a decree for an account of the administration of the personal estate of Lloyd M Lowe, & a decree against the administrator *pendente lite* & the excx of said personal estate, for the mal-administration of said estate, for the rents & profits of the real estate of said deceased, for increase & hires of that portion of the personal estate to which the cmplnt is entitled under the last will & testament of Lloyd M Lowe; & a decree against the legatees & devisees under said last will & testament for contribution, & so forth. The bill states that Lloyd M Lowe, late of said county, departed this life on Aug 28, 1949, having before that time executed in due form of law his last will & testament in writing, which has since been duly admitted to probate; by which among other things, he devised & bequeathed unto the cmplnt, in fee simple, the plantation called *Belleview*, lying & being in said county, upon which he then resided, with the lands adjoining thereto, containing in the whole 500 acres, together with the following negroes: Frank, Geo, Jim, Henry, boy Bob, woman Mary & her increase, Nanny, Nell, & girl Emily & her increase; also, his stock of cattle, horses, sheep, & hogs; his plantation utensils & all his books. That the said testator, by a codicil to his last will & testament, bearing date Jul 18, 1849, which was also admitted to probate as a part of his last will & testament, among other things revoked the aforesaid devise & bequest of the said land & negroes made to the cmplnt in his said last will & testament in fee simple, & in lieu thereof devised & bequeathed to the cmplnt a home at the place called **Belleview** for 7 years after his death & the use of all the land & negroes devised to him in his said will, with the exception of negroes Geo & Bill; & after the expiration of said years he devised & bequeathed the said land & negroes to his son John H Lowe, in trust for his grandson Lloyd M Lowe; & in case the said John H Lowe should die before the expiration of the said 7 years he directed that his son-in-law, John M Steed, should take charge of said property for the use of said Lloyd M Lowe, & appointed John H Lowe & Sophia A Lowe as the excs of said last will & testament. That immediately after the death of said testator the said John H Lowe & Sophia A Lowe took possession of the whole of said estate, both real & personal, & on Nov 24, 1849, a contest having arisen in the Orphans' Court of PG Co touching the validity of said will, letters *pendente lite* on the personal estate of said deceased were granted by said court to the said John H & Sophia A Lowe, who kept possession of both the real & personal estate, which they cultivated, & took to their own use the rents, issues, & profits thereof, without having up to this time accounted for the same either to the said Orphans' Court or to the cmplnt. That on Aug 19, 1851, the said contest touching the validity of said will having been finally determined in favor of the validity thereof, said letters *pendente lite* were revoked by said Orphans' Court, & full letters testamentary on said personal estate were committed to the said Sophia A Lowe, who took possession of all of said property, both real & personal, & has taken to her own use the rents, issues, & profits thereof ever since, whereby the cmplnt was excluded from all benefit therefrom, although he frequently demanded the possession of the said real & personal estate devised & bequeathed to him by the said last will & testament; but the said John H & Sophia A Lowe, adms *pendente lite* as aforesaid, & the said Sophia A Lowe, excx aforesaid, refused to deliver possession thereof, but unjustly withheld the same. That the said real estate, under the injudicious & improper cultivation of the said John H & Sophia A Lowe, has been greatly depreciated in value; they have permitted said land to become very poor by constant cultivation without the use of either clover or plaster, or any other system of improvement; the houses have been permitted to fall into decay & ruin, & the fencing taken away & destroyed, where the interest of the cmplnt in said real estate has been greatly lessened. That they have by great mismanagement & neglect permitted a large portion of the very valuable stock of horse, cattle, & sheep, which was bequeathed to the cmplnt, to die for want of proper attention; other portions thereof they have suffered to be taken away from said premises. That the farming utensils bequeathed to said cmplnt have been either taken from said premises or abused & worn out in the cultivation of said land. That the said Sophia A Lowe, excx as aforesaid, has sold several of the most valuable negroes bequeathed to the cmplnt for 7 years as aforesaid, for the purpose as she alleged of paying the debts of said testator & the costs of said administration; having befoe that time delivered to all the other legatees & devisees under the said will the property devised & bequeathed to them respectively, instead of selling a portion of the property devised & bequeathed to all of said legatees & devisees, so that they might contribute rateably to the payment of said debts, if any, & to the cost of said administration. The bill prays that a decree may be passed requiring the said John H & Sophia A Lowe to account for the rents & profits of said estate to the cmplnt from the death of said testator, & for any loss sustained by the cmplnt by reason of the improper cultivation, mismanagement, & neglect of said real estate; & for the annual hires & increase of the aforesaid negroes bequeathed to the cmplnt; also, for the horse, cattle, sheep, & hogs, & their usual increase; farming utensils & books bequeathed as aforesaid to the cmplnt, or account to him for the value thereof at the death of said testator; & if any of said personal property has been sold for the purpose of paying the debts of said testator or the cost of said administration, to require the said excx to exhibit an account of the sales thereof & the manner in which the proceeds thereof have been appropriated; & to require the said Sophia A Lowe, John H Lowe, Bradley S A Lowe, Jas M Steed & Leonora his wife, Lloyd M Lowe, Enoch L Lowe, Lloyd McC Lowe, Enoch M Lowe, & Rebecca Lowe, all of whom are legatees & devisees under said last will & testament, & who have received the property devised & bequeathed to them respectively in said will, to contribute in a rateable proportion towards re-imburseing the cmplnt in the sum or sums of money which may have been realized from the sale of any of said property sold by said excx & applied to the payment of the debts of the testator & the cost of said administration. It futher states that the said Jas M Steed & Leonora his wife, Lloyd M Lowe, Enoch L Lowe, Lloyd McC Lowe, Enoch M Lowe, & Rebecca Lowe reside out of the State of Md, & prays an order of publication against them. Said absent dfndnts to appear in this Court, in person or by solicitor, on or before the first Mon in Nov next. –Edw W Belt, Clerk of the Circuit Court of PG Co.

MON JUN 25, 1855
Murderers sentenced. In the First District Court of New Orleans, on Jun 16, Judge Robertson pronounced sentences of death on Jas Costello, D Callinghan, John Shields, & Patrick Kennedy. Patrick Haggarty, accessory to Callinghan, was sentenced to the penitentiary for life, also Richd Scott. John Johnson, convicted of manslaughter, was sentended to 18 years' imprisonment. Appeals were taken in the cases of Costello, Kennedy, Scott, & Johnson.

Notice: our accounts will be ready for delivery on Jun 28 to our customers, & we trust that they will promptly settle the same. –Geo W Hinton, 406 Pa ave

Boston Journal: Miss Harriet S Russell appointed Postmaster at Great Falls, N H, vice Hon Richd Russell, deceased. Miss Russell has had charge of the ofc during the time her father held the appointment, & has proved herself a faithful & efficient public servant.

Notice to all whom it may concern: our accounts will be ready for delivery on Jun 26 to our customers, & we trust that they will promptly settle the same. —Wm R Riley, corner 8th st, opposite Centre Market.

The penchant for collecting specimens of the cryptography of great men still manifests itself. A correspondent of the Times gives us an instance. Charlotte Corday's signature brought 770 francs, one of Murat 81, of Robespierre 27, Lamennais 25. A very republican letter by Josephine Beauharnais, written while she was still the wife of Alex'r Beauharnais, brought 200 francs.

Wm H Cryss, aged about 13 years, a son of Mr Henry Cryss, of Alexandria, lost his life by accidentally falling overboard from a boat in the river opposite that place on Fri last.

Two small frame houses, occupied as shops by different tenants, & owned by Mr Geo C Grammer, on Pa ave, near 13th st, were destroyed by fire yesterday evening.

Mrd: on May 31, in Augusta, Ga, by Rev Dr A Means, Lawson P Hoover, of Wash, D C, to Miss Indie V, daughter of John Jackson, of the former place.

Mrd: on Jun 20, in the Presbyterian Church at Chapel Hill, N C, by Rev Prof Mitchell, Jas M Spencer, of Clinton, Ala, to Miss Cornelia Ann, only daughter of Rev Prof Phillips.

Died: on Jun 24, Cornelia Rosaline, infant daughter of W Wallace & Virginia Kirby, aged 1 year & 7 months. Her funeral is this afternoon at 5 o'clock, from the residence of her grandfather, Isaac Beers, on E st, between 3rd & 4th sts.

TUE JUN 26, 1855

Mr Walker, at Dripping Springs, 40 miles west of Austin, was attacked & killed by what appeared to be 5 Indians. A negro who was with him at the time escaped & reported the crime. A party pursued & caught them, killing 4 & wounding one, & they all turned out to be white men with their faces painted in disguise. The prisoner said that in the mountains a party of 100 had been committing depredations on the frontier, all of which had been charged upon the Indians. [No dates given-current item.]

Five prisoners confined in the jail at Louisville, Ky escaped on Wed. They are: Saml Bryant, alias Luke O'Brien, charged with robbery; M B Garman, alias Geiger, & Jas Jones, charged with passing counterfeit money; Wm Yearnes & Thos McCauley, alias John Fitzgerald, charged with obtaining money under false pretences. The jailor offers a reward of $300 for their arrest & delivery to him, or $50 for the arrest of each.

The German Yagers, commanded by Capt Schwarzman, made a handsome parade yesterday for target shooting. The new hat, or helmet, of the Yagers is a very excellent & picturesque feature in their uniform.

Died: on Jun 23, in Wash City, Mrs Charity Powell, wife of Wm C Powell, in her 63rd year. She was a native of S C, & for 20 years of her life was a member of the Baptist church, & fulfilled devotedly the duties of wife, mother, & friend.

Died: on Jun 25, at Portsmouth, N H, Alex'r Ladd, aged 70 years, an eminent merchant & esteemed citizen, for many years connected with the Branch Bank of the U S for N H, & its last Pres.

Died: on Jun 14, in Wilkesbarre, Pa, at the residence of her father, Rev John Dorrance, Frances G, wife of Lt John C Beaumont, U S Navy, aged 24 years.

WED JUN 27, 1855
The Democrats of Louisiana held their State Convention at Baton Rouge on Jun 18 & nominated the following candidates for State officers, viz:

Robt C Wickliffe, for Govn'r.   Saml F Marks, Auditor.
Chas H Mouton, Lt Govn'r.   C E Greneaux, Treas
Andrew S Herron, Sec of State.   E Warren Moise, Atty Gen
Saml Bard, Superintendent of Education

Household & kitchen furniture at auction on: Jul 2, by order of the Orphans Court of Wash Co, D C, at the residence of the late Fred'k Hager, on the corner of F & 25th sts. —Theresa Hager, admx -C W Boteler, auctioneer

San Francisco election: on May 28, resulted in the choice of the following ofcrs: Mayor, Jas Van Ness, Dem, 65 majority; Treas, Wm McKibben, Dem, 104 majority; Comptroller, Andrew J Moulder, Dem, 185 majority; Tax Collector, Edw T Batturs, K N, 503 majority; Harbor Master, Geo B Schaffer, Dem, 141 majority; City Marshal, Hampton North, K N, 3 majority; Clerk Superior Court, J B McMim, K N, 217 majority; City Atty, Balie Peyton, K N, 54 majority; Surveyor, J J Hoff, Dem, 314 majority.

Boston Transcript of Sat: the venerable Saml Sumner Wilde, L L D, died at his residence in Boston yesterday, in his 85th year. He died full of years & honors, leaving behind a spotless character & an example worth the emulation of all.

Railroad accident at N Y on Jun 15, killed Saml Anderson, from Jefferson Co, N Y, who was sitting on the platform. The coupling on one of the cars broke or became disconnected & ran into the platform.

Mr Rezin Hammond, of Anne Arundel Co, Md, has 100 acres of land set in strawberries. He has employed as many as 200 pickers this season, consisting of men, women, boys, & girls. The price paid for picking is one & a half cents per quart, at which rate good pickers can make some $3 a day.

A Revolutionary Patriot Dead. The Warsaw New Yorker announced the death of Peter Besancon, at the advanced age of 98 years. It says the deceased was one of the band of noble spirits who crossed the ocean with Lafayette to assist the Colonies in the struggle for independence. He was born in or near the city of Besancon, in France, in 1762, came to America at the age of 16, was present at the execution of Maj Andre, & remained in the army until the end of the war.

$100 reward for runaway negro carpenter Sandy, about 26 years old, who left on Tue. –B I Gardner, adjoining the village of Upper Marlboro', Md.

Gas in the kitchen. Mr Willard, of the Nat'l Hotel accompanied me to his kitchen. Here, connecting a portable tube, one end of which terminated in a hollow gridiron & the other end with the gas pipe for the ordinary use of the house, the hollow of the gridiron was filled with gas, which, being ignited, displayed numeorus rows of brilliant little lights. These were covered over by a corrugated iron place, under which the gas burned, & by which it was soon heated sufficiently to allow the process of broiling a beef-steak to begin. The slice of meat was placed on the raised parts of the plate, which answered the purpose of the bars of a gridiron, while the hollows between them conducted off the juice to a receiver. In this simple manner things continued for 8 minutes, when the steak was taken off as juicy & as tender as I never saw exceeded. In other apparatus, Mr Willard boils, roasts, & bakes with equal promptness & facility. –A Wayfarer

Pittsburgh, Jun 25. The ceremonies attending the consecration of St Paul's Roman Catholic Cathedral in this city, on Sunday, were highly imposing. The services commenced at 5 o'clock in the morning. Archbishop Hughes, of N Y, & Archbishop Kenrick, of Balt, with 13 other bishops & 35 priests participated, & over 5,000 persons were present. [Jul 4th newspaper: Catholic Cathedral in Pittsburgh, Pa, was commenced 4 years ago: estimated to seat from 4,000 to 5,000 within its wall; & if necessary, additional pews can be set upon the space now left free for processions.]

Norfolk, Jun 26. Mr Hunter Woods was elected Mayor of Norfolk on Jun 25.

N Y, Jun 26. A warrant having been issued for the arrest of Chas H Stanley, Sec of the British Consulate, charged with enlisting troops within the U S for the British army, he appeared today & gave bail.

Wanted, John Boyle, or his heirs, of Wash, D C, may hear of something to his or their advantage by calling on J Wagner Jermon, Atty at Law, 46 South 6th st, Phil.

THU JUN 28, 1855

Mademoiselle Rachel is to leave Paris for America about Aug 1, & will give her first performance in N Y about Sep 1. Monsieur Raphael Felix has engaged her services. –N Y Courier

Brvt Col J N Gardner, of the 1st Regt of Artl, has assumed command of that regt in consequence of the absence of Col Crane, & has established his headquarters at **Fort McHenry**, where he has commanded for some time back. The light batteries stationed there are commanded by Brvt Maj W H French, 1st Artl, & 1st Lt A Merchant, 2nd Artl.

Ex-Govn'r Collier, of Ala, died a few days since in Tuscaloosa Co. He had been previously ill from an attack of jaundice, & had started for Blount Springs, & died on the road from a sudden & violent attack of the disease. –Montg Journal, 22nd. [Jul 9th newspaper: Gov Collier not dead. There are strong hopes of his recovery.]

Annual Commencement of the Columbia College was held yesterday at the E st Baptist Church. Addresses were made by Mr Geo F Bagby, of Stevensville, Va; Mr Jos J McCree, of Clarke Co, Ga; Mr Albert E Carter, of East Feliciana, La; & Mr Chas A Councill, of Suffolk, Va: all of the graduating class.

House for rent: 3 story brick dwlg in *Cox's row*, 1st st, Gtwn. –Bladen Forest, corner F & 20th sts.

Died: on Jun 27, after a protracted & painful illness, in his 56th year, Mr John W Clarke, formerly of Balt, but for the last several years a resident of Wash City, where he was esteemed by all who knew him.

FRI JUN 29, 1855

Mr Francis Chas Stainback, who held the ofc of Flour Inspector at Petersburg, Va, & was esteemed as an accomplished business man, committed suicide at that place on Wed night. He had been subject for several years past to fits of mental aberration.

Foreign Items: The British lost in their attack on the quarry works nearly 700 men. Col Shearman, Majors Bayley & Dickson, Capts Muller, Forster, Corbett, Wray, Lts Laurence, Stone, Machell, Lowrey, & 150 privates were killed. The wounded number 510 & the missing 15. A French correspondent on Jun 2nd from before Sebastopol writes that 44 boxes of explosive materials were found, all connected by means of tubes, buried about 6 inches in the ground. [Jun 30th newspaper: the quarry work, the capture of which is ascribed to the brave troops in Gen Pelissier's dispatch of the 7th is situated between what on the 6th were our advanced works on Frenchman's Hill & the Redan.]

Boston Journal: painful accident at Edgeworth 2 or 3 days age. A little girl about 8 years old, the child of Mr Walch, of that place, was instantly killed on the Boston & Maine railroad. Her father is a watchman in the rubber factory, where she had been to carry his supper. She was returning to her home, & did not see the single engine approaching upon the other track. Her father, hearing his loss, exhibited the most painful anguish.

SAT JUN 30, 1855
Mrd: on Jun 28, by Rev S A H Marks, Mr Robt Henry Jordan to Miss Mary E Mattingly, all of Wash City.

Died: on Jun 28, in Wash City, Miss Charlotte Ewell, in her 17th year. Her funeral will take place from the residence of her uncle, N M McGregor, at 10 o'clock, this morning.

Died: on Jun 26, in Gtwn, at the residence of her son, after a lingering illness, Mrs Letitia Brooks, wife of Jos Brooks, aged 78 years & 11 days.

Phil, Jun 29. The locomotive attached to a freight train on the Columbia road exploded near Columbia, killing Geo Sergler, engineer.

MON JUL 2, 1855
Conviction of mail robbers at the U S Court for the northern district of N Y, held at Canandaigua, on Wed, the following sentences were pronounced:
Wm Gillmore & Wm Fowler, for robbing the post ofc at Sodus, Wayne Co, sentenced to imprisonment in the Auburn prison for 1 year, & fined $400 each.
Adam Wheeler, Amaziah Storms, & Alex O Dell, for robbing the mail at Binghamton, Broome Co, sentenced to 1 year each in the penitentiary.
Geo Johnson, for robbing the mail at Binghamton, sentenced to 1 year in the Auburn prison.
Friend Kenyon, for robbing the mail at Syracuse, sentenced to 3 years in the Auburn prison.
Jas H Wilbur, for robbing the mail while a clerk in the post ofc at Fonda, Montg Co, sentenced to 10 years' imprisonment in the Auburn prison.

S Wells Williams has been appointed by the Pres to be Intrepreter & Sec of the Legation of the U S in China.

We had the pleasure of a visit yesterday from one perhaps of the oldest men in Md, Mr Richd Crandell, who was born in this county on Jul 16, 1747, &, therefore, will be 108 years of age on Jul 16th next. He has the appearance of a man not more than 80 years of age, & even last fall he sowed nearly all the grain on his farm. He served as a pivateersman during the Revolution, & relates many interesting facts connected with the struggle for American Independence. –Annapolis Republican of Sat.

Three boys drowned on Sun, in a lake, when they were amusing themselves in a rickly old boat that capsized. They were Patrick Tige, about 18 years of age, Jas O'Neal, aged about 12, & Horace White, about 10. –Steuben [N Y] Advocate

Mason & Dixon Line. Through the research of Mr John H B Latrobe, of Balt, this subject was chosen by him for an address before the Historical Society of Pa. Chas Mason & Jeremiah Dixon, who, 86 years ago, ran a line through the forest, until the Indians forbade the further progress of chain & compass, & whose greatest merit seems to have been that of accurate surveyors, have obtained a notoriety for their names as lasting as the history of our country. It was in 1763 that the proprietaries of Pa & Md agreed with Mason & Dixon to survey the boundary between their respective grants. They landed in Phil in Nov, 1763, & entered at once upon their work. In a note Latrobe tells us that Lalande, in his Bibliographie Astronomique, says that Dixon was born in a coal mine. He died at Durham, England, in 1777, but Mason survived him 10 years, & according to the Encyclopedia Americana died in Pa in 1787. One of the stones, that which marked the n e corner of Md, being undermined by a brook, in the course of time fell, & was removed to form part of a chimney to a neighboring farmhouse. Upon the stone being missed Mr Latrobe says the Legislatures of Pa, Md, & Dela took the matter in hand, & a joint commission was appointed, obtaining the services of Lt Col Jas D Graham, a distinguished ofcr of the Topographical Engineers of the U S, that caused the work of Mason & Dixon to be reviewed. Col Graham's work corroborated in all important particulars the work of his predecessors. Some errors were discovered, however. By the correction of one of these errors the State of Md gained an addition to her territory of one acre & eighty-seven hundredths of an acre, but whether the loss fell upon Pa or Dela does not appear. Mr W Smith, who once resided a full half mile within the State of Pa, & Christian church, by the same resurvey, was found to be in Pa.

Earthquake at Balt on Thu was confined to within a space of 10 miles east & west of Balt, though to the north it extended through a range of country of about 60 miles. The Howard Gazette, published at Ellicott's Mills, say: On Wed last, about 12½ o'clock P M, an earthquake startled the citizens by a violent shock, causing doors & windows to rattle, for the space of about a minute & a half; shaking the houses in some localities to their foundations. The Balt Co Advocate alludes to a second shock 15 minutes later.

On Fri last, at E O Brigham's saw mills, a young man named John Spooner was sawed in two by a circular saw. He was stooping to pick something up and fell on the carriage. –Montreal Herald

Dr John B Blake, the new Com'r of Public Bldgs, has entered upon the duties of his ofc, & appointed R J Roche as his clerk & W P Mohun superintendent of the out-door work.

A Javenese paper contains the following matrimonial announcement: Married, Theodore Poland, pensioned titular colonel, knight of the two orders of the Netherlands, to the mother of his children, the Javanese woman Fien. This marriage contracted in gratitude, & as a reward for the heroism she exhibited in his behalf in 1833, on his return from the fortress of Amerongen, when she rescued him, already severely wounded, from certain death, by carrying him, with the assistance of a servant, a distance of 3 furlongs, wrapped in a sheet, & suspended to a bamboo, while pursued by the enemy, & by safely bringing him through the enemy lines.

Treasury Dept. Clerical changes: P R Van Wyck promoted to 2nd class clerkship in the Sec's ofc, vice Isaac Strohm, removed. Salary, $1,400 per annum.
Register's Ofc: John R Nourse, 2nd class clerk, removed.
Edgar Patterson promoted to 3rd class clerkship, vice John B Blake, resigned. Salary, $1,600 per annum.
John H McIlvaine promoted to 2nd class clerkship. Salary, $1,400 per annum.
Third Auditor's Ofc. John S Duke promoted to 2nd class clerkship, vice J B Pleasants, removed. Salary, $1,400 per annum.
Chas T Hull, of Va, appointed to 1st class clerkship. Salary, $1,200 per annum.
Fifth Auditor's Ofc. J C Pickett appointed to chief clerkship, vice T Mustin, reduced. T Mustin appointed to 3rd class clerkship, vice J H Houston, removed. Salary, $1,600 per annum.
Sixth Auditor's Ofc. W H Sullivan promoted to 3rd class clerkship, vice J A M Duncanson, removed. Salary, $1,600 per annum.
J H Somerville appointed to 2nd class clerkship. Salary, $1,400 per annum.
J H McGlaughlin, of Pa, appointed to 1st class clerkship. Salary, $1,200 per annum.

Opening of the *Saut Canal*. At a meeting held on Jun 23, 1855, on board the steamer **Illinois**, on her return trip from Lake Superior, being the first boat through the ship canal around the Falls of St Mary, Hon Danl Goodwin, of Detroit, was appointed chairman, & Philip Hunt, of the same place, was chosen secretary. Cmte consisted of: H G Spafford & Theodore Williams, of Detroit; Hon S M Burroughs, of N Y; Z Hosmer, of Boston; & E C Rahin, of Ontonagon.

Mrd: on Jun 21, in St Peter's Church, Pittsburg, Pa, by Rev T B Lyman, Jesse Turner, of Van Buren, Ark, to Rebecca J, 2nd daughter of Edw Allen, of that city.

The large dwlg house well known as the residence of the former British Minister, Mr Fox, on the lower approach to Gtwn, beyond the circle, was destroyed by fire yesterday. This property is understood to belong to the estate of the late Gen Gratiot. The loss is estimated from five to eight thousand dollars; but may have been insured. There is little room to doubt that it was fired by the hand of an incendiary.

Navy Yard, Wash, Jun 27, 1855. The withdrawal of Cmdor Paulding from the Wash Navy Yard occasioned correspondence from his friends, connected to him by official ties at the yard, trusting long life, health, happiness, & prosperity. Signed:

Richd Barry	Abel G Davis	L Gaddis
D McComb	H N Ober	J F Dobbin
R D Beale	John H Pecke	Geo Herold
Francis Barry	John Clapham	C Jos Ihrie
John H Smoot	E Foster	J D Brandt
J C Clark	W P S Sanger	Jas Tucker
Edw Evans	S M Pook	J R McCathran
Chas H Gordon	F McNerhany	J Philips
A Woodward	M Hunt	J M Padgett
J J White	T E Williams	

Died: on May 30, at the residence of her son-in-law, Mr Jenkin Thomas, on Gay st, Gtwn, Mrs Eliz Meem, in her 86th year. She was a resident of Gtwn during the whole period of her life.

Died: on Jun 9, at Boston, Mass, Mr Washington Blanchard, aged 45 years. Mr Blanchard was deservedly eminent as a miniature painter. He had long been greatly depressed & saddened by the chronic affection which finally terminated his life. He was well known in Wash City, where he will long be affectionately remembered by his many friends.

Country situation for sale: the subscriber offers at private sale **Ellaville**, on the Wash & Balt Turnpike Road, one mile from Bladensburg: lots that vary from 1 to 10 acres. There has been erected on one of the lots a very handsome house, containing 13 rooms, & having water fixtures, & modern improvements. –Chas B Calvert

Chicago, Jun 9. The special mail agent Mr Pinkarton, this morning arrested Theodore P Denniston, a clerk in the Post Ofc here, for robbing the mails. $4,000 in bank notes were found in his room. It is the general belief that ten to fifteen thousand dollars have been lost from the mails. The brother of Dennison was arrested in Apr last for the same offence. Dennison is now in jail. [Jul 10th newspaper: Perry Denniston, nephew of the Postmaster at Chicago, arrested for abstracting money from the mails, has absconded. He was held in bail in the sum of $2,500. Since his arrest the robbery of letters continuing, suspicion fell upon his brother, Theodore F Denniston, who was observed to be in the habit of changing money at various brokers-$1,310 on Tue week being only one morning's plunder. He was arrested, & nearly $4,000 found in his room. He had since confessed his guilt.] [Aug 16th newspaper: Dennison was sentenced last Monday to 10 years' imprisonment, by Judge Drummond, in the U S District Court at Chicago.]

Obit-died: on Jun 19, at *Ayre Hall*, Northampton Co, Va, John Eyre, aged 87. He was born on the spot on which he died, & which had been the residence of his ancestors for several generations. It was here that he passed almost the whole of his long & meritorious life, dispensing the revenues of an ample fortune in elegant hospitality, & in act of kindness, liberality, & beneficence. He was called by his romantic admirers Sir Chas Grandison. He was married to an accomplished lady, whose death preceded his by 26 years. They had no offspring. For about two years he was affected with blindness & impaired hearing; his reason was unclouded. –G T

TUE JUL 3, 1855
N Y Evening Post. The Memoirs of Sydney Smith, by his daughter, Lady Holland, [edited by Mrs Austin,] have appeared at last.

Fatal effects of the heat in N Y on Sat. Coroner's inquests was held in the cases of: Anthony Kohl, a German, about 52; Mary O'Brien, native of Ireland; Eliz Ahern, a native of Ireland, aged 19; Richd Fitzgerald, a laborer, aged 22; Jos Fraser, a resident of Oak st, about 36; & Michl Costello, of West 32nd st.

Deaths from the heat, in Balt, on Sat: John Hogan; John Barker, & Jos Hamilton, [formerly a police ofcr.]

On Wed night last the residence of Chas Somerville, at Point Patience, Patuxent river, Calvert Co, Md, was entirely destroyed by fire, together with out houses, embracing the negro quarters; but a very small amount of the contents were saved. The house was a very large frame one, with all the conveniences of a country residence. Mr Somerville & his lady were absent on a visit to a neighbor, & direction had been left to keep a light burning until their return, & it is supposed that from this light the fire originated. The loss will be about $5,000. A negro boy, about 12, was burnt to death.

The house of Capt Lindsay Walker, in Albemarle Co, Va, was destroyed by fire on Jun 28. A daughter of Dr Gilmer, of Lynchburg, was burnt to death at the time. Capt Walker lost all his furniture.

The Board of Trustees of Union Academy at Snow Hill, Md, wish to employ a competent teacher to fill the place of Principal. He will be expected to teach Latin & Greek languages & the usual English education. –Geo M Upshur, sec

Furnished rooms for rent: Pa ave, opposite Willard's Hotel, No 215. –Th Friebus

Mrd: on Sabbath evening, by Rev John C Smith, Mr Benj P B Wood to Miss Sarah Catherine Cissell, all of Wash City.

Died: on Jul 2, in Wash City, at the Nat'l Hotel, Edward, son of Jas H & Susannah Horbach, aged 2 years & 5 months.

N Y, Jul 2. Bloody affray at Brooklyn on Sunday morning, between a party of drunken rowdies left Chas Johnson dead on the street; Robt Johnson, his brother, mortally wounded; & Patrick McDonough severely cut. Three men, Michl Gorman, Michl McGee, & Patrick Sorley, were arrested & charged with being the murderers.

Orphans Court of Wash Co, D C. Letters of administration on the personal estate of Eliz Slater, late of Wash Co, deceased. –S A Peugh, adm

WED JUL 4, 1855
Wash Corp: 1-Nominations made by the Mayor: for Atty, Jos H Bradley; Tax Clerk, Joshua L Henshaw; Bookkeeper, Andrew J Larner; Messenger, Jacob Kleiber.
Com'rs of Improvement: Geo W Harkness, Francis B Lord, Jos S Martin, Henry D Gannell, Com'rs of Asylum: Theordore Wheeler, John P White, B W Reed
For Intendant of the Asylum: Wm Dixon; physician to the Asylum, Dr Geo M Dove Resident Medical Student, Chas M Hammett.
Com'r Eastern Section of the Canal, T M Fugett.
Com'r of the Western Section of the Canal: Frank Little
Sealer of Weights & Measures, Wm M McCauley;
Inspector of Fire Apparatus, Caleb Buckingham
Inspector of Flour & Salted Provisions, Jacob Kleiber
Chief of Police, John Davis
Police Ofcrs:

Washington Hurley	R R Burr	Josiah Adams
Jos B Peerce	Wm Martin	John A Willett
Wm H Barneclo	A R Allen	Isaac Stoddard
Wm A Boss	J Simonds	U B Mitchell
J F Wollard	J H Wise	
E G Handy	J M Busher	

Clerks of Markets:

Leonard Storm	Peter Little	Wm B Wilson
H B Robertson	F B Poston	

Com'rs of Markets:

P F Bacon	Lemuel Barnes	J L Rider
Ephraim Wheeler	M H Grimes	J McKnew
Alex'r Lee	J W Lelaway	R H Rawlings

Inspectors & Measurers of Lumber:

John G Robinson	Wm Bird	Henry Lyles
Wm H Hamilton	John W Stevens	Wm Burroughs

Wood & Coal Measurers:

Henry Haliday	John P Hilton	Jno E Lewis
Wm P Ferguson	Wm Baun	

Measurers of Grain, Brain, etc: Jas Gaither & Wm P Ferguson
Com'rs of the West Burial Ground: Wm Wilson, John Wilson, J C Harkness, & Guy Graham, Sexton.
Com'rs of the Eastern Burial Ground: F Y Naylor, J P Ingle, & Benoni Jones, Sexton.

Superintendent of Sweeps:
John Lewis
B L Bowen

Wm A Robinson
W H Lusby

Jas Burgess
P C Bartlett

Scavengers:
G T McGlue
O McBee
Jos Whitney
Basil Benson

John Taylor
L Childers
Jas Tucker
Hanson Brown

J B McFarland
Francis Ballinger

Physicians for the Poor:
Dr S A Storrow
Dr A H Lee
Dr W F Lippett

Dr S J Radcliff
Dr J M Grymes
Dr S A H McKin

Dr J D Stewart

Apothecaries to Furnish Medicines for the Poor:
A G Ridgely
W T Evans

W H Gilman
H H McPherson, jr

John E Bates
Atho Boswell

Recently elected ofcrs of the Patriotic Bank: J P Ingle, Pres; Wm Orme, Jas C McGuire, A E Perry, J F Caldwell, T B Blagden, W J McDonald, D Saunders, & John Purdy, directors.

Elected ofcrs of the Bank of the Metropolis: Thos Carbery, Pres; Lewis Johnson, Geo Parker, Geo W Graham, Chas Hill, Jas Thompson, Wm B Todd, Stephen P Franklin, Geo Lowrey, & Robt P Dunlop, directors.

Household & kitchen furniture at auction on: Jul 6, at the residence of Mr H H Whaley, 255 Pa ave, between 12th & 13th sts. -J C McGuire, auct

Commencement of the Univ of Va in Charlottesville on Thu. Degrees conferred: Bacherlor of Arts: J E Jones, of Charlottesville, Va; Henry M Matthews, Lewisburg, Va; Wm G Strong, Albemarle, Va.
Masters of Arts: Gray Carroll, Isle of Wight, Va; E T Fristoe, Rappahannock, Va; Edwin L Taliaferro, Gloucester, Va; Wm D Thomas, Richmond City, Va; Powell Harrison, Leesburg, Va; David Watson, Louisa, Va; Thos H Malone, Athens, Ala.

Mrd: on Jul 2, at the Capitol Hill Parsonage, by Rev Gideon H Day, Levi T Hyatt to Ann L Wolfe, all of Wash City.

Died: on Jun 30, at Moss Neck, Caroline Co, Va, in her 47th year, Jane Catharine, wife of Jas Parke Corbin & eldest daughter of the late John Spotswood, merchant.

Chas W Mixon, of Chowan Co, N C, took $6,000 from the Bank of the State, at Eliz city, & while it was locked in his bureau it was stolen by a gipsy woman who was doctoring Mrs Mixon, & replaced with a brown paper. They disappeared with the money from the vicinity.

St Louis, Jul 1. 1-A party of 7, on the route from *Fort Union* to *Fort Sarpy*, were attacked on May 1 by a band of armed Sioux, & Geo Sikes, of Quincy, Ill, was killed. The remainder of the party were detained some time by the Indians, but were finally permitted to proceed. 2-From *Fort Leavenworth*: McCrea, who shot Malcolm Clarke, has been committed to jail on the charge of murder, & bail was refused. 3-Violent personal rencontre occurred in Kansas between Gov Reeder & Stringfellow, & the Govn'r was badly beaten.

Orphans Court of Wash Co, D C. Letters of administration on the personal estate of Collins Bayliss, late of Wash Co, deceased. –M A Bayliss, admx

[There was no newspaper for Thu Jul 5, 1855.]

FRI JUL 6, 1855
Destructive floods on Wed last. Hornellsville Tribune: we understand the wife & one child of Mr Jas Halloway were drowned about 2½ miles west of this village. A mill-dam belonging to Mr Hart was swept away. The dwlg-house & barn of L Stephens & the cooper shop of J L Truair were carried away.

Mary J Anderson, of 22 Minnetta pl; Cornelius A Hearns, of 223 Eliz st, a native of Ireland, age 23 years; & John Schreiden, of 49 Avenue B, a German, 40 years of age, died on Monday from the effects of the excessive heat of Sat. –Journ of Commerce

Cincinnati Gaz: Mrs Catharine G Ray, widow of the late Dr Ray, of that city, died suddenly on Jun 29. She became giddy & lost her balance while at the window of the 3rd story of her residence, & fell breaking her thigh & probably her neck. She died in a few minutes after being taken into the house. She leaves a large circle of relatives to lament her untimely death.

A son of Thos French, of Pembroke, N H, accidentally blew a portion of his head off while gunning & was found dead. At Portsmouth, R I, a similar fate befell Albert C Brown, aged 19 years.

Wash, Jul 5, 1855. Letter to Vespasian Ellis. Dear Sir: the Cmte of Arrangements of the American party for the celebrating the 4th of July request a copy of you eloquent oration delivered on that day for publication. S Yorke AtLee, J N Craig, John L Smith, F A Tucker, T Brown, W E Waters, Cmte of Arrangements.

Land for sale. The subscriber will dispose of 150 acres of his land, in Pg Co, Md, about 2 miles from Alexandria. Address me at Alexandria. –John H Bayne

We regret to learn that a little boy, son of Mr Keenan, living on the Island, was fatally injured by the explosion of gunpowder with which he & other boys were playing on Jul 4. He has since died. His brother & Geo Freer, son of Mr Barrow Freer, of the Island, & a son of Mr Ross, of 13½ & D sts, were seriously injured.

$250 reward for runaway negro boy Abraham Jones, about 20 years of age. He has relatives in Balt. –B W Reed, Wash City, D C, corner of 14th & F sts, No 231.

Mrd: on Jul 4, in Wash City, by Rev J E Weems, Almanza Tufts, of Collinsville, Ill, to Miss Mary Slade, daughter of Rev J E Weems.

Died: on Jul 5, Edwin, infant son of Richd W & Jane Polkinhorn. His funeral will be today at 9½ o'clock, from the residence of his parents, D st, between 6th & 7th sts.

Died: on Jul 2, in Phil, Fanny L, aged 3 years & 10 months, only child of Emily L & Purser H M Hieskell, U S N.

Died: on Jun 28, in N Y C, aged 84 years, Mr John MacLeod, for many years a resident of Wash & a clerk in the Gen Post Ofc Dept where he continued for 10 years since. At an advanced age, he sought, with his family, a home & employment elsewhere. He met his end with the intelligent serenity & assured hopes conferred by a humble trust in the merits of his Redeemer. He was a native of Glen-Fruin, Scotland, & emigrated to this country in 1793; enrolled himself as a citizen of his adopted country, he settled in Alexandria, but moved to Wash in 1812. His body was brought here & interred in the family burial place, *Congressional Cemetery*.

Literary Notice. The Annual Exhibition of the Wash Seminary will take place at Carusi's Saloon on Jul 9, at 9 A M. No boys will be admitted unless accompanied by their parents. –H J Deneckerl, S J, Pres

SAT JUL 7, 1855
Trustee's sale of brick house & lot at auction: on Jul 13, by deed of trust from Beedy Wise dated Aug 29, 1850, recorded in Liber J A S No 56, folios 93 thru 95, of the land records for Wash Co, D C: sale of all of lot 34 in square 411, in Wash City, with a brick house: fronts on 8th st west, between D & E sts. –J Fitz Bartlett, trustee –Green & Scott, aucts

Hon John I Guion, Judge of the 7th judicial district of Mississippi, died at Vicksburg, in that State, on Jun 26.

Circuit Judges chosen Circuit Judges at the late election:

D M Woodson	Geo Manierre	Isaac G Wilson
Sidney Breese	David Davis	B R Sheldon
Wm K Parrish	M E Hollister	Jos Sibley
Justin Harlan	John S Thompson	Onslow Peters
P H Walker	S W Randall	Chas Emerson
J W Drury	Edwin Beecher	

Mr Alex'r D Duval was elected Treasurer of the city of Louisville on Sat last. He had no competition for the office.

N Y-usual number of accidents: 1-Gen Hall was thrown from his horse & one of his legs badly broken. His horse was frightened by an explosion of fireworks. 2-Mrs Phillips, residing at 32 King st, was shot through the thigh with a ball from a gun or pistol, which is supposed to have been discharged by some person from the rear of another house. A brother of Mrs Phillips had, nearly about the same time, a pistol ball shot through the leg of his pantaloons. 3-Ferdinand Smith was arrested for carelessly firing off a pistol, loaded with a ball, which came near shooting Mrs Ward, 187 Franklin st, while she was at the window. 4-Wm Maher, a lad residing at 71 Henry st, was severely injured by an explosion of powder in a sarsaparilla bottle. He had applied a slow match to the bottle, but, the powder not immediately igniting, he took hold of it, when the accident occurred. 5-Jos Martin, an Italian boy, was killed by falling from a window in house 46 Baxter st.

Ladies School, Fairfax Court House, Va. Mrs H M Baker informs her patrons & friends that her School will re-open in Aug 28, 1855.

Magnificent residence for sale. I will now sell the place upon which I reside, adjoining the village of *Tennallytown*, on the Gtwn & Rockville turnpike, about 2 miles above Gtwn: contains 63½ acres, divided into small & convenient lots. The dwlg is brick, 32 by 40, with a wing 25 by 31, each 2 stories, with the necessary outbldgs, all new. There is also a 2 story brick house on the turnpike corner of the place, now rented as a grocery store at an annual rent of $75, which will be sold with the place or separate if desired. Apply on the premises or by letter directed to *Tennallytown*. –Thos Marshall

Windsor Forest for sale. The subscriber offers for sale his farm, lying in the upper part of Stafford Co, Va, about 18 miles from Fredericksburg: contains 392½ acres of land; with a pleasant & convenient dwlg house in good repair, & all other bldgs necessary or useful. Address Jefferson Spindle, Garrisonville Post Ofc, Stafford Co, Va. Mr John E Tackett or Mr Wm W Spindle, of Fredericksburg, may be consulted with regard to terms.

The Lynchburg Virginian mentions a rumor that Dr Averett, of Halifax, Va, formerly a member of Congress, went to his study, a few days ago, with a lighted cigar & laid down on a lounge, when, probably falling to sleep, his cigar set fire to a thickly wadded dressing gown which he had on. He was soon enveloped in flames, &, either from suffocation or the inhaling of flame, expired.

Valuable farms for sale: in execution of the decrees of the Circuit Court of Alexandria Co, rendered at the Nov term, 1854, & the May term, 1855, the undersignd will again offer at public sale, in front of Rufus Smith's Hotel, in Middleburg, Va, on Aug 11, the balance of real property belonging to the estate of Dr Wm L Powell, deceased, viz: the farm called *Oakendale*, in Fauquier Co; originally contained about 675 acres, but by a recent sale has been reducted to 469 acres, 3 rods, & 4 poles; the bldgs consist of a small stone dwlg & the usual out-houses. Also, the *Coon-skin tract*, containing about 610 acres, in Loudoun Co, near Carter's mill, on Goose Creeks. –L B Taylor, B P Noland, Com'rs

MON JUL 9, 1855
Fatal accident at Clarkson Corners on Jul 3 at Goodrich's tavern. A small cannon was cast at the Lower Furnace, Brockport, under the superintendence of the foreman, Mr Merrill, who with his wife was at the 4th of July ball, held at the tavern. As the gun was about to be discharged he stepped to an upper window to see the affair, when the match was applied, the cannon burst, & a piece weighing about 3 pounds struck him in the face, tore away his chin & right cheek, & a portion of his forehead, causing instant death. His age was between 30 & 35 years. He was an industrious & respectable man. -Rochester Democrat

Trustee's sale of a valuable farm at Ball's Cross Roads: by 2 deed of trust made & recorded among the land records for Alexandria Co, Va, with instructions from the parties interested, the subscriber will sell, at Public Auction on Jul 19, at the auction rooms, a tract of land containing 122 acres, adjoining Ball's Cross Roads, said tract being a portion of the *Glebe Farm*, formerly owned by Gen J P Van Ness. It is to be divided into 4 lots; one of which, 34 acres, has a good substantial farm house, overseer's dwlg, barn, & other out-bldgs. -Jas C McGuire, auct

Admiral Boxer, venerable English Admiral, died of cholera on ship-board, at Balaklava, on Jun 2, after a short illness. It is said that he had been depressed by the death of a nephew bearing his name & attached to his person, which took place from the same cause 3 days previously on board ship.

Viennia, Jun 16. The Grand Boyard, Constantine Balsh, step-son of the reigning Prince, has been killed in a duel by Count Stelberg, a major in the Austrian Hussars. We do not know yet the details or the cause of this affair.

List of the graduated Cadets who have been appointed Brevet 2nd Lts in the several arms named from July 1, viz:

Corps of Engineers
1-Cyrus B Comstock
2-Godfrey Weitzel

Dragon Arm:
6-Ebenezer Gray, co C, 1st regt
8-David McM Gregg, co C, 2nd regt
18-Jas Wheeler, jr, co E, 2nd regt
20-Lewis Merrill, co D, 1st regt

Cavalry Arm:
3-Cornelius Van Camp, co F, 1st regt
5-Junius B Wheeler, co F, 2nd regt
16-John R Church, co I, 1st regt
17-Albert V Colburn, co D, 2nd regt

Regt of Mounted Riflemen:
10-John V D DuBois, co G
26-Wm W Averell, co C

Artillery Arm:
4-Geo H Elliott, co A, 4th regt
7-Saml Breck, jr, co H, 1st regt
9-Fred'k L Childs, co F, 2nd regt
11-Michl P Small, co G, 3rd regt
12-Francis R T Nicholls, co L, 2nd regt
13-Alex'r S Webb, co K, 4th regt
14-John W Turner, co L, 3rd regt
15-Francis A Shoup, co A, 1st regt

Infantry Arm:
19-Geo D Ruggles, co D, 1st regt
21-Alfred T A Torbert, co K, 2nd regt
22-Chas W Thomas, co C, 5th regt
23-Jas H Hill, co F, 10th regt
24-Edw L Hartz, co K, 7th regt
25-Clarence E Bennett, co A, 3rd regt
27-Timothy M Bryan, jr, co C, 9th regt
28-Wm B Hazen, co D, 4th regt
29-Henry W Freedly, co K, 9th regt
30-Henry M Lazell, co G, 1st regt
31-Wm R Pease, co G, 10th regt
32-Jesse K Allen, co F, 5th regt
33-Robt C Hill, co B, 6th regt
34-Geo McG Dick, co G, 8th regt

The long-pending assault & battery case between Mr N P Willis & Mr Edwin Forrest, the actor, was decided during the June term of the Court of Appeals of N Y, the judgment of the court appealed from being affirmed.

Mr Andrew Haymaker, of Charleston, who has been blind in one eye for 54 years, from a film growing over it, was suddenly restored to sight a short time since. He was standing on the steps of the court-house in that village while a number of men & boys were playing ball. The ball, projected with great force, struck him in the blind eye, completely removing the film & restoring sight. Considerable inflammation followed, but is now getting better, & the sight is good. -Chicago Journal

Died: on Jul 7, at **Cole Brook**, PG Co, Md, Jas Lingan Addison, late of New Orleans, in his 42nd year. His funeral will take place this afternoon at 4 o'clock.

Orphans Court of Wash Co, D C. Letters of administration, with will annexed, on personal estate of Saml J Little, late of Wash Co, deceased. –John Little, adm w a

TUE JUL 10, 1855
Mrd: on Jul 2, in the Vestry of St Matthew's Church, by Rev Jas P Donelan, John H Haviland, of N Y, to Theresa Belmonte, only daughter of Wm Wilkinson, of Wash City.

Mrd: on Jul 3, by Rev Dr Cole, Mr John A Foos to Miss Martha Ann Young, all of Wash City.

Died: on Jul 5, at Mount Hope, Balt, Miss Matilda Wathen, aged 65 years, a native of Chas Co, Md, but for the last 2 years a resident of Wash City.

Died: on Jul 6, Charles Hardesty, aged 2 years, 10 months & 9 days, second son of Wm & Anna R Berry, late of Balt.

Horse for sale: a gentle family horse at J R Sutton's stables, 8th st, between D & E.

WED JUL 11, 1855
Clerks in the State Dept were recently examined & classified as follows:
Chief Clerk: R S Chew, of Va
Fourth Class: Edw Stubbs, of N Y, disbursing agent; Francis Markoe, of Pa; L F Tasistro, of N Y; Jas S Mackie, of Ohio; Henry D Johnson, of Mass; R W Young, of Va; G J Abbott, of N H; R S Chilton, of N Y.
Third Class: A H Derrick, of Pa; W C Reddall, of Va; John P Polk, of Dela; Geo Chipman, of Vt; W E Stubbs, of Md; A C Gillett, of Fla; Wm Hogan, of N Y.
Second Class: C V Gordon, of Va; W J Bromwell, of Md.
First Class: H D J Pratt, of Mass; Geo Bartle, of Va; John C Nevins, of the Dist of Columbia

On Friday, while Mr Jas Lancelott & wife, of Cranston, & Mrs Stephen Sturgeon, of N Y C, a sister of Mrs Lancelott, & Mr Burdett, of this city, a brother of the 2 ladies, were bathing at Field's Point, an accident occured by which the ladies were drowned. The women were unaware of the great depth of the water a short distance from the shore, & were unable to save themselves. The men did what they could to rescue them. Mrs Lancelot was 20 years of age & Mrs Sturgeon 31. All of them are natives of England. –Providence Journal

Mr Robt Reid, of the firm of Robt Reid & Co, of Mobile, lost his life on Sat. While riding along the Shell road he was met by a horse running away with the shafts of a wrecked buggy attached to him. One of these struck Mr Reid in the breast. He got home & lingered until Sunday, when he expired. –Mobile Register, Jul 3

Two sons of Mr McClure, merchant, of West Troy, aged 9 & 12 years, were drowned in the State basin, near the Mohawk bridge, in West Troy, on Friday. The younger brother was bathing & shouted to his brother for help. He reached his brother, & in the struggle both were drowned. –Troy Whig

Savannah Republican: Dr Wm Terrell died on Jul 4, at his residence in Sparta, Hancock Co. He was one of the most accomplished gentlemen & useful citizens in Ga. Our readers will remember his munificent donation last year of $20,000 for the establishment of an agricultural professorship in the Univ of Ga. That professorship bears the name of its founder. -Republican

Mr Clark S Brown, the principal of an academy, was lately murdered at Pontotoc, Miss. A few days previous to the murder he punished, for some misdemeanor, a lad named Carey Wray, about 12 years of age. John, an elder brother of the lad, who attended the same school, was subsequently expelled for having at the time, it is alleged, twice threatened Prof Brown if he whipped his brother again. Three days after another brother, aged 18, who was studying medicine in a ofc in the city, armed himself with a revolver & bowie knife, went to the academy, & wanted Brown called out, but the assistant refused the request. Wray then accosted him rudely at the public park & Wray inflicted 7 fatal wounds on Brown, which caused his instant death. The murderer was arrested & committed to prison.

Two Mormons were drowned at Baptism on Jul 2: Alex'r Williams & his son. Williams, after the baptism struck out into the river for a swim, & his drawers slipped down over his feet, causing him to sink. His son was drowned in going to rescue him.

Application will be made to the Com'r of Pensions for the issue of a duplicate Warrant No 73,800, for 160 acres, act of Feb 11, 1847, issued to Jas W Sier, late a private in Capt Phelps' company B, 4th Regt, U S Artl, in the war with Mexico, said warrant having been assigned to P Keen, & by him assigned to John E Garey, & the same having been lost, & a caveat against its location entered in the Gen Land Ofc, dated Jul 5, 1855. –Birchett & Downing, Attys for John E Garey.

Dissolution of the copartnership between Williamson & Osgodby by mutual consent. Either is authorized to settle the business of the firm. –Jno B Williamson, Thos W Osgodby

Died: on Jul 7, Wm Clark, in his 59th year.

Died: on Jul 10, Mrs Eliza Marshall, consort of the late Jas B Marshall. Her funeral will take place from her late residence, Garrison st, Navy Yard, today at 4 o'clock.

Orphans Court of Wash Co, D C. Letters of administration on the personal estate of Christopher Byrne, late of Wash Co, deceased. –Jos Mundell, adm

THU JUL 12, 1855
Intelligence received at the War Dept of the death of Lt Saml T Shepherd, of the 2nd dragoons, at *Fort Leavenworth*, on Jun 27, of cholera.

U S sloop-of-war **Constellation** about to be attached to the Mediterranean squadron: Capt, Chas H Bell; Lts, Cicero Price, Wm M Walker, Lardner Gibbon, John P Bankhead, C M Fauntleroy; Surgeon, John A Lockwood; Assist Surgeon, Wyatt M Brown; Purser, John Johnson; Master, Richd L Law, Passed Midshipmen, Edw T Spedden, O F Stanton, Franklin Shepperd; Midshipmen, Philip Porcher, R W M Graham, T McK Buchanan; Boatswain, John Burrows; Gunner, Eugene Mack; Carpenter, John Jarvis; Sailmaker, Francis Boom.

Geo Raglan, a mulatto man, on trial before the Criminal Court for this District, was convicted on Tue of the crime of murder in the first degree in causing the death of Francis Fitzpatrick, in May last, by blows inflicted with a swingletree. Notice given of a motion for a new trial.

During the recent thunder storm in Minnesota the lightning struck the house of a widow lady named Wright, killing the oldest daughter, [a young lady,] & a boy some 7 or 8 years of age. The family were strangers, having but lately arrived in the Territory.

Notice is given that Stanislaus Murray retired from the Wash City Savings Bank on Jul 2 by mutual consent. The business will hereafter be conducted by the undersigned. -Lewis Johnson, Edw Simms, John Purdy

Mrd: on Jul 10, by Rev Mr Holmead, Henry Stark, of N H, to Emma B, daughter of Wm B Randolph, of Wash City.

Mrd: on Jul 10, at Wesley Chapel Parsonage, by Rev R L Dashiell, Mr Chas Williams to Miss Alice Moore, both of Wash City.

Mrd: on Jun 30, in Wash City, by Rev Mr Stanley, Mr J Meiere to Miss Maria B French, both of Wash City.

FRI JUL 13, 1855
Died: on Jul 12, in Wash City, Mary, aged 27 months, eldest daughter of Annie & Capt Sutherland, of the Marine Corps. Her funeral is this evening at 5 o'clock from the residence of her father.

Wash, Jul 10, 1855. Mr Thos Champion, of this city, lately obtained a patent for an improvement in steam boilers & furnaces of such a nature to admit of all the water in the boiler being evaporated & the steam exhausted by the engine, & it stopped for want of steam, & yet no explosion takes place, nor even the boiler be injured, provided the fire be extinguished as soon as the engine shows signs of stopping.

Eastwood School, near Staunton, Va, by Pike Powers: will open on Aug 15 & close on Jun 15 following. References: Faculty of the Univ of Va; Col Francis H Smith, Va Military Institute; Rt Rev Wm Meade & Rt Rev John Johns, Bishops of Diocese of Va. Hon John Letcher, Lexington, Va. Hon Alex'r H H Stuart, Staunton, Va.

Family School for Boys will commence at his residence near Alexandria, Va, on Sep 17. Address E R Lippitt, Alexandria, Va.

U S Patent Ofc, Wash, Jul 12, 1855. Ptn of Benj Fatham, of N Y, & Geo N Fatham, of Phil, praying for the extension of a patent granted to them Oct 11, 1841, for an improvement in machinery for making pipes or tubes of lead, tin, & other metallic substances, for 7 years from the expiration of said patent, which takes place on Oct 11, 1855. –S T Shugert, Acting Com'r of Patents.

SAT JUL 14, 1855
N C election next month; candidates for Congress in various districts of the State:

Know-Nothing	Edw G Reade, W
Robt T Paine, Whig	R C Puryear, Whig
Thos J Latham	S N Stowe, Dem
David Reid, Dem	L B Carmichael, Whig
Jas B Shepard, Dem	
Anti-Know Nothing:	
H M Shaw, Dem	John Kerr, Whig
Thos Ruffin, Dem	A M Scales, Drm
Warren Winslow, Den	Burton Craige, Dem
L O'B Branch, Dem	T L Clingman

Some of the British ofcrs who were slain in the assault upon Sebastopol of Jun 18:

Maj Gen Sir John Campbell	Lt Adj Hobson
Col Yea	Lt Muerant
Lt Col Shadforth	Lt Davies
Capt Forman	Lt Ashwin
Capt Jesse	Lt Bellow
Capt Shiffner	Lt Hurt
Capt Robinson	Lt Alt
Capt Fenwick	Lt Murray
Capt Hon C Agar	Lt Graves
Capt Caulfield	

Americans in Europe: we find the following in the Paris American of Jun 23. Gen Dix & family, of N Y, arrived last week from Italy. They propose sailing in the ship **Arago** from Havre on Jul 4 next for the U S. Maj Lewis Cass, jr, left Paris for a water-cure establishment in Germany. Miss Anna M Ware, bearer of important dispatches from the U S, arrived last Sat. Mr Marshal Woods, Com'r & juror, has been for some days on a visit to London. Mr Wales, editor of the Scientific American & Com'r, returned from a short tour on the Rhine. Mr Elliott, from S C, & Mr Thos Maskell, from Louisianna, Com'rs for the Universal Exhibition, arrived here a few days ago. Messrs Pringle, Morgan, Washburn, & Grow, members of Congress, & Mr Harrington, late under Sec of Treasury, left on Monday last for Italy. Wm D Bowie, jr, Com'r for the State of Md, recently arrived in Paris. We regret to announce the resignation of the Chairman of the American Com'rs, Maunsell B Field, who, in consequence of urgent private business, is obliged to visit the U S. Mr Valentine, of Mass, has been chosen to fill the vacancy. G W Farant & O Pegram, of Va, are also in Paris.

The Court of Claims met yesterday, present, Judges Gilchrist, Blackford, & Scarburgh. Gentlemen who were desirous of being admitted as attys: when the Clerk read their names, & those present were sworn by the Clerk, a part with uplifted hand & a part upon the Holy Bible, & some at their request, were affirmed. The following named gentlemen were admitted:

*W H F Gusling, of Iowa
A H Evans, of Wash
Jos S Williams, of Tenn
J H Peters, of Wash
Richd K Meade, of Va
John L Pendleton, of Va
Thos M Blount, of Fla
Ezra W Dean, of N Y
N C Fowle, of Wash
Abram Waheman, of N Y
Timothy Fitch, of N Y
Erastuss T Montague, of Va
John O Sargent, of N Y
Nathan Sargent, of N Y
Jos Howard, of Ohio
S S Baxter, of Va
Israel Williams, of Ohio
Richd T Burchell, of Va
Wm H Miller, of Ohio
Jos H Coombs, of Ohio
C W Downing, of Wash
Saml L Lewis, of Va

C H Stewart, of Wash
Saml F Vinton, of Ohio
Jos B Stewart, of Ky
Rd J Cox, of Wash
B B French, of Wash
John H Rockwell, of Conn
J M Carlisle, of Wash
John H Craig, of Wash
Chas Abert, of Wash
Robt C Schenck, of Ohio
G H McCutchen, of Wash
Jos T Stevens, of Wash
Jos H Bradley, of Wash
Saml Chilton, of Wash
Luke Lea, of Wash
Wm Hunt, of Wash
Wm B Webb, of Wash
Wm M Merrick, of Wash
Richd H Clarke, of Wash
M Thompson, of Wash
[*Aug 1st newspaper: correction- Gusling should be Gurley.]

[Jul 16th newspaper: sworn Attys, but were omitted in our list on Sat:]
F P Stanton, Wash   Nathan Sargent, Pa
A H Lawrence, Wash   John S Tyson, Md
Chas E Sherman, Ala   Wm H Philip, Wash
N Titus Wakeman, N Y

Teacher wanted: I desire to employ a single gentleman, of liberal education, to board in my family & to fill a situation about to become vacant in my school.
–Caleb S Hallowell, Alexandria, Va.

Mr Hugh Auchincloss, an old & highly respected merchant of N Y C, died at his residence on Staten Island after a short but painful illness. He was a native of Scotland, where he was born in 1780, & migrated to this country in 1803. He established himself in business in N Y in 1805, & for 50 years has been continually engaged in trade, being at his death, the oldest dry good merchante in N Y actually engaged in business, his early contemporaries, John Haggerty, John Steart, & other old business men, having long since retired. –Evening Post [No death date given, current news item.]

From private letter written on board the U S ship **John Adams**, at Panama, Jun 28, Lt Mooney, of the ship **Independence**, on Jun 3, came suddenly to his death by drowning. The Lt was insane, & had been the object of constant vigilance on the part of ofcrs & men for some days. On Jun 3 he rushed from his room through the ward room & up the ladder to the deck, his fellow-ofcrs in full pursuit, &, although arrested in his progress by the master–at-arms, he thew him off & jumped overboard from the starboard side of the forecastle. He was sought for, but without recovering the body. He was regarded as a competent ofcr, & was popular on board ship. The cause of his insanity is not mentioned, but it is stated that he was temperate in his habits. –Journal of Commerce

By virtue of 2 writs of fieri facias, issued by John L Smith, justice of the peace in & for Wash Co, D C, at the suit of Henry Thorn against the goods & chattels of Jas A Wise: sale on Jul 21, in front of the Centre Market: sale of the property seized of Jas A Wise. –Wm D Bell, constable

Mrd: on Jul 12, by Rev L J Gilliss, John A Linton to Jeannette H, daughter of Wm A Bradley, all of Wash City.

Mrd: on Jul 12, by Rev Byron Sunderland, T Robinson Rodgers, of N J, to Margaret M, daughter of Josiah F Caldwell, of Wash City.

From Alta Calif, Jun 7: Col T J Henley, the Superintendent of Indian Affairs in Calif, left town on Sat, by the steamer **America**, for the purpose of visiting the Tejon Reservation.

Indian Creek, May 16, 1855. One of the 7 miners of this place was yesterday, Sunday alone in the camp. He was J B Hills, of Wash, & the Indians are supposed to have broken through the window, dragged him out, & stabbed & killed him. J W Bucks was elected captain of a company of volunteers & are going out in pursuit of the Indians. Yours, Jas H Taylor.
+
Killed by the Indians, at Indian Creek, Calif, May 13, Mr Josiah B Hills, of Wash. Mr Hills had won for himself the respect & esteem of all who knew him.

Montgomery White Sulphur Springs, Montg Co, Va, is opened for the reception of visiters. It is on the western slope of the Alleghanies, in said county. The services of Mr Thompson Tyler, who is well known in the Atlantic cities, have been procured. A fine band of music is also engaged. –Robt H Mosby, President Montg White Sulphur Springs Co, Shawlesville, Va.

MON JUL 16, 1855
Trustee's sale: by deed of trust from R H Hoffman, & at the request of the creditors named therein, I will sell at auction east half of lot 11 in square 653, in Wash City, containing 4,775 square feet, & also part of the lot at the s w interestion of 1st & Potomac sts, in Gtwn, which lies next the residence of Jeremiah Orme, fronting on the south line of 1st st about 30 feet. –W Redin, trustee -Green & Scott, aucts

The last steamer from Europe brings intelligence of the death of Maj Gen J Brecknall Estcourt, Adj Gen of the forces in the Crimea. He died of cholera on Jun 23.
-Portland [Me] paper

In the case of Thos Gallagher, tried at Detroit on Thu for selling a glass of brandy, it was proved to have been imported, where upon the jury rendered a verdict of not guilty, declaring the sale of imported liquors in any quantity is not prohibited by law.

Academy of the Visitation, B V M, Mount de Sales, near Balt, Md: annual distribution of premiums took place on Jul 12. The premiums were presented by the Most Reverend Archbishop. Premiums distributed to the following students:

Maria Orendorf, Balt, Md
Mary Moore, N Y
Va Scott, Wash, D C
Mgt Bogus, Balt, Md
Mgt Fusting, Catonsville, Md
Cornelia Read, Balt, Md
Kate Costigin, St Mary's Co, Md
Eliz Posey, Woodville, Miss
Mary Hamilton, Chas Co, Md
Helen Carroll, Balt Co, Md
Edmonia Maddox, St Mary's Co, Md

Eliz King, Wash, D C
Alice & Rebecca Hewlett, Balt
Susan Conolly, Balt, Md
Bessie Lee, Balt, Md
Ellen A Jenkins, Balt, Md
Rebecca Jenkins, Balt, Md
Josephine C Laub, Wash, D C
Fannie Mortimer, Balt, Md
Fannie Fowler, Balt Md
Susan Davis, Portsmouth, Va
Eliz Smith, Balt Co, Md

Anna Jenkins, Balt, Md
Mgt Murray, Balt, Md
Kate Hamilton, Chas Co, Md
Eliza Whyte, Petersburg, Va
Rosalie Bourke, Portsmouth, Va
Annie Hussey, Pottsville, Pa
Bessie Ferrall, N C
Anna Ward, Norfolk, Va
Jane Slevin, Phil, Pa
Maria Lujan, of Dona Ana, New Mexico
Anna Morgan, St Mary's Co, Md
Annie Kerns, Pottsville, Pa
Va Clare, Wash, D C
Ellen Jenkins, Balt, Md
Mary Teresa McKee, Balt, Md
Adeline Neale, Balt, Md
Estelle Claxton, Richmond, Va
Martha & Mgt Green, Portsmouth, Va
Mary Cummiskey, Balt, Md
Laura D Laub, Wash, D C
Emily S Mathews, Chas Co, Md
Cecilia Young, Balt, Md
Maria Tilghman, Queen Ann Co, Md
Augusta McLaughlin, of Balt Co, Md
Marion Black, Charleston, S C
Jeanette Sanders, Balt, Md

Alice & Kate Gautier, Wash, D C
Roberta McLaughlin, Balt, Md
Eliza Waiger, Calif
Va Sollers, Calvert Co, Md
Chareilla Price, Balt, Md
Cezarina Wiger, Balt, Md
Josephine McKee, Balt, Md
Ione Burke, N Y
Dolored Pacetti, Havana, Cuba
Lamarcita Martinez, Corpus Christi, Texas
Melitona Martinez, Corpus Christi, Texas
Alexandrine Godfroy, Detroit, Mich
Regina Keenan, Balt, Md
Mary Dunlevy, Balt, Md
Laura Stuart, Balt, Md
Emma Vallett, Balt, Md
Josephine Beard, Balt, Md
Sarah Fusting, Catonsville, Md
Louise Trumbo, Charleston, S C
Minnie Worthington, Balt Co, Md
Eliza Walbach, Balt, Md
Fannie Clay James, Balt, Md
Gertrude Jenkins, Balt, Md

A freshman student at Waterville College, by the name of Woodward, belonging to New Gloucester, was found drowned in the Kennebec river, near Waterville, Me, on Jul 9.

The Balt papers relate the painful partriculars of the death of a soldier last week, at **Fort McHenry**, whilst he was undergoing punishment for a high military offence. His name was Louis Loup, a Swiss, who had served 18 or 20 years in the army of the U S. He was found drunk upon guard last Wed night, arrested, & placed in the guard house, & the next morning he was tied by his hand to the flag-staff, where he was found dead 2 hours afterwards. Dr Webster, the surgeon of the fort, testified that the deceased came to his death by congestion of the brain, superinduced by intemperance. The verdict of the jury was that he came to his death from maltreatment & intemperance. A sgt who chastised him during the night, has been delivered over to the civil authorities for trial & the ofcr of the day at the time, Lt Griffith, has applied for & been granted a court of inquiry, composed entirely of ofcrs who are not on duty at that fort.

Mrs Catharine Devine has been arrested in N Y as party to a heavy robbery of silks, $4,000 worth, from Auffren, Ordt, Hessenberg & Co. Mrs Devine's grosser half is wanted also, but cannot be found.

At Kingston, Canada, on Fri last, whilst the Nat'l Guard, a visiting military company from N Y, were going through their exercises of firing, a heart-rending cry fell upon the ears of all present. It was soon found that a young country woman with her child had been shot by a ball from one of the muskets. She was the wife of Jeremiah Cassel, a farmer, who lives about 10 miles from Kingston. Her child, an infant 6 months of age, was picked up when the mother fell, covered with blood, which flowed profusely from a wound in the head. The husband, who was standing near his wife at the time, escaped unhurt. The woman was expected to survive, but the child cannot survive. To atone for the mischief, a collection in aid of the woman was taken up, & nearly $1,000 was collected.

Sundry persons were arrested last week at Cincinnati upon the charge of recruiting soldiers for the Crimea. They are Chas Rowecroft, British Consul; Fred'k Poshner, Hungarian capt; David Rady, Irish capt; Jas Turnhill, paymaster, Wm Hamilton, surgeon, Robt Mackay, agent of the British Gov't; & a party of privates with unmistakeable German names. Mr Rowecroft was released under a parole of honor, while the other dfndnts were each held in $300 bail to appear. The company were under command of David Rady, capt, who had the through tickets by cars & steamer for each dfndnt in his possession.

The London correspondent of the Boston Post writes that the cmte of the Nelson memorial fund, organized about a year ago by a number of gentlemen, who had discovered that the last request of Nelson that "he left his daughter Horatia as a legacy to his country," had been utterly neglected, have just made their report. The eight children of Mrs Ward, the Horatia alluded to, have all been provided for. The eldst son has been presented to a living by the Countess of Waldegrave, the 2nd appointed a surgeon in the navy; the 3rd receives a Gov't clerkship; the 4th & 5th receive a cadetship; & the 3 daughters have a pension of L100 each year for life settled upon them by her Majesty. This daughter, Horatia, it will be remembered, is the only child of Lord Nelson by Lady Hamilton, & who, whatever may have been the character of the mother, is a most estimable & deserving wife & mother.

A lad named Johnson, & Francis Noble, age 9 years, were drowned at Albany on Tue.

For rent: a large bldg at the corner of 7th & Pa ave, over the stores of Messrs Carter, Bartholow, & Etchison. It contains about 60 rooms; improved with gas, tanks, bath-rooms, & with hot & cold water conveyed through each story in the house. Apply at 295 G st north, between 13th & 14th sts. –Anne R Dermott

The first bronze statue of Washington ever made was cast on Thu last in the city of Richmond. Mr Hubbard & the workmen were present when the metal was tested.

The Phil Ledger announces the death of Dr Thos C Bunting, who died at Llangollen, Wales, on Jun 28, to which country he had gone for the benefit of his health. Dr Bunting accompanied the Pennsylvania volunteers to Mexico.

Lt Saml Kinsey, of the 1st Regt of U S Artl, who came to Wash from **Fort McHenry**, on Jul 3 with the light battery of his regt, died on Sat of typhoid fever. His remains were taken to Rhode Island, accompanied by his parents.

By order of distrain from Robt Beall against the goods & chattels of John N Morhiser for house rent due & in arrears & to me directed, I have seized & taken sundry property of the said Morhiser, & shall expose said goods at public sale for cash, on Jul 19, in front of the Centre Market. –Chas Kemble, bailiff

Died: Chas Bradford, son of Seraphim & Catharine Masi, in his 15th year. His funeral will take place from his father's residence, 455 10th st, on Mon, at 9 o'clock. [No death date given.]

Died: on Jul 14, William Shugert, infant son of Anthony & Eliz J Buckly, aged 5 weeks. His funeral is this evening, at 4 o'clock, from the residence of Mr Wm Martin, 396 D st, between 5th & 7th sts.

Died: on Jul 13, in Gtwn, D C, after an illness of 3 days, Benjamin Latimer Tompkins, aged 8 years & 8 months, only son of Juliet L & the late Benjamin G Tompkins, of Mathew's Co, Va.

TUE JUL 17, 1855
Mr Jas Bryan, father of Wm Bryan, of Annapolis, died on Thu last, in Queen Anne's Co, Md, in his 99th year. He was the youngest of 3 brothers who served during the Revolutionary war under Gen Washington.

John C Nichols, charged with an extensive system of swindling & forgery at Charleston, S C, has been arrested at Brussels, in Belgium.

The Catholic College of Worcester: the college of the <u>Holy Cross</u> at Worcester, Mass, which was burnt down 3 years ago, having been rebuilt & enlarged, has been got under way again with favorable prospects, & on Tue there was a public commencement on the grounds of the college that extends over 100 acres. There are about 50 or 60 students, young men, from 12 to 20 years. The degree of A M was conferred on Henry F Brownson, a graduate of this college, son of O A Brownson.

Dr R L Bohannon, the oldest professor of the **Medical College** of Va, died at Richmond on Sunday last. He had reached an advanced age. He was one of the first professors in the college & he was the last of those who founded the institution that remained in the faculty. –Dispatch

Court of Claims: gentlemen sworn attys of the Court yesterday:
Chas A May, of N Y
Willie P Mangun, jr, of Wash
H L Stevens, of Pontiac, Mich
Nathl Hatch, of Wash
Chas Lee Jones, of Wash
Danl Webster, of Phil
Asbury Lloyd, of Wash

L G Brandebury, of Pa, was sworn in on Sat.

The tailoring store of Mr E C Eckloff, on the south side of Pa ave, near 9th st, was, on Sat night, robbed of several hundred dollars' worth of goods; & the adjoining tobacco store, kept by a relative of Mr Eckloff, was also robbed of about $300s' worth of cigars & fancy articles.

Jos Peck, Butcher, Centre Market, notifies his cutomers & friends that he can be found at the stall opposite to those he has been occupying for the last 8 months. The best Beef always on hand.

Wanted, after Sep 1, by the subscriber, a situation as instructor in Music & French in a Female Seminary or as Assistant in a Male Academy. He has had some years' experience in teacher. Unexceptionable references given. Address E F Foster, c/o R Baylor, Loretto, Essex Co, Va.

Died: on Jul 16, in the triumph of the Christian faith, Eliza Sandiford Anderson, wife of Mr C A Anderson, & daughter of the late Thos Sandiford, of Wash City.

Died: on Jul 14, Ovid V, infant son of Jas S & Eliz J Holland.

Died: on Jul 16, in Wash City, William Thomas, the only child of Wm & Mary Goods, aged 4 months. His funeral will take place from the residence of his parents, this evening, on 11th st, between I & K sts, at 5 o'clock.

Six cents reward for runaway black boy Alex'r Brown about 18 years old, sometimes he calls himself Davis. –Douglass Moore, 412 F st north, between 6th & 7th sts.

Buffalo, Jul 16. Jas Thompson's house, in the village of Brant, was fired by incendiaries on Sat night, & Mr Thompson, with his 3 daughters & 2 grand-daughters, perished. [Jul 19th newspaper: 1 o'clock on Sunday the most horrible calamity occurred in the town of Brant, the firing of Mr Jas Thompson's house, where 6 persons perished in the flames, Mr T, 3 daughters, & 2 grand-daughters. The ladies were aged between 18 & 24. Mr Thompson was quite elderly.]

The College of St James, Md, will open on Oct 1. The grammar school receives pupils when not less than 12 years of age & prepares them for college. The college embraces the full course of collegiate training & education. –Rev John B Kerfoot, D D, Rector, P O College of St James, Md.

WED JUL 18, 1855
Academy of the Visitation, B V M, Gtwn, D C. Annual distribution of premiums on Jul 11, distributed by Rev Bernard A Maguire, S J, Pres of Gtwn College, assisted by Rev Chas F King, S J. Premiums awarded to the following students:

Isabel Burns, of Alexandria, Va
Agnes Montague, Fayetteville, N C
Ellen O'Donoghue, Gtwn, D C
Frances Beckham, Warrenton, Va
Victoria Philips, Warrenton, Va
Louisa Benson, Montg, Ala
Alice Murray, Gtwn, D C
Rosa Cole, Balt, Md
Martha Smith, Middleburg, Va
Martha Anderson, Montg Co, Md
Bettie Whitworth, Petersburg, Va
Martha Rice, St Paul, Minn
Ada Semmes, Gtwn, D C
Caroline Davis, N Y
Lydia Robinson, Montg, Ala
Martha Bisselle, Gtwn, D C
Priscilla Neale, Chas Co, Md
Caroline Philips, Warrenton, Va
Mary Duncan, Montg, Ala
Mary Pizzini, Richmond, Va
Louisa Buckner, Fauquier Co, Va
Laura Lancaster, Chas Co, Md
Caroline Massi, Wash, D C
Eliza Baasen, Milwaukie, Wisc
Amelia Lancaster, Wash, D C
Amanda Payne, Gtwn, D C
Adelaide Frederick, Augusta, Ga
Kate Potter, Binghamton, N Y
Jane Poe, Gtwn, D C
Anita & Dolores Ansoatigui, Mexico
Maria Sosa, Panama
Maria Briscoe, Wash, D C
Martha Easton, Greenville, N C
Louisa Jamieson, Martinsburg, Va
Caroline Lancaster, Chas Co, Md
Susan Plowden, St Mary's, Md
Louisa Rabe, San Francisco, Calif
Kate Miller, Raleigh, N C
Teresa Baasen, Milwaukie, Wisc
Sarah Gross, Gtwn, D C
Kate Blackford, Gtwn, D C
Augusta McClelland, Gtwn, D C
Augusta Winter, Wash, D C
Ada O'Donnell, Clarksville, Md
Fannie Turner, King Geo Co, Va
Ann Miles, St Mary's, Md
Kate Smith, Reading, Penn
Florence Poe, Gtwn
Agnes Hayes, Opelousas, La
Hibernia Ferrall, Halifax, N C
Annie Goldthwaite, Montg, Ala
Rosa Rabe, San Francisco, Calif
Victoria Moreno, Pensacola, Fla
Beverly Rudd, Fredericksburg, Va
Caroline Hickey, Wash, D C
Celestia Semmes, PG Co, Md
Helen May, Gtwn, D C
Virginia Anderson, Montg Co, Md
Ella Bibb, Gtwn, D C
E J Rice, St Paul, Minn
Florence Brent, Alexandria, Va
Genevieve Carusi, Gtwn, D C
Virginia Hempstone, N Y
Maria Bradley, Wash, D C
Cecilia Coad, St Mary's, Md
Carlotin Moreira, Rio Janeiro, SA
Mary Jane Robinson, Montg, Ala
Mary Bowie, PG Co, Md
Catharine McGarrity, Gtwn, D C
Sallie Major, Phil

Eliza L White, N Y
Mary E Smith, Gtwn, D C
Catharine Tierney, Gtwn, D C
Lavinia Philips, Warrenton, Va
Lizzie Philips, Warrenton, Va
Eliz Bellinger, Charleston, S C
Ellen Posey, Chas Co, Md
Emma Malbon, Gtwn, D C
Eugenia Moore, Columbus, Ga
S Savage, Wash, D C
Victoria Pizzini, Richmond, Va
Carlota Moreira, New Orleans, La
Ann Atwell, New Orleans, La
Josephine Hurdle, Gtwn, D C
Lucia Bellinger, Charleston, S C
Victoria Hicks, Gtwn, D C
Isadora Homiller, Gtwn, D C
Mary Frances Garrett, Gtwn, D C
Ada Ward, Pittsylvania, Va
Teresa Favier, Wash, D C
Mary Moxley, Gtwn, D C
Catharine McWilliams, Chas Co, Md
Margaret Kengla, Gtwn, D C
Agatha O'Neill, Gtwn, D C
Mary Warring, Montg, Md
Dolores Madan, Havana, Cuba
Margaretta Kieckhaefer, Wash, D C
Mary E Baker, Wash, D C
Eliz Woolard, Gtwn, D C
Clara Kidwell, Gtwn, D C
Josephine Clarke, Gtwn, D C
Arabella Grimes, Gtwn, D C
Mildred Nowton, Gtwn, D C
Hattie Essex, Gtwn, D C
Bettie Hurdle, Gtwn, D C
Romain Goddard, Wash, D C
Annie Pickrell, Gtwn, D C

Lucinda Clements, Chas Co, Md
Mary Jane Cannon, Wash, D C
Mary Clary, Wash, D C
Eliza Newman, Gtwn, D C
Mary Clementine McWilliams, Cobb Neck, Md
F Petit, Gtwn, D C
Teresa Keegan, New Orleans, La
Martha Stone, Gtwn, D C
Josephine Dannell, Anne Arundel Co, Md
Caroline Hickey, St Mary's, Md
Alice Edelen, St Mary's, Md
Louisa Keegan, New Orleans, La
Eva Eve, Augusta, Ga
Francilia Alexander, Wash, D C
Virginia Coolidge, Gtwn, D C
Mary Bellinger, Charleston, S C
Emma Woolard, Gtwn, D C
M J Herron, Gtwn, D C
Mary Clements, Gtwn, D C
Maria Devereux, Gtwn, D C
Henrietta Wetzell, Gtwn, D C
Helen Brooks, Gtwn, D C
Harriet Stanton, Memphis, Tenn
Albinia Gilliam, Dinwiddie, Va
Mary A Gallagher, Wash, N C
Octavia Prudhomme, Oupelousas, La
Lavinia Clements, Gtwn, D C
Alice Penrice, St Louis, Mo
Alice Youlee, Wash, D C
Bettie Watson, Richmond, Va
C Sauve, New Orleans
Isabel Burns, Alexandria, Va
Frances Beckham, Warrenton, Va
Ellen O'Donnoghue, Gtwn, D C

Wash Corp: 1-Ptn of S H Steigruff for the remission of a fine: referred to the Cmte of Claims. 2-Ptn from Isaac Ten Eyck, asking additional compensation for numbering the city: referred to the Cmte of Claims.

For rent & possession immediately: a 3 story brick house, with attic & basement, on D st, between 2nd & 3rd sts. Apply to Oliver Whittlesy, Indiana ave, between 3rd & 4 ½ sts, south side.

Died: on Jul 17, William C I, aged nearly 12 months, son of Lt John J & Louisa S Guthrie. His funeral will take place at 5 o'clock P M, Jul 18, from the residence of his father, 54 Frederick st, Gtwn.

Died: on Jul 17, Philip Hopkins, in his 40th year. His funeral is today at 10 o'clock A M, from his late residence, 573 H st north.

Died: Jul 17, Danl Parker Porter, of the Treasury Dept, in his 67th year. His funeral will be from the residence of Mrs James, 291 F st, between 12th & 13th sts, this afternoon, at 5 o'clock.

Buffalo, Jul 16. The prisoner Mayberry was hanged by a mob at Janesville, Wisc, last week. The prisoner had been found guilty by Judge Doolittle, but the law only prescribes imprisonment for life. The sheriff undertook to remove the prisoner from the court-house to the jail, with his posse, but a cry arose "Hang Him!' The ofcrs were overpowered by the crowd, the prisoner seized, a rope placed around his neck, & he was dragged to a cluster of trees & hung till dead. A band of 300 men had been organized to execute the deed.

THU JUL 19, 1855
House servant & waiter wanted: I wish to purchase for my own use a negro man, not exceeding 30 years of age, with his wife & children. The man must be a good waiter & house servant, sober & trustworthy. The negroes to be warranted sound, healthy, & slaves for life. Any gentleman having such servants to dispose of can obtain a liberal price for them & secure to them a comfortable & permanent home by applying to me at *Mount Vernon*, near Alexandria, Va. –John A Washington

The remains of Mr Chas B Masi, aged nearly 16 years, son of Mr Seraphim Masi, of Wash City, were yesterday conducted to the grave & buried with military honors by the Scott Guards, Capt Jamison, of which he was a member, & the Marion Rifles, Capt Shekell. These 2 companies are composed of youths & very young men.

Mrd: on Wed, by Rev John C Smith, Dr Danl McFarlan to Miss Mary A, daughter of Wm W Moore, all of Wash City.

Mrd: on Jul 17, in Wash City, by Rev Mr French, Capt Geo W Lay, U S Army, of Va, to Henrietta, daughter of Hon J A Campbell, of the U S Supreme Court.

Died: last night, Wed, at his residence in Wash City, Maj Augustus A Nicholson, Quartermaster of the U S Marine Corps.

Teacher wanted: Trustees of the Alleghany Co Academy, Cumberland, Md, desire to obtain the services of a Principal. –Thos J McKaig, Pres of Board of Trustees

The Trustees of <u>Warren Academy</u>, Warrenton, Va, will elect a Principal on the first Monday of Aug next. –H A White, Sec, Warrenton, Va.

FRI JUL 20, 1855
An arrival at N Y brings intelligence of the loss of the schnr **Emma** on which Col Kinney, with some 20 men, took passage for Central America. The vessel was wrecked on the Caycos Islands on Jun 19; passengers & crew were saved; all the stores of the expedition were lost.

The frig **Congress**, bearing the broad pennant of Cmdor Breese, dropped down from the navy yard last evening to her present anchorage. She will proceed to sea early this morning. List of her ofcrs: Cmdor, Saml Breese; Cmder, Thos T Craven; Flag Cmder, Geo A Magruder; 1st Lt, Luther Stoddard; 2nd Lt, Wm May; 3rd Lt, W C Bolton Porter; 4th Lt, Baise N Westcott; 5th Lt, Saml Marcy; Flag Lt, J B Carter; Fleet Surgeon, Wm F Patton; Purser, Jas A Semple; Capt of Marines, Benj E Brooke; Lt of Marines, John R F Tattnall; Master, J P Jones; Chaplain, Mason Noble; Passed Assist Surgeon, Chas Eversfield; Assists Surgeons, D B Corwin & W T Hoard; Cmdor's Sec, Mr Lansing; Passed Midshipmen, B P Loyall, W H Cheever, W Ward, E P McCrea; Midshipmen, Geo E Law, Edw Lull, A Hopkins, A F Crossman; Capt's Clerk, Wm H Evans; Purser's Clerk, G C Breemater; Cmdor's Clerk, J Smith; Boatswain, Geo Willmuth; Gunner, Geo Sirian; Sailmaker, T C Herbert; Carpenter, Jas Meads.

The framed cottage on 9th st which was owned & occupied by Mrs Humphries, was destroyed by fire on Thu. The new frame dwlg on the adjoining lot, owned & occupied by Mr Isaac Hill, was somewhat injured. The former was insured to the amount of $600, which will not cover the loss. It was the work of an incendiary.

Mr Richd Isaacs, an old & respectable citizen of the *Forest of PG*, was at 4 o'clock yesterday morning conveyed from the market-house to the Infirmary, almost exhausted from the loss of blood. A common bile on his leg, with which he had been troubled for a few days, had impaired the substance of a large vein, which was ruptured at this moment. He was dong very well yesterday, under the kindly care of the medical attendants & nurses of the Infirmary.

Jas Myers, a clown, & one of the proprietors of Myers & Madigan's circus company, met with an untimely death while performing on the slack rope at Geneva, N Y, a few days since. [Jul 23rd newspaper: the report of the death of Myers is said to be unfounded, & the only truth in it is the breaking of the ring by which the rope was fastened to his feet.]

Family School for Boys will commence near Alexandria, Va, on Sep 17, to be taught by himself at my residence, with the aid of teachers. –E R Lippitt, Alexandria, Va

Mr Jas M Boyd, of Lynchburg, Va, lost his life under the most painful circumstances on Tue last. A gas chandelier in the hall of his residence became detached from its fastenings & fell. Mr Boyd replaced the chandelier & took the light from a servant to apply to the burner. In the mean time the gas had escaped to such an extent that as soon as the light was raised so as to come in contact with the stratum the gas ignited, entirely enveloping Mr Boyd in the flame, & he was burnt in so shocking a manner as to cause his death in a few hours. He was esteemed by all who knew him.

Mrd: on Jul 17, at the Univ of Va, by Rev Wm H McGuffy, J J Hoge, of Wheeling, Va, to Mary S Calhoun, of the Univ of Va.

Died: on Wed, in Wash City, Maj Augustus A Nicholson, Quartermaster of the U S Marine Corps, aged 53 years. His brother ofcrs of the Army & Navy & his friends & acquaintances are invited to attend his funeral, from the family residence, this afternoon, at 5 o'clock, punctually.

Died: on Jul 11, at Bluffton, Beaufort District, S C, Lewis T Hamilton, the youngest surviving son of Gen Jas & Eliz Hamilton, in his 23rd year.

Family School for Boys will commence near Alexandria, Va, on Sep 17, to be taught by himself at my residence, with the aid of teachers. –E R Lippitt, Alexandria, Va

SAT JUL 21, 1855
Household & kitchen furniture at auction on: Jul 27, at the house next door to Mr Purdy, on Pa ave, between 1st & 2nd sts. -Green & Scott, aucts

Exchange Ins Co, 11 Merchant's Exchange, Phil: Capital $200,000. John M Hale, Pres; E P Hinds, Sec. Directors: John P Wetherill, Jas J Duncan, Jacob H Lex, Jas W Riddle, John M Pumroy, R C Hale. –Jas J Miller, Agent, Columiba Pl, Corner 7th st & La ave, Wash.

Gtwn Female Academy will be resumed on Sep 3. Terms for boarding pupils $250 per session. –Wm J Clark, corner of Gay & Wash sts.

Died: yesterday, of bilious dysentery, in his 29th year, Rev Jacob W Winans, a native of Elizabethrown, N J. His funeral will be from the Presbyterian Church on F st, where a discourse will be delivered by Rev Dr Gurley, at 4½ o'clock, this afternoon.

Died: on Jul 18, in Gtwn, Ellen Ray, only child of Robt H & Sarah E Watkins, aged 11 months & 2 weeks.

Died: on Jun 28, at Port au Prince, Francis Horace, son of John & Caroline Wadsworth, of N Y, & grandson of Francis Masi, of Wash City.

One of the best Grocery Stands in Wash City at Public Sale: on Jul 26, on the premises, that valuable property on the corner of B & 11th st, near 12th st bridge, formerly kept as a grocery store by Sengstack & Clark, & late by Wm H Clark. Can be seen at any time by application to C P Sengstack, D st, between 12th & 13th. -J C McGuire, auct

Hon Edw Everett, of Mass: extracts from an oration given by Everett on the last national anniversary, at the celebration of the day in his native town of Dorchester.
1-It is 225 years since the commencement of the settlement of our ancient town, the first foothold of the pioneers of Gov Winthrop's expedition.
2-It is the 79th anniversary of the Declaration of the Independence of the U S.
3-In the year 1841 I occupied, with my family, the Villa Careggi, near Florence, a mansion, once, as its name imports, Casa Regia, a princely residence, belonging to the Grand duke of Tuscany, but of late years private property & occasionally leased to travellers. Half fortress, half palace, it was built by Cosmo de Medici in 1444, 9 years before the capture of Constantinople by the Ottomans in 1458.
4-The Platonic Academy was established in the arcades of the Villa Careggi; the stores of learning & thought accumulated by the mind of antiquity were thrown open to the world. The first book ever printed with a date appeared in 1455, & in 1462, 9 years only after the Koran began to be read at Constantinople, the Bible went forth on the wings of the press to the four quarters of the world.
5-On Monday, Nov 22, 1773, the cmtes of Dorchester, Roxbury, Brookline, & Cambridge met the Boston cmtes in Faneuil Hall. On Nov 28 the ship **Dartmouth**, the first of the tea ships, arrived. On Dec 16 a party of persons disguised as Mohawk Indians boarded the tea ships & threw into the water 342 chests of tea.
6-As early as 1619 **Thompson's Island** is known to have been occupied by an Englishman. In 1624 as many as 50 vessels were employed on this coast. Among the leading non-conformists in that quarter none was more active influential than Rev John White, of Dorchester.

Mrd: Jul 17, by Rev A Holmead, John A Shields to Miss M King, both of Wash City.

A dispatch from Reading, Pa, Jul 10: Arthur Hughes, the special agent of the Post Ofc Dept, arrived here this afternoon with Adam Smith, of Clark post ofc, in Richmond, Northampton Co, charged with robbing the mails. Smith confessed to taking one letter containing $400, mailed at Stroudsburg, for the Eastern Bank.

MON JUL 23, 1855
Wanted a teacher well qualified to act as an assistant in a select classical & mathematical academy. -P A Bowen, Gtwn, D C

We learn that a letter containing a note for $500 has been found by Mr Peter Shunck, of Howard Co, among some waste paper purchased at the Balt post ofc. The letter was directed to the cashier of the Exchange Bank of Va, at Abingdon, & was for Mr Alex'r Brog, of N Y. -American

Death of 2 English writers: Mr John Black & Jas Silk Buckingham, the traveler. Mr Black was for many years the editor of the Morning Chronicle, & Mr Buckingham, was the editor of the Athenaeum. Both have recently died.

Fatal recontre on Jul 13 at Fairmount, Clark Co, Mo, between J H Childress & Dr J B Craven. The latter was killed. The affray grew out of an old difficulty. The Dr threw a weight at Childress, & while in the act of throwing another the latter struck him over the head with a scythe he happened to have his hand to grind.

The funeral of Maj Augustus A Nicholson, Quartermaster of the U S Marine Corps, took place from the family residence of the deceased, on Capitol Hill, on Friday. The impressive service for the burial of the dead was conducted by Rev Smith Pyne.

Wash, Jul 20, 1855. J D Hoover, Marshal: in the cases of Richd Biddle, Saml Keys, Davis Hazard, & John McNenny, 4 seamen & ordinary seamen, confined in the U S Penitentiary in this District, under sentences of naval courts martial, I have thought proper to remit the residue of the punishment awarded against them, so far as regards confinement. You will therefore have them discharged from confinement. I am, respectfully, your obedient servant, Franklin Pierce. [On Sat they were discharged from imprisonment.]

Mrd: on Jul 17, in Trinity Church, Gtwn, by Rev Mr Ashwanden, A Pierce Shoemaker, of Wash Co, D C, to Martha L, daughter of Lewis Carbery, of Gtwn, D C.

Died: on Sat, in Montg Co, Md, Andrew Lawrence, aged 12 years, 2nd son of Jos & Charlotte L Thompson, formerly of Wash City. His funeral is this day, at 2 o'clock, at *Oak Hill Cemetery*, Gtwn.

Died: on Jul 19, in Wash City, John Howard Stewart, only son of John McFarland, aged 9 months.

TUE JUL 24, 1855
Public sale of cargo of anthracite coal: on Jul 26, on board the schnr **Devothea Haynes**, lying at Riley's wharf. –John W George, Master -Green & Scott, aucts

Household & kitchen furniture at auction on: Jul 30 at the residence of Geo Butler, near the Navy Yard, S C ave, at Pa ave, between 6th & 7th sts. -Green & Scott, aucts

Now is the time to lay in your fuel. The undersigned will now deliver good oak wood, 5 cords or upwards, at $5.50 per cord, cash. –T Drury, 165 Pa ave, between 17th & 18th sts, south side.

Capt Geo F Lindsay, Assist Quartermaster U S Marine corps, has been ordered from the Brooklyn Navy Yard, where he has been stationed for some years, to the Marine Barracks in Wash City, vice the late Maj Nicholson, deceased, until the President may make a permanent appointment.

Mr Martin F Conway, late of Balt, has refused to take his seat in the Kansas Legislature, & has returned his certificate of election to Gov Reeder, alleging as a reason that the members have been elected, not by the free suffrages of the actual residents of the Territory, but by fraud & force of arms, employed & brought into exercise by a number of Missourians.

Sgt John Morrow, who is alleged to have caused the death of soldier Loup at **Fort McHenry**, was taken before the U S Com'r at Balt recently for examination. The Com'r decided that the examination must be private. The prisoner protested & insisted it be made public. In this state of the case the District Atty moved the commitment of the prisoner on a charge of murder, to take his trial before the U S District Court in Nov next; & the case was so disposed of.

The famous steamboat **Martha Washington** conspiracy has turned up at Boston, where Saml J Cheney has been arraigned before Com'r Loring on a charge of perjury, in falsely swearing to a certain shipment of goods on board that vessel.

Prof Richardson, Principal of the Female Seminary at Freehold, N J, met with an accident on Sat. While superintending some arrangements for giving an exhibition, he stooped down over a place where a carpenter was boring a hole to suspend a chandelier, & just at that instant the auger came up through the floor & took away one of his eyes. Mr Richardson had previously lost the use of the other eye, so that now he is blind.

On Jul 13 Danl Callaghan was hung at New Orleans for murder. He made no confession & met his doom with indescribable coolness & composure. David Stoddard, who was executed on the same day at Rock Island, Ill, for the murder of his wife, manifested considerable motion. He made a speech from the gallows, stating that 14 years ago both himself & wife were professed Christians, living happily together, but unfortunately he took to drinking, by which his family were broken up & became wanderers & outcasts. He confessed to killing his wife.

Locomotive explosion at Milton, Vt, on Thu last, killed Mr Richd R Bush, the conductor, & Mr French, the engineer.

Died: on Jul 23, Robert, youngest son of the late John Brereton, aged 2 years & 2 months. His funeral will take place from the residence of his mother, near Baldensburg, this afternoon, at 3 o'clock.

Died: on Jul 19, at the residence of her father, in St Mary's Co, Md, Lela Penn, the 2nd daughter of Wm H & Caroline P Hebb.

Died: on Jul 16, at Emmitsburg, Md, Kate, infant daughter of Col B B & Mary Simmes, at Point Coupee Parish, La.

Died: on Jul 21, at Staunton, Va, Ann Ogle, infant daughter of Henry H & Anne Ogle Lewis.

Cape Island, N J, Jul 23. A party of 5 persons who went on a sailing excursion on Sat from Somer's Point to Beesely's Point drowned when their boat was upset. Drowned were G Tully, Chas T Wabon, his wife & child, & L Young.

For rent: a 2 story brick dwlg on East Capitol st, between 1st & 2nd sts east, & next the residence of B B French. –Jas Lynch, Capitol Hill

WED JUL 25, 1855
Trustee's sale of all of square 596, with improvements, at auction: on Aug 26, by deed of trust from John Downs & Wm Downs to the subscribers, dated Nov 4, 1848, recorded in Liber J A S No 1, folios 330 thru 337, of the land records for Wash Co, D C: all of square 596, in Wash City, with improvements. –Walter Lenox, Henry Naylor, trustees -Green & Scott, aucts

Trustee's sale of part of square 534, with improvements, at auction: on Aug 27, by deed of trust from Chas B Church & wife, dated Nov 3, 1848, recorded in Liber J A S No 3, folios 28 thru 34, of the land records for Wash Co, D C, being part of square 354, with a good dwlg house. –Walter Lenox, Henry Naylor, trustees -Green & Scott, aucts

Wash Corp: 1-Ptn from Wm Guinand, asking to be refunded the amount paid for a wagon license: referred to the Cmte of Claims. 2-Ptn from Robt Earl & others for paving the footway on 21st st west: referred to the Cmte on Improvements. 3-Ptn of John Trader, praying for the refunding of certain taxes erroneously assessed: referred to the Cmte of Claims. 4-Ptn of Robt Devereux, praying for the remission of 2 fines: referred to the Cmte of Claims.

A son of Mr Wm A Wilson, of Brunswick Co, N C, died on Thu last. He died suddenly from the accidental discharge of a gun. He was only 10 years old

Chas Louis Chapman, a porter & watchman at the Riggs & Co Bank, was arrested on Monday & accused of fraud or robbery committed upon that institution, & that $5,000 worth of coupon bonds, on deposite, & $5,000 in gold had been abstracted therefrom. Three of the missing coupons were found in a book upon his premises, & he confessed the crime.

Obit-died: on Wed last, at his residence, Woodsfield, Monroe Co, Ohio, Hon John Davenport. He had attained a good old age; was among the earlier settlers in Barnesville; a Christian & member of the Methodist Episcopal Church. –Balt Patriot

Cleveland Leader: The celebrated Alex'r Campbell, of Bethany, Va, died in New Orleans on Jun 27, of disease of the heart. He was the founder of the sect of Christians known as the Disciples, now very numerous & powerful. [Jul 31st newspaper: the statement that Alex Campbell, of Bethany, Va, is dead, is not correct. The mistake arose by confounding him with Alex Campbell, M D, of New Orleans, who died there more than a month since of heart disease.]

Died: on Jul 19, Mrs Rebecca C Craver, aged 61 years, wife of Mr P Craver, formerly of St Mary's Co, Md, but for the last few years a resident of Wash.

Cow lost: $5 reward. Anyone returning said Cow to the subscriber will receive a reward of $5. –John Bohn, Pa ave, Capitol Hill

THU JUL 26, 1855
Suicides: Geo Schank, of Waynesborough, Pa, hung himself on Jul 7, for grief at the death of a favorite horse. Jos Buffington, a highly respectable citizen of Bealsville, Pa, who was engaged to be married on Jul 4, rendered the ceremony unnecessary by shooting himself through the heart on Jul 3. –Newark Advertiser

Mrd: Wed, by Rev John C Smith, Felix K Sutton to Miss Lucy J Wright, both of Va.

Mrd: Jul 19, in Wash City, at the residence of G W McKnew, by Rev Gideon H Day, Dr Elisha J Cook, of New Windsor, Carroll Co, Md, to Miss Minerva McKnew, of Howard District, Md.

Died: Jul 24, Andrew Hoover, infant son of F B, jr, & Matilda C Lord, aged 9 months.

FRI JUL 27, 1855
Trustee's sale of a part of square 450, with improvements: on Aug 29, by deed of trust from Fred'k Honsum & wife, dated Jan 15, 1852, recorded in liber J A S No 41, folios 319 thru 325, all of lot 3 in square 450, with a house. –Walter Lenox, Henry Naylor, trustees -Green & Scott, aucts

Household & kitchen furniture at auction on: Aug 2, at the residence of Mr John King, on High st. –Barnard & Buckey, aucts

Trustee's sale of brick house & lot at auction: on Aug 30, by 2 deeds of trust from Jos Radcliff & wife, one dated Apr 16, 1850, recorded in Liber J A S 14, folios 240 to 246, of the land records for Wash Co, D C, & the other dated May 3, 1851, recorded in Liber J A S 30, folios 389 thru 394, of the land recorded of Wash Co, D C: part of lots 1 & 22 in square 455, with a fine brick house. Property is at the corner of 6th st west & F st north, in Wash City, D C. –Walter Lenox, Henry Naylor, trustees -Green & Scott, aucts

A young man named John Barnes, aged 17 years, bled to death on Monday in Buffalo, from the effects of a tooth which had been extracted some days previous.

On Sunday last Catharine Hobin, a girl of 11 years, died at Boston from the effects of swallowing a quantity of pins.

A little daughter of Mrs Russell, while in a daguerrean gallery at Boston on Monday for the purpose of having her portrait taken, fell backward out of the window, 40 feet to the pavement, & was killed.

Pawnee, Kentucky Territory, Jul 6, 1855. On Jul 2 an election of ofcrs was gone into by both Houses, with the following result:
In Council: Speaker, Thos Johnson; Chief Clerk, John Haldeman; Assist Clerk, C H Grover; Sgt-at-Arms, C S Whitehead; Doorkeeper, Wm H Godfroy; Engrossing Clerk, T C Hughes; Enrolling Clerk, ___ Waful.
In House: Speaker, J H Stringfellow; Chief Clerk, J M Lyle; Assist Clerk, John Martin; Sgt-at-Arms, T J B Cramer; Doorkeeper, P B Campbell; Engrossing Clerk, J M Fox; Enrolling Clerk, B F Simmons; Public Printer, John T Brady.

Wm Kinney, an Irish laboring man, was accidentally drowned in the canal, near the Little Falls, above Gtwn, on Tue night.

Lots of ground on K st, near 12th, were sold on Wed, at fifty cents per square foot, that at the corner bringing 65 cents. Mr J C McGuire, was the auctioneer, & Lt B W Hunter, U S Navy, & Mr Wm Dogherty were the purchasers.

Bishop Doane, of N J, has confirmed more than 600 persons during the ecclesiastical year, an increase of 40% over any previou year. Bishop Whittingham, of Md, confirmed 950 last year, more than twice the average of previous years. The membership of the Episcopal Church in Md has doubled in 15 years.

Died: yesterday, after a painful illness, borne with pious resignation, Eliz Jane, the beloved wife of Jas S Holland. Her funeral will take place this afternoon at 4½ o'clock, from her late residence, 412 9th st.

Died: on Jul 16, in PG Co, Md, at the residence of Mrs Mary Hall, Mrs Mary E Mullikin, relict of the late Dr B O Mullikin, & eldest daughter of the late Col Wm T Wootton, in her 35th year.

I certify that Geo W Dunlop, of Wash Co, D C, brought before me as a stray trespassing on his enclosures, a black mare. –B K Morsell, J P [Owner is to prove property, pay charges, & take her away. –Geo W Dunlop, Md av & 6th st.]

SAT JUL 28, 1855
Army General Order: Gen Orders, No 10: War Dept, Adj General's Ofc, Wash, Jul 19, 1855. Promotions & Appointments in the U S Army made by the Pres:
I-Promotions. Corps of Engineers:
1st Lt Zealous B Tower, to be Capt, Jul 1, 1855, having served 14 years continuous service as Lt.
1st Lt Horatio G Wright, to be Capt, Jul 1, 1855, having served 14 years continuous service as Lt.
2nd Lt Andrew J Donelson, to be 1st Lt, Mar 3, 1855, vice McClellan, appointed Capt in 1st regt of cavalry.
2nd Lt Jas C Duane, to be 1st Lt, Jul 1, 1855, vice Tower, promoted.
2nd Lt Walter H Stevens, to be 1st Lt, Jul 1, 1855, promoted.
Brvt 2nd Lt Wm P Craighill, to be 2nd Lt, Mar 3, 1855, vice Donelson, promoted.
Brvt 2nd Lt Geo W Custis Lee, to be 2nd Lt, Mar 3, 1855, the date of Capt R E Lee's appointment as Lt Col of 2nd Cavalry.
Corps of Topographical Engineers:
1st Lt Amiel W Whipple, to be Capt, Jul 1, 1855, having served 14 years continuous service as Lt.
2nd Lt Francis T Bryan, to be 1st Lt, Jul 1, 1855, vice Whipple, promoted.
Brvt 2nd Lt Geo H Mendell, to be 2nd Lt, Mar 3, 1855, the date of Capt Johnston's appointment as Lt Col of 1st Cavalry.
Brvt 2nd Lt Geo W Rose, to be 2nd Lt, Mar 3, 1855, the date of Capt Emory's appointment as Major in 2nd Cavalry.
Brvt 2nd Lt Jos C Ives, to be 2nd Lt, Apr 30, 1855, the date of Capt T J Lee's resignation.
Ordnance Dept:
1st Lt Josiah Gorgas, to be Capt, Jul 1, 1855, having served 14 years continuous service as Lt.
1st Lt Thos J Rodman, to be Capt, Jul 1, 1855, having served 14 years continuous service as Lt.
2nd Lt Wm T Welcker, to be 1st Lt, Jul 1, 1855, vice Gorgas, promoted.
2nd Lt John W Todd, to be 1st Lt, Jul 1, 1855, vice Rodman, promoted.

1st Regt of Dragoons:
Maj Benj L Beall, to be Lt Col, Mar 3, 1855, vice Sumner, appointed Col of 1st Cavalry.
Capt Chas A May, of the 2nd Dragoons, to be Major, Mar 3, 1855, vice Beall, promoted.
2nd Lt Wm T Magruder, to be 1st Lt, Mar 3, 1855, vice Sacket, appointed Capt in 1st Cavalry.
2nd Lt Robt Johnston, to be 1st Lt, Mar 3, 1855, vice Sturgis, appointed Capt in 1st Cavalry.
2nd Lt Isaiah N Moore, to be 1st Lt, Mar 3, 1855, vice Stoneman, appointed Capt of 2nd Cavalry.
Brvt 2nd Lt Milton T Carr, to be 2nd Lt, Mar 3, 1855, vice Magruder, promoted.

2nd Regt of Dragoons:
1st Lt Richd H Anderson, to be Capt, Mar 3, 1855, vice May, promoted Major in the 1st Dragoons: Co A.
1st Lt Alfred Pleasanton, to be Capt, Mar 3, 1855, vice Hardee, appointed Major in 2nd Cavalry: Co C-transferred to H.
2nd Lt Beverly H Robertson, to be 1st Lt, Mar 3, 1855, vice Wood, appointed Capt in 1st Cavalry.
2nd Lt Jonas P Holliday, to be 1st Lt, Mar 3, 1855, vice Oakes, appointed Capt in 2nd Cavalry.
2nd Lt Chas E Norris, to be 1st Lt, Mar 3, 1855, vice Anderson, promoted.
Brvt 2nd Lt John Pegram, of the 1st Dragoons, to be 2nd Lt, Mar 3, 1855, vice Robertson, promoted.
Brvt 2nd Lt Thos J Wright, to be 2nd Lt, Mar 3, 1855, vice Holliday, promoted.
Brvt 2nd Lt John B Villipigue, to be 2nd Lt, Mar 3, 1855, vice Norris, promoted.

1st Regt of Cavalry:
1st Lt Wm N R Beall, to be Capt, Mar 3, 1855, vice Garnett, appointed Major in 9th Infty. Co A
2nd Lt David S Stanley, to be 1st Lt, Mar 27, 1855, vice Beall, promoted.

Regt of Mounted Riflemen:
2nd Lt Geo W Howland, to be 1st Lt, Mar 3, 1855, vice Palmer, appointed Capt in 2nd Cavalry.
Brvt 2nd Lt Jas Wright, to be 2nd Lt, Mar 3, 1855, vice Howland, promoted.
Brvt 2nd Lt Wm M Davant, to be 2nd Lt, Mar 3, 1855, vice Carr, appointed 1st Lt in 1st Cavalry.

1st Regt of Artl:
Capt Francis Taylor, to be Major, Mar 3, 1855, vice Smith, appointed Lt Col of 10th Infty.
1st Lt Abner Doubleday, to be Capt, Mar 3, 1855, vice Taylor, promoted. Assigned to Co E.
2nd Lt Alvin C Gillem, to be 1st Lt, Mar 3, 1855, vice Bowens, Commissary of Subsistance, who vacates his regimental commission.

2nd Lt Henry W Slocum, to be 1st Lt, Mar 3, 1855, vice Williams, Assist Adj Gen, who vacates his regimental commission.
2nd Lt Jas W Robinson, to be 1st Lt, Mar 3, 1855, vice Doubleday, promoted.
2nd Lt John M Scofield, to be 1st Lt, Mar 3, 1855, vice Patterson, appointed Capt in 9th Infty.
2nd Lt Geo Bell, to be 1st Lt, Jun 30, 1855, vice Coppee, resigned.
Brvt 2nd Lt Geo H Elliot, of the 4th Artl, to be 2nd Lt, vice Bell, promoted, to date from Jul 1, 1855.
Brvt 2nd Lt Saml Breck, jr, to be 2nd Lt, to date from Jul 1, 1855.

2nd Regt of Artl:
1st Lt Saml S Anderson, to be Capt, Mar 8, 1855, vice Sedgwick, appointed Major in 1st Cavalry. Assigned to Co D.
2nd Lt John Mullan, jr, to be 1st Lt, Feb 28, 1855, vice Moore, resigned.
2nd Lt Geo L Hartsuff, to be 1st Lt, Mar 8, 1855, vice Anderson, promoted.
[Promotion to date from Mar 31, 1855, vice Van Buren, resigned-cancelled.]
2nd Lt Matthew M Blunt, to be 1st Lt, Mar 31, 1855, vice Van Buren, resigned.

3rd Regt of Artl:
1st Lt John F Reynolds, to be Capt, Mar 3, 1855, vice Steptoe, appointed Major in 9th Infty. Co H
1st Lt Edw G Beckwith, to be Capt, May 12, 1855, vice Thomas, appointed Major in 2nd Cavalry. Co A
2nd Lt Edw H Day, to be 1st Lt, Mar 3, 1855, vice C S Winder, appointed Capt in 9th Infty.
2nd Lt Sylvester Mowry, to be 1st Lt, Mar 3, 1855, vice Reynolds, promoted.
2nd Lt Geo R Bissell, to be 1st Lt, May 12, 1855, vice Beckwith, promoted.

4th Regt of Artl:
1st Lt Albion P Howe, to be Capt, Mar 2, 1855, vice Hunt, appointed Paymaster. Co G
2nd Lt Rufus Saxton, jr, to be 1st Lt, Mar 2, 1855, vice Howe, promoted.
2nd Lt Edw McK Hudson, to be 1st Lt, Apr 30, 1855, vice Couch, resigned.

1st Regt of Infty:
Capt Saml P Heintzelman, of 2nd Infty, to be Major, Mar 3, 1855, vice Morris, promoted to 4th Infty.
2nd Lt Saml B Holabird, to be 1st Lt, May 31, 1855, vice Hamilton, resigned.

2nd Regt of Infty:
1st Lt Nelson H Davis, to be Capt, Mar 3, 1855, vice Casey, appointed Lt Col 9th Infty. Co C
1st Lt Wm M Gardner, to be Capt, Mar 3, 1855, vice Heintzelman, promoted to 1st Infty. Co D
2nd Lt J P Roy, to be 1st Lt, Mar 3, 1855, vice Davis, promoted.
2nd Lt Jas Curtiss, jr, to be 1st Lt, Mar 3, 1855, vice Jones, Assist Adj Gen, who vacates his regimental commission.
2nd Lt Adolphus F Bond, to be 1st Lt, Mar 8, 1855, vice Gardner, promoted.

Brvt 2nd Lt Robt F Hunter, to be 2nd Lt, Mar 3, 1855, vice Frazer, appointed 1st Lt in 9th Infty.
Brvt 2nd Lt John O Long, to be 2nd Lt, Mar 3, 1855, vice Roy, promoted.
3rd Regt of Infty:
2nd Lt Andrew Jackson, to be 1st Lt, Mar 3, 1855, vice Bee, appointed Capt 10th Infty.
Brvt 2nd Lt Richd V Bonneau, to be 2nd Lt, Mar 3, 1855, vice Jackson, promoted.
4th Regt of Infty:
Maj Thompson Morris, of the 1st Infty, to be Lt Col, Mar 3, 1855, vice Wright, appointed Col 9th Infty.
1st Lt Lewis C Hunt, to be Capt, May 23, 1855, vice Prince, appointed Paymaster. Co C
2nd Lt Henry C Hodges, to be 1st Lt, May 23, 1855, vice Hunt, promoted
5th Regt of Infty
 2nd Lt Saml Archer, to be 1st Lt, Mar 3, 1855, vice Lugenbeel, appointed Capt in 9th Infty.
2nd Lt Wm H Lewis, to be 1st Lt, Mar 3, 1855, vice Dent, appointed Capt in 9th Infty.
Brvt 2nd Lt Alex'r Chambers, to be 2nd Lt, Mar 3, 1855, vice English, appointed 1st Lt in 9th Infty.
Brvt 2nd Lt Lucius L Rich, to be 2nd Lt, Mar 3, 1855, vice Beall, appointed 1st Lt in 1st Cavalry.
Brvt 2nd Lt Archibald Gracie, jr, of the 4th Infty, to be 2nd Lt, Mar 3, 1855, vice McArthur, appointed 1st Lt in 2nd Cavalry.
Brvt 2nd Lt David H Brotherton, to be 2nd Lt, Mar 3, 1855, vice Lewis, promoted.
6th Regt of Infty:
1st Lt Lewis A Armistead, to be Capt, Mar 3, 1855, vice Walker, appointed Major in 10th Infty. Co F
1st Lt Richd B Garnett, to be Capt, May 9, 1855, vice Monroe, resigned. Co K
2nd Lt Daruis D Clark, to be 1st Lt, Mar 3, 1855, vice Armistead, promoted.
2nd Lt Wm P Carlin, to be 1st Lt, Mar 3, 1855, vice Nelson, appointed Capt in 10th Infty. [Promotion to date from Mar 26, 1855, vice Buckner, resigned-cancelled.]
2nd Lt Jas L Corley, to be 1st Lt, Mar 3, 1855, vice Heth, appointed Capt in 10th Infty.
2nd Lt Elisha G Marshall, to be 1st Lt, Mar 26, 1855, vice Buckner, resigned.
2nd Lt John C Kelton, to be 1st Lt, May 9, 1855, vice Garnett, promoted.
Brvt 2nd Lt Benj F Smith, of the 1st Infty, to be 2nd Lt, Mar 3, 1855, vice Clark, promoted.
Brvt 2nd Lt Silas P Higgins, of the 8th Infty, to be 2nd Lt, Mar 3, 1855, vice Carlin, promoted.
Brvt 2nd Lt Henry H Walker, of the 3rd Infty, to be 2nd Lt, Mar 3, 1855, Shaaff, appointed 2nd Lt in 2nd Cavalry.
Brvt 2nd Lt Jas A Smith, to be 2nd Lt, Mar 3, 1855, vice Fleming, appointed 2nd Lt in 9th Infty.
Brvt 2nd Lt Chas G Sawtelle, of the 2nd Infty, to be 2nd Lt, Mar 3, 1855, vice Corley, promoted.

Brvt 2nd Lt John M Cleary, of the 3rd Infty, to be 2nd Lt, Mar 26, 1855, vice Marshall, promoted.

7th Regt of Infty:
1st Lt Saml B Hayman, to be Capt, Mar 3, 1855, vice Garnett, appointed Capt in 1st Cavalry. [Co A-transferred to C.]
1st Lt John M Jones, to be Capt, Mar 3, 1855, vice Holmes, promoted to 8th Infty. [Co C-transferred to A.]
2nd Lt Peter W L Plympton, to be 1st Lt, Mar 3, 1855, vice Van Dorn, appointed Capt in 2nd Cavalry.
2nd Lt Robt R Garland, to be 1st Lt, Mar 3, 1855, vice Gardner, appointed Capt in 10th Infty.
2nd Lt Nicholas B Pearce, to be 1st Lt, Mar 3, 1855, vice Hayman, promoted.
2nd Lt Wm L Cabel, to be 1st Lt, Mar 3, 1855, vice Jones, promoted.
2nd Lt Gurden Chapin, to be 1st Lt, Mar 3, 1855, vice Smith, appointed Capt in 2nd Cavalry.
Brvt 2nd Lt Andrew W Evans, to be 2nd Lt, Mar 3, 1855, vice Pearce, promoted.
Brvt 2nd Lt Edmund C Jones, of the 2nd Infty, to be 2nd Lt, Mar 3, 1855, vice Plympton, promoted.
Brvt 2nd Lt Augustus H Plummer, of the 6th Infty, to be 2nd Lt, Mar 3, 1855, vice Cabell, promoted.
Brvt 2nd Lt David P Hancock, to be 2nd Lt, Mar 3, 1855, vice Chapin, promoted.
Brvt 2nd Lt Edgar O'Conner, to be 2nd Lt, Mar 3, 1855, vice Forney, promoted.

8th Regt of Infty:
Capt Theophilus H Holmes, of the 7th Infty, to be Major, Mar 3, 1855, vice E B Alexander, appointed Col of 10th Infty.
2nd Lt Richd J Dodge, to be 1st Lt, Mar 3, 1855, vice Snelling, appointed Capt in 10th Infty.
2nd Lt Thos K Jackson, to be 1st Lt, Mar 3, 1855, vice Pickett, appointed Capt in 9th Infty.
2nd Lt Wm T Mechling, to be 1st Lt, Apr 23, 1855, vice Crozet, deceased.
Brvt 2nd Lt Thos M Jones, to be 2nd Lt, Mar 3, 1855, vice Dodge, promoted.
Brvt 2nd Lt Wm Craig, of the 3rd Infty, to be 2nd Lt, Mar 3, 1855, vice Jackson, promoted.
Brvt 2nd Lt Zenas R Bliss, of the 1st Infty, to be 2nd Lt, Mar 3, 1855, vice Stockton, appointed 2nd Lt in 1st Cavalry.

II-Appointments:
Subsistence Dept: Brvt Capt Marcus D L Simpson, 1st Lt in the 2nd Regt of Artl, to be Commissary of Subsistence with the rank of Capt, vice Buckner, resigned, to date from Mar 26, 1855.
Medical Dept: Jas T Ghiselin, of Md, to be Assist Surgeon, vice Moses, resigned, to date from Jun 1, 1855.
Pay Dept:
Brvt Maj Henry Prince, Capt in the 4th Regt of Infty, to be Paymaster, vice Johnston, appointed Col of 2nd Cavalry, to date from May 23, 1855.

Ordnance Dept:
Wm R Andrews, of N Y, [late Capt 10th Infty,] to be Military Storekeeper, vice Webber, deceased, to date from May 19, 1855.

1st Regt of Dragoons:
2nd Lt Wm D Pender, of the 2nd Artl, to be 2nd Lt, Mar 3, 1855, to stand next below 2nd Lt M T Carr.
2nd Lt Alfred B Chapman, of the 3rd Artl, to be 2nd Lt, Mar 3, 1855.
Brvt 2nd Lt Benj F Davis, of the 5th Infty, to be 2nd Lt, Mar 3, 1855.
Brvt 2nd Lt John T Mercer, of the 6th Infty, to be 2nd Lt, Mar 3, 1855.
Brvt 2nd Lt Horace Randal, of the 8th Infty, to be 2nd Lt, Mar 3, 1855.
Brvt 1st Sgt John Williams, of Co G, Regt of Mounted Riflemen, to be 2nd Lt, Jun 18, 1855. [Transferred to 2nd Cavalry.]
John A Thompson, of Va, to be 2nd Lt, Jun 25, 1855.

2nd Regt of Dragoons:
2nd Lt Abner Smead, of the 1st Artl, to be 2nd Lt, Mar 3, 1855, to stand next below 2nd Lt John B Villepigue. [Declined.]
2nd Lt Geo A Gordon, of the 2nd Artl, to be 2nd Lt, Mar 3, 1855.
Brvt 2nd Lt Saml T Shepperd, of the 2nd Infty, to be 2nd Lt, Mar 3, 1855.
Brvt 2nd Lt John Mullins, of the 7th Infty, to be 2nd Lt, Mar 3, 1855.
Francis C Armstrong, of Texas, to be 2nd Lt, Jun 7, 1855.
Henry B Livingston, of N Y, to be 2nd Lt, Jun 18, 1855.
1st Sgt John Green, of Co B, Regt of Mounted Riflemen, to be 2nd Lt, Jun 18, 1855.

1st Regt of Cavalry:
Brvt Maj John Sedgwick, Capt in the 2nd Artl, to be Major, vice McCullough, declined, to date from Mar 8, 1855.
Wm S Walker, of Miss, [late of the Voltigeurs,] to be Capt, vice Wilkins, declined, to date from Mar 3, 1855, & to stand next below Capt De Saussure. Co G
Edw W B Newby, of Ill, to be Capt, vice Reynolds, whose appointment is cancelled, to date from Mar 3, 1855, & to stand next above Capt Geo T Anderson. Co H
2nd Lt Robt Ransom, jr, of the 1st Dragoons, to be 1st Lt, [with a view to his appointment as regimental Adjutant,] to date from Mar 3, 1855, & to stand next below 1st Lt E A Carr.
2nd Lt Elmer Otis, of the 4th Infty, to be 2nd Lt, vice Hight, declined, to date from Mar 3, 1855, & to stand next below 2nd Lt Jas E B Stuart.
Brvt 2nd Lt Jas B McIntire, of the 7th Infty, to be 2nd Lt, to date from Mar 3, 1855, & to stand next below 2nd Lt Otis.
Richd H Riddick, of N C, to be 2nd Lt, vice Stanley promoted, to date from Mar 27, 1855.

2nd Regt of Cavalry:
Brvt Maj Geo H Thomas, Capt in the 3rd Artl, to be Major, to date from May 12, 1855.
Chas Radziminski, of Louisiana, [late of the 3rd Dragoons,] to be 1st Lt, to fill an original vacancy, & to date from Jun 30, 1855.

Brvt 2nd Lt John B Hood, of the 4th Infty, to be 2nd Lt, vice G B Anderson, declined, to date from Mar 3, 1855, & to stand next below 2nd Lt W W Lowe.
Jas B Witherell, of Mich, to be 2nd Lt, vice Merrifield, declined, to date from Mar 3, 1855, & to stand next below 2nd Lt J B Hood.

Regt of Mounted Riflemen:
1st Sgt Christopher H McNally, of Co D, to be 2nd Lt, May 23, 1855.
Sgt Edw Tracy, of Co F, to be 2nd Lt, May 23, 1855.

1st Regt of Artl:
Chas H Webber, of Mass, to be 2nd Lt, May 29, 1855.
Waterman Palmer, jr, of Pa, [late of the 8th Infty,] to be 2nd Lt, Jun 7, 1855.
Douglas Ramsay, of the District of Columbia, to be 2nd Lt, Jun 7, 1855.
Wm M Graham, of the District of Columbia, to be 2nd Lt, Jun 7, 1855.
John Sergeant, of Pa, to be 2nd Lt, Jun 30, 1855. [Declined.]

2nd Regt of Artl:
John G Taylor, of Ky, to be 2nd Lt, Jun 7, 1855. [This appointment cancelled, & Lt T appointed in 8th Infty.]
Wm Butler, of Kansas, to be 2nd Lt, Jun 7, 1855.
Sgt Major Thos Grey, [2nd Lt in 9th Infty during war with Mexico,] to be 2nd Lt, Jun 7, 1855.
Geo Garner, of Md, to be 2nd Lt, Jun 30, 1855.
Raymond Fairfax, of Va, to be 2nd Lt, Jun 30, 1855.
Venerando Pulizzi, of the District of Columbia, to be 2nd Lt, Jun 30, 1855.

3rd Regt of Artl:
Francis B Schaffer, of Calif, to be 2nd Lt, Jun 7, 1855.
Dunbar R Ransom, of Vt, to be 2nd Lt, Jun 7, 1855.
Wm Wilkins Harding, of Pa, to be 2nd Lt, Jun 7, 1855.
Wm K Lear, of ___, to be 2nd Lt, Jun 7, 1855.
Geo P Ihrie, of N J, to be 2nd Lt, Jun 18, 1855.
John Drysdale, of Fla, to be 2nd Lt, Jun 30, 1855.

4th Regt of Artl
Jas J Dana, of N Y, to be 2nd Lt, Jun 18, 1855.
Wm Stretch Abert, of the District of Columbia, to be 2nd Lt, Jun 18, 1855.
J Thos Goode, of Va, to be 2nd Lt, Jun 18, 1855.

1st Regt of Infty:
Jas E Powell, of Maine, to be 2nd L, Jun 7, 1855.
John D McCall, of Iowa, to be 2nd Lt, Jun 18, 1855.
Jas A Morrow, of Conn, to be 2nd Lt, Jun 18, 1855.
Walter Jones, of Va, to be 2nd Lt, Jun 30, 1855.

2nd Regt of Infty:
A S Coolidge, of Mass, to be 2nd Lt, Jun 7, 1855.
Henry A Sargent, of Mass, to be 2nd Lt, Jun 18, 1855.
Wm C Spencer, of Md, to be 2nd Lt, Jun 18, 1855.
Wm F Lee, of Va, to be 2nd Lt, Jun 30, 1855.

3rd Regt of Infty:
Edwin A Morrison, of New Mexico, to be 2nd Lt, Jun 18, 1855.
4th Regt of Infty:
St Clair Dearing, of Ga, to be 2nd Lt, Jun 7, 1855.
Murray Randolph, of Miss, to be 2nd Lt, Jun 30, 1855.
Arthur Shaaff, of Ga, to be 2nd Lt, Jun 30, 1855.
Beall C Compton, of N Y, to be 2nd Lt, Jun 30, 1855.
5th Regt of Infty:
Edmund Freeman, of Mass, to be 2nd Lt, Jun 7, 1855.
Chas J Lynde, of Texas, to be 2nd Lt, Jun 30, 1855.
6th Regt of Infty:
Wm B Reynolds, of Ill, [late 2nd Lt in 16th Infty,] to be 2nd Lt, May 29, 1855.
Aaron B Hardcastle, of Md, to be 2nd Lt, Jun 7, 1855.
Ralph Abercrombie, of Pa, to be 2nd Lt, Jun 30, 1855.
7th Regt of Infty:
Thos B Edelin, of Md, to be 2nd Lt, Jun 7, 1855.
Edw J Brooks, of Mich, to be 2nd Lt, Jun 30, 1855.
Jesse B Wharton, of Md, to be 2nd Lt, Jun 30, 1855.
8th Regt of Infty:
John G Taylor, of Ky, to be 2nd Lt, Jun 7, 1855.
John R Cooke, of Mo, to be 2nd Lt, Jun 30, 1855.
Thos F Smith, of Mo, to be 2nd Lt, Jun 30, 1855.
9th Regt of Infty:
Brvt Maj Robt S Garnett, Capt in 1st Cavalry, to be Major, vice Benham, declined, to date from Mar 27, 1855.
Alonzo Loring, of Va, to be 1st Lt, vice Harrison, declined, to date from Mar 3, 1855, & to stand next below 1st Lt A T Palmer. [Declined.]
Edwin R Merrifield, of Mich, to be 1st Lt, vice Loring, declined, to date from Mar 3, 1855, & to stand next below 1st Lt A T Palmer. [Declined.]
Robt H Davis, of Miss, to be 1st Lt, vice Ten Broeck, declined, to date from Mar 3, 1855, & to stand next below 1st Lt G W Carr.
Nathl Wickliffe, of Ky, to be 2nd Lt, vice Webb, declined, to date from Jun 30, 1855.
10th Regt of Infty:
1st Lt Anderson D Nelson, of 6th Infty, to be Capt, vice Clarke, declined, to date from Mar 3, 1855, & to stand next below Capt J G S Snelling. Co A
1st Lt Henry Heth, of 6th Infty, to be Capt, vice Symmes, declined, to date from Mar 3, 1855, & st stand next below Capt B E Bee. Co E
John Dunovant, of S C, to be Capt, vice Barker, whose appointment has been revoked, to date from Mar 3, 1855, & to stand next below Capt J A Gove. Co K
III-The 2nd Lts appointed from civil life, whose commissions are of the same date, will take rank relatively, as follows: to rank from May 29, 1855:
1-Chas H Webber, 1st Artl
2-Wm B Reynolds, 6th Infty

To rank from Jun 7, 1855:
1-Waterman Palmer, jr, 1st Artl
2-Francis B Schaffer, 3rd Artl
3-John G Taylor, 8th Infty
4-Douglas Ramsay, 1st Artl
5-Wm Butler, 2nd Artl
6-Dunbar R Ransom, 3rd Artl
7-Wm M Graham, 1st Artl
8-Thos Grey, 2nd Artl
9-Wm Wilkins Harding, 3rd Artl
10-Wm K Lear, 3rd Artl
11-Francis C Armstrong, 2nd Dragoons
12-Jas E Powell, 1st Infty
13-A S Coolidge, 2nd Infty
14-St Clair Dearing, 4th Infty
15-Edmund Freeman, 5th Infty
16-Aaron B Hardcastle, 6th Infty
17-Thos B Edelin, 7th Infty

To rank from Jun 18, 1855:
1-Henry B Livingston, 2nd Dragoons
2-John Green, 2nd Dragoons
3-John Williams, 1st Dragoons
4-Jas J Dana, 4th Artl
5-Wm Stretch Abert, 4th Srtl
6-Geo P Ihrie, 3rd Artl
7-J Thos Goode, 4th Artl
8-Edwin A Morrison, 3rd Infty
9-John D McCall, 1st Infty
10-Henry A Sargent, 2nd Infty
11-Jas A Mower, 1st Infty
12-Wm C Spencer, 2nd Infty

To rank from Jun 30, 1855:
1-Nathl Wickliffe, 9th Infty
2-John Sargeant, 1st Artl
3-Edw J Brooks, 7th Infty
4-Geo Garner, 2nd Artl
5-Raymond Fairfax, 2nd Artl
6-John R Cooke, 8th Infty
7-Murray Randolph, 4th Infty
8-John Drysdale, 3rd Artl
8-John Drysdale, 3rd Artl
9-Arthur Shaaff, 4th Infty
10-Ralph Abercrombie, 6th Infty
11-Jesse B Wharton, 7th Infty

12-Chas J Lynde, 5th Infty
13-Wm F Lee, 2nd Infty
14-Walter Jones, 1st Infty
15-Beall C Compton, 4th Infty
16-Thos F Smith, 8th Infty
17-Venerando Pulizzi, 2nd Artl

IV-Transfers:
Maj Wm H Emory, 2nd Cavalry, transferred, May 26, to 1st Cavalry.
Capt Oscar F Winship, 2nd Dragoons, transferred Mar 27 from Co H to Co C.
Capt Alfred Pleasanton, 2nd Dragoons, transferred Mar 27 from Co C to Co H
Capt Wm H French, 1st Artl, transferred May 1st from Co E to Light Co K.
Capt Horace Brooks, 2nd Artl, transferred from Co D to Light Co A. [No date.]
Capt Saml B Hayman, 7th Infty, transferred Jun 22 from Co A to Co C.
Capt John M Jones, 7th Infty, transferred Jun 22 from Co C to Co A.
2nd Lt John Williams, 1st Dragoons, transferred Jul 19 to 2nd Cavalry.

V-Casualties:
Resignations, 13.
Capt Jas Monroe, 6th Infty, May 9, 1855.
Capt Thos J Lee, Corps of Topographical Engineers, Apr 30, 1855.
Brvt Capt Schuyler Hamilton, 1st Lt 1st Infty, May 31, 1855.
Brvt Capt Henry Coppee, 1st Lt 1st Artl, Jun 30, 1855.
Brvt Capt Simon B Buckner, Commissary of Subsistence, & 1st Lt 6th Infty, Mar 26, 1855.
1st Lt Darius N Couch, 4th Artl, Apr 30, 1855.
1st Lt Danl T Van Buren, 2nd Artl, Mar 31, 1855.
1st Lt John C Moore, 2nd Artl, Feb 28, 1855.
2nd Lt Austin N Colcord, 2nd Infty, May 31, 1855.
2nd Lt Henry F Witter, 5th Infty, May 20, 1855.
Brvt 2nd Lt Thos H Ruger, Corps of Engineers, Apr 1, 1855.
Brvt 2nd Lt Chas G Rogers, 2nd Dragoons, Feb 1, 1855.
Assist Surgeon Israel Moses, May 31, 1855.

Commissions vacated under the provisions of the 7th section of the act of Jun 18, 1843:
1st Lt Isaac Bowen, 1st Art, Commissary Subsistence, his regimental commission, [only,] Mar 3, 1855.
1st Lt Seth Williams, 1st Artl, Assist Adj Gen, his regimental commission, [only,] Mar 3, 1855.
1st Lt David R Jones, 2nd Infty, Assist Adj Gen, his regimental commission, [only,] Mar 3, 1855.

Commissions Vacated by New Appointments:
Adj General's Dept:
Edw R S Canby, commission of Assist Adj Gen, [brvt capt,] Mar 3, 1855, being appointed Major 10th Infty.

Pay Dept:
Albert S Johnston, commission of Paymaster, Mar 3, 1855, being appointed Col 2nd Cavalry.

Corps of Engineers:
Robt E Lee, commission of Capt, Mar 3, 1855, being appointed Lt Col 2nd Cavalry.
Geo B McClellan, commission of 1st Lt, Mar 3, 1855, being appointed Capt 1st Cavalry.

Corps of Topographical Engineers:
Jos E Johnston, commission of Capt, Mar 3, 1855, being appointed Lt Col 1st Cavalry.
Wm H Emory, commission of Capt, Mar 3, 1855, being appointed Major 2nd Cavalry.

1st Regt of Dragoons: [Date-Mar 3, 1855.]
Edwin V Sumner, commission of Lt Col, being appointed Col 1st Cavalry.
Delos B Sackett, commission of 1st Lt, being appointed Capt 1st Cavalry.
Sanl D Sturgis, commission of 1st Lt, being appointed Capt 1st Cavalry.
Geo Stoneman, commission of 1st Lt, being appointed Capt 2nd Cavalry.
Robt Ransom, jr, commission of 2nd Lt, being appointed 1st Lt 1st Cavalry.
Kenner Garrard, commission of 2nd Lt, being appointed 1st Lt 2nd Cavalry.
Benj Allston, commission of 2nd Lt, being appointed 2nd Lt 1st Cavalry.
Wm W Lowe, commission of 2nd Lt, being appointed 2nd Lt 2nd Cavalry.

2nd Regt of Dragoons: [Date-Mar 3, 1855.]
Wm J Hardee, commission of Capt, being appointed Major 2nd Cavalry.
Thos J Wood, commission of 1st Lt, being appointed Capt 1st Cavalry.
Jas Oakes, commission of 1st Lt, being appointed Capt 2nd Cavalry.
Nathan G Evans, commission of 2nd Lt, being appointed 1st Lt 2nd Cavalry.
Geo H Steuart, commission of 2nd Lt, being appointed 1st Lt 1st Cavalry.
Chas W Field, commission of 2nd Lt, being appointed 1st Lt 2nd Cavalry.
David Bell, commission of 2nd Lt, being appointed 1st Lt 1st Cavalry.
David S Stanley, commission of 2nd Lt, being appointed 2nd Lt 1st Cavalry.

1st Regt of Cavalry:
Robt S Garnett, commission of Capt, Mar 8, 1855, being appointed Major 9th Infty.

Regt of Mounted Riflemen: [Date-Mar 3, 1855.]
Innis N Palmer, commission of 1st Lt, being appointed Capt 2nd Cavalry.
Eugene A Carr, commission of 2nd Lt, being appointed 1st Lt 1st Cavalry.
Geo B Cosby, commission of 2nd Lt, being appointed 2nd Lt 2nd Cavalry.
Jas E B Stuart, commission of 2nd Lt, being appointed 2nd Lt 1st Cavalry.

1st Regt of Artl: [Date-Mar 3, 1855.]
Chas F Smith, commission of Major, being appointed Lt Col 10th Infty.
Francis E Patterson, commission of 1st Lt, being appointed Capt 9th Infty.
Henry E Maynadier, commission of 2nd Lt, being appointed 1st Lt 10th Infty.

2nd Regt of Artl:
John Sedgwick, commission of Capt, Mar 8, 1855, being appointed Major 1st Cavalry.

Wm D Pender, commission of 2nd Lt, Mar 3, 1855, being appointed 2nd Lt 1st Dragoons.
Geo A Gordon, commission of 2nd Lt, Mar 3, 1855, being appointed 2nd Lt 2nd Dragoons.

3rd Regt of Artl: [Date-Mar 3, 1855.]
Edw J Steptoe, commission of Capt, being appointed Major 9th Infty.
Geo H Thomas, commission of Capt, being appointed Major 2nd Cavalry.
Chas S Winder, commission of 1st Lt, being appointed Capt 9th Infty.
Jas Van Voast, commission of 2nd Lt, being appointed 1st Lt 9th Infty.
Jas Deshler, commission of 2nd Lt, being appointed 2nd Lt 10th Infty.
Alfred B Chapman, commission of 2nd Lt, being appointed 2nd Lt 1st Dragoons.

4th Regt of Artl:
Franklin E Hunt, commission of Capt, Mar 2, 1855, being appointed Paymaster.
Cuiver Grover, commission of 2nd Lt, Mar 3,1 855, being appointed 1st Lt 10th Infty.

1st Regt of Infty: [Date-Mar 3, 1855.]
Richd W Johnson, commission of 2nd Lt, being appointed 1st Lt 2nd Cavalry.
Chas R Woods, commission of 2nd Lt, being appointed 2nd Lt 9th Infty.
Peter T Swaine, commission, of 2nd Lt, being appointed 2nd Lt 10th Infty.

2nd Regt of Infty: [Date-Mar 3, 1855.]
Silas Casey, commission of Capt, being appointed Lt Col 9th Infty.
John W Frazer, commission of 2nd Lt, being appointed 1st Lt 9th Infty.
Lyman M Kellogg, commission of 2nd Lt, being appointed 2nd Lt 10th Infty.

3rd Regt of Infty: [Date-Mar 3, 1855.]
Barnard E Bee, commission of 1st Lt, being appointed Capt 10th Infty.
Louis H Marshall, commission of 2nd Lt, being appointed 1st Lt 10th Infty.

4th Regt of Infty:
Geo Wright, commission of Lt Col, Mar 3, 1855, being appointed Col 9th Infty.
Henry Prince, commission of Capt, May 23, 1855, being appointed Paymaster.
Wm Myers, commission of 2nd Lt, Mar 3, 1855, being appointed 2nd Lt 9th Infty.
Lawrence A Williams, commission of 2nd Lt, Mar 3, 1855, being appointed 2nd Lt 10th Infty.
Elmer Otis, commission of 2nd Lt, Mar 3, 1855, being appointed 2nd Lt 1st Cavalry.

5th Regt of Infty: [Date-Mar 3, 1855.]
Pinkney Lugenbeel, commission of 1st Lt, being appointed Capt 9th Infty.
Fred'k T Dent, commission of 1st Lt, being appointed Capt 9th Infty.
Wm N R Beall, commission of 2nd Lt, being appointed 1st Lt 1st Cavalry.
Thos C English, commission of 2nd Lt, being appointed 1st Lt 9th Infty.
Jos H McArthur, commission of 2nd Lt, being appointed 1st Lt 2nd Cavalry.

6th Regt of Infty: [Date-Mar 3, 1855.]
Wm H T Walker, commission of Capt, being appointed Major 10th Infty.
Anderson D Nelson, commission of 1st Lt, being appointed Capt 10th Infty.
Henry Heth, commission of 1st Lt, being appointed Capt 10th Infty.
Jos L Tidball, commission of 2nd Lt, being appointed 1st Lt 10th Infty.
Adlen Sargent, commission of 2nd Lt, being appointed 1st Lt 9th Infty.

John T Shaaf, commission of 2nd Lt, being appointed 2nd Lt 2nd Cavalry.
Hugh B Fleming, commission of 2nd Lt, being appointed 2nd Lt 9th Infty.

7th Regt of Infty: [Date-Mar 3, 1855.]
Robt S Garnett, commission of Capt, being appointed Capt 1st Cavalry.
Earl Van Dorn, commission of 1st Lt, being appointed Capt 2nd Cavalry.
Franklin Gardner, commission of 1st Lt, being appointed Capt 10th Infty.
Edmund K Smith, commission of 1st Lt, being appointed Capt 2nd Cavalry.
Henry M Black, commission of 2nd Lt, being appointed 1st Lt 9th Infty.
Alfred Cumming, commission of 2nd Lt, being appointed 1st Lt 10th Infty.
John H Forney, commission of 2nd Lt, being appointed 2nd Lt 10th Infty.

8th Regt of Infty: [Date-Mar 3, 1855.]
Edmund B Alexander, commission of Major, being appointed Col 10th Infty.
Jas G S Snelling, commission of 1st Lt, being appointed Capt 10th Infty.
Geo E Pickett, commission of 1st Lt, being appointed Capt 9th Infty.
Jas McIntosh, commission of 2nd Lt, being appointed 1st Lt 1st Cavalry.
Philip Stockton, commission of 2nd Lt, being appointed 2nd Lt 1st Cavalry.
Henry Douglas, commission of 2nd Lt, being appointed 2nd Lt 9th Infty.

Cancelled:
Wm B Reynolds, appointment of Capt 1st Cavalry, to date from Mar 3, 1855.
Jas P Barker, appointment of Capt 10th Infty, to date from Mar 3, 1855.
Wm W Kirkland, appointment of 2nd Lt 1st Cavalry, to date from Mar 3, 1855.

Declined:
Brvt Lt Col Braxton Bragg, Capt 3rd Artl, the appointment of Major 1st Cavalry, to date from Mar 3, 1855.
Capt Henry W Benham, Corps of Engineers, the appointment of Major 9th Infty, to date from Mar 3, 1855.
Benj McCullough, the appointment of Major 1st Cavalry, to date from Mar 3, 1855.
Brvt Capt Henry F Clarke, 1st Lt 2nd Artl, the appointment of Capt 10th Infty, to date from Mar 3, 1855.
1st Lt John C Symmes, Ordnance Dept, the appointment of Capt 10th Infty, to date from Mar 3, 1855.
Wm D Wilkins, the appointment of Capt 1st Cavalry, to date from Mar 3, 1855.
Saml R Harrison, the appointment of 1st Lt 9th Infty, to date from Mar 3, 1855.
Alonzo Loring, the appointment of 1st Lt 9th Infty, to date from Mar 3, 1855.
Alex'r P Ten Broeck, the appointment of 1st Lt 9th Infty, to date from Mary 3, 1855.
2nd Lt Geo B Anderson, 2nd Dragoons, the appointment of 2nd Lt 2nd Cavalry, to date from May 3, 1855.
2nd Lt Thos Hight, 2nd Dragoons, the appointment of 2nd Lt 1st Cavalry, to date from Mar 3, 1855.
2nd Lt Nelson B Sweitzer, 1st Dragoons, the appointment of 2nd Lt 1st Cavalry, to date from Mar 3, 1855.
2nd Lt Wm A Webb, 6th Infty, the appointment of 2nd Lt 9th Infty, to date from Mar 3, 1855.

2nd Lt Abner Smead, 1st Artl, the appointment of 2nd Lt 2nd Dragoons, to date from Mar 3, 1855.

Edwin R Merrifield, the appointement of 2nd Lt 2nd Cavalry, to date from Mar 3, 1855; & the appointment of 1st Lt 9th Infty, todate from Mar 3, 1855.

John Sergeant, the appointment of 2nd Lt 1st Artl, to date from Jun 30, 1855.

Deaths:
Maj Saml B Dusenbery, Quartermaster's Dept, at Santa Fe, New Mexico, Apr 5, 1855.

1st Lt Alfred Crozet, 8th Infty, at Cincinnati, Ohio, Apr 23, 1855.

2nd Lt Saml Kinsey, 1st Artl, in the City of Wash, D C, Jul 14, 1855.

2nd Lt Saml T Shepperd, 2nd Dragoons, at **Fort Leavenworth**, Kansas, Jun 27, 1855.

Military Storekeeper John A Webber, Ordnance Dept, at Watertown Arsenal, Mass, May 6, 1855.

VI-The ofcrs promoste & appointed will join their proper companies & stations without delay; those on detached service, or acting under special instructions, will report, by letter, to the cmder of their respective regts & corps. By order of the Sec of War: S Cooper, Adj Gen

Memorandum-Correction of Names.
1-1st Lt David, 9th Infty, to be borne on Register as Robt H instead of Robt W.
2-2nd Lt Thompson, 1st Dragoons, to be borne on Register as John A, instead of Jas A Thompson.
3-2nd Lt Armstrong, 2nd Dragoons, to be borne on Register as Francis C, instead of Francis N Armstrong.
4-2nd Lt Clarke, 1st Cavalry, to be borne on Register as Hartford T, instead of Henry T Clarke.
5-2nd Lt Powell, 1st Infty, to be borne on Register as Jas E, instead of John E Powell.
6-2nd Lt Compton, 4th Infty, to be borne on Register as Beall C, instead of Beall Compton.
7-2nd Lt Wharton 7th Infty, to be borne on Register as Jesse B, instead of Jesse Wharton.
8-2nd Lt Harvie, 9th Infty, to be borne on Register as Edwin J, instead of Edward J Harvie. –S Cooper, Adj Gen

The stable & carriage house of Dr G Bailey, Editor of the Nat'l Era, on C st, between 3rd & 4½ sts, was destroyed by fire yesterday; strongly felt it was the work of vicious boys. The adjoining stable of Edw Semmes was injured.

Ex-Pre Martin Van Buren, accompanied by Maj Van Buren, his eldest son, arrived at Kinderhook on Jul 20 from Europe, after an absence of 2 years, in the enjoyment of excellent health.

Groceries & store fixtures: at auction, on Aug 1, at the Grocery Store of Mr Lewis Lepreux, at 11th & F sts. -Green & Scott, aucts

Henry M Tucker has been committed in default of $10,000 bonds, on the charge of having attempted to blow up his father's house, in Providence, on Jul 12. The evidence was entirely circumstantial, but very strong.

The Navy Dept have advices of the recent death of Master Francis G Clark, U S Navy, at the Naval Hospital, Norfolk, Va.

Recent letter from Havana mentions the failure of Jose Ricardo O'Farrel, one of the largest property-holders in Cuba, with liabilities to the amount of $1,400,000. It is alleged that his property is worth $3,000,000, & all productive.

Mrs Homer, wife of Russell Homer, of Cambridge, took her little daughter, 2½ years of age, to the daguerreotype rooms of Messrs James & Co, at Boston, on Wed, to obtain a likeness of the child. After the picture had been taken, the mother's attention was diverted, & the child fell out of the window into the street, striking upon her head, & died soon after.

Mrd: on Jul 26, by Rev Mr Duncan, Geo E Kessler, of Fred'k Co, to Miss Anna C Jarbo, formerly of St Mary's Co, Md.

Mrd: on Thu, by Rev John C Smith, Mr John T Chancey to Miss Emily Jane Keene, all of Wash City.

Died: on Jul 25, Elbert, aged 20 months & 18 days, son of Elijah & Mary Edmonston.

Died: on Jul 27, in her 24th year, Mrs Mgt Rebecca, wife of Wm H Gorbutt, & daughter of the late John & Mgt Keith.

Died: on Jul 27, in the hope of a blessed immortality, Mrs Eliz Pennington Martin, in her 70th year.

Obit-died: on Jun 27, at **Fort Leavenworth**, K T, of cholera, Lt S Turner Shepperd, of the U S 2nd Dragoons. He was a son of Hon A H Shepperd, of N C, & a graduate of West Point in the class of 1854. Though nursed during his short & sudden illness of only 24 hours with all the care which the constant anxiety & watchfulness of his comrades, 3 of whom were his classmates, could bestow, the malignant disease rapidly sapped the fountain of life, baffling the untiring efforts of the most experienced surgeons. Young, active, & vigorous as the noblest oak, he was cut down in the midst of life.

<u>Urbana Female Institute</u>, Urbana, Fred'k Co, Md, will commence on the 1st Monday of Sept & continue 10 months. –Geo G Butler, A M, Principal, Urbana, Md.

St Louis, Jul 26. A cmte, appointed by the Kansas Legislature to draw up a memorial to the Pres for the removal of Govn'r Reeder, reported yesterday. The memorial sets forth various cmplnts against Reeder, calling him a clog to the wheels of Gov't & praying his speedy removal.

Chancery Sale: Philip T Berry & John S Berry vs John Lee. Be decree of Circuit Court of Wash Co, D C, passed in the above cause, dated Nov 9, 1854, public auction on Aug 20, 1855, on the premises: lots 25 thru 26, on the west side of Montg st; lots 32 & 33, on the west side of Green st; lot 43, & 6 feet of the north side of lot 44, making one lot of 46 feet, on the east side of Green st; lots 11 & 101, fronting 40 feet each on the east side of Green st; all in Lee, Deakins & Casenove's addition to Gtwn, D C. –Henry King, trustee -Barnard & Buckey, aucts

For sale on Aug 20, at the Fairfax Court House, that being Court day, that valuable & well known Farm called **Green Springs**, lately the residence of Jas Sheriff, [formerly *Moss' farm*,] in Fairfax Co, on both sides of the Little River Turnpike Road, adjoining the lands of Danl Minor, John Withers, & others, containing 341 acres; with a 2 story dwlg house, kitchen, smoke, spring, & other out houses. –Wm Sheriff

U S Patent Ofc, Wash, Jul 27, 1855. Ptn of Pearson Crosby, of Fredonia, N Y, praying for extension of a patent granted to him on Nov 3, 1841, for an improvement in saw-mills for re-sawing boards, for 7 years from the expiration of said patent, which takes place on Nov 3, 1855. –S T Shugert, Acting Com'r of Patents.

MON JUL 30, 1855
Jenny Lind & her husband, it is said, are harmoniously & actively engaged in carrying out her plans for the establishment of public schools in Sweden.

On Monday the locomotive Hercules left the foot of Plane No 8, taking on board before starting a large huckleberry party on their way home, when the locomotive was thrown down an embankment 30 feet. Wm Berry, son of Jacob Berry, of Graysport, aged about 14, was instantly killed. –Holidaysburg [Pa] Standard

Recent commencement at Harvard College: degree of A B was conferred on 84 graduates; the degree of medicine on 33; the degree of Bachelor of Science on 14, [among whom, near the head of the list, were Messrs E L Force & H C Force, of this city;] the degree of Bachelor of Laws on 58; the degree of A M on 24; the honorary degree of D D on 4 distinguished divines; & the degree of L L D on Govn'r Gardner, Hon Nathan Appleton, Hon R C Winthrop, & Nathan Bishop.

Mr F Michie, a graduate of the Univ of Va, will take charge of the school at my house for the ensuing year, commencing Sep 3 & terminating Jul 3. Terms: $200 per session of 10 months. I wish to fill 3 vacancies with boys from 11 to 14 years of age. -Jas K Marshall, Leeds, Fauquier, near Markham Station.

Legislature proceedings in Kansas: bill entitled "An act to remove the seat of gov't temporarily to the Shawnee Manual Labor School, in the Territory of Kansas: the bill passed. Mr McMeekin introduced a bill establishing the statues of Missouri in Kansas for the time being: passed. The Council consists of 13 members & the House of Reps of 26 members. The names & politics of the latter, as now constituted, are as follows: [All pro-slavery except Houston, Ohio, 36, farmer, mrd, freesoiler.]

Anderson, Ky, 24, lawyer, single
Banks, Ky, 36, farmer, mrd
Blair, Tenn, 47, farmer, mrd
Brown, Md, 34, farmer, single
Croysdale, Missouri, 26, physician, single
Harris, Va, 32, physician, mrd
Heeskill, Va, 47, merchant, mrd
Houston, Ohio, 36, farmer, mrd, [freesoiler]
Johnson, Kansas, 22, farmer, mrd
Kirk, Ky, 37, farmer, single
Marshall, Va, 39, merchant, mrd
Mathias, Md, 28, lawyer, single
McGee, Ky, 36, merchant, mrd
McMeekin, Ky, 33, merchant, mrd
Payne, Ky, 36, farmer, mrd
Scott, Ky, 36, farmer, mrd
Scott, Ky, 52, farmer, mrd
Tebbs, Va, 32, mrd
Wade, Missouri, 27, farmer, mrd
Ward, Ky, 55, farmer, mrd
Waterson, Pa, 54, farmer, mrd
Weadle, Va, 28, teacher, single
Whitlock, Missouri, 37, farmer, mrd
Williams, Ky, 35, farmer, mrd
Wilkinson, Tenn, 35, farmer, mrd
Younger, Missouri, 42, farmer, mrd

Fatal affray between Seaborn Collins & 3 brothers named Anderson, in Rankin Co, Miss, on Jul 17. Anderson having abused one of Collins' children, Collins got his gun & started for Anderson's house, but before reaching there he met 3 of the Anderson's in the woods, hunting, & walking within gun-shot he raised his rifle & shot Wilburn Anderson, killing him instantly. John Anderson shot Collins in the shoulder, wounding him, it is thought, fatally.

W F Bayly has removed to 13th & Pa ave, over R Tweedy's Grocery Store, where he will be glad to see his friends & customers who want Stationery & Fancy Articles at cost prices.

A Roman Catholic Convent Case occupied the attention of the Court at Chicago Jul 19. A habeas corpus was issued to Sister de Sales, one of the Sisters of the Convent, otherwise **Sisters of Mercy**, so called, of Chicago, commanding that they bring the body of Mary E Parker before the Judge of the Cook Co Circuit Court. The young lady was brought into Court, where she appeared to remain under constraint, but conversed with her counsel a few moments without removing from the neighborhood of the lady superior. The Court took the young lady aside, conversed with her for some time, & then stated that Miss Parker, although on some accounts unwilling to remain in the convent, was not willing to leave it until her father returned to the city, & that she was not in the fear of returning thither; that the writ of habeas corpus had been issued solely for the benefit of the young lady, &, as she declined to avail herself of the liberty asked for therein, the Court would merely state that she was at liberty to go where she pleased. Miss Parker & the respondent then retired together, & the young lady returned with the lady superioress to the Convent.

Mr Wm R Riley, dry goods merchant, at 8th & La ave, has for a year past been the victim of a series of depredations amounting to a couple thousand dollars. He had employed a youth, John W Moore, whose father, Spalding C Moore, has been living & keeping a store at Tebee, PG Co, Md. On Fri last the father & son were arrested in this city charged with stealing & the former with receiving the missing goods. The value of those then found in a trunk belonging to John W Moore is valued about $500. The culprits were both committed to jail by Capt Burch; & Mr Riley found stolen goods on the premises of the elder Moore. The Moore family was always regarded as being poor, but an amount of gold coin was found in their house that greatly surprised their neighbors.

Mrd: on Jul 24, in the first Baptist Church, by Rev Stephen P Hill, Jas Overton Sanderson to Ellen C Barnes, all of Wash.

Died: on Jul 29, at the residence of her son-in-law, Mr John Varden, Mrs Mgt L Tolmie, consort of the late Robt Tolmie, in her 81st year. Her funeral will be this evening, at 5:30 P M, from 397 10th st, between H & I sts.

Died: on Jul 18, at the residence of his brother, N Chapman Hunter, in Fairfax Co, Va, Fred'k A Hunter, a man of cultivated mind, generous feelings, & high sense of honor.

Died: on Jul 26, in Wash City, in her 31st year, Mrs Prudence Ann Patterson, wife of Geo C Patterson, of Md, beloved by all who knew her.

Died: on Jul 24, at **Chilolmwood**, D C, of dysentery, Mary Elizabeth, in her 3rd year, daughter of John B & Mary E Wiltberger.

Died: on Jul 25, at **Oak Mount**, Fairfax Co, Va, Rozier Grafton, young son of Lt D F Dulany, U S Navy.

Died: Jul 29, after a short illness, Mary Roberta, infant daughter of John E & Sarah V Porter.

TUE JUL 31, 1855
Household & kitchen furniture at auction on: Aug 2, at the residence of the late Rev J W Winans, on H st, between 12th & 13th sts, by order of the Orphans Court of Wash Co, D C. –J R Nourse, exc -Jas C McGuire, auct

Star: the President has removed Mr Reeder from the post of Govn'r of the Territory of Kansas, & has offered the appointment to Hon John L Dawson, of Pa. [Aug 1st newspaper: Gov Reeder says he thinks he has been treated unfairly, because the Pres has called upon him for his defence against charges of violating rules which are not specified, & asks for their specification. In relation to the charge of having purchased half-breed Kansas lands, that he has purchased no such lands.]

At N Y, on Sat, while 2 painters, Jas Dougherty & John Lane, were painting the front wall of the N Y Hotel, on a scaffold put up at the 6th story, the fastenings gave way & both men fell nearly 70 feet. Dougherty was instantly killed, & Lane was taken to the hospital in a dying condition.

New Bedford [Mass] Mercury: on Fri, Philip H Wing, house carpenter, fell some 26 feet from a staging attached to a new bldg where he was working, & was taken up alive but insensible.

A camp meeting of the Methodist Protestant Church, is to be held on the grounds of Wm Minor, in Alexandria, Va, commencing on Aug 2.

Orphans Court of Wash Co, D C. Letters testamentary on the personal estate of Jacob W Winans, late of Wash Co, D C. –John R Nourse, exc

Died: on Jul 28, after a short & painful illness, John Henry, infant son of David & Christiana Hines, aged 11 months & 28 days.

Episcopal High School of Va, Rev John P McGuire, Rector, will commence on Sep 12. Pamphlets sent to those who request it: Post Ofc, Theological Seminary, Fairfax Co, Va.

Select School for Young Ladies, by Mrs Sheffey & Daughters, Kalorama, Staunton, Va: will be resumed on Sep 17.

U S Patent Ofc, Wash, Jul 30, 1855. Ptn of Jas Gamble & Jos S Hill, of Cincinnati, Ohio, praying extension of a patent granted them Dec 30, 1841, for an improvement in apparatus for moulding candles, for 7 years from the expiration of said patent, which takes place on Dec 30, 1855. –S T Shugert, Acting Com'r of Patents.

WED AUG 1, 1855

Obit-died: on Sunday last, at the Warm Springs, near Staunton, Va, whither he had gone for his health, Hon Wm Frick, Judge of the Superior Court of the City of Balt.

Huntsville [Texas] item of the 14th ult says: Dr Steiner, who killed Col Arnold last year, has been acquitted by the district court of Hill Co, & a troop of soldiers, who were in attendance to arrest him on leaving the court, were prevented from carrying out their orders by a party of men, who carried the prisoner off to a place of safety. We shall think it strange of the Doctor be not court-martialed & shot yet.

Mr Wm A Moody, conductor on the Va Central Railroad, was caught between a freight car & a water tank, at Gordonsville, on Sunday, & so severely crushed that he expired on the same day. He had been employed on the road for 14 years.

Meeting of the Grand Encampment of D C was held last week & the following were elected ofcrs: Chas Calvert, Grand Patriarch; W D Stewart, G H Priest; G F Henning, Senior Warden; A H Jones, Junior Warden; Wm Cooper, Scribe; Jno H Bartlett, Treasurer; A Jackson, Sentinel; R Adams, Marshal; Thos Rich, Grand Rep.

Mrd: on Jul 30, at Foundry Parsonage, by Rev E Phelps, Mr John W Houck to Catharine M Perrie, all of Wash City.

Died: on Jul 30, Caroline, aged 3 years & 10 months, daughter of J Bayard H & Henrietta Smith.

Havre de Grace, Jul 31. A disease resembling cholera is prevailing here very fatally, the deaths numbering about 10 per day. The wife & children of J T Bradbury have died in the last 48 hours.

Superior candle moulds, of hard Britannia Metal & warranted, manufactured by John Caverley. Also, syringes, surgical instruments, & Britannia Ware. –John Caverley, 169 Race st, Phil, Pa.

Six first class dwgls for rent: on I st, between 15th & 16th sts: 4 stories, besides basement & attic. They are on the same square with St John's Church, & the large stone front houses occupied by Mr G W Riggs & Gov Marcy. Apply to the subscriber, at Riggs & Co's banking-house. –A Hyde

THU AUG 2, 1855
Trustee's sale of valuable lots: by deed of trust from Geo E B French, dated Dec 29, 1854, recorded in Liber J A S No 92, folios 57 thru 60, of the land records of Wash Co, D C: sale on Sep 3 next, of lot 2 in square 43, & lot 7 in square south of square 104. –Wm P Williams, trustee -Jas C McGuire, auct

Stock of stoves & tin ware at auction: on Aug 3, at the store of Mr H Lisberger, on Pa ave, between 19th & 20th sts.

The U S frig **Potomac**, bearing the broad pennant of Cmdor Hiram Paulding, commanding the home squadron, sailed from Norfolk for N Y on Sat last. List of her ofcrs: Com Levin M Powell, commanding; Com Jas L Lardner, Capt of the Fleet; Melancton Smith, Wm L Herndon, L B Avery, D M Fairfax, Edw Brinley, Lts; Maxwell Woodhull, Flag Lt; Thos Dillard, Fleet Surgeon; H M Hieskell, Purser; Moses P Chase, Chaplain; Geo E Morgan, Master; Wm A Harris & Henry O Mayo, Passed Assist Surgeons; Capt Benj Macomber, commanding Marine Guard; Geo R Graham, 2nd Lt; Geo M Robinson, Cmdor's Sec; Jos S Skerrett, H M Garland, Jesse Taylor, Jas G Maxwell, Henry Erben, Passed Midshipmen; M Secard, C S Norton, H H Dalton, Edw Lea, Midshipmen; Robt W Tucker, Capt's Clerk; L Henriques, Purser's Clerk; Amos Colson, Boatswain; Wm H Hamilton, Gunner; J G Thomas, Carpenter; Jas Ferguson, Sailmaker.

Mr W R H Scott, of Paris, Ky, while returning from the Nat'l Theatre to the Spencer House, Cincinnati, on Friday last, was knocked down & robbed of $1,530. He was not much hurt, but was handled very roughly.

Fauquier White Sulphur Springs: reports that a malignant disease now prevails at the Springs must have originated in a malignant design to injure the proprietors. We reside at Warrenton & have practiced at these Springs for the last 16 or 18 years & find them perfectly healthy. –John A Chilton, M D; Saml B Fisher, M D

Information wanted of Wm Townley, aged about 13 years, left his parents' residence a fort-night ago, & has not since been heard from. Any information concerning him will be thankfully received by his father, John Townley, living in Wash st, Wash City.

Mrd: on Jun 20, in Mecklenburg Co, N C, by Rev H B Cunningham, D D, Mr J W McGinn to Miss Christian A Henderson.

Died: yesterday, G W Utermehle, sr, in his 79th year. His funeral will be this afternoon at 4 o'clock, from his late residence, corner of 7th & M sts.

Died: yesterday, Henry Taylor, son of John H & Mgt Thorn, aged 2 years & 5 months. His funeral will take place today at 10 o'clock, from the residence of his parents, 387 5th st.

The family of Marshal St Arnaud have published, at Paris, a selection from his correspondence: 1-Writing to his brother, Aug 9, 1854: If I were to give way to my impressions, to my turnoff mind, & the feelings of my heart, I should never have written to you a sadder letter. I am in the midst of one vast tomb, resisting the scourge that is decimating my army, seeing my bravest soldiers succumb at the very moment I most want them. God strikes me with one hand, raises me up with the others. 2-Writing to his wife 2 days later, from Varna: God spares us no misfortune, no calamity, my dear. I seek all my energy in the dept of my soul; I wish I could find there more resignation. A violent fire broke out yesterday at Varna & a seventh part of the town no longer exists. 3-He writes to Madame St Arnaud: Old Fort, [Crimea] Sep 7, 1854. My Beloved Wife; The English are not ready, & make me lose precious time. I shall stop for the night at the Bulgansk, so that I may be quite fresh on the 19th, & force the passage during the day. If I can I will drive the Russians to the other side of the Katcha. May God protect us yet a few days & all will go well. I heard mass this morning under my large tent, & I prayed for you. Four abbes breakfasted with me. As I have to endure all my pains, I have two cutting ones above my left breast which agonize me. Cabrol says it is my health. I could strangle him. Prince Menschifoff may do what he likes, but I shall be before Sebastopol between the 10th & 22nd. I only think of the moment when we shall be very quiet at home. In the spring we will take a trip to Italy, & we will return by Switzerland & Germany. We will travel with only 2 servants & like plain folks. Do not let us build too many castles in the air, for that brings bad luck. 4-On the next day he writes:I have just written to Lord Raglan that I could not wait any longer; nothing shall stop me longer. 5-To his brother he writes from the field of battle on Alma, Sep 22, 1854. Today everyone thinks as I do in the armies & the fleets. The change has been rapid. It began on the 14th, broke out into acclamations on the 20th, & today I am a great man. Such is the world. 6-Four days after writing this the Marshal resigned his command, & on the 29th, 3 days later, died.

Obit-died: on Monday last, Hon John Woods, a distinguished citizen of Ohio, at his residence in Hamilton, near Cincinnati. –Cin Gaz

Univ of Nashville, Collegiate Dept, Western Military Institute: the next session will commence on Sep 10, 1855. Address J Berrien Lindsley, Chancellor of the Univ, or V R Johnson, Superintendent of the Instutite.

FRI AUG 3, 1855
Univ of Va: the past session of the Univ was its 31st; among her foster children are A H H Stuart, of Staunton; Henry Winter Davis, of Balt; & Toombs of Ga, & a host of others. The Univ was founded by Thos Jefferson. –Sigma

Dr W R Whitehead, an American Surgeon, is in the employ of the Russians. He writes that he was indebted to Prince Gortschakoff for the peculiar advantages that he enjoyes as to rank--- superior physician of a regt of 5,000 men. –Sebastopol, Apr 14, 1855.

Alexandria Gaz: the remains of a person found on Sat in PG Co, Md, has been identified as those of Dr Grant, of Balt, who was in the county for the purpose of purchasing a farm. He had stopped at the public house of Mr Surrat, who identified his clothes. He stopped later at another house kept by Mr Thorn, on the Piscataway road, & in whose company he was last seen. Warrants have been issued for the arrest of 2 men suspected of having murdered the deceased. He had considerable money with him at the time he was murdered. Also, a fine gold watch & other valuables not yet found. Dr Grant left a family in Balt, Md. [Aug 7th newspaper: H C Thorn denies any knowledge of the Doctor or that he ever stopped at his house. The whole matter is still wrapped in mystery.]

Homer Ruggles, late Assist Postmaster at Nathfield, Vt, has been convicted at Montpelier of mail robbery, & sentenced to 10 years' imprisonment in the State prison at hard labor.

The farm advertised by Chas McNamee, Trustee, to take place this day, will not take place today, the business having been fully settled to the satisfaction of the Trustee. By order of the Trustee. -Green & Scott, aucts

The unknown man who died at the Infirmary on Wed proved to be Isaiah Rice, who very recently removed from Balt to Wash City. His remains were yesterday identified by his friends, & at 3 o'clock conveyed to Balt, where it was understood the Hebrew Society would receive & inter them. He had been in feeble health, & strayed from his friends without their knowledge.

On Sat last Tucker Jones, residing near Dinwiddie Court-house, Va, had difficulty with his son Benjamin, a boy, during which the latter inflicted upon his father a wound which resulted in instant death. The boy was arrested & held to bail.

Mr Wm Haynes, an esteemed citizen of Trenton, Me, was killed on the 25th ult by a kick from one of his cows, which he was milking.

The murderers of Thos B Estabrook, of South Reading, Vt, have all been convicted & sentenced in Michigan, where the murder was committed. A G Estabrook, brother of the murdered man, has returned from the West, where he has been engaged for 18 months, in great danger of his own life, in prosecuting the murderers of his brother. [T B Estabrook went to Mich to marry a young woman he had been some time engaged to, &, making his business known at a tavern near the bride's residence, was followed & murdered for his money.]

Fatal affray at Millikin's Bend, La, on Sat. Mr Jas Cavalier, clerk in the store of Messrs Cavalier & Rathman, & brother to one of the firm, had a dispute with Mr E F Moreland about some freight. Moreland & Cavalier exchanged shots the next day. Moreland died in about 24 hours; Cavalier will recover, as both balls were extracted.

Mrs Doyle & her 4 year old child were burnt to death at Michigan city, last Fri, by the use of camphene.

Mrd: on Jul 19, at Frog Level, Parish, St James, La, by Rev N G North, Wm Preston Gibson, of Terrebonne, to Miss Elodie Mary Humphreys, daughter of the late Alex'r & Emilie Perret Humphreys, of St James.

Died: on Jul 17, at St Louis, Mo, of cholera, Sister Mary Serena, [Miss Caroline T Noyes,] formerly of Wash City. She fell a victim while nobly striving to save the lives or alleviate the sufferings of others, thus happily illustrating in her death the beauties of a life devoted to acts of charity & benevolence.

Died: on Aug 2, in Gtwn, Louisa, wife of Dr J B Gibbs, & daughter of the late John Burbridge, of Allegany Co, Md. Her funeral will take place at 5 o'clock P M, this day, from her late residence on Montg st.

N Y, Aug 2. Admiral Nachimoff was killed at Sebastopol during the attack of Jul 11, 1855.

Notice: I desire to sell the lot which I own on K st, being the 3rd lot from 13th, fronting on Franklin Square. Its width is 25 feet on K, & extends back 147 feet to a 30 foot alley. The price is .65 per foot, & the terms of payment may be learned from Cmdor Smith, at the Navy Dept. –Albert Smith

The very highest point. I offer for cash the one-quarter west on 10th st & 100 feet on O st. The title is perfect. –Estwick Evans, near the corner of 9th & I sts.

SAT AUG 4, 1855
Trustee's sale of valuable real estate in Montg Co, Md, by decree of the Circuit Court for said county, as Court of Equity, in the case of Chas H Anderson & others vs Thos O Smith & wife, the subscriber will expose to public vendue at the Court House door, in Rockville, on Aug 28, the following real estate, of which Richd S Anderson, late of Montg Co died seized & possessed: **The Home Farm**, at present occupied by Chas H Anderson, on Rock Creek: contains 400 acres of land: with a comfortable dwlg, kitchen, stable, & other out-houses. On the same day will be offered a wood lot, containing 20 acres, about a mile north of Rockville. Also, a lot of 84 acres, adjoining the lands of John Brewer, L A Dawson, & John W Spates. –Thos O Smith, trustee

Wash Corp: 1-Cmte of Claims: adverse report on the bill for the relief of Mrs B H Cheever: laid on the table. Same cmte: bill for the relief of John Tradu: passed.

Mrd: on Aug 2, by Rev P D Gurley, D C, Mr John V Douglass, of Richmond, Va, to Miss Georgia M Rawlins, of Wash.

Mrd: on Jul 31, at the residence of Judge Gardiner, in Chas Co, Md, by Rev Mr Wright, J D Gardiner, of Louisiana, to Miss Mary C Gardiner, of the former place.

Died: on Aug 3, in Wash City, Mr Eldred Rawlins, a clerk connected with the Gen Post Ofc. His funeral is this afternoon at 4½ o'clock, from his residence on H, between 13th & 14th sts. Interment at **Glenwood Cemetery**.

Died: on Aug 3, Percy, young son of Wm H & M D Gilman, aged 16 months & 25 days. His funeral is this afternoon at 5 o'clock, from the residence of his father, No 6 4½ st.

Milwaukee, Aug 3. On Wed at West Bend, Wash Co, Milwaukee, Geo Debar called at the house of a German, John Muebet, & murdered him, together with his wife & hired boy, under circumstances of the most horrid cruelty. He robbed the house & set it on fire, & fled. He was arrested shortly afterwards, & has barely escaped lynching at the hands of the citizens.

Powder Mill explosion at Wilmington, Aug 3, at Garesche's powder mills, near this city: thru the carelessness of a workman. Killed at once were Frenchmen: Eugene Perene, Jos De Peane, & Francis Fisler. A boy named John Pugh was also employed in the house at the time & was killed. Mr Garesche had cautioned one of the Frenchmen to quit the premises or to quit smoking a pipe. This house had been in operation for 40 years without an accident. [Aug 20th newspaper: Mr Garesche has determined not to rebuild his powder mill, & has sold his stock of materiel to E I Dupont & Co.]

Classical teacher wanted at Greene Academy, Huntsville, Ala: apply to Jas J Donegru, Wm Echols, jr, S D Cabaniss, or J Withers Clay, Cmte Board of Trustee

MON AUG 6, 1855

Dissolution of copartnership under the firm of Burns & Cochran by mutual consent. Harmon Burns will continue the business at the old stand, 408 Pa ave. –Harmon Burns, Geo W Cochran [Cochran recommends his former partner & friend.]

Appointments by the Pres: 1-Thos A Hendricks, of Indiana, to be Com'r of the Gen Land Ofc vice John Wilson, removed. 2-Josiah Minot, of N H, to be Com'r of Pensions vice Loren P Waldo, resigned. 3-Murray McConnell, of Ill, to be Fifth Auditor of the Treasury vice Josiah Minot, appointed Com'r of Pensions.

Dr John C Calhoun, 3rd son of the late Hon J C Calhoun, died on Jul 24 in Winnsboro, SC, where he had recently arrived from Florida afflicted with consumption. His remains were conveyed to *Fort Hill* for sepulture.

Distribution of premiums at *St Mary's Female Institution*, near Bryantown, Chas Co, Md, on Jul 26, 1855. Entrance music: "Grand Russian March", [C P Frances,] on 2 pianos, by Misses Fitzpatrick, Kelly, O'Brien, & Mattingly. Hymn, "O, Maria," sung by Misses Gwynn & Conlan, accompanied by Miss Fitzpatrick. "When the Day with Rosy Light,: duet, [variations by Hewitt,] by Misses Fitzpatrick & Kelly. Premiuns distributed to the following students:

Frances Kelly, of Balt
Jance C Gwyan, PG Co, Md
Hortense J Digges, Chas Co, Md
Constance E Miles, Chas Co, Md
Kate J Lloyd, Chas Co, Md
Imogen T Miles, Chas Co, Md
Harriet M Kelly, Balt, Md
Eliza C Matthews, Chas Co, Md
Mary C Sanders, Chas Co, Md
Matilda D Smith, Balt
Mary A Arnold, Wash, D C
Lizzie R McGarr, Wash, D C
Emily T Boone, Chas Co, Md
Rose E Mudd, Chas Co, Mc
Sarah M Gough, St Mary's Co, Md
Anna M Surratt, PG Co, Md
Estelle P Neal, St Mary's Co, Md
Frances R Richards, Wash, D C
Clodine J Miles, Chas Co, Md
Bettie W Tyler, Wash D C
Sarah E Sollers, Wash, D C
Celestia S Warren, Chas Co
Kate D Queen, Chas Co
Mgt M Marshall, Chas Co
Matilda D Smith, Balt, Md
Mary A Bowling, Chas Co, Md
Marian M Fenwick, Wash
Louisa McLean, Wash
Isabela McLennan, Balt, Md
Mgt E Keleher, Wash
Jane M McGarr, Wash
Mary R Broome, Calvert Co, Md
Martha E Miller, Balt
Honorah Fitzpatrick, Wash, D C
Mgt Bowling, Chas Co
Laura C Higdon, Chas Co
Kate Montgomery, Chas Co
Rosetta E Scott, St Mary's Co
Celestia M Mattingly, St Mary's Co, Md

Recently the ship **Colchis**, Capt Douglass, was leaving New Orleans for Phil, & 5 men went out to furl the jib & were knocked overboard by the parting of a rope. Those who lost their lives were John Schmidt, Karl Davids, & John Trainor.

Died: on Sunday, of consumption, Mrs Ruth A Peaco, relict of the late Wm H Peaco, in her 33rd year. Her funeral will take place this afternoon at 4 o'clock, from the residence of Mr L Etchison, 6th & H sts.

N Y, Aug 4. The Danish brig **Jennette** drifted ashore at the Bahamas on Jul 14 with all the crew dead on board, supposed to have been murdered by pirates, as a schnr was seen alongside on the day previous.

N Y, Aug 4. Chas Wheeler, agent of the Commercial Express Co, a bogus concern, was arrested this morning for embezzling $8,000 belonging to the Kensington Bank of Lansingburgh.

TUE AUG 7, 1855
Public sale on Aug 24, parts of the land of which Thos Fisher, late of Montg Co, died seized, below the mouth of Watt's Branch, which passes directly through said tract. Lot 3, containing 159¾ acres of land; Lot G contains 94½ acres of land, near the mill of Mr Gamble. Purchasers are referred to the subscribers, or to the family of Mrs A C Fisher, who reside on the premises. –W H Offutt, Saml Hardesty, N O Chappell

Petersburg Express: about a fortnight ago Mr Tucker Jones, who resided in the neighborhood of Dinwiddie Court-house, Va, while in a fit of passion seized a loaded gun & fired off one barrel at his wife & son through the door of his house, with the intent to kill them. Some of the shot took effect in Mrs Jones' arm, but before a second barrel could be discharged, the son, Ben Jones, seized a chair & struck down his father. The old man died from the effects of the wound about 10 days later. Jones was admitted to bail to answer the charge & is now at large.

A singular trial just terminated in the Oneida Circuit Court of N Y. Emily C Day vs two brothers named Roth. It appears that Volkert Roth won the heart of Miss Day in England, which is her home, & formed an engagement of marriage with her. She had about L2,500 in money which Volkert persuaded her to entrust to his keeping, in order that he might come to America & establish himself & return & marry her. He later represented to Miss Day that he had lost the money when his business failed. She came to the U S to hunt her faithless swain. She found him at Utica, N Y, where he had bought, with his brother, the Museum, & was carrying it on as a place of entertainment. She sued them both, & claimed the Museum in part payment of the money due her. The jury rendered a verdict for the plntf of $8,435.25, being the full value of the Museum, we presume. The money taken from Miss Day was all the property she had in the world.

Trustee's sale of valuable real estate: by decree of the Circuit Court of Wash Co, D C, in Chancery, in a cause wherein H B Sweeney, Treasurer, & others are cmplnts, & Dowling's heirs are dfndnts: sale on Sep 5 of lots 10 & 11 in square 566, fronting on north F, between 2nd & 3rd sts. –John F Ennis, trustee -Green & Scott, aucts

Phil Inquirer: on Sat night near the Quarantine Ground, the fine steamer **General McDonald**, with an excursion party on board for Cape May, estimated at from 100 to 150 in number, came into collision with the schnr **A G Pease**, at anchor off the Lazaretto & showing a light. But a few days have passed since the drowning of Mr & Mrs Watson & child, of Camden, & 2 young men of Phil. -Inquirer

Dr Amstrong, an eminent homoeopathic physician of Louisvill, Ky, has fallen victim to the cholera, after an illness of 24 hours. [No death date given-current item.]

Notice. No person is authorized to sign my name but myself. –Wm Noyes, Wash

$150 will be paid for the apprehension & conviction of the party or parties who set fire to the bldg at the corner of Pa ave & 22nd st west on Aug 4. –H N Lansdale

Order of distrain against the goods & chattels of E Brown for house rent due & in arrears to H Moran: sale on Aug 11, of sundry articles of furniture. –Wm Cox, blf

Died: on Aug 3, at Fauquier White Sulphur Springs, Va, of a disease of the heart, Maj H J Dean, Atty at Law, of Spartanburg District, S C, aged 49 years. He died surrounded with those dear to him, & with perfect resignation to the will of God.

Died: on Aug 6, Lydia Ann, the only daughter of Saml & Lydia Ann Hoover, aged 5 months. Her funeral will be from the corner of 6th & P sts on Aug 7, at 4 o'clock.

N Y, Aug 6. At a fire in Chatham st last night 2 children of Mr Isaac Jacobs were burnt to death. He has been arrested on susupicion of having fired the store, the insurance upon which was $4,000. [Aug 8th newspaper: Mr Jacobs was absent at the time, but in the upper part of the bldg were Mr Jacobs' wife & 4 children, the servant girl, an errand boy, & a cutter; also Mrs Hecht & 4 year old daughter. These were all rescued from the upper windows, but most of them were dreadfully burnt. The two eldest sons of Mr Jacobs were taken from a bed burnt to a crisp; one about 4½, the other 1½ years. Five persons were seriously injured; the servant, errand boy, & one child escaped without injury. Mr Jacobs' state of mind is described as most painful to witness. There are suspicious circumstances connected with the fire, Jacobs was arrested & detained to await the investigation of the Fire Marshal.] [Aug 9th newspaper: There being no evidence to warrant the detention of Jacobs, he was discharged from arrest. The child Hecht, aged 4 years, died at the City Hosspital last night. The mother of the child, it is feared, is fatally injured. Mrs Jacobs, it is thought, cannot recover.]

Saratoga, Aug 6. Robt Halsey, of Ithaca, has been robbed at Congress Hall of $9,000 in railroad bonds, jewelry, & diamonds. The burglars have been arrested, but the property has not been recovered.

Mossy Creek Academy, Mossy Creek, Augusta Co, Va: will commence its 3rd annual session on the 1st Wed of Sep next, under the management of Messrs Jno Hotchkiss & J T Brodt as Associate Principals, assisted by a competent corps of teachers.
-J M McCue, Pres of Board of Trustees

Utica Female Academy will commence its 18th year on Sep 7, for the reception of pupils: Miss Kelly as Principal. –T Pomeroy, Chairman of Board of Trustees. –J Watson Williams, sec, Utica, N Y.

Riverside Institute, at Aubwindale, Newton, Mass, will commence on Sep 6. Address at Aubwindale: A F Hildreth, J E Woodbridge, G F Walker.

WED AUG 8, 1855

The London papers announce the death of Dr Archibald Arnott, of her Majesty's twentieth regt of foot, in his 84th year. Dr Arnott enter the army upwards of 60 years ago, & retired from active service in 1826, during which time he shared the perils & exploits of his regt on the Nile, in Calabria, Portugal, Spain, & Holland. After the war he accompanied his brave companions to St Helena & India, & at the former station became the medical attendant of Bonaparte, by whom he was regarded with the warmest affection & esteem. Napoleon expired with his right hand in that of Dr Arnott.

Appointments by the Pres: 1-Andrew B Moore, of Ala, to be Associate Justice of the Supreme Court of the Territory of Kansas, vice Rush Ellmore, removed. 2-Townsend Harris, of N Y, to be Consul General of the U S to Japan.

On Friday the fine, solid, & liberal old family mansion of Henry B Pearson, of Harvard, was totally destroyed by fire. The Transcript says that it was built in 1736 for the first minister of Harvard, Rev John Seccomb. It reminded one of the lonely halls of merry England. In 1770 it became the seat of the Bromfields, being occupied at the close of the last & beginning of the present century by Col Henry Bromfield, & then by his descendents. The origin of the fire is not known. -Boston Post

Thos H Kent, of Joseph, Agent, 44 Fayette st, Balt City, Md, will attend to buying & selling property on commission; also will pay the highest rpice for Land Warrants.

Orphans Court of Wash Co, D C. Letters of administration on the personal estate of Philip Hopkins, late of Wash Co, deceased. –Ann M Hopkins, admx

N Y C: 1-On Sat Michl Driscoll, a child, was run over & instantly killed by a horse & cart, driven by Wm Devoy. The occurrence was purely accidental. 2-Mary Black, a child 3 years of age, was killed on Sat by falling from a 3rd story window. 3-Wm Clare, a carman, was drowned on Sat by accidentally falling into the dock at Pier 5, North River. 4-Two promising lads, aged about 13 years, sons of J C Andrews & the late Rev Jos Tyler, were drowned in the river near Hartford on Sat.

Mrd: on Aug 7, in Wash City, by Rev G W Samson, Mr Coffer Mayhugh to Miss Ann E Bradley, both of Va.

Mrd: on Aug 7, at M E Church South, by Rev Jas A Duncan, Mr H F Zimmerman to Miss Sarah Virginia Caldwell, all of Wash City.

Orphans Court of Wash Co, D C. Letters testamentary on the personal estate of Jos Furgerson, late of Wash Co, deceased. –Letticia Furgerson, excx

Orphans Court of Wash Co, D C. Letters testamentary on the personal estate of Ruth A Peaco, late of Wash Co, deceased. –Lemuel Etchison, exc

THU AUG 9, 1955
Catherine Manning, John Canary, & Patrick Murphy were yesterday arrested on suspicion of being about to issue a batch of counterfeit notes of $3 of the Mercantile Bank, Providence, R I. The police also arrested Mgt Riley, Mgt Calahan, & Mgt Cary, said to be bold operators in pushing bad money. –N Y Mirror

Accounts, says an English paper, have reached London of the death of Mr John McClintock, of Drumear, in the county of Louth, Ireland, formerly Sgt-at-arms in the Irish House of Commons, for the loss of which ofc he has been in receipt of a pension of L2,000 a year for upwards of half a century. He was 85 years old.

Assignee's sale: public auction on Aug 15th, one undivided sixth part of the house & lot on 8th st, between E & F sts, formerly owned & occupied by Jacob B Moore, & subject to the life estate of the widow of said Moore. Said estate is sold per order of the assignee of Frank Moore, an insolvent debtor. –Cheever Newhall, assignee -Green & Scott, aucts

Trustee's sale of part of square 545, with improvements, at auction: on Sep 10, by deed of trust from John Phipps, dated Jul 26, 1848, recorded in Liber W B No 147, folios 58 thru 64, of the land records of Wash Co, D C: all that parcel of ground, being part of lot 10, in Joel W Jones' subdivision of square 545, in Wash City, D C, fronting 16 feet on 4½ st, between south M & N sts, running back 130 feet; with a good dwlg house. –Walter Lenox, Henry Naylor, trustees -Green & Scott, aucts

Late English papers announce the death at the city of Ems, in Germany, on Jul 7, of Rear Admiral Sir Wm Edw Parry, R N, one of the most daring & successful of modern Arctic explorers. In 1803 Wm Edw Parry, son of Dr Parry, of Bath, England, entered the naval service os his country as midshipman, in which capacity, as well as that of lt, which rank he attained in 1810, he served several years on the coast of North America.

Mrd: on Aug 7, by Rev Mr Hodges, John P Ingle to Mrs Eliza B Baker, all of Wash.

Mrd: on Aug 7, at Christ Church, Gtwn, by Rev Mr Norwood, Mr John T Whitaker, jr, of Wash, to Miss Eliza Jane Craig, of Gtwn.

Died: Tue, Walter Simms, in his 20th year. His funeral will take place from the residence of his father, 486 north L, between 10th & 11th, Fri morning at 9 o'clock.

Died: on Aug 8, Francis Ignatius Peerce, in his 48th year. His funeral will take place at 4 o'clock P M, this day, from the residence of Wm T Herron, Gtwn, 76 Fayette st.

Died: on Aug 7, of cholera infantum, William C H, only child of C & M E Miller, aged 16 months & 28 days.

U S Patent Ofc, Wash, Aug 8, 1855. Ptn of Abraham Howe & Sidney Grannis, of Hudson Co, N Y, praying for the extension of a patent granted to them on Oct 11, 1841, for an improvement in the manufacture of wire heddles for weavers' harness, for 7 years from the expiration of said patent, which takes place on Oct 11, 1855. -S T Shugert, Acting Com'r of Patents

Cincinnati, Aug 7. The cornice of a new bldg in process of erection for the Ohio Life Ins & Trust Co, fell this afternoon, crushing to death Robt Cameron, master builder, & W B Curtis, superintendent of the bldg. John S Chambers & B Waldron, who were passing by, also were killed. [Aug 11th newspaper: Killed when the stone cornice fell were: Robt Cameron, master bldr; B Walden, of the firm of Walden & Vance; John T Chambers, boss carpenter; Wm Grawson, stonecutter; M Donheen & J Gillan, laborers.]

FRI AUG 10, 1855
Milwaukee "Wisconsin" gives details of the murder committed in the night of Aug 1, about a miles from West Bend, Wisc. A young man, Geo Debar, who had labored for different farmers in the vicinity, called at the house of Mr John Meyer, saying he would like the money for his labor done a few days previously. The money was given to him by Meyer from a package of about $100. Debar then asked for a drink of water. Meyer said he had none that was fresh but could give him a mug of beer. Debar went to the cellar to get the beer, & when he was coming up through the trap-door, Debar dealt him a blow on the top of his head which prostrated him to the cellar's bottom. Mrs Meyer, seeing her husband thus struck, ran for the woods to call a neighbor. The murderer chased her, armed with a knife, & overtaking her, aimed a stab at her neck, cutting her head half off. A small boy set up a cry, but Debar rendered him senseless with a blow, & then rifled the house & fired it. The boy has since died. Mr Meyer's wound, though serious, was not dangerous. Some reports are that Mrs Meyers is dead, & another, that she will recover. The murderer was arrested at Milwaukee on Aug 2. Debar was pronounced guilty, & whilst he was being reconveyed to prison he was wrested from the police & became the victim of torture & of a terrible death, by hanging, at the hands of the mob.

The Navy Dept has advices of the death of Lt Wm Decatur Hurst, U S Navy, who died on Aug 7 at Mendham, N J, & of Master Augustus Ford, U S Navy, aged 84, who died at Sackett's Harbor, N Y, on Aug 4.

Mr John H Bartlett, late Clerk to the Collector of Taxes of the Corp of Wash, has been appointed to a first class [$1,200] clerkship in the ofc of the First Auditor of the Treasury. –Star

Trustee's sale: by deed of trust from John A Grimes, recorded in J A S 29, folios 864, of the land records of Wash Co, D C: public sale on Aug 27 of the lot of ground on the south side of Water st, between the warehouses recently occupied by Edw Shoemaker & Messrs Wheatley & Morrison. –Hugh Caperton, trustee -E S Wright, auct, Gtwn

Mr Geo Hamlin, a machinist & for a long time a foreman at Winans' machine shops, together with some 5 other Baltimore mechanics, start this morning for N Y, en route for Russia, where they go to take charge of important positions on the great Russian railroad. A half dozen other Balt machinists are already in England on their way out.

Fire last night in the upper part of the bldg, at 7th & E sts, occupied by Mr Johnson as a grocery store. Mr Thos Dulany, who has a room there, ventured upon the dangerous experiment of replenishing a camphene lamp whilst it was burning. The result was an explosion, & he was seriously burnt. The room was set on fire.

Mrd: on Aug 7, by Rev Gideon H Day, Mr Wm Armijer to Miss Mary Ann Campbell, both of PG Co, Md.

Mrd: on Thu, by Rev John C Smith, John West to Miss Jane Gibbs, both of N Y.

Died: on Aug 1, at *Leeds*, Fauquier Co, Va, George Hatley, infant son of Geo H & Nannie B Norton.

Died: on Aug 8, at *Mount Oak*, PG Co, Md, the residence of his grandfather, John B Mullikin, William Livingston Gunton, son of the late Wm A & Mary R M Gunton, aged 2 years & 6 months.

Philadelphia College of Medicine will commence early in Oct, 1855, & terminate in Mar, 1856. Address or apply to B Howard Rand, M D, Dean, at the College, 5th st, below Walnut, Phil, Pa.

SAT AUG 11, 1855
Cottage Seminary for Young Ladies, Brookeville, Montg Co, Md. The 22nd session will open on the 2nd Mon in Sept next. -Mrs M E Porter, Principal

Salem Reg: The pulpit of the South Church was occupied yesterday, forenoon & afternoon, by 2 brothers, Rev Brown Emerson, senior pastor of the church, & Rev Reuben Emerson, of South Reading. The former is in his 78th year, & the latter in his 84th, & both have been pastors of churches more than half a century each.

The Shepherdstown [Va] Register: On Aug 1, at Middlekauff's culver, the canal boat **David Seigle**, belonging to Wm Brown, of Antietam Iron Works, loaded with coke, was on her way from Cumberland; when nearing the culvert the capt discovered a breach in the canal. He jumped ashore & urged the crew & 2 passengers to do so also. The two passengers, Wm Dunham, of Cumberland, aged about 70 years, & Miller Cole, from Wmsport, both drowned.

Trustee's sale: by deed of trust from Messrs Hiram F Clarke & Geo B Clarke, & by direction of J H Howell: sale on Aug 24, of the east half of lot 7 in square 496, with the improvements & appurtenances. –W Redin, trustee -Green & Scott, aucts

French Seminary, Wash, D C. Mrs R W Young, with an efficient corps of Professors, will, on Sep 17, establish at her residence, 436 G st, a French Seminary for Young Ladies.

Upperville Academy, Fauquier Co, Va, will commence on the 1st Mon of Sep, & continue for 10 months. –J Welby Armstrong, Principal

Died: on Aug 10, Mary Helen, aged 1 year & 9 days, daughter of T & M E McCloskey. Her funeral will take place from the residence of her parents, 382 13th st north. [No date or time given for the funeral.]

Orphans Court of Wash Co, D C. In the case of Nathl P Causin, adm of Col John H Stone, deceased, the administrator & Court have appointed Sep 11 next, for the final settlement of said estate, of the assets in hand. –Ed N Roach, Reg/o wills

MON AUG 13, 1855
Estimated cost of a **Metropolitan Railroad**-Washington: Gtwn to the Balt & Ohio Railroad: distance in miles: 41.24: cost: $1,850,000. Balt & Ohio Railroad to Hagerstown: distance in miles 34.91: cost: $1,865.00. –Wm H Grant, Acting Chief Engineer

Household & kitchen furniture & superior Rosewood Grand Pianoforte at auction on: Aug 21, at the residence of J C Fremont, on C st, between 3rd & 4½ sts.
-Jas C McGuire, auct

Desperate attempt to escape. David Wright, confined in jail at Columbus, Ga, under conviction of murder in the 1st degree, committed about 18 months ago, set fire to his cell on Sat night week & burnt himself to death.

Piney Point: delightful retreat. Col Dix, the enterprising proprietor took advantage of the recess to thoroughly improve the premises. The tables literally grown under the daily varieties of fish, fowl, & meats, to say nothing of the luxuries carefully prepared by the estimable lady of the Pavilion-together such as to elicit commendation from the most fastidious epicure. At present we have about 280 guests, amongst whom are Cmdor Shubrick, U S N, & family; Gen Gonzales, of Cuba; Dr Clymer, U S A; Dr Edwards, U S A; Hon Judge Crawford & family; J M Carlisle & family; Dr Duhamel & family; Wm B Todd & family; Wm A Bradley & family, & Col J H Riley, all from Wash; Mr Megallon, of the Spanish Legation, & family; & Prof Gibson, of the Univ of Pa. Md & Va are also well represented, with Col Jenifer & Col Dedrick ar the head.

Appointment by the Pres: Wilson Shannon, of Ohio, to be Govn'r of the Territory of Kansas, vice John L Dawson, declined.

Household & kitchen furniture at auction on: Aug 15, at the residence of Mrs E Cropley, on 3rd st, between High & Market, all her household effects.
-Barnard & Buckey, aucts

Died: on Sunday, Dr Henry Lee Heiskell, Surgeon U S Army. His funeral will be at the Church of the Epiphany, [Rev Mr French's] this afternoon, at 5 o'clock.

Died: on Jun 25, at the residence of her husband, in Chowan Co, N C, Mrs Corissande E Dixon, wife of Alex'r Dixon, formerly of Fauquier Co, Va, & daughter of Gen Duncan McDonald, of Edenton, N C, in her 29th year.

The corner-stone of the German Reformed Church will be laid today at 5½ o'clock, on 4½ st, between Md & Va ave, on the Island. Addresses will be delivered in English & also in German by different clergymen. The public are invited.
-P A B Meister, Pastor

I hereby tender my sincere thanks to those firemen & other gentlemen who promptly aided in the suppression of the fire which originated in the attic over my store on Thu evening. It was caused by the dangerous practice of filling camphene lamps whilst burning by the gentleman occupying the room, who was much injured thereby.
-Jno H Johnson, 7th & C sts

TUE AUG 14, 1855
Trustee's sale: by decree of the Circuit Court of Wash Co, D C, passed in a cause, No 989 on the equity docket, wherein Geo McCallion & others are cmplnts, & Jos Peck, John Walker, & others are dfndnts: sale on Sep 7 next, of: two undivided third parts of lots 7, 22 thru 25, & 27, in square 106, in Wash City, upon which are several good dwlg houses. –W Redin, Chas S Wallach, trustees -Green & Scott, aucts

Frank Wheeler, a bright Mulatto, aged 16 years, disappeared from Wash City on Jul 31. His distressed mother, Mary Wheeler, corner of 13th & H sts, Wash, will be exceedingly grateful to any one who will give her information concerning him.

Young Ladies Boarding & Day Seminary, Leesburg, Loudoun Co, Va: will re-open on Sep 3. –Mrs M L Edwards, Principal

Reports from Ky indicate that the majority of Chas S Morehead, for Govn'r, will be from 7,000 to 8,000 votes. His colleagues of the Know-Nothing State ticket are of course also elected. They are as follows: Jas G Hardy, Lt Gov; R C Wintersmith, Treas; Jas Harlan, Atty Gen; Thos S Page, Auditor; Andrew McKinley, Land Reg; J D Mathews, Sup Pub Ins. The Congressional Districts render it probable that the following have been elected to Congress:

Henry C Burnett, Dem
John P Campbell, K N
W L Underwood, K N
A G Talbott, Dem
Joshua H Jewett, Dem
J M Elliott, Dem
Hump Marshall, K N
Alex K Marshall, K N
Leander M Cox, K N
S F Swope, K N

Alabama election: Govn'r Winston [Dem] is re-elected by a large majority. According to the latest reports the following have been elected to Congress:
Percy Walker, K N
Eli Shorter, Dem
Jas F Dowdell, Dem
Sydenham Moore, Dem
Wm R Smith, K N
W R W Cobb, Dem
Sampson W Harris, Dem

The latest catalogue of *Wm & Mary College* gives a brief sketch of the progress of the College. In age it is next to *Harvard*. It was chartered in 1693 by King Wm III & Queen Mary, who gave out of their private means nearly L2,000 sterling towards erecting the necessary bldgs. This, with 20,000 acres of land, the ofc of Surveyor Gen, [in virtue of which one-sixth of the fees received by public surveyors in the colony & the sole power of appointing them were given,] & one penny a pound on all tobacco exported from Va & Md, granted in the charter, L2,500 raised by subscription in the colony, & a gift of L200 from the House of Burgesses, constituted the endowment of the college. A full list of the Alumni cannot be made out. Incomplete as it is it contains such names as Theodoric Bland, Peyton Randolph, Carter Braxton, Geo Wythe, Thos Jefferson, John Page, Edmund Randolph, Jas Monroe, John Marshall, Jas Barbour, Philip P Barbour, Wm B Giles, Benj Watkins Leigh, Chapman Johnson, John Randolph of Roanoke, Spencer Roane, Littleton W Tazewell, Wm C Rives, John J Crittenden, Wm S Archer, John Nelson, John Tyler, & Winfield Scott, among the most distinguished in American history.

Died: on Aug 13, Wm Wallace Ingman, printer, in his 24th year, eldest son of Wm & Julia A Ingman. His funeral will take place from his late residence, 10th st, near H, this morning at 10 o'clock.

Died: on Aug 13, Mrs Eliz McCafferty, aged 73 years. Her funeral is this evening at 4½ o'clock, from the residence of her nephew, B B Curran, Navy Yard, corner of South Carolina ave & 6th st.

Died: on Aug 13, after a long & severe illness, Frederick, infant son of Frederick & Josephine S Koones, aged 1 year, 2 months & 18 days. His funeral is this morning at 11 o'clock, at the residence of his parents, 4th st, 3 doors below G st.

Died: on Aug 12, William Thomas, aged 13 months & 24 days, only son of Isaac & Roberta Barrett. His funeral will take place from the residence of Jenkin Thomas, Gtwn, at 5 o'clock, today.

Fair Hill Boarding School for Girls: the 9th session will commence on Sep 10. Apply to R S Kirk, or Wm H Farquhar, at Olney post ofc, Montg Co, Md.

Presbyterian High School, Brownsburg, Va: in Rockbridge Co, Va, will commence on Sep 1. –Rev Jas Greer, A M, Principal

Young Ladies Classical Institute, a select boarding & day school, 490 E st, between 5th & 6th sts, [removed from No 9 Indiana ave,] Wash. The school, formerly under the care of Rev R W Cushman, D D, but for the last 2 years in charge of the present principal, will commence on Sep 10. –Stephen H Mirick, A M, Principal

WED AUG 15, 1855
Auction sale of the large & commodious brick house & lot on Capitol Hill: on Aug 21, the well built 3 story house lately occupied by Hon Judge Cranch, on Delaware ave, next to north B st. The lot being half of lot 6 in square 686. There is a pump of excellent water near the door. -Green & Scott, aucts

Midshipman John Cain, of Indiana, died of yellow fever on board the ship Falmouth, during her passage from Key West to N Y. He graduated at the naval school at Annapolis last year.

Land warrant lost. Notice is given that the undersigned, assignee of Land Warrant 63,174, [160 acres,] issued Jul 16, 1849, to the heirs of Bolivar W Jones, deceased, private of Capt P S Brooke's company South Carolina regt of volunteers, Mexican war, intends applying to the Pension Ofc for a duplicate of said Warrant, the original having been lost or stolen. A caveat has been filed against patenting said warrant. –Abner Perrier, Edgefield District, S C.

$250 reward for runaway mulatto, my servant woman Ellen Carroll, about 22 years old. –Louisa Sommers, 6th st, Island, Wash, D C.

THU AUG 16, 1855
Rittenhouse Academy, corner of 3rd & Indiana ave, will commence on Sep 3. O C Wight, Principal; A T Taylor, Assist; T R Raoult, Teacher of French; R Gibson, Teacher of Drawing.

Jos Wagner was arraigned before the U S Com'r at Boston, on Sat, on a charge of enlisting soldiers for the British army. He was discharged on the ground that the offence, if committed, came under the jurisdiction of N Y. He was immediately re-arrested, & will be sent to N Y. Orders from the British Gov't have been received to enlist no more recruits in the U S.

Mr Stapleton, an Irishman, about 2 years in the country, employed in the navy yard, died of yellow fever on the Sabbath, at Norfolk. There have been 8 deaths in Norfolk, from yellow fever, in the 48 hours ending on Monday.

Mr D Tafft, of Charleston, S C, & a person named Brecker, of Albany, N Y, were sitting with their arms out of the express train car window, when air, raised by the passage of a train, blew open the side door of a freight car at the depot, breaking the arm of Mr Brecker & cutting the left arm of Mr Taft clean off between the shoulder & elbow, the part cut off fallingon the track. Mr Taft was on a tour of pleasure to Niagara Falls, accompanied by his wife & young son. He is a strong muscular man, about 35 years of age, & being in good health will probably survive his injuries. -Albany Journal

The Nebraskian of Aug 1 appeals to the Gov't for protection against the Indians, who recently murdered Geo Denmaree & Jackson Porter, on Bell Creek, & severely wounded Mrs Porter. Gov Izard set a military force under Gen Thayer to the scene to act on the defensive, without pursuing the Indians. The Omahas had agreed to co-operate with the Territorial volunteers in defence of the frontier.

Valuable Albemarle land for sale: in pursuance of a trust deed made to me by Col Jno R Jones & wife, of record in Albemarle Clerk's Ofc: sale on Sep 17, upon the premises, at public auction: the highly desirable Farm, the property of said Jones, containing about 700 acres of land in Albemarle, on Meadow Creek; with a large barn, corn-house, stables, negro-houses, & ice house, the mansion house being recently burnt. Apply to Col John R Jones, Mr Jas H Daniel, or myself, at Charlottesville, Albemarle, Va. –V W Southall, trustee

Petersburg Female College will commence on Sep 26. Apply to Rev Geo W Carter, or to any one of the Directors: D'Arcy Paul, Chairman, W T Davis, J H Cooper, Weley Grigg, E P Nash, Wm Lea, John Lyon, Petersburg, Va.

Public sale of a farm containing 328 acres of land, at the Cross Roads Tavern; adjoins the lands of Mrs Noland, Wm C Pierce, & others: with a frame dwlg & barn & other out-bldgs. The land is owned by Mgt & Sarah Donohough. –Patrick Lyddane
+
Public sale on Sep 11 next, of the Cross Roads Farm & Tavern: contains 172 acres: large brick dwlg, used as a tavern, & all necessary out-bldgs. It lies on the Plank & Union Turnpike Road, about 9 miles from Wash. –Patrick Lyddane

Teacher wanted to teach 3 or 4 small children. One who can teach French & Music, & a Southern lady is preferred. –Robt Beverley, Broad Run Sta, Fauquier Co, Va.

The Trustees of the Bladensburg Academy desire to employ a gentleman to take charge of the Institution. Situated about 5 miles from Wash. –B O Lowndes, sec

For rent: dwlg house No 6, 4½ st, the former residence of the subscriber, recently occupied by Thos Blagden, being in complete order. Inquire at the store of White & Sons, 321 Pa ave. –W G W White

$100 reward for runaway negro man Joe, who calls himself Gallaway: age about 35 years. He has a wife living at Mr Henry Jones' near Queen Anne, PG Co; a number of relatives in Anne Arundel Co, some of whom live at Messrs John & Albert Clagett's, near the South River Bridge. –Grace H Clagett, living near Mount Pleasant Ferry, PG Co, Md.

FRI AUG 17, 1855
The Buffalo Commerical of Sat give an account of the exploit of Mrs S Becker, who resides on the Canada shore of Lake Erie, who saved the lives of 8 seamen who were wrecked near her residence on Nov 21, 1854. The schnr **Conductor** left the port of Amherstburgh, bound for Totonto, when a hurricane came up & the vessel struck bottom. The sea made a clear breach over the vessel & forced the crew into the rigging, where they remained from 5 in the morning until 2 in the afternoon. Ice was fast making all the time. The crew then described a woman & 2 little boys approaching along the beach. They built a fire on the shore & made signs to the sailors to swim ashore. She aided the captain from the water, having walked up to her neck in the water to save the exhausted man. She drew him to the fire and resuscitated him. Five times she went into the raging waters to rescue one of the crew. Mrs Becker has received a purseof $690 raised by private subscriptions in Canada. She knew how to save the lives of 8 perishing sailors in six feet of water. Mrs Becker is a large, masculine woman, about six feet high, weighs 200 pounds, was born in Canada, & is 30 years old. She lives on the island of Long Point with her husband, & they gain their subsistence by fishing. He was away trapping at the time.

Norfolk: the fever is still very bad here at Portsmouth. Mr Nash Tatem, the Chief Inspector in the Navy Yard is dead. Mayor Woodis, of this city, is ill. Cmdor Barron is supposed to be dying, & Dr Sylvester is dying. T S Broughton, jr, son of the editor of the Herald, is dying. Great difficulty in getting nurses, & as high as $10 per night is charged for attendance upon the sick. Col John Harper, John B Davis, Nathl Manning, & Emily Wilson are dead.

Died: on Aug 16, Lambert, infant son of L F & Mary C Clark, aged 16 months. His funeral will be this afternoon at 4 o'clock.

Died: on Aug 11, at Aldie, Loudoun Co, Va, Mrs Cynthia Berry Smith, widow of the late Gen Thos A Smith, of Missouri.

Mortality at **Fort Riley**, in Kansas Territory of Aug 6. Maj Ogden died last Fri. The wife & 2 children of Maj Woods, the wife of Maj Armistead, 6th Infty, & 45 or 46 citizens died. The Quartermaster Sgt of the 6th Infty also died. [No name given.]

Kansas: Lecompton is named from Judge Lecompton, of the Supreme Court of Kansas. Yesterday shares in the Lecompton Town Co could have been bought for $100; today they cannot be bought for less than $1,000.

Valuable tract of land near Beltsville at public sale: on Aug 23, a tract containing 100 acres, adjoining the farms of Messrs Soper, Marlow, & Parker. There is on the place a good log-house. -Jas C McGuire, auct

Orphans Court of Wash Co, D C. Letters testamentary on the personal estate of Geo W Uttermuehle, late of Wash Co, deceased. –Chas Uttermuehle, Augustus Uttermuehle, Geo W *Uttermuhle, excs.]*Uttermuhle as written.]

Mrd: on Jul 24, in St George's Chapel, Harford Co, Md, by Rev Mr Crampton, Gen Thos F Bowie, of PG Co, Md, to Virginia, only daughter of Luke Griffith, late of Harford Co, deceased.

SAT AUG 18, 1855

Letter received at the ofc of the New Bedford Mercury from Capt Mooers, of the barque **Maria**, of that port, dated Bay of Islands, Mar 16, 1855, reports the loss of ship **Griminesia**, of Callao, Capt Penney, on Jul 3, 1854, on a reef to the westward of New Caledonia, in lat 19 45 south, lon 161 45 east, not laid down on the charts. She went on at 2 A M. The captain, with the mate, doctor, & 4 seamen, left her in a boat, & saw nothing of her after & thinks she went to pieces. She had on board 650 coolies from China, & a crew of 50 men, & all must have perished with the exception of the 7 in the boat.

Trustee's sale of house & lot at auction: on Sep 17, on the premises, by deed of trust from Edw Lockery & Wm T Hook to the subscribers, dated Jul 23, 1850, recorded in Liber J A S No 15, folios 393 thru 395, of the land records of Wash Co, D C: sale of the west part of lot 5 in square 378, containing 4,407 square feet, more or less, with improvements appertaining thereto; fronts on north D, between 9th & 10th sts. -Walter Lenox, Henry Naylor, trustee. -Green & Scott, aucts

Chancery sale: by decree of the Circuit Court of Wash Co, D C, made in the cause of Wm Bird et al vs Horatio Maryman, exc of Zachariah Hazel et al, #886, Chancery: public auction on Sep 11, of lots 3 & 4 in square 784, fronting on Md ave & north B st. –Walter S Cox, trustee -Green & Scott, aucts

The trial of the 2 brothers, Mask, charged with the murder of Miss Smith, in Marshall Co, Miss, terminated at Holly Springs. They were found guilty & one is sentenced to be hung & the other to 15 years' imprisonment in the penitentiary.

Unknown remains. The Marlboro [Md] Gaz says that in the investigation held on Wed at Mr Elial Palmer's tavern, before Messrs Lee & Brookes, two Justices of the Peace, no facts were elicited to cast any light upon the supposed murder case on the farm of Mr Abram Beall. There is no identity to the remains of the deceased, recently discovered on Mr Beall's farm.

On Jul 21 Henry T Walls was killed at the town of Woodbury, Tenn, in a drunken row, whereupon the citizens assembled together & adopted a most stringent prohibitory law. They resolved that they would not sell liquor themselves, would not rent their property to a liquor seller, & wound not sell property to a man who would use it for such purpose. They then made up a purse & bought all the liquor in the place, rolled the barrels into the street, poured out the contents, & set fire to them.

Rewards amounting to $1,200 have been offered by the Gov'r of N J & other individuals for the arrest & conviction of the man who murdered Conrad Bauer, in the city of Newark, on Aug 7.

Dr Allen Potter, of Blackstone, was taken furiously insane on Aug 11. The cause must be attributed to the spirit rappings, in which he has been deeply engaged the past year. The prospect of his recovery is doubtful. –Woonsocket Patriot, 14th.

Fatal accident in Carroll Co, Md. The Western Sentinel states that 3 persons, an Irishman named Kanally & 2 children, were burnt to death, at Rouse's Point, last week, by coming in contact with a barrel of whiskey which had caught fire. The mother was also so badly burnt that it is thought she cannot recover.

Obit-died: on Jul 20, Mrs Matilda Grammer, wife of Mr G C Grammer, of Wash City. She lived chiefly for the immortal interests of her husband & children; pain was the familiar companion of her daily thoughts & of her nightly pillow.

Died: in Elizabethtown, N J, of congestion of the brain, Margaret Magruder, consort of T Robinson Rodgers, & youngest daughter of Josiah F Caldwell, of Wash City. [No death date given-current item.]

Died: on Aug 14, Laura McP, in her 18th year, 2nd daughter of Henry & J Catherine Thecker.

Died: on Aug 15, after a lingering illness, Danl Bogan Robertson, youngest son of Danl & Mary Eliz Robertson, aged 1 year & 4 months.

Died: on Aug 10, Thos Sessford, in his 36th year, son of Mgt & the late Jas Sessford.

MON AUG 20, 1855

Telegraphic intelligence from Boston. Hon Abbott Lawrence died on Sat of congestion of the liver. As a well-known member of an enterprising, wealthy, & munificent family, the loss of this universally respected gentleman will be deeply felt in his own State. He was born in 1792 in the village of Groton, Mass, & was therefore 63 years of age at the time of his decease. His father was a respectable farmer of Middlesex Co, of limited means, who was too poor to give his large family of children any better education than the village common school afforded. In 1808 he went to Boston, whither his elder brother Amos had preceded him, & engaged in business on a limited scale as a retail merchant. In a few years he went into partnership with Amos: the firm did a large business in British fabrics; for several years Mr Lawrence resided in England; he left the importing business & invested largely in the calico mills of Lowell; he amassed a princely fortune, & aided largely in the bldg up of the city of Lowell. Mr Lawrence was married many years ago to a daughter of Col Bigelow, of Middlesex Co, & leaves, besides his widow, 3 sons & 3 daughters, all of whom are married. [Aug 23rd newspaper: Abbott Lawrence was the 5th son of Saml Lawrence, & was born in Groton Mass, Dec 16, 1796. His father was one of those patriotic citizens who rallied at Concord to oppose the progress of the British troops. He originated the institution which is called Lawrence Academy, where his sons received their early education. He died in Groton, Nov 8, 1827, aged 73 years, & his widow May 2, 1845, aged 89 years. He was the father of 9 children, 6 of whom survived him, viz: Luther, who resided in Groton & Lowell, & died in 1839, being the Mayor of the city; Wm, a merchant, who died in Boston in 1850; Amos, above named, died in Boston in 1853; Abbott, the subject of the above notice; Eliza, who married Dr Joshua Green, now resident in Groton; & Saml, the only surviving son, a merchant & capitalist, now residing in Boston. Mr Lawrence was married on Jun 26, 1819, to Katharine daughter of Hon Timothy Bigelow, of Groton, afterwards of Metford. His wife survives him. He has left 3 sons & 2 daughters.

His sons have all been graduated at Harvard College.] [Aug 25th newspaper: The funeral took place on Wed: the following gentlemen served as pall-bearers: Hon Edw Everett, Hon Wm Sturgis, Hon Robt C Winthrop, Hon Judge Sprague, Pres Walker, of Harvard College, Hon Nathan Appleton, Hon Wm Appleton, & Hon David Sears. The body was conveyed to Mount Auburn.]

Hon John Rowan, of Ky, brother-in-law of Jas M Buchanan, of Balt Co, has died. He was the son of the late Judge Rowan, of Ky, & was Charge to Naples during the administration of Pres Polk. [No death date given-current news item.]

Maj C A Ogden of the U S Army is stationed at Boston. The gentleman who recently died at **Fort Riley** is supposed to be Maj E A Ogden, of the Paymaster's Dept.

Upwards of 300 members of the Cushman family, the descendants of the first agent of the Leyden pilgrims, the purchaser of the immortal ship **Mayflower**, the Plymouth colony's right hand in England, the principal patentee of one of the first charters on Mass Bay, the advocate from the press at home of the aboriginal population, & the Christian pleader from the pulpit among the colonists here in behalf of peace & concord, assembled from different parts of the country at Plymouth, Mass, on Wed, the 235th anniversary of the sailing of the Pilgrims, for the purpose of acting in the matter of erecting a monument to the memory of their illustrious ancestor. An address was delivered by Rev Robt W Cushman.

New Orleans papers announce the death in that city, on Aug 11, of Saml J Peters. He had held a number of offices of trust & responsibility & secured the respect, esteem, & regard of all. New Orleans Bulletin

Gored to death by a bull: yesterday Mr Solomon Childs, a farmer in the north part of Waltham, was gored by a bull he had chained in his barn, which either had got loose or had caught & thrown down Mr Childs as he passed him. The family was absent at a funeral & returned home to find him dead. He was about 40 years of age, & leaves a family. Boston Journal

Household & kitchen furniture & a grand Piano, at auction on: Aug 30, at the residence of Lt S Chase Barney, on E st, between 6th & 7th sts. –C W Boteler, auct

Last Tue, as Randall Hanson, son of Wm Hanson, of Minneapolis, was returning from Mr N Jenkins, in Hennepin Co, he drove his horse on the margin of Crystal Lake for the purpose of watering him. All at once the horse commenced sinking, the quicksand giving way, & before Mr Hanson could rescue him, he was drowned. Mr Hanson had his mother in the buggy at the time; she escaped. Mr Hanson says the sand in some portions of Crystal Lake moves almost in the same manner as the water. –St Anthony's Express, Aug 11.

Capt Titus, an old captain in the city of Buffalo, in command of the propeller **Montezuma**, was drowned at the mouth of the Kalamazoo river, Lake Michigan, on Fri of last week. He started to ashore in a yawl, which capsized, & not being a swimmer, Capt Titus sunk. His body washed ashore in about 3 hours.

The undivided half interest in the **Mountain House** at Capon Springs, with its furniture was bought at public sale on Wed of last week for $11,750 by Thos B P Ingram, one of the landlords of the establishment.

Mr Bushnell's School will commence on the first Monday in Sept: located on 13th st, between F & G sts, Wash.

Drug Store, corner of 9th & I sts. R C Dyson & Co have bought out the above named establishment, & are prepared to furnish the public with fresh drugs & medicines.

At Richmond, on Fri, while Mr David E Sharp & 2 or 3 of his employees were loading a lighter in the dock with plaster, the boat, after being loaded, capsized while tied to the wharf, & Mr Geo Rogers & Mr Richd Enroughty were drowned.

The capsizing & sinking of the barque **L M Hubby**, off Point Betsy, a week ago. She left Chicago the Sunday previous in ballast for a cargo of lumber at Saginaw. She was lost in the county of Leclanan, in the water 10 miles off that shore in at least 500 feet of water. He capt was Lyman Roberts, of Edinburgh, near Erie, Pa. Her mate was Jas Cotterell, of Cleveland, & was the only one of the 12 comprising her crew who was saved.

The Patapsco American states that a difficulty having occurred in Clarksville district, Md, between Messrs Benj Blowers & Greenway Garther, originating in a dispute about a small tract of land, an altercation took place between them on Wed, during which Garther shot Blowers, inflicting a possible fatal wound. Garther has been arrested & held in $5,000 to answer.

Died: on Aug17, Miss Ann Frances Hickey, in her 38th year. Her funeral will be from the residence of her brother-in-law, J C Fitzpatrick, south B st, Capitol, on Aug 20, at 9 o'clock, precisely.

Died: on Aug 19, Wm T Porter, in his 42nd year.

Died: on Aug 19, James Gales Gibson, youngest daughter of Francis & Sarah Jane Gibson, aged about 11 months.

Richmond, Aug 16. Yellow fever at Richmond. Names of persons who have as yet died here of yellow fever: S T Lynan, Thos Toddy, Eden Casey, Jas Muld, & Dennis Murphy. They were every one from Gosport. There are 3 cases sick at the hospital.

Md Military Academy, Oxford, Talbot Co, Md: will commence on Oct 1 next. -John H Allen, Superintendent, graduate of the U S Military Academy, West Point.

TUE AUG 21, 1855
In less than 2 months, we shall be within 6 days of England, & indeed of all Europe. The steamer **James Adger** left N Y last week to take in tow the vessel from which the submarine telegraph wire is to be laid across the Gulf of St Lawrence, & we learn by telegraph that she left Halifax on Fri. No one doubts the practicability of laying a submarine telegraph cable across the Gulf of St Lawrence to St Johns, in Newfoundland, however incredulous some may be as to the remainder of the enterprise, that of laying a similar wire across the Atlantic. In about 6 weeks, or 2 months, then, we may calculate upon being in telegraphic communication with St Johns, in Newfoundland. But that point is within 6 days by steamer of Liverpool, & indeed the distance has been done in 5½ days. Across the Atlantic it is proposed to have 6 telegraphic wires, each independent of the other & enclosed in a substantial cable of twisted iron wire. The cable now being laid across the Gulf of Lawrence contains but 3 communicating wires, but another wire is to be put down as soon as the Atlantic cable is laid.

Jon Philo C Fuller died last week at Rose Hill, near Geneva, N Y. To his numerous trusts Mr Fuller was always faithful. –Albany Journal

It is now generally believed that it was Mr Saml N Gant, of Michigan, whose body was recently found in PG Co, Md. He was in Washington in June, & previously visited this State to see his relatives & look up some land claims. His son publishes the Cass Co [Mich] Tribune. –Sun

Mrd: on Sabbath, by Rev John C Smith, Mr Richd H Moore to Miss Eliza Jane Haller, all of Wash City.

Died: on Aug 16, Wm Roche, in his 35th year.

Died: on Aug 19, Robert Alexander, infant son of John L & Eliz C Hawkins, aged 8 months & 8 days.

Mr Jacob Hall, of PG Co, Md, who has been a sojourner in this city for several months past, was thrown from his buggy a few miles out on 7th st road on Sunday & his right leg was broken below the knee. He may have fractured one or more of his ribs. Mr Hall weighs nearly 300 pounds, & there is of course greater difficulty in determing the precise nature & extent of his wounds than in ordinary cases. He will remain in the Wash Infirmary until his recovery.

Died: yesterday, Sallie Houston, infant daughter of C E & Jessie M Weaver, formerly of Meadville, Pa. "A lovely flower cropped in the bud."

Mr Horatio Browning, of Wash City, was injured by the upsetting of a stage, in which he was returning from Montg Co, Md, on Sunday afternoon. He had 3 of his ribs broken, but he is reported to be doing well.

Cottage Home School for Young Ladies, Mass ave, between 10th & 11th sts: 6th academic year will commence on Sep 3. Miss M A Cox, Principal; Madam Dorman, Teacher of Franch; Mr Gibson, Teacher of Drawing & Painting; Mr Scheel, Teacher of Music. Circulars may be obtained at the Bookstore.

I will sell the Farm upon which I reside, on the road from Gtwn to Rockville, containing about 150 acres, more or less. Apply on the premises, or to Geo R Marshall, Tenallytown, D C.

For rent: the most western house in *Cox's Row*, Gtwn, D C. Apply to Bladen Forrest, corner of F & 20th sts.

Norfolk-: Aug 14. Mayor Woodis is not ill & Cmder Barron is convalescent, & is now out of danger, at the Naval Hospital. Mr Wm Broughton is convalescent. –Norfolk Beacon

WED AUG 22, 1855
Flood in Rickingham, Va. On Aug 14, a flood occurred in the northern branch of Cook's Creek, a few miles west of Harrisonburg, & Mrs Eliz Simmers, about 75 years old, was drowned while attempting to get from her dwlg to her barn, which is situated on more elevated ground.

Wash City Ordnance: 1-Act for the relief of Thos W Jones: the sum of $45.37 be paid to him for wood furnished District School No 3 during the winter of 1854-55. 2-Joint resolution to pay A J Larner $20, for his services as Clerk to the Cmte on Elections.

Intelligence from Norfolk exhibit no abatement of the yellow fever there. Deaths from yellow fever reported by the Board of Health for 3 days of last week: Thu: Wm Baten, aged 40; Mr Hudgen, 52; Geo Billups, 19; Columbus Rhea, 23; Dr R W Sylvester; Mr Christian; Jas Henderson, 28; Mrs Curtin, 67; Caroline Phillips, 23. No deaths in the hospital. Fri: Oliver Ellsworth, 45; Josephine Allen, 28; Sarah Pugh, 25; Wm Sclater, 28; ___ Gregg, 28; W Banks, colored, 25; Alfred Trader, 19. Sat: Miss Lizzie Barron, daughter of Cmder Sam Barron, aged 15; Mrs Taylor, wife of W V Taylor, 22; Josiah Ship, 55; Mary Maser, 42; Thos Keeling, 22; Wm Hess, 66; Mrs Fallon, 38; Mrs Jakeman, 36; Mrs Hughes, 36; Philip, mulatto, 24; Geo, colored, 50.

Dr Thos S Waring, of Richmond, Va, was killed by the Indians, on Jul 8, at La Ventura, in the State of Coahuila, Mexico, about 17 miles from Saltillo.

Obit-died: the Savannah Courier announces the death of Hon Isaac H Bronson, Judge of the U S Circuit Court for the northern district of Florida. He died at Pilatka, of pulmonary consumption, on Aug 13. He was a native of the State of N Y, from which he was for 1 or 2 terms a Rep in Congress. About 1839, appointed one of its Territorial judges, he removed to Florida. At the time of his death he was 47 or 48 years of age.

Mr Emig tried an experience to see whether lager beer is or is not intoxicating. He drank 3 gallons in 12 hours & died the same night.

Capt Wm E Stark, of the U S Marine Corps, died at Norfolk on Sat last of apoplexy. The Norfolk Herald says of him: Capt S was a native of this city, & leaves an amiable & estimable family. He entered the Marine Corps in 1831, since which time he has been actively employed in the service. He was an ofcr & gentleman beyond reproach.

Genoa, Jul 26-Madame Maubourg, eldest daughter & last surviving child of the Marquis Lafayette, is dead. She died a few days ago, aged about 75, at her princely residence in Turin, where she has lived many years, [& since the death of her noble husband, at one time Ambassador to the Holy See,] with her daughter, the Baroness Perrone, widow of the Piedmontese General killed at the fatal battle of Novara in 1849. Madame Maubourg often spoke gratefully of her family relations with the U S.

On Aug 9, Mrs Sarah Hevener, wife of John Hevener, of Pendleton Co, Va, was bitten twice upon the leg by a rattlesnake, which she subsequently killed. Death ended her sufferings that night.

On the East river on Sunday, a row boat, with 6 persons, was upset near the head of Cherry st. John Mahers & his son were drowned, but others were rescued by Mr Campbell, a boat-keeper, at the foot of Grand st.

Mrd: on Aug 16, at St Paul's Church, Boston, by Rev J P Robinson, Mr J B Bryan, of Wash City, to Miss Louisa Hammond, of the former place.

Died: on Tue, after a short illness of 8 days, Edw Mahony, a native of the county Kerry, Ireland. His funeral will take place from St Patrick's Church, this evening, at 4 o'clock.

Died: on Aug 21, in her 81st year, Mrs Matilda Latly. Her funeral will be from the residence of her son-in-law, on F st, between 19th & 20th sts. [See death notice for Mrs Matilda Lally below.]

THU AUG 23, 1855
Two little children of O W Wilcox, of Springfield, & two children of Elijah Stebbins, jr, of Vernon, Vt, at which latter place the first two were visiting, were poisoned on Aug 11, by eating the seed of the spotted cowbane, or musquash, which closely resembles caraway. The children remained insensible for 8 hours.

Mrd: on Aug 21, by Rev F Israel, Jas Riggles to Miss Eliza Tinkler, all of Wash City.

Mrd: on Tue, by Rev John C Smith, John D DeBell to Miss Annie W Daniel, both of Fairfax Co, Va.

Died: on Aug 21, in Wash City, Gwinn H Maddox, of St Mary's Co, Md, in his 22nd year. His funeral will take place from the residence of his parents, 21 4½ st, this afternoon, at 3 o'clock.

Died: on Aug 21, in her 81st year, Mrs Matilda Lally. Her funeral will be from the residence of her son-in-law, on F st, between 19th & 20th sts, on Thu at 4 o'clock.

Died: on Aug 19, at Stafford Hall, Wash Co, Md, Robt Wyatt Dodge, eldest son of R P & Caroline R Dodge, in his 13th year. His funeral will take place from the residence of his parents, 89 Montg st, Gtwn, this morning at 10½ o'clock.

Died: on Aug 20, in Fred'k Co, Md, James Robert, infant son of Edw & Maria L Swann, of Wash City, aged 13 months.

Teacher wanted to take charge of 4 children in a private family. Address E Pliny Bryan, Piscataway, PG Co, Md.

FRI AUG 24, 1855
Trustee's sale: by deed of trust recorded in Liber J A S No 34, folios 299 thru 302, of the land records of Wash Co, D C, we will sell, on Sep 28, lot 18 & part of lot 17, in square 466. –E C Morgan, W E Howard, trustees -Green & Scott, aucts

Chancery sale of valuable improved & unimproved property: by decree of the Circuit Court of Wash Co, D C, made in the cause of Selby B Scaggs & Sarah Ann Scaggs, Francis O Brady & Eliz Ogden, vs Susan Brady & Nathl B Fugitt, the subscriber will proceed to sell, as trustee in the above cause, the following: lot 3 & 4 in square 834; parts of lots 11 & 12 in square 823; parts of lots 2 & 3 in square 825; part of lot 3 in square south of square 825; part of said lot 3 between parts of lot sold by the late Nathl Brady to Wm Venable & Sarah McDaniel, fronting 3 feet on 4th st east; part of lot 1 in said square south of square 825; part of lot 3 in square north of square 853; the whole of lot 4 in square 535, of which the late Nathl Brady died seized. Sales to commence on Sept 17 thru Sep 19. –Henry Naylor -Green & Scott, aucts

Yellow fever at Norfolk: Capt Geo Chamers is dead. Cmder Barron, Drs Schofield & Parker are out of danger. In Portsmouth, Patrick Williams, master joiner, & Newton Ashton, keeper of the magazine in the navy yard, are both dead. Rev T G Keen, of the Baptist Church, formerly a resident of Mobile & now of Petersburg, arrived in Norfolk to aid in taking care of the sick. Wash, Aug 22: Mrs C S Jones volunteered to go to Norfolk & nurse the sick without remuneration. She will go there tomorrow.

The barn of Mr Theodore Mosher, a couple miles north of Wash City, was destroyed by fire on Wed. No doubt the work of an incendiary.

Mrs Capt Reid died at Wheeling, Va, on Aug 19. She was the wife of Capt Saml C Reid, distinguished for his defence of the brig **General Armstrong** against the English squadron at the port of Fayal in 1814. Mrs Reid was the daughter of Capt Nathan Jennings, of Fairfield, Conn.

The U S practice ship **Preble**, J F Green, Lt Commanding, arrived at Boston on Tue. She left Annapolis on Jun 22 last with about 80 midshipmen belonging to the Naval School, on a cruise for practice, & have touched at Norfolk, Eastport, Portland, & Provincetown. She will remain at Boston for a week or 10 days, & then return to Annapolis. The **Preble** carries eight 32 pounders. List of her ofcrs: Lt Com Jos F Green; Lt, Robt H Wyman; Purser, B Frank Gallagher; Passed Assist Surgeon, John Ward; Masters, Wm H Parker & Sam R Franklin; Acting Master, Wm K Mayo; Passed Midshipman, Wilson McGunnagle; Carpenter, H P Leslie; Sailmaker, H W Frankland; Gunner, John Wilson.

Stock of 2nd-hand furniture at auction: on Aug 29, at the store of the Messrs Hines, opposite the West Market, their entire stock in trade. –Wall, Barnard & Co, aucts

One of the famous Jewish banker brothers, Solomon Rothschild, has lately died at Paris. He leaves a fortune estimated at forty-five millions of dollars, to be enjoyed henceforth by 2 heirs, who will divide between them.

From the file of the Norwich Weekly Register, published in the years 1792-93.
Gtwn, [M] Aug 8, 1792. On Aug 4 the corner stone on the western abutment of the Federal bridge was laid in due form by Uriah Forrest, Mayor of this town. After the ceremony the company returned to Mr Suter's Fountain Inn, where a handsome entertainment was given by the Mayor to the workmen & others concerned in erecting the bridge.
Norwich, Oct 30, 1792. A Gtwn account mentions that the public sale of the lots in the city of Wash turned out highly satisfactory to the Com'rs. Those made by single lots averaged at 90 odd pounds, those by squares nearly 75 pounds each. The corner-stone of the President's house is to be laid this day at 12 o'clock, & the greater part of the materials being ready on the spot.

Wash, Apr 10, 1793: Wed was the day appointed by the Com'rs for their decision on a plan for the hotel, in conformity to the terms of the lottery scheme. Ten were presented, so varied in their beauties as to astonish the collection of gentlemen who were present at the pleasing exhibition. After due consideration the drawing of Mr Jas Hoban, of Charleston, S C, was preferred. The workmen are already at the foundation on square 430, central between the President's house & the Capitol

Consulate of the U S, Marseilles, Mar 9, 1855. Tribute of respect to Capt Mitchell, of the American barque **Florence**, of Bath, Maine, who rescued from imminent peril the ofcrs & crew of the Neapolitan ship **La Lucie**, Capt Doleberte, of Palermo, near the coast of the U S & brought them to this port on Mar 6. Capt Mitchell declines the acceptance of any gratuity or remuneration of expenses. -H M John L Hodge, Consul of the U S, Marseilles. [Letter from Raimond De Gayzucha, Le Consul General, Consulate of H M the King of the Two Sicilies, Marseilles, Mar 13, 1855.]

Died: on Aug 23, in Gtwn, Hamilton, son of Anna H & A H Dodge, aged 6 years & 6 months. His funeral will be from the residence of his parents, West & Greene sts, this afternoon at 5 o'clock.

Died: on Aug 13, in Wash City, after 2 weeks' illness, Miss A B Anthony, formerly of N Y, but for several years last past a resident of Wash City.

Rugby Academy, 14th st, west of Franklin Square, will be resumed on the 2nd Mon in Sept. Number of pupils is limited. Circulars can be obtained at the residence of the Principal on N, between 12th & 13th sts. –G T Morison

SAT AUG 25, 1855

3,500 acres of land for rent: on Stauton river, Halifax Co, Va. I am bldg comfortable brick dwlgs for small farmers upon the land, dividing the land into small tracts or farms for persons of small capital to farm upon. Direct letters to Barksdale post-ofc, Halifax Co, Va. –Chas A Clark

Gen Thos Metcalfe died at his residence, **Forest Retreat**, in Nicholas Co, Ky, on Aug 18. He was a native of Fauquier Co, Va, where he was born on Mar 20, 1780. When quite young his parents emigrated to Ky & settled in Fayette Co, where he had the restricted advantages of a few months' attendance on a country school. At age 19 years his father died, & he set about making a livelihood for his mother & sister. In 1813, during the war with Great Britain, he commanded a company at the battle of **Fort Meigs** & distinguished himself by his gallantry. He had been previously a member of the Legislature of Ky, & while absent on this campaign, he was re-elected to that body, receiving every vote in the county but 13. In 1848 he was appointed to fill Mr Crittenden's unexpired term in the Senate. Since then he chiefly confined himself to his farm, situated half-way between Maysville & Lexington.

N Y, Aug 23. Mr Alex'r H Petrie was arrested here today, charged with a fraudulent attempt upon certain insurance companies by means of running a steamer ashore. The dfndnt recently purchased the steamer **G W P Custis** at Wash, & immediately insured her for $7,500, merely to cover her trip from Wash to this city. He engaged a captain to run her ashore at the most advantageous point. The captain, instead of coming on here, he ran the steamer to Alexandria & started overland for this city, where he gave the information of the affair at one of the insurance offices interested, & a warrant was at once obtained for Petrie's arrest. Since an **attempt** was made to perpetrate a swindle, the prisoner cannot be legally held by the State courts. The U S District Atty has it under advisement. A bill of sale of the steamer, dated Wash, Jul 25, 1855, from Chas C Mills, was found in Petrie's possession, & in it the purchase money is set down at $8,000; but it is insinutaed that the real value of the vessel is not more than $3,000.

Household & kitchen furniture at auction on: Aug 28, at the late residence of Mr Wm Frush, on Green st, below Bridge, the entire household furniture & effects.
-Barnard & Buckey, aucts

A number of colored citizens who had organized under the name of Massasoit Guards, with the intention of forming & appearing as a military corps, recently applied to the cmder-in-chief for a loan of State arms, & yesterday they received notice that their application was refused. A letter from Gov Gardner to Robt Morris, 1st Lt of the organization, contained the opinion of Atty Gen Clifford in the matter, which was in accordance with the refusal of his Excellency.
--Boston Transcript, Wed

Mrd: on Aug 24, by Rev John C Smith, Mr John Hancock to Mrs Mary D Dudley, both of Alexandria, Va.

Mrd: on Aug 21, at **Woodlands**, Montg Co, Md, Wm Rich Hutton, of Wash City, to Mary Augusta, daughter of Francis C Clopper, of the former place.

Died: on Thu, Emma Theresa, eldest child of John & Eliz Wagner, in her 9th year. Her funeral will take place on Sunday at 3 o'clock, from the residence of her parents, 330 K st, between 13th & 14th sts. "While gathering jewels for his diadem my Saviour whispered, come!"

Died: on Aug 21, James Ernest, aged 22 months, son of James & Annette Travers.

Montgomery Land at public sale: on Sep 18, 2 lots of land in said county. One contains 72 acres, 2 miles below Rockville; the other contains 112½ acres & lies off the pike a short distance. Both are wooded but unimproved, & are portions of the real estate of the late Jas B Higgins. –W Viers Bouic, John M Kilgour, trustees

For sale: a first-rate Family Horse, warranted sound. Buggy & harness will be sold with him, if desired. –A Gladmon, 9th & M sts.

MON AUG 27, 1855

From Calif: The will of Capt Jos L Folsom, U S Army, whose death was announced a few days ago, was admitted to probate at San Francisco on Jul 25. He gives to his mother $5,000 during her natural life; all his other personal property to be equally divided between his mother & his sister, Mrs Forrest; one-third of his real estate to his nephew, Gustavus Decatur Folsom, now in Ohio; & the other two-thirds of the real estate to go to the children of Mrs Forrest-one third of the two-thirds to go to the male child. Messrs A C Peachy, H W Halleck, & P W Van Winkle are the excs. Capt Folsom had been closely identified with San Francisco since its birth as a city.

Household & kitchen furniture at auction on: Aug 29, at the residence of the late Eldred Rawlins, on H st, between 13th & 14th sts, 2nd door east of the Demenou bldgs. The furniture is excellent & well kept. -Jas C McGuire, auct

Capitol Dome: Mr Pringle Sleight, the master carpenter of the Capitol Extension, has nearly completed the various parts which are to compose the massive scaffolding to be erected in the Rotundo to facilitate the removal of the dome, [as authorized by the last Congress,] which is to be replaced by one of iron, of far higher & of graceful proportions, & in architectural keeping with the appearance of the Capitol, improved by the 2 additional wings. Congress appropriated $100,000 for the erection of the iron dome, the present one being of combustible materials & not graceful in its proportions. -Sentinel

Obit: the death of Hon Jabez D Hammond took place on Aug 18, at Cherry Valley, N Y, where he had resided for many years. His was a life of untiring industry. He leaves behind him a wide circle of relatives & friends to mourn his loss.
–Albany Argus

The Misses Koones will re-open their Seminary for Young Ladies on Sep 3. Residence 450 D st, between 2nd & 3rd sts.

Gtwn Classical & Mathematical Academy: the undersigned, having rented the bldg in which the late Wm R Abbott, so long & so favorablt conducted his Academy, will receive an additional number of pupils. The exercises will be resumed on Sep 3.
–P A Bowen, Principal, 94 West st, Gtwn, D C.

On Friday, in Elm st, N Y C, a deliberate murder was perpetrated. Robt Bulins shot Henry Bloomer with a pistol, & he died soon after. Bulins confessed the deed. He charged Bloomer with having robbed his trunk 2 years ago, & swore falsely against him on a recent trial for assault. He is in prison.

On Aug 20 Peter Dowling was killed at Chalfin Bridge, in Monroe Co, Ill, by John Leiper, who immediately fled. They were engaged in a social game of cards & had a dispute about the paltry sum of 80 cents. As Dowling rose from his seat he was shot.

Died: on Aug 25, in Balt, of yellow fever, Mr Thos H Greene, in his 32nd year. He was a resident of Norfolk, in which place he contracted the disease which terminated his life, while using his utmost endeavors to afford relief to the afflicted. Ardent in his attachments, he proved a firm friend, & died lamented by those he knew & loved.

New Orleans, Aug 25. Santa Anna has abdicated! He left the city of Mexico on Aug 9 with an escort of 2,500 men, signed his abdication at Perote, & embarked on Aug 17 at Vera Cruz for Havana. [Aug 28th newspaper: Santa Anna came into public life in 1821.]

Phil, Aug 25. We much regret to learn that Cmdor Stewart fell from a pear tree yesterday & was taken up insensible. He was alive at 10 o'clock today, but has not since been heard from. [Aug 31st newspaper: Cmdor Stewart is out of all danger.]

Orphans Court of Wash Co, D C. Letters of administration on the personal estate of Patrick White, late of Victoria, Texas, deceased. –Morris S Miller, adm

TUE AUG 28, 1855
New Bedford: the Mercury has a list of those paying a tax of $50 & upwards, from the Assessors' books: John A Parker's estate, $631,700; Wamsutta Mills, $600,000; Thos S Hathaway, $160,900; F S Hathaway, $156,800; Jas Arnold, $544,500; O & G O Crocker, $251,500; Isaac Howland, jr, & Co, $1,500,000; Sylvia Ann Arnold, $342,600; Edw M Robinson, $464,600; & Edw C Jones, $314,900.

Household & kitchen furniture, family carriage & matched horses, rockaway, & farming utensils at auction on: Sep 11, at the country seat of Thos Marshall, near the village of ***Tennallytown***, on the turnpike to Rockville, about 2 miles from Gtwn.
+
Splendid Country Seat, near Wash, at Public Sale: on Sep 11, the residence belonging to Thos Marshall, adjoining the village of ***Tennallytown***, 2 miles above Gtwn, on the Gtwn & Rockville turnpike. It contains 63½ acres, divided into small & convenient lots. The dwlg is of brick, 21 by 40, with a wing 25 by 31, each 2 stories, with the necessary outbldgs, all new, & built under the personal superintendence of the owner, with gas fixtures throughout; 450 feet above tidewater. There is a 2 story brick house on the turnpike corner of the place, now rented as a grocery store at an annual rent of $75, which will be sold with the place or separate if desired. -Jas C McGuire, auct

Stock of groceries at auction: on Fri next, in the store of J M Cost, on the corner of Bridge & Jefferson sts, Gtwn. –Barnard & Buckey, aucts

Mrs Henry A Burr informs her pupils that their studies will re-commence on Sep 24: 391 H st, between 13th & 14th sts.

Stock, fixtures, & furniture of a Confectionery Establishment at Public Auction: on Sep 4, at the establishment of Messrs Ryder & Plant, on 7th st, opposite Odd Fellows' Hall, I shall sell their entire stock & fixtures. –Jas C McGuire, auct

Death of a man who voted for Pres Washington. Mr Benj Blackford died at the residence of his son, Mr Wm M Blackford, in this city, on Monday. He was one of the few men living who enjoyed the proud recollection of having voted for the Father of his Country for Pres; & he has also voted in every succeeding Presidential election. Mr Blackford was a gentleman of fine intellect & very extensive information, both of which he retained to the last. He has left a name without reproach. –Lynchburg Virginian of Aug 22.

Died: on Aug 26, in Wash City, Bridget, wife of Wm H Hayward, in her 37th year.

Died: on Aug 25, Mrs Jessie Magaw Weaver, wife of Chas E Weaver, late of Meadville, Pa. She was the daughter of the late Dr Jesse Magaw, of Mercersburg, Pa, & in all the relations of child, wife, & mother her conduct was so fine & so exemplary as to win the admiration & esteem of all who formed her acquaintance. She died in communion with the Episcopal church, & has left, in her 32nd year, a bereaved husband & 4 children to mourn their untimely & irreparable loss.

Died: on Aug 27, Clara Matilda, daughter of Jas T & Lucinda L McIntosh, aged 5 years. Her funeral is today at 11 o'clock.

WED AUG 29, 1855
Yellow fever at Norfolk: Hunter Woodis, Mayor of Norfolk, died Aug 26. He was but 34 years of age. He leaves a wife & 2 children, whom he had sent to Wash no later than Wed last. [35 have died in Norfolk in the last 48 hours-Aug 27.]

Explosion of the boiler of the U S steamer **Hetzel**: on Aug 24, near the Capes of the Chesapeake, a short distance from **Head Hog Island**. Killed were: Saml C Latimre, 3rd assist engineer, U S N; Wm Bulger, 1st class fireman; Wm Gardner, 1st class fireman; John T Knight, 2nd class fireman; Bernard Moran, seaman. Injured: Michl Scanlon, ordinary seaman, badly; Benj F Vanhorn, 2nd class fireman, slightly. -Star

Mr Wm G Busey has been appointed assistant to the City Surveyor of Wash.

The N Y papers announce the death, in that city, of Dr Horatio G Jamieson, long known as an eminent surgeon in Batl, where he had been a practioner for nearly half a century. His age was 76 years. He had just published a new work on cholera, in the preparation of which he had been long engaged.

Military movements in Texas: letter dated Jul 31. 1-Lt John Williams, 1st Dragoons, was murdered by private Dunn, of Co G, Regt Mounted Riflemen, at *Fort Davis*, on The 30th ult. The Lt was shot 3 times causing instant death. Lr Williams was an ornament to the service, a good & faithful soldier, & had won his way step by step from a private soldier to the rank of 2nd Lt. 2-Our commanding ofcr, Col W W Loring, Mounted Riflemen, U S Army, when in the act of stepping from his carriage on Jul 26, fell, breaking his right arm & otherwise injuring him, a casualty that is deeply deplored by all particularly at a time when his services & wise counsel are so much needed. Should he be deprived of the use of his right arm he will be almost powerless, having been deprived of his left during the Mexican war, at the head of his regt.

An Eastern genius has succeeded in harnessing steam to a musical instrument which will out-sax Mr Sax's noisy inventions most decidedly. His name is Joshua C Stoddard, of Worcester, Mass. It consists of a horizontal steam-chest or cylinder some 6 feet in length & from 4 to 6 feet in diameter, which is fed with steam from the large boiler in the establishment where it is located. One of these instruments can be heard from 10 to 25 miles on the water, & every note will be perfect & full. We heard the inventor play Rosalie on it, & it looked like getting off tail notes mechanically. This invention is so completely under the control of the operator that, were it arranged with a key-board similar to a piano, it would obey the slightest touch, & a child could play slow or quick tunes, every note of which might be heard several miles. It would appear rather novel to John Bull to hear Yankee Doodle from one of our ocean steamers as she was about to enter a British port.

Rockville Academy, Montg Co, Md, will re-commence on Sep 1. –O W Treadwell, Principal; Jas Andrews, jr, Assist.

The *Methodist* of Boston had a grand celebration yesterday, Aug 28, at the First Church in Hanover st, to commemorate the 60th anniversary of the laying of the corner stone of the first Methodist church in Boston. The first was a small church in old Methodist alley, built by contributions of 6d sterling & upwards & costing about $1,000.

Obit-died: on Aug 22, after an illness of several months, Hon Abrhahm M Schermerhorn. He was a native of Schenectady, N Y, where he graduated at Union College, studied law, & was admitted to the Bar. However, he engaged in Banking, in which business he afterwards became eminent. Many friends will feel saddened when they hear of his death. –Rochester American

John Tine, alias Jones, was on Monday arrested by ofcrs Mockbee, Stanley, & Thomas, in the act of setting fire to a small tenement in Wash City. He has been committed for trial.

The Lynchburg [Va] Republican learn of the death of a man named Thompson, by the hand of one named Lester, in Bedford, last week; also of the murder of a man named Woodson by a negro named Jones, owned by Mr Bedford. Also, a man named Granville Tucker was fatally injured by a man named Goff in a affray in the same county.

Mrd: on Aug 28, by Rev Andrew G Carothers, Mr Chas Carver to Miss Frances Crump, both of Va.

Mrd: on Monday, by Rev John C Smith, Mr Thos Harry to Miss Mgt Harnett, all of Wash City.

Died: on Aug 27, George Jacob Warder, only child of Geo J & Helen C Seufferle, aged 11 months & 27 days. His funeral will be at 10 o'clock this morning from the residence of Geo S McElfresh, 420 6th st, between F & G sts.

Musical Class: instruction in the Piano Forte. Apply to me by note at Mrs Smith's, 233 F st. –W Henry Palmer

THU AUG 30, 1855
Meeting of the Columbia Hose Co, No 2, held on Aug 23, the following ofcrs were elected: H C Purdy, Capt of Hose; C Robinson, 1st Assist; L Dowell, 2nd Assist.

On Sunday last the steamer **Elm City**, coming through Hurl Gate, going from New Haven to N Y, ran over a small 14 foot sail boat, containing 3 persons, who had started from this city for Flushing Bay on a fishing excursion. It is supposed that all in the small boat were drowned, as they have not been seen nor heard from since. Their names were Jas Lester, Richd Roberts, & Jos Stratton.

Yellow fever at Portsmouth: Dr Trugien is now at the hospital, worn out with exhaustion. Among the deaths are those of Mr L W Boutwell, brother of Capt Boutwell, U S Navy, & of his daughter, Emma. The daughter died on Fri, the father on Sun. Mr D D Fiske, the Mayor, was taken ill with the fever on Mon, & is thought to be better. Jas H Saunders, sec of the Howard Association, is down this morning. Of the Protestant Clergymen 3 are still at their posts: Rev Messrs Chirholm, Eskridge, & J U K Handy.

Capt Snelling, of the U S Army, died at Cincinnati on Sat. He has been stationed at Dayton & engaged in the recruiting service. Capt Snelling was the son of a distinguished ofcr in the army, & was educated at West Point. He was promoted for his gallantry during the war in Mexico, & received a severe wound at the capture of the city, from which it is probable he never entirely recovered. Since that time, until last fall, he has been mostly in service upon the Western frontier.

Died: on Aug 26, at Princess Anne, Md, in her 23rd year, Mrs Margaret C, wife of Dr Wm Stewart, of Somerset Co, Md, & daughter of S W Handy, of Wash City.

PG Co land for sale: the Farm of the late Thos Hall, of said county: on Sep 10 next: this farm contains about 440 acres of land; adjoins the lands of Messrs Geo W Duvall, Dennis Duvall, & others, & nearly by the side of **Good Luck**. The improvements are a comfortable 2 story dwlg-house, kitchen, quarter, & other necessary out-houses. Title clear. –Absolom A Hall, R D Woodward. Millersville, Anne Arundel Co, Md.

Obit-died: on Aug 20, at the residence of his son, Wm M Blackford, in Lynchburg, Va, Benj Blackford, in his 88th year. Mr Blackford's mental faculties retained their full vigor down to a late period of his last illness, when they yielded to disease rather than to age.

Died: on Aug 26, Mr Thos Campbell Young, aged about 38 years. He was born in Lochmaben, Dumfrieshire, Scotland, & was the eldest son of the late Rev Andrew Young, for many years pastor of the U P Church in that burgh. It will be a rich consolation to an aged mother, called upon to mourn the death of her wandering son, to be assured that he died professing the faith of his parents. She is also assured that American & Scottish friends watched around the couch of her son. Rev Dr Gurley, pastor of the old school Presbyterian Church of Wash City, was unremitting in his attention, ministering things spiritual & eternal. -Scotus

The train from N Y C met with a serious accident near Burlington by running over a horse. The train was thrown from the track, & the following were killed: Catharine Bigelow; John Dallam & Thos J Meredith, Balt merchants; Maj Boyce & wife, U S Coast Survey; Mrs Mgt Prescott, wife of Rev Mr Prescott, of Salem, N J; Baron De St Andre, the French Consul at Phil; D F Haywood, G W Ridgeway, C M Barclay, Edw C Bacon, Wm Kent, Alex'r Kelly, of Phil; M J Stoughton; Martin Connell, of Wilmington, Dela; Jacob Howard, Lebanon, Tenn; Harry Rush, Gtwn College; Jas Lincoln, Ellicott's Mills; Mrs Barclay, wife of Clement C Barclay, of Phil, who was on her way to Europe. Persons wounded: the daughters of Major Boyce; Wm C McClay, a member of Congress from N Y, seriously; Mrs King, of Charlestown, Va; Mr Ingersoll, son of Lt Henry Ingersoll, of Phil; Hon Wm Whelan, of the Naval Bureau, Wash; Cmder Jos M Smith; Spencer McCorkle, of the Coast Survey; & Dennis O Kane, of Wash. [Aug 31st newspaper: the train came in collision with a light pleasure wagon, driven by Dr * *Hannegan, of Columbus, N J, who attempted to cross the track in front of the cars. Dr Hannegan said the carriage contained his wife, her father, Thos Antrim, his wife, my child, & myself. My family was only slightly injured. It is said that *Dr Hannegan is hard of hearing. [Sep 3rd newspaper: Dr * *Heneiker was not deaf, as was first reported.] He has been practicing medicine for the last 32 years. Coroner Saml W Earl, on Wed, had all the bodies of the dead collected & conveyed to the Lyceum Hall, for their friends to identify.

Killed: Mr Geo W Ridgeway, oil merchant, Phil
Alex Kelley, queensware store, Phil
Baron de St Andre, French Consul, Phil
Edw P Bacon, Spring Garden st, Phil
Wilson Kent, of the firm of Dyott & Co, Phil
Mrs Clement Barclay, of Phil, on her way to Europe
Mrs Mgt Prescott, of Salem, N J, wife of Rev Mr Prescott & sister-in-law of the historian.
Thos J Meredith, merchant, Balt
Mr Jacob Howard, Lebanon, Tenn
John Dallam, merchant, Balt
Mrs Boyce, wife of Capt Boyce, U S Coast Survey, Wash
Rev John M Connell, Presbyterian clergyman, Wilmington, Del.
Miss Jane Lincoln, aged 32
D T Haywood, Charleston, S C
*Henry Rush, Gtwn College, D C
Chas Bottom, of the firm of Bottom & Co, iron building manufacturer, Trenton, N J
M J Stoughton, residence unknown
Catharine Bigelow, Phil
Catharine Brown, colored servant of Com Smith
Mr Geo Ingersoll, son of Lt Harry Ingersoll, of Phil
Wounded:
Capt Boyce, U S Coast Survey, Wash
Two daughters of Capt Boyce, one badly
Hon Wm Wheelan, Naval Bureau, Wash
*Dennis O'Kane, D C
Cmdor Jos Smith, U S Navy, Wash
Spencer McCorkle, U S Coast Survey, slightly
Henry L Bennett, Phil, slightly
John F Gillespie & wife, Memphis, Tenn, badly
Mrs King, Charleston, S C, rib fractured
John Kelly, Pittsburgh, badly injured in the back
___ Lukins, flour dealer, Phil
Wm H Newbold, broker, Phil, badly
Thos Finley, Phil, collar bone broken & otherwise hurt
Miss Lincoln Phelps & mother, from Ellicot's Mills, Md, injured
Mrs Lukins & servant, badly
___ Packer, Phil, leg broken & otherwise injured
Mrs Pringle, N Y, slightly
Hon Wm B McClay, N Y, severely
T Morgan, fancy dry goods dealer, Phil
Caroline Hyman, colored, slightly
Mr Fisk, Conn, leg broken
Mr Kay, Haddonfield, N J, both legs broken-not likely to recover

Dennis O'Phelan, badly-both legs fractured
Philip Oren, Schuylkill Co
Rev Mr Parvin, Episcopal clergyman, severely
J M Little, Pittsburgh, slightly
Saml Lahm, Canton, Ohio, badly
Geo H Harlan, Cecil Co, Md, collar bone broken & badly bruises
Jas M Patton, Phil, compound fracture of thigh
Mr Leeds, Phil, slightly
Mr Sargeant, Phil
Geo F Harlan, Conn
Jas C Wheaton, Phil
___ Shankland, express agent
Dr A Porter, Harrisburg, slightly
Chas Dickessey, Phil
Judge Reeves, Ohio, slightly
Chas W Oldenburg, Phil
Wm Clarke, Delaware Co, Pa
Mrs Haslan, Jersey City
Jos Burk, Phil, back broken
Rebecca Phillips & daughter, Phil
Abigail Phillips
Ford Frazier, laborer, Manayunk, slightly
Chas Le Bouttillier, Phil, slightly
J D Fisher, Phil
Danl Saurbeck, Ohio, considerably]
[*See Sep 1st newspaper: Rush & O'Kane.]
[* *Hannegan changed to Heneiker in later coverage.]

FRI AUG 31, 1855
Col Thos Shadforth, of the English army wrote to his wife & children on the evening of Jun 17, just previous to the attack upon the defensive works of Sebastopol. He writes his last farewell to those he so dearly loved. Six hours had not passed, his letter was yet but a few miles on its way to his family, & the noble man had passed away from the earth. Extract: " God ever bless you, my beloved Eliza & my dearest children; &, if we meet not again in this world, may we meet in the mansion of our Heavenly Father, through Jesus Christ. God bless & protect you! And ever believe me." Your affectionate husband & loving father, Thos Shadforth

Mr Geo West, of Baily & Co's Circus Co, undertook to correct the elephant for killing a horse, when the elephant became enraged & killed Mr West. It took place between Camden & Columbia on Monday.

Norfolk Herald of Wed: Dr Trugien died in Portsmouth on Wed, & Dr Bilesola is the only resident physician that is able to be out, the others being with the fever or so over-worked that they cannot visit their patients.

Obit-died: on Aug 21, in Burlington Co, N J, Capt Chas Gauntt, of the U S Navy, in his 61st year. He entered the navy in 1811, & in 1812 was appointed to the U S ship **Wasp**, Capt Jones. He was in the action of the **Wasp** & the ship **Frolic** in 1812; was taken prisoner to the Island of Bermuda, from whence he was exchanged by transfer of prisoners. He was afterwards in the frig **Macedonian** & the frig **Mohawk**, & also on Lake Erie. In 1827 he was appointed to the ship **Warren** as 1st Lt to search the Mediterranean & Archipelago in quest of pirates, which arduous duty he continued until 1829, when the object of the cruise was satisfactorily accomplished & the ship returned to the U S. He was afterwards in the Pacific, in command of the ships **Raritan & Dale**, besides shore duty at the Phil navy yard.

Fatal affray last week at Helena, Ark, in which Walter B Cleveland & John Neal were killed & a man by the name of Jopes seriously wounded. Cleveland shot Neal, when he in turn was stabbed by the latter, & death ensued in both case after the lapse os some 24 hours.

Norfolk, Wed. In Portsmouth: on Aug 7, Dr Robt Thompson, of Balt, & Dr Cannon, of Norfolk, are among the dead. A private letter names, as among the deaths reported today, Jas Harrison, of the firm of Capps & Harrison; Capt Fatherly, Mr Scott, Mrs Small, & Dr Tunstal.

I offer for sale my Farm in PG Co, Md; adjoins the lands of Capt Gibson, Mr Berry, & others: contains 120 acres. It is remarkably healthy. A large family dwelt upon the farm the past 6 years, during which time there was not a case of bilious fever or ague & fever. The dwlg contains 6 rooms & a cellar. Apply to the subscriber, at Alexandria, or to Jas Lee, Mount Welby post ofc, PG Co, Md. Mr Wm Allen, who lives adjoining, will show the farm. –W Tasker Weir

Died: on Aug 29, with the resignation of a true Christian, Sarah B, wife of Andrew Hoover. Her funeral will be from her late residence, 238 I st, between 18th & 19th sts, this afternoon at 4 o'clock.

New Orleans Picayune of Aug 22: Lt Chas N Underwood, 1st U S Infty, died at **Fort Duncan** on Aug 7. He was much esteemed by his brother officers.

SAT SEP 1, 1855

The paper mill of Mr W S Whiteman, near Nashville, Tenn, was destroyed by fire on the 22nd ult. Loss estimated at $42,000, on which there was $14,000 in insurance.

At the Women's Rights Convention at Saratoga a few days since, while Mrs Lucy Stone Blackwell was speaking, some facetious opponent of Lucy's theory asked her "who would take care of the babies when mothers went to Congress?" "I will reply to that everlasting query," rejoined Lucy, "by asking who takes care of them when their mothers come to Saratoga?"

From Norfolk. New cases of yellow fever as of Thu afternoon: Lts Richd L Page & Jas Henderson, U S Navy; Mrs Tazewell, G W Camp, Miss Holden, Miss Dodd, Miles P Butcher, P Sharpley, Dr Constable, Dr McFaddin, of Phil; Dr Wm Selden, of Norfolk; Dr Sylvester, jr, & his brother, Dr Rose, a member of the Howard Assoc; Dr Junius Briggs, Mrs J R Small, Capt Thompson, of Phil, Penn; & Mrs Maul, of New Orleans. Mr Whittle, wife of ComWm Whittle, & daughter of the late Com Sinclair, died on Wed. The deaths for 36 hours ending on Thu afternoon: Dr Thompson, of Balt, Miss Todd, Mr Mallory Todd, Miss Spratt, two Misses Camp, Thos Beverage, & his mother-in-law, Mrs Beetly, Francis Tarrant, Jos Tatem, Mrs Amos Small, Mrs Capt White, Thos Lewis, jr, & his sister Martha Lewis, Mrs Walter Jones, Jas Dowre, John G Hatton, Saml Forbes, Mrs Nathl Manning, Mrs Wm Gwynn, & Miss Marrisetti. The following person arrived on Thu from the South, to tender their services at Portsmouth & Norfolk: E E Jackson, Mr & Mrs Parker, & a colored boy, from Charleston, S C; Dr Campbell, Capt Ives, Treasurer of the Howard

Assoc, & 10 female nurses from New Orleans; Drs J B Read & R J Flinn, also T J Charlton, J E Godfrey, J J McFarland, & R W Skinner, medical students, & Wm Ebbs & John White, assistants, from Savannah.

Advices from Lisbon to the 9th ult mention the death of Gen Arista, ex-Pres of Mexico, who died suddenly on the steamer **Tagus**, whilst on his way to Southampton.

Col Hart, the American Consul at Santa Cruz, Island of Teneriffe, died suddenly at that place of apoplexy on Jul 23, & was buried with military honors by a force of marines & seamen from the U S flag-ship **Jamestown**. The Spanish authorities & foreign Consuls attended his funeral. Col Hart was the author of "Marian Coffin" & other literary works known to the public.

A dispatch from St Louis announces the death of Lt Gov Brown, of Missouri. [No other details.] [Sep 6th newspaper: Dr Wilson Brown, Lt Govn'r of Missouri, died on Aug 27, the 51st anniversary of his birth. He was a native of Anne Arundel Co, Md. He emigrated to Missouri in 1827, & represented Scott Co in the Legislature in 1836. Subsequently he held the ofc of Auditor of State, which position he held until he was elected Lt Govn'r.]

The Public Schools of Wash City will be re-opened on Sep 3. –Geo J Abbott, sec

Portsmouth, Va, Aug 29. Dr Trugien died at the U S Hospital this morning. The fever tended to the brain, & he had two attacks of apoplexy, the last of which carried him off. Though not yet in the prime of life, he had attained a practice & reputation rarely enjoyed by many of his seniors. –Rev I W K Handy, of the Middle st Presbyterian Church.

The reports from the scene of the N J railroad disaster represent Mr Harry Rush as among the killed & Mr Dennis O Kane as severely injured. These names should have been printed Mr Hugh Rush & Mr Dennis O'Kane. The former was 19 & the latter 25 years of age. They were both natives of Ireland & schoolmates of Gtwn College, on their way to Worcester, Mass, in company with 4 other Jesuits, to enter upon their duties as professors in the College of the Holy Cross at that place.

St Andrew's Society of Washington was organized during the present month, & the following were elected ofcrs for the ensuing year: Gilbert Cameron, Pres: Wm Ballantyne & John Smith, Vice Presidents; Fred'k D Stuart, Treasurer; Jas McWilliams, Sec; Chas Sword, Jas Henderson, Jas Anderson, Jas Batchen, Wm R Smith, & A B McFarlan, Managers. This Society is composed of Scotchmen & the lineal descendants of Scotchmen.

Information wanted of Chas & Mgt Devlin or their heirs. They lived in York, Penn, in 1835, but subsequently removed West. Any information that can be given of them will be thankfully received by Mrs Bridget Richardson, at Mrs Culverwell's, on L st, between 9th & 10th sts, Wash.

For sale: a valuable & improved farm, within 3 miles distance from Wash City: about 110 acres, adjoining the farms of Messrs Henry Willard, Hugh B Sweeney, & Mrs McDaniel. It has a good frame dwlg house, containing 12 rooms, a barn, stable, carriage & corn houses, & the other usual necessary bldgs on a well conducted farm. Apply on the premises to the subscriber, or to John C Brent, Atty-at-law, 30 La ave. -Edw Fenwick

Mrd: on Aug 30, at the Assembly's Church, by Rev Andrew G Carothers, Benj Franklin, M D, of Wash City, to Miss Mary V Davis, of Gtwn, D C.

Died: on Aug 31, Mary Jane, wife of C E Walker, in her 34th year. Her funeral will take place at Wesley Chapel, corner of 5th & F sts, on Sunday at 3 o'clock.

Died: yesterday, in Wash City, very suddenly, Mrs Serene, consort of A L Hazleton, in her 35th year. The friends & acquaintances of Mr & Mrs Hazleton are requested to attend the funeral of the latter, from the residence of Mrs Bannerman, corner of E & 9th sts, at 3 o'clock on Sep 2.

Died: on Aug 17, at Stroudsburg, Pa, Ellia Lewis Hamersly, son of the late Robt Hamersly, of York, Pa, in his 30th year.

MON SEP 3, 1855
Died: on Sep 1, at his residence in Wash City, Hon Wm Cranch, Chief Judge of the Circuit Court of D C, & one of the oldest residents of the Federal city, having removed here with his family from Mass in 1796 or 1797, three or four years before the Gov't was transferred from Phil. His funeral will take place from his late residence, Capitol Hill, corner of East Second & South D sts, on Tue, at 4 o'clock. [Sep 4th newspaper: Judge Cranch died at about the age of 86 years; he was a native of Mass] [Sep 5th newspaper: the funeral of the lamented Judge Cranch took place yesterday afternoon, attended by the Pres of the U S & other distinguished ofcrs of the Gen Gov't, by the Bench & Bar of our several Courts, & by a very large number of citizens & friends. The religious service was conducted by Rev Wm Furness, of the Unitarian Church, Phil.]

Died: yesterday, in Phil, Mrs Harriet Smith, wife of Cmdor Jos Smith, U S Navy. Her funeral will take place this morning, at 9 o'clock, from St John's Church.

Wm H Fry, an old esteemed citizen of Phil, died on Fri last, in his 79th year. He was one of the pioneers of the present Phil press, having founded the Nat'l Gazette.

The fine ship **Lightfoot**, Capt Pierce, owned by Messrs Howes & Co, of N Y, was wrecked near Sands Head, Jun 19, & shortly after became a total loss. She was from London, bound to Calcutta, with a valuable cargo. The cargo was on English account, & insured in Europe.

More on the N J railroad disaster found in the Aug 30th newspaper. The death of Capt Boyce occurred immediately after he was extricated from the ruins of the demolished cars. His daughter, Emma, 22 years of age, after suffering the amputation of a limb, also expired. His wife it was for a time hoped would recover, but before their friends had reached Gtwn with the remains of the father & daughter the mother also expired. Capt Boyce was formerly an ofcr in the U S Army, but in 1836 resigned his commission to accept a position in the Coast Survey, to which branch of service he was attached at the time of his death. While in the army he was promoted 2nd Lt 1st Infty Jul 1, 1822; 1st Lt Jun 30, 1825; Aid-de-Camp to Maj Gen Macomb 1825-29; Capt Oct 25, 1835. [Gtwn Advocate: Capt Boyce had been for some time one of the owners of the largest flour mill in Gtwn, built by Mr Jas Davis. The death of his daughter, Miss Emily Boyce, has caused much regret. We had hope for the recovery of Cmdor Jos Smith & lady; but we heard yesterday that Mrs Smith had expired. Cmdor Smith, his niece, & Dr Whelan, of the Navy Dept, & a son & daughter of Capt Boyce, & Mr Dennis O'Keene, of Gtwn College, comprise all from this District of the wounded who have survived the accident. The dead are those we have here named & Mr Hugh Rush, a scholastice of Gtwn College.]

Mrs Taylor, residing near Brooklyn Lake, Dinwiddie Co, Va, & a son 9 years old, were drowned last Fri. The lad fell into the water trying to reach a hat that had fallen in & a younger brother gave the alarm to the parents, which caused Mrs Taylor to hasten into the lake, but went too far, & was also drowned. Mr Taylor plunged into the lake & swam to Mrs Taylor, but being seized with a cramp, came near perishing with the others. –Sussex Herald

Parlor Mirrors of any size; fancy bracket tables, portrait & picture frames, constantly on hand. –Francis Lamb, 237 Pa ave, opposite Gautier's Saloon.

Norfolk-yellow fever. The Norfold Herald of Fri announced the death of Dr Thos Constable, a practicing physician & member of the Board of Health; Dr Thos Nash, a zealous member of the faculty; & Mrs Eliz Whittle, wife of Cmder Whittle, of the U S Navy, & daughter of the late Cmdor Sinclair. It names as among the sick Messrs Camp, Cashier of the Exchange Bank; Hatton, Teller of the Farmers' Bank; & Higgins, Teller of the Va Bank-the two latter said to be very ill. Dr Wm Selden was taken ill on Tue & Dr Geo J Halson on Wed. There were 18 deaths at Norfolk on Thu, 20 deaths on Fri, & 12 deaths on Sat. Among them were Mrs Capt Starke, J L Hodges, Jno G H Hatton, a child of Cmder Whittle, Rev Mr Dibbrell, a Methodist clergyman, Ignatius Higgins, teller of the Bank of Va, & R R Dove. From Portsmouth: deaths in this town for the days mentioned: Aug 28: Jas Hanrahan, Mrs Burhan, Mrs Johnson, Mrs Martha Rozier, Thos Wrenn, Mrs Godfrey, Mrs Randolph's child, orphan at the academy, Nathl Brittingham, Chas C Patem, 3 children names not received. Aug 29: son of Mr Buckner, Mr Trapple, son of Malachi Williams, negro child at Dr Peete's, Colemen Donahoe, child of Chas Myers, Mrs Chas Avery, Robt Powers, Mrs Harwood, Miss Sophronia Gwynn,

Mrs N Manning. Aug 30: Mr Cooke, of Newtown, negro man of Mrs Brickey, Mrs Mintas, Capt Saml Forbes, Mrs Francis Gwynn, Miss Bilisoly, negro child at Mr Bohannon's, negro child at Dr Peete's, Wm Pebworth, son of Mr Broughton, negro man Bill of John Cocke, Miss Morrisett, Mary Jane Nosay, & 4 at the hospital. In Portsmouth on Fri & Sat there were 35 deaths.

TUE SEP 4, 1855
The Pres appointed B Squire Cottrell, U S Commercial Agent at San Juan, Nicaragua, vice Jos W Fabens, removed. -Star

Official item. The Pres removed, some days ago, Maj Richd P Hammond, Collector of the Port of San Francisco, & appointed Hon Milton S Latham, a member of the last House of Reps, in his stead. The cause of this change has not been made known.

Among the late fatalities at Norfolk from the yellow fever, are Dr Nash, Dr Constable, & the Rev Mr Diberl, & others. –Balt Sun

The body of Miss Jane Lincoln, daughter of Mrs Phelps, of Ellicott's Mills, killed by the late railroad disaster, has been taken to Balt for interment. Mrs Phelps was not so seriously injured as reported. She received only a sprain. Her youngest daughter was not bruised as reported. They were both extricated from beneath a mass of ruins.

The Phil Ledger gives the following correct list of those who have been killed in the late railroad disaster: [Mrs Boyce, of Gtwn, reported to have died is not only not among the killed, but in a fair way to recover.]
Killed:

Capt Boyce, Wash, D C
Emily Boyce, Wash, D C
Mrs Cmdor Smith, Wash, D C
Catharine Brown, colored, Wash, D C
Henry Rush, Gtwn, D C
Alex Kelley, Phil
Geo W Ridgeway, Phil
Baron de St Andre, Phil
Wilson Kent, Phil
Mrs Clement Barclay, Phil
Edw C Bacon, Phil
Geo Ingersoll, Phil
Thos G Meredith, Balt
John Dallam, Balt
J Howard, Lebanon, Tenn
Mrs Mgt Prescott, Salem, N J
Wm Humphries, Peoria, Ill
John F Gillespie, Natchez, Miss
Chas H Bottom, Trenton
Hugh B Jervis, Neward, Del
Rev J M Connell, Wilmington, Del
Miss Jane Lincoln, Ellicott's Mills, Md

[Some doubt appears to exist as regards the body said to be that of Mr Humphries, of Ill. The name P Loveland was found written in pencil on the watch-pocket of his pantaloons. There are no other marks by which to recognize the body, & no baggage checks were found upon him.]

Died: on Aug 29, at Burlington, N J, Capt Wm M Boyce, of Gtwn, D C.
+
Died: on Aug 29, at Burlington, N J, Emily M Boyce, eldest daughter of Capt Boyce, of Gtwn, D C.

Mrs Cmdor Jos Smith, so long a resident of Wash City, died shortly after the dreadful railroad catastrophe in which she was a sufferer to the extent of being bruised & shocked by concussion. She died in the Naval Hospital, in Phil, on Sat, having been taken to the residence of its cmder, a family friend, when able to leave Burlington. Her remains were taken to **Oak Hill Cemetery** [near Washington] on Monday, followed by a large concourse of mourning friends. -Star

$20 reward for the return of a Bay Mare stolen from the subscriber's premises on Sep 2. –Geo McCeney, near Wash City.

Orphans Court of Wash Co, D C. Letters of administration on the personal estate of Gollibt Jacob, late of Wash Co, deceased. –Heinrika Jacob, admx

WED SEP 5, 1855

Excellent & nearly new household, & kitchen furniture at auction on: Sep 10, at the residence of Walter Lenox, 411 F st, between 6th & 7th sts. -Jas C McGuire, auct

Monument to a Black. The Richmond Enquirer advocates the erection of a monument to the memory of Peter Francisco, a colored man, born a slave in Va, but emancipated at the commencement of the Revolution, & enlisted as a soldier. He served all through the war, & was subsequently Sgt-at-Arms of the Va Legislature. The above paragraph met out eye & according to his biography, which we published a short time ago, he was not a colored man, as therein stated. He knew nothing of his birth or parentage, but supposed he was born in Portugal, whence he was stolen when a child & carried to Ireland. His earliest recollections were those of boyhood in the latter country. While yet a lad he apprenticed himself to a sea-capt for 7 years, in pay for a passage to this country. On his arrival his time & services were sold to a Mr Winston, of Va, in whose service he remained until the breaking out of the Revolution. He obtained permission of his master to join the army & was engaged in active & effective service during the whole contest. He became the father of a respectable family in Va, & died in 1836, whilst holding the station of Sgt-at Arms of the Va Legislature.

Coroner Wilhelm held an inquest at N Y on Sat upon the body of Frances Young, a young married woman, 27 years of age, born in Ireland, who died on Sat from burns from a camphene lamp which exploded, the flames of which were fatal. In the same city, on Sun, Jos Frazer, age 4 years, died from burns received by his clothes catching fire from matches, which he ignited to amuse himself.

Norfolk, Sep 1. Mr L R Gibson died a day or two since in Princess Anne from fever; also, Parker Sharpley, at Ocean View. Six physicians are down at Norfolk: Drs Wm Selden, Geo J Halston, Sylvester, jr; McFadden & Quigenfeuse, of Phil, & Dr Baird, of New Orleans. Dr Rose is up & doing very well. Rev Jos Ashwanden, Catholic minister from Gtwn College, who went down to fill temporarily the place of Rev Mr Devlin, [also sick,] has been carried to the hospital sick with fever.

Died: on Sunday last, in Richmond, Va, after a few days' illness, Wm C Shields, for many years one of the editors of the Norfolk Beacon.

R A Worrell, Dr McCabe, Finley F Ferguson, Dr Francis Mallory, & Capt Hicks, of Norfolk, & Dr Jos N Schoolfield & Wm H Peters, of Portsmouth, arrived in this city yesterday, their mission being to obtain from the Gen Gov't permission to use **Fortress Monroe**, at Old Point Comfort, as a refuge for the afflicted people of Norfolk & Portsmouth. They were to meet with the Pres yesterday, which they did: but no decision had then been had upon the subject. [Sep 7-Permission refused.]

The Norfolk Herald of Sep 3. The following have been struck down by the yellow fever, since our last issue. Rev Mr Dibbrel, pastor of the Methodist Episcopal Church, died at his post, following the command of his Divine Master. John G H Hatton, Pres of the Common Council & teller of the Farmers' Bank of Va, aged 44. Ignatius Higgins, teller of the Va Bank, aged 39. Alex'r Feret, chief book-keeper of the Exchange Bank. Dr Geo J Halston, aged 38. Wm H Garnett, a most devoted & efficient co-worker with the Howard Assoc, aged 36. Wm Sylvester, son of the late Dr R W Sylvester, aged 20. Jas M Brooks, grocer, aged 45. Dennis O'Brian, undertaker, aged 39. Edw Daly, grocer, aged 60. Wm H Hallett, of the firm of Dixon & Hallett, grocers. Wm Doyle, aged about 50. Miss Sarah Freeman, daughter of Capt Wm G Freeman, aged 40. Miss Martha C Holden, a much-esteemed teacher, aged 44. Miss Bettie Baylor, daughter of Mrs Catharine Baylor. Miss Evelina Fitzhugh, aged 44. Wm K Storrs, keeper of the City Prison. Wm E Cunningham, senior editor of the Beacon, is no more. Compelled to suspend his editorial duties, he devoted himself to attending on the sick, & has fallen a martyr to the cause of humanity.

Fort Pierre. The Indians were quiet, & Laframbeau, one of the interpreters, reported having had a conversation with some of the Sioux Indians, in which they professed a willingness to give up the murderers of the mail party last fall, but thought it was not right to give up those who had killed Lt Grattan & his party. That, they contend, was a fair fight.

Marshal's sale: by writ of fieri facias under the lien law, issued from the Clerk's ofc of the Circuit Court of Wash Co, D C: public sale on Oct 4, for cash, all the right & title of John Rynex of, in, & to certain bldgs erected on lots 2 & 3 in Peter's Beatty's, Threlkeld's, & Deaken's Addition to Gtwn, or that piece of ground in front of said lots 2 & 3, measuring 126 feet & 8 inches on the south side of Water st; on the piece of ground lying in front of lot 4, in said addition; & on that part of Fayette st which extends from water st to the channel of the Potomac river; & on the western half of all that pary of Fayette st which lies between Water st & the Chesapeake & Ohio Canal; & on that part of Water st, 20 feet wide, north of Water st, entending along the line of the premises purchased by said Rynex from Miller & Duvall, consisting of a large brick moulding-house, 2 stone stacks for melting iron ore, 1 large brick wheel-house & connecting shed; seized & levied upon as the property of John Rynex, & sold to satisfy judicials No 68 to Mar term, 1849, in favor of Wm C & Simon J Temple. –Thos Woodward, Deputy of the late Marshal of the D C, Robt Wallace

Died: on Aug 18, after a long & painful illness, in her 13th year, Mary Adelaide, youngest daughter of Jas & Mary Keck.

THU SEP 6, 1855
Richmond Enquirer: Col Stockton, of Fayette Co, has recently sold 40,000 acres of land in that county to Dr Salisbury, of one of the Northern States, for $105,000, the money to be paid some time this month.

Constables sale: by writ of fieri facias, issued by Jno S Hollingshead, J P in Wash Co, at the suit of C Evans, against the goods & chattels of Chas Sampson, I have seized & taken in execution all the right, title, claim, interest at law & in equity of the said Chas Sampson in & to one long boat **J Lambirc Washington**; & give notice that on Sep 8 I will offer for sale the property so seized, by public auction, for cash. Sale to take place at 7th st & the canal. –A E L Keese, Constable.
–S C Davison & H Yeatman, constables

Mrd: on Sep 4, at West River, Anne Arundel Co, Md, by Rev Jos E Nourse, Dr Hamilton P Howard, of Wash City, D C, to Miss Maria E, daughter of A C Gibbs.

Verdict on the late Railroad Accident: Burlington, Sep 5. The coroner's jury returned a verdict this morning delaring that the deaths were caused by running the cars backward, & that the immediate cause was their coming in contact with the pair of horses drived by Dr Heineken, whose conduct is censured as careless & reckless; & that the engineer did not observe the rules of the company relative to blowing the whistle on approaching cross-roads. The verdict exonerates the conductor, who, it states, acted in accordance with the company's rules; but it declares that the company should adopt some more efficient mode of preventing the recurrence of such accidents.

FRI SEP 7, 1855
The War Dept has received intelligence of the death, on Sep 4, of Brvt Capt Chas G Merchant, 1st Lt 8th Infty U S Army, at East Pascagoula, Miss, after a brief illness.

Capt Geo F Lindsay, Assist Quartermaster U S Marine Corps, who has for some time past been discharging the duties of the Quartermastership of the Corps in Wash City, made vacant by the death of the late Maj Nicholson, has been promoted by the Pres to that position, with the rank of Major.

Railroad disaster. The last body that has been remaining at Burlington unrecognized since the sad accident of Wed last has been identified as that of T Loveland, of the firm of Messrs Green, Loveland & Co, merchants at Laconia, Ill. Mr Green, the partner of the deceased, came from Boston & at once recognized the remains.

Eben Lipscomb, indicted for the murder of his wife, [the mother of 7 children,] in June last, was tried a few days since before the Superior Court of Preston Co, Va, Judge Camden presiding. The jury rendered a verdict of murder in the first degree, & the Judge sentenced Lipscomb to be hung on Dec 14 next.

On Friday last an accommodation stage capsized near Ashville, N C, in which were Hon Wm Cain, [late Lt Govn'r of S C] & wife, & the wife, 2 daughters, & a son of Dr Elias Horlbeck, of Charleston. Mrs Cain was killed, dying in a few minutes, & all the others were much injured & bruised. The driver lost control of the horses.

Orphans Court of Wash Co, D C. Letters of administration on the personal estate of Marcelus Gallaher, late of Wash Co, deceased. –Edw A Gallaher, adm

Mrd: on Sep 6, by Rev Dr Pyne, W Geo Anderson, of Louisville, Ky, to Nannie, daughter of Josiah Colston, of Wash City.

Died: on Sep 6, Mary K, wife of Philip C Johnson, aged 59 years.

Died: on Sep 1, in Leesburg, Va, at an advanced age, Mrs Nancy Mason, relict of the late Westwood T Mason, of Loudoun Co, Va.

Charleston, Sep 6. The jury of inquest on the death of Capt Ayres, of the ship **Ariel**, have returned a verdict of murder against the 1st mate & the 2 apprentices.

SAT SEP 8, 1855
Circuit Court of Worcester Co, Md: in Equity. Saml S McMaster vs John Williams & others. The bill states that a certain Ann P White, late of said county, deceased, by her last will & testament, dated May 20, 1839, & duly proved, now on file in the ofc of the Reg/o Wills for said county, among other things, bequeaths the residue of her money to remain in the hands of Lewis West & David H White, with directions to them to pay over the interest thereof to her mother every year while she was a married woman, & in the event of her said mother becoming a widow, then the whole to her absolutely; & if her said mother should die a married woman, then she leaves the whole of said fund in the hands of her executor to be applied to the support of missionaries in India, under the direction of the Genr'l Assembly Board of Missions of the Presbyterian Church in the U S, & all the rest & residue of her property she gives to her mother. By said will Geo Hudson was appointed executor thereof, & letters testamentary were granted to him by the Orphans' Court of Worcester Co, by virtue whereof he possessed himself of the personal estate of said Ann P White, but died before he had completed the administration; & letters of administration, de bonis non, with a copy of the will annexed, were granted unto the cmplnt, Saml S McMaster, who, after giving bond, proceeded to complete said administration, & paid off the debts of said testatrix & all the legacies required to be paid off before the death of said testatrix's mother, after the payment of which there remains in his hands $4,521.88, $500 of which are to be paid to John White, son of Ambrose J White, a legatee under said will, leaving a balance of $4,021.88, which was invested, by order of the Orphans' Court of Worcester Co, before it came into the hands of cmplnt, & still remains invested in the same securities. The cmplnt further states that during the life of the mother of said testatrix, to wit, Sarah K

Williams, wife of John Williams, of said county, he paid over to her the interest on said money annually; by order of said Orphans' Court he retained $300 to meet anticipated expenses, & still has $125 undisposed of, to be added to the amount above mentioned; that the said Sarah Williams died in 1854, leaving her husband, John Williams, surviving her, & that since her death several persons claim said funds, to wit: the said John Williams, who hath instituted suit for the same; Wm Townsend, Justus M Bratten, Arra Clayvell, wife of Wm Clayvell, Mary Odell, Esther Dix wife of John Dix, & Joshua Atkinson, all of the State of Md; Geo Atkinson, whose residence is unknown, & Mary Chapman wife of Jas Chapman, of the State of Va, who are the next of kin of said testatrix, & threaten to institute suit for said funds against said cmplnt; also the Board of Foreign Missions of the Presbyterian Church in the U S of America, & the Board of Missions said to be incorporated under the laws of the State of N Y, who also threaten to institute legal proceedings against said cmpnt for said funds, claiming under said last will & testament; by reason of which conflicting claims the cmplnt, unable to determine to whom the funds belong, & being willing; & ready to pay the same to the party legally entitled, asks that the parties may be restrained from proceedings at law against him, & that they may interplead, & offers to being the money into court for the benefit of those entitled, & that subpoenas might issue against the residents of the State of Md commanding them to appear in said court. To this bill John Williams, one of the dfndnts, answers, admitting the charges in cmplnt's bill in regard to himself, & claims said fund as the surviving husband of Sarah K Williams, who survived said Ann P White, setting forth the death of said Ann, & the subsequent death of his said wife, Sarah, mother of said Ann, & that the bequest for the support of missionaries in India is void & of none effect; that said Ann left no child descendant, father, brother, sister, or descendant of a brother or sister, whereby, & by reason of said residuary devise & bequest to said Sarah K Williams, his deceased wife, he claims that said fund has devolved upon him the said John, with the interest & dividends which have accrued, or may accrue, from the death of Sarah K Williams, & he prays the court to decree accordingly. The other parties residents of the State of Md, & dfndnts in said cause, have also answered said bill, admitting the various matters & things in said cmplnt's bill alleged against them, & submitting to such decree as the court may think it proper to pass; but the said Board of Foreign Missions of the Presbyterian Church in the U S A, & the Board of Missions, & the said Geo Atkinson, & Jas Chapman & Mary Chapman, his wife, non-residents of the State of Md, as alleged in said bill, have not, nor hath either of them, appeared in said court. The absent dfndnts are warned to appear in this court, in person or by solicitor, on or before the 3rd Tue of May next. –Jas A Stewart -Edw D Martin, Clerk of the Circuit Court of Worcester Co.

Alex'r Ray purchased at the price of $13,500, the property sold on Sep 5, in Gtwn, by Barnard & Buckey, aucts. It is to be used as a coal depot by a company of which Ray is president. We may expect to have an extensive coal company in operation before the close of the year.

Died: on Sep 6, Wm King, in his 17th year. His funeral will take place from the family residence this afternoon at 3 o'clock.

Three ladies, well known in Boston, were drowned in the Kennebec river, near Swan Island, yesterday afternoon. As Mrs Dumaresque, of Roxbury, Mass, with her daughter, Miss Fanny Dumaresque, & Miss Richards, of Gardiner, Me, were sailing on the Kennebec, the boat was upset & the 3 ladies drowned. Mrs & Miss Dumaresque were the wife & daughter of Capt Dumaresque, the well known master of the ship **Romance of the Seas**. –Boston Traveller [Sep 10th newspaper: correct account: Miss Sarah Richards, daughter of F Richards, of Gardner, & Miss Fanny Dumaresq, daughter of Capt Philip Dumaresq, of this city, went in the water to bathe. Miss Richards getting alarmed, Miss Dumaresq went to her assistance, when both of them got into the current, & cried for help. Mrs Capt Dumaresq rushed to assist them, & they were all borne into the current & drowned. Mrs Dumaresq was in the house when she heard the cries of those in the water, & went to the shore to their aid. Her little daughter endeavored to dissuade her, but she said, "It is my duty." Those were her last words. She was formerly Miss Deblois, & belonged to the family of that name in this city. –Boston Courior]

Tutor wanted: must be an elderly gentleman of strict moral character, capable of teaching Latin & French, & all the higher branches of a thorough English education, to superintend the studies of 2 young gentlemen, age 20 & 17, & a boy of 10. Also, to be their companion out of study hours. Address me by mail: F S Key, Poolesville, Montg Co, Md.

A Wilmington, Del paper says that an Irish weaver, John Brown, who emigrated to the U S in 1794 & set up his loom in Wilmington, in the same place it now occupies, has ever since been engaged in weaving carpets there, & still continues it, as happy as the day is long, after a lapse of 61 years.

Wash Corp Ordinance: 1-Act for the relief of B C Wright & C G Klopfer: to pay to them the sum of $1.96, the amount of taxes they erroneously paid in 1854 on lots 1 & 21 in square 499.

New & used pianos for sale & to rent at 498 11th st, above Pa ave.
–Fr C Reichenbach

MON SEP 10, 1855
On Sat ofcrs arrived in town with John Fitzgerald, the murderer of his father, mother, & brother. He confesses that he alone did the dreadful dead, & that he also meant to murder his brother Patrick & set the house on fire. Fitgerald is confined in a cell in the jail in this city. His trial will be held next month. –Auburn American, Sep 3

Shooting affray on Aug 9: a man named Craine has been paying attention to Miss Susan M Newham, & wanted to marry her. She declined & he drew a revolver & killed her. The populace seized Craine, & organized a court for the purpose of trying him for murder. During this time Sheriff Buel rescued Craine & put him in jail.

The house of Wesley Vanaman, Hamilton township, N J, was destroyed by fire on Fri, & 2 sons of Mr Vanaman, aged 10 & 18 years, & Albert Schley, perished in the flames.

Orphans Court of Wash Co, D C. Letters of administration on the personal estate of Maj Augustus A Nicholson, late of the U S Marine Corps, deceased. –Somerville Nicholson, Nicholas Callan, adms

Orphans Court of Wash Co, D C. Letters of administration, with the will annexed, on the personal estate of Henry U Goodrich, late of Wash Co, deceased. –Marietta B Goodrich, admx, W A

Election to fill the vacancy in the Board of Common Council, occasioned by the resignation of W H Edes, [elected to the Board of Aldermen,] came off on Thu last. There were 618 votes, of which Mr Jas Goddard [K N] received 256, Mr David English 354 votes, & 4 blanks. Mr English's majority 96. -Advocate

Mr O Fisk, who was wounded in the late terrible railroad accident at Burlington, N J, & who suffered the amputation of his foot, died in that city on Fri from the severity of his injuries.

Mr Robt J Lawrenson died on Sat from injuries received by an accident on the Stonington Railroad a few days since. He was well known & highly esteemed in Wash City, where his parents & friends reside. He was employed as an agent of the Post Ofc Dept at the time of his death. [Sep 14th newspaper: a post morten examination of the body of R J Lawrenson, mail agent between Boston & N Y, showed his lungs to be badly inflamed & other injuries sufficient to cause his death. His remains were taken for interment to Washington, his native place, accompainied by his bereaved family & father. His life was insured for $1,000, & ofcr & employees on the railroads are collecting a purse to be tendered to his bereaved wife. –Boston Transcript] [Sep 15 newspaper: Mr Lawrenson leaves a widow, children, & afflicted parents & their family.]

Died: on Sep 8, in South Boston, of injuries sustained by the late accident on the N Y & Stonington Railroad, Rev Robt J Lawrenson, U S Mail Agent, & eldest son of Jas Lawrenson, of Wash City. His funeral will take place from Wesley Chapel, 5th & F sts, this afternoon at 4 o'clock.

Died: on Sep 6, at **Blakely**, her residence, in Jefferson Co, Va, Mrs Jane C Washington, aged 69 years, widow of the late John Augustine Washington, of **Mount Vernon**, Va. Her funeral will take place today at 11 o'clock A M, at **Mount Vernon**. The steamer **Thomas Collyer** will leave Washington at 9 o'clock A M for **Mount Vernon**, to afford such friends of her family as may desire to attend an opportunity of doing so.

Died: on Sep 7, in Wash City, in his 24th year, Mr Henry U Goodrich, formerly of St Albans, Vt, & for the last 16 months a resident of Wash City.

Died: on Sep 5, at Springdale, Fairfax Co, Va, of congestive fever, Geo Dale, in his 62nd year.

Yellow fever: partial list of the deaths reported: Sep 6-Mrs G W Camp, Mrs Chandler, Miss Chandler, Mr Boothy, Mrs John Allmand, Mrs T F Owens, Mr Small, custom-house, Mrs Ferret, Miss Baylor, Mrs W C Whithead, Mrs Harwood, Dr Sylvester, Wm D Robert, Whitting, Solomon. Dr Howe, from Balt, was sick with the fever, but doing well. Dr Campos, of Norfolk, also sick, but improving. Mayor Fiske is better. Dr Gooch, who was reported dead by the Richmond papers, was in an improved condition, so as to give hopes of his recovery. Two nurses from Balt died, also, Dr Bryant, of Phil. In Portsmouth on Fri: Dr Morris, of Balt was sick, & Dr Marshall was dying.

$100 reward: Information wanted. My father, Matthew Markland, left his boarding house on C st, between 3rd & 4½ sts, on Sep 2 last, & has not been seen or heard of. He was 60 years of age, 6 feet 2 inches high, heavy frame, & remarkably straight for one of his age. I will cheerfully give the reward to any person who will furnish information by which I will be enabled to find him. –A H Markland, 480 north L st.

TUE SEP 11, 1855
Accident on the Camden & Amboy Railroad on Sat. John Holland, the engineer, was so badly injured that amputation of one of his limbs became necessary, & he died shortly after the operation was performed.

Extensive sale of groceries, wines, & liquors: on Sep 17, at the Grocery Store of Shekell Brother, No 40, opposite Centre Market. –Jno T Towers, B O Shekell, trustees -C W Boteler, auct

First class bldg lot for sale on Sep 15: adjoins the newly built residence of Capt J B Montgomery, being lot 6 in square 218, fronting 50 feet on I st, running back 30 feet 7 inches to a 20 foot alley. -J C McGuire, auct

Died: on Sep 9, Jas C Eslin, in his 29th year. His funeral will take place from the residence of his father, near the Columbian College, this afternoon, at 4 o'clock.

Died: on Sep 4, Mary, wife of Purser Edw Fitzgerald, U S Navy.
+
Died: on Sep 2, Frank T, aged 23; & on Sep 5, Charles H, aged 26, sons of Purser Fitzgerald, all of Norfolk, Va.

$50 reward for runaway negro girl Margery Arnold, about 16 or 17 years old. Her mother lives with Mr Rowe; one sister with Mr Angues, on I st; one with Mr Polk, on F st; & one belongs to Mr John Smith, but is living to herself. She has an uncle living with Mr John C Rives & an aunt living at Mr C B Calvert's piggery, on the Balt road. She has a brother living at the Kirkwood House & 2 sisters living at the residence of the late Govn'r Sprigg, PG Co. Her father lives at Mrs Sanders', near Rock Creek. –Tilgman Hilleary, Post Ofc, Buena Vista, PG Co, Md.

WED SEP 12, 1855
Mrs Evans, of Balt, after washing an infant 10 months old in a tub of water, laid it on the floor while she left the room. A larger child put the infant back in the tub, & attempted to resume the washing of it; but the poor baby's head was kept under water so long that when the mother returned she found it dead.

Latest from Norfolk. Deaths at Norfolk during the 24 hours ending at noon on Monday were the following: Physicians deceased on Sunday:

Dr Craycroft, of Phil
Dr Smith, of Columbia, Pa
Dr John S Marshall, Balt
Dr Fleas, a German physician of Balt
Dr Gooch, a promising physician of Richmond
Dr Morse, of Richdmond
Dr Balfour, of Norfolk, died at the Springs

Deaths at Portsmouth: Dr Williams, Pres of the S & R Railroad; John Collins brother of Dr Collins; & Geo W Chambers

<u>Victims of the fever at Norfolk:</u>
R S Barnard, druggist
Jas Harris
Mr Jackson
Miss Woodeard
Miss Whitehead
Mr Daudler
Mr Steaten
Two Miss Hambureys
Miss M Huchings
John Hammer
Barbara Suddeway
David Christopher
Jane Simpson
___ Lewis, aged 10
Miss John Saunders, aged 15
Wife of Rev Leonidas Smith
Wm B Sorey, U S Marshal
Jasper Menser, watchman
Fred'k Johnson, How Assoc
Miss Gieslin, aged 16
Miss Hetty Revel, aged 45
Son of N B Wilroy
Mr Baker
Solomon Spratt
E Balance & 7 of his family
Mrs B B Walters
Mrs John Seldon
Miss Virginia Seldon
Mr Alex Ferret
Mrs Alex Ferret

Mrs Holden	Jas Cherry, jr
Miss Martha Holden	Wm Mehegan
Mr Richd Hall	Mr Robinson
Mr Wall	John Granberry
Master Granbury	Miss Mary Woodward
Mr Geo Barnes	Theodore Cunningham
Mr Nelson Meyer	Miss Susan Nimmo
Jas Chearney	Mrs Adams
A Briggs	Wm Doyle
Jas N Myers	Mrs J M Smith
Susan Flanagan	Theodore Owens
Wm D Dunbar	Mrs Henry Harwood
Jos Barron, aged 15	Mrs Wm C Whitehead
Dulton Wheeler, How Assoc	Mrs Stikes
Mrs Aristides Smith	Thos Fentress
Archibald Briggs	Mrs John Alaband

There was excitement at Suffolk, Va, on account of the death of Mr Riddick, who had been at neither Portsmouth or Norfolk since the disease commenced. The physicians pronounced his disease typhoid fever, but rumor made it yellow fever.

By an arrival from **Fort Davis** the San Antonio Ledger has the following account of a fight with a party of savages. Lt Randal, on his way to his post with Maj Ruff, volunteered to take command of 20 riflemen & followed a fresh Indian trial. He discovered a party of 15 Indians in a canon. He succeeded in killing 8 of them, mortally wounded 2, & force 2 off a precipice of 60 feet. One child was taken prisoner. Of the 15 Indians only 2 escaped. The Indians only fired one shot, & that was by the chief from a Gov't rifle. He was killed immediately after he fired by the guide, & scalped by Lt Randal. More than one half the party were females dressed as males. 8 horses & all their property fell into the hands of Lt Randal.

Obit-died on Aug 28, at Bailey's Springs, in Alabama, after a protracted illness, Hon Henry W Collier, Ex-Govn'r of the State of Alabama. He was a native of Va, was raised & educated in S C, & emigrated to Alabama about the time he attained his majority. He was for 12 years Chief Justice of his adopted State, & more recently served 4 years [2 election terms] as its Chief Magistrate.

On Thu, Sep 6, Michl Kennedy, a laborer on the aqueduct, near the Great Falls, was beaten by some of his drinking companions & then left alone in the woods. He was seen wandering about the next morning, bruised & bleeding, & taken to the laborers' quarters, where he died an hour later. Hugh & John Bruniham have been arrested on the charge of having caused his death, & committed to jail at Rockville.

Sale of retail stock of dry good: on Sep 17, at 12 North Chas st, Balt, Md, the entire stock belonging to Mr Thos R Crane, who is closing his business preparatory to removing to the country. –Taylor & Gardner, Aucts, Balt, Md

Died: on Sat, at Fredericksburg, Va, after an illness of 4 weeks, Frank Taylor Smith, only child of Henry Smith, of Washington, in his 18th year.

Harrisburg, Sep 11. Mail train going West was thrown off the track by running over a cow near New Cumberland. Wm Able, a fireman, was instantly killed, & John G Miller, mail agent, John Struly, engineer, Quinten Ratcliffe, conductor, & ___ Falls, agent of Adams' express, were seriously injured.

THU SEP 13, 1855

Norfolk & Portsmouth-yellow fever. The steamer **Georgia**, Sep 11, 1855. Among the passengers who come to fill up the vacancies of those who have passed away, consist of Dr De Castro; Dr Wilson, of Cuba; Dr Freeman, who returns from Phil after a brief visit; Drs Moore & Hintze, of Balt. In addition to this valuable medical aid, Messrs Hersel, Gordon, Beard, & Parker, of Phil, come as nurses, & Townsend, of Phil, as druggist. From Portsmouth: among the dead are Richd Eskridge, son of Ray Vernon Eskridge; Rev Vernon Eskridge, U S Navy; & Rev Jas Chisholm, of the Episcopal Church. Dr Smith, of Columbia Pa, & Dr Marshall, of Balt, died yesterday, & were buried side by side. Of a party of 11 doctors & nurses who went down in the steamer **Georgia** on Aug 29 of 6, viz: Drs Miller, Smith, Fleeas, Marshal, & nurse Craven, are dead. The houses of citizens who have fled are, it is believed, pretty generally respected. Few cases of theft are reported, & burglaries are not common. The plague fly disappeared on Thu. They are insects very much like mosquitoes, escept with large wings, & their bites greatly inflame the flesh & raise great knots on it. When they came here their bellies were red, & when they left they had become yellow. –Petersburg Express

Obit-died: on Sep 2, 1855, at Richmond, Va, Wm C Shields, aged about 64 years. He was a native of Phil, & the 3rd son of John Shields, deceased, a prominent & wealthy merchant of that city. In 1809 he was appointed a midshipman in the U S navy by Pres Madison, &, serving with distinction in the war of 1812, he became a prisoner under Sir Jas Yeo. Due to the harships he experienced during his captivity he contracted hemorrhage, which compelled him to resign his commission & leave the service soon after regaining his libery by an exchange of prisoners. He then made his permanent abode in Va & became the founder of the Richmond Compiler. In 1844 he established the Norfolk Courier, which he continued to conduct until a year or two previous to his death. He died of yellow fever, soothed at the last moments by the presence of two of his devoted children & the attentions of Drs Snead & Marks, of Richmond.

John T Houchins, accused of robbing the mail between Patrich C H & Pittsylvania, Va, was arrested in Salisbury, Sat last. He confessed the crime. –North Carolinian

Next to Jul 4, 1776, Sep 17, 1787, is the most memorable epoch in our history, the celebration of the anniversary of the adoption of the *Federal Constitution* in Wash City & in Balt, Md.

Died: on Sep 12, at his residence, E st, between 6th & 7th sts, John Hall, aged 55 years. His funeral will take place from his residence, this day, at 4 o'clock.

Died: Sep 3, in Norfolk, Va, of yellow fever, Mrs Eliz E Chandler, relict of J R Chandler, Surgeon U S Navy. On Sep 5, Alice Lee, eldest daughter; & on Sep 10, Augustus Page, eldest son of J R & Eliz E Chandler.

Died: on Sep 10, in Norfolk, of the yellow fever, Thos Briggs, a resident of Wash City, aged 40 years. He was a native of Cambridge, England, & left that country in 1836. He served in the U S Army as sgt in Capt Kirby's company of the 2nd artl during the Fla war, & in the N E boundary commission under Maj Graham. He afterwards followed his business [that of a tailor] in Wash City. When the fever broke out he volunteered his services as a nurse & left for Norfolk without pecuniary assistance. He died a martyr in the cause of humanity. –B

Died: on Sep 11, at the Marine Barracks, in Wash City, Elizabeth Ellen, only daughter of Sgt Robt & Briget Hamilton, aged 15 months.

Died: on Sep 11, Edward, the youngest child of Geo S & Ellen E Noyes, aged 18 months.

Font Hill for sale: a beautiful bldg site of about 10 acres, overlooking Gtwn, Wash, & the Potomac river, 10 minutes' walk from the omnibus stand in Gtwn. Price to one who will build $1,000. Also, *Rock Hill*, immediately adjoining, of about 20 acres. Price $3,000. The quarry on it alone is worth the money. –Lloyd & Co, opposite the Treasury bldg.

Proposals will be received for the erection of a brick church & school house attached on the s w corner of Prince & Paine sts, in the city of Alexandria, Va.
–Chas Haskins, Architect, ofc Pa ave, between 10th & 11th sts.

Orphans Court of Wash Co, D C. In the case of Benj L Jackson, adm of Harriett E Jurdine, deceased: the administrator & Court have appointed Oct 2 next, for the final settlement of the personal estate of said deceased, of the assets in hand.
–Ed N Roach, Reg/o wills

FRI SEP 14, 1855
Dr Chaloner, of Phil, still continues in attendance on the wounded by the railroad accident at Burlington. The body of Mr Otis Fisk was removed on Sat to Conn, where he leaves a widow & 10 children. The wounded remaining are Mrs Gillespie, Mr & Miss Newbold, Mrs Hulseman, Mrs Boyce, Mrs Caroline Pringle, & Messrs Kelley, Finley, O'Kane, Pew, Dixey, Taylor, Mrs Phelps, & servant girl Caroline.

Groceries, liquors, & store fixtures at auction: on Sep 19, at the Grocery Store of W A Orme, 7th & I sts. –A Green auct

Extensive sale of musical stock, instruments & fixtures: on Sep 28, at the Music Store of Hilbus & Hitz, 327 D st. –John Carroll Brent, trustee -A Green, auct

The purchaser of the property herein named having failed to comply with the terms of sale made on Aug 27, I will resell, at his risk & cost, by deed of trust from John A Grimes, recorded in J A S No 29, at Folios 364, of the land records of Wash Co, D C: sale on the premises, in Gtwn, Sep 20th, the lot of ground on the south side of Water st, between the warehouses recently occupied by Edw Shoemaker & Messrs Wheatley & Morrison. –Hugh Caperton, trustee -Edw S Wright, auct, Gtwn

The crew of ship **Ariel** have been examined before the Coroner's Jury at Charleston in regard to the murder of Capt Eayres on that ship on passage from N Y for Bombay. On the night of the murder Mr Pratt, 2nd mate, had the first watch, from 8 to 12, & Mr Lakeman, 1st mate, the second, from 12 to 4. Mr Pratt spoke to him at 12, & that was the last time that he was seen alive. From some inexplicable cause Mr Lakeman neglected to awaken him at 4, & at about 7 the next morning he was found by the steward dead in his bed. He had been killed by blows inflicted with an axe & a knife. A boy named Giraud confessed to another boy, Anderson, that he had murdered the captain. The crew testified that blood stains had been found on Giraud's clothes & a bloody knife in his chest.

Murder a few days ago in Fletcher, Vt, 20 miles north of Milton Falls. A son of Mr Chase went into the garden of Mr Fulton & took a melon which Mr Fulton had forbidden him, whereupon he caught the boy & whipped him severely. Mr Chase, with the boy, went to see Fulton, argument ensued, & he stabbed & killed him. Before the ofcrs could secure him he committed suicide.

Yellow fever. Increasing mortality at Norfolk & Va: among the dead are Mr Cunningham, of Farmers' Bank; Mr Johnson, apothecary, stated to be from Wash; Mrs Walke, wife of the Episcopal minister; Mrs Geo Loyall; & Mrs Dr Sylvester.

Orphans Court of Wash Co, D C. In the case of Wm M Mann, adm of Susan Davenport, deceased, the administrator & Court have appointed Sep 29, for the final settlement of the personal estate, of the assets in hand. –Ed N Roach, Reg/o wills

Mrd: on Sep 13, in Wash City, by Rev G W Samson, Mr John W Davis to Miss Sarah A Dove, both of Fairfax Co, Va.

Mrd: on Sep 11, in the M E Church South, by Rev Jas A Duncan, Mr Wm Gethrell, of Montg Co, Md, to Miss Maria Louisa Zimmerman, of Alexandria, Va.

Died: on Sep 12, in Wash City, Miss Eliza N Jackson, formerly of Va. Her funeral will be from the Foundry Church this morning at 10 o'clock.

Closing out our Stationery & Fancy Goods to make room for our immense stock of fine goods for the fall & winter trade. –John F Ellis, 306 Pa ave, between 9th & 10th.

SAT SEP 15, 1855

Norfolk & Portsmouth: Correspondence of the Balt American. The steamer **Georgia**, Sep 13, 1855. For the 3 days ending with Tue last there were 149 deaths. Dr Marsh, of Phil; Dr Nunn, of Savannah; & Dr West, of N Y, are on the street today for the first time since their sickness. Dr J F Powell, our surgeon, saw Dr Morris, of Balt, today, & found him doing well, & his physician advises him to return to Balt as soon as he is able to do so. Dr Whitehead, acting Mayor of Norfolk, is convalescent. Interment in the cemeteries in Norfolk: Catholic cemeteries: 120; Jewish cemeteries: 12; Potter's Field; 17. Interment at Julappi: 32. The Doctor Briggs reported dead should have been his father Archibald Briggs. Dr Briggs has not been sick. Rev Mr Hume is to remove the children of the Portsmouth Orphan Asylum to Richmond in a few days.

Family groceries at auction: on Sep 21, at the Grocery Store of R D'Tweedy, Pa ave & 13th st, the entire stock & store fixtures. –C W Boteler, auct

Workmen are now engaged in taking down the old town house of Gen Washington, on Cameron st, between Pitt & St Asaph sts, Alexandria, Va, & it will very shortly be numbered with the things that were. Tradition says that Washington was the architect & his family servants performed the work; the same measurably true at **Mount Vernon**. Christ Church, where the Father of his Country worshiped, & which is still in possession of his family Bible, stands in the middle of the street, a short distance above, & in full view from the door to this house, where, it is said, the venerable chief might so often be seen sitting on the frequent occasions that business or pleasure called him to Alexandria. The house for nearly 20 years & until a few months past has been occupied by a worthy family, the Misses Jordan, whose grandparents were neighbors of Washington, & who still show, with just pride, an ancient candlestick & other relics that were presented to their ancestors in token of friendly regard by Washington himself. –Alexandria Gaz

Mrd: on Sep 10, at Trinity Church, N Y, by Rev John F Young, Lewis Cruger to Louisa E Williamson, both of Charleston, S C.

Phil, Sep 14. Capt Saml W Downing, late of the U S Navy, died yesterday at his residence near Bristol, Pa. [Sep 17th newspaper: He was but recently deprived of his command by a court martial, owing to his conduct in South America, in receiving Cmdor Coe on board of a U S ship after Coe had betrayed the cause in which he was engaged. The Phil Inquirer says that Capt Downing, was a gallant ofcr who possessed many fine qualities. He was a midshipman under Decatur.]

Died: yesterday, in her 39th year, Mrs Susan Ingle, wife of Mr Jos Ingle. Her funeral will take place tomorrow at 4 o'clock P M, from her husband's residence.

MON SEP 17, 1855

Trustee's sale of *Exchange Hotel*: by deed of trust from David A Hall, dated Aug 1, 1842, recorded among the land records of Wash Co, D C, in Liber W B No 95, folios 160 thru 163: public auction on Oct 1: part of lots 4 & 5 in square 490, being the same property which was conveyed by the Bank of Wash to said David A Hall by deed bearing even date with the deed of trust aforesaid, with improvements thereon. This property fronts on C st, between 4½ & 6th sts, well known as the *Exchange Hotel*. –Jas Adams, trustee -Jas C McGuire, auct [Sep 19th newspaper: Frank Selden states that he will protest against & contest said sale, inasmuch as he is not bound for any rent whatever, but, on the contrary, entitled to damages, because the said eating house & the appurtencnces have been & are in a dilapidated condition, & very far from being in the state of repair guaranted by the lease under which he holds the said premises, having been out of repair the whole time.]

Mrs Gillespie, relict of the late John F Gillespie, a victim of the late railroad catastrophe, died on Fri at Burlington, N J, where she has been a sufferer ever since the amputation of her limb. This makes the 24th death by this sad calamity.

Ky Statesman: there is an old citizen living in Pulaski Co, Elijah Denney, who is perhaps the oldest man in Ky. He will be 118 years of age on Sep 10, & is as active as many men at 40. He served 7 years in the war of the Revolution, & was wounded at the siege of Charleston; was at the siege of Savannah & in the battle of Eutaw Springs. He was also present at the battles of Camden, King's Mountain, & Monks' Corner. He served under Cols Horry & Marion, & was an eye wtiness of the sufferings & death of Col Isaac Hayne, of S C, an early victim of the Revolution. He is a strict member of the Baptist Church, & rides 6 miles to every regular meetingof his church. He has 4 sons & 5 daughters, all living; the eldest is now in his 78th year & the youngest son is 51. He is perhaps the only surviving soldier of Francis Marion, Sumter, & Horry.

Died: yesterday, Mrs Mary Boyd, wife of Mr Geo Boyd. Her funeral will take place this afternoon, at 3 o'clock, from her husband's residence, 262 F st.

On Fri evening the Balt & Wilmington railroad ran over Mrs Updyke near Newport, Dela, killing her instantly. The unfortunate woman was walking on the track, & being very deaf did not hear the train.

A daughter of Mr Geo Hood, employed in the factory at Mechanicsville, in Attleboro, met with an accident on Thu. As she was combing her hair while at work, her tresses were caught in the machinery, & with a portion of her scalp, torn from her head. In attempting to extricate herself one hand & arm were also much lacerated.

Burlington Railroad accident. Among the passengers were Mrs Lincoln Phelps, Principal of the Parapsco Female Institute, near Ellicott's Mills, Md, two of her daughters, & a female servant. Her eldest daughter was killed almost instantly. Mrs Phelps & her youngest daughter were much bruised, & the servant had the fingers on one of her hands cut off. The death of Mrs Phelps would be felt as a great loss by the community, as the Patapsco Institute is unquestionably among the best schools in the U S for finishing the education of young ladies. There are usually about 80 scholars at that school, which are as many as Mrs Phelps desires to teach. Mrs Phelps is still at Burlington, & able to walk about her room, & expects to open the school on Sep 27. She will be assisted in her duties as Principal by her daughter, Mrs O'Brien. -Globe

Com'rs sale: by decree rendered in the suit of John P Dulany vs Selden, Withers & Co, in the Alexandria Circuit Court, on Jun 1, 1855, the undersigned will sell at public auction, in front of Saml Catts' Tavern, at West End, Alexandria, on Nov 15, the following real & personal property: farm known as *Morvin*, adjoining the lands of Messrs Daingerfield, Corbett, & others, on Four-Mile Run, Alexandria Co; contains 272 acres; with a brick dwlg house, containing 8 rooms, brick ofc, ice house, large barn, & servants' house. Also, 2 horses, 2 mules, several head of cattle, one 4 horse wagon, ploughs, & other farming utensils. To examine this property call on Mr S J Merchant, the manager on the farm. -Fairfax H Whiting, Thos M Monroe, David Funsten, Com'rs

Died: on Sep 15, aged 17 days, Matthew St Clair, infant son of John G & Bertha M Clarke.

Died: on Sep 7, in Portsmouth, Va, of yellow fever, Miss Alyda M Vermillion, eldest daughter of Mr John Vermillion.
+
Died: on Sep 11, in Portsmouth, Va, of yellow fever, Mr John Vermillion, in his 55th year.

Balt, Sep 16. Miss Patterson, of Phil, is not dead, as heretofore announced.

TUE SEP 18, 1855
Chancery sale: by decree of the Orphans Court of Wash Co, D C, in the case of Offutt & Co vs R Davis' administrator & heirs, No 1,045 equity, dated Nov 16, 1854: public auction on Oct 10, on the premises, part of lot 43 in Old Gtwn, about 33 feet east from Market Space, & fronting 24 feet on the south side of Bridge st, with a 3 story brick house. –Walter S Cox, Trustee -E S Wright, auct

Cmdor S H Stringham, who had been for the last 3 years in command or our naval squadron in the Mediterranean, has received preparatory orders to take command of the navy yard & station at Boston.

Trustee's sale: by deed of trust, executed by Benj E Green, dated Mar 27, 1845, recorded in the land records of Wash Co, D C, in Liber W B 115, folios 327 thru 330: public auction on Oct 17, in front of the premises, square 729 in Wash City; that is to say, all that part of lot 13 in said square. Also, lot 14 & part of lot 13, in said square. This property fronts on First st east, between East Capitol & A sts south, facing Capitol square, & is improved by substantial 2 story brick bldg. -Johnson Hellen, Jas Adams, trustees -Jas C McGuire, auct

Trustee's sale of unexpired term of lease, good-will, & furniture of *Nat'l Eating House*, 6th & Pa ave, by deed in trust from Frank Selden, dated Oct 13, 1854, recorded in Liber J A S 87, folios 297: public sale on Oct 1, at the Eating House: the said lease expires on Dec 1, 1856. –Wm B Webb, trustee -J C McGuire, auct

The American Order in the city of Balt has made the following nominations for Judicial ofcrs, viz: Z Collins Lee, for Judge of Superior Court; Milton Whitney, for Prosecuting Atty; Saml S Gaskins, for Sheriff; Chas G Griffith, Saml G Spicer, & Edw D Kemp, for Judges of Orphans' Court; & Wm J Hamill, for Clerk of Court of Common Pleas.

S Eaton, of Syracuse, N Y, has been arrested for forging pension papers. He was held in $5,000 bail to appear before the U S Court at Albany in Oct next. –Albany Journal

Mrd: on Aug 13, at *Locust Grove*, Taliaferro Co, Ga, by Rev Peter Whelan, Dr Rogers Semmes, of Canton, Miss, to Miss Sarah A Griffin, of *Locust Grove*.

Mrd: on Sep 13, at Grace Church, [Island,] by Rev Alfred Holmead, Mr Wm W Turner to Miss Mary M Randolph, daughter of Col Wm B Randolph, all of Wash City.

Died: on Sep 5, at McConnellsville, Ohio, Emma, wife of Henry C Derrick, of Wash.

Gorham, N H, Sep 10. Mr Bourne, of Kennebunk, Me, with his wife & daughter, left the **Glen House**, at Mount Washington, yesterday, to ascend the mountain on foot without a guide. They lost their way & remained without shelter all night. All suffered extremely, & the daughter died during the night. Mr & Mrs Bourne were discovered this morning, & are now doing well. [Sep 22nd newspaper: on Sep 13, Miss Bourne, of Maine, together with her uncle & his daughter, determined to go up **Mount Washington**, & to remain during the night at the house upon the summit. They were told at the half-way house not to proceed. The advice was disregarded. They lost their way & his niece Miss Bourne died during the night. She had promised her father she would return home by Sat, & the coffined body was carried home as promised. –Corr Evening Post.]

Wash Stove Manufactory, 267 Pa ave & 11th st, Wash. -Jas Skirving, agent

Miss Ann Young, having returned to Wash after a short absence, will resume the duties of her Academy at the old location in the West End, corner of I & 18th sts, on Oct 1.

Teacher wanted: a single gentleman to take charge of a small private school. Address Dandrige Sale, Loretto, Va.

WED SEP 19, 1855
From Norfolk & Portsmouth-yellow fever: among the deaths we are sorry to see the name of Rev Mr Chisholm, struck down while faithfully discharging his duty. Another son of the French Consul, Mr Sehisano, is dead in Norfolk, & also dead are Mrs Bernard & child. She is the relict of the late Robt S Bernard, the apothecary, who died of the fever very recently. She was the daughter of T G Broughton, the venerable editor of the Herald. Also dead is Rev Mr Bagnell, Baptist clergyman. Dr Selden is not dead. Dr Upshur is very ill. Dr D M Wright has entirely recovered.

There will be a meeting of the descendants & collateral relations of Gen Israel Putnam, of Revolutionary memory, at the Putnam Station, on the Norwich & Worcester Railroad on Oct 24. The next day there will be a public address & dinner. The object of these meetings is to raise $3,000, required by the Legislature of Conn to obtain from it a grant of a like sum to erect a monument over the remains of Gen Israel Putnam.

Sad occurrence in Henrico Co, Va, on Sat last: Mrs Martha E Stevens had paid a visit to one of her neighbors, & while there Mrs Sarah Garrison, the lady on whom she had called, took a pistol in her hand & left the house to shoot a bird for a sick child, Mrs Stevens accompanying her. When they saw some one approaching them, Mrs Garrison attempted to conceal the pistol behind her, but the hammer caught in the folds of her dress, causing immediate explosion, & lodged the entire load in Mrs Stevens' side. Her injuries are beyond the power of medical skill to heal.

Albany Argus: Judge Mitchell, of the Supreme Court of N Y, decided in the case of John P Beekman, adm with the will annexed of Wm Barthrop, deceased, against the people of the State of N Y & others, which involved the validity of certain trusts for charitable purposes created by the will of the deceased. The validity of the will is sustained, & the trusts directed to be carried into execution. The amount involved is said to be near $300,000. The administrator, Dr Beekman, has been in possession of this estate since 1839, during all which time the charitable purposes of the testator have remained unexecuted. The administrator is now to account for this large fund. The administrator claimed that the will was void, in which event one half of the estate would fall to him & his brother, Thos Beekman, & the residue to a sister of Dr Barthrop in England; & the suit now decided was prosecuted upon that theory, with, as appears, a disastrous result.

Household & kitchen furniture at auction on: Sep 24, at the residence of Mrs Ennis, A st, between Delaware ave & 1st st: all her furniture. -Jas C McGuire, auct

Wash Corp: 1-Ptn from Honora Fitzpatrick for the remission of a fine: referred to the Cmte of Claims. 2-Act for the relief of Jacob F King; & act for the relief of Robt Devereux: referred to the Cmte of Claims. 3-Cmte appointed to examine into the eligibility of the Assessors elect beg leave to report: Mr Douglass is duly qualified; Israel Wayson is duly qualified; Wm H Clampett, returned as Assessor, is not, in the opinion of your cmte, qualified for said ofc, inasmuch as he was born in a foreign country & has not been naturalized, as required by the 5th section of the charter of 1820: John L Smith, John P Pepper, Thos J Fisher, J H McCutchen, J H Peters, & John Bayne. Report read & ordered to lie on the table. 4-Ptn of John T Davis; ptn of Bazell Bell: both for the remission of a fine: referred to the Cmte of Claims. 5-Act to erect a foot bridge across **Tiber creek** at a point of its intersection with the canal: passed.

New music: "What is Home without a Mother," by Alice Hawthorne, author of 'Listen to the Mocking Bird; My Cottage Home; Song of the Farmer; Let us Live with Hope; How Sweet are the Roses; I set my Heart upon a Flower; & Pet of the Cradle." Price 25 cents each. –Winner & Shuster, Music Publishers, 110 north 8th st, Phil, Pa.

Fatal accident: Mrs Jane Williams, living in N Y, was accidentally burnt on Sunday night by the bursting of a camphene lamp.

Teacher wanted in a Classical Academy of high order in Va. Apply to Mr Robt Bell, Bookseller, Alexandria.

For rent, the spacious new store & cellar in the bldg lately erected by the subscriber on the corner of 9th & D sts. Apply to S P Franklin, Pa ave, between 9th & 10th.

Mrd: on Sep 18, at the Assembly's Church, by Rev Andrew G Carothers, Mr Uriah F Lansdale to Miss Anne E Spates, both of Montg Co, Md.

Died: on Sep 17, at the residence of her son-in-law, Thos Thornley, in Wash City, Mrs Mary McComb, aged 69 years. Her funeral will take place from the Warden's apartments of the U S Penitentiary today at 10 o'clock.

THU SEP 20, 1855
On Aug 7 Mr Alfred Marsh, residing about 9 miles east of Notasulge, Miss, had 3 of his children killed by lightning. They were 16, 10, & 2 years of age. They were returning to the house when they were killed by lightning. The eldest had the youngest on his shoulders when death overtook them.

Toronto Leader of Sat says: information was laid before the police magistrate last Wed, by a resident of that city, to the effect that he recognized Jas McNally as having been the perpetrator of a murder committed in Boston 4 or 5 years ago. A merchant named Smith was owed some money by McNally, who kept a grocery store in Boston, & he reproached him for not paying the money. McNally drew a knife & stabbed Smith, who died almost immediately, & escaped. He had been residing for some years in Totonto. He confessed that he was the party that murdered Mr Smith, & is now in jail awaiting the examination.

Yellow fever: among the deaths recently, in Norfolk, were Dr Geo L Upshur, Ex-Mayor Delany, & another son of Rev A Smith. Josiah Wills, Pres of the Va Bank, & John Tunis, sr, are ill.

Hon W B W Dent, late a member of Congress from Ga, died at his residence in Newnan, Ga, on Sep 9, after a long illness.

Health report: ofc of the Board of Health, Wash, Sep 19, 1855. Interments during the month ending Aug 31, 1855: total 170. –H P Howard, M D, Pres.

Orphans Court of Wash Co, D C. Letters testamentary on the personal estate of Raphael R Triay, late of Wash Co, deceased. –Francis R Triay, exc

The undersigned will offer at public sale, on the premises, the house & lot of land at the Anacostia Bridge, now in the occupancy of the bridge keeper, Mr Bailey Brown, for cash to the highest bidder. Possession to be given Jan 1, 1856.
–Margery Darnall, Richd N Darnall, adms of the late F L Darnall.

Mrd: on Sep 18, in the First Presbyterian Church, by Rev Byron Sunderland, D D, Mr F L Moore to Miss Ginnie Campbell, youngest daughter of Wm H Campbell, all of Wash City.

Mrd: on Sep 18, by Rev J G Butler, Wm H Mills to Mary A Millington, both of Wash City.

Mrd: on Sep 18, in Wash City, by Rev Mr Sunderland, Lt Junius B Wheeler, 2nd Regt of Cavalry, to Miss Emily T Beale, of Wash.

Died: on Sep 18, suddenly, in Rockville, Montg Co, Md, Dr Turner Wootten.

Died: on Sep 19, suddenly, in Wash City, S B Knox, 2nd Assist Engineer U S N. His funeral will be from the residence of his mother-in-law, Mrs Selden, on N Y ave, between 9th & 10th sts, this evening, at 4 o'clock P M.

Died: yesterday, Caleb Pike Smith, late Editor of the Belknap [N H] Gaz, & at the time of his decease a clerk in the Gen Land Ofc in Wash City. His funeral is this day at 12 M, at his late residence, at the corner of D & 15th sts.

T F Cronin informs his neighbors that he will open school on Oct 1. Apply at 79 Washington st, between 4th & 5th sts.

For rent: desirable brick dwlg house on N Y ave, next door to 2nd Presbyterian Church, between 13th & 14th sts. Apply to Dr Sam E Tyson, 10th & I sts.

FRI SEP 21, 1855
Excellent household & kitchen furniture at auction on: Oct 2, at the residence of Capt Magruder in one of the bldgs known as Gadsby's Row, on Pa ave, between 20th & 21st sts. -Green & Scott, aucts

Died: on Sep 9, in New Orleans, Lucius C Duncan, suddenly struck down by a fit of apoplexy. He had nearly recovered, when on Jul 28, the same terrible malady returned upon him with fatal severity. He was a native of Louisiana, & being left an orphan at an early age, he was sent by a generous patron to the North to be educated. He was placed at school at Munson, Mass, completed his studies, & entered Yale College in 1817, the last year of Pres Dwight & the first of Pres Day. He returned to New Orleans in 1821, & practiced law. In later life he indulged his love of foreign travel by several visits to the Old World. –New Haven Palladium

Orphans Court of Wash Co, D C. Letters of administration on the personal estate of John Hall, late of Wash Co, deceased. All persons indebted to the estate to settle as soon as possible; all having claims against said deceased to exhibit the same.
–Eleanor Hall

Mrd: on Sep 19, in Wash City, by Rev G W Samson, Mr Wm H Beardsley, of Wash, to Miss Maria S O Schiebler, of Balt.

Mrd: on Sep 5, in Gtwn, by Rev B F Brooke, Thos Rich to Mrs Mgt S Miller, both of Wash City.

Meeting of the Union Guards on Sep 18, preamble submitted by H C McLaughlin, address by Jas Donnelly. Meeting regarding the death of 2nd Lt Thos Briggs. –J Lackey, sec Union Guards. Portsmouth & Norfolk papers please copy.

SAT SEP 22, 1855
Steamer **North Carolina**, Sep 20. The noble Pres of the Howard Association, Wm B Ferguson, is prostrated with yellow fever.

Household & kitchen furniture, rare oil paintings, china, & glassware at auction, on Oct 4, at the residence of Mr Gevers, Minister from the Netherlands, who is about to remove from the country. -J C McGuire, auct at auction on:

Dr John A Briscoe, the U S Navy Agent at Balt, died in that city on Thu.

Notice is given of the loss of Land Warrant 63,041, for 160 acres, issued in the name of Wm R Waugh, late of Chilton's Co U S Dragoons, dated Jul 13, 1849. Application will in due time be made to the Com'r of Pensions for a duplicate of said warrant. -Jno D McPherson

White Peach Brandy. John Douglas, near Anacostia Bridge, Eastern Branch, is now distilling from his orchard Peach Brandy of excellent quality. Those who want a nice article will avail themselves of this opportunity.

From the Binghamton [N Y] Democrat: obit-died: in Elizabethtown, N J, of congestion of the brain, Mgt Magruder, consort of T Robinson Rodgers, & youngest daughter of Josiah F Caldwell, of Wash. She was an intimate friend of the family of Mr D S Dickinson, & spent a few weeks with them in the society of Binghamton about a year since. She was best known at the fireside of the home she had cheered by her presence, discharging the sacred ofcs of sister & daughter. She was united in marriage Jul 12, & departed this life on Aug 16. Many hearts will long bleed over the recollections of her too early & painful death.

For rent: the house on the Island, containing 8 rooms & basement, now in the occupancy of Mr Anthony Holmead. Inquire of Rev Alfred Holmead, Island.
-J B Holmead

Died: on Sep 21, in Wash City, John M Krafft, for many years a citizen of Wash. His funeral will take place tomorrow from his late residence, F & 12th sts, at 2 o'clock.

Died: on Sep 12, in St Louis, at the residence of Mr A E Orme, Mr Wyatt S Berry, of Vandalia, Ill.

MON SEP 24, 1855
Judge Dyer, of the U S Court in Iowa, died at Woodstock on Sep 14. He was a native of Pendleton Co, Va.

Trustee's sale: by deed of trust executed by Wm T Hook, dated Jun 9, 1854, recorded in Liber J A S, 89, folios 247 thru 250, of the land records of Wash Co, D C: sale on the premises, on Oct 9, of the west part of lot 5 in square 378, fronting 23 feet & 5½ inches on north D st, by 187 feet deep to a wide public alley; improved by a large coach factory & shops. –H C Spalding, trustee -Jas C McGuire, auct

Wm Tuckerman, for many years a hardware merchant in Boston, died on Thu. The Traveller says he had not particular disease, but the dishonesty of his son, the defaulting treasurer of the Eastern Railroad, weighed very heavily on his mind, & mortification & distress which it caused was one of the causes of his death.

Sister Mary Susannah Richards died at Richmond, on Fri, of yellow fever. She came up a week previously in charge of the Portsmouth orphans. She was from Phil, had been 14 years a Sister of Charity, & was in her 42nd year. She had been in Norfolk 6 weeks nursing the sick, & has fallen a martyr doing good to her fellow-creatures.

Masonic Meeting this evening at their Hall, 9th & D sts. –W S McNairy, sec pro tem

Jos Gawler, Undertaker, between 17th & 18th sts, No 182. Coffins of every style & finish, with suitable silver-plated mountings; names, plates, & handles. Hearse & Carriages furnished, & all calls promptly attended to by day or night.

Norfolk-yellow fever: Mr Ferguson died on Sat. Portsmouth: Dr Walters, of Balt, & Riger, of Phil, were very ill. Drs Asperil & Kennedy, of Phil, are convalescent. Acting Mayor Halliday was taken to the hospital yesterday. The bells tolled in Balt in respect to the memory of Mr Ferguson, Pres of the Howard Assoc of Norfolk. He was formerly a citizen of Balt.

Balt, Sep 23. Wm Fowler, of Balt, was killed today by jumping off the cars at Monocacy.

TUE SEP 25, 1855
Administrator's sale of the personal effects of Augustus A Nicholson, deceased, by order of the Orphans Court of Wash Co, D C: on Oct 1, at the late residence of Maj Nicholson, deceased, on 2nd st, between E st & South Carolina ave.
–Sumerville Nicholson, Nicholas Callan, adms -A Green, auct

Improved property known as ***Flint's Hotel***, at public auction: on Oct 23: sale of part of lot 6 in square 254, fronting 37 feet 3 inches on Pa ave, between 13th & 14th sts, running back 159 feet to a 30 foot paved alley, with a handsome 3 story brick house with back bldgs. This property has been occupied for the past 3 years by Mr C W Flint as a first class restaurant. -Jas C McGuire, auct

Retired Naval ofcrs: Captains on leave pay:

Chas Stewart	Chas W Skinner	Chas Boarman
Stephen Cassin	Jos Smith	Wm Jamesson
Geo C Read	David Geisinger	Henry W Ogden
Thos Ap C Jones	Wm D Salter	Hugh N Page
David Conner	John Percival	Stephen Champlin
John D Sloat	Wm V Taylor	

Captains on furlough pay:

Jesse Wilkinson	Jos Smoot	Wm Inman
Foxhall A Parker	Benj Page	Lewis E Simonds
Philip F Voorhees	Wm K Latimer	Harrison H Cocke
Thos M Newell	Henry Henry	Horace B Sawyer
Thos Paine	John H Graham	

Captains dropped:

John P Zantzinger	Uriah P Levy	Wm Ramsey

Cmders on leave pay:

John J Young	Jas Glynn	T Darrah Shaw
Jos R Jarvis	Jos Myers	Robt D Thorburn
Wm M Armstrong	Robt Ritchie	Saml Lockwood
Wm F Shields	Elisha Peck	Lloyd B Newell
Edw W Carpender	Timothy G Benham	John Manning
John L Saunders	Oscar Bullus	John Colhoun
John S Paine	Cadwallader Ringgold	Amassa Paine

Cmders on Furlough pay:

Chas T Platt	Thos J Manning	Geo Adams
Thos R Gedney	Andrew K Long	Isaac S Sterett
Henry Bruce	Wm Green	Fred'k A Neville
John S Nicholas	Chas H Jackson	Murray Mason

Cmders dropped:

Fred'k Varnum	Thos Petigru	Zach F Johnston
Saml W Le Compte	John S Chauncey	Wm S Ogden

Lts on leave pay:

Jonathan W Swift	Henry Darcantel	Jas B Lewis
Jonathan D Ferris	Geo M White	John Hall
Mathew F Maury	Geo M Selden	Francis Lowry
Jas S Palmer	Stephen Decatur	Melancton B Woolsey
Geo Hurst	Richd L Love	
Jas F Miller	Wm Reynolds	

Lts on furlough pay:

Frank Ellery	Geo R Gray	Fabius Stanly
Jas M Watson	Bernard J Moeller	John N Maffitt
Junius J Boyle	Henry Walhe	Jas A Doyle
Wm E Hunt	John P Parker	Mathias C Marin
Peter Turner	Montgomery Lewis	Alex'r Murray
Wm D Porter	Albert A Holcomb	Robt B Rich
Gabriel G Williamson	Richd Forrest	Mathew C Perry
John C Carter	Henry C Flagg	V R Morgan
Simon B Bissell	E C Bowers	Henry Rolande
John J Glasson	Dominick Lynch	John S Taylor
Henry A Steele	Horace N Harrison	Foxhall A Parker
Robt Handy	Chas Thomas	John F Abbott
A H Kilty	Augustus S Baldwin	Wm B Fitzgerald
Wm Chandler	Wm B Whiting	Maurice Simmons
Jas M Gillis	Chas Hunter	Robt M McArann
Alex'r Gibson	Saml R Knox	
Bushrod W Hunter	Lewis C Sartori	

Lts dropped:

W A C Farragut	John L Ring	S Chase Barney
Hillary H Rhodes	Danl F Dulany	Thos H Stevens
Lawrence Pennington	J J B Walbach	Israel C Wait
Wm H Noland	L B Avery	Abner Read
Jas Noble	Thos Brownell	Alex'r C Rhind
J T McDonough	Wash A Bartlett	
Richd W Meade	A Davis Harrell	

Master in the line of promotion on leave pay: Wm M Low

Masters in the line of promotion dropped from the Navy:

Julius S Bohrer	Geo A Stevens	David Ochiltree
John Walcutt	Peter Wager, jr	Augustus McLaughlin
John Madigan, jr	John P Hall	

Passed Midshipmen on furlough pay:

Saml Pearce   Edw C Grafton

Passed Midshipmen dropped from the Navy:

J Howard March	Allen T Byrens	Geo S King
Jas S Thornton	Edmund Shepherd	Jos A Sewall
Edw A Selden	Wm R Mercer	Chas B Smith
Nathl T West	Chas Gray	Jas Bruce

Masters not in the line of promition on leave pay:

Robt Knox	Fred W Moores	Chas V Morris
Wm Vaughan	H A F Young	John Pearson
Francis Mallaby	Jas Ferguson	Edmund F Olmstead
John Robinson	Wm N Brady	
John Quinn	Saml C Reid	

Masters not in line of promotion on furlough pay:
A Cunningham   Michl Clear   R Clarendon Jones

Texas: a court-martial was in session at **Fort Davis**, Texas, for the trial of Private Dunn, of Co G, Mounted Riflemen, for the murder of Lt John Williams.

Augustus M Vaughan, appointed Postmaster at Norfolk, Va, vice Dr Gault, deceased.

A convict named Lightfoot, confined in the penitentiary for this District, escaped on Sat last by boring through the wall of the hospital, where he had been placed because of real or feigned sickness.

Mrd: on Sep 18, at Trinity Church, Parkersburg, Va, by Rev Jas Craik, of Louisville, Ky, Edw F De Selding, of the former place, to Miss Bettie M, eldest daughter of the late Joel Shrewsbury, of Kanawha Co, Va.

Mrd: on Monday, by Rev John C Smith, the Rev Matthew Smith, Pastor of the Presbyterian Church, Centerville, Iowa, to Miss Mary Frances, eldest daughter of John R Nourse, of Wash City.

Dissolution of copartnership existing between Wm H Brereton & Saml Brereton, of the firm of Brereton & Bro, engaged in the grocery business, by mutual consent. Wm Henry Brereton will conduct the business at the old stand, F & 7th st.
-Wm H Brereton, Sam Brereton

WED SEP 26, 1855
Wm Gooseman was found last night in the yard of 15 west 35th st, with one of his legs broken. It was ascertained that he had entered the house with false keys. & after stealing $200 worth of jewelry, became alarmed & jumped out of a 3rd story window. He was taken to the hospital where his leg had to be amputated. -Mirror

Norfolk & Portsmouth-yellow fever. Within a few days some of the best citizens of those places have fallen, including Josiah Wills, Dr Galt, Wm B Ferguson, Wm Reed, Chas Beale, Caleb Johnson, John D Gordon, & Dr Richd Tunstall. In the two cities on Sat 4 physicians died, viz: Dr Capry, of N Y, Dr Dilliard, of Montg, Ala, & Dr Burns, in Norfolk; & Dr Walters, of Balt, in Portsmouth.

Household & kitchen furniture at auction on: Oct 3, at the residence of Capt H L Benham, 407 3rd st, between Pa ave & C st. -Jas C McGuire, auct

The wife of Hon Theodore S Fay, our Minister Resident near the Federal Gov't of Switzerland, died at Berne on Aug 31.

The Trenton Gaz understands that Dr Heineken has commenced an action in Phil to recover damages from the Camden & Amboy Railroad Co for the destruction of his horses & carriage at Burlington. He went before the grand jury at Mount Holly & made formal cmplnt, for the purpose of having the directors of the company indicted for manslaughter. The same day Mr Shreve, of Bordentown, made a similar cmplnt before the jury against Dr Heineken, for the purpose of having him indicted. The grand jury will make a rigid investigation of the affair. Israel Adams, the engineer, was required on Fri to enter into sureties for his appearance, when required, in the sum of $4,000. On Sat the grand jury came into court with a bill against him for manslaughter. No bill had been found against Dr Heineken or the company. Jabez Kingdom, ticket agent at the Burlington Railroad depot, was indicted for keeping a watch & some money, the property of Mr Loveland, of Ill, whose body remained at the Lyceum several days unrecognized, & was claimed by several persons. Still recovering from their injuries are Mrs Boyce, Mrs Newbold & daughter, Mr Pew, Hon Mr Maclay. Mr Danl O'Kane is said to be in a critical condition. His right leg was fractured near the thigh & below the knee. Mr O'Kane will be removed to Phil.

H G Sothoron Key, of Md, appointed Navy Agent at Balt, vice Briscoe, deceased.

Isaac F Miller left Albany, on Sep 3, to go to N Y to receive a pension, he having lost his arm in the Mexican war. He was to return next day, but has not since been heard of. He was 35 years of age, & of steady habits. Can any one tell of him?

Mrd: on Sep 20, at Wesley Chapel Parsonage, by Rev R L Dashiell, Mr Alfred D Farmer to Miss Susan Dugan, both of PG Co, Md.

Mrd: on Sep 25, by Rev R L Dashiell, Mr John H Bird to Georgiana Cookman, daughter of Rich Polkinhorn, all of Wash City.

Mrd: on Sep 24, at St Matthew's Church, by Rev Jas B Donelan, Mr Edw Dolan, of Providence, R I, to Mary Ann Maher, youngest daughter of Jas Maher.

Died: on Sep 24, of consumption, Miss Mary Ella Craven, in her 21st year. Her funeral will be from the residence of Mr Parish, H st, between 10th & 11th, this afternoon, at 3½ o'clock.

Richmond, Sep 25: among the dead in Portsmouth are Mrs Webster, mother of N B Webster, Miss Mary Riley, John C Godwin, clerk to naval storekeeper, Mrs M Taylor, J Whitmore, Jos Haydon, M Parsons, Jesse Anderton, Jas Brownley, C Harvey, Wm Proctor, & Benj Newton. Mr Holliday is ill; H Stokes is recovering. Letter dated this morning: Drs Rizer & Hatton & Wm R Singleton are recovering. In Norfolk Dr Richd Tunstall & John D Gordon [banker] are dead. Dutton Wheeler is dying.

The subscriber wishes to engage a lady to reside in his family as Governess. She must be competent to teach all the branches of English, French, & Music. –C H Carter, near Queen Anne, PG Co, Md.

Plumbing in all branches. –P H Sims, Practical Plumber, 512 7th st.

THU SEP 27, 1855
The Buffalo Commercial Advertiser announces the death, on Sep 21, at his residence in Attica, N Y, of Hon Harvey Putnam. He was 62 years of age.

Capt John S Nichols, who had command of the U S steamer **Michigan** on the Lakes, has been retired on furlough pay. He addressed the crew & ofcrs: "My lads, you perceive that after nearly forty years' service it has been decided that I am incompetent to command this ship-the fifth that I have commanded. I believe that your feelings towards me are kindly, &, if so, I wish to show them by your obedience, activity, & general good conduct under my successor, & prove that I am still competent to leave behind me a ship in good order & a well-disciplined crew. My lads, farewell."

During the present term of the Court of Common Pleas for Delaware Co, Ohio, Mr Terry, of Ashley, recovered a verdict of $3,000 against the Cleveland, Columbus, & Cincinnati Railroad Co for injury sustained by his wife from being struck last fall by one of the locomotives running on the road.

On Thu last Geo Haight was committed to jail in Troy, N Y, to answer a charge of stealing $100 from a letter abstracted from the post ofc at Dryden, N Y, where Haight was deputy postmaster, on Aug 25.

The Nashville papers announce the death in that city, on Sep 21, of E P McGinty, who was Editor of the Nashville True Whig, at the time of his death.

Francis Connolly, aged 3 years, residing at 48 Suffolk st, died from severe injuries received by the explosion of a camphene lamp in his parents' residence.

I certify that John Brady Camp, of PG Co, Md, brought before me as a stray trespassing upon the enclosure of Henry C Matthews, a red Ox. –Jno W Scott, J P Owner is to come forward, prove property, pay charges & take him away.
-John Brady Camp, near Bladensburg Depot

FRI SEP 28, 1855
Orphans Court of Wash Co, D C. Letters testamentary on the personal estate of Patrick Moran, late of Wash Co, deceased. –Owen Murray, adm

New Grocery, Wine & Liquor Store: 474 Pa ave, between 3rd & 4½ sts. -Jonas P Levy

Mrd: on Sep 26, by Rev Mr Hodges, Dr Christopher Johnston, of Balt, to Miss Sallie L Clay, daughter of Col B P Smith, of Wash, D C.

Mrd: on Sep 20, at Afton, Albemarle Co, Va, the residence of David Hansbrough, by Rev Saml Blain, Thos W Wood, of Albemarle, to Miss Lydia Gates, youngest daughter of the late Gen J D Learned, of St Louis, Mo.

Mrd: on Sep 25, by Rev P D Gurley, D C, Mr Nicholas B Ray to Miss Laura E Ratcliff, both of Wash City.

Mrd: on Sep 25, by Rev C F McCauly, at the residence of Henry McDuell, Fred'k Co, Md, Geo W E Kennedy to Miss E S McDuell, both of Wash City.

Died: on Sep 27, in Wash City, after a lingering illness, Rosanna Bowen, in her 73rd year. Her funeral is this afternoon, at 3:30 o'clock, from the residence of her son-in-law, Elijah Edmonston, on H st, between 4th & 5th sts.

SAT SEP 29, 1855
Extensive sale of superior rosewood, walnut, mahogany, cherry & maple cabinet furniture: on Oct 16, at the Cabinet Warerooms of Saml Kirby, on 8th st, between Pa ave & D st. -Jas C McGuire, auct

At a meeting held at Boston on Mon, for the purpose of choosing delegates to the American Convention, Dr Henry Willard was one of the speakers, & almost immediately after concluding his remarks dropped on the floor & instantly expired. The deceased had been afflicted some years with an organic affection of the heart.

Household & kitchen furniture at auction on: Oct 2, at the residence of Mr Thos Knowles, on 1st st. -Barnard & Buckey, aucts

Died: on Sep 28, Arthur Howard, the 4th son of Wm & Eliz A Hoover, in his 9th year.

MON OCT 1, 1855
Promotions in the Navy:
Cmders promoted to be Captains:

G J Pendergrast	Stephen B Wilson	Wm W McKean
Wm C Nicholson	T Aloysius Dornin	Franklin Buchanan
Jos B Hull	Robt B Cunningham	Saml Mercer
John Kelly	Victor M Randolph	Chas Lowndes
Wm H Gardner	Fred'k Engle	L M Goldsborough
David G Farragut	John Rudd	Geo N Hollins

Duncan N Ingraham
Jon Marston
Henry A Adams
Wm S Walker
Geo F Pearson
Saml F Dupont
Lts promoted to be Cmders:
John W Livingston
Archibald B Fairfax
Henry K Thatcher
Jas H Rowan
Wm McBlair
John S Missroon
Richd L Page
Fred Chatard
Benj J Totten
Arthur Sinclair
Robt B Hitchcock
C H A H Kennedy
Thos W Brent
Jos Lanman
John K Mitchell
Thos Turner
Chas H Poor
Jas Findlay Schenck
Timothy Hunt
Sylvanus Wm Godon
Wm Radford
Saml F Hazard
John M Berrien
Geo A Prentiss
Alfred Taylor

Wm L Hudson
Geo A Magruder
John Pope
Levin M Powell
Chas Wilkes
Thos O Selfridge

Saml Phillips Lee
John P Gillis
Saml Swartwout
Raphael Semmes
Jas P McKinstry
Oliver S Glisson
John A Dahlgreen
Stephen C Rowan
Edw R Thompson
Guert Gansevort
Chas Green
Edw L Handy
Melancton Smith
Cicero Price
J R Goldsborough
Chas S Boggs
Theodore P Green
John R Tucker
Thos J Page
Geo Minor
Percival Drayton
Robt F Pinkney
Thos R Rootes
Edw M Yard
Wm S Young

Henry Eagle
G J Van Brunt
Wm M Glendy
Geo S Blake
Saml Barron
Andrew A Harwood

Jos F Green
John DeCamp
Chas W Pickering
Overton Carr
Luther Stoddard
Wm M Walker
John A Winslow
Benj More Dove
Thornton A Jenkins
John Rodgers
John B Marchand
Wm Rogers Taylor
Henry J Hartstene
Benj F Sands
Henry French
Saml Larkin
Henry S Stellwagon
Jas L Henderson
Danl B Ridgely
Wm T Muse
Chas Steedman
Wm Lewis Herndon
Jas Alden
Augustus L Case
Roger Perry

Masters Promoted to be Lts: Chas W Aby; Edw C Stout
Passed Midshipmen Promoted to be Lts:
Reuben Harris
Jas B McCauley
Thos S Phelps
Alex F Warley
Garrit V Denniston
Leonard Paulding
Francis S Conover
Edw Barrett
Colville Terrett
John W Bennett

Homer C Blake
Calrk H Wells
S P Quackenbush
Earl English
Jos M Bradford
Reigart P Lowry
Jonathan H Carter
Wm H Parker
J Pembroke Jones
David A McDermut

Wm P Buckney
Geo E Morgan
Rcihd L Law
Wm H Wilcox
John T Barraud
Thos Roney
John H Upshur
John Van N Philip
Saml R Franklin
Wm D Whiting

Wm L Powell	Wm M Gamble	John C Spretson
S Ledward Phelps	Jonathan Young	Bancroft Gherardi
Edw Y McCauley	Wm K Mayo	Danl L Braine
Theodoric L Walker	Thos Young	John Taylor Wood
Wm Mitchell	Jas E Jouett	L Howard Newman
Francis A Roe	T Scott Fillebrown	Chas E Thorburn
Jos D Smith	Jos Fry	Richd T Bowen
Wm H Murdaugh	Leonard H Lyon	Chas W Flusser
John M Brooke	Milton Haxton	Wm S Lovell
Wm Gibson	Robt Selden	John R Eggleson
Edw Renshaw	Albert Allmand	Adns B Cummings
Jos D Daniels	Robt Stuart	Bayard E Hand
John T Walker	Theodoric Lee	Geo E Belknap
J C P DeKrafft	Geo H Bier	Edw P Williams
John Van McCollum	Pend G Watmough	Jared P K Mygatt
John E Hart	Geo W Young	John D Rainey
Oscar C Badger	John H Russell	David B Harmony
Thos C Harris	Edw E Stone	Wm Gwin
John Kell	Thos C Eaton	John J Cornwell
John L Davis	Dawson Phenix	Jas P Foster
Alex A Semmes	Robt F R Lewis	Henry Wilson
John B Stewart	Chas P McGary	A E K Benham
M Patterson Jones	Hunter Davidson	Robt T Chapman
Watson Smith	Andrew W Johnson	Wm P A Campbell
Alex M DeBree	Stephen B Luce	Wilson McGunnegle
Jos E De Haven	Dulany A Forrest	John Irwin
Alex W Habersham	Robt W Scott	J S Skerrett
Wm T Truxton	Walter W Queen	Jas A Greer
John K Wilson	Robt R Carter	Chas H Greene
Greenleaf Cilley	Edmund W Henry	Francis H Baker
Horace N Crabb	Thos T Houston	Isaac W Hester
Saml Magaw	Ralph Chandler	E T Spedden
Jas H Rochelle	John R Hamilton	E K Owen
Robt D Minor	Jas Parker	Wm T Glassell
Wm C West	Philip C Johnson, jr	Aaron Ward Weaver
Nich H Van Zandt	John Watters	Austin Pendergrast
Francis G Dallas	K Randolph Breese	Jos P Fyffee
Simeon S Bassett	Oscar F Johnson	Wm P McCann
Robt C Duvall	Lewis A Kimberly	J S Stillwell
David P McCorkle	Beverly Kennon	Julius G Heileman
Geo H Hare	S Livingston Breese	Jos D Blake
Wm Sharp	Geo U Morris	Eugene H Oakley
Jas I Waddell	Edwin F Gray	Jas H Gillis

Passed Midshipmen Promoted to be Masters:

DeGrass Livingston	Wm H Cheever	Jesse Taylor, jr
Wm E Fitzhugh	H A Adams, jr	J G Maxwell
Trevott Abbott	B B Taylor	Henry Erben
B P Loyall	W H Ward	F E Shepperd
C H Cushman	J W Dunnington	T P Pelot
O F Stanton	H M Garland	E P McCrea

At Boston, on Tue, a son of Mr Otis Churchill, aged 11 years, whilst playing with a loaded gun, accidentally discharged it & killed himself.

Hon Benj Gorham, of the city of Boston, died suddenly in that city on Thu at the advanced age of 80 years. He was the son of Nathl Gorham, who assisted in forming the Constitution of the U S. He graduated at Harvard College in 1795; representative in Congress; & was one of the oldest members of the Suffolk bar at the time of his death.

Died: on Sep 29, Mr Jas Coolidge, in his 51st year, leaving a disconsolate widow & 4 small children to mourn his loss. He was for many years a clerk in the Sixth Auditor's Ofc. His funeral is this day at 3 o'clock P M, from Trinity Church, Gtwn.

TUE OCT 2, 1855
Geo Knight, postmaster at Dryden, N Y, has been committed to jail in Troy to answer a charge of stealing $100 from a letter received at that ofc.

Died: on Sep 24, in Norfolk, Va, after an illness of 7 days, Anna Maria Truxton, only daughter of Lt J L Henderson, U S Navy, aged 15 years. Until herself stricken down she ministered to others. No victim of the pestilence that has desolated her native city was more beloved.

Died: on Sep 22, after a few days' illness, Sarah Eliza, eldest daughter of Geo & Catharine Bohrer, & grand-daughter of Mr Phlip Otterback, in her 16th year.

Died: on Aug 3, at **Fort Riley**, Kansas, of cholera, Mrs Clayonie Woods, wife of Maj Saml Woods, 6th Infty, & their 2 children, Clifford & Mary. Mrs Woods was a native of Balt, a daughter of the late Wm B Barney, & a grand-daughter of Judge Chase & Cmdor Barney. Within a short space of 3 hours, deprived by absence of the protecting care of the husband & father, though happily ignorant of each other's fate, they breathed their last amid a scene of horror seldom paralleled. In the quarters jointly occupied with the family of Maj Woods by Maj Ogden & the Chaplain 7 persons lay deceased or dying, while throughout the Fort raged the wildest & most fearful confusion-here the sick untended, the dead unburied; there ghastly fear, cowardly desertion of duty, & riotous insubordination.

Geo W Cochran has resumed the Cigar & Tobacco business at the old stand, 514 7th st, opposite the Nat'l Intelligencer ofc.

For sale: a pair of dun carriage horses, the property of a gentleman in the country who has no further use of them; gentle in either single or double harness. Also, a second-hand family carriage. Refer to H L Chapen's Wood Yard, 9th & H sts, Wash.

WED OCT 3, 1855
Yellow fever. In Portsmouth, on Sat, Dr Cole, of Phil, & Dr Hunter, of N Y, were among the dead. In Norfolk on Sat there were 4 deaths, on Sunday 7, & on Monday, 3 deaths. Miss Catharine Redman, matron of the Orphans' Asylum, is dead.

Boston Courier: the trustees of **Mount Auburn Cemetery** have contracted 4 monumental statues to be placed in the chapel now in process of reconstruction in the cemetery. Illustrative of the history of Mass, they will represent Govn'r Winthrop, Jas Otis, John Adams, & Judge Story. The statue of Winthrop will be by Richd Greenough; it will be a sitting figure in the costume of the colonial times. The statue of John Adams is already executed; that of Jas Otis will be by Thos Crawford, & that of Judge Story by his son. Adams & Otis, being orators, will be standing, while Winthrop & Story, being magisterial personages, will be represented sitting.

Yellow fever. In Portsmouth, on Sat, Dr Cole, of Phil, & Dr Hunter, of N Y, were among the dead. In Norfolk on Sat there were 4 deaths, on Sunday 7, & on Monday, 3 deaths. Miss Catharine Redman, matron of the Orphans' Asylum, is dead.

Richmond Dispatch: steamer **Curtis Peck**, Oct 1, 1855. The venerated & estimable wife of Chief Justice Taney breathed her last on Sat at Old Point. She has been in feeble health for some days past, &, though her disease had none of the marks of yellow fever, soon after her decease the skin bore the unmistakeable evidence, by its hue, that the insidious destroyed had been lurking in the system. Would that I could pause her in my record of the sorrows of her distinguished husband; but, alas! The same pen traces the sad story of this bereavement must also convey the melancholy intelligence that in a few brief hours after the spirit of the mother passed away the eyes of her eldest single daughter, Miss ___ Taney, were also closed in death. Her's was a decided case of yellow fever; & on yesterday Mother & daughter were committed to the same dark grave, to the solemn measure of the dirging waves. The eulogy of Mrs Taney must be written by those who knew her amid the sanctities of her home; & the gentle memories of the daughter must be treasured by the circle in which she moved respected & beloved. Mrs Taney was a sister of the late Francis S Key, the immortal author of The Star Spangled Banner. It is also reported that another single daughter of the venerable Chief Justice is quite ill at Old Point. The Judge has been occupying for some 2 or 3 summers the cottage at Old Point opposite the former residence of Col DeRussy, & himself & his whole family had won upon all who were brought into social contact with them.

Miss Clara Haskins was found dead in her bridle dress & chamber near Natchez, Miss, on Sep 2. She was found by her bridesmaids lifeless upon her couch, with an empty vial which had contained prussic acid still clasped in her hand. She committed suicide rather than marry a man she could not love in obedience to parental authority.

The advertiser wishes to obtain a situation as Gardner. He can produce most satisfactory references. He is a married man without children. Address Wm Hughes, Florist, B & 7th sts, on the Island, Wash, D C.

Local Item. On Monday two young men, Robt Warren & Thornton Avery, visited a disreputable house in the n e part of Wash City, where they in some manner offended the owner of the premises, W B Edwards, who regarded himself as protector of the house & its inmates. Edwards order them to leave, & upon their refusal, fired upon them & killed Avery & Warren is believed to be mortally wounded. Edwards was promptly arrested & committed to prison by Justice Birch.

Wm Darran, a rigger, was on Fri last injured [fatally it is feared] by a fall, while at work on the aqueduct near the Great Falls, some miles from Wash.

Orphans Court of Wash Co, D C. Letters of administration on the personal estate of John M Krafft, late of Wash Co, deceased. –Mary C Krafft, admx

Mrd: last evening, by Rev Mr Eckard, Mr Henry Weaver to Miss Eliza Ann Linkins, both of Wash City.

Died: on Oct 2, at *Mount Pleasant*, the residence of her grandfather, Isabella Ritchie Stone, aged 19 months, the youngest child of Dr Robt K & Mgt Ritchie Stone. Her funeral will take place today at 12 o'clock. Hacks will be in readiness at J F Harvey's wareroom at 11 o'clock to convey the friends of the family.

St Andrew's Society will meet at Temperance Hall this evening.
–Jas MacWilliams, sec

Strayed or stolen this day from the subscriber a black & white Pointer Puppy. Suitable reward for return of the same. –M G Emery, 418 F st

THU OCT 4, 1855
Irving Ellsworth, son of Hon J Ellsworth, of N Y, was recently standing in front of a buzz saw, in Pleasantville, Iowa, when a piece of oak lath, sharp at one end, was thrown by the saw with such force that the sharp end struck him under the left eye, & pierced the brain to the depth of 2 inches. He lived half an hour.

Household & kitchen furniture at auction on: Oct 5, at the residence of C L Lombard, 607 H, between 4th & 5th sts. –A Green, auct

Memphis News: rencontre occurred in that place on Sat week between Mr Q K Underwood, editor of the Shield, & Mr J M Cleveland, editor of the Star, in which the former was mortally wounded. The difficulty grew out of a newspaper controversy. The combatants used pistols & knives.

Dissolution of copartnership existing under firm of M Snyder & Sons was dissolved by mutual consent on Oct 1, 1855. The business will be conducted at the old stand, under the firm of M Snyder & Son. –M Snyder, A M Snyder, M Snyder, jr

Furniture & house-keeping goods, now on sale at the new store, 7th st, next to Odd Fellows' Hall. –A Rothwell

Gen Harney's report of his battle with the Sioux Indians: dated Headquarters Sioux Expedition, camp on Bluewater Creek, Nebraska Territory, Sep 5, 1855. I arrived at Ash Hollow on Sep 3, ascertained that a large portion of the Burle band of the Sioux nation, under Little Thunder, was encamped on Blue-water Creek, about 6 miles north. I ordered Lt Col P St Geo Cooke, 2nd dragoons, with companies E & K of same regt, light company G, 4th artl, & company E, 10th infty, all mounted, to move on Sep 3, secure a position which would cut off the retreat of the Indians to the Sand Buttes; movement was executed in a most successful manner, not having excited the suspicion of the enemy. I left my camp with companies A, E, H, I, & K, 6th infty, under immediate command of Maj A Cady, of that regt, & proceeded towards the principal village of the Brules. Before reaching it, the lodges were struck & their occupants commenced a rapid retreat up the valley of the Blue water, precisely in the direction from when I expected the mounted troops. They halted short of these & a parley ensued between their chief & myself, in which I stated the causes of the dissatisfaction which the Gov't felt towards the Brules; I did not wish to harm him personally, but he must either deliver up the young men, whom he could not control, or they must suffer the consequences of their past misconduct & take the chances of a battle. Little Thunder returned to his band to warn them of my decision. I ordered the infty to advance, the leading company [Capt Todd's] as skirmishers, supported by company H, 6th infty, under Lt McCleary; the remaining companies of the 6th being held in hand for ulterior movements. The cavalry pursued & killed a large number of them: 86 killed, 5 wounded, about 70 women & children captured, 50 mules & ponies taken. The amount of provisions & camp equipage must have comprised nearly all the enemy possessed. The casualties of the command amount to 4 killed, 4 severely wounded, 4 slightly wounded, & 1 missing, supposed to be killed or captured by the enemy. Killed: Alex Lyall, private, Co K, 2nd dragoons; Chas McDonald, do; Robt Fitzpatrick, private, Company G, 4th artl; Thos Carroll, do. Wounded: Thos Heally, sgt, Co E, 2nd dragoons, in several places; Geo Fink, cpl, Co K, 2nd dragoons, severely; Wm Walsh, private, do, severely; C E Rutherford, do, severely; Theopholite Morff, do, slightly; Francis Larken, do, slightly; Jas Kennedy, do, slightly. Missing: Marshall Ryder, private, Co K, 2nd dragoons, without doubt killed. Mentioned for fine military spirit & service: Capt Todd, 6th infty; Capt Steele & Lt Robinson, 2nd dragoons; Capt Heth, 10th infty; Capt Howe & his Co G, 4th artl; Brvt Maj Woods, Capt Wharton, & Lt Patterson, 6th infty; Lts Buford & Wright, regimental quartermaster & adj of the 2nd dragoons; Lts Drum, Hudson, & Medenhall, 4th artl; Lts Hight & Livingston, 2nd dragoons; Lt Dudley, 10th infty; also, Mr Jos Tesson, one of my guides who conducted the column of cavalry to its position in the rear of the Indian villages. Mr Carrey also, chief of the guides, rendered good service in transmitting my orders. My personal staff rendered me most efficient service in the field: Maj O F Winship, Asst Adj Gen & chief of the staff, & Lt Polk, 2nd infty, my aid-de-camp; Assist Surgeon Ridgeley, of the medical staff; Lt Warren, topographical engineers, was engaged to & during the combat reconnoitering the country & the enemy, & has subsequently made a sketch of the former, which I enclose herewith. There are also in the possession of ofcrs & others, in camp, the scalps of 2 white females, & remnants of the clothing, carried off by the Indians in the Grattan massacre, all of which in my judgment sufficiently characterize the people I have had to deal with. I am, Colonel, very respectfully, your obedient servant, Wm S Harney, Brvt Brig Gen [Report to: Lt Col L Thomas, Assist Adj Gen, Headquarters of the Army, N Y.] [See Oct 29th newspaper.]

Mrd: on Oct 3, at Foundry Church, by Rev E P Phelps, Mr Wm E Waters, of Wash City, to Miss Abby J, daughter of Wm A Evans, formerly of Maine.

Died: in Troy, Md, Mrs Mary Isabella Osbourne, in her 19th year, 3rd daughter of Isaac Reed. Her funeral will take place from her father's residence on 1st st west, this afternoon, at 4 o'clock. [No death date given.]

Died: on Oct 3, in Wash City, Florence Lengair, aged 5 year, 3rd daughter of Lorenzo & Anna H Dorsey.

Managers of the Union Benevolent Society will meet on Oct 5 at the usual hour & place. –Emma E Gurley, sec

Montgomery, Oct 2. Yellow fever at Montgomery: 24 cases since the first report on Sep 25th to last Sat. Among the dead are Mathew Harris, an eminent lawyer, Mr McNutt, a school teacher, Tridman Woodruff, F Balling, & John H Knox.

Dissolution of copartnership in the Painting business. Jno W Mankins, Geo H Varnell [Geo H Varnell will continue the business at the old stand of the late firm, 51½ La ave, between 6th & 7th sts. Having retired from the firm I take pleasure in recommending my late partner. –Jno W Mankins]

Intending to change my location, I offer for sale the valuable property upon which I reside, located in the n e suburbs of Staunton: commodious brick dwlg, servants' houses, stabling, & all other necessary out-bldgs; 8 acres of highly improved grounds. Possession given on Jan 1, 1856. –Thos P Eskridge

Hog Island at public auction: on Nov 13 next: in Surry Co, on the James river, a few miles below Jamestown; contains nearly 2,000 acres of land. Also, 700 or 800 acres of mainland adjacent to the island. There will be a survey made & a plat of all prepared & offered for examination in Petersburg, at the ofc of Messrs David & Jno P May, & upon the place on the day of sale. Also, 40 or 50 slaves. Also, cattle, buggy & harness, household & kitchen furniture. –T B Robertson, exc of Wm Robertson, deceased.

FRI OCT 5, 1855
Trustee's sale of valuable bldg lots: on Oct 22, by deed of trust from Estwick Evans & wife, dated Sep 15, 1854, filed in the clerk's ofc for Wash Co, D C: all that part of lot 8, in square 531, in Wash City. Terms cash. All conveyance at the cost of the purchaser. –Hugh B Sweeny, trustee -A Green, auct

Sale of blacksmith's tools, by order of the Orphans Court of Wash Co, D C: on Oct 8, on 18th st, between Pa ave & H st, the tools & stock in trade of the late John Poor. -Jas C McGuire, auct

Magnificent Rosewood Grand Piano, parlor furniture, French plate mirrors, lace curtains, family carriage, & matched gray horses: at auction on Sep 23, at the residence of his Excellency Gen Almonte, Minister from Mexico, on F st, between 11th & 12th sts. -Jas C McGuire, auct

The Floyd [Va] Intelligencer announces the death of Hon Archibald Stuart, at his residence in Patrick Co, on Sep 17, of disease of the heart.

N Y, on Tue, Coroner Kidder held an inquest on the body of the wife of Mr John Lewis, who died when her husband, Mr Lewis, who had been delirious with fever, tried to leap through the window on the 3rd floor. In her effort to stop him, she seized him & they both fell about 25 feet. Mrs Lewis was instantly killed. Mr Lewis in at the city hospital in a precarious condition. He is a daguerreotypist, doing business in Chatham st. His mother who resided downstairs, & was not present.

In the case of Clark for the deliberate & premeditated murder of Willard W Wight, at New Haven, the jury on Thu last, brought in a verdict of acquittal, on the ground of insanity. –Buffalo Courier

Died: on Wed, in Wash City, of typhoid fever, Wm H P, only son of John G Schott, in his 18th year. His funeral is this afternoon, at 2 o'clock, from the residence of his father, Capitol Hill.

Died: on Oct 4, suddenly, Mrs Rosetta M Tschiffely, in her 46th year. Her funeral is this afternoon, at 4 o'clock, from St Paul's English Lutheran Church.

Died: on Oct 2, at Orange Court-house, Va, after a brief illness, Willis Kennard, youngest son of Francis B & Helen M Clark, of Mobile, Ala, aged 3 years, 4 months & 17 days.

Supreme Court of the U S, No 60, Dec Term, 1854. Appeal from the Circuit Court of the U S for the District of Maine. Nehemiah Carrington, appellant, vs the brig **Ann C Pratt**, Leonard B Pratt, claimant. Mr Fessenden, of counsel for the appellee, having filed a suggestion that Nehemiah Carrington, the appellant, had departed this life since the last continuance of this cause, now here moved the Court for an order to make the proper reps parties, & for the usual order of publication. It is now ordered by the Court, that unless the proper reps of the said appellant shall voluntarily become parties within the first 10 days of the ensuing term, the appellee shall be entitled to have the appeal in this cause dismissed.
–Wm Thos Carroll, C S C U S

Supreme Court of the U S, No 117, Dec Term, 1854. Appeal from the Circuit Court of the U S for the Eastern District of Louisiana. John B Craighead & al, appellants, vs Jos E Wilson & al. Mr Janin, of counsel for the appellees, having suggested the death of John B Craighead & Jas E Robertson, two of the appellants, & that Thos Brown Craighead, another of the appellants in this cause, has been found a lunatic, & that a guardian has been appointed to him, now here moves the Court for an order, to make the proper reps parties, for the usual order of publication. The Court orders that, unless the proper reps of the said appellants shall voluntarily become parties within the first 10 days of the ensuing term, the appellees shall be entitled to have the appeal in this cause dismissed. –Wm Thos Carroll, C S C U S

SAT OCT 6, 1855
Mrd: on Sep 20, in Trinity Church, Shepherdstown, Va, by Rev C W Andrews, D D, Mr Geo R Robinson, of St Louis, Mo, to Miss Annie Andrews, eldest daughter of the officiating clergyman.

Mrd: on Oct 4, by Rev T H Busey Dr Geo W Anderson, of Bedford Co, Pa, to Miss Caroline M Morsel, of PG Co, Md, daughter of Saml Morsel.

Died on Oct 4, Edward Miller, eldest son of Edw W & Mary Devall. His funeral will take place, from the residence of his parents, near Bladensburg, today at 3½ o'clock.

Died: on Oct 5, in Gtwn, A P Waugh, age 54 years. His funeral will be from his late residence, on Bridge st, at 2 o'clock Sunday afternoon.

For sale or rent: the house corner of N Y ave & 18th st, commonly called "**The Octagon.**" For terms apply to Jos H Willard, Willard's Hotel. –Benj Ogle Tayloe, Wm H Tayloe

For sale, 3 small farms, within 4 miles of Wash: 80,000 feet on the Island; 30,000 in the Northern Liberties; 60,000 on Capitol Hill; a house on 11th st, $6,000; one on L st, $2,500; two on 8th st, $900 each; one on G, $3,000; five on Mass ave, $3,250; & several others. –N Titus Wakeman, Real Estate Agent & Broker, 514 7th st, opposite Nat'l Intelligencer ofc, over Geo Cochrane's Tobacco Warehouse.

For rent: desirable residence on G, between 20th & 21st sts. It has recently been thoroughly repaired, there are gas & fixtures in the house. Inquire of Saml Stott.

MON OCT 8, 1855
Taking the veil. A double religious ceremony was performed at the Convent of the **Sisters of Mercy** in this city on Sep 25. Miss Madeline Coster [sister Marie Leguori] took the white veil of the novices, & the black veil of the **Sisters of Mercy** was taken by Miss Alicia Cecilia Shubrick, [sister Marie Jerome.] Miss Coster is a grand-daughter of Adm De Grasse, & Miss Shubrick is the daughter of Capt Shubrick, of the U S Navy. –N Y Mirror

The undersigned have formed a copartnership in the practice of law in all the Courts of D C, & will attend to professional business generally. Ofc corner of 6th st & La ave. –Rich H Clarke, A Austin Smith

Mrd: on Sep 20, by Rev John R Hendrick, the Rev John T Edgar, D D, of Nashville, Tenn, to Mrs Ann Innes Crittenden, daughter of John Morris, residing near Frankfort, Ky.

Mrd: on Oct 2, at Canandaigua, N Y, by Rev Dr Daggett, John Eliot Thayer, of Boston, Mass, to Cornelia Adeline, only daughter of Hon Francis Granger.

Died: on Fri last, at the residence of her father, Mr Thos Foster, in Wash City, Mrs Ann E Dinkle, consort of H W Dinkle, of Alexandria, & formerly of Winchester, Va. She has left a disconsolate husband & 3 infant daughters & a large concourse of realtives & friends to mourn their loss. She was a consistent member of the Methodist Episcopal Church.

Died: on Sep 23, at his residence near Lexington, Ky, Col Alfred G Carter, of Wash Co, Miss, in his 59th year.

Wash City Ordinances: 1-Act for the relief of R W Dove: the sum of $160 be paid to him for placing a window in the Council Chamber, as ordered by the Common Council. 2-Act for the relief of Jacob F King: the fine of $10, imposed on him in forestalling the market, is hereby remitted: provided he pay the costs.

TUE OCT 9, 1855
The fine ship **William Penn**, of New Bedford, Capt Cole, from the Chincha Islands, bound to Balt, was lost on Sep 30, & all on board, with the exception of one man, a seaman, Francis Dixon, were drowned. The captain's wife, who was on board, also drowned. –Balt Patriot

Mrs M A Hills will open Fall Millinery on Oct 11: Pa ave, between 9th & 10th.

Wash Navy Yard, Sep 18, 1855. Cmdor Chas S Morris, U S Navy. Dear Sir: Having learned that you are among those placed on the reserved list of the navy, & consequently detached from this yard, the undersigned, who have for many years been associated with you on duty therein, avail themselves of the occasion to bear cheerful testimony to the prompt, efficient, & faithful manner in which you have performed every duty assigned to you. Signed:

W P S Sanger, Com Eng	A G Herold
S M Pook, N C	Francis Barry
F McNerhany, N S K	John H Smoot
Jas Tucker, M Smith	Edw Evans
Abel G Davis, M Plumber	Henry N Ober
C A Woodward, M Blockmaker	John C Clark
Edw Foster, M Carpenter	Chas H Gordon
Jas Phillips, M Mason	John P White
Jno H Peake, M Painter	Jas R McCathran
B B Curran, M Joiner	M E Bright
Wm H Bland, M Founder	L Marceron
Jos M Padgett	John F Tucker
D W McComb, Clerk to Cmder	John D Brandt
Trustun D Beale	John Holroyd
Lemuel Gaddis	N Lewis
John F Dobbyn	Danl Kleiss

Suits against the Camden & Amboy Railroad Co have commenced in the Supreme Court of Pa for damages by the following persons, survivors of the late terrible calamity at Burlington: Mrs Phelps, principal of the Patapsco Institute, at Ellicott's Mills, Md, brings suit in her own name, & that of Miss Jane P Lincoln, who was killed; Miss Myra L Phelps, daughter of the above, brings suit in her own name; seven children of Mr Alex'r Kelly, of Phil, who was killed; Lambert A Phillips & Rebecca Phillips, his wife, in right of said Rebecca, who was seriously injured; Jas E Wheeden & Catharine Holsman, also injured.

Letter in the Christian Advocate from Rev Beverly Waugh, senior Bishop of the Methodist Episcopal Church, to the Rev Dr Lucket, descriptive of the state in which he found his family on his recent return from an official visit to Western N Y. Letter is dated Balt, Sep 17. Mrs Waugh had a sister residing in poor stricken Norfolk. She, with 3 sons, had come to Balt a week before my return, & was immediately attacked by yellow fever, & in 3 days she was in her grave, & in 24 hours was followed by her son, age about 23 years old. My dear wife was in bed sick when her sister arrived. Our son, Alex'r Townsend, had been quite unwell, which gave rise to a report that he had yellow fever. Our neighbors were too much alarmed to come in, & the hired woman became so alarmed that she went off. Fortunately Mrs Waugh's oldest sister was with her. As soon after my return as my son was able to travel with safety, I got them all off for the country, 120 miles from Balt, at the house of Mrs Waugh's sister. My poor afflicted brother-in-law is still in Norfolk, if living. Since his wife left home another of their sons, who remained in Norfolk, has fallen a victim to the epidemic, & an old servant likewise.

Yellow fever. At Trinity, La, the fever is raging. Dr Quail is among the victims. At Memphis, Tenn, Dr Geno Harris has died of the disease. E F Gibbs, C O Jackson, & Wm H Hampton, 3 prominent merchants of Vicksburg, have fallen victims to the fever; also Wm E Francis.

Died: after a long & painful illness, I F Barry, aged 23 years & 6 months. His funeral will take place from the residence of his mother, Mrs C Barry, corner of 10th & C sts, this afternoon at 4 o'clock. [No death date given.]

Died: on Oct 5, Mary Eliz, infant daughter of Henry & Maria M Smith, aged 1 year, 10 months & 20 days.

Mrd: on Oct 4, by Rev R L Dashiell, Branlon B Jeffers, of Loudoun Co, Va, to Kate C Taylor, of Wash City.

Died: on Oct 7, after a short illness, Mr John S Stillings, in his 57th year. His funeral is this day at 3 o'clock, from his late residence on L st, at the Navy Yard.

Died: on Oct 5, in Wash City, of cholera infantum, Walter Hill, youngest son of Mr & Mrs I A Hopkins, aged 1 year & 2 months.

Boston, Oct 8. The passenger train on the Boston & Maine railroad was thrown from the track this morning by running over a cow. The engine fell down the embankment, & E Abbott, of Andover, & Chas Richardson, of Haverhill, express messengers, were killed instantly. R Gleason was badly injured, & Geo Richardson, fireman, was so badly crushed that he was thought to be dying. Two brakemen each lost a leg. None of the passengers were injured.

Obit-died: on Aug 12, 1855, at Wash City, Henry Lee Heiskell, M D, Surgeon U S Army. He was born in Winchester, Va, Mar 16, 1803; graduated in medicine at the Univ of Pa in 1828; appointed an assist surgeon in the army on Jul 13, 1832, & on Jul 7, 1837, promoted to the rank of surgeon; served several years at Southern stations, sharing in the dangers of the Florida war; he was ordered to Madison Barracks, Sackett's Harbor, N Y; from whence, in Sep, 1840, he was called to Wash City & assigned to duty in the Medical Bureau as assist to the Surgeon-General. He remained there for 15 years, until his death. In Jun, 1842, he married Eliz K Gouverneur, the daughter of Saml L Gouverneur, & grand-daughter of Pres Monroe, who, with 4 children survives him. During the last 3 years of his life Dr Heiskell's failing health served to withdraw him, to a certain extent, from the busy cares of office.

Orphans Court of Wash Co, D C. Letters of administration on the personal estate of Catharine Brown, late of Wash Co, deceased. –Jos Smith, adm

WED OCT 10, 1855
In the U S Court, Hon John W Brockenbrough presiding, at Staunton, Va, John M Meek was convicted on Sat last of robbing the U S mail & sentenced to the penitentiary for 10 years. At the time he was engaged in carrying the mail in Augusta Co, Va, & opened one of the mail bags & rifled the letters of their contents.

Wash Corp: 1-Interrogation of Wm H Clampitt: [Assessor elect, regarding whether he is a citizen of the U S or not.] I heard my father was born in a foreign country. Mr Christopher Cammack says he first formed an acquaintance with Clampitt's mother when she was a widow, about 1822 or 1823, then Wm was a very small boy, 3 or 4 years old. The next youngest child was in infant in the arms. From that period to the present, with intermission of 1 or 2 years, he has been a resident of D C. Clampitt declined to answer question 3: Have you, or not, heard your mother or father say you were born in a foreign country? I decline to answer this question by the advice of counsel. Clampitt answers question 5: Have you, or not, said you thought your father was naturalized, & that consequently you were a naturalized citizen? I never did say so. Resolved: That the ofc of Assessor of the 2nd Ward be & the same is hereby declared vacant.

Messrs C L Coltman & J A M Duncanson have commenced the erection of a fine brick merchant gristmill, to run five pairs of stones by a sixty-horse engine, now being built for them at the establishment of the Messrs Ellis. It is to be on the canal basin, between 13th & 13½ sts, & adjoining the machine works of the firm named above. -Ibid

Mrd: on Oct 4, by Rev Mr Sutherland, A Jackson Beall to Georgie, eldest daughter of Geo Hill, jr, all of Gtwn, D C.

Public sale on Oct 24, of Jefferson Machine Shop & Iron & Brass Foundry: by deed of trust by Geo F S Zimmerman & others, dated Sep 14, 1855, recorded in the clerk's ofc of the court of Jefferson Co, Va. Foundry is near the depot of the Winchester & Potomac Railroad, on the borders of Charlestown. –N S White, trustee

Died: on Oct 8, in Gtwn, after two weeks' illness, Pedro Antonio Daunas, Prof of Music at Gtwn College, in his 38th year. His funeral is this morning at 9 o'clock, at Mrs Rhodes', corner of Market & Bridge sts.

Middleton, Conn, Oct 9. Hon Saml D Hubbard, an ex-member of Congress, & subsequently Postmaster General during Pres Fillmore's administration, died at this place last night.

Died: on Oct 9, in Wash City, in his 46th year, John Ennis, a native of Wexford, Ireland, but for the last 25 years a resident of Wash City. His funeral is this afternoon, at 4 o'clock, from his late residence, on Wash st, between 4th & 5th sts.
+
Members of the Northern Liberties Fire Co are to meet at their hall, in full uniform, to attend the funeral of their late fellow-member, John Ennis, sr, at 1 o'clock. -J T Halleck, sec

Orphans Court of Wash Co, D C. In the case of the administrators, with the will annexed, of Wm McKinstry, deceased, the administrator & Court have appointed Oct 30 for the second settlement of the personal estate of said deceased, of the assets in hand. -Ed N Roach, Reg/o wills

THU OCT 11, 1855
Gilmor House, Monument Square, Balt, Md, now open for the reception of guests. -J Mildeberger Smith, Proprietor. W S Warner, late of St Nicholas Hotel, N Y, Superintendent

Superior Rosewood Chickering Piano Forte, excellent cabinet furniture & house-keeping effects at Public Auction: on Nov 1, at the residence of Capt G S Blake, U S Navy, on Pa ave, between 17th & 18th sts. -Jas C McGuire, auct

Promotions & appointments in the Marine Corps.
1st Lt Fred'k B McNeill, to be a captain from Aug 19 last, vice Stark, deceased.
2nd Lt Israel Green, to be 1st Lt, vice Sutherland, promoted.
2nd Lt Jacob Read, to be 1st Lt from Aug 19 last, vice McNeill, promoted.
Alex'r W Stark, of Va, to be 2nd Lt from Aug 19 last, vice Green, promoted.
David M Cohen, of Md, to be 2nd Lt from Aug 19 last, vice Read, promoted.
Jas Lewis, of Pa, to be a 2nd Lt from Sep 25 ult, vice Dallas, resigned.

At the late term of the Berkeley Superior Court an action was brought by Wm T Herring against Geo Lemmon to recover damages in a case of slander. In 1853, from testimony given by Mr Lemmon, Mr Herring was indicted for forgery; but he was honorably acquitted. Hence the present suit. The jury gave a verdict for the plntf, assessing the damages at $1,500. –Richmond Whig

On Fri last, Dr Chas Broadfoot Baker, formerly of Fayetteville, but for several years past a practicing physician of Elizabethtown, N C, was found in the road a short distance below that place in a dying condition. He expired in a few minutes. The cause of his death was not certainly known. His sulky was standing in the road near him & his horse met half a mile off, having broken loose from the traces, that he had been thrown out; but there were no bruises upon the body, except very slight ones on the face & knee. –Fayetteville Observor

Mrs W L Davison, 303 Pa ave, between 9th & 10th sts, announces that she will open a splendid assortment of French Hats & Head-dresses on Oct 13.

$5 reward for the recovery of a sorrel Poney, stolen from my meadow.
-Wm H Gunnell, C st, between 4½ & 6th st.

An estray came to my premises on 7th st Plank Road, a large black horned Cow. Owner can have by proving property & paying charges. –Harriet White

Mrd: on Oct 9, by Rev Mr Hodges, Jas H Wilson to Miss Mary Frances Salisbury, all of Wash.

Mrd: on Sep 20, by Rev G H Day, Chas F M Larkin to Mary M Hazlup, all of Va.

Mrd: on Sep 30, by Rev Mr Boyle, Mr J H Middleton to Miss E Brannan, both of Wash City.

Died: on Oct 8, Annie Eliz Harvey, eldest daughter of Danl & Matilda B Smith, aged 8 years & 7 months.
+
Died: on Oct 9, William Edward, son of Danl & Matilda B Smith, aged 2 months & 11 days.

FRI OCT 12, 1855
The steamer **Union**, from Havre, which arrived at N Y Oct 11, reports having spoken yesterday, 60 miles south of Sandy Hook, a steamer under command of Lt Harstene, who had on board Dr Kane & his party of Artic Explorers. Dr Kane sailed from N Y in the brigantine **Advance** on May 31, 1853, for the Polar Seas, in search of Sir John Franklin & his companions. His entire ship's company consisted of: Elisha M Kane, Surgeon in the U S Navy, commanding the expedition; J Wall Wilson, 1st mate;

Henry Brooks, 2nd mate; Amos Bronsell, 3rd mate; Jas McGeary, 4th mate; Christopher Ohlsen, carpenter; J J Hayes, surgeon; Augustus Sontag, astronomer; Henry Goodfellow, naturalist; Geo Stephenson, Jefferson T Parker, Geo J Whittell, Wm E Godfrey, Geo Reilly, & C Blake, seamen; Wm Morton, steward; Peter Sheppard, cook. This expedition consisted of 2 vessels, the propeller **Arctic** & the barque **Release**, which were officered as follows: Ofcrs of the **Release**: Henry H Hartstene, Lt commanding; Wm L Lovell, acting master; Jos P Fyffe, passed midshipman; Elisha R Kane, assist surgeon; Van Rensselaer Hale, boatswain. Ofcrs of the **Arctic**: Chas C Simms, Lt commanding; Watson Smith, acting master; Harman Newell, engineer; Saml Whiting, acting boatswain. Three of Dr Kane's party have died, viz: Christopher Ohlsen, carpenter; Peter Sheppard, cook; & Jefferson T Parker, seaman. The remainder were more or less frostbitten. On Sep 4 the barque **Rescue** narrowly escaped shipwreck by coming in contact with an iceberg, which stove in her bulwarks & carried away her boats. No traces whatever were discovered of Sir John Franklin's party. [Oct 15th newspaper: Christian Ohlsen, carpenter, died of lockjaw, produced by intense cold; Jefferson Baker, seaman, died of the same complaint; Pierre Schubart, cook, [French,] died from the effects of amputation of his foot, which was rendered necessary from being frostbitten.]

Extensive sale of real estate & valuable wharf property: at the south end of 7th st west, under deed of trust, dated May 1, 1854, recorded in Liber J A S No 73, folios 5, 6, et seq: sale on Nov 12, the property in Wash City, D C, known as square 472, with improvements, [excepting a certain lot of ground therein belonging to the heirs of the late Simon Frasier;] the entire wharf property west of square 472, known as *Page's wharf* property; the whole of square 471; lots 3 thru 6, in Page's subdivision of square 390. –John F Fenwick, Richd Wallach, trustees -Jas C McGuire, auct

Mrd: on Sep 30, by Rev Mr Boyle, Mr J H Middleton to Miss Mary E Brannan, both of Wash City.

SAT OCT 13, 1855
Trustee's sale of 3 valuable brick dwlg-houses & unexpired term of lease of lots, with privilege of purchase, on 9th st west of N st north. By deed in trust, dated Sep 12, 1854, recorded in Liber J A S, No 85, folios 97: public auction on Nov 5, all the unexpired term of a certain lease from Ulysses Ward to Aloysius N Clements, dated Jun 19, 1854, of lots 2 & 3, in Saml Norment's subdivision of square 399, with the privilege of purchase; & also all the bldgs on said lots: which face 50 feet on 9th st, with 3 well built brick dwlg houses. –Chas S Wallach, trustee -Jas C McGuire, auct

Another of the pioneers of the water cure system is dead. Joel Shew, M C, died at Oyster Bay on Oct 6. For several years it has been evident to his friends & to himself, that his lease of life was short at longest. –Life Illustrated

Elisha Bartless, a Revolutionary soldier, died in Georgia, Vt, on Sep 30, at the advanced age of 100 years, 9 months & 13 days. He was born in Chatham, Conn, Dec 16, 1754, the son of a clergyman, & youngest of 10 children. He served 13 months in the Continental army under his brother, Capt Saml Bartlett, marched with his company for Boston, & arrived just after the battle of Bunker Hill; was in the division that fortified Dorchester Heights; present at the evacuation of Boston; was in the battles of Brooklyn Heights, of White Plains, & of the capture of Burgoyne. Mr Bartlett was a farmer by profession, & labored more or less till the last 2 years. He was fond of the company of children, & the friend of all. He retained his faculties in an eminent degree to the last. A few days previous to his death he affirmed, & it is believed, that he had walked unaided every day for 100 years.

Fruit Trees for sale: John Saul, corner of 7th & H sts.

Robt Rogers, aged about 8 years, died at the house of his widowed mother, near 5th & Wash sts, Thu. He was assaulted on Friday week, by a schoolmate, age 10, who had frequently attacked him before. He was arrested & committed to prison. Rogers was a quiet inoffensive child, the other boy maltreated & abused him.
-Phil Bulletin

Died: on Oct 11, at the residence of Mr Jas Mankin, 398 9th st, Mr Jos N Jones, of Chas Co, Md, in his 23rd year. His funeral will be from St Patrick's Church, F st, on Sat at 4 o'clock.

Died: on Oct 12, Paulus Cromwell Thyson, infant son of Paulus & Parthenia Thyson, aged 15 months. His funeral is today at 10 o'clock, from the residence of his parents, on 7th st, between H & I sts.

Mrs Allen Thompson, formerly of F st, has removed to the s e corner of Pa ave & 4½ st, where she will be happy to accommodate gentlemen with furnished rooms, with or without board.

MON OCT 15, 1855
Powder Mill at Gorham, Me, exploded on Fri, killing Franklin Hawkes, Geo Whipple, Jas Whipple, Saml Phinney, & John Sweet. The present owners are G G Newhall & Co, of Boston. The mill was formerly owned by Oliver Whipple, of Lowell, Mass, whose brother & son are among the killed.

Public sale of bldg lot on Indiana ave: sale on Oct 19, of lot 3, in square 573, fronting 24 feet on Indiana ave, between 1st & 2nd sts, adjoining the handsome residence recently built by the late Jno W Gibbons. –Chas S Wallach, atty -J C McGuire, auct

The Washington House is now renovated & fitted up for public reception.
-Coban Baker, Proprietor, Wash, D C.

Mr Ralph Landon, a worthy citizen of this place, was killed on the Vt & Canada Railroad at Swanton Falls on Monday. In attempting to get on the cars he seized the upright iron stancheon with his right hand, & appeared to succeed in placing his feet on the step, but a heavy carpet bag which he held in his hand seemed to swing him around between the cars, & he fell upon the track face downwards. The wheels of the car, 4 in number, passed over his body just above the hips, nearly severing it. –Burlington Sentinel

Two Revolutionary veterans gone. 1-Henry Spohn, aged 90 years, died in Herkimer Co, N Y, on Aug 20. He commenced his military career at age 16, & served as a substitute. His sister was shot by the Indians at the time of the war, near the bridge between Mohawk & Herkimer. 2-Mr Casler, aged 95 years, died at German Flats on Sep 18. He was present when Butler, the Tory, was shot by an Indian. He also helped to set the picket about the fort at Herkimer.

Cumberland Coal: just landed at my wharf on the Canal. –F L Moore, West side 9th st, between D & E sts.

Died: on Oct 13, in Wash City, Henry S Addison. His funeral will be today at 3 o'clock, from the residence of Mrs Barker, on 10th st, next door to the corner of C.

Died: on Oct 13, Emma Georgiana, daughter of Geo & Emma Poe, in her 27th year. Her funeral will be today, at 4 o'clock P M, from the residence of her parents, Gtwn.

Died: on Sat, at the residence of her mother, Mrs Magill, Mrs Maria L B Isaac, in her 26th year, wife of Mr Jos C Isaac.

Died: on Oct 13, at the *Vineyard*, near Wash City, Mrs Hannah Murray Blackford, of Birmingham, England, aged 81 years, widow of the late Edw Blackford, for many years a merchant in N Y.

TUE OCT 16, 1855
On Sep 14 the Nicaragua steamer **Uncle Sam** arrived at her wharf at the foot of Jackson st. Rumors were raised that cholera had raged on board of the boat. The captain reports at the custom-house the death of 103 adults, 8 children, & 9 seamen. –Times

N W Richardson has sold to John Glaize, for $77.50 per acre, the farm of 190 acres lying on the plank road, one mile n w of town. It is the residue of the Baldwin tract bought by Mr Richardson 3 years ago, & cost him altogether $56 per acre, being $4,000 less than is now obtained. The prospective of railway improvements is making its mark in the increased value of Fred'k Co lands.

Hon Wm T Nuckolls, of S C, died at his residence in that State about Sep 25, in his 55th year. He was for 6 years a Rep in Congress from S C, his service terminating some 20 years ago, at which time he was stricken down by sickness, & has since been the victim of continued affliction & suffering.

Wanted: information of Christopher Hillman, formerly a soldier in Co A, 6th Infty, U S Army. Said Hillman left his family in Illinoistown, [opposite St Louis,] in pursuit of work in the State of Missouri, about Jun 1, & has not since been heard of. Hillman is about 50 years of age, has light hair, eyes, & complexion, & is bald. Any information about him addressed to his wife, Sarah Hillman, 400 20th st, Wash, D C, will be thankfully received.

For rent: dwlg part of house 332 Pa ave, between 9th & 10th sts. Immediate possession given. Apply to Chas H Lane, Gentlemen's Furnishings Store, 424 Pa ave, Wash.

Rooms for rent in house No 1 Union Row, corner of 7th & F sts. Apply to Z C Robbins.

Mrd: on Sep 8, at the residence of Mr Jos Jordon, by Rev Jacob Schough, Saml B McKenney, of the city of Norfolk, to Miss Eliza F Guy, daughter of the late Talbot Guy, of Norfolk Co.

Died: on Oct 14, Mr Geo A D Clarke, in his 39th year. He was a native of N Y C, & had been for some years previous to his death a clerk in the Interior Dept. He was at one time Disbursing Agent for the Census Ofc, & subsequently the assistant to the Disbursing Agent of the Interior Dept. His funeral will take place this evening at 3½ o'clock, from his late residence at Mrs Paris', corner of 13th & F sts.

Died: on Oct 14, John Foy, in his 64th year. He was a native of Castlereagh, county of Roscommon, Ireland, but for the last 28 years a resident of Wash City, where he has many devoted friends to mourn his death. His funeral will take place on Oct 16, at 2½ o'clock, from his late residence, opposite the Railroad Depot, to which the friends & acquaintances of the family are invited.

Died: on Sep 25, of congestion of the brain, Susan Colby, aged 3 years & 6 months, daughter of the late Z W & M A Cherry.

Chicago, Oct 15. Judge Thos Clingman, of Carroll Co, Misouri was murdered on Oct 9 by a field slave. The neighbors lynched the slave immediately.

WED OCT 17, 1855
Extensive stock of groceries, liquors, & teas at auction, on Oct 22, at the store of Messrs Berry & Bowie, on 7th st. –Perry & Bowie. –Wall, Barnard & Co, aucts

Fire on Sunday night at the farm of Mr J Hill Carter, of Falkland, Prince Wm Co, Va, in which 6 negroes resided, was discovered to be on fire, & so enveloped in flames that no ingress could be had. Five were burnt to death, 2 young men, one woman, past middle age, one boy of 10 or 12 years of age, & a girl some 2 years younger. This calamity is said to have had its origin in intemperance, as the adults were known to be in a state of intoxication at bed time.

Orphans Court of Wash Co, D C. In the case of Edw Shaw, administrator with the will annexed of Francis N Shaw, deceased: the administrator & Court have appointed Nov 6 next, for the final settlement of the personal estate of said deceased, of the assets in hand. –Ed N Roach, Reg/o wills

The yellow fever epidemic has been painfully fatal to <u>Ministers of the Gospel</u>. Rev Wm M Jackson, Pastor of St Paul's P E Church, died on Oct 3. He was the last of 7 victims of the destroyer, viz: Rev Mr Dibrell, of the M E Church in Granby st; Rev Mr Chisholm, St John's P E Church, Portsmouth; Rev Vernon Eskridge, M E Church, Chaplin U S Navy; Rev Mr Jones, M E African Church in Bate/Bute st; Rev W Cadogan Bagnall, Baptist Church; & Rev Mr Devlin, Catholic Priest, Portsmouth. <u>Physicians deceased</u>: Dr R W Silverter, Dr Geo I Halsen, Dr Thos N Constable, Dr Junius A Briggs, Dr R G Sylvester, Dr Geo L Upshur, Dr Richd Tunstall, Dr Thos Nash, & Dr Cannon-the two last Thompsonians. Dr Francis L Higgins had the fever in Norfolk, & when convalescent went to Phil, where he relapsed & died. Dr Henry Selden went with his family to Hampton towards the close of Sept, his own health being greatly impaired, & there took the fever & died on Oct 2. <u>Husbands & wives deceased.</u> They are given from memory, & there may be others: Capt W E Stark, Dr R W Sylvester, J G H Hatton, R S Bernard, Mr Lewis, Elkanah Balance, Alex'r Feret, Horace Drewry, John D Gordan, Jos H Robertson, Wm P Burnham, Alex Watt, John Shuster, Mr Doyle, Benj Quick, F A Johnson, E Bryant, Wm B Ferguson, Richd Dove, John R Wyatt, Mr Rudder, Thos Jenning, Thos H Beveridge, & Edw Daley. A letter by N C Whitehead, J P, Acting Mayor of Norfolk, rendering the thanks of the city to the stranger physicians & nurses who came to its relief: Norfolk, Sep 27, 1855. To Dr A B Williman, Chairman: The spirit that prompted you to your work of martyrdom would retain you at your posts so long as there might be aught to be accomplished. The plague is at length in a degree stayed. A list prepared from the original entries has been handed to me by Franklin H Clack, of New Orleans, [our efficient temporary Chief of Police,] shows that, out of 87 physicians & assistants who visited us during the space of 33 days preceding the 19th, 20 physicians are numbered with the dead. This is exclusive of the mortality among our resident physicians, more than half of those abiding here having died.

Orphans Court of Wash Co, D C. Letters of administration on the personal estate of Wm M Boyce, late of Wash Co, deceased. –M M Boyce, excx

N Y Typographical Society meeting on Oct 6, for an election of ofcrs for the ensuing term, with the following result: Pres, Danl L Northup; V Pres, John W Forbes; Sec, Thos C Faulkner; Treas, Jas Narine; Trustees, C C Savage, John Thomas; Dirs of the Library, Chas McDevitt, Henry J Crate, J P Nesmith. The roll book shows some 250 members. The library contains 4,000 volumes, with constant additions. -Mirror

Powder explosion at Gorham on Oct 12. The Portland Argus says: S Phinney, after the explosion, walked several rods until he met a man who spoke to him, & he instantly fell dead. John Swett was thrown nearly a quarter of a mile. F Harkes had his bowels blown out & one side of his head blown off. Geo O Whipple, E C Hardy, & Mr Robinson, of Lowell, were instantly killed.

Wash Corp: 1-Act granting permission to Allen S Dorsey to convert a certain bldg into a livery stable: referred to the Cmte on Police. 2-Ptn from Thos Bayne & Matthew Trimble, asking to be refunded certain moneys: referred to the Cmte on Finance. 3-Names of Ward Apothecaries: A G Ridgely; S N Sylvester; Wm T Evans; W H Gilman; H H McPherson, jr; John E Bates; O Boswell.

Mrd: on Oct 16, at the residence of her uncle, Robt W Lathan, by Rev R L Dashiell, Miss Jane E Latham to Chas B Young, of Wash City.

Mrd: on Oct 11, by Rev Mr Day, Richd F Cole to Frances V Byrne, both of Wash City.

Mrd: on Oct 4, at the residence of S Newton Dexter, Whitesboro, N Y, by Rev Pres North, Jas G Farwell, of Utica, to Gertrude Walton, daughter of the late Thos R Gold.

Mrd: on Oct 15, by Rev T N Haskell, Mr John Priest, of Vicksburg, Miss, to Miss Helen Jane Anderson, of Wash City.

Mrd; on Sep 15, in Espirito Santo Church, Havana, Mr J B Belt, of Wash, to Miss Carmen Munoz, of Havana.

Died: on Oct 9, at Summit Point, Jefferson Co, Va, in her 26th year, Mrs Ellen G Moore, wife of Saml J C Moore, & daughter of Dr Saml Scollay, of Middleway, Va.

Mrd: on Oct 1, at Dranesville, Va, Sarah Hannah, the only child of Jos & Elizabeth Eliza Davison, of Wash, in her 11th year.

Died: on Oct 15, John A Lloyd, aged 36 years. His funeral is this day at 2 P M, from his late residence, foot of Anacostia bridge, near the Navy Yard.

Orphans Court of Wash Co, D C. Letters of administration on the personal estate of Martha A Sanderson, late of Wash Co, deceased. –Wm Sanderson, adm

Orphans Court of Wash Co, D C. Letters of administration on the personal estate of John F Kahl, late of Wash Co, deceased. –Johanna Kahl, admx

Cumberland, Oct 16. The body of a young man named Henry Graff was found last evening in the mountains as short distance from the city, having been shot & his body mutilated. A stranger, Fred'k Miller, who had been living in the vicinity, a German from Pittsburg, was arrested on suspicion of being the murderer. In his possession were found articles belonging to the deceased, & also the clothing, watch, & pocket-book of Dr J F C Hadel, who was also missing, & in whose ofc young Graff was a student. After a search was made the body of Dr Hadel was found in the mountains horribly mutilated. Dr Hadel was formerly Health Com'r of Balt. The head of Dr Hadel was found buried at some distance from the body. The murderer is a German peddler who recently broke jail at West Alexander. [Oct 19th newspaper: Splg: Graff is named as Henry Graeff. Both victims were shot in the back, near the neck. It seems that Dr Hadel was going to attend to professional duties at the insistance of Mr Miller, of someone needing him. After killing Dr Hadel, he then returned & lured Graeff to go with him, telling him that Dr Hadel had an accident & needed him. The murderer, Fred'k Miller, was found in the house the Doctor occupied, asleep in the upstairs apartment, where Hadel & Graeff usually slept, especially during the absence of Mrs Hadel. Among the effects of the accused were found a box full of the Doctor's effects, his watch & chain, seals, & rings.]

THU OCT 18, 1855

Stock of new & second-hand furniture at auction: on Nov 2, at the Furniture Store of J W Hauptman, 405 9th st, 3 doors from Pa ave. –A Green, auct

Hon Thos W Cumming, who represented the second district of N Y in the last Congress, died at his residence in Brooklyn on Saturday last.

Public sale of a delightful country seat or market farm, with stock, household furniture, on the Rockville Turnpike, containing about 86 acres, known as the **Burnett Farm**, about 5 miles from Gtwn, & within 5 minutes' walk of the Bethesda Church, on Oct 31: joined by the lands of Saml Perry & Robt Dick. There are 2 dwlgs, barn, stable, corn-house, & a pump at the door. Also, all household & kitchen furniture. -Jas C McGuire, auct

Orphans Court of Wash Co, D C. In the case of Gottleib C Schneider, adm of Mary Kelley, deceased, the adminstrator & Court have appointed Nov 10 next for the final settlement of the personal estate of said deceased, of the assets in hand. –Ed N Roach, Reg/ wills

Robbery of railroad cars: Rochester, Oct 15. On Sat a visit made to the residence of 2 conductors residing in this city, Wm Hopper & Geo R Lyon, & to the boarding house of Saml Huntington, brakeman, at those places a large quantity & variety of goods were found stored. Martin Hillon, a brakemen, lived at Lyon's house, & some of the articles were found in his bed & in trunks belonging to him. W A Tracy & W H Tomer, brakemen, living at Niagara Falls, also suspected, had their boarding places searched, & valuable articles, not usually found in the wardrobe of single gentleman, were found. The stolen goods have been returned to the police ofc. When the ofcrs were at Hopper's house, his wife presented a cashmere shawl to a neighbor's daughter, telling her to claim it as her own in case she was questioned about it. Eight prisoners were arrested on Sat & Sun & lodged in jail. Today 4 more were arrested: John McLane, John Handy, Wm Hagadorn, & M Grave, brakemen. –Corr N Y Times

Army news. The War Dept has received advices of the death, at **Fort Tejon**, Calif, on Sep 8, of 1st Lt Thos F Castor, 1st Regt of Dragoons. 1st Lt Alpheus J Palmer, 9th Regt of Infty, has resigned his commission.

Orphans Court of Wash Co, D C. Letters testamentary on the personal estate of Hannah Blackford, late of Wash Co, deceased. –Geo W Riggs, exc

For sale or exchange for Wash City property, a valuable farm, containing 130 acres, in Montg Co, Md, about 8 miles from Wash. Apply to Pollard Webb, ofc on Pa ave, 7 doors east of the Nat'l Hotel.

$5 reward for return of strayed Red Cow. –Jos Peregoy, 444 F st, between 5th & 6$^{th.}$

Mrd: on Oct 16, by Rev Andrew G Carothers, Mr Jos Plowman to Miss Mgt Ann Wilson, daughter of Wm B Wilson, all of Wash City.

Court of Equity, Fall Term, 1855. North Carolina, Randolph Co. Alfred H Marsh, Henry B Elliott, Julius Pagenstecher, against The Occee Mining Co & Wm Hikok, & F W Allen. In this case the Court having ordered the clerk & master to take an account of all the partnership dealings in the pleadings mentioned, of the outstanding debts against the copartnerhship, & of any indebtedness between the partners, & also of the property belonging to said partnership & the value thereof; it appearing that the dfndnts are not inhabitants of this State. Said dfndnts are notified that I shall take said account at my ofc in Asheboro on Dec 1st next. Witness, Jonathan Worth, Clerk & Master of said Court. –J Worth, C M E

FRI OCT 19, 1855
A fire occurred in Wash City on Wed, a frame house in the n w suburbs, occupied by Mr Isaiah Stuart, having been destroyed. It is believed to have been purposely fired.

The copartnership existing under the firm of Boyce & Taylor, is dissolved by the death of Wm M Boyce. –Vincent J Taylor, surviving partner of Boyce & Taylor.

Orphans Court of Wash Co, D C. Letters testamentary on the personal estate of Wm Cranch, late of Wash Co, deceased. –W G Cranch, exc

Mrd: on Oct 18, by Rev R L Dashiell, Washington B Williams to Miss Jane E Johnson, all of Wash City.

SAT OCT 20, 1855
Mrd: on Oct 18, by Rev Geo Hildt, of McKendree station, Wm H Johnson to Miss Anna Eliz Littleton, both of Wash City.

Mrd: on Oct 18, by Rev John Lanhan, Jas E Ford, of Bourbon Co, Ky, to Harriet, daughter of Presley Simpson, of Wash City.

Died: on Oct 19, of typhoid fever, Mr Elisha Woodbury, in his 56th year, a native of N H. His funeral is this evening at 3½ o'clock, from the residence of his son, Mr Henry E Woodbury, 424 11th st, near H st.

Died: yesterday, Mary Alice, youngest daughter of Valentine & Ellen Harbaugh, aged 4 years. Her funeral will be this evening at 4 o'clock, from the residence of her parents.

U S Patent Ofc, Wash, Oct 18, 1855. Ptn of Robt Piggot, of Balt, Md, praying for the extension of a patent granted to him on Jan 17, 1842, for an improvement in apparatus for teaching geography, for 7 years from the expiration of said patent, which takes place on Jan 17, 1756. –S T Shugert, Acting Com'r of Patents

Dancing & Waltzing Academy, at Copp's Assembly Room, will open on Oct 27. -Mons J Cocheu

MON OCT 22, 1855
Advices from the East India squadron, dated Hong Kong, Aug 8, 1855. An engagement had taken place on Aug 4 between divisions of boats from the U S steam frig **Powhatan** & her British Majesty's steam sloop **Rattler**, & a large fleet of piratical junks which had for some time previously infested the neighboring waters & committed extensive depredations on commerce. The **Powhatan**'s boat expedition was in command of senior Lt R B Pegran; that of the **Rattler** was commanded by Cmder Wm A Fellows. The fight was severe, & ended in a complete route of the pirates. Capt Fellows having engaged a large war junk with his gig's crew & 5 musketeers, Lt Rolando came to his assistance, & captured the junk by boarding her, after encountering a hand to hand resistance. Immediately after the capture she was blown up by one of the piratical crew, who, fighting courageously,

was forced below, & is supposed in his desperation to have fired a train communicating with the magazine. The effects were most disastrous, capsizing the **Rattler**'s gig, blowing Capt Fellows overboard, together with Lt Rolando & a number of the **Powhatan**'s men, killing 2 & severely wounding others, one of whom has died. Pvt Adamson, of the marine, who had fought gallantly during the day, was shot severely in the groin, after being one of the first to gain the enemy's deck. From the "Friend of China" we find the following detail of the **Powhatan**'s division engaged in the action:
First Launch: Lt R B Pegram; Boatswain, Geo Briley
Second Launch: Lt Henry Rolando; Master's Mate, Saml R Craig
First Cutter: Master Edw T McLauley; Assist Surgeon, Albert Schriver; Assist Engineer, Mortimer Kellogg; 1st Lt, Jas H Jones, commanding U S Marines.
The same paper give the following list of killed & wounded:
On the side of the British ship **Rattler**:
Killed: John Massey, gunner, R M A; Geo Mitchell, able seaman; Jas Silvers, carpenter's mate..
Wounded: John Lindsay, B M A, burnt severely; David Lloyd, R M A, burnt severely; Richd Clark, slightly wounded & burnt; Jas Poulter & John Earle, able seamen, burnt severely; Jas Paull, B I C, burnt badly; Wm Robinson, gunner, R M A, contused head.
U S Boat Division:
Killed: Jos A Halsey, landsman, of Newark, N J; Isaac Coe, landsman
Wounded: Lt Pegram, contusion hand; Lt Rolando, burnt on hand; John Pepper, seaman, mortally; Benj Adamson, marine, gunshot, dangerously; Jere Pendergast, landsman, fracture of left clavicle & burns; Saml Mullard, marine, burnt very severely; Fred Hommell, marine, burnt very severely; P Waldersmidt, marine, burnt very severely; Joshua Lewis, seaman, burnt every severely; Wm Taylor, Cap A Gd, burnt very severely; Chas Tingwell, seaman, cutlass wound. John Pepper, seaman, died a few hours after the action. The wounded were taken to Hong Kong.

Household & kitchen furniture at auction on Oct 24: also carriage & harness, cows & hogs, at the late residence of John Agg, deceased, 3 miles north of Wash City, adjoining the Military Asylum, all the personal effects of the late John Agg & Hannah Blackford, deceased. –A Green, auct

Pensacola Gaz: correction of a statement going the rounds of the papers that Prince Lucien Murat, heir slightly apparent to the throne of Naples, was formerly a resident planter of this State. This is all a mistake. It was Prince Achille Murat, who married the daughter of Col Byrd Willis, of Va, & settled on a plantation somewhere near Talahassee. Prince Murat was well known as a courteous gentleman, where the father & family of his lady resided. It is now many years since his demise. His widow still resides on the plantation, & is blessed with fortune, health, troops of friends, all of which she is most deserving.

Trustee's sale of lot 20 in square 626, with 2 frame houses thereon: on Nov 12, by deed of trust from John T B Suit, dated Jul 3, 1852, recorded in Liber J A S No 44, folios 160 & 161, of the land records of Wash Co, D C: sale of above lot 20 in square 626, known as Walter C Johnson's subdivision. This property fronts 25 feet on Mass ave. –John Y Donn, trustees -C W Boteler, auct

Orphans Court of Wash Co, D C. Letters of administration on the personal estate of John Sciferline, late of Wash Co, deceased. –Michl Pock, adm

Orphans Court of Wash Co, D C. Letters of administration on the personal estate of Thieleman Engle, late of Wash Co, deceased. –Catharine Engle, admx

A noble woman, Margaret M Smith, of Burlington, N J, died in that town on Monday last, aged 64 years. She was noted for her charities, & after the recent railroad disaster she opened her house to the sufferers & nursed them with the utmost care. It was in her house that Mr & Mrs Gillespie died. The excessive fatigue & excitement of that period of trial were too much for the weak frame of the noble woman. No one in Burlington was ever more mourned.

On Friday a fire broke out in a 4 story frame bldg, 12 State st, N Y, occupied as a dwlg by 4 families, & 5 persons perished by burning & suffocation. The 3rd floor was occupied by Oliver D Vandeburg, wife & 2 children, his mother-in-law, Mrs Catharine Peacock, aged 50 years, & his sister-in-law, Miss Mary Peacock, aged 19 years. Mr Vandeburg awoke to the cry of fire, awoke his wife, got her & his 5 year old daughter, & infant child to the window, where he told them to remain until he jumped out on the front piazza to catch them. His wife dropped the infant, which he caught, & threw herself out of the window, breaking her wrist. Miss Peacock also dropped herself out of the window. The little daughter, Almeda, & Mrs Peacock, were not seen or heard of until their charred remains were found on the stairway. It is evident that the heroic little girl had gone back for her grandmother, had found her, & in the attempt to escape by the stairway, both were burnt to death. The 4th floor was occupied by Mrs Brown, aged 20 years, & her 9 year old nephew. Their bodies were found in bed in a sleeping position without any signs of having struggled. They must have died from suffocation before the flames reached them. The attic was occupied by Julia Recus & a German girl named Reca, & Miss Baker, as sleeping apts. Julia escaped by jumping on the piazza. Miss Baker made her way to the hall of the 1st floor, where she was rescued in a terribly burnt condition, but there are no hopes of her recovery.

Local Matters. Danl Mahoney, a laborer, was instantly killed by accidentally falling from a scaffold in the new hall of the Representatives at the Capitol on Sat last. He has left widow & a child.

Dissolution of partnership under the title of Hilbus & Hitz, by mutual consent.
-Geo Hilbus, John Hitz, jr

Mrd: on Oct 18, by Rev F Israel, Alex'r Duehay to Miss Pauline Harley, both of Wash City.

Mrd: on Oct 17, by Rev N P Tillinghast, Prof M Yarnall, U S Navy, to Miss Eliza J Hepburn, of Gtwn, D C.

Mrd: on Oct 18, in Wilmington, Dela, by Rev Mr Crooks, Mr Edw S McPherson, of Wash, to Miss Sallie P McCauley, of Wilmington, Dela.

Died: on Oct 18, after a brief illness of chronic croup. Sarah B, youngest daughter of John H & Sarah G Johnson, aged 3 years & 3 months.

Charleston, Oct 20. A duel took place near Savannah last Sat, between John Chaplin, an ex-Lt of the U S Navy, & Dr Kirk, his brother-in-law. Kirk was killed by the 3rd shot, & Chaplin was slightly wounded. [Oct 26th newspaper: The difficulty is said to have originated in the distribution of some property. Dr Kirk was from Savannah, while Mr Chaplin was from S C. –Balt American] [Oct 30th newspaper: the Virginia & other papers are copying the statement sent to Charleston by telegraph in regard to a duel fought near this city by Dr Kirk & a Lt Chaplin. The whole story is an unmitigated Roorback; there is not a word of truth in it. –Savannah Courier]

Cumberland, Oct 21. Fred'k Miller was tried on Sat for the murder of Dr J F C Hadel. The verdict was guilty of murder in the first degree. The testimony on the trial indicated that the accused was also guilty of the murder of Henry Graeff, for which he will be tried on a separate indictment. [Oct 24th newspaper: Miller was tried today for the murder of Mr Graeff, & was convicted of murder in the 1st degree. The evidence was nearly the same as in the case of Dr Hadel.]

TUE OCT 23, 1855
Mount Vernon Association: the Ladies of Virginia seem to be determined to raise a sufficient fund to purchase *Mount Vernon* for the State. Though Mrs Washington at one time consented to the request of Congress to have the remains of her venerated husband removed to the Capitol, it is now well understood that they are not to be disturbed. Hence the anxiety of the Virginians to secure *Mount Vernon* to the State, & to give the tomb of Washington the care appropriate to the sacred spot.

Mrd: on Oct 18, by Rev W F Speake, Chas W Mitchell to Miss Sarah Ashton, daughter of C H B Ashton, all of Wash City.

Mrd: on Oct 18, by Rev Dr Morris, Edw D Miller, formerly of Wash, D C, to Mary E, eldest daughter of Wendell Bollman, of Wash City.

Died: on Oct 19, in her 14th month, Emmeline Sophia Macleod, infant daughter of Jas Mandeville Carlisle.

Died: on Oct 22, after a brief illness, Mrs Catharine Purdon, in her 50th year. Her funeral will be from her late residence on 14th st, near Pa ave, on Oct 23 at 3 o'clock.

Obit-died: on Oct 14, 1855, John Foy. The writer of this expresses the feelings of his many friends when he declares that Washington did not possess a nobler hearted, more generous, or better man than John Foy. His heart was open as the day; To melting charity. None knew him but to love him, None named him but to praise him. Mr Foy was in his 64th year at the time of his death, having been born in Castlereagh, county Roscommon, Ireland, but was for the last 28 years a resident & citizen of Wash City. He died in the faith of his fathers, thus leaving the best consolation for his deeply afflicted widow, relatives, & numerous friends. May he rest in peace.
-A Friend

WED OCT 24, 1855
Twenty-five years ago *Iowa* was a wilderness, tenanted only by the savage. Now she has a civilized population estimated at about 600,000, & constantly increasing. The emigration to the State this year has been very heavy.

N Y Historical Society lately laid the corner-stone of a Library Bldg, to be erected at the corner of 2nd ave & 11th st, N Y. In an address Mr Bradish, the Pres, gave the reasons for the selection of the site as having: The recommendation of being rich in its historical associations & its memories of the past. It is a part of the Farm, & is but a few hundred feet from the ancient residence of Peter Stuyvesant, the early & distinguished Govn'r of the then Dutch colony of New Netherlands. It is still nearer to the tombs of the Govn'rs of 3 distinct dynasties: the Dutch Colonial, the English Colonial, & the Independent Constitutional of N Y. In the churchyard repose the remains of Govs Stuyvesant, Slaughter, & Tompkins.

Prof Tyler enumerates the 40 physicians who perished at Norfolk & Portsmouth since Jul 8 of yellow fever, as follows:

Sylvester	Selden	Booth
Constable	Burns	Howe
Halson	Trugien	Bache
Sylvester, jr	Parker	Dillord
Higgins	Lovett	Gooch
Briggs	Walters	Jowle
Upshur	Thompson	Gelbardt
Tunstall	Fliess	Blow

Jackson	Craycroft	Smith
De Besane	Mierson	Marshall
Obermuller	Handy	Craven
Decapry	Cole	Berry
Hunter	Moore	
Schell	Rizer	

An accident occurred at the Oneida Depot on Fri last. Mr Saml Vanch, residing near Poughkeepsie, was with his wife & 5 children. At Oneida Mrs Vanch left the train, & before her return the cars started. In attempting to get upon the moving train she fell below the cars, & was run over, cutting off one leg & otherwise so injuring her that she died shortly after.

New Orleans Daily Delta; The blood of the Butlers, as an old writer says, is hot & bold, but it is always true to the truth. Americans are familiar with the glorious Butlers, "the gallant band of patriot brothers," as Washington called them, who fought with such signal courage in the cause of the Revolution, & even to this day their children & their children's children display the hereditary passion for military glory & for liberty. In our own State, as in S C, the old stock has bourgeoned plenteously & born splendid fruit. The following paragraph, which appeared in one of the late numbers of the N Y Albion, commorates the gallant fate of the 3 sons of the future head of the house in Great Britian: Lt-Gen the Hon H E Butler is about to erect a handsome mural tablet in Thomastown Church, county Kilkenny, to the memory of his 3 gallant sons, Capt H T Butler, [55th Regt,] & D A A G, who was killed at Inkermann; Capt C G Butler, [86th Regt,] who served in Scinde, & who died of fever at Bombay in Dec last; & to Capt J A Butler, of the Ceylon Rifles, killed at Silistria, whose intrepid daring in the successful defence of that fortress has been the theme of universal admiration. The tablet was just completed by Gaffin, the sculptor. Within a laurel wreath are the names of the several places at which the gallant ofcrs had distinguished themselves, namely, China, Alma, Inkermann, Scinde, Kaffirland, & Silistria. In the inscription to the young volunteer at Silistria an honorable mention is made of his gallant friend & brother ofcr, Maj Nasihyth.

Murder in Milwaukee. On Oct 15, H C Adams, a banker of Milwaukee, was shot by Johan Finier. The murderer went into his ofc & demanded money of Mr Geo Papendick, deposited in the Germania Bank, which had failed last year. Mr P offered $25 on account; $50 was demanded. This was refused, when the German drew a pistol, which Mr Adams observing, asked Mr Jos Colt to go for a police ofcr. The German fired at him, then fired a second time at Mr Geo Papendick. Mr Adams died on Oct 17. The ball missed Mr Papendick. The coroner's jury brought in a verdict of willful murder against Finier.

Died: on Oct 23, after a protracted illness, Miss Sarah F Bartlett. Her funeral will be from the residence of her mother, 423 H st, near 11th, this afternoon at 3½ o'clock.

Died: on Oct 23, at his residence, on the Heights of Gtwn, D C, John H King, aged about 54 years. Unambitious of public fame, he devoted himself to the welfare & prosperity of his own town & vicinity, where he was well known for his public spirit & unspotted moral character. Few men may hope to leave behind them a more enviable reputation for enterprise, probity, & pure unobtrusive Christian charity. His funeral will take place this afternoon [24th] at half past three o'clock. His friends are invited to meet the remains at the *Oak Hill Cemetery*, Gtwn, D C.

THU OCT 25, 1855
Officers of the Ladies' **Mount Vernon** Association of Pa: Pres: Mrs Mgt Lamb. Vice Presidents: Mrs John W Claghorn, Mrs Maj Geo H Crosman, Mrs Franklin Peale, Mrs Maria Heyward Drayton, Mrs Hutter. Secs: Mrs Anna Lex, Miss Mary E Lawson. Treasurer: Edmund Wilcox. Ofcrs of the Ladies' Mount Vernon Association of Phil: Pres: Mrs Dr Thos Harris, U S N. Vice-Presidents: Mrs Robt Newlin, Miss Ann Leamy, Mrs Thos J Perkins, Mrs Edw Mitchell, Mrs B H Moore. Sec: Esther Rittenhouse Barton. Treasurer: Edmund Wilcox. Honorary members: Mrs Ed Gaskill, Miss R Glentworth.

Jas Naysmith, the inventor of the steam hammer, has effected an improvement of great value in pudding iron. It consists in the disengagement of the carbon from the molten metal in the pudding furnace by subjecting it to the action of currents of steam, introduced as near as possible at the lowest portion of the molten metal, thence diffused upwards, so as not only to mechanically agitate the metal, & thereby keep exposing fresh surfaces of it to the action of the oxygen of the air passing through the furnace, but also to remove the sulphuric & other deleterious substances in the iron, by making the oxygen of the air & also the hydrogen of the water combine with them, & carry them off in the state of acid gas.

Foreign Obits: 1-Rt Hon Sir Henry Ellis, K C B, died recently at Brighton, having been in declining health for some months. The deceased was Minister Plenipotentiary ad interim in Persia in 1814, prior to his going to China. In 1835 he was appointed Ambassador to Persia, which post he relinquished in Nov the following year. He was sent on a special mission to the Brazils in 1842, & in 1849 appointed by the Govn't to attend the conference at Brussels on affairs of Italy; since which he had been unemployed. 2-The venerable diplomatist, Rt Hon Sir Robt Adair, died recently at his residence in London, at the great age of 92 years. He was the son of Robt Adair, the eminent surgeon, by a daughter of the 2nd Earl of Albermarle. Sir Robt was appointed Minister Plenipotentiary at Vienna, Apr 5, 1806; appointed Ambassador at Constantinople in Apr, 1809; in Jul, 1831, sent on a special mission to Brussels, & also to Berlin, & remained so employed until the latter part of 1835, when he returned to England. 3-John Adam Von Itzstien, one of the most eminent of the political reformers of Germany, died on Sep 14 last, at his residence near Hallgarten, on the Rhine, aged 81 years. He entered political life in 1822.

Died: on Oct 24, Mr Beniah Willett, in his 57th year. His funeral is this evening at 3 o'clock, from his late residence on 13th st.

Household & kitchen furniture, horses & cows, farming utensils, & the personal effects of the late John Agg & Hannah Blackford, deceased, postponed because of rain, will positively take place on Oct 26, at the late residence of John Agg, deceased. –A Green, auct

At Boston on Sunday, David Merrill, a returned Californian, stabbed his wife, Catharine M Merrill, in a most shocking manner, & then stabbed himself, as is supposed, fatally. No less than 13 wounds were inflicted upon the person of the wife & 5 upon the husband himself. She died on Tue.

Circuit Court of Wash Co, D C: Chancery Docket: No 706. Oct Term, 1855. Wm S Nicholls vs Eliz Frere, widow, Ann Conner wife of Hugh Conner, & others, heirs-at-law of Jas B Frere, deceased. The bill of cmplnt, which was filed in the case on Oct 25, 1850, states that the cmplnt sold to the said Jas B Frere in his lifetime lot 14 in square 86, in Wash City, D C aforesaid, for the sum of $195.84, & received from him in payment on account from time to time an aggregate sum of $175, most of which was applied in payment of interest accrued on the unpaid portion of the said purchase money, leaving a balance of $121.13, with interest still unpaid, as is shown by exhibit A, filed with said bill, & which the dfndnts have neglected & refused to pay; that the cmplnt retained the title to the said lot of ground as security for the payment of said purchase money. The cmplnt, in his amended bill, further states that Ann Frere, one of the children & heirs-at-law of the said Jas B Frere, & one of the dfndnts to the original bill, has, since the same was filed, attained her full age & married one Hugh Conner, who is not an inhabitant of D C & lives in parts unknown to the cmplnt, & the cmplnt asked that the said Hugh Conner may be made dfndnt to said bill & may answer the matters therein contained. The object of the bill is to obtain a decree for the sale of the said lot of ground for payment of the said balance of purchase money & the interest thereon & cost of this suit; & it appearing to the Court that the said Hugh Conner does not reside within D C & is in parts unknown to cmplnt; it is by the Court ordered that he appear in this Court on or before the 3rd Monday in Mar next. –Jno A Smith, clerk

No 896-Equity: Circuit Court of Wash Co, D C. John Blackburn & wife & others, cmplnts, vs John A Scott & others, dfndnts. Morris Adler, trustee, reported to this Court that on Sep 4, he offered for sale at public auction parts of lots 32 thru 35, in the original plan of Gtwn, D C; & lots 43 & 44, & part of 45, lying south of Water st, being part of the estate of Allen Scott by said decree directed to be sold; & that at said sale Alex'r Ray was the purchaser of the whole of the said property in one lot for the sum of $6,000, & he has complied with the terms of the sale.
–Jno A Smith, clerk

Mrd: on Oct 24, at Grace Church, by Rev Mr Holmead, H Bowlsby Willson, of Canada, to Miss Harriott Conway Ladde, of Wash City.
+
Mrd: on Oct 24, by Rev Mr Holmead, Wiley P Mangum, jr, to Miss Fanny Vaulx Ladde, of Wash City.

Wash City Ordinances: 1-Act to refund Wm Hogan certain money: the sum of $5.37; & $75.27, the same having been paid by him for lot 5 in square 51, improperly sold at a tax sale on Apr 11, 1853, with 6% interest. 2-Act for the relief of Jas Barnes: fine imposed on him for the alleged violation of the law in keeping a livery stable without a license is remitted: provided he pays the costs of prosecution. 3-Act for the relief of John Allen: 2 fines imposed for keeping & harboring 2 dogs contrary to the laws of this Corp, are remitted: provided Allen pay the costs of prosecution. 4-Act for the relief of F B Poston: to pay him the sum of $15.19, for cleaning away snow, repairing benches & stands, & furnishing bell & other articles for the Western Market.

Died: on Oct 24, David Finch, aged 56 years, a native of Newtown, Conn, but for 11 years past a resident of Wash City. His funeral will be from the Foundry Church tomorrow at 3 o'clock P M.

FRI OCT 26, 1855
Household & kitchen furniture at auction on: Oct 31, by order of the Orphans Court of Wash Co, D C: at the late residence of John M Krafft, deceased, at the corner of 12th & F sts north. –Mary C Krafft, admx -A Green, auct

Jackson, Miss: on Oct 6th is was stated that there were 150 cases of yellow fever. At Napoleon, Ark, there were 35 cases on Oct 7. Robt Mayson & Mr Hibbard, two merchants, had died. J Watt Smith, assistant editor of the Memphis Eagle, & his wife, & her sister, Mrs Ward, have all fallen victims to the epidemic in that city.

On Wed Mr Jas A Lovelace, a respectable carpenter of Wash City, aged probably between 35 & 40, was conveyed to the Infirmary severely injured by being shot on one side of the face with a gun in the hands of John Harmon, his brother-in-law. His jaw was broken & his cheek much torn, & a large number of shot, which had passed around under the integuments, were removed from the back of his neck. We fear his case is critical. Harmon was arrested by ofcr Boss & committed to prison by Justice Hollingshead, to be further examined after the result of his act shall be determined. . [Oct 31st newspaper: John L Harman, charged with shooting Jas A Loveless on Oct 24, was yesterday admitted to bail by Justice Hollingshead in the sum of $500. The wounded man still lies at the Infirmary, but, though his jaw is broken & his face disfigured, the appearances indicate his probable recovery.]

Henry Levy, a native of France, met his death, a few days ago, on Hunter Point, L I, while under the water in a submarine armor. He used armor of India-rubber, dispensing with air-tubes & force-pumps. He had an India-rubber receiver attached to his body which contained a supply of oxygen gas, the flow being regulated by a tube & faucet. In his last experiment, after walking in the water a short distance, he returned, complaining of being unwell & feeling heated. Against advice he returned to the water, remaining under water 30 minutes, all the time signaling he was alright, but when drawn up it was found that he was dead. The signals, it is believed, were made by the motion of the water.

Died: on Sep 23, 1855, at **Fort Clark**, Texas, Jas G Stanly, brother of Hon Edw Stanly, of N C. He received the kind attention of a friend of his family.

Died: on Oct 13, at Memphis, Tenn, of the prevailing fever, Eleanor, wife of Wm J Delano, [formerly of Wash City, but recently of Dayton, Ohio,] aged 32 years.
+
Died: one hour after, of the prevailing fever, at the residence of Wm J Delano, Miss Emily Stewart, [late of Dayton, Ohio,] aged 22 years.

Obit-died: on Oct 19, at his residence in Watertown, the venerable Dr Walter Hunnewell, aged 86 years. He was born in Cambridge, Mass, Aug 10, 1769; was graduated at Harvard College in 1878, being a classmate with John Quincy Adams, Judge Cranch, Rev Thaddeus Mason Harris, D D, of Dorchester, Hon Jas Lloyd, & Judge Saml Putnam. He passed the greater part of his professional life in Watertown, a highly respected citizen & skilful physician. –Boston Transcript

Died: Hon Robt H Morris, Judge of the Supreme Court of the State of N Y, in N Y C, on Wed. [Oct 27th newspaper: Judge Morris died at the residence of his father-in-law at Astoria. Had he lived, his term of ofc would not expire until Dec 31, 1860. He occupied a number of official postions. He was formerly Recorder & afterwards Postmaster of this city. His death was caused suddenly by the rupture of a blood vessel. –Commercial Advertiser]

English & Classical School for Boys, at Sterling, Mass, 40 miles from Boston & 12 from Worcester, on the Fitchburg & Worcester Railroad. –John L Graves, Principal

Circuit Court of Wash Co, D C-in Chancery. Mary Hoffman, admx & heir at law of Thos Moore, deceased, vs Hannah Moore, & Jas Moore & Laura Ann Moore his wife, heirs at law of said Thos Moore, deceased. The trustee reported that he sold to Edw Cowling, for $2,000, the property named & described in the above cause on Jul 13, 1855; & that said Edw Cowling has complied with the terms of said sale.
-Jno A Smith, clerk

Obit-died: Mr Herman C Adams, the banker who was recently assassinated in Milwaukee, was a son-in-law of one of our most respected & esteemed citizens, David H Burr, lately appointed Surveyor-Genr'l of the Territory of Utah. The published accounts of this sad tragedy do not state so clearly & distinctly as they should do [to make the matter understood by persons at a distance] that Mr Adams never had any connexion whatever with the Germania Bank, which was indebted to the murderer, Feiner. That bank was owned by Germans, & failed some time before Mr Adams thought of removing to Milwaukee. Mr Adams rented the rooms formerly occupied by that concern, & this will account for the presence of Papedick, [who was the principal manager of the broken bank] in Mr Adams's ofc at the time the demand was made upon him which led to the murder. In every relation of life Mr Adams was without reproach. Of him it can be truly said: None knew him but to love him, None named him but to praise. [See Oct 24th newspaper.]

St Louis, Oct 25. Dates from *Fort Laramie* to Sep 19th have been received. Capt A P Howe, of the 4th Artl, was on trial before a court-martial for disobedience of orders at the battle of Blue Water. Gen Harney arrived at the Fort on 17th. The Sioux Indians were committing depredations, & had sent a defiance to Gen Harney. Capt Cady had arrived, & will accompany the General, as Col Hoffman is sick.

In Chancery. Wm McL Cripps vs Robt J Brent et al. The bill states that the said Chas Gratiot, in his lifetime, was indebted unto the said Wm McL Cripps in the sum of $190.63, with interest thereon from Sep 1, 1852; that the said Chas Gratiot has lately died, leaving a widow, Ann Gratiot, & two children, Julia Chouteau, the wife of Chas P Chouteau, & Victoria de Montholon, the wife of Chas de Montholon, all of whom are non-residents of D C; that the said Chas Gratiot left no personal estate, & that his said real estate is therefore liable to be sold for the payment of the aforesaid debt & interest. The bill also states that Robt J Brent, survivor of Wm L Brent, on or about May 14, 1849, recovered a judgment against the said Chas Gratiot for $500 damages, to be released on payment of $300, with interest thereon from Dec 11, 1844, till paid, & also $10.92 costs; & that the said Robt J Brent is also a non-resident of D C. It is ordered that the absent dfndnts appear in the Court, in person or by solicitor, on or before the 4th Monday of Mar next. –Jas S Morsell, Assist Judge -Jno A Smith, clerk

SAT OCT 27, 1855
Announcement of the resignation of the distinguished ofcr, Brig Gen Ethan A Hitchcock. The Springfield Republican explains the reason of his resignation. It seems that he was the ofcr to whom Gen Scott gave temporary leave of absence a short time ago, & whom the Sec of War ordered back to his post. Gen Hitchcock then threw up his commission. He entered the army in 1817 as a 3rd lt, & had reached almost the highest rank known to the army, having been brevetted a brig general for gallant & distinguished services in the storming of Molino del Rey, Mexico, Sep 8, 1847.

Died: on Oct 25, Dr Anthony Holmead, in his 32nd year. His funeral is this afternoon at 3 o'clock, from his late residence on 4½ st.

Died: on Oct 26, Amy Chilton, infant daughter of Robt S Chilton, aged 2 years & 6 months. Her funeral will be on Sunday next at 4 o'clock, from the residence of her parents, 501 N Y ave, near H st.

Died: on Oct 24, at N Y, Catharine, widow of the late Cmdor J Chauncey, U S Navy, aged 76 years.

St Louis, Oct 25. The court martial for the trial of Capt Howe has been dissolved without action, in consequence of some irregularities in the proceedings.

Phil, Oct 26: cholera at Carraccas. The passengers by the ship **Thomas Dallett**, from Caraccas, report that the cholera was raging there fearfully, the death averaging 50 per day. One-tenth of the population has been carried off, & business was almost suspended.

Prof Agassiz's School in Cambridge, Mass. The domestic character of the school, in his own house, under a supervision which mades the school-house as much like home life as possible, & that a great part of the instructions are given by members of his own family, whose familiarity with French & German gives great facility to the instruction in those languages, French being made the medium of communication. The school has been in operation for some time. The second term opens on Feb 15.

MON OCT 29, 1855
Circuit Court of Wash Co, D C. Offutt & Co et al, vs R Davis; heirs & administrator. The trustee reported he has sold part of lot 43, in Old Gtwn, being the dwlg & store of R Davis, deceased, to Saml Cropley for $2,250, & that the purchaser has complied with the terms. –Jno A Smith, clerk

1069-Equity. Sweeny et al vs Dowling's heirs. John F Ennis, trustee, in the above cause, reported that on Jun 4, 1855, he sold parts of lots 10 & 11 in square 566, in Wash City, to John Rover, for $730; & on Sep 5, 1855, he sold the western portion of said lot 11 to the said John Rover, for the sum of $900; & on the same day he sold the eastern part of lot 10 to the said John Rover, for the sum of $800, & that due notice was given of the time, place, & terms of said sales; & that the said purchaser has since complied with the terms of the said several sales. –Jno A Smith, clerk

From *Fort Laramie*. Gen Harney sent word to Little Thunder, the chief of the party engaged in the battle of Blue Water, that if he behaved himself he should not be molested. It has been generally supposed that Little Thunder was killed in the battle of Blue Water, but this was not the case. He escaped unhurt. All the prisoners taken in that battle, some 70 women & children, have been sent to *Fort Kearny*.

In our issue of Sat last, says the Thibodeau [La] Minerva, we referred to a storm which passed over the parish of Terrebonne on Oct 5, blowing down the sugar-house of Mrs Pierce, & killing the child of Dr Jennings. We have since learned that Mr Jos Toupe, living on Little Caillou, had his house blown down & 3 of his children instantly killed, & himself & wife severly wounded, Mrs T having since died. Mrs Pierce, her eldest son, & a servant girl were also severely wounded, but we are happy to say, are not dangerously so.

Orphans Court of Wash Co, D C. Letters testamentary on the personal estate of Grace A Fox, late of Wash Co, deceased. –Alfred H Parry, exc

Mrd: on Oct 25, by Rev A F N Boyle, Wm H Compton, of Wash, to Sarah W, daughter of H C Scott, of Upper Marlboro, PG Co, Md.

Mrd: on Oct 25, at the Cathedral, Balt, by Rev Thos Foley, Col John J Hughes, of Chas Co, Md, to Victorine, only daughter of P Davis, of the same county.

Mrd: on Oct 18, at Rochester, N Y, by Rev Mr Story, Geo C Morgan, of Md, to Miss Alice, daughter of the late Dr Baltzell, of Fred'k, Md.

Obit-died: on oct 13, in her 27th year, Emma Georgina, daughter of Geo & Emma Poe, of Gtwn. Disease early marked its victim, sapping the sources of life, & leaving the flower to wither which had bloomed once so fairly & with such promise. Her illness, long & painful, was born with the resignation of the saint & the fortitude of the martyr. Her death was in the arms of an aged father & devoted mother, with the fond embraces of sisters, brothers, & friends.

TUE OCT 30, 1855
Household & kitchen furniture at auction on: Nov 5, at the residence of Mrs Taylor, on 12th st, between F & G sts north. –A Green, auct

Hon Justin Butterfield, formerly Com'r of the Land Ofc under Gen Taylor, & for many years one of the most prominent jurists in Ill, died at Chicago a few days ago.

Rear-Admiral W Percy, of the British Navy, died in London on Oct 5. In 1814 he was appointed to the command of the vessel **Hermes**, 20 guns, which having 25 men killed & 24 wounded in an unsuccessful attack on **Fort Boyer**, Mobile, was set on fire & destroyed, to prevent her falling into the hands of the Americans, in Sep of that year. Capt Percy had under orders at the time, besides his own, the ship **Canon-**20, the ships **Sophie** & **Childers**-18 each. He was honorably acquitted of all blame in the loss of the **Hermes** by a court-martial.

Orphans Court of Wash Co, D C. Letters testamentary on the personal estate of Henry L Heiskell, late of Wash Co, deceased. –E R Heiskell, excx

Hon Chas W Whipple, one of the Justices of the Supreme Court of Michigan, died at Detroit on Oct 25 after a lingering illness. He earned a high reputation as a faithful ofcr & an accomplished jurist.

Chas Higgins, about 15, on Oct 25 near Alton, Ohio, took his gun into the yard to kill a chicken. Not observing his mother on the other side of a fence, he fired, the ball killed the chicken, & glancing upwards struck her in the head & killed her almost instantly. She was a widow about 45 years of age, & leaves a family of 7 children.

Died: on Oct 29, Cara Ella, infant daughter of J C & M McKenna. Her funeral will be this afternoon at 3 o'clock, from the residence of her parents, 416 F st.

WED OCT 31, 1855
Trustee's sale of a valuable square of ground at auction: on Nov 7, by deed of trust from Walter A True, dated Feb 10, 1855, recorded in Liber J A S, 93, folios 135 thru 137, all of square east of square 590, bounded by Delaware ave, 1st st west, I st south, & Public Space. Terms cash. –H B Sweeny, trustee -A Green, auct

Brvt Maj Francis Woodbridge, captain 2nd artl, died suddenly on Oct 20 at Barrancas barracks, Pensacola harbor, Fla. He was a native of the State of Vt, & entered the Army Jul 1,1 837.

The resignation of Don Platt, of his position as Sec of the American Legation at Paris arrived in Wash by the last foreign mail, & we understand that O Jennings Wise, [son of Hon Henry A Wise, of Va,] now the American Legation at Berlin, has been transferred & appointed to fill the vacancy at Paris thus created. -Star

Rev Wm Case, the oldest Wesleyan clergyman in Canada, died at Alnwick, Canada West, in the early part of last week, at the advanced age of 75 years. He was a member of the Methodist Eiscopal Church for nearly 60 years, &, in connexion with Rev Dr Bangs, of N Y, planted the Methodist church in Canada.

Wash Corp: 1-Ptn of Fred'k Lakemeyer, praying for the remission of a fine: referred to the Cmte of Claims. 2-Letter from Geo Deas on the joint resolution in relation to the alley in square 105: ordered to lie on the table. 3-Joint resolution to continue the arch on <u>Tiber creek</u>: adopted. 4-Ptn of Mgt King, for the remission of a fine: referred to the Cmte of Claims.]

Mrd: on Oct 30, by Rev Gideon H Day, Mr Richd Oliver Polkinhorn to Miss Hannah M Thompson, daughter of John Thompson, all of Wash City.

Died: on Oct 29, at Balt, Com John D Daniels, in his 73rd year. In early life he filled a large space in the public eye from being identified with the revolutionary struggles in Columbia, S A.

THU NOV 1, 1855
Stock of new furniture at auction: on Nov 5, at the Warerooms of Mr C O Wall, on 7th st, between D & E sts. –Wall, Barnard & Co, aucts

For sale: that desirably located House on Missouri ave, 3rd house east of 4½ st. Apply to T Pursell, 341 Pa ave, opposite Brown's Hotel.

Stock of family groceries at auction: on Nov 5, at the store of H W Blunt, High & Gay sts. –Barnard & Buckey, aucts

First class farm for sale in Fauquier Co, Va. I am authorized by the owner to dispose, by a private sale, of a farm about 6 miles from Warrenton, in Fauqier Co, Va, late the property of Jas H Fitzgerald, & known as *Rock Hill*. This farm contains by estimation 1,287 acres: the mansion house is commodious & comfortable, with all necessary out-bldgs. –Jas V Brooke, Warrenton, Fauquier Co, Va

Mrd: on Oct 25, by Rev F H Richey, Wm H Barbour, formerly of Balt, Md, to Miss Elvina N, eldest daughter of Rev S A H Marks, of Wash City.

Mrd: on Oct 21, at Havre-de-Grace, Md, by Rev Septimus Tustin, D D, of Wash, John T Moore, to Miss Louisa Wareham, both of the former place.

Mrd: on Monday last, at the country-seat of the late Hon Levi Woodbury, in N H, Capt G V Fox, of the U S Navy, to Miss Virginia L Woodbury, a daughter of the deceased statesman.

Died: on Oct 30, at his residence in Wash City, Andrew Coyle, in his 73rd year. His funeral services will be this afternoon at 3 o'clock, at the First Presbyterian Church.

C Warriner, Watchmaker & Jeweller, has removed to 370 Pa ave, under Brown's Hotel, Wash, D C.

The partnership under the name of E Wheeler & Co is this day dissolved by mutual consent. –E Wheeler, F J Harvey. We have this day sold to Messrs Harvey & Adams all our stock of goods in the Hardware line of business. They will open at the old stand, 345 Pa ave. –Harvey & Adams

FRI NOV 2, 1855
Excellent work horse at auction: will be added to the sale to take place at the farm of the late J M Kraft, deceased, near the Columbian College, on Nov 2. –A Green, auct

Hon Edw B Dudley, formerly Govn'r of N C, died at Wilmington on the 30th ult, in his 65th year. He was universally esteemed.

Portland Advertiser: letter dated **Glen House**, White Mountains, Oct 28, says Dr B S Ball, who attempted to go up the mountains on Wed last, was found on Sat alive, but with his feet & 2 fingers on one hand badly frozen. He was very much exhausted & standing up when found. He appeared to know what he was about; had laid 2 nights with nothing but his umbrella over him, in sight of the Glen House all the time.

The banking-house lately occupied by Messrs Selden, Withers & Co, on 7th st, 4 stories high, 28 feet front, running back 80 feet, on a lot 100 feet deep, was yesterday sold by Mr A Green, auct, to Mr Henry Bradley, for $15,100.

Mrd: yesterday, by Rev J G Butler, Mr John Tredway, formerly of Balt, to Miss Mary M, daughter of Andrew Noerr, of Wash City.

Mrd: on Oct 31, in Wash City, by Rev Wm T Eva, Mr H L Offutt, of Gtwn, D C, to Miss Anna Maria Fisher, of Montg Co, Md.

Mrd: on Nov 1, in the Foundry M E Church, by Rev J Thos Ward, of Phil, Mr Ulysses B Ward to Miss Anne Waters, both of Wash City.

Mrd: on Nov 1, at the residence of W H Gilman, by Rev Dr Sunderland, Edw Jackson, of Boston, to Nannie B, only child of Jeremiah O'Brien, of Wash City.

Mrd: on Oct 1, at Pleasant Valley, Va, by Rev J Hall, Mr John Maxwell to Miss Lydia E Shannon.

Mrd: on Oct 16, in Springfield, Hempstead Co, Ark, at the residence of J W Finley, A D Fowlkes, of Lafayette Co, Red River, formerly of Va, to Josephine, daughter of Wm S Derrick, late of Wash City, deceased.

Mrd: on Oct 29, in Troy, N Y, by Rev Dr Kennedy, G W Shields, of Wash, to Susan, daughter of the late Richd P Hart, of the former place.

Died: on Oct 31, in Gtwn, D C, of consumption, Harriet, wife of Jas Murray, in her 50th year. Her funeral is today at 10 A M, from her late residence 158 High st.

Geo E Badger, of N C, & J M Carlisle, of Wash, have extended their professional association [heretofore restricted to the U S Court of Claims] to embrace the argument of causes in the Supreme Court of the U S. They may be addressed at Raleigh, N C, or at Wash City.

Orphans Court of Wash Co, D C. In the case of Leigh R Holmead, adm of Thos Hall, deceased, the administrator & Court have appointed Nov 24 next, for the distribution of the personal estate of the deceased, of the assets in hand.
–Ed N Roach, Reg/o wills

SAT NOV 3, 1855

Judge Chas Mason, of Iowa, late Com'r of Patents, has returned to Wash & resumed the discharge of the duties of the position named. –Star

Mr Jos S Walter, the father of the architect of the Capitol, died on Thu at his residence in Phil, in his 74th year.

On Sat last, on motion of A H Lawrence, Mr Wm Q Force, of Wash City, was admitted an atty of the Circuit Court of Wash Co, D C.

Govanstown Female Seminary, at Govanstown, Balt Co, Md. Dr Wm T Jones, Principal; Mrs Catharine M Rivers & Mrs Catharine M Jones, Assist Principals; Miss Adelaide C Wildgoss, Teacher in English Dept & Assist in Music; Miss Margaretta C Bordley, Teacher of Drawing & Painting & Oil Colors; Prof L R Gawronski, Teacher of Modern Languages & Music. This institution is situated in the village of Govanstown, on the York road, 4 miles from Balt. The winter session will commence on Nov 12.

In the Empire, of Sydney, [N S W] of Jul 11, are details of the seizure of the ship **John**, of New Bedford, & of the murder of the captain, first & 2nd mates, & a number of the crew. The account was by Capt Bowles, of the schnr **Black Dog**, which arrived at Sydney Jul 8 from the South Sea Islands. Murdered by pirates: the captain of the **John**, Otis Tilton, of Edgartown; the 1st mate Henry C Allen, son of Jos Allen, jr, of New Bedford; 2nd mate Isaac W Gallop, of New London. The ship is owned by Fred'k Parker, of New Bedford, & was last reported at Paita, Jan 24, bound to the Sandwich Islands, with 350 sperm & 350 whale oil.

Mrd: on Nov 1, by Rev Geo Hildt, Mr John C Harkness to Mrs Maria Lare, daughter of H G O'Neale, all of Wash City.

Mrd: on Nov 2, at the Steamboat Hotel, by Rev E P Phelps, Mr Walter Roberts to Miss Martha Jane Richards, both of Va.

Died: on Nov 1, of consumption, in his 27th year, Wm H Jones, formerly a merchant. His funeral will take place today at 10 o'clock A M, from the residence of his sister, Mrs Peirce, on 8th st, between I & K sts.
[Peirce copied as written.]

Died: on Nov 2, in Wash City, Lydia Vanderbilt Wurdeman, wife of Wm Wurdeman, in her 37th year. Her funeral will be from her late residence, Sunday, at 3 o'clock.

MON NOV 5, 1855
Household & kitchen furniture at auction on: Nov 9, at the residence of Fred D Steuart, on K st, between 8th & 9th sts, all his furniture & effects. -Jas C McGuire, auct

Executor's sale of household & kitchen furniture, at auction, on Nov 13, at the residence of the late Capt Easby, Pa ave & 9th st east. -Jas C McGuire, auct

Statement of Lt Gen Scott's account, as settled by the War Dept, in accordance with the decision of the Pres.
Pay for Gen Scott from Mar 29, 1847, to Aug 31, 1848-17 months 3 days, at $50 per month: $855.
Pay from May 10, 1849, to Sep 30, 1855-76 months 22 days, at $50 per month: $3,836.67.
Subsistence from Mar 29, 1847, to Aug 31, 1848-522 days-10 rations per day, 5,220 rations, at 20 cents: $1,044.
Subsistence from May 10, 1849, to Sep 30, 1855-2,335 days, 10 rations per day, 23,350 rations, at 20 cents: $4,670.
Difference between pay, etc of lt gen & maj gen: $10,405.67

The Buffalo "Republic" of Fri contains a letter from Mr John Van Buren to Mr Israel T Hatch, in which Mr Van Buren states: the purpose of my father, if he lives till next Tue, is to vote the entire Democratic ticket, at the head of which you stand. This has never been concealed from his friends from the day the nominations were made. I declare the conduct of the Editors of the N Y Evening Post, in reference to the Democratic cause in the present canvass base, cowardly, & dishonest. [It will be seen that the witty politician is losing his temper, which is much to be regretted in one who is so agreeable as long as he keeps his gentle mood. We should think he will always find the Attic sale more effective in political warfare than saltpeter.]

The Govn'r of Pa has appointed John S Hollingshead, of Wash City, Com'r for that State to take acknowledgment of deeds & all other instruments of writing to be used in that State. The ofc of Mr H is open for the transaction of all kind of business connected with the duties of a magistrate as late as 11 o'clock every evening.

Md State Agricultural Society meeting at Balt on Thu, the following were elected ofcrs for the ensuing year: Pres, Jas T Earle, of Queen Anne's Co.
Vice Presidents:
St Mary's Co, H G S Key
Chas, John Hamilton
PG, Clement Hill
Calvert, A Somerville
Anne Arundel, Thos S Iglehart
Howard, C Carroll
Montg, R Dick
Carroll, S T E Brown
Fred'k, Anthony Kimmel
Wash, David Brumbaugh
Allegany, Saml P Smith
Balt, John Merryman, jr

Balt City, J C Brune
Harford, Ramsay McHenry
Cecil, M G Eldridge
Kent, Dr Kennard
Queen Anne's, J R Emory
Caroline, Wm Hardasctle
Dorchester, Wm L Hearne
Pa, Aaron Clement
Corr Sec: J Howard McHenry
Rec Sec: Saml Sands
Curators:
St Mary's Co, E Plowden
Chas, Chas H Wills
PG, Oden Bowie
Calvert, Dr J A Chesney
Anne Arundel, N B Worthington
Howard, Geo Y Worthington
Montg, Geo Brook
Fred'k, O Horsey
Carroll, W H Herring
Wash, J Newcomer
Allegany, Norman Bruce

Talbot, Matthew T Goldsboroug
Somerset, Wm H Jones
Worcester, Thos W Hargis
Dist of Col, J H Bradley
Delaware, Bryan Jackson
Va, J W Ware
Eastern Va, Thos R Joynes

Treas: Robt Bowie

Balt, Jas Carroll, jr
Balt City, Frank Cooke
Harford, J Carroll Walsh
Cecil, G M Eldridge
Kent, Geo Gale
Queen Anne's, Jos Tilghman
Talbot, Jas N Goldsborough
Caroline, Arthur J Willis
Dorchester, John R Martin
Somerset, John L Crocket
Worchester, Z P Henry

Yesterday 3 boys with 2 girls attempted to cross the Maumee river at Buttonwood Island, above Maumee City, in a 2 horse wagon. The boys Chas French, 15; Chas Creed, 12; Geo Skinner, 6; the girls were daughters of Isaac Hull, aged 10 & 15 years. The horses got into deep water & the wagon overturned. The girls were drowned, not being seen by the men who came to the rescue. They were the only daughters of Mr Hull. –Toledo Blade, Oct 31

Cmdor Gregory has been ordered to the command of the new steam frig **Merrimac**, recently launched at the Boston yard, & now rapidly fitting for sea.

For sale or rent: the desirable residence of the late Maj A A Nicholson, near **Duddington**. Apply to John C Brent, Atty at Law, 30 La ave, or to Buckner Bayliss, Mo ave, between 4½ & 6th sts. The key of the house will be found at **Duddington**.

Henry Hopkins, a lawyer at Island Pond, Vt, & lately postmaster at that place, was arrested for mail robbery. Recently a letter mailed to Quebec, enclosed in which was $200, failed to reach its destination. Suspicion fell on Hopkins. He was arrested & committed to the Portland jail. $170 was found upon his person. The money was easily identified, as the sender had stamped his business card upon the back of each bill. -Boston Traveller

Orphans Court of Wash Co, D C. Letters of administration on the personal estate of Saml Perkins, late of Wash Co, deceased. –Saml F Perkins, adm

Mrd: on Oct 31, by Rev Jas B Donelan, Mr Jas Ward to Miss Catharine Tuomy, both of Wash City.

St Louis, Nov 2. Horrible railroad accident this morning. The excursion train of 11 cars, which left here yesterday to celebrate the opening of the Pacific Railroad to Jefferson City, met with an accident at the Gasconade river, 100 miles west of this city. As the train was crossing the bridge fell, precipitating 10 of the cars, with all their passengers, nearly 30 feet into the river. There were, without doubt, about 700 persons in these cars, & not more than 200 escaped uninjured. The following persons are known to be among the dead:

Thos Gray
Capt O'Flaherty
E Church Blackburn
Henry Chouteau
Rev Dr Bullard
Mr Mott, [Rep of Dunklin Co]
Mr McCullough, of Dunklin

Capt C Case
E C Yosti [firm of Shields & Yosti]
B B Dayton
Mann Butler
Jos Harris, of St Louis Co
Mr Chappell, father of J T Chappell
Geo Ebeele

Thos S O'Sullivan, [Chief Engineer of the road] [Nov 6th newspaper: Information from Mr David H Bishop & Wm Rumbold, citizens of this place: excursion train had 12 or 14 cars; passengers had come down the Missouri river on the steamer **Ben Bolt**; the water was about 20 feet deep; also died-Judge Lackland & Geo Eberll.

Wounded:
Geo K Budd
Dr Post
Thos C Chester
Mr Littlejohn
Heber Livermore
Henry C Hart
Rufus K Lewis
Mr Griswold
Frank Lane
Mr Hitchcock
John C Richardson
Oliver Quinette
Capt Couzins
John B Carson
John M Wimer

W Lingo
F L Billon
Mayar King
Col D H Armstrong
Dr Vansant
Mr Hendle, druggist
Jos White, rep from Ripley
Peter Brown, of Jefferson
Mr Radcliffe, brakeman
Mr Roberts, paymaster
Mr Jecko, firm of Hart & Jecko
Mr Layton, rep of Perry Co
Mr Taylor, firm of Warren & Merritt
Wm Edge McClean, of CapeGirardeau
Mr Moore, of St Genevieve, [will die]

[Nov 8th newspaper: the masonry of this bridge was the work of Saler, Schulenburg & Co; the wooden superstructure, trestle work, was put up by Stone, Boomer & Co. All men of great experience in bridge bldg in the West.]

For rent: large 4 story brick dwlg house on North Capitol st, near the Depot. Possession given immediately. Inquire of Baruch Hall, 521 7th st.

Orphans Court of Wash Co, D C. Letters testamentary on the personal estate of John H King, late of Wash Co, deceased. –Ellen J King, excx

Died: on Nov 4, of consumption, Priscilla C, consort of Denton S Porter, in her 28th year. Her funeral will be from Mrs Bates', s w corner of Pa ave & 9th st, this afternoon at 2 o'clock.

Died: on Oct 18, at Laporte, Indiana, Mrs Rebecca W Parker Fraser, aged 52 years.

Wash City Ordnance. 1-Act to grant permission to Jos Barber to lay a foot pavement in the alley in square B, between 4½ & 6th sts; along the line of his property on the alley, on south side of Pa ave; pavement not to exceed 2 feet 6 inches in width; the same to be done at his own expense.

TUE NOV 6, 1855
The English papers announce the approaching marriage of Sir Thos Trowbridge & Miss Louisa Gurney, of Norwich. Sir Thomas was in the battles of Alma & Inkermann, & at Inkermann he contributed essentially to the defeat of the Russians. But during the terrible fight a cannon ball carried away both of his feet. Expecting to bleed to death, he refused to be carried to the rear, & directed his men to raise him upon a gun-carriage & take him to the front, that he might see the issue of the battle; & in that position he continued coolly to direct the fire of his battery until permitted to share in the shouts of final victory. The wounded man's life has been spared, & he was about to be rewarded by the happy consummation of a long-cherished attachment with the beautiful & amiable lady who is to share his titles & honors while she consoles & repays his sufferings. –Boston Traveller

Died: on Nov 5, Josephine, daughter of Wm A Linton. Her funeral will be from the residence of her father on Nov 7, at 3 o'clock.

Orphans Court of Wash Co, D C. Letters of administration on the personal estate of John S Stillings, late of Wash Co, deceased. –Eliz Stillings, admx

Orphans Court of Wash Co, D C. Letters of administration on the personal estate of Geo A D Clarke, late of Wash Co, deceased. –Mary V Clarke, admx

Mrd: on Oct 23, by Rev Mr Barber, Jas Steele to Mattie E, eldest daughter of Capt R B Cunningham, U S Navy.

Died: on Nov 4, at the residence of her son-in-law, J W Brown, of Wash City, Mrs Eliz B Scott, widow of the late Alex'r Scott, of Wash City. Her funeral will be this day at 3 o'clock, 512 12th st, near Pa ave.

Died: on Sep 22, at Texana, Texas, Mrs Georgiana Hughes, wife of Dr John M Bronaugh, formerly of Wash City, & daughter of the late Hon John P Morris, of Missouri.

Orphans Court of Wash Co, D C. Letters of administration on the personal estate of Beniah Willett, late of Wash Co, deceased. –Richd H Willett, adm

WED NOV 7, 1855
Auction of the personal effects of Jos Elgar, deceased, by order of the Orphans Court of Wash Co, D C: sale on Nov 9, at his residence, west side of 3rd st west, near Pa ave, [the flag will designate the house.] -A Green, auct

Utica Observer: excessive drinking in that city. On Thu, Mrs Catharine Sullivan, a wife, & the mother of 5 children, died in her sleep from excessive drinking. Her 11 year, the oldest boy, found her cold & dead.

St John [N B] papers of Nov 1. A patient, John E Clarke, who has been an inmate of the asylum upwards of 3½ years, & had at times been very docile, was employed in various way, frequently attending upon the family of Dr Waddell. In a fit of insanity he seized an axe & struck 2 attendants with repeated blows, killing them both. The murdered men were Wm Carroll & Barry Mills. The former was nearly 70 years of age, & an attendant for 14 years. The latter was 42, & employed there for 4 years.

Charlestown, Jefferson Co, Va: last week a Miss Beall sued a Mr Miller for breach of marriage promise, & the case must have been an aggravated one, for the jury found a verdict of $8,000 for the plntf, Messrs J M Mason & A Hunter for the plntf, & Messrs R Z Conrad & Wm Lucas for the dfndnt. We believe it was the first case of the sort ever tried in that county, & hence the unusual interest.

John McCarron, convicted of the murder of Jas O'Brien, in the village of Boonville, on Jul 18, 1853, was executed in the jail yard in the village of Rome on Friday. He had previously confessed the crime.

Died: on Nov 3, in Phil, Maria, wife of Lt Madison Rush, U S Navy, & daughter of the late Geo Blight, of that city, aged 23 years.

N Y, Nov 6. Fatal disturbance at Albany between Michl Brennan, a fighting man, having assaulted Wm M Crossen, the latter drew a pistol & shot Brennan through the heart, killing him instantly.

Home Hill for sale: this residence is in Falls Church, Fairfax Co, Va, 10 miles from Wash City: comprises 10 acres of land, a dwlg-house, & barn. Apply to John Gilbert, Pa ave, Wash, D C, or to the subscriber, on the premises. –R F Judson

$5 reward for information that will lead to the recovery of 2 horses, strayed or stolen, from the commons, on Sunday last. –Michl O'Sullivan, 252 Capitol st.

Nat'l Eating House: Wm Coke & Co have taken the above old & well-known stand on the corner of 6th & Pa ave, for many years kept by Wm Walker. He trusts that his friends & the public will not forget Old Billy Coke, who is ready to serve them.

THU NOV 8, 1855

A writ, issued by the Court of Delaware Co, at the suit of Passmore Williamson, on a complaint of false imprisonment, was served on Tue on Judge Kane, while on a visit at the house of his brother-in-law, Judge Lieper, near Chester. The case will come up for trial at Media, in the adjoining county. –Phil American

Gen Timothy Upham, formerly of Portsmouth, N H, died at his residence in Charlestown, Mass, on Fri last. He served as Col of U S troops in the last war with Great Britain, was for many years Collector of Portsmouth, afterwards followed mercantile pursuits, & was at one time a candidate of his party for Govn'r of his State. He was a gentleman of the old school, a man of noble & generous impulses, & had a host of personal friends. His age was 72. –Boston Courier

For schnr **Fairview**, 64 tons burden, lying at Page's wharf. Please call on Wm Greenwell, on board the vessel. –A Green, auct

$150 reward for runaway negro man Lewis Bond, age about 37 years; ran off in company with his brother Peter. Address Edw M Clark, Wash.

Foreign Item: Sir Wm Molesworthy, [age 45 years,] Sec of State for the Colonies, died on Oct 22 of a low gastric fever. He had been ailing for some time. He is the last of his race, we believe, with his death the baronetcy expires.

Gen Tacon, formerly Govn'r Gen of Cuba, died of cholera. [No date-current item.]

Battista Lorino, LL D, late Prof of Languages in N Y Conf Sy, having arrived in Wash, is desirous to commence himself in the above quality with some Southern Institution of standing. Being also a distinguished English scholar & musician, he had no objection to live in a private family. Apply at his residence, Pa ave, between 1st & 2nd sts, at Mr C Aigler's.

Died: on Nov 3, Sarah A, wife of R B Griffin, in her 39th year.

Maj Gen Walker's raid into Central America. On May 4, he left San Francisco with 62 men, on board the brig **Vesta** for San Juan del Sur to join the Democratic party of Nicaragua. In Tola he encountered some 30 of the enemy. At the battle of Virgin Bay the Americans did not lose a single man, had but 2 wounded, Lt B T Williamson & private J Small. On Oct 3 the ship **Cortes** arrived at San Juan, having on board Lt Col Gilman, Capt Davidson, & 35 recruits. Gen Walker & his forces remained at San Juan until Oct 10. Passengers from N Y came up & arrived at **Fort San Carlos** about one hour after the ship **Virgin** had left. The steamer **San Carlos**, Capt Slocum, was hailed from the fort, when Capt S came to & let go his anchor some distance before passing the fort. An 18 pound ball was fired at the steamer & struck her forward, instantly killing Mrs Alex'r White, of Clinton, Almeda Co, Calif, & taking both legs off her child, who lived some 5 or 6 hours. Another child of the same family had his foot injured with the same shot, but would recover. The mother & child were buried ashore at San Carlos. Killed at the attack on Virgin Bay, viz: John L Boyd, of Wayne Co, Ind; his body was robbed of $700. Wm Fitz, iron factory, Chattoga Co, Ga; died a few days after the affray. Wm Howard, of Lexington, Mo; body robbed of $2,000. Henry B Davis, of Vernon, Van Buren Co, Ohio; body robbed of $2,000. The wounded: Cornelius Cross, of Boonville, Mo; a gunshot wound in the hip. He will recover. Came home.
Rev D B Henry, of West Brookville, Maine; a gunshot wound in the thigh, but will recover. He is at the Irving House. N Y.
Thos Williams, of Phil; a bayonet wound in the shoulder & arm & a heavy blow from the butt of a gun. Will probably recover. Came home.
Chas Stanwood, of Lowell; a gunshot wound, but not dangerous. Came home.
Theron Wales, South Weymouth, Mass; left arm badly fractured. May lost his arm & possibly his life. He was left in the hospital at Granada.
J G Kendrick, of Cincinnati, has a gunshot wound in the left breast, but will recover. Left in the hospital in Granada.
Michl Foncannon, Tiffin, Ohio, has a slight wound. His life was saved by a twenty-dollar piece in his pocket. Came home.
[Note: The paper had 3 columns of coverage. Extracts taken where a person or people, were mentioned.]

FRI NOV 9, 1855
Nearly new household & kitchen furniture at auction on: Nov 12, at the residence of Maj Drake, 411 H st, between 12th & 13th sts. –A Green, auct

Mr Henry Franklin, of North Attleboro, was accidentally killed by the discharge of a gun, while loading it, on Tue last. The charge, with the ramrod, passed into his brain, & killed him instantly. –Taunton Gazette

Mrd: on Nov 8, by Rev Dr Sunderland, at the First Presbyterian Church, Col M Thompson, of Wash City, to Miss Mary G, daughter of John Douglass, formerly of Alexandria, now of Wash City.

Died: on Nov 8, Mrs Mary David, aged 54 years. Her funeral is this afternoon, at 3 o'clock, from the residence of Mr Thos Conner, corner of K & 7th sts.

For rent: one of the new block of 5 story bldgs on Indiana ave, near the City Hall, adjoining the residence of the Peruvian Minister, with closets & all the modern conveniences of gas, furnace range, bath & other water fixtures, with a stable & coach house, if desired. Apply to J E Weems, on the premises, or at his residence, 562 Pa ave.

SAT NOV 10, 1855
Pacific Railroad Disaster. The St Louis Intelligencer of Monday furnishes the following complete list of the killed by the accident on the Pacific railroad on the preceding Fri: B B Dayton, lawyer; Wm L Chappel, ticket agent O & M R E C Blackburn, Pres City Council; Cyrus Melvin, policeman; Mann Butler, Justice of the Peace; Rev Dr A Bullard, Pastor First Presbyterian Church; J A Ross, firm of Ross & Gillum; Thos Gray, firm of Gray & Clark; Calvan Case, proprietor omnibus lines; E C Yosti, firm of Shields & Yosti; Henry Chouteau, firm of Chouteau & Valle; Thos S O'Sullivan, chief engineer P R R; Capt O'Flaherty, firm of McAllister & Co; W L Lynch, son of the undertaker; Elisha B Jeffrees, Rep Franklin Co; Jos Harris, brother of the rep from St Louis Co; Saml Bast & Patrick Barry, firemen on locomotive; Adolphe Abeles, merchant; Rev Mr Teasdale, Baptist minister; R M Dubois, firm of L & C Speck; Wm Hume, merchant; Geo Eberle, livery stable keeper; T Jefferson Mott, Rep from Dunklin Co; Jos Finnegan, Lt Night Guard; Mr McCullough, of Dunklin Co; Wm Athey, late clerk in Assessor's ofc; one body, left at the Gasconade, name not known; one body identified at Hermann, name not known. The bridge on which the train was to cross the Gasconade was a superstructure of scaffolding, put up in lieu of the regular bridge contracted for. The Boeuff bridge, which has been used since the road was opened to Hermann, in Aug, was a similar erection. [Nov 14th newspaper: three bridges broken on the Pacific Road. Scarcely had the news reached us that the bridge over the Gasconade had fallen, when the telegraph brought intelligence that the bridge across Boeuff creek had also fallen, just after a portion of the train containing those who had been wounded at the Gasconade had passed over it! The St Louis Democrat of Tue says that on Fri night the bridge across the Moreau river gave way, & is now a mass of ruins.]

Obit-died: It is with pain, says the Savannah Republican of Nov 3, that we announce the death of Dr J C Habersham. He died at his residence in this city yesterday, after a long & painful illness, aged 65 years. He belonged to one of the oldest & most respectable families in the State. His ancestors were of that heroic band who accompanied Oglethorpe to these shores, & assisted in laying the foundations of the colony of Georgia on the spot where he breathed his last. He carries with him down into the grave the respect & regrets of all who knew him.

Navy Yard, Gosport, Nov 3, 1855. Eulogy upon the lives & characters of our friends & fellow citizens who have departed. I first speak of Cmdor Isaac McKeever, who day after day the death of one civil ofcr after another was reported to him, men quitting their posts, his own clerks falling around him, amid appeals from those less considerate than himself to close the yard, you would have seen not only the man who has borne aloft in triumph the flag of his country, but one willing to sacrifice health & even life for the cause of suffering humanity, rather than contribute to the alarming calamity around him. There has never been a commandant on this station more universally respected as an ofcr or beloved as a man than Cmdor McKeever. Capt Barron, our then Executive ofcr, who had recently returned from Wash, was in the early stage of the epidemic forced from the bed-side of his dying companion & hurried to the hospital with the fever upon him. What a touching scene was this! To be torn from the fond though deathly embrace of an affectionate wife with the expectation of soon meeting her in the spirit-land! We deeply sympathize with him in the loss of his devoted wife & accomplished daughter. Mr Hartt, our able naval constructor, passed through the thickest of the fight unscathed, leading where any dare to follow, being both night & day engaged in attending the wants of the living & burying the dead. Of the 11 civil ofcrs who remained steadfastly to their duty, 7 have fallen-N N Tatam, timber inspector, recently appointed; Patrick Williams, master house-joiner; John Vermilion, master boat-bldr; John B Davis, master spar-maker; Richd Williams, master mason; Chas Myers, master plumber; Chas Cassels, master sailmaker. The families of some of these gentlemen are almost broken up. Only the son of Mr P Williams' family is let. Four grown daughters soon followed their father. All depts of the yard suffered: the spar-makers lost 7 out of 12 who remained; the smithery, out of 34 who remained, lost 19. One among the many victims in this shop's crew that deserves more than a passing notice. I allude to Mr Wm Jones, foreman more than 30 years, a more faithful & engergetic man never walked inside the gate. When Mr Allen, the head of the dept was taken sick, Mr Green was acting foreman; & he, too, the next day was stricken down. Then Mr Totterdill, Mr Ballentine, & Mr Snead, each in rapid succession, fell at his post; & all, except Mr A & Mr Snead, quickly followed one another to the grave. As many as 9 died in Mr Totterdill's family, leaving only 3 helpless orphans. There are upwards of 1,000 men now at work. But I see by the Argus today that there are perhaps 900 men, who, short a time since, mustered at roll call, whose cordial grasps of the hand & familiar faces we will see & feel no more.

Died: on Sep 20, at Point Coupee, La, in his 25th year, after an illness of 3 days, Dr John Hubbard Minor, son of Dr Jefferson Minor, Essex Co, Va. Thus has been cut down by this desolate disease, in early manhood, the first-born of devoted parents.

Died: on Nov 9, Richd Henry Rawlings, in his 36th year. His funeral is this afternoon, at 3 o'clock, from his late residence, 429 Mass ave.

Died: on Nov 7, at Boscage, Montg Co, Md, Mrs Helen Watkins, wife of G M Watkins, & daughter of the late Z H Gatton, of said county.

London Herald: we hear from Kiel of the death of Lt John R Ouseley, of H M S Pemborke, son of Sir Wm Gore [formerly British Minister in Brazil & the River Plate] & Lady Ouseley. This promising young ofcr, aged 21, was landed from the Pembroke on account of the extreme weakness to which he was reduced by illness brought on by exposure during the bombardment of Sweaborg; & although his father, who had been summoned by telegraph, procured the best medical aid, which for some days gave hopes of his recovery, the disease when he landed had advanced too far to be overcome. His funeral took place of Oct 9 at Kiel, in the presence of his father, the British & French Consuls, & some English residents. Sir W Gore Ouseley, father of the gallant deceased, was attaché to the British Embassy at Wash in 1825. While at that capital he married the daughter of Govn'r Van Ness, formerly Govn'r of the State of Vt, & subsequently Envoy Extraordinary at Madrid.

Troy Whig. Mrs Mgt Martin, who is stopping at the residence of her grandson, in this city, is 98 years of age. She is one of the few remarkable women of the Revolution who took part in the struggle for American independence. Her husband, Gilbert Martin, was a sgt in the army of Gates, & was in the battle at Saratoga. Mrs Martin, then a very young woman, was on the field during both struggles constituting this battle & terminating in the defeat of the splendid army which Burgoyne had transported from Canada, confidently anticipated that he would be able with it to divide the army of the patriots & secure Sir Henry Clinton in possession of the southern line of defences. Mrs Martin represents the struggle as most terrific. Mr Martin was wounded in the shoulder, & while his wife was in the act of affixing a bandage she herself was wounded in the hand. "Gilbert sprang up like a chafed lion. Peggy, said he, I'll go & teach those cowardly fellows better manners than to shoot at a woman." I saw him no more till the fight was over.

Orphans Court of Wash Co, D C. Letters of administration on the personal estate of Louis J Kennedy, late of Wash Co, deceased. –R C Morgan, adm

$50 reward for return of buggy & horse stolen from the stable of the subscriber, on Sep 27, an iron gray horse; the buggy was painted an olive green color, with leather top, & lined with white & drab trimming, with wooden dash board. The person by whom the above is supposed to have been stolen is a stout genteel looking man, about 60 years old, & registered his name at Ball's Cross Roads, & at Rockville, Md, as E S Ott, of Bedford, Pa. Deliver to my stable on Pa ave, between 13½ & 14th sts.
-Thompson Naylor

Mrd: on Nov 8, by Rev Jas A Duncan, Mr Harman Newell, U S Navy, to Miss Ann M Duvall, of Wash City.

Mrd: on Nov 6, at Cleveland, King Geo Co, Va, by Rev Mr Friend, Alfred N Bernard to Miss Mgt B Mason, daughter of W R Mason.

MON NOV 12, 1855
At Waterford, Mich, on Nov 1, four sons of Jesse Chapman, living in different parts of the State, all made their appearance at the paternal mansion with a lady accompaniment, followed by a clergyman, who joined the whole quatern in the bonds of matrimony. After a chat with the "old folks" they left on their wedding trip.

Mohawk Courier: inquest held by Coroner Waite, at Little Falls, on the body of Thos Stafford, at the village of Van Hornsville, Herkimer Co, on Nov 3. The deceased bathed his head every morning in a cistern near his house. He slipped in head first & was found with his legs hanging over the edge of the cistern. It is supposed he remained in that position an hour before he was discovered. He was 43, & leaves a wife.

Mr John Van Buren. $50 reward. The last seen of this gentleman was on Tue, when he was observed making his exit from Tammany with the Softshell platform sticking out of his pocket. –N Y News

For rent: good 3 story brick dwlg-house on west side of 11th st, between G & H sts, recently occupied by Mr Francis Hume. –Apply to Lewis Johnson.

Mrs Mary Adams, on Pa ave, opposite Browns' Hotel, has several unoccupied rooms suitable for families.

Mrd: on Nov 3, by Rev Mr Hodges, David W Garet to Susan E Collison, all of Wash City.

Died: in Brunswick Co, Va, Mrs Ariana W Smith, relict of the late Capt Richd Smith, of that county. [No death date given-current item.]

Jas M Cunningham & Washington Altemus, alias Geo Wash Kane, were on Thu arrested by ofcrs Davis, Handy, & Kimble, at the Railroad Dept in Wash City, charged with passing counterfeit.

Phil, Nov 10. The locomotive of a freight train on the Pa Railroad exploded yesterday near Pa, killing Mr Chandler, the fireman, & severely wounding John Wilhelm, the engineer, who was blown up above the telegraph wire, which broke with his weight. His thigh was fractured & he received serious internal injury.

The Board of Managers of the Wash City Protestant Asylum gratefully acknowledge the following donations: Mrs Susan Ireland, $500; Mrs Ogle Taylor, $50. By order of the Board: Susan R Coxe, sec

In Chancery: 929. Aaron O Dayton vs Jas P McElfresh & Jas A Watson. Wm B Webb, trustee, reported he has sold part of lot 18, in square 453, with bldgs & improvements thereon, to Aaron O Dayton, for $570. The trustee reported that the said premises were sold, for the purpose of foreclosing the equity of redemption in a certain mortgage of said premises, & were purchased by the mortgagee; that the said purchase money has been credited upon the debt secured by said mortgage, leaving a balance still due to said mortgage. –Jno A Smith, clerk

TUE NOV 13, 1855
Naval Intelligence. Portsmouth [N H] Navy Yard, Cmder Pickering, recently promoted, takes the place of Capt Pearson, also recently promoted & detached. Lt A G Cleary ordered to that yard vice Pickering, promoted.
Boston: Cmder Theo P Green, recently promoted, takes the place of Capt Selfridge, also recently promoted & detached. Lt Chas S McDonough ordered to that yard, vice Green, promoted. Lt Johnson B Creighton ordered to the Boston yard vice Cmder Henry French, recently promoted & detached. On the Boston receiving ship, Cmder S F Hazard, recently promoted, ordered to take the command, vice Capt Wm S Walker, recently promoted & detached. Cmder Chas Green, recently promoted, has been detached from that ship.
N Y Navy Yard: Cmder John DeCamp, recently promoted, takes the place of Capt Hudson, also recently promoted & detached. Lts T M Brasher & J W A Nicholson have been ordered to that yard. Cmder Alfred Taylor, Lt A F V Gray, Surg Robt T Barry, & P A Surg Ashton Miles have been ordered to the rendezvous. Cmder T G Benham, Lt J G Carter, Surg S Jackson, & Assist Surg Geo Peck, detached.
Phil: Cmder S W Godon, recently promoted, has been detached. Lts Wm Ronkendorff & Wm W Roberts have been ordered to that yard.
On the receiving ship, Cmder Wm S Young, recently promoted, has been ordered to the command vice Capt Fred'k Engle, recently promoted & detached. Lt J Hogan Brown & Wm E Hopkins have been ordered to that vessel
At the rendezvous, Cmder John Goldsborough recently promoted, takes the place of Capt Hollins, also recently promoted & detached.
At the Balt rendezvous, Cmder Fred'k Chatard, recently promoted, takes the place of Cmder Murray Mason, detached. Cmder Roger Perry has also been detached from that rendezvous. Lt Edmund Lanier has been ordered there.
Washington Yard: Cmder Jos Lanman, recently promoted, takes the place of Cmder Pettigru, detached.
Norfolk Yard: Cmder Chas H Poor ordered to take the place of Capt Saml Barron, recently promoted & detached. On the receiving ship at Norfolk, Cmder John R Tucker takes the place [in command] of Cmder John Manning, detached.
–U S Nautical Magazine

Deacon Danl Fitch, a soldier of the Revolution, died in West Killingly, Conn, on Nov 3, at the aged of 93 years, 9 months & 27 days.

The robbery of the house of Mr P G Murray, at Pa ave & 4½ st, of about $100 worth of silver-ware, on Sunday, should admonish housekeepers to increased vigilance.

A **Steam Fire Engine** has been purchased by the city of Columbus, Ohio. Pittsburgh has recently had one built on a plan invented by one of her own mechanics. The steam fire-engine is now to be found in Cincinnati, New Orleans, Pittsburgh, Columbus, Phil, & Boston.

Among the most recent issues of the Patent Ofc was a patent of Mr J P Heacock, of Ohio, for a boring, drilling, & screw-cutting machine. There is more done by the machine & less by the attendant than by any combination of machinery for like purposes we have ever looked upon.

Brvt Maj Israel B Richardson, Capt 3rd Infty, U S Army, has resigned, to take effect on Sep 30th last. Lt Winfield Scott Hancock, of the 6th Infty, U S Army, has been appointed Assist Quartermaster in the service, vice Reynolds.

Died: on Nov 12, in Gtwn, Martha Edes, youngest daughter of Wm H Edes, in her 18th year. Her funeral will be from her father's residence, 113 Gay st, Wed, at 3 o'clock.

Union Association regular monthy meeting at Harmony Hall, on Nov 13. Speakers to be Hon A E Maxwell, Dr Sherrett, & Robt Ould. –Z K Offutt, Rec Sec

Madame Paul Paillard, who has just arrived from Paris, where she was a pupil of the most celebrated Professors & herself a Teacher of Music with much success, informs the ladies & families of Wash that she proposes to give instruction on the Piano. For information call at 256 Pa ave, or at Gautier's Saloon.

On Tue last a man by name of Maples, living in Preston, near Norwich, struck his wife on the head with a cleaver, & then his 4 year old child. Supposing them dead, he went to a tree back of his barn, &, taking an ox chain, succeeded in hanging himself by the neck until he was dead. At last account the wife & child were alive, but not expected to survive. Maples was a temperate man, & possessed some property. No cause has been assigned for the crime. –New London Star of Tue

WED NOV 14, 1855
Circuit Court of Wash Co, D C. A Jardin et al, vs A Favier's heirs & adm. The trustee reported he has sold to A Jardin certain parts of original lots 1, 2, & 13, in square 119, fronting in all 72 feet & 2 inches on 19th st, for $5,171.41, & that he has complied with the terms of the sale. –Jno A Smith, clerk

Wash Corp: 1-Ptn from Sarah Roberts, asking to be refunded certain money erroneously paid for a license: referred to the Cmte of Claims: passed. 2-Ptn from Jonas P Levy, asking that a part of his license may be remitted to him: referred to the Cmte of Claims. 3-Cmte on Unfinished Business: ptn of Jos T Totten, asking for the transfer of the 6 foot alley marked B, in square 165: referred to the Cmte on Improvements.

For rent: comfortable 4 story brick house, 16 K st, between 8th & 9th sts; pump in the yard; & gas will be introduced. Apply at 446 6½ st, between E & F sts. -Francis Mohun.

From Nicaragua: Don Mateo Mayorga, Sec of State, was executed on the plaza of Granada, his party having fired into the American passengers of the steamer **Uncle Sam** & the steamer **Star of the West**.

The Court of Inquiry of which Brig Gen Henry Stanton was Pres, recently in session at *Fort Columbus*, after due investigation, reported that there exists no grounds for the trial of Lt Henry M Lazelle, of the 1st Infty, by court-martial, under virtual [but mistaken] charges made against him by Lt Alex'r S Webb, 4th Artl, further proceedings are not to be taken in the case.

To be hung. Private Wm J Dunn, of company G, mounted riflemen, U S A, was recently tried by court-martial at *Fort McIntosh*, Texas, Capt Thos Claiborne, jr, of the mounted rifles, being Pres of the Court. The charges were for mutiny & the murder of Sgt John Williams, of the same regt & company, by shooting him with a revolver. The Court found the prisoner guilty as charged & sentenced him to be hung at such time & place as the Pres may appoint. The murder, which was an atrocious one, was committed at the camp of the company at Limpa Creek, El Paso road, Texas, on or about Jun 30th last. The Pres has directed the sentence to be carried out at *Fort McIntosh* on the 4th Fri next succeeding the reception of his confirmation of it [the sentence] at that post. -Star

Mrd: on Nov 6, at the Capitol Hill Parsonage, by Rev G H Day, Mr Geo T Mangenn to Miss Jane Collins, all of Wash City.

Mrd: on Nov 7, by Rev G H Day, Mr Isaac Bridewell to Mary Jane Roctor, all of Va.

Died: on Nov 10, in Gtwn, Alice Dallam, youngest daughter of Chas S & Ellen D English, aged 2 years & 29 days.

Orphans Court of Wash Co, D C. In the case of Richd P Jackson, adm of Richd Davis, late of Gtwn, D C, deceased, the administrator & Court have appointed Dec 4 next, for the settlement of the personal estate of the deceased, of the assets in hand. -Ed N Roach, Reg/o wills

Orphans Court of Wash Co, D C. Letters of administration on the personal estate of Anthony Holmead, late of Wash Co, deceased. –Eliz Holmead, admx

Orphans Court of Wash Co, D C. Letters testamentary on the personal estate of Stepney Forust, late of Wash Co, deceased. –Basil Brooks, exc

THU NOV 14, 1855
The steamship **Sierra Nevada**, on board of which 45 persons died of cholera on her last trip up from San Juan to San Francisco, had 862 passengers. –North American

Mr Wm Wymann, a machinist, residing in this city, has been sent to the mad-house at Cambridge, a victim of the spiritual rappings, on complaint of the City Marshal. Wymann, for some months past, has neglected his business & his family, so that the latter separated from him & returned to the home of the wife in Providence. -Charlestown [Mass] Aurora

Wash City Ordinances: 1-Act for the relief of Wm Rupp: fine imposed for keeping open his bar after the lawful hours is remitted. 2-Act for the relief of John Barthol: the sum of $25 be paid to him for the destruction of his bedding, by order of the Mayor, as a preventive to the propagation of the yellow fever.

The Albany Express train on the Harlem Railroad, which left Chatham Four Corners on Mon, about midway between Copake & Boston Corners, an elevation of some 35 feet above the level ground, the entire train, with the exception of the engine & tender, was suddenly precipitated down the embankment by a violent gust of wind, landing upside down with their load of human freight snugly secured within. The dead are: Mr Rathbone, a paper manufacturer at Boston Four Corners, & Mr Gaylord, brakeman of the train. The injured are doing as well as can be expected.

A youth named Robt Johnson died on Tue at the residence of Mr McCullom, bricklayer, whose apprentice he was, from a blow he had received a few hours previous from a companion with whom he had been sparring in the vicinity of the Northern Liberty market-house.

Mrd: on Nov 13, by Rev Dr Holmead, Geo F Barrett to Miss Mgt J McAlwee, of Wash City.

Mrd: on Nov 14, in St Alban's Church, D C, by Rev Smith Pyne, D D, Rev Wentworth L Childs to Louise, eldest daughter of W C D Murdock, of Belle-Vue.

Died: on Nov 14, in Wash City, Dr Tobias Watkins, in his 75th year. His funeral will take place from his residence on 9th st, tomorrow, at 3 o'clock P M.

Died: on Nov 13, in Wash City, Mr Beverly W Bell, in his 37th year. His funeral will be this afternoon at 3 o'clock, from his late residence, 510 I st, between 6th & 7th sts.

SAT NOV 17, 1855

Lt Jonathan D Ferris, of the U S Navy, died at his residence in Norfolk on Tue last. He was upwards of 80 years of age, & had been gradually declining for some months past. He was a native of the State of N Y, but for many years a resident of Norfolk. He entered the navy as Sailing Master on Feb 28, 1809, & received his commission as a Lt Jul 13, 1832, from Pres Jackson, as an acknowledgment of his gallant services at the battle of New Orleans.

On Oct 18 Mr Thos Stephenson, while on his way to the new saw-mill on the north branch of the Minneishka for lumber, was overtaken by a prairie fire, & so badly burnt that his life is almost despaired of. Should he live he will be disabled & disfigured for life.

Cincinnati Inquirer: about 6 years since Mrs Martha Wood, with her son, his wife, & a couple of children, arrived in that city from New Bedford, Mass. She stated that she was a widow of 24 years' standing, her husband having been mate of a whaler which had been lost at sea. The family had resided for the greater part of the time on Liberty st, Mr Wood, the son, working at his trade, that of a cooper. A few days ago a gray-headed & toil worn man called at the residence of the family, &, seeing Mr Wood, inquired for the widow, who, being called into the room, while gazing intently at the stranger, whose eyes were fixed mournfully upon her, requested to know his business. "Do you not know me, Martha?" said he. She gave vent to an hysterical cry, & fainted in the arms which were open to receive her. The tale is soon told: the ship in which he had made his last voyage from New Bedford was cast away in the South Sea Islands, & he was one of the few who escaped a watery grave. After enduring almost unheard of privations he succeeded, after 30 years' absence, in reaching his native city. From a brother of his wife he learned their present location, & arrived here to find her. How many hopes & fears must have agitated the old mariner as he again set foot, after his long pilgrimage, upon his native soil.

Mrd: on Nov 15, by Rev Stephen P Hill, of Wash City, Richd T Halley to Clara M Cipperley, daughter of Hiram & Mgt Cipperley, all of Fairfax Co, Va.

Mrd: on Nov 15, by Rev Mr O'Toole, Thos F Powers to Miss Mary M Slater.

Mrd: on Nov 14, at N Y, by most Rev Archbishop Hughes, Thos Francis Measher to Eliz, daughter of Peter Townsend, of Southfield, Orange Co, N Y.

Mrd: on Nov 13, at Charlestown, Mass, by Rev Mr Lambert, Albert B Powers, of Wash City, to Virginia, daughter of Purser Levi D Slamm, U S Navy.

Mrd: on Nov 14, in the city of Poughkeepsie, N Y, by Rev Mr Buel, of the Protestant Episcopal Church, Thos Moore, of Fairfax Co, Va, to Miss Priscilla Haviland, only daughter of Mr D Haviland, of the former place.

Died: on Nov 16, at his father's residence, of consumption, Wm Pinkney King. His funeral will be tomorrow at 4 o'clock.

Dissolution of the copartnership under the firm of Kirkwood & McGill by mutual consent. The business will be carried on as usual at the old stand, 9th & D sts, by J Kirkwood. –Jos Kirkwood, Thos McGill

By a decree of the Circuit Court of Fauquier Co, Va, pronounced on Sep 17, 1855, in a suit in chancery therein pending, styled Kemper vs Annan, it was, amongst other things, ordered that one of the Com'rs of said Court should inquire & report to the Court who are the distributes of the estate of Eleanor McCormick, deceased, late of said county, & to what share thereof they are entitled. On Jan 5, 1856, at his ofc in Warrenton, in said county, a Com'r will inquire as directed by said decree. -Jas O Brooke, Com'r

In Equity. Iardella et al vs Bulger's heirs. John F Ennis, trustee, reported that on May 23, 1855, he sold lot 13 in square 517, in Wash City, D C, to Patrick O'Donoghue, for $1,230, & that the said purchaser has since complied with the terms of sale. –Jno A Smith, clerk

MON NOV 19, 1855
Household & kitchen furniture, & Rosewood Chickering Piano Forte, at auction on: Nov 23, at the residence of Jas L White, on the west side of 6th st, between D & E sts. -Jas C McGuire, auct

The St Louis Democrat announces the death of Bishop Vaudevelde, Catholic Bishop of Natchez, formerly of St Louis & Chicago. He died of yellow fever on Nov 13.

Sale by order of the Orphans Court of Wash Co, D C, on Nov 21, of the personal effects of the late John S Stillings, deceased, at the shop of Stillings, 7th & L sts, near the Navy Yard. –A Green, auct

The tunnel beneath the English Channel, it is said, will in 5 years' time connect Dover & Boulogne; & M Favre, a distinguished French engineer, has lately been employed in surveying the neighboring coasts & taking soundings, with a view of immediately carrying out this magnificent project. The tunnel will be about 18½ miles, & its cost per yard $539, amounting in round numbers to $20,000,000.

Mrd: on Nov 15, at Woodbury, Fairfax Co, Va, by Rev Jas A Duncan, Rev Wm E Judkins, of the Va Conference, to Miss Mary G, daughter of W W Ball.

Alexandria Sentinel [extra] of Sat. On Friday smoke was issuing from the roof of John T Dowell's china store on King st, near Water st. The pipe of the Star fire company had been introduced into the bldg & was playing upon the fire when the west wall of the bldg fell upon the pipemen & their assistants & others who were below, burying them in the ruins & causing a frightful loss of life. John Dogan, a colored man, is perhaps the sole survivor, & he is severely wounded. Lying in a heap were the bodies of: David Appich, a young man, only son of Gotlieb Appich, Star Fire Co. Wm S Evans, plumber, Pitt st, near the Marshal House. Robt I Taylor, street paver, Star Fire Co. Geo Plain, painter, member of the City Council, Star Co. Jas W Keene, bricklayer, Friendship Co. A little distance from the above was found the body of J Carson Green, son of Edw Green, & partner of Chas J Wise in a plaster mill. Injured were Dr Richd E Stone, burnt & bruised. He had to be cut out by his friends. Robt P Henry, left hand badly cut. Chas J Wise, face cut, Relief Co. J A Shinn, stunned by a falling beam, & bruised, Relief Co. Wm H Lambert, bruised on the leg, Relief Co. Francis A Marbury, caught in the rubbish, but extricated himself, flesh wounds. David Williams, cut in the face, Sun Co. The bldg belonged to Mr Jas P Smith & was partially insured in the sum of $5,600. The stock belonging to John T Dowell, the proprietor of the store was fully insured for $20,000.

+
Five of the victims of the calamity, viz: Geo Plain, Robt I Taylor, Jas W Keene, Wm S Evans, & David Appich, jr, were interred yesterday afternoon. Mr John A Roach & Jas Carson Green are to be buried today.

In Equity. John Iardella & others against Mgt Bulger & others. On Nov 26th at the Court-house, City Hall, Wash, I shall state the account of the trustee with the trust fund & distribute the same among the parties entitled. –W Redin, auditor

In Equity. Armand Jardine against Henry Naylor, Jas C McGuire, Thos Berry, W S Cox, Wm Emmert, Honorine Jardine, Albertine Favier, Louisa Favier, Miriam Favier, Agricola Favier, Malvina Favier, & Theresa Favier. The parties above named, the trustee, & the creditors of the late A Favier are notified that on Nov 26, at the Court-house, City Hall, Wash, I shall state the trustee's account with the trust fund & distribute the same among the parties entitled. –W Redin, auditor

Obit-died: Mrs Wm Boyd Ferguson, of Norfolk. In the death of this estimable woman the family circle sustains an irreparable loss. Turning to her only relative, who in despairing grief exclaimed, "Oh, Georgie, if you leave me what will become of me?" she said, "Trust in God." -C S J [No death date given-current item.]

Died: on Oct 11, at his residence in Clark Co, Va, Mr Thos Briggs, aged 73 years. The deceased leaves a large family & an extensive circle of friends & relatives to mourn his loss. Though confined to his room for a number of weeks, yet, a few days previous to his death, his family & himself had high hopes of his ultimate recovery. The father, husband, & friend has gone forever from the earth.

Died: on Nov 7, in Montg Co, Md, Helen, wife of G M Watkins.

Died: on Sep 16, at Elgin, near Natchez, Mrs Annis Dunbar, wife of Dr John C Jenkins, & daughter of the late Dr Wm Dunbar, a victim of the prevailing epidemic. On Oct 2 she would have completed her 35th year. When death came, it came suddenly with violent pain which convulsed the body & deranged the reason. In the discharge of duty she seemed to have exposed herself to the fatal disease. From the bedside of a sick relative she went to the chamber where she was to die. [Another of the church & community, died but 2 days before Mrs Jenkins: Mrs Susan Gillespie.]

Ordered by the Orphan's Court for Chas Co, this Nov 13, 1855, that Geo H Gardiner, adm of Wm Jameson, late of said county, deceased, give 3 weeks' notice in the Nat'l Intell, for a certain Alfred H Dent to be & appear in this Court on the second Tue in Dec next & receive the amount due him as the creditor of the deceased. –T A Smith, Reg of Wills for Chas Co, Md. –Geo H Gardiner, adm of Wm Jameson

In Chancery. Christopher S O'Hare & others against Mary W Prather, admx, & Emily Prather, Sarah Ann, Martha, Geo, & Henry Prather, heirs of Overton J Prather, deceased. By an interlocutory order of the Circuit Court of Wash Co, D C, I am directed to state an account of the personal estate of said Overton J Prather, & to report whether the sale of his real estate be necessary for the payment of his debts. Meeting on Nov 28 at the Court house, City Hall, Wash. –W Redin, auditor

TUE NOV 20, 1855
New Book. The Studies & Teaching of the Society of Jesus, at the time of its suppression, 1750 & 1773. Translated from the French of M L'Abbe Maynard, Honorary Canon of Poictiers. Balt: John Murphy & Co, 1855. The abbe fixes our view upon the society as it was at the time when Clement XIV put an end to its corporate existence & its public labors.

Another trouble in Missouri. Some time ago Mr Geo S Park, one of the editors of the Parkville Luminary, was compelled to leave the place owing to some excitement against him on the slavery question. He has lately been invited to return for the purpose of settling some business involving his own interest & that of many of the citizens of Parkvile.

Brvt Col Wm Fenwick Williams, of the Royal Artl, has, by the Queen's commands, been promoted to the rank of Maj Genr'l in the army, for his distinguished conduct in the defence of Kars, & of the position in front of that town, when attacked on Sep 29 by a large Russian army, which on that occasion sustained a signal defeat by the Turkish troops.

Local: Rachel W Barker, a minister of the Society of Friends preached on Sunday at Carusi's Saloon to a densely crowded but perfectly orderly assemblage of persons.

The choldera continues to rage at Rome. Amongst its victims have been the Marquis Gagliati, Minister Plenipotentiary of Sicily; The Count Liederkerke de Beaufort, Envoy Extraordinary of the King of Holland; & M Matranga, a learned Orientalist of the Vatican library.

Capt Nye has piloted the good steamship **Pacific** across the Atlantic for the last time, & when next she leaves this port she will be under the command of Capt Asa Eldridge, in whose hands she will doubltess maintain the high fame which has attached to her under her late skilful captain.

An old & well-tried veteran of the stage, Mr Geo H Barrett, after a career of nearly half a century, finally retires to private life on Tue, when a farewell benefit is to be given him at our Academy of Music. –N Y

Chicago Times: E B Ames, of Hennepin, Putnam Co, in this State, has been appointed by the Pres to the post of Consul at Hamburg, one of the three free cities of Germany.

Mrd: on Oct 9, in Downieville, Calif, by Rev E M Hagar, Mr Robt G Keefer, of Thorold, Canada West, to Miss Augusta Virginia Langton, of Wash, D C.

Phil, Nov 19. E Debust, an eminent mineralogist of N C, committed suicide at his hotel in this city this morning by cutting his throat. Is is said the act was caused by pecuniary embarrassments.

First class hotel in the First Ward for sale: on H, between 17th & 18th sts, nearly opposite Senator Fish's residence, within a few hundred yards of the Pres' Mansion. It was built 3 years ago, with all modern improvements; contains 17 rooms. Apply to D D Addison, on the premises, or to N T Wakeman, opposite the Nat'l Intell ofc.

WED NOV 21, 1855
Household & kitchen furniture at auction on: Nov 26, at the residence of Mrs Bell, 510 North I st, between 6th & 7th sts, an excellent assortment. –A Green, auct

Chas White, age 21, was apprehended by Messrs Bell & Eckloff, of the Auxillary Guard, on Tue, after a protracted race & an immersion in the canal, into which he had plunged to escape his pursuers. He had just robbed the boot & shoe store of Mr Wall, on 9th st. He was committed for trial by Capt Birch.

Bakers, look out! For rent, that well established Business Stand, 12th & F sts, that 3 story brick house, with basement, cellar, & garret, with a large bake-house & oven, all complete, with a large lot & stable attached. These premises have been used as a bakery by John M Krafft for many years past. Apply, adjoining the premises, to Mary C Krafft, admx.

Remarkable man-from the Ky Statesman. Elijah Deny, an old citizen in Pulaski Co, who is perhaps the oldest man in Ky, was 118 years of age on Sep 10 & is as active as many men of 40. He works daily upon a farm; had never drank coffee, but one cup in 1848; served 7 years in the war of the Revolution, & was wounded at the siege of Charleston; was at the siege of Savannah & at the battle of Eutaw Springs; present at the battles of Camden, King's Mountain, & Monk's Corner. He served under Col Horry & Col Marion, & was an eye-witness of the sufferings & death of Col Isaac Hayne, of S C, an early victim of the Revolution. He is a strict member of the Baptist Church, & rides 6 miles to every meeting of his church. He had 4 sons & 5 daughters, all living, the eldest now in his 78th year, & the youngest in his 51st year. He is perhaps the only surviving soldier of Francis Marion, Sumpter, & Horry.

Washington Riding Academy, 1st Ward Livery Stable, G st, between 17th & 18th sts, is now open for the reception of pupils, under the direction of Mr Louis Douglas, the well known riding master from Balt. –Friedereck Lakemeyer, Agent

The trial of Mr W G Dendall, late Postmaster at New Orleans, on charge of embezzling money sent through the mails, took place on Nov 15. 11 jurors voted for his acquittal; the 12th declined concurrence, on the alleged ground of inability to come to any decision in view of the testimony. The Gov't resisted the motion of dfndnt's counsel for the immediate trial of another case of a similar nature, & had it postponed till the Aug term of the Court.

Wash Corp: 1-Ptn of Mrs Anna Maria Stone & others for a change of an alley in square 686: referred to the Cmte of Improvements. 2-Ptn of Mary Carroll for the remission of a fine: referred to the Cmte of Claims. 3-Ptn of Anne Nash for the remission of a fine: referred to the Cmte of Claims.

Died: on Nov 19, in Wash City, Mr John Hamilton Alexander, aged 26 years. His funeral will be this afternoon at 3 o'clock, at the Unitarian Church.

Large 2 story brick house on 21st st west, for rent, gas fixtures, burners, & chandeliers complete. Inquire of Saml Drury, 73 Pa ave.

House for rent on 7th st, handsomely furnished, with all the modern improvements, gas, furnace, hot & cold water for bathing & washing purposes. Apply to Maj T L Smith, First Auditor's Ofc.

Orphans Court of Wash Co, D C. In the case of John H King, adm of John A King, deceased, the administrator & Court have appointed Dec 11 next, for the final settlement of the personal estate of said deceased, of the assets in hand.
–Ed N Roach, Reg/o wills

Independence Hall Restaurant, Columbia Pl, corner of 7th & La ave. Messrs Doniphan & Bevans will open this day, Nov 21.

$100 reward for runaway negro man Tom Sprigg, about 23 years old. –Dennis Duvall, living near Buena Vista Post Ofc, PG Co, Md.

THU NOV 22, 1855
Beautiful country seat for sale: the *Vineyard*, the residence of the late John Agg, on the heights north of Wash, about 3 miles from the Capitol, adjoining the farm attached to the Military Asylum, within half a mile of Rock Creek Church: contains about 75 acres; good water near the dwlg, & good roads leading to it. Apply at the City Hall, or at his residence near the *Vineyard*, E J Middleton, exc of John Agg.

Dr Theodoric Romeyn Beck, for many years Sec of the Board of Regents of the Univ of the State of N Y, & an eminent man of science, died at Albany yesterday, at age 64 years.

The marriage of Sophia, second daughter of Sir Allan McNab, Premier of the Canadian Ministry, to Wm Coutte, Viscount Bury, only son of the Earl of Albemarle, took place at Dundurn Castle, the residence of the bride's father, on Thu last, with great éclat. The affair caused quite a flutter in the quiet city of Hamilton.

U S Patent Ofc, Wash, Nov 21, 1855. Ptn of Andrew Ralston, of West Middletown, Pa, praying for the extension of a patent granted to him for an improvement in threshing machines, for 7 years from the expiration of said patent, which takes place on Feb 21, 1856. –Chas Mason, Com'r of Patents

U S Patent Ofc, Wash, Nov 21, 1855. Ptn of John J Grenough, of N Y, N Y, praying for the extension of patent granted to him for an improvement in sewing machines, for 7 years from the expiration of said patent, which takes place on Feb 21, 1856. –Chas Mason, Com'r of Patents

Orphans Court of Wash Co, D C. Letters of administration on the personal estate of Wm E Stewart, late of Wash Co, deceased. –Mary E Stewart, admx

On Monday last, a youth named Saml T Hicks, son of Mr Saml Hicks, of Richmond, was shot & killed by Geo Wade, son of Mr Thos Wade, while the two were hunting on Quarle's farm, about 2 miles from Richmond. It was an accident, witnessed by another boy who was present. –Richmond Whig

Mrd: on Nov 16, at N Y, by Rev Dr Taylor, Jas Lorimer Graham, jr, to Josie A, daughter of Thos Garner.

Mrd: on Nov 15, in Newark, N J, by the Bishop of N J, assisted by Rev Dr Henderson, J M Gevers, Envoy Extraordinary & Minister Plenipotentiary of his Majesty the King of the Netherlands to the Court of St Petersburgh, to Miss Catharine Maria Wright, the only daughter of Hon Wm Wright, U S Senator.

Mrd: on Nov 21, by Rev Geo Cummins, Chas A Sherman, of N Y C, to Sarah D, daughter of Jos H Bradley, of Wash City.

Block Island is so isolated from the rest of the world that the intermarriages of those more or less nearly related by blood are more common then elsewhere. The Providence Journal mentions the death, at that place, of Mrs Nancy Dodge, wife of John F Dodge, leaving 3 deaf & dumb sons. A great proportion of the inmates of the asylums for the deaf & dumb, the blind & idiotic, are found to be the product of the intermarriage of cousins.

FRI NOV 23, 1855
New Work. The Song of Hiawatha, by Henry Wadsworth Longfellow. Foston: Tickner & Fields $1.55. For sale by Taylor & Maury. We have in this newest Poem of Mr Longfellow perhaps the only American Epic.

At the Nov term of PG Co Court, Md, a German, who was indicted for an assault with intent to kill & rob Mr John Higgins, of Bladensburg district, was acquitted of the charge of an attempt to kill, but found guilty on the other count. He was sentenced to 9 year & 8 months' confinement in the penitentiary. The prisoner is quite a young man. [Name not given.]

In Chancery. Mary Hoffman against Hannah Moore, Jas Moore, & Laura Moore, heirs of Thos Moore. The parties named, the trustee, & creditors of the late Thos Moore, are notified that on Dec 1 next, in the City Hall, Wash, I shall state the trustee's account with the trust fund & distribute the same among the creditors & parties. –W Redin, auditor

U S Patent Ofc, Wash, Nov 16, 1855. Ptn of Wm C Grimes, of Phil, Pa, praying for the extension of a patent granted to him Feb 12, 1842, for an improvement in spark arresters, for 7 years from the expiration of said patent, which takes place on Feb 12, 1856. –Chas Mason, Com'r of Patents

Wash Corp: 1-Act authorizing the Mayor to refund certain money to Sarah Roberts: $20, erroneously deposited by her in the Bank to the credit of the Corp. 2-Act for the relief of John T Davis: fine imposed for firing a gun in the public streets is remitted, with the provision that he pay the costs of prosecution.

Died: on Nov 21, Mary Augusta, eldest daughter of the late Jas & Margaretta France. Her funeral is today at 3 o'clock P M, from the residence of her mother, 501 7th st.

Promotions & Appointments in the Army. General orders of Jul 19.

I-Promotions:

Assist Surg Josiah Simpson to surgeon. Brvt 2nd Lt C B Comstock, eng, to be 2nd Lt.

Topographical Engineers:
2nd Lt Geo H Derby to be 1st Lt.
Brvt 2nd Lt Henry L Abbot to be 2nd Lt.

First Regt of Dragoons:
1st Lt Richd C W Radford to be Capt.
2nd Lt Robt Williams to be 1st Lt.
2nd Lt Nelson B Sweitzer to be 1st Lt.
2nd Lt Benj Allston to be 1st Lt.
[Lt Allston restored to former position in 1st dragoons, not having accepted the appointment tendered him in the 1st cavalry.]
Brvt 2nd Lt David McM Gregg, of the 2nd dragoons, to be 2nd Lt.
Brvt 2nd Lt Jas Wheeler, jr, of the 2nd dragoons, to be 2nd Lt.

2nd Regt of Cavalry:
2nd Lt Philip Stockton to be 1st Lt.
Brvt 2nd Lt John R Church to be 2nd Lt.
Brvt 2nd Lt Albert V Colburn, of the 2nd cavalry, to be 2nd Lt.

2nd Regt of Cavalry.
Brvt 2nd Lt Cornelius Van Camp, of the 1st cavalry, to be 2nd Lt.
Brvt 2nd Lt J B Wheeler to be 2nd Lt.

Regt of Mounted Riflemen:
Brvt 2nd Lt John V D Dubois to be 2nd Lt.

1st Regt of Artl:
Brvt 2nd Lt Fred'k L Childs, of the 2nd artl, to be 2nd Lt.

2nd Regt of Artl:
1st Lt Jas Totten to be Capt.
2nd Lt Thos M Vincent to be 1st Lt.
Brvt 2nd Lt Michl P Small, of the 3rd artl, to be 2nd Lt.
Brvt 2nd Lt A S Webb, of the 4th artl, to be 2nd Lt.

3rd Regt of Artl:
Brvt 2nd Lt F R T Nicholls, of the 2nd artl, to be 2nd Lt.

1st Regt of Infty:
2nd Lt Thos G Williams to be 1st Lt.
Brvt 2nd Lt Chas W Thomas, of the 5th infty, to be 2nd Lt.

2nd Regt of Infty:
Lt Col Francis Lee, of 6th Infty, to be Colonel.
Brvt 2nd Lt Geo D Ruggles, of the 1st infty, to be 2nd Lt.

3rd Regt of Infty:
1st Lt Geo Sykes to be capt.
2nd Lt Lawrence W O'Bannon to be 1st Lt.
Brvt 2nd Lt Henry W Freedly, of the 9th infty, to be 2nd Lt.

5th Regt of Infty:
1st Lt Henry R Selden to be capt.
2nd Lt Henry C Bankhead to be 1st Lt.
2nd Lt Donald C Stith to be 1st Lt.
Brvt 2nd Lt Alfred T A Torbert, of the 2nd infty, to be 2nd Lt.
Brvt 2nd Lt Robt C Hill, of the 6th infty, to be 2nd Lt
6th Regt of Infty:
Maj Geo Andrews, of the 7th infty, to be Lt Col.
7th Regt of Infty:
Capt Isaac Lynde, of the 5th infty, to be Major.
2nd Lt T J C Amory to be 1st Lt.
Brvt 2nd Lt Wm R Pease, of the 10th infty, to be 2nd Lt.
8th Regt of Infty:
2nd Lt Milton Cogswell to be 1st Lt.
2nd Lt Robt G Cole to be 1st Lt.
Brvt 2nd Lt Edw L Hartz, of the 7th infty, to be 2nd Lt.
Brvt 2nd Lt Wm B Hazen, of the 4th infty, to be 2nd Lt.
Brvt 2nd Lt Henry M Lazell, of the 1st infty, to be 2nd Lt.
9th Regt of Infty:
2nd Lt Chas R Woods to be 1st Lt.
Brvt 2nd Lt Jesse K Allen, of the 5th infty, to be 2nd Lt.
10-Regt of Infty:
1st Lt Jos L Tidball to be capt.
2nd Lt Peter T Swaine to be 1st Lt.
2nd Lt John B Forney to be 1st Lt.
Brvt 2nd Lt Jas H Hill to be 2nd Lt.
Brvt 2nd Lt Clarence E Bennett, of the 3rd infty, to be 2nd Lt.
Brvt 2nd Lt Timothy M Bryan, jr, of the 9th infty, to be 2nd Lt.
II-Appointments:
1st Lt Julius P Garesche, of the 4th artl, to be assist adj gen, with brevet rank of capt.
1st Lt John C McFerren, of the 3rd infty, to be assist quartermaster, with the rank of capt.
1st Lt Eugene E McLean, of the 2nd infty, to be assist quartermaster, with the rank of capt.
1st Lt Winfield S Hancock, of the 6th infty, to be assist quartermaster, with the rank of capt.
Pascal A Quinan, of Md, to be assist surgeon.
9th Regt of Infty:
John G Read, of Michigan, to be 1st Lt.
John C Howard, of Texas, to be 1st Lt.
III-Transfers:
Maj Enoch Steen, 2nd drag, transferred to 1st drag.
Maj Chas A May, 1st drag, transferred to 2nd drag.
2nd Lt John A Thompson, 1st drags, transferred to 1st cavalry.

Resignations:
Brvt Brig Gen E A Hitchcock, colonel 2nd infty.
Brvt Maj Israel B Richardson, captain 3rd infty.
1st Lt Thos Henry, 7th infty.
1st Lt Wm G Peck, corps of topog engineers.
1st Lt Alpheus T Palmer, 9th infty.
1st Lt Jas F Harrison, 10th infty.
2nd Lt Fred'k M Follett, 8th infty.
2nd Lt Geo L Andrews, corps of engineers.
2nd Lt Lyman M Kellogg, 10th infty.
2nd Lt Peter Parkinson, jr, 1st cavalry.
2nd Lt Geo Hartwell, 2nd cavalry.
2nd Lt Wm W Harding, 3rd artl.
2nd Lt Venerando Pulizzi, 2nd artl.

Declined:
John G Read, the appointment of 1st lt, 9th infty.
2nd Lt Benj Allston, 1st dragoons, the appointment of 2nd lt, 1st cavalry.
A S Coolidge, the appointment of 2nd lt, 2nd infty.

Deaths:
Brvt Maj Francis Woodbridge, capt 2nd artl.
Brvt E A Ogden, capt & assist qm.
Capt Jos L Folsom, assist qm.
Capt Jas G S Snelling, 10th infty,
Brvt Capt Chas G Merchant, 1st lt, 8th infty.
1st Lt Thos F Castor, 1st drags.
1st Lt Chas N Underwood, 1st infty.
1st Lt Edw J Dummett, 1st cavalry.
2nd Lt Wm M Davant, mounted riflemen.
2nd Lt John Williams, 2nd cavalry.
Surgeon Henry L Heiskell, at Washington.

Honora Sullivan, wife of Michl Sullivan, aged about 30 years, & a resident of Wash City during the past 5 years, was yesterday fatally injured. She was crossing 4½ st at its intersection with the north side of Pa ave, & was within 10 or 11 feet of the west side, when she was struck & knocked down by a horse, & run over by a buggy attached to the horse, driven violently down 4½ st by a boy to the jurors unknown, & that, falling, she struck her head against the pave stones, causing concussion of the brain, of which she died in about 1¾ hours. We learn that she was the mother of 5 or 6 children.

Mr Clark Mills has finished the equestrian statue of Gen Jackson [similar to that which adorns Lafayette Square] for the city of New Orleans, where it will be inaugurated on Jan 8 next with much pomp & ceremony.

Claiborne [La] Advocate of Oct 31. About 5 weeks ago there eloped from Terryville, Claiborne parish, Dr Clement & Sarah T Wafer, an orphan heiress of a wealthy Lousiana planter, being at the time at school at Terryville. They proceeded to Arkansas where the nuptial ceremony was duly performed. On their return the happly couple were met by the brother of the bride, who chastised the groom for the abduction of his sister. Finally they were allowed to proceed to the Dr's residence in Arcadia, Bienville parish, whence, a few days afterwards, the bride was summoned to the bedside of a sick sister. While at her house Mrs Clement signed a letter written by her brother-in-law, in which she accused her husband of deception, cowardice, age, & ugliness, avowing her determination not to live with him. They then went with her sister to Red River, in the parish of Rossiter, & took up residence in another sister's residence. Dr Clement followed in pursuit with 15 stalwart friends armed, & demanded the person of Mrs Clement, who yielded, on condition that she should be taken to the residence of her uncle, Rev Mr Wafer. Her brother raised a force of armed men & took to rescue his sister, but on approaching the house of his uncle found it surrounded by the Dr's army, with cocked guns. He proceeded to Homer & caused the issuance of a warrant for the arrest of Dr Clement & party for the forcible abduction & imprisonment of his sister. The Deputy Sheriff summoned a posse, to whom the Dr's party submitted. Next morning, Claiborne was thrown into violent commotion by the sudden appearance on horseback, with double barreled guns, of the entire body of men, some 60 in number. Blood shed was caused by the accidental discharge of one of the guns of this party, wounding a lawyer who was standing in his ofc. It appeared on the trial of one of the writs that Miss Wafer had been engaged to a brother of her sister-in-law; but, some person unknown forged a letter purporting to be from her fiance where she was discarded. Her elopement with the Doctor was precipitated, & the unfortunate girl soon found that she was linked to a man whom she could not love, &, in fact, positively disliked.

SAT NOV 24, 1855
Portraiture of Washington, being an appendix to the Custis Recollections & Private Memoirs. The earliest original of the Pater Patriae is the portrait of Col Washington painted by Chas Wilson Peale in 1772, & now in fine preservation at **Arlington House**. It was in the parlor at **Mount Vernon** for 27 years. Dr Jas Craik pronounced it to be a faithful likeness of the Provincial Colonel in the prime of life. The venerable Jas Craik was the associate & bosom friend of the chief from 1754 to the last days at **Mount Vernon**. Next we have a full-length of the Cmder-in-Chief, painted by Peale in 1779, during the Revolution. In 1790 appeared the equestrian portrait of the Chief by Col Trumbull. There is a copy, size of life, of this portrait in the City Hall of N Y. In 1789 the first Pres lost his teeth, & the artificial ones with which he was furnished answering very imperfectly the purpose for which they were intended, a marked change occurred in the appearance of his face, more especially in the projection of the upper lip, which forms so distinguishing a feature in the works of Stuart & others who painted portraits of the great man subsequent to 1789. It annoyed Washington to sit-he was a bad sitter; after every sitting, he was wont to

declare this must be the last. The last original [profile in crayons] was by Sharpless in 1796, & is now at *Arlington House*. The Chief admired this portrait & ordered the same artist to do every member of his domestic family, including Geo W Lafayette. Of the first Pres there was also a portrait by Rembrandt Peale, son of the soldier artist.

[Dec 27th newspaper: There appears to be one error of date; at least it wholly overlooks one or two pictures, known to be originals, as well as those painted from life & now lost sight of. Mr Custis says the earliest original of Col Washington was painted by Chas Wilson Peale in 1772, & is now in fine preservation at *Arlington House*. Rembrandt Peale, the son, published two memoris of his father, in which he states [Dunlap's quotation] that he proceeded to London in 1770, & remained there till 1774. He of course could not have painted in America in 1772. In 1774 he found constant employment at portrait painting in Annapolis. In 1776 he painted in Phil, & then joined Washington's forces, & was present at the battles of Trenton & Germantown. During his leisure hours, while in camp, he painted a miniature head of Washington & the portraits of his ofcrs. This head was executed at a farm-house in N J. In 1779 he painted the full-length portrait of Washington. In 1794 Stuart painted his first portrait of Washington, which he destroyed, not being satisfied with it. Washington sat again & subsequently for the picture presented by him to the Marquis Lansdowne. "The last Original," says Mr Custis, was the profile likeness by Sharpless. He then adds: We have enumerated all the reliable originals of the Pater Patriae from 1771 to 1796. There can be no question but that other original pictures of Washington exist at the present time, & Mr Custis has failed to give us a correct list of the artists who were so fortunate as to obtain sittings. There was Jos Wright, commissioned in 1783 by Washington to paint his portrait, who addressed him upon the subject thus: *Mount Vernon*, Jan 10, 1784. Sir: When you have finished my portrait, which is intended for the Count de Solms, I will thank you for handing it to Mr Robt Morris, who will forward it to the Count de Bruhl,]Minister from his electoral Highness of Saxe, at the Court of London,] as the channel pointed out for the conveyance of it. Be so good as to forward the cost of it to me, & I will remit you the money. –Geo Washington. The above picture was painted at *Rocky Hill*, near Princeton, & was commenced Oct, 1783. At this time & place Wright painted both the Genr'l & Mrs Washington; & Dunlap, who was present, says that he also was favored with a sitting from Washington, but failed to make a picture. At this time Wright painted a half-length of Washington, by the request of the latter, who presented it to Mrs Eliz Powel, a particular friend of the General's & his family. That portrait is still in Mrs Powel's family. At the suggestion of Hon Francis Hopkinson, Washington gave sittings to Robt Edge Pine, in 1785. In 1789 Washington sat to Edw Savage for a portrait to be placed in the Harvard collection. The picture is described as every way deficient. In 1792 Arch Robertson obtains sittings from the General, at the request of the Earl of Buchan. Mr Robertson sent the picture to England by Col Lear, & received the thanks of the Earl of Buchan. I have been led to recall the history of the portraits of Washington to correct any impression that might be received from Mr Custis' letter, that the number of originals was limited to the six he enumerated; & I trust that patient inquiry will establish the fact whether the Wurtmuller picture is an original or not. –Aquidneck]

J U Wright, mail agent on the Ga Railroad, was arrested on Nov 6 charged with robbing the U S mail. He made a full confession of the crime. Wright has been lodged in the Cobb Co jail to await his trial. –Altanta [Ga] Intelligencer

1-Three sons were born to John Havens, of Wethersfield, Conn, on Nov 17, all doing well. 2-An English woman, an emigrant passenger on one of the Hudson river boats, gave birth to 3 boys at Albany on Monday.

Mrd: on Nov 15, in Wash City, by Rev S A H Marks, John Smith to Miss Martha Lucinda Allen.

Mrd: on Nov 22, by Rev S A H Marks, Joshua Brightwell to Miss Malvina Jones.

Mrd: on Nov 22, at N Y, at St James' Evangelical Lutheran Church, by Rev Jas L Shock, Mr Philip A Keller, late of Wash, D C, to Miss Sarah Davy, of N Y.

Mrd: on Nov 20, in Wash City, by Rev Jas Donelan, Sivannus Trunnell to Miss Elizabeth, daughter of Thos Robbins, all of Wash City.

Mrd: on Nov 22, at **Wood Lawn**, PG Co, Md, by Rev Geo A Leakin, of Balt, Dr W Miller, of Gtwn, D C, to Sophie R, daughter of the late Henry Tolson.

Mrd: on Nov 1, in St James' Church, Greenville, Tenn, by the Rector, Mr John C Marshall, of Knox Co, to Miss Martha W, daughter of Gen Thos D Arnold, of Greeneville, Tenn.

Died: on Nov 23, Mrs Missouri J Loudon, wife of J F Loudon, of Wash City, aged 27 years.

Died: on Nov 13, at Dubuque, Iowa, at the residence of his brother, Geo O Karreck, Mr Jos Karreck, formerly of Wash City, in his 43rd year.

Horrid Affair: Charlotte [N C] Whig: in the Lancaster district on Nov 11, a young man named Edw Lewis, living in Lancaster district, S C, near the N C line, was shot through the head with a rifle as he was sitting by the fire reading. The murderer is supposed to be his brother-in-law, B F Therrell, who was seen round the house of his mother-in-law with the gun on his shoulder, who walked in & dragged out his wife from the corpse of her brother. He has not been arrested, though many are in pursuit.

Obit-died: on Oct 30, in N Y C, Peter Augustus Jay, well known in thie district, where he resided for a long time. Although aware of his feeble hold on life, the shock was as painful as if it had been unexpected.

MON NOV 26, 1855

Trustee's sale of valuable country seat near Wash City: by deed of trust from Geo T Massey, as trustee, & Ann Brown to the subscribers, dated Dec 13, 1853, recorded in Liber J A S 68, folios 505 thru 510, of the land records for Wash Co, D C: public auction at the auction rooms at Mr McGuire, on Dec 27: part of the land whereof Anthony Holmead, sr, died seized & part of the tract called **Pleasant Plains**, & part of the land which Anthony Holmead, jr, conveyed to Boltzell & Mayhew, which they conveyed to John Pickrell, the piece of land aforesaid lying east of the Washington & Rockville Turnpike Road, containing 5 $1/16^{th}$ acres, more or less, being lot 2 of Geo Taylor's subdivision, adjoining the land of Geo Taylor, near a lot sold to J C Lewis; conveyed to the said Ann Brown by John F Sharretts by deed duly recorded in 1853, with improvements. –Francis J Middleton, Richd H Clarke, trustees -Jas C McGuire, auct

A little boy, son of Mr Cumberland, residing opposite Christ Church, in Gtwn, was accidentally burnt to death yesterday. Being in a room with several other children, he set fire to his clothing whilst he was amusing himself by burning paper.

Seventy-five years after his death Geo Taylor, one of the signers of the Declaration of Independence, has been honored with a monument to his memory by the citizens of Northampton Co, Pa, where he spent the greater portion of his useful life & among whom his ashes repose. This is the first monument erected to a signer of the Declaration of Independence.

Mr Josiah B Kilbourn, of the firm of French, Wells & Co, crockery merchants, Boston, has been missing from home since Wed. He left a note at his house in Brookline addressed to his wife, concluding as follows: "Before you read this I shall have gone off Cambridge bridge." He was about 35 years of age, very active in business. It has been intimated that he left for Europe in the ship **Asia**, which sailed from this port on Wed, but his nearest friends & business associates believe he took the course intimated in his letter. His accounts are found to be all right.

The case of Dr F L Zemp, of Camden, vs the Wilmington & Manchester Railroad Co, was tried at Sumterville, S C, last week, & the jury brought in a verdict of $10,000 damages for the plntf. He was standing on the platform of the car while the train was in motion, & the accident occurred by which he lost a leg & received other injuries.

Mrs C Russ, Milliner, lately from N Y, has taken a store, 3 East Capitol st, where she has the latest syles of Winter Bonnets & Cloaks.

I have this day constituted Messrs Ford & Brother, Druggists, 11th & Pa ave, sole Agents for the sale of my Life Preserver & Cordial. Each bottle will bear my signature in writing. —Richd Thompson, Proprietor of the Life Preserver & Cordial.

Mrd: on Nov 22, by Rev Jas A Duncan, Wm C Murphy to Miss Laura Ann Pierce, both of Rappahannock Co, Va.

Died: on Nov 24, in his 49th year, Henry Ellis, a native of the County Meath, Ireland, but for the last 22 years a resident of Wash City. His funeral is this afternoon, at 3 o'clock, from his late residence, 434 Mass ave, between 6th & 7th sts.

Died: on Nov 24, after a short illness, Mrs Frances Emily D, 3rd daughter of the late Alex'r C Draper, M D, & wife of Alonzo R Fowler. The relatives & friends of the family & of Mrs Susannah Draper are invited to attend her funeral this afternoon, at 2 o'clock, from her late residence on 12th st, between M & N sts.

TUE NOV 27, 1855

Sunnyside for sale: the subscriber, desiring to remove South, offers this beautiful & highly improved farm, in Alexandria Co, Va, for sale: contains 200 acres; with a good dwlg house of 8 rooms, besides garret & basement; a house for overseer & hands, stabling for horses & cattle, with necessary sheds, usual to a dairy & market farm. Apply to Burke & Herbert, Alexandria, Va, or to the subscriber, on the premises. —Edw B Powell

Circuit Court of the U S in Balt, Md, engaged in the trial of Capt Jos L White, charged with abandoning the ship **James Cheston** at sea for the purpose of defrauding the insurers, came to a close on Sat last by his acquittal. The Atty for the U S then asked permission to enter nolle prosequis in the case of Chason & Packwood, which were granted, & they were discharged from prison, where they have been confined for nearly 6 months. -Patriot

Died: on Sunday, after a lingering illness, in her 6th year, Ada Beall, youngest daughter of Saml & Mary E Norment, of Wash City. Her funeral is this morning at 10 o'clock, from the residence of her parents, 42 Missouri ave.

Died: on Nov 25, Danl G Hickey, in his 59th year. His funeral is this afternoon, at 2 o'clock, from his residence on 4½ st, near F, Island.

Died: on Nov 18, at **Fort Moultrie**, Sullivan's Island, S C, after but a few weeks' illness, Lt Waterman Palmer, U S Army, in his 23rd year.

Orphans Court of Wash Co, D C. Letters testamentary on the personal estate of Beverly W Beall, late of Wash Co, deceased. —C E Beall, excx

Calif & Central America: Corral had been found guilty of treason & shot. Espinosa had vanished.

Mrs Trippe, No 6 4½ st, can accommodate a few boarders. She would also take table boarders. The location is convenient, the rooms large & comfortable.

In Chancery. A F Offutt & Co against John Davis, R P Jackson, & others. The parties named & trustee in the cause, & creditors of the late Rich Davis are notified that on Dec 5, at my ofc, City Hall, Wash, I shall state the trustee's account with the trust fund & distribute the same among the creditors & parties. –W Redin, auditor

Kirkwood House, City of Wash, D C: improvements made to their Hotel, in accordance with the advancement & refinement of the age. –J H & A W Kirkwood

The subscriber will open his new & elegant Drug Store on the site for several years occupied by him on Pa ave, between 6th & 7th sts, on Dec 1. –Z D Gilman

WED NOV 28, 1855
Sale at auction of a Stationery & Fancy Store, by order of a deed of trust, executed on Sep 29, 1853, & at the request of all parties interested, the subscriber will, on Dec 10, sell out in detail all articles in the store of Mrs Garrett Anderson, on Pa ave, between 11th & 12th sts. -Jas C McGuire, auct

Death in the Genr'l Land Ofc. On Sat, Mr Abram Hines, one of the packers, while discharging his duties, was struck with paralysis, & has since died. He was upwards of 60 years of age, & was an old resident of Wash City. He has been employed in this Ofc since Apr, 1844, & has been faithful in the discharge of his duty.

In the Circuit Court of this county on Monday a verdict was rendered for $5,000 in favor of Jos L Scroyer, of Ohio, against Messrs Frink & Walker, late stage proprietors of this city, for an injury to plntf by the overturning of a stage coach at Hennepin, in 1852, by the drunkenness of the driver. –Chicago Journal, Nov 21

Wash Corp: 1-Cmte of Claims: discharged from the consideration of the ptn of Anne Nash for the remission of a fine. 2-Ptn of Chas Frankenberger for the remission of a fine: referred to the Cmte of Claims. 3-Ptn from Philip Krafft, asking to be refunded certain moneys erroneously paid at a tax sale: referred to the Cmte of Claims.

Mrd: on Nov 21, at St John's Church, Hagerstown, Md, by Rev Walter Ayroult, Thos J D Bowie, of Montg Co, to Eliz, eldest daughter of Edw W Beatty, of the former place.

Mrd: on Nov 20, in New Brunswick, N J, at the residence of her parents, by Rev Bishop Janes, E M Patterson to Henrietta, only daughter of Judge S G Deeth & Eliz Ogden Deeth, all of that city.

At Balt, on Sunday night, 5 young men entered the Wash Hotel, a tavern at the corner of Eutaw & Camden sts, & having drank freely they refused to pay for the liquor. The proprietor's brother, Eugene Broader, attempted to help the barkeeper put them out. One of them, John Farring, drew a pistol & shot Eugene, killing him instantly. Another of the gang, Chas Robinson, attempted to murder the proprietor of the house, but both balls fired by him lodged in the floor. All the party were arrested & committed to jail.

Boston, Nov 25. Jas McNally was committed to jail today, charged with the murder of Chas S Smith, a trader in Boston, about 5 years ago. After the murder McNally fled to Canada, where he escaped suspicion until within a short time. He was arrested in Toronto.

Boarding: Mrs E Cudlip, south side of Pa ave, between 3rd & 4½ sts.

Boarding: the Misses Keech, 325 Pa ave: for families or single gentlemen.

New Boarding House, 28 4½ st, a few doors north of Pa ave: Mrs Wm Irving.

Farm at private sale: the subscriber, intending to leave Montg Co, Md, is desirous of selling his Farm, on the Plank road, 6 miles from Wash, containing 100 acres of land: with a comfortable dwlg house & suitable out-bldgs. –Thos O Wilson

THU NOV 29, 1855
News from Central America: Gen Corral, who lately made a treaty with & surrendered to Walker, was tried & shot in the plaza at Granada on the 7th instant for having corresponded with some of the officers of the late Gov't. His arrest, trial, & execution all took place within 80 hours. Gen Rivas is the newly-elected Pres of the Republic. [Dec 5 newspaper: The shooting of Corral by Walker was not a judicial act, as represented. Admitting the legality of Walker's gov't in Nicaragua-which is in itself preposterous-he had no right to court martial any man for treason, it being a political & not a military offence. The shooting of Corral was unmitigated murder, & nothing else. –Star.]

The father of Hon Howell Cobb died on Wed last, in Athens, Ga, at age 72 years.

Hon Dudley Selden, formerly a member of Congress, & a prominent practitioner at the N Y bar, died in Paris on Nov 8.

An inquest was held on Monday upon the body of Ashbel D Crane, who was shot while on a target excursion the day previous. He was with the Amity Guard as a guest, & acted as one of the judges on this occasion. The company was at the large shooting gallery at Klos' Hotel. In the evening after dinner, Mr Crane was leaving, when a bullet, fired by a lad named Geary, passed through a wall & killed him upon the spot. –N Y Courier

Jacob Lorman, a soldier of the Revolution, died at the residence of his son, in Montg Co, Md, on Nov 13, in his 110th year of his age. He entered the army in 1776 as one of the Pa line, & served through the whole of the war of Independence-was at the capture of Yorktown, & the battles of White Plains & Trenton, besides several other engagements. He possessed remarkably good health, & was able to go about until within a day or two of his death.

Mrd: on Nov 27, at Foundry Parsonage, by Rev E P Phelps, Mr Chas Makibben to Miss Mary Delaney, all of Wash City.

Mrd: on Nov 18, at St Dominick Church, by Rev Fr Clarkson, Mr Jas T Lloyd to Miss Louisa R Locke, 2nd daughter of the late Andrew R Locke, all of Wash City.

Mrd: on Nov 22, at Cincinnati, Hon Geo E Pugh, a Senator in Congress from the State of Ohio, to Miss Theresa Chalfant, of Cincinnati.

A Card. Wm Tucker, Merchant Tailor, 426 Pa ave: latest styles, which he is prepared to make up at the shortest notice.

FRI NOV 30, 1855

Art matters in Washington. Personal friends of our talented townsman, Mr W D Washington, will be pleased to learn that he has sent home from Dusseldorf a number of new paintings. They are to be seen at the residence of his father on F st. The subjects delineated are "Entrance to a Castle," "The Student,' & Commencement of the Huguenot War.' It affords us pleasure to announce the return from Europe of the well-known Washington artist, Mr E Johnson; he has taken a room in the new bldg adjoining Browns' Hotel, & intends to spend the winter in Wash. Mr Osk Bessau, though occupied with his duties as a teacher of drawing & painting, is still producing some of his beautiful pictures in water colors. The admirers of the late Judge Cranch will find at the studio of his son, Mr John Cranch, [Adams' Express Bldg,] a very faithful portrait of that eminent jurist & sage. Mr Cranch, the painter, will spend the winter in Wash. Mr Stanley is also still a resident of Wash, & has recently completed a number of his spirited pictures of frontier life.

Dr Francis Mallory, some years ago in Congress from the Norfolk district of Va, has been elected without opposition as delegate from Norfolk City to the Legislature of Va, to supply the vacancy occasioned by the death of Wm D Roberts.

Morgantown [Va] Union: the 2 year old child of Franklin Gray, in Preston Co, was missing & a search was instiued, but the child was not found. On Sat, Mr B Hawley, as he was returning home, & within a half mile of Mr Gray's home, found the child, but it was dead from exposure, having been without food from Friday morning.

Boston Journal of Tue. Rev Henry Mills Haskell, a highly-esteemed young Minister, died of typhus fever, at St Petersburgh, on Oct 31. He was ordained in Mar last at the Central Church in this city, & immediately afterwards departed to enter upon his charge as minister of the British & American Congregational Church & Society in St Petersburgh, via England & Prussia. Gov Seymour, U S Minister at St Petersburgh, has communicated the tidings of his death to his parents.

The Greenbrier [Va] Era stated that a little son of Thos Maddox, some 19 months old, wandered from home on Nov 17, & got lost in the woods. Some 15 men searched for the child until Sunday, when the father found him. The child was alive, but chilled & insensible. At last accounts it was doing well.

Mrd: on Nov 28, by Rev Dr Fuller, D H Tebbs, of Wash City, to Miss Mattie E Stewart, of Balt.

Mrd: on Thu, by Rev John C Smith, Wm Smith to Miss Rachel Mary Parker, all of Wash City.

Mrd: on Nov 27, by Rev Jas Donelan, Mr Chas Forrest to Miss Caroline Hartman, both of Wash City.

Mrd: on Nov 27, at Waverley, Va, by Rev John Towles, Dr R Stuart Lomax, of King Geo, to Jeannie, daughter of Fred'k Foote, of Prince Wm Co, Va.

Died: after an illness of 2 weeks, Josiah Reed Bailey, in his 33rd year. His funeral will be this afternoon at 2 o'clock, from his late residence, 435 7th st, between G & H sts. [No death date given.]

Phil, Nov 29. The remains of the Baron de St Andre, the late French Consul, who was killed at the Burlington railroad disaster, were yesterday removed to the Catholic cemetery in presence of a brother of the deceased, who lately arrived from France.

SAT DEC 1, 1855
The new work of our fellow townsman, Mr Geo Wood, "Modern Pilgrims," appears to have experienced an uncommon degree of popularity. It was first issued on the 10th ult, & we find by the Boston Transcript of the 27th that the whole edition had been already sold, & a fresh one was in the press.

Miss Eliza Logan is to appear this evening at the Nat'l Theatre in the drama of Lucretia Borgia. She will also sing la Marsellaise.

A man named Wooster has been fined $1,000 & forfeited 6 slaves, at New Orleans, for selling them in such a manner as to separate mother & child, contrary to the laws of Louisiana.

Trustee's sale: by deed passed by the Circuit Court for PG Co, Md, sitting as a Court of Equity, in the case of Mary A Markwood & others vs Stephen W Markwood & others, the trustee will expose to public sale, on Dec 20th, on the premises, at the late residence of Wm Markwood, deceased, the real estate of which he died seized & possessed, containing about 88 1/8 acres. It is located in said county, & adjoins the land of Messrs Wingard, Buel, & Sargeant, about 2½ miles from Wash City. The improvements consist of a very comfortable frame dwlg, store-house, & all bldgs necessary for farming operations, with a fine well of water in the yard adjoining the dwlg. It will be sold free of the widow's right of dower. –J Contee Mullikin, N C Stephen, trustees

Lloyd's forthcoming Steamboat Directory gives a singular account of a man, Mr J C Dent, of N Y, being frightened to death on board the steamer **Jas Robb**, during her trip up the Mississipi river in 1852. The boat took fire in the night & Mr Dent rushed to his state room, snatched up his trunk, which contained $12,000, carried it a few steps, then fell dead in the cabin from excessive fright. The fire was subdued.

On Nov 17, Mr Thos J Boyd, while riding on horseback in Lawrence Co, Pa, was crushed to death by a dead tree falling on him. His horse was also killed.

Mrs Sweetman, of Medina, N Y, has been killed by an apothecary, who put up strychnine for her instead of morphine.

Circuit Court of Wash Co, D C-in Equity. Henry Toland, Thos Biddle, Henry J Williams, Benj Gerhard, & Geo P Meade, vs Geo Stewardson, Alfred Ingraham, Eliz M Ingraham, Mgt G Meade, Richd W Meade, Wm Patterson, Salvadora Patterson, Hartman Bache, Maria C Bache, Thos B Huger, Mariamne Huger, Alex'r J Dallas, Jas D Graham, Salvadora Graham, Wm M Meade, Jas D Graham, jr. The above cause has been referred to me as special auditor to inquire & state the amount of the debt due to the cmplnts, secured upn the mortgaged property; the value of the lots included in the mortgage; & the value of the improvements erected thereon by the late Mgt C Meade, & when so erected. Meeting on Dec 8, at the Auditor's room, City Hall, Wash, regarding said property. –Walter S Cox, Special Auditor

John H Gibbs' Hair Dressing & Furnishing Room, 218 Pa ave, Willard's Hotel. The attention of gentlemen requiring Wigs, Toupees, or Scalps, is particularly directed to Gibbs' Saloon, as especial care is given to their manufacture & a natural appearance.

Mrd: on Nov 19, at the Cathedral, Balt, by Rev Thos Foley, Augustus O Burch, jr, of Chas Co, to Mrs Jane C Wilkinson, of St Mary's Co, Md.

Died: on Nov 15, in Charleston, S C, of consumption, Priscilla Clark, wife of N M Porter, in her 35th year, a native of Balt, Md.

Wash Corp Ordinances: 1-Act for the relief of Hanson Brown: the sum of $240.60 be paid to him for grading north O st. 2-Act for the relief of Edmund Wheeler: the fine of $10 imposed on him for being found in the Perseverance engine-house after night, is remitted, the said Wheeler, paying the costs of prosecution.

Boston, Nov 30. The store of Chas M Paine, optician, was robbed yesterday of property to the amount of $6,000.

New Store & New Goods: Hat, Capt, & Gentlemen's Furnishing Establishment, 332 Pa ave, between 9th & 10th sts, Eash. –Geo H B White & Co's

Great bargains in embroidery. Mrs R G Etchison, [successor to Mrs R A Peaco,] No 12 Market Space, between 8th & 9th sts.

MON DEC 3, 1855
The aggregate ages of 3 sisters & 2 brothers Brindle residing at St Thos, Pa, is 426 years: Molly Brindle is 91 years 5 months old; Melchoir, 89; Catherine 87 years 2 months ; Jacob 80 years 3 months; & Eliza 76 years 10 months.

Col J C Fremont has taken a house in N Y for the accommodation of himself & family during the winter, that he may enjoy greater facilities in preparing & publishing the results of his Pacific railway explorations.

The Montg [Ala] Journal mentions the death of N H Clanton, Senator from Macon Co, on Nov 27.

Mr Wm Mohler, the owner of the celebrated **Weir's Cave** in Augusta Co, Va, has sold it to Messrs Davis Craig & John Parkins for $10,000. There are 60 acres of land included in the sale. The cave is still to be kept open to the public. –Richmond Despatch, Nov 29.

On Nov 27 a horrible murder was committed in Haywood's Billiard Saloon, Monument Square. Frank Hyatt, the bar-keeper, was shot dead by hands unknown. Mr Haywood was absent at the time. It is thought it might be a sea captain to whom the deceased refused to give liquor, being then intoxicated. –Savannah Georgian, 28th. [Dec 4th newspaper: Nathl Lewis has been committed to jail at Savannah on the charge of murder, for having shot & killed Francis Hyatt on Tue.]

Last Sat Mr Peter Conaffee, of Pawtucket, Mass, died of hydrophobia after terrible sufferings. About 7 weeks previously he had been bitten slightly by his own dog. –Boston Journal, Fri

Appointment by the Pres: Jas Dunlop to be Chief Judge of the Circuit Court of the U S for the District of Columbia.

The steamer **Minnesota** was launched into the Potomac from the Navy Yard in Wash City at twenty minutes past two o'clock on Sat last. Miss Susan L Mann, a young lady of Wash City, baptized the noble vessel, giving her the name of **Minnesota**.

Mrd: on Nov 22, at **Loch Willow**, near Staunton, Va, by Rev John Hendren, D D, Magdalen M, daughter of Jas Addison Cochran to John B Cochran, of Ky.

TUE DEC 4, 1855
S B Waite, Chemist & Pharmacist, will open at 528 7th st, between D & Pa ave, lately in the occupancy of Mr Z D Gilman. –S B Waite

Criminal Court-Wash, commenced this morning. The following are the grand jurors:

Thos Carbery, foreman	Darius Clagett	Geo W Riggs
Geo S Gideon	Wm F Bayley	Matthew G Emery
Buckner Bayliss	Thos Miller	Amon Baldwin
Wm Thompson	Judson Mitchell	Thos Berry
Wm Wilson	Stephen P Franklin	Saml Pumphrey
Benedict L Semmes	Selby Scaggs	Aaron W Miller
Saml Drury	Robt White	Jehiel Brooks
C W Pairo	Edw M Linthicum	Thos Blagden

Names of the Petit Jury:

Jedediah Gittings	Edw Tolson	Michl Quigley
Theodore Meade	Patrick McKenney	E H Edelin
Leonidas Bowen	J W Barnaclo	W A Wallace
Jacob Smull	H S Williams	K Mitchell
John W Ott	Wm Golding	Thos Tanner
Deanl Lightfoot	Joshua Higton	Thos A Stott
Anton Grinder	John J Joice	J Simmons
Fras J Murphy	John Harrison	Ezekiel Young
Humphrey O	John W Burns	Jas A Burns
Whitmore	A Davis	
J B Holmead	W T Drury	

The copartnership existing under the name of Chas Stott & Co is this day dissolved by mutual consent. The business will be conducted in future by Chas Stott, at the old stand, who will settle the affairs of the late concern. –Chas Stott, S B Waite

Choice Clarke Co land for sale: my Farm, on the Winchester & Berry's Ferry Turnpike road, known as **Glen Owen**: 284 acres. –John Joliffe, Clarke Co, Va.

Va farm for sale by decree of the Circuit Court of Fairfax Co, pronounced at its Nov term, 1855, in the suit of Fish vs Fish & others: public sale on Jan 21, of the valuable Farm on which the late Ruth Scot resided at the time of her death: 191½ acres: in Fairfax Co; with a comfortable house, barn, stable, spring-house & orchard. Mr Archibald Sherwood, living adjoining, will show the premises. –Henry W Thomas, Francis Fish, Com'rs.

WED DEC 5, 1855
It is announced in yesterday's Washington Union that John W Forney, late Clerk of the House of Reps, is joint editor & proprietor of that paper.

Trustee's sale: by deed of trust recorded in Liber J A S 101, of the land records for Wash Co, D C, we will sell on Jan 10, in Wash City, D C: part of lot 9 in square 582, with a frame house & bakery. –E C Morgan, H B Sweeney, trustees -A Green, auct

The case of Malinda Winn vs the Macon & Western Railroad Co [Ga] was tried last week at Macon. The engine coming in collision with a carriage containing Mrs Winn, with 3 children & a negro driver, the consequence was that 2 of the children & driver were killed outright, & Mrs Winn sustained a fracture of the arm, & the 3rd child, the plntf in this case, sustained a very serious fracture of the skull, from the effects of which she has never wholly recovered. The jury returned a verdict of $7,000 against the road.

Dudley Selden, who died at Paris on Nov 7, was taken ill on the 5th, while walking with his servants on the Boulevards. On the 6th he was to give a grand dinner to Mr Fillmore, Mr Mason, Mr Thorndike, & other distinguished gentlemen. The following day he died.

The elegant mansion of Ex-Govn'r Hunt, of Lockport, N Y, was entirely consumed by fire on Fri. It was completed during the past year at a cost of about $10,000. There was no insurance on it. The fire originated in the garret, where a tinner was employed in repairing the pipes connected with a cistern, which was surrounded by cotton batting to guard against freezing. The workman accidentally dropped the candle he was using. Most of the furniture & books were saved.

Died: on Dec 3, at Phil, Pa, Oliver Whittlesey, of Wash City. His funeral will be on Dec 6, at 11 o'clock, from his residence, Indiana ave.

Died: on Dec 1, in Wash City, Catherine Alicia, aged 5 years & 6 months, 2nd daughter of Cecilia Kenny & Thos J Boyne.

Died: on Dec 1, Anne Maria, aged 1 year & 4 months, the youngest child of John R & Margaret Zimmerman.

Execution of a murderer in Calif. A man named Crane, a printer, who 7 or 8 years ago published a newspaper at Richmond, Va, was on Oct 26 legally executed upon the gallow at Coloma, Calif, for the murder of a young woman, Susan M Newman, whom he shot with one of Colt's revolvers near Ringgold, El Dorado Co, on Aug 10 last, & who died on Aug 15. He had a wife & 4 children in the Atlantic States, but regarded himself as married to this young woman, by God & myself, for full 15 months, & shot her because her parents preferred another who was addressing her. He went to the gallow gaily dressed, behaved with great levity, sang a hymn of his own composition, & died exclaiming: Susan receive me; I'll soon be with you.

Albany, Dec 4. The house of Mrs Spelman, at Palmer Hill, Essex Co, was burnt on Sunday, & 3 small children perished in the flames.

THU DEC 6, 1855

An old soldier condemned for murder: the trial took place in Burlington, Iowa, in Nov last. The accused was a man named John J Jones, 73 years of age, who had been a soldier under Gen Jackson, & was with the old hero in several of his campaigns against the Indians. Jones was charged with murdering Horatio W McCardle, a neighbor, some 15 years ago. Capitol punishment having been abolished in Iowa, the prisoner was sentenced to hard labor in the penitentiary during the remainder of his life. Jones, through his atty: I had a family & home, a rude home, a plain & humble family. The deceased robbed me of the one & invaded the sanctity of the other-two small sons, a lovely daughter & a cherished wife. The day of the fatal deed I had no fixed design. He met me with a club; I shot him; & though I claim not to have acted in defence, I do assert that there was mutual combat. I fled; my family followed. For 15 years I have lived at Lockland & made no secret of the deed I had done. That lovely daughter is now a hopeless cripple, wearing a haggard face. One boy has gone to join his injured mother, the other lives, but not to me, he comes not near me. Judge Lowe: the story of your crime is a short one: you set up a claim to land occupied by Mr McCardle, upon which he had raised crop, & was engaged in gathering the same for himself & family, & you walked into his field with your gun, & sent a bullet to his heart in presence of his son. I shall limit your punishment to hard labor in the penitentiary during the remainder of your life on earth.

Newark Advertiser: A son of Hon Wm L Dayton, of Trenton, was struck on the head a few days since with a bandy stick while playing & injured so as to cause his death on the following day.

N Y, Fri. Michl Butler, age 12 years, died from injuries received in a fight with another boy, Hugh Dyer. Inflammation of the brain was the cause. –Com Adv

Mrd: on Nov 29, at the Wesley Chapel Parsonage, in Wash City, by Rev R L Dashiell, Mr Jno Atwell to Miss Lucinda C Simpson, both of Alexandria.

Mrd: on Nov 29, at the Wesley Chapel Parsonage, in Wash City, by Rev R L Dashiell, Mr Ebenezer Humphreville to Miss Frances Grigsby.

Mrd: on Dec 4, by Rev R L Dashiell, Mr Wm W Beard, of PG Co, Md, to Miss Ann J Hopkins, of Anne Arundel Co, Md.

Died: yesterday, at the residence of Col A G Sloo, Mrs Catharine Forman, of Cincinnati, Ohio, aged 73 years. Her funeral will be today at 12 o'clock, from **Franklin Row**.

Died: on Nov 14, at N Y, Mrs Anne E Ullmann, widow of the late John J Ullmann.

For sale: a new 3 Wakeman, 7th st, or on the premises, 512 M st.

Orphans Court of Wash Co, D C. Letters of administration on the personal estate of Josiah R Bailey, late of Wash Co, deceased. –Ann E Bailey, admx

Orphans Court of Wash Co, D C. Letters testamentary on the personal estate of John C Clark, late of Wash Co, deceased. –Robt Clarke, adm

Orphans Court of Wash Co, D C. Letters of administration on the personal estate of Wm Duran, late of Wash Co, deceased. –Robt Clarke, adm

FRI DEC 7, 1855
Moses, a slave belonging to Mr Otterback, of Wash City, was committed to prison on Wed, charged with attempting to kill a German in the employ of that gentleman, having stabbed him in the side with a knife & then attempted to shoot him.

Boston Courier of Wed. Saml Kettell, the late senior editor of that veteran journal, has died. [No death date given-current item.]

Orphans Court of Wash Co, D C. Letters testamentary on the personal estate of Henry Ellis, late of Wash Co, deceased. –Eliz Ellis, Peter Conlan, excs

Mrd: on Dec 4, in Wash City, by Rev F L Knight, Mr Robt Thomas, of N Y, to Miss Frances Crawford, of Wash City.

Died: yesterday, in Wash City, after protracted suffering of disease of the lungs, Mr Wm Ball, eldest son of Robt Ball, of Alexandria Co, Va, in his 51st year.

SAT DEC 8, 1855

Sad accident at Balt on Sat: four men were engaged upon a scaffolding painting St Alphonsus Church, at a height of 50 feet, supported by slats of plank nailed against the wood work of the windows, when the supports gave way & the whole were thrown to the ground. Their names are John Mortimer, Jas Connolly, Thos Burns, & John Gifford. Mortimer & Gifford have since died.

1st Lt Danl M Beltzhoover, 1st Regt of Artl, & 2nd Lt Raymond Fairfax, 2nd Regt of Artl, have resigned their commissions in the U S Army. -Star

Warrenton Female College, Warrenton, N C, will being on Jan 16, 1856. Apply to Rev Thos S Campbell, Pres

There are at the present time in the parish prison in New Orleans, under sentence of death, persons convicted of capital crime last winter & spring in the First District Court of that city. Their names are Jas Henry Costlow, Jas Shields, Patrick Kennedy, John Melvin, & Manuel Obregon. The last named was convicted of arson, the rest of murder. In all their cases appeals have been taken to the Supreme Court of the State, & will be decided upon this month or next.

The Frankfort Commonwealth announces the death, on Sat last, at the residence of her father in Scott Co, Ky, of Mrs Wright, wife of Govn'r Wright, of Indiana.

Mrd: on Dec 6, by Rev F H Richey, Mr Enos E Berkley to Miss Sarah M McCathran, all of Wash City.

Mrd: on Dec 4, by Rev P D Gurley, D D, Mr Wm Storey to Miss Jennette Henderson, both of Wash City.

Mrd: Dec 6, at **Morton View**, Culpeper Co, Va, by Rev B Grimsley, Thos H Gibbs, of West River, Md, to Helen, daughter of the late Marshall Ashby, of Fauquier Co, Va.

Died: on Dec 6, in his 23rd year, Joseph Lovell Johnson, youngest son of Dr Richmond Johnson. His funeral will be today at 12 o'clock, from the residence of his father, K & 25th sts.

Died: on Dec 6, after a sudden illness, Mr A S Loughery, aged 43 years, formerly of the Treasury Dept. His funeral is today at 11 o'clock, from his late residence, at Mrs Robinson's, 558 Pa ave.

Mrs Burghalter is desirous of commencing again to give instructions on the Piano to a few pupils at their residences. Term, $15 per quarter. Communications left at Mrs Clitch's Fancy Store, between 9th & 10th sts, will meet with prompt attention.

Died: on Dec 7, at the ***Highlands***, in Montg Co, Md, Robt Y Brent, in his 67th year. His funeral will be Dec 9 at 2 o'clock, from his late residence. [Dec 24th newspaper: Mr Brent was no ordinary individual. He was descended of highly influential parents. His father was the first Mayor of Wash City & Paymaster Genr'l of the U S Army. Mr Brent, though residing a few miles north of Wash, was closely identified with its interest; preferring the retirement of a farmer's life to the excitement of politics, he refused the higher places tendered him by his friends. He well performed the multitudinous vocations of son, husband, father, friend, neighbor, & citizen.]

Orphans Court of Wash Co, D C. In the case of Mary A Miller, admx of Michl Miller, deceased, the administratrix & Court have appointed Dec 29, for the settlement of the personal estate of said deceased, of the assets in hand.
–Ed N Roach, Reg/o wills

MON DEC 10, 1855
The Cincinnati "Commercial" gives particulars of the explosion of the steam fire-engine "Joe Ross," in that city, on Wed, whilst undergoing a trial for the satisfaction of a cmte of gentlemen from Chicago. When the greatest power of the engine was being tested, the receiving chest exploded, instantly killing the engineer, John Winterbottom, & wounding A B Latta, inventor of the engine, Jeremiah Brant, carpenter, Horace English, & one or two others. The force threw Mr Winterbottom some distance in the air. The steam was at 180 pounds; the highest point in trials heretofore only about 145.

Appointments by the Pres:
Jas Dunlop, of D C, to be Chief Judge of the Circuit Court of the U S for said District.
Wm M Merrick, of D C, to be Assoc Judge of the Circuit Court of the U S of the said District, vice Jas Dunlop.
John R Parham, to be Surveyor & Inspector of the revenue for the port of Columbia, Mississippi, under the authority given in the act approved Mar 3, 1855.
John R Parham, Surveyor of the Customs at Columbus, Mississippi.
[John R Parham written 2 times.]

Trustee's sale: by decree of the Circuit Court of Wash Co, D C, passed in a cause, No 989, wherein Geo McCallion & others are cmplnts, & Jos Peck, John Walker, & others are dfndnts: auction on Jan 3, 1856, of: two undivided third parts of lot 7, 22 thru 25, & 27, in square 106, with several good dwlg houses, in Wash City.
-W Redin, Chas S Wallach, trustees -A Green, auct [I am authorized by the owners of the other undivided third part in the above lots to say that it will be offered for sale at the same time, so that purchasers will be able to buy the entirety of each lot.]

Oliver Pillsbury, who died at West Newbury last week at the age of 81 years, has been a subscriber to the Newburyport Herald for 61 years, & what is still better, had always cheerfully paid for it when the bill was presented.

Oregon & Wash Territories. Letters received by Com'r of Indian affairs from Superintendent Joel Palmer, dated Oct 9, 16, & 19, state a large number of citizens have been killed by the Indians. Indian Agent Thompson, in a letter which accompanies the above letters, gives the information respecting the fate of Agent Boland: letter dated Dalles, Sep 28. Mr Boland left this place for the Catholic mission on the Yakamah river some 10 days ago, to learn the truth of the reported murder of several citizens by the Yakamah tribe of Indians. He said he would return in 3 days. Nothing has been heard from him except the Indian rumor of his murder, which rumor is made by friendly Indians. A squaw, who was taken captive & afterwards escaped, states that Mr Boland reached the Catholic mission & was midway on his return, when he was overtaken by 3 or 4 Indians, who seized & bound him, & afterwards put him to death by cutting his throat. It was stated that the Indians, under the control of Scloo, plan to attack & destroy Mr Joslyn & family, who reside at White Salmon river, 20 miles below this place; take his stock & make a large feast, that their hearts may be made strong; then descend upon the people at the Cascades, cutting off communication with the Dalles; & destroy the people. Mr Agent Olney was dispatched to the Walla-Wallas, Cayuses, & Umatillas, with instructions to remain among them till matters were quiet. A battle between the troops under Maj Haller & the Yakamah Indians took place at Top-in-ish, on Oct 7. Our troops lost one man killed & 5 or 6 wounded.

Counterfeiter arrested. Robt F Weddell was arrested at Pittsburg last week on a charge of altering bank notes.

U C Court: the case of Harriet Smith vs Zalmuna Phillips was given to the jury yesterday. The suit was brought by Miss Smith to recover a note for $25,000. She alleged that Reuben Smith, aged 60 years, formerly a servant in the family of Theodore Lyman, of Waltham, had accumulated property to the amount of $30,000, & that in his last & fatal sickness in West Roxbury, the plntf, Miss Smith, his niece, attended him as nurse, & in consideration of her services, he gave her his note for the amount claimed. The note was produced at the trial. The heirs at law, who contested the suit, reside in Ohio. The jury returned a verdict awarding Miss Smith $8,060.14, which is presumed to be just one-fourth of the value of the property of the deceased.
-Boston Journal of Thu

Rev Jas B Donelan, who for the past 9 years has been the Pastor of St Matthew's Church, in Wash City, announced yesterday to his congegation that he had resigned his place as their pastor, & that, at his request, the Archbishop had appointed Rev John B Byrne his successor. Mr Donelan also announced that he would remain in the Church as an assistant to Fr Bynre.

Mrd: on Dec 6, by Rev Jas McIntire, Rev Isaac W K Handy, Pastor of the First Presbyterian Church, Portsmouth, Va, to Miss Rebecca H Dilworth, daughter of John D Dilworth, of Newcastle Co, Dela.

Mrd: on Nov 14, at **Fort Riley**, [Kansas Territory,] by Rev Mr Clarkson, Lt Jas E B Stuart, U S Cavalry, to Flora, eldest daughter of Col P St Geo Cooke, U S Dragoons.

Died: on Dec 1, at the Western Hotel, N Y, Jas Mahony, in his 41 year, a native of the county Cork, Ireland, for the last 2 years a resident of this Wash City. He served gallantly his adopted country as a volunteer during the Mexican war. He leaves a wife & 2 children to lament their sad bereavement.

Died: on Sat, William Edgar, infant son of John T & Ann Virginia Moss, of Wash City.

Estray cow came to the premises of the subscriber. Owner is to come forward, prove property, pay charges, & take her away. –Jas Owens, over the upper bridge of the Anacostia.

TUE DEC 11, 1855

Obit-died: on Sat, at Phil, in his 81st year, Col Saml Miller, of the Marine Corps, which he entered about 45 years ago, & for a number of years thereafter was stationed at the headquarters of that corps in Wash City. He commanded the detachment of the Marine Corps which, with Cmdor Barney's pieces of artillery & the other troops there present, made a stand between Wash City & Bladensburg against the invading army of the enemy in Aug, 1814. In this brief engagement Col Miller was severely wounded. For some years previous to his death he had been stationed at the Phil navy yard. He has yet left in Wash City many friends who lament his death.

The Watchman & State Journal of Montpelier, Vt, announced the death of its esteemed editor, Ezekiel P Watson, who was connected with the paper first as an apprentice & then as editor for 50 years. He was generous to a fault, & no object of charity ever went unrelieved from his door.

Azariah H Simmons, one of the proprietors of the Phil Ledger & of the Balt Sun, died at Phil on Sunday last. He was a practical printer, was one of the pioneers of the penny press system in both Phil & Balt, & by his industry & attention to business, amassed a large property.

Private Boarding House, 303 G st, between 13th & 14th sts: most eligible accommodations for either married or single persons. –Mrs Emma Bryant

Catharine Cooper, of Lancaster, Pa, recovered a verdict of $5,500 against the Ohio & Pa Railroad Co for the loss of her husband by an accident on the road, resulting from carelessness on the part of the employes of the company.

Estray Red Cow came to the subscriber, on the Wash Plank Road. Owner is to come forward, prove property, pay charges, & take her away. –Harriet White

Circuit Court of Wash Co, D C-in Chancery. Robt Cruit against Edwin Walker & others. The bill charges that the cmplnt, at the Mar term, 1847, of said court, recovered a judgment against one John Walker for $2,400, with interest thereon from Jul 26, 1845, & $50.45 costs of suit; that an execution was issued on said judgment, & was returned to the Oct term of said Court *nulla bona*, & is still unsatisfied; that said John Walker has no property upon which an execution can be levied, but is the owner of certain property in Wash City, among which are lots 5 thru 17, in square 555, which said lots, with other property, he has conveyed away for the purpose of hindering, delaying, & defeating said cmplnt in the recovery of his said debt; that said John Walker did, by deed dated Jan 23, 1846, convey the above property to certain trustees to secure certain debts therein mentioned as due to said Edwin Walker & others; that the said debts in said deed mentioned were not real, & if so have been wholly or for the most part paid; that no sale of the said property has been made under said deed, but said property has been ever since, & still is, in the possession of the said John Walker, & the rents thereof received by him; that cmplnt has a right & offers to redeem said Edwin Walker of any amount that may be due him of said debt; & the object of the bill is to obtain a sale of the said property & other premises, under the order of the Court, & out of the proceeds thereof to pay, first, whatever of the said debts in said deed & others may be due; second, all incumbrances prior to said cmplnt's debt, & afterwards cmplnt's debt. It appearing that said Edwin Walker does not reside in the District, but beyond the limits of the same. He is to appear in said Court on or before the third Monday of April next. -Jno A Smith, clerk

The funeral of Oliver Whittlesey was on Thu last, & his remains were consigned to their last resting place on earth, in the new & beautiful **Glenwood Cemetery**. The eloquent ceremonies at the dwlg of the deceased were performed by Rev Mr Eckhardt & Rev Mr Sunderland. At 12 o'clock the procession moved for **Glenwood**, Federal Lodge of F & A Masons, with its Master, J W Nairn, accompanied by the Grand Master of Masons of the District, Chas S Frailey, leading the procession, Wash Encampment of Knights Templars, under the command of B B French, performing the duites of pall-bearers & escort, the deceased being a member of each of these bodies. Thus we buried Oliver Whittlesey-a man who for years we have loved & honored; upon whom disease, in its most melancholy & appalling form, fell heavily within the two of three past years, & which has now laid him in the grave in the very meridian of his manhood. -F

Mrd: on Dec 9, by Rev Andrew G Carothers, Mr Thos Stone to Miss Josephine Eliz Smith, both of Wash City.

Died: on Dec 10, of typhoid fever, Jas P Burroughs, in his 23rd year. His funeral will be this afternoon at 3½ o'clock, from the residence of John H Smoot, 1st st, Gtwn.

Wash City Ordinance: 1-Act for the relief of Robt Porter: the fine of $10 imposed on him for keeping a dog without a license is hereby remitted; provided he pays the costs of prosecution.

WED DEC 12, 1855

"One evil of **old age** is, that as your time is come you think every little illness is the beginning of the end." When a man expects to be arrested, every knock at the door is an alarm.

Senate: 1-Memorial of Mrs Catharine Van Rensselaer Cochran, only living child & immediate rep of Gen Philip Schuyler. Mr Seward presented it early because of the advanced age of the lady, now in her 79th year. She sets forth that in her memorial that when Gen Burgoyne was advancing along the valley of the Hudson toward Albany it became necessary for her father, who then commanded the American army, to construct a bridge across the river over half a mile in length, the whole cost of which was furnished from her father's private purse; that when Gen Burgoyne was retreating he caused the mansion house, stores, mills, etc, of her father to be destroyed, involving a loss of $20,000, according to Lossing's field notes, & according to the statement of Gen Burgoyne of ten thousand pounds sterling. She states that her declining life is embittered by the inconvenience & sorrow attendant upon poverty, together with the trials imposed by an invalid & helpless son, dependent upon her for support; that the recognition by the last Congress of the meritorious acts of the noble De Kalb has emboldened her to ask a similar acknowledgment of her father's self-sacrificing devotion upon the altar of his country; & that she confidently relies upon the patriotism & justice of Congress to vindicate her father's merits. Mr Seward gave notice that he would at an early day bring in a bill for her relief.

From Calif. 1-Wm H Richardson, U S Marshal for the northern district of Calif, was murdered at San Francisco on Nov 17 by an Italian gambler named Cora. Cora was arrested & put in jail. 2-Isaac B Wall, Collector of the Post of Monterey, was murdered near San Louis Obispo, together with a companion, Thos Williamson, Assessor of Monterey Co. Their murderers were supposed to be a party of Mexicans under one Garcia. They were overtaken at Salina, & a fight ensued, in which 2 of the sheriff's party were killed. 3-Capt Archibald McRae, of the revenue cutter **McLean**, committed suicide in a fit of insanity. 4-The banking-house of Saunders & Brennan, at San Francisco, has failed. Their liabilities were $80,000, & their assets nothing.

Household & kitchen furniture at auction on: Dec 18, at the residence of J M Donn, 12th st, between G & H sts. -Jas C McGuire, auct

The steamship **America** brings us the intelligence of the death of Lady Emmeline Stuart Wortley. She died on Oct 29, at Beirut, Syria, where she had resided for several years past. This lady was the 2nd daughter of the Duke of Rutland, & the widow of the late Chas Stuart Wortley. She visited the U S twice, & in 1851 published a volume of travels, giving her impressions of the society & institutions which came under her observation. —Journal of Commerce

Orphans Court of Wash Co, D C. Letters of administration on the personal estate of Adam Dulaney, late of Wash Co, deceased. —Caleb Dulaney, adm

Circuit Court of Wash Co, D C-in Chancery. John A Fraser vs John Walker & others. Chas S Wallach & Edw Swann, trustees in the above cause, sold lot 4 in square 388, to J W Birch, for $775, & part of square 472 to John Walker, for $1,100; that said purchasers had complied with the terms of sale. —Jno A Smith, clerk

Application has been made to the Mayor of Wash City for deeds to be given for lots 22 & 23 in square A, to be subscriber, by virtue of two bonds of conveyance, executed by the Com'rs of Low Grounds, dated on or about Apr 22, 1825, to Archibald McIntyre, who, at a public sale made by said Com'rs on said day, was the purchaser of said lots; which said lots, by subsequent assignment & conveyance, duly recorded in the clerk's ofc, have beome the property of the undersigned, & the said bonds properly belong to him, but have been lost or mislaid, so that they cannot be found. —W W Corcoran

Circuit Court of Wash Co, D C-in Chancery. The trustee reported the sale of lot 3, in square 11, in 4 several parcels, on Aug 9, 1852: that one parcel was purchased by Henry Eld for $240; another of them by John B Magill for $24; another of them to Francis Bayle for $97; & the remaining one to Elkanah Denham for $225; that the purchase money, with the interest chargeable thereon, has been paid & satisfied unto the trustee. -Jno A Smith, clerk

Mrd: on Dec 11, in Trinity Church, by Rev Dr Cummins, Thos S Scrivener to Catherine, daughter of E French, all of Wash City.

Mrd: on Dec 10, at Brown's Hotel, by Rev Jas S Petty, Hanson Jordan, of Front Royal, Va, to Miss Mariam D Hoye, of Preston Co, Va.

Mrd: on Dec 6, near Bethesda, Montg Co, Md, by Rev Wm T Evan, Mr Jacob L Bohrer to Miss Mgt C Perry, daughter of Saml Perry.

Mrd: on Dec 11, in Gtwn, by Rev W F Speake, Mr Percy W Hall to Miss Martha A T Fowler, of Montg Co, Md.

Died: on Dec 10, at Pittsburgh, Pa, aged 73, Mrs Clara Bomford, widow of the late Col Geo Bomford, U S Ordnance. Her remains are expected in Wash City today, by train from the West, arriving at 11 o'clock A M.

Died: on Monday, in Balt, of a lingering illness, & in Christian peace, Laura Matilda, wife of Thos E Dell, & daughter of Mrs Eliz Kleiber, of Wash City.

Died: on Nov 26, at Springfield, near Middleburg, William Wellford, infant son of Jno D & Parke Farley Rogers.

U S Patent Ofc, Wash, Dec 11, 1855. Ptn of Thos Woodward, of N Y, praying for the extension of a patent granted to him on May 7, 1842, for an improvement in shielded pins, for 7 years from the expiration of said patent, which takes place on May 7, 1856. –Chas Mason, Com'r of Patents

THU DEC 13, 1855
The project of connecting the Red Sea with the Mediterranean by a ship canal cutting the **Isthmus of Suez** is one of vast importance to the commercial interests of the world, & has already excited much attention among the scientific & intelligent commercial men in the U S. Mr Ferdinand de Lesseps has just published a pamphlet upon the subject in France. He was formerly Minister of France at the Court of Spain, afterwards, in 1849, Envoy from the French Republic on a mission to Rome, & then Director of the Commerical Dept in the Ministry of Foreign Affairs at Paris.

House for rent & furnishings for sale: desirable 3 story brick dwlg, 422 D st, between 6th & 7th sts. Apply to H F Loudon & Co, under Browns' Hotel.

To his Excellency the Pres of the U S: May it please your Excellency: we, the undersigned citizens of Doniphan Co, respectfully petition your Excellency to remove the present chief excutive ofcr of this Territory, Govn'r Wilson Shannon, & replace him by a gentleman of judgment & ability, who, while a friend of law & order, will refuse to recognize as law-abiding men ruffians who have invaded our boarders & violated our ballot-boxes repeatedly, or residents who have invited such outrages & publicly defended them as just, necessary, & even constitutional.
[Note: Those who signed were not listed in the newspaper.]

Died: on Dec 12, in Wash City, Elizabeth Starr, daughter of Robt & Jane Farnham, in her 9th year. Her funeral will be on Friday morning at 10 o'clock, from the residence of her father, 11th & M sts.

Died: on Dec 8, at the residence of her father-in-law, in Milroy, Mifflin Co, Pa, in her 24th year, Mrs Janet Dellett, formerly of Wash City.

Large sale of land: by decree of the Circuit Court of PG Co, Court of Equity: public sale on the premises, on Jan 7 next, all the real estate of the late John Townshend, near Brandywine, PG Co, Md, comprising several tracts & parcels of land, in the aggregate about 1,500 acres. –C C Magruder, Saml H Berry, trustees

FRI DEC 14, 1855
Alex'r Mahon died at Harrisburg on Sunday last, at age 75 years. He formerly held a prominent position in Pa; but age & blindess [which he had been efflicted with for 8 or 10 years,] incapacitated him for any kind of business. We believe he was a native of Cumberland Co. He resided at Washington, when holding a prominent public ofc. -Phil Bulletin

John Walker's Provision Store: Louisiana ave near 6th st: fresh beef, mutton, veal, dried beef, beef tongues, & salted provisions.

Died: on Dec 9, at Gloucester Point, N J, Michl Pepper, aged 71 years.

Mrd: on Dec 13, by Rev Andrew G Carothers, Mr Wm M Mills to Miss Virginia C Nalls, both of Fairfax Co, Va.

Mrd: on Dec 6, at **Greenwood**, PG Co, Md, by Rev W Pinkney, Mr D R Wall to Miss Sarah J Crawford.

Senate: 1-Memorial from Lt John J Glasson, a lt in the navy, complaining of the decision of the Naval Board appointed under an act of Congress of Feb 28, 1855, & asking to be restored to the active service list. 2-Memorial from Zadoc Thompson, asking compensation for his services in preparing an historical article to the census returns of Vt at the request of the Superintendent of the Census Bureau. 3-Ptn from Stephen Tuthill, asking remuneration for losses sustained by his father, John Tuthill, during the Revolutionary war. 4-Ptn from Franck Taylor, asking the return of duties on articles imported by him for the use of the U S, which were exempt by act of Jan, 1849. 5-Ptn from Capt L C Hunt, asking remuneration for losses sustained by the burning of the steamship **City of Pittsburgh**, on board of which he was a passenger under an order to join his company in Calif. 6-Ptn from Mrs A R Linn, of Missouri, & widow of the late Dr Linn, formerly of the Senate, asking the commutation & interest due the reps of the late Col Wm Linn, of the Revolution.

SAT DEC 15, 1855
Sale by order of the Orphans Court of Wash Co, D C: on Dec 19, Groceries, Cigars, Store fixtures, etc, at the store lately occupied by the late Josiah R Baily, on 7th st, between G & H sts. –A Green, auct

Chickering & Sons' Pianos. Since his late advertisement the subscriber has received 10 more Square Pianos & 1 Parlor Grand Piano, which, with the Pianos in store, fills up his usual large & complete assortment. By the steamer **Joseph Whitney**, which will leave Boston on Dec 15, will be received a further supply of Chickering Pianos. Second-hand pianos taken in part payment. –Richd Davis, Pa ave

Mrd: on Dec 13, by Rev Wm Hodges, Lt A W Johnson, U S Navy, to Miss E Marion Moore, of Wmsburg, Va.

Mrd: on Dec 13, at the Church of the Epiphany, by Rev J W French, John W Magill to Kate C, daughter of F S Myer, all of Wash City.

Senate: 1-Ptn from Sarah B Hobbins, sole heir & lineal descendant of Michl Jackson, an ofcr of the Revolutionary army, asking to be allowed the half-pay to which her ancestor was entitled. 2-Ptn from Wm M Brooks & Eliza M Priest, asking to be allowed the amount due Col David Brooks as pay & commutation for his services during the Revolution. 3-Ptn from Peyton G King, late Receiver of Public Moneys at Monroe, La, asking to be relieved from liability incurred in consequence of loss of certain public moneys by robbery. 4-Ptn from Cezaere Wallace, asking the confirmation of his title to a tract of land. 5-Ptn from Randall D Livingston, asking confirmation to a title to a tract of land in the Bastrop grant.

Furs at Seymour's. I have just completed a few sets of dark Canada Mink Sable mantillas, which are now ready for inspection: are cheap at $150, but will be sold much lower for cash by calling early at the Fur manufactory in Gtwn.
-W F Seymour

Died: on Dec 13, Lura Sophia Paynter, wife of Abraham Paynter, & only daughter of Geo & Sophia Page, in her 28th year. Her funeral is today at 2 o'clock, from the residence of her father, F & 7th st.

Died: at Upperville Academy, Fauquier Co, Va, in his 17th year, of typhoid fever, Julius, son of Rezin H & Mgt Snowden, of Birmingham, Anne Arundel Co, Md. [No death date given-current item.]

MON DEC 17, 1855
Orphans Court of Wash Co, D C. Letters testamentary on the personal estate of John Foy, late of Wash Co, deceased. –Sarah Foy, excx

Kickapoo City [Mo] Pioneer of Nov 3<u>1</u>. [31-copied as written.] Incendiarism is abroad in the land. An effort was made by one or more black-hearted abolitionists last night to destroy Mr B D Hamilton & his family, residents of Salt Creek, by fire. Mr Hamilton is an undoubted pro-slavery man, & this is the only cause that can be assigned for setting fire to his premises.

Hon Chas Jackson, for several years one of the Justices of the Supreme Judicial Court, died on Thu, at his residence in Bedford Pl, at age 80 years. He was born in Newburyport, May 31, 1775. His father was Hon Jonathan Jackson, who was a member of the Continental Congress in 1780. Judge Jackson graduated at Cambridge in 1793, studied law with Theophilus Parsons, & in 1813 was appointed a Judge of the Supreme Court by Govn'r Strong. He held this ofc until 1824, when his bad state of health compelled him to resign it. He has been for several years past lived in retirement. –Boston Atlas

Land Warrant No 52,004, dated Jun 26, 1852, to Humphrey Keyes, private in Capt Humphrey's company of Va militia, war of 1812, for 40 acres, has been lost or destroyed. A caveat has been entered at the Land Ofc, & an application will be made in due time for a duplicate warrant. –Humphrey Keyes

Obit-died: on Thu last, at Troy, Maj Oscar F Winship, of the Adj General's Dept U S Army, of congestion of the brain, after a very brief illness. He entered the Military Academy at West Point in 1836, & graduated in 1840; was appointed 2nd Lt 2nd Dragoons in 1840; 1st Lt 2nd Dragoons in 1844; in 1846 was brevetted captain for gallant & meritorious services at Palo Alto & Resaca de la Palma, & also in 1846 appointed assist adj genr'l with rank of captain. In 1847 he was brevetted major for gallant services at Churubusco, & the same year promoted to assist adj genr'l with rank of major, & in 1851, he was promoted captain of 2nd Dragoons. The deceased, for 2 years of more, was chief of the staff of Maj Gen Wool while commanding the eastern division of the army. Maj Winship had recently left Gen Harney's command at *Fort Pierre* for a brief period to recruit his health & visit his family; & if life & health had been spared him he would have been at St Louis in a few days actively engaged in the preparation of the material & requisites for an early opening of the spring campaign by the army to which he was attached, which is now in winter quarters near the base of the Rocky Mountains, not far from the source of the Missouri river. He was a native of N Y, & was about 40 years of age. –Troy Whig

Saml E Arnold, of Wash Co, D C, brought before me as strays, two oxen, trespassing upon the premises of the *Congressional Burial Ground*, Wash City. –Jas Crandell, J P [Owner is to prove property, pay charges, & take them away. –Saml E Arnold, at the *Congressional Burial Ground*.]

Died: on Sunday, in Wash City, Mr Geo Cox, formerly of Wash City, but for some years past a resident of Balt. His funeral is today, at 2 o'clock, from the residence of his sister-in-law, Mrs Cornelius Cox, 357 Mass ave, between 10th & 11th.

Confectionary. Thos Potentini has recently purchased the establishment of John Miller, 279 Pa ave, between 10th & 11th st, which he will carry on with increased facilities for ministering to the tastes of those who may favor him with their patronage.

TUE DEC 18, 1855
The Louisville papers contains notice of the death of Col Wm Riddle, of that city, in his 40th year. He was a prominent & useful citizen. During the Mexican war he was Adj of the Louisville Legion, & proved himself an efficient & popular ofcr. He was present at the capture of Monterey, & enjoyed in high degree the confidence of Gen Taylor.

Oliver King & Warren C Ayres have been arrested in Lawrence, Mass, charged with having robbed the Express Co at the West of $50,000 in gold belonging to the Gov't.

Senate: 1-Ptn from J H Graham, a post-capt in the U S navy: wounded on the Canada shore in the war of 1812 & had to have his leg amputated; in Sep, 1814, was on board the flag-ship of the late Cmdor McDonough when vanquishing the British fleet on Lake Champlain; was on board the frig **United States**, which sailed for the Mediterranean under Com Shaw for the purpose of compelling the Algerines to do justice, but that Com Decatur had already anticipated the object, & dismissed the subject; in 1816 he was appointed acting-lt, & ordered by the Dept to the recruiting service in N Y, where he was on actve duty about 12 years; under Pres Tyler, he was deputed to the same service as cmder, where he remained 2 years, when, by orders of Sec Bancroft, he was detached, since which period, for want of orders, he has been unemployed. He asks that he may not be denied the privilege of being placed with the ofcrs of his rank on the honorable retired list, with full leave of absence pay.
2-Ptn from Ozmand Peters, a lt in the revenue service, asking that the bounty law of Mar, 1855, may be so amended as to embrace all those who served in any war of the U S. 3-Memorial of W C McDongas, asking compensation for assisting to take the census of Calif. 4-Ptn from Catharine Newington, asking the right of pre-emption to the land upon which certain public bldgs purchased by her at **Fort Atkinson** are located. 5-Ptn from Chas Stearns, of Springfield, Mass, asking indemnity for damages sustained in consequence of illegal prosecutions by the U S. –Ptn from Wm Foster, asking compensation for his services in opening the port of Manzanilla, Mexico.

Died: on Dec 9, after a very protracted illness, Mr Lewis Smith, of Gtwn, in his 69th year. He was one of the oldest & most esteemed of the District. He died as he lived, by faith in the Divine Redeemer, in joyful hope of a blissful immortality.

WED DEC 19, 1855
New Hampshire Veterans: last Monday the N H visiters, the District veterans of 1812, & the ofcrs of our military btln marched to the President's Mansion. There, in the great East Room, they were received by the President, who was attended by members of the Cabinet & several distinguished ofcrs of the Army. The following is the muster-roll of the ofcrs & members of the btln of Veterans:

Col C E Potter   Capt S T Langley   Hon T T Abbott
Lt Col Wm Patten   Capt B P Cilley   Fife-Maj G W Parker
Maj H Brown   Lt B F Agnew   Drum-Major J Clark

1st Co: Capt, S W Parsons; Lt J Wallace; 1st Sgt, A F Patten

Privates:
E W Herington   S Dunn   J P Moore
S G Rollins   J Bliss   J Kennara
W S Berry   Wm Gray   Saml Patton
W F Chamberlain   C Poor   J Campbell
L Sargent   T W Little   A L Hutchinson
J H Denison   C Stinson   J L Bradford
M Hill   J Craig   W Stinson
B F Straes   D Hall   Wm Richardson

2nd Co: Capt, B D Moores; Lt, D C Gold; Sgt, J M Bonell; Sgt, A S Roby

Privates:
Wm D Stokes   G W Riddle   W Neal
J Peavy   W Advance   J E Smith
D L Robinson   J W Moore   J Eastman
A Walker   G H Kimball   H Dennison
N Parker   J O Parkes   A Chandler
J C Young   J L Kelly   J W Smith
D B Nelson   A Kimball   C F Gold
J H Moore   S C Morrill   W P Riddle
P V Putney   E Hall

Col W P Riddle; Maj E T Stevens

Privates:
S Andrews   W W Brown   S Gamble
J S Elliot   J Hussey   W Whittle
Capt B M Tilotson

Privates:
T Rundell   J A Hains
J Harbell   J Doten

3rd Co:
Capt, S M Daws; Lt, S C Hall; Sgt, G W Converse; Sgt, J C Ricker

Privates:
J A Ellis   H C Parker   C Richardson
D W Fling   B B Quimby   M W Allmer
D A Bunton   F Fennay   H Clouth

H Dickey	E B Edwards	D Kennard
H F Monatt	B F Martin	S Simons
H G Lowell	W P Newell	Wm Walker
W H Hill	M Lyons	C Holmes
J A Page	G Kennard	

4th Co: Capt, J G Cilley; Lt J M Baum; Sgt, W C Knolton
Privates:

C Shedd	J M Parker	J Currie
E H Davis	J Don	F H Pike
J Rogers	C Cheney	A Kidder
S Hall	B Nutt	G Kidder
A W Thompson	A C Wallace	H W Brown
F A Brown	S Measury	D L Robinson
S Palmer	W Dignum	J F Langley
D Spofford	N Head	M Hitchinson
J J A Sargent	Mr Proctor	L Pattridge
J Sawyer	H Murphy	S Hall
A G Tucker	J Iansbee	M Don
D Cross	E Dustin	J A Potter
H H Ladd	P S Brown	D B Kebby
S P Chase	F A Lane	J Yough
C G W Bartlett	J T Spofford	___ McCabe

City Item: Mr Jas E Murdock will appear at the Nat'l Theatre this evening as Hamlet, supported by Mrs Malinda Jones as Queen Gertrude, & by Miss Devlin as the fair Ophelia.

New Orleans, Dec 17. The Supreme Court this morning made a decision in the Mrs Gen Gaines' case, reversing the decision of the Second District Court, & decreeing that Danl Clarke's will of 1813 be probated, & that Mrs Gaines be put in possession of the property she has so long contended for. [Dec 27th newspaper: The decision in the matter of Myra Clarke Gaines, on the application to allow the olographic will of her father, Danl Clarke, made in 1813, to be probated, which will constitute Mrs Gaines the universal legatee of her father, & Delachaise & Delacroix his executors. The estate involved in this litigation is estimated to be one of the largest in the U S. The property is now generally held by wealthy persons, & consists mostly of sugar plantations & some of the best property in the city of New Orleans. The olographic will was made 2 years after the will under which the other heirs hold possession of the property was made; the other heirs will have the right to contest her title.]

$10 reward for return of a strayed or stolen bay Mare, or secure her so that I get her again. –Wm Coates, near Bladensburg, PG Co, Md.

The Savannah papers announce the death in that city, on Fri last, of Robt H Griffin, in his 33rd year; a distinguished member of the Order of Odd Fellows, & lately its chief ofcr. At the time of his death he was clerk of the U S District Court & Pres of the Gas Works, responsible posts, which he filled acceptably. The Georgian eulogizes him as a faithful citizen & good lawyer.

U S Patent Ofc, Wash, Dec 15, 1855. Ptn of Fred'k E Sickels, of N Y, N Y, praying for the extension of a patent granted to him for an improvement in valves of steam engines, for 7 years from the expiration of said patent, which takes place May 20, 1856. –Chas Mason, Com'r of Patents

Circuit Court of Wash Co, D C. Jno B Kibbey & Jno C Whitwell, vs Eliz F Marceron, Jos B Marceron, & others. The parties above & creditors of Philip T Marceron, deceased, are notified that the cause has been referred to me, as special auditor, to state the Trustee's account with the trust fund & the proper distribution of the same. I will attend for this purpose at the Auditor's room, City Hall, Wash, on Jan 2, at 12 o'clock M. –Walter S Cox, Special Auditor

Died: on Dec 17, in Wash City, at the residence of his relative Mrs Isabella Walker, Thos Jones Johnston, of Mississippi, in his 35th year. He had been a resident of Wash City for the past 8 or 9 years, & connected with some branch of the Gen Gov't, holding at the time of his death the position of Chief Clerk in the ofc of the Auditor of the Treasury for the Post Ofc Dept. He has left a wife & several children widowed & fatherless. For some time he had been a sufferer from general disease, but few thought it would terminate so suddenly & fatally. He was in his usual place in the church on the last Sabbath. His funeral will be attended from the First Presbyterian Church, 4½ st, this day at 1 o'clock P M.

Senate: 1-Ptn from Eliz V Lomax, only surviving child of Capt Wm P Lindsay, of Lee's legion of the Revolution, asking 5 years' full pay of a capt of dragoons, with interest. 2-Ptn from Susan T Lea, admx of Jas Maglennen, asking compensation for property lost in the service of the U S during the war of 1812. 3-Ptn from Jonas P Levy, asking a revision by Congress of the action of the First Comptroller of the Treasury upon the act for the relief of the petitioner. The petitioner requests Congress to call upon the Comptroller for all the documents in the case, including especially that to which he had been denied access, or which have been surreptitiously suppressed. When the documents are produced & examined the petitioner believes that they will clearly establish all the grave charges which have been preferred, & that Congress will come to the conclusion that the dignity of Congress requires that the laws of Congress should be enforced against the ministerial ofcrs of the Govn't, & that the petitioner is fully entitled to ample renumeration for the losses originally sustained, to indemnification for the delays, expenses, & outrages to which he has been exposed by the illegal & oppressive conduct of the Comptroller.

THU DEC 20, 1855

Senate: 1-Ptn from Uriah P Levy, late a capt in the U S navy, complaining of the action of the Naval board, appointed under the act of Feb, 1855, in his case. Under said act he had been ignominiously dismissed the service of his country. 2-Ptn from Peter Wager, late a master in the U S navy, remonstrating against the action of the naval board in his case. 3-Ptn from Jas Harrington, belonging to the Smithsonian grounds, asking to be allowed the same extra compensation as was allowed to other laborers on the public grounds by resolution of Mar 3, 1855. 4-Ptn from John Dick, asking that a patent may be issued for land settled under a permit by the Register of the Land Ofc at St Augustine, Fla. 5-Ptn from Capt Jno B Montgomery, of the U S Navy, asking to be released from liability for an unpaid balance of public money entrusted to him for recruiting purposes, & lost by failure of the bank in which it was deposited.

John Elda & his wife, in making the round of the dry goods stores in Albany one day last week, succeeded in purloining & attaching to Mrs Elda's dress, in such as manner as to escape observation, over $500 worth of silk goods. They were afterwards arrested. Elda is a cigar merchant in N Y C. –N Y Sun

Trustee's sale of valuable real estate at auction: on Jan 22 next: by deed of trust from Lemuel Williams & wife, dated Oct 10, 1848, recorded in Liber W B No 147, folios 70, 71,of the land records of Wash Co, D C: west part of lot 1 in square 166, in Wash City, D C; with improvements thereon. –Walter Lenox, Henry Naylor, trustees -A Green, auct

Trustee's sale of house & 2 lots: by deed of trust from Saml Byington, dated Apr 18, 1850, recorded in Liber J A S No 14, folios 246 thru 251, of the land records of Wash Co, D C: sale on Jan 20 next, of lots 1 & 2 in square 502, with a good frame house, situated at the corner of 4½ st west & south N st. –Walter Lenox, Henry Naylor, trustees -A Green, auct

From the Mercer Whig: Hon John Findley died at his residence in that county on Dec 9, aged 82 years. He was a son of Hon Wm Findley, of Westmoreland Co, who had been so long a member of Congress from this State that in 1815 he was called the "Father of the House," & was elected & served one term as Govn'r of Pa. He was one of the earliest settlers of Mercer Co, having moved in 1796 to the farm upon which he has ever since lived & is now buried. -Pittsburgh Gaz

The N Y Mirror narrates an impromptu marriage in that city: Rev Mr Gillett last evening united in the holy bonds Mr Chas E Adams to Miss Jessie M, daughter of the late Hon Thos M Woodruff, at the residence of the bride's mother. It was an unusually sudden but we trust will prove none the less a happy move.

Mr Wm Palmer, Prof of Singing & the Flute, has a few vacancies in his time yet unfilled. Apply at his residence, H st, corner of 18th st.

Hammond st, N Y, Dec 13, 1855. Letter to Mr Sam C Reid, jr, on the last moments of Col Aaron Burr, written by P J Vanpelt, D D. In the summer of 1836, Col A Burr came to Port Richmond Hotel, [Staten Island,] where he took board, near where I then resided, as also did the relative & friend of Col Burr, Judge Ogden Edwards. The colonel being a valetudiarian, in feeble health, Judge Edwards solicited me to visit him, which he said was desired by Col Burr. On Sep 13, 1836, the day on which he died, I found Col Burr as usual, pleased to see me, tranquil in mind, & not disturbed by bodily pain. He said he did not feel well. I then said, Col, I do not wish to alarm you, but, judging from the state of your pulse, your time with us is short. He replied, I am aware of it. His mind & memory were perfect. We kneeled in prayer before the throne of heavenly grace, imploring God's mercy & blessing. He turned in his bed & put himself in a humble devotional posture, & seemed deeply engaged in the religious service, thanking me for the prayer made for him. He breathed his last without a groan of struggle. Thus died Col Aaron Burr. His first funeral service was performed by me in the Port Richmond House where he died. Thence we took his remains to the Chapel of Princeton College, N J, where Dr Carnahan, the Pres, & myself performed his last funeral service before the students, the faculty, the military, & a numerous assemblage, & he was buried, as he requested, in the sepulchre of his ancestors. –P J Vanpelt, D C

Montpelier for sale: contains 717 acres, in Loudoun Co, facing the Blue Ridge; bldgs are large & commodious. I will take $30,000 for it, $10,000 in hand & the balance to suit the convenience of the purchaser. The estate is offered considerably below the price at which lands of equal quantity are rating in the immediate neighborhood, & is considered by those who best know it to be a sacrifice; but, for the purpose of accomplishing specific objects, I am desirous of effecting a sale. –Ludwell Luckett, Middleburg Post Ofc, Loudoun Co, Va.

Died: on Dec 19, in his 73rd year, Wm Williams, born in Merthyr Tidvil, Glamorganshire, Great Britain. His funeral will be this afternoon at 3 o'clock, from his late residence on 12th st, near Pa ave.

Died: on Dec 11, at his residence, in Culpeper Co, Thos Beckham, in his 85th year. He lived honored & respected, & died lamented by all who knew him. He was always regarded as an old Va gentlemen, proverbial for his hospitality, honesty, & strict veracity.

Academy of Music for enabling all classes to obtain a good musical education. Apply to W Henry Palmer, Director, corner H & 18th sts. Terms $5 per quarter.

Miss E E McDonald, 70 Bridge st, Gtwn, is now selling off her handsome stock of Millinery. For rent, a large parlor & other rooms.

In Chancery: No 924. Levin M Powell & Jeannette C Powell vs W A Bradley, Sydney A Bradley, Chas M Thruston, Wm T Thruston, & others. Wm B Webb & Jos H Bradley, jr, trustees in the above cause, have sold the real estate by the said decree ordered to be sold, as follows: lot 1 in square 528 to Thos Croggan for $630; lots 2, 3, 16 & 17 to Moses Kelly for $1,851.50; lots 4 & 5 in square 528 to Geo Emmert for $956.66; lot 6 in square 528 to Geo R Hall for $490; lot 7 in square 528 to Elijah Edmonston for $536.66 2/3; lot 8 in square 528 to Chas Ball for $669.45; lots 9 & 10 in square 528 to Jos S Boss for $805; lot 13 in said square to Wm Tucker of A for $1,073.25; lots 18 thru 21 to Chas S Wallach for $1,606.50; lots 22 & 23 to Chas Hibbs for $708.30; lot 24 in said square to Rudolph Buckley for $393.15½; lots 25 & 26 in said square to Jas A Fletcher for $842; part of original lots 7 & 8 in square 690, & a brick house thereon, to John S Meehan for $2,100; another part of lot 7 in square 690 to Fannie C Thruston for $758.91; another part of lot 8 & part of lot 19 in square 16 to Geo W Mitchell for $3,025; that the said purchasers have complied with the terms of the said sale. –Jno A Smith, clerk

FRI DEC 21, 1855
Senate: 1-Ptn of Peter Wager, jr, late a master in the U S Navy: referred to the Cmte on Naval Affairs. Same for the memorial of Uriah P Levy.

Prof Francis Lieber, LL D, has resigned his place of Professor of History & Political Economy in the S C College at Columbia, where he has been for 20 years. -Boston Courier

In the Supreme Court of the U S, this morning the cause of Wm Wells, now imprisoned in the penitentiary of Wash City, will come up for argument on his petition, in which he states that, having been convicted of murder in 1851, & sentenced to be hanged in Apr, 1852, he was pardoned by the Pres, on condition that he should be imprisoned for life in the penitentiary; but that, being advised by counsel that this pardon was absolute & the condition void, the petitioner was in Apr last, upon his own petition, brought before the District Court upon a writ of habeas corpus, & by that Court re-committed to prison, upon the ground that the power of conditional pardon was vested in the Pres. The petitioner now asks for a like writ to be issued by the Supreme Court, & for his dismissal from custody for the reason heretofore assigned. Chas Lee Jones is counsel for the petitioner.

Mrd: on Dec 20, by Rev M D Conway, Abram C Wayland to Mgt Kennedy, all of Orange Co, Va.

Mrd: on Dec 11, by Rev Lemuel Wilmer, Mr Walter H Marlow, of Wash, to Miss Eliza A Turner, of Chas Co, Md.

Mr Jonas Crane, of Luray, Page Co, Va, writes to the Editor of the Alexandria Sentinel, stating that it was not his brother, Jas M Crane, who was executed for murder in Calif. This gentleman published a paper some years ago at Richmond, & is now in the editorial management of the Calif Weekly Journal. It was J V Crane, from Lexington, Ky, who was executed in Calif & left a wife & 4 or 5 children near Lexington. Mr Crane, formerly of Richmond, never was married, & is not the sort of man to get into unlawful scrapes or to commit murder. His friends will be happy to read this contradiction.

The proceedings of a Court-martial held at Jefferson Barracks in July last for the trial of Brvt Lt Col Wm R Montgomery, Major in the 2nd Regt of Infty, have been officially published. He was sentenced to dismissal from the service for allowing improper locations of land in the military reserve of the Pawnee Indians, & the creation of a town site thereon, in violation of his public duty, & for joining the parties concerned in the appropriation of said lands. The Pre of the U S has approved the finding of the Court.

Trustee's sale of improved property: by deed of trust from Jas Muntz & Mary his wife, dated May 2, 1854, recorded in Liber J A S No 76, folios 129, of the land records of Wash Co, D C: public auction on Jan 5 next of the west half of lot 24 in square 625, with 2 story frame house. –P M Pearson, trustee -A Green, auct

House of Reps: 1-The House resumed the business of voting for a Speaker-the $\underline{67^{th}}$ vote results: Mr Banks, of Mass: 104; Mr Richardson, of Ill: 73; Mr Fuller of Pa: 34; scattering: 10. Necessary to a choice: 111.

Margaretta Button, widow & admx of Thos Button, who was killed on the Hudson River Railroad on Nov 4, 1853, has recovered $5,000 damages. Evidence proved it was negligence on the part of the company in driving their cars at too great a rate of speed, & in neglecting to expose lights on the outside & hang bells from the horses.

Mann Beckwith, the notorious character, was killed at Louisville on Dec 17 by a police ofcr. The ofcr, upon arresting Beckwith for a misdeameanor, was resisted & knocked down. He then drew his pistol, shot his assailant, & delivered himself into the hands of the law.

Mrd: on Dec 20, at the parsonage of the M E Church, by Rev Geo Hildt, Mr Geo H Perrie, of Wash City, [formerly of Chas Co, Md,] to Miss Helen Parker, of the latter place. [Dec 22nd newspaper: same notice.]

Mrd: on Dec 17, by Rev Fred'k Fitzgerald, John L Peyton, of Staunton, Va, to Miss Bettie Washington, of Vernon, Lenoir Co, N C, the residence of her father, John C Washington.

Folsom's History of Saco & Biddleford. Origin of the Alden Family. Mrs Rose Standish, consort of Capt Standish, departed this life on Jan 29, 1621. In a very short time after the decease of Mrs Standish the captain was led to think that, if he could obtain Miss Priscilla Mullins, a daughter of Mr Wm Mullins, the breach in his family would be happily repaired. He therefore, according to the custom of those times, sent to ask Mr Mullins' permission to visit his daughter. John Alden, the messenger, faithfully communicated the wishes of the captain. The old gentleman did not object on account of the recency of Capt Standish's bereavement. The damsel was called into the room, & John Alden, who is said to have been a young man of most excellent form, with a fair & ruddy complexion, arose, & delivered his errand. Miss Mullins listened, fixing her eyes upon him, with an open countenance, "Prithee, John, why do you not speak for yourself?" The young man blushed, bowed, & took his leave. However, he soon renewed his visit, & it was not long before their nuptials were celebrated in ample form. From this couple were desceneded all of the name of Alden in the U S. What report he made to his constitment after the first interview tradition does not unfold; but it is said, how true the writer knows not, that the captain never, to the day of his death, forgave him.

Letter on board the U S ship **Vincennes**, of the North Pacific Expediton, which states that off the coast of Kamtschatka, with Maury's line & Brooke's lead, bottom was obtained from a depth of 1,700 fathoms, & the specimen was immediately put under the microscope of 500 linear, there were seen infusoria that were probably alive before being relieved of the enormous pressure at that depth. Many of them were fresh & clear. Lt John M Brooke, of the U S Navy, is the author of the simple instrument that makes it possible to secure a specimen of the bottom. The enormous pressue of the water upon the ball always broke the line when sounding of any great depths were attempted.

Washington Market & Grass Farm for sale: ***Lower Gisboro***, the best farm in the District, on the Potomac river, containing 200 acres; improved by a fine brick house of 10 rooms, large barn, new corn house, overseer's house & negro quarters, all in good condition. Refer to Hugh Bernard Sweeny, of the Banking-house of Sweeny, Rittenhouse & Co.

SAT DEC 22, 1855
Private School for Boys: at Winston, Alleghany Co, Md, will commence on Jan 14 & close on the last day of Nov, 1856. –P Pendleton, Winston, Alleghany Co, Md.

Mrd: on Dec 20, by Rev A G Carothers, Mr Thos F Sands to Miss Ann E Davis, both of Wash City.

Died: last evening, in Wash City, Wallace Murray, son of Benedict & Martha Milburn, in his 8th year. His funeral will take place tomorrow at 2½ o'clock, from the residence of his father on 5th st west.

Norwich [Mass] Courier: result of a trial before the Superior Court of that city, in which a handsome young lady, Miss Ellen R Wheeler, was plntf, & Ralph Coates was dfndnt, both parties belonging to North Stonington. A year ago Coates lost several pieces of veal, as he believed, through the carnivorous propensities of the fair Ellen's dog, a noble Newfoundland. Armed with a gun, Coates went to a neighbor's, where Ellen & her dog were visiting, & seized the dog by the throat to drag him out. Ellen threw her arms around the dog & was dragged out with him & lacerated in going over the door steps. Coates then shot the dog, & this suit was for $500 damages. The Jury gave the full sum sued for, & would have given it had it been twice as much.

To the heirs of the late John White, late of Armagh, Ireland. Inquiry has been made for the heirs, excs, & administrators of John White, who was born in the county of Armagh, & emigrated, it is supposed, in 1814-15 to the U S. It is said he left two sons, Wm & Abner. Persons applying as heirs will please to state the names in full of their parents & grand-parents & of such of their relatives as emigrated to this country, with all other particulars, to show their descent from or relationship to said John White. Excs or adms of said John, of Wm, or Abner White are requested to give full descriptions of the family of the parties whose interest they may represent. All communications & proofs must be post-paid, & addressed for transmission to Henry M Morfit, Counsellor-at-Law, 4½ st, Wash.

Obit-died: on Tue last, at **Mulberry Grove**, near Port Tobacco, Hon Danl Jenifer, at an advanced age. Col Jenifer has filled high & honorable stations both in the Nat'l & State Legislatures. He was sent as Minister to Austria under the administration of Gen Harrison, & represented the country at the Court of Vienna. His death was caused by a violent attack of pneumonia, superinduced by taking cold while attending the funerals of two deceased friends on Dec 8.
–Port Tobacco Times of Thu.

Appointments: the Va Conference of the Methodist Episcopal Church South, lately in session in Richmond, have made the following amongst other appointments of ministers: Washington District-Wm W Bennet, P E; Wash City, D S Doggett; Alexandria, Jas A Duncan; Rock Creek, John K Littleton; Howard, David Wallace; Fairfax, A G Brown; Mission, to be supplied; Potomac, W P Twyman; Leesburg, J S R Clarke; Loudoun, P F August, J F Poulton; Warrenton, W E Judkins, one to be supplied; Springfield, E A Gibbs; South Branch, J E Potts; Clark, R S Nash.

Mrd: on Dec 20, by Rev A G Carothers, Mr John T Hoover to Miss Cecilia J Nailor, both of Wash City.

Mrd: on Dec 20, at the Chapel of the Theological Seminary of Va, by Rev Wm Sparrow, D D, Rev Julius E Grammer, of Wash, to Bessie, daughter of the officiating minister.

Mrd: on Dec 20, at the parsonage of the M E Church, by Rev Geo Hildt, Mr Geo H Perrie, of Wash City, [formerly of Chas Co, Md,] to Miss Helen Parker, of the latter place.

Died: on Dec 21, suddenly, M Frank Howard, aged 13 months, infant son of T J & Sallie Magruder. His funeral is today at 2½ o'clock, from the residence of his parents, 422 F st, between 6th & 7th sts.

Died: on Dec 13, in his 33rd year, Dr Wm Lowndes Hamilton, the 5th son of Gen Jas & Eliz Hamilton, of S C. He lived fondly beloved & died deeply regretted.

Administrators sale: by order of the Orphans' Court of PG Co, the undersigned, as adm c t a, of Francis Edelen, late of said county, deceased, will expose at public sale, at the residence of Mrs Christiana Edelen, in Spalding's District, in said county, on Dec 31, all the residue of the personal estate of said deceased, consisting of a number of young & valuable negroes, household & kitchen furniture, & a lot of farming utensils. –Saml H Berry, Adm c t a of F Edelen

MON DEC 24, 1855
New Orleans Picayune: Susan B Anthony & the rest of the discontented sisterhood of strongminded women, in the State of N Y has already got up their annual petition to the Legislature of that State for the restoration of woman's legal & political rights. Restoration does not seem to be exactly the proper word, by the by, there being no time that we have ever heard of when woman was supposed to have any such legal & political rights as those she is now invoked to aid Miss Anthony in demanding at the hands of the Legislature.

Hon Thos H Bayly was recently at Charleston, S C, on his way to Havana for the benefit of his health.

Trustee's sale of valuable & eligibly situated real estate: by 2 several deeds in trust from Jas A Wise & Harriet Ann Wise, his wife, dated Apr 7 & Sep 8, 1855, duly recorded: public sale on Jan 24, 1856, part of lot 12 in square 429, with a 3 story brick dwlg house thereon: located on 7th st west, between G & H sts, & rapidly enhancing in value. –Chas S Wallach, Jno C C Hamilton, trustees
-Jas C McGuire, auct

I return my sincere thanks to Friends & the Firemen & the Police for their kind exertions at the fire in my residence on last Fri night. –J W French

Orphans Court of Wash Co, D C. Letters testamentary on the personal estate of Geo Cox, late of Wash Co, deceased. –Caroline Cox, excx

Rev Robt Montgomery, an English poet of inferior merit but wide celebrity, better known as Satan Montgomery, from a religious poem of his on Satan, died recently at Brighton, England. His original name was Gomery, & he was the son of a minor actor of that name attached to the Surrey Theatre, London. He added the prefix "Most" to his name in imitation of the famous Sheffield poet, Jas Montgomery. He was educated at Oxford Univ, at the expense of a London merchant, & was ordained as a minister in the English church. In this capacity he became quite popular as preacher at Percy Chapel, London. –North American

Orphans Court of Wash Co, D C. Letters of administration on the personal estate of Wm McFadden, late of the U S Army, deceased. –Ellen McFadden, excx

Mrd: on Nov 15, in Calvert Co, Md, by Rev J Newton Watson, Mr Geo C P Wilkinson to Miss Henrietta, daughter of Jos Blake.

Mrd: on Dec 19, at Madison, N J, by Rev Mr Merritt, Hillary B Schreiner, of Gratz, Pa, to Augusta M Martin, daughter of the late Dr Joel Martin, U S Army.

Died: on Dec 23, in Wash City, Mrs Araminta Pickrell, of Chas Co, Md, in her 54th year, after a protracted illness of 5 months. Her funeral will take place this afternoon at 3 o'clock P M, from the residence of her brother Stanislaus Murray, 5th st, between D & E sts.

Died: on Dec 23, suddenly, Chas Tschiffely, aged about 70 years. His funeral is today from his late residence, near the corner of 8th & N sts, at 3½ o'clock.

TUE DEC 25, 1855
Senate: 1-Ptn from Hannah F Niles, daughter of & only surviving child of Capt Robt Niles, asking compensation for the martime services of her father during the Revolutionary war. Capt Niles died in extreme poverty in 1818, before any beneficiary laws were passed, having received nothing for his acts of patriotism save his mere pittance of pay. His daughter is now advanced in years & poor. 2-Ptn Cezaire Wallace, asking confirmation of his title to a certain tract of land.

Robt Bunyan, aged 80 years, the last male descendant in a direct line from John Bunyan, the author of the "Pilgrim's Progess," died at his residence in Grecian Place, Lincoln, England, on Nov 17. The English paper says: "The last male descendant of John Bunyan died 167 years after the glorious old dreamer, & the last male descendant of Sir Walter Scott died just 20 years after the illustrious novelist.

Hon Hiram Bell, a member of the last Congress from Ohio, died last Fri at his residence in Greenville, Darke Co.

Portrait gallery of the 6 wives of Henry VIII: 1-Katharine of Arragon, the first wife, was the youngest daughter of Ferdinand & Isabella of Spain: betrothed at an early age to Arthur, elder brother of Henry, & heir apparent to the English throne, & was actually wed to him on Nov 14, 1501, Arthur dying soon after. Katharine was in her 18th year & Henry but 12 years of age. The match was consummated. Divorced by the arbitrary edict of her royal husband repudiated, maligned, & crossed in her love for the child, her daughter Mary, whom she was not allowed to see. Katharine of Arragon was recorded by Mr Herbert as being so near to perfection. 2-Anne Boleyn, Henry's second wife, was of noble ancestry; she perished beneath the sword of the headsman. 3-Jane Seymour, was the third wife, but her reign was brief; for, having given birth to a son the following year, she expired soon after. 4-His fourth wife, Anne of Cleves, was painted by Hans Holbein, as surpassingly fair & a lady of charms. Henry was disappointed & dismayed when his destined bride arrived. He found her positively ugly, ungainly in person, dark in complexion, & pitted with the small-pox. He married her then divorced her. 5-The fifth wife was Katharine Howard. She was found guilty of adultery & duly executed. 6-Katharine Parr, the sixth wife of Henry had the good fortune to survive him. She was herself four times married & four times a widow. She said it was safer to be his mistress than his wife. She married Henry less than 2 months into her second widowhood. Henry died not long afterwards & she happily escaped repudiation or execution.

Appointments by the Pres: 1-Franck Roulhac, Surveyor of the Customs at Hickman, Ky. 2-W Irving Crandall, Surveyor of the Customs at Chattanooga, Tenn.

Queen Victoria has acceded to the request of the Colony of *Van Dieman's Land* to change the name of that island & colony to *Tasmania/*

Admiral Bruat, cmder of the French fleet in the Black Sea, whose death off Messina was announced by the last steamer's papers, was but 59 years of age, & enjoyed a high reputation in the French navy. He was an Alsatian, born at Colenar May 26, 1796, educated at the Naval School at Brest, & in 1815 entered the navy: became a lt in 1827. Later in life he became Govn'r of the French islands in the Pacific.

Mr Ernest Von Herringen committed suicide yesterday at his lodgings in Wash City, by shooting himself in the head with a pistol. He had been confined to his room for 2 or 3 weeks by sickness & was known to be in a despondent frame of mind. He left a will dated Dec 12. From his appearance he was between 40 & 50 years of age. He leaves a widow, now residing in Va.

Mrd: on Dec 18, by Rev Geo D Cummings, of Trinity Church, Bainbridge S Clarke, of N Y C, to Miss Armedia, daughter of M Snyder, of Wash.

Mrd: on Dec 19, by Rev Richd G Temple, of St John's Church, Troy, N Y, Lt Wm R Boggs, of the Ordnance Corps, to Mary S, daughter of Maj J Symington.

Died: on Dec 23, Ella Burns, aged 2 years, 9 months & 14 days, eldest child of Mrs Eliz Sanders & the late Francis Sanders.

St Paul's, Minnesota, Dec 23. A party arrived here yesterday from Red River, on their way to Canada, bring intelligence of the death of Sir John Franklin & his party. They perished on the coast opposite to Montreal Island, where their bones now lie. They died of hunger. A party of Esquimaux reached them just as the last man perished. The party brings home several relics of Franklin's expedition.

Circuit Court of Wash Co, D C-in Chancery. John Blackburn & wife & others, devisees of Allen Scott, against John D Scott & others, also devisees. The above parties & trustee are to meet at my ofc in Gtwn, on Dec 31. –W Redin, auditor

THU DEC 27, 1855
Clearing out sale at Mrs Anderson's store on Pa ave: stationery, music, books, fancy goods, ink, pens, & crayons, etc. -Jas C McGuire, auct

The trial at Cincinnati, some time ago, of Wm H Arrison, for the murder of the Allison family by an infernal machine, was convicted of murder, sentenced to death, but these proceedings were deemed to be invalid; the second trial concluded last week, but there had been some improper conduct on the party of one of the jurymen, Spencer Cooper, the offending individual. Arrison was remanded to jail, & will undergo a third trial.

At Louisville, Ky, on Sat last, Juudge Bullock sentenced Geo Bennett to death for the murder of Thos Mullen; the execution to take effect on Feb 1. An appeal had been taken to the Court of Appeals. It is stated to be the first appeal ever taken in Ky in a case of murder.

Wash Corp: 1-Act for the relief of Mrs Ann Laporte: passed. 2-Ptn from Philip Aldorffer for the remission of a fine: referred to the Cmte of Claims. 3-Ptn from Lewis F Skidmore for the remission of a fine: referred to the Cmte of Claims.

Mrd: on Dec 11, at Lynchburg, Va, by Rev Wm H Kinckle, John Royall Holcombe to Matilda T Lee, only daughter of Lt John Hite Lee, U S Navy, deceased.

Died: on Dec 24, in Wash City, at the residence of Col C K Gardner, Capitol Hill, Alida Gardner, infant daughter of Emma K & Alex'r Mouton, of Louisiana.

Died: on Dec 21, in Richmond, Va, at his residence, John G Mosby, in his 70th year.

Died: on Dec 26, Aldebaran Semmes, son of John W & Georgiana Wade, in his 4th year. His funeral is today at 2 o'clock, from their residence, 612 H st.

Balt, Dec 26. Judge Dorsey, formerly Chief Justice of Md, died at his residence at Ellicott's Mills today of paralysis. [Dec 29: Hon T B Dorsey resided near Ellicott's Mills, in possession of a very large estate, & surrounded by a numerous list of relations & friends, with whom we sympathize in their sudden bereavement. No man was more highly esteemed when living than Judge Dorsey. –Balt Pat]

FRI DEC 28, 1855
Senate: 1-Ptn from Geo M Weston, an authorized agent of the State of Maine, asking remuneration for certain lands taken by the U S under the treaty of Washington. 2-Ptn from Jacob Carlton, for himself & owners & sharers in the fishing schnr **Brandywine**, employed in taking fish, asking to be allowed fishing bounty for the time so employed. 3-Letter from Lt Alex Gibson, complaining of having been placed on the furlough list by the Naval Board & urging redress for his grievance at the hands of Congress. 4-Ptn from A C Rhind, late a lt of the U S Navy, complaining of having been dropped from the navy by the action of the Naval Board at Wash, & asked Congress to investigate his case, & more particularly the action of the board. 5-Ptn from the Rector of St Andrew's Church, Staten Island, N Y, & 35 citizens of Richmond Co, N Y, asking that Lt John C Carter be restored to the active list of the Navy.

Brookeville Academy will be resumed on Dec 31. -E B Prettyman, A M, Principal, Brookeville, Md.

Mr Arnold Lewis was found murdered, in a field in West Greenwich, on Wed last. On Tue, Dec 18, he stopped at the house of Gorton W Briggs, in Exeter to pay for an axe, & remarked that he had $50 in his pocket-book. This was said in the hearing of a woman named Sybill Corey, who was in the house at the time. He went off to Connell's, & then to the house of Jeremiah Franklin, across some lots, & was waylaid & murdered. A young man, Shubael Corey, alias Baker, & his mother, the Sybill Corey above named, were both arrested on Thu. Corey had confessed to the murder. Mr Lewis leaves 9 children. He was formerly a highly respectable citizen of Exeter & Brig Gen of the State Militia. Of late years he has been irregular in his habits. Corey, the murderer, is only 19 years old. –Providence Post

Mrd: on Dec 24, at the residence of Thos C Haynes, in Warwick Co, Va, by Rev Humphrey Wynne, Thos E Milstead, of Richmond, Va, formerly of Chas Co, Md, to Miss Sarah K Randle, of the former place.

Duelling pistols for sale: remarkable for their fine balance & accurate shooting, have been left with the subscriber for sale. –C H Munck, Pa ave near 6th st.

SAT DEC 29, 1855
A horrible murder was perpetrated at New Haven, Conn, on Sunday, by a band of fanatics who called themselves Wakemanites; meetings are held at the house of Mr Saml Sly, who has no wife or family, but has a woman living in the house with him named Rhoda Wakeman, who is the founder of the Wakemanites. At the meeting last Sunday were Almeron Sanford & his wife, Justus Matthews, Betsey Keeler, a Mrs Davis, & a colored man named Josiah Jackson, & others. On Monday morning a young son of Justus Matthews began to search for his father, wondering why he had not made his appearance at so late an hour. He went to one of the rooms & found his father lying dead upon the floor. The boy gave the alarm to Justice Bennett, & he with a number of men repaired to the scene of blood. They found Justus Matthews, a pistol maker, who works at Whitneyville, but lived in Hampden, with his throat cut from ear to ear. Arrested & lodged in jail, charged with committing or in some way being accessory to the crime: Israel Wooding, Almeron Sanford & wife, Abigail Sables, Thankful S Hersey, the widow Wakeman, [the prophetess,] Saml Sly, & Josiah Jackson. Saml Sly confessed that he alone committed the murder. Thankful S Hersey was an accessory. Since the inquest Mrs Wakeman, Miss Sable, & Jackson remain in prison. Mr & Mrs Sanford, Mrs Julia Davis, & Mr Wooding have been discharged.

P J Steer, Merchant Tailor, 488 7th st. Bills have been made out, in anticipation of a general settlement on the first of the year.

Assassinations in N C. 1-The Murfreesboro Gaz learns that on Wed, John Freeman, ex-Sheriff of Bertie, was shot by some person unknown. 2-Mr B W Thatch was waylaid & shot on Dec 8, near his residence, in Chowan Co. David Morriss has been arrested on suspicion. 3-The Raleigh Standard learns that on Monday last a young man by name of Peebles was murdered at his place, 5 or 6 miles from Smithfield.

A handbill, describing the murder of R G Watson, of New Madrid Co, by two men named Phillips & their nephew, Dr Ross, has been received in this city. Mr Watson was one of the most prominent citizens of that county, & worth nearly $100,000. The friends of the deceased have offered a reward of $3,000 for the apprehension of his murderers. –Alton[Ill] Dem of Dec 21.

Macon [Miss] Beacon of Dec 12 states that 2 ladies of that county were burnt to death on the same day by their clothes taking fire. One was the wife of Mr R Barnhill, who, at the time, was playing with her sister's child, with her back to the fire. The other was Miss Mitchell, who died in a similar accident.

Mrd: on Dec 27, at Trinity Church, Upper Marlboro, PG Co, Md, by Rev Mr Rolfe, Levin Wailes, of Natches, Miss, to Nannie, daughter of Dr Jas Harper.

Mrd: on Dec 25, at South Berwick, Maine, by Rev Saml M Gould, Wm P Blake, of Wash City, to Charlotte H L Hayes, daughter of the late Hon Wm A Hayes, of South Berwick.

Mrd: on Dec 27, in Phil, at St Luke's Church, by Rev Dr Howe, Cmder Jno R Goldsborough, U S Navy, to Mary Lawrence, daughter of John Penington, of that city.

Died: on Dec 23, Wm Alexander, of Gtwn, in his 71st year, a native of Ireland, but for the last 18 years a resident of the District of Columbia.

MON DEC 31, 1855
Household & kitchen furniture at auction on: Jan 4, at the House-furnishing Store of Mr A H Lee, on north K, between 7th & 8th sts. –A Green, auct

Orphans Court of Wash Co, D C. Letters testamentary on the personal estate of Wm Ball, late of Wash Co, deceased. –Robt Ball, jr, exc

Circuit Court of Wash Co, D C-in Chancery. Thos Redden, exc of Jas Ratrie, against John Ratrie, Wm J Redden, Sarah E Redden, Ann M Redden, & Jas C Haviland. Jas Ratrie, late of D C, died intestate in 1853; in his last will he willed his estate to Thos Redden [whom he made executor] & to John Ratrie, subject, however, to the payment of 3 legacies, of $100 each, to Wm T Redden, Ann M Redden, & Sarah E Redden, these legacies to be paid within 5 days after said Jas Ratrie's death. The bill further states that said Thos Redden administered in D C on said Jas Ratrie's estate, but found no personal estate of said Jas Ratrie. The exec therefore asks in said bill that the real estate of said Jas Ratrie, deceased, in said District, may be sold to pay said legacies, & to pay off a mortgage to Jas C Haviland, which is coming due on part of said real estate for $335, & also to pay off such other debts as may be due from said estate; it appearing that John Ratrie, one of the parties interested, resides beyond the jurisdiction of this Court. Said John Ratire to appear in the Clerk's ofc of this county, on the first Monday of Jun next. –Jno A Smith, clerk

Two children of Patrick Ryan, one about a year old, & the other about 2 years old, were burnt to death in their shanty on Tue. Mr Ryan was at work & his wife had gone to a neighbors to get some milk. All their little property was of course destroyed. –Albany Register

Died: on Dec 29, Miss Lucy Goldsborough, in her 25th year. Her funeral will be this afternoon at 2½ o'clock, from the residence of her mother, corner of 18th & I sts.

Died: on Dec 17, at his residence in Macon, Miss, in his 34th year, Geo H Foote, a prominent member of the Mississippi Bar, & a young gentleman of great promise. He was a native of Fauquier Co, Va.

Fort Brooke, Fla, Dec 23. An exploring party, under command of Lt Geo L Hartsuff, 2nd Artl, consisting of one sgt, one cpl, & 7 privates, were suddenly attacked by a party of Seminole Indians at daylight on Dec 29, about 16 miles s e from *Fort Simon Drum*, about 40 miles s e from *Fort Myers*. On Dec 21 three men of the command arrived at *Fort Myers*, & it is supposed that Lt Hartsuff, with the remainder of the party, have been killed. Lt Hartsuff, when last seen, had one arm broken, & was thought to be wounded in the side. Private Hanna, Co G, 2nd Artl, one of the party, brought the above information to *Fort Myers*. Hanna was wounded in the abdomen, but not seriously. He left private Baker, who was also wounded, about 18 miles from *Fort Myers*. Baker gave out at that point, & could come no further. The Indians making the attack were some 25 or 30. Two companies of the 2nd Artl were to leave *Fort Myers* on Dec 22 in search of Lt Hartsuff & his missing men.

The newspapers state that Miss Jenny Campbell, aged 115 years, died in Orange Co, Va, on Dec 6.

A

Abbot, 133, 166, 437
Abbott, 10, 29, 80, 99, 259, 331, 340, 369, 376, 385, 467
Abeles, 421
Abercrombie, 98, 288, 289
Abert, 178, 217, 228, 263, 287, 289
Able, 355
Aby, 374
Academy of the Visitation, 265
Accardi, 58
Achille, 398
Acken, 29, 90, 103
Acton, 233
Adair, 403
Adams, 1, 5, 9, 29, 43, 56, 63, 127, 135, 145, 150, 158, 174, 184, 202, 231, 233, 252, 300, 354, 355, 359, 361, 368, 371, 374, 376, 377, 402, 406, 407, 411, 424, 447, 470
Adamson, 398
Addison, 29, 83, 91, 173, 231, 258, 391, 433
Adlen, 223
Adler, 188, 404
Adrian, 29
Advance, 467
Agar, 262
Agassiz, 408
Agg, 157, 174, 398, 404, 435
Agnew, 467
Aguierre, 123
Ahern, 251
Ahrend, 232
Aigler, 419
Aiken, 53
Akin, 97
Alaband, 354
Albritten, 64
Albritton, 70
Alby, 179
Alden, 374, 474

Aldorffer, 479
Aldrich, 218
Alexander, 29, 43, 96, 123, 140, 160, 271, 285, 293, 434, 482
Alexandrovina, 136
Alexandrovitch, 136
Allen, 11, 26, 28, 29, 60, 93, 94, 101, 129, 140, 166, 169, 185, 214, 249, 252, 258, 324, 325, 339, 396, 405, 413, 422, 438, 442
Allerton, 132
Allison, 29, 210, 479
Allmand, 352, 375
Allmer, 467
Allston, 123, 291, 437, 439
Almonte, 381
Alt, 262
Altemus, 76, 424
Amazeen, 113
Ambler, 18, 54
Ambrose, 74
American Portrait Gallery, 47
Americus, 150
Ames, 433
Amey, 70
Amidon, 157
Amory, 438
Amstrong, 308
Anderson, 14, 29, 50, 80, 121, 122, 195, 215, 244, 254, 269, 270, 282, 283, 286, 287, 293, 297, 304, 341, 348, 357, 382, 394, 445, 479
Anderton, 371
Andre, 145, 245
Andrew, 93
Andrews, 11, 42, 45, 46, 96, 101, 166, 286, 309, 334, 382, 438, 439, 467
Angues, 353
Angus, 14, 51, 57, 65
Ankrim, 123
Anna, 332
Annan, 430
Annis, 75

484

Ansoatigui, 270
Anthony, 329, 476
Antrim, 336
Antwerp, 102
Apis, 16
Appich, 431
Appleby, 212
Appleton, 29, 296, 322
Appointments by the Pres, 42, 72, 73, 74, 96, 101, 202, 217, 305, 309, 456, 478
Appollo Hall, 91
Apreece, 210
Archer, 38, 71, 119, 136, 284, 315
Argenti, 87
Arista, 340
Arlington House, 189, 440, 441
Armijer, 312
Armistead, 284, 319
Armitage, 29
Armstrong, 17, 29, 87, 143, 178, 209, 214, 286, 289, 294, 313, 368, 416
Arnold, 11, 46, 53, 60, 83, 168, 300, 306, 332, 353, 442, 465
Arnott, 309
Arnow, 106
Arrison, 225, 479
Arrott, 102
Ashby, 455
Ashdown, 145, 182, 233
Ashe, 166
Ashley, 3, 54
Ashmun, 176
Ashton, 126, 328, 400
Ashwanden, 276, 345
Ashwin, 262
Asperil, 367
Atchinson, 29
Athey, 421
Atkinson, 11, 29, 60, 198, 349
Atlantic cable, 324
Atlee, 213
AtLee, 217, 254
Atwell, 271, 454

Auchincloss, 264
Auchinloss, 113
August, 475
Aulick, 83
Austin, 29, 148, 155, 251
Avelyn, 210
Averell, 214, 258
Averett, 257
Avery, 224, 301, 343, 369, 378
Awl, 140
Awong, 210
Ayer, 12
Aymer, 88
Ayrault, 143
Ayre Hall, 251
Ayres, 348, 466
Ayroult, 445
Ayton, 138, 162

B

Baasen, 270
Baber, 210
Bache, 401, 449
Bachman, 45
Backus, 185, 215
Bacon, 25, 166, 183, 227, 252, 336, 337, 344
Baden, 29, 94
Badger, 375, 412
Bagby, 246
Bagnall, 393
Bagnell, 362
Bailey, 29, 77, 294, 448, 454
Bailie, 74
Baily, 338, 464
Bain, 183
Baird, 94, 345
Baker, 29, 30, 54, 89, 108, 115, 145, 164, 182, 186, 220, 233, 256, 271, 310, 353, 375, 388, 389, 390, 399, 480, 483
Balance, 353, 393
Balch, 139, 191
Balcher, 221

Baldwin, 157, 182, 217, 369, 391, 451
Balfour, 353
Ball, 9, 29, 30, 95, 154, 161, 197, 217, 227, 412, 430, 454, 472, 482
Ballantine, 14
Ballantyne, 341
Ballard, 16, 204
Ballentine, 422
Balling, 380
Ballinger, 253
Balsh, 257
Baltimore, 29, 133, 168
Baltzell, 409
Baltzer, 29, 142
Bamberger, 13
Bammistle, 234
Bancroft, 466
Bangs, 410
Bankhead, 261, 438
Banks, 72, 73, 297, 325, 473
Bannerman, 341
Barber, 417
Barbour, 25, 114, 315, 411
Barclay, 22, 202, 336, 337, 344
Bard, 244
Baring, 1
Barker, 29, 118, 195, 235, 251, 288, 293, 391, 432
Barkley, 234
Barlow, 217
Barnaclo, 451
Barnard, 18, 66, 99, 160, 182, 235, 280, 314, 328, 330, 349, 353, 392, 411
Barneclo, 252
Barnes, 15, 16, 30, 44, 115, 133, 252, 280, 298, 354, 405
Barney, 64, 184, 322, 369, 376, 458
Barnhill, 481
Barnhouse, 30
Barnum, 165
barque **Clara Winsor**, 176
barque **Florence**, 329
barque **Grapeshot**, 186

barque **L M Hubby**, 323
barque **Maria**, 319
barque **Oriole**, 28
barque **Release**, 212, 220, 389
barque **The Lily**, 26
Barraud, 158, 374
Barrell, 28
Barrett, 29, 59, 316, 374, 428, 433
Barron, 30, 214, 238, 319, 325, 328, 354, 374, 422, 425
Barry, 29, 30, 84, 109, 125, 182, 185, 250, 384, 385, 421, 425
Barsahlin, 30
Barscht, 29
Barth, 161
Barthol, 428
Bartholow, 267
Barthrop, 363
Bartle, 259
Bartless, 390
Bartlett, 144, 253, 255, 300, 312, 369, 390, 402, 468
Bartol, 202
Barton, 12, 80, 403
Barziza, 73
Bascom, 100
Bashlott, 106
Basset, 131
Bassett, 78, 82, 375
Bast, 421
Bastianelli, 112
Batay, 220
Batchen, 341
Bate'er, 30
Bateman, 30, 105
Baten, 325
Bates, 29, 30, 50, 70, 145, 166, 174, 196, 253, 394, 417
Battle, 30
Batturs, 244
Bauer, 29, 126, 320
Baum, 207, 468
Baun, 252
Baxter, 263

486

Bayard, 53, 60
Bayle, 461
Bayley, 227, 246, 451
Bayliss, 254, 415, 451
Baylor, 269, 346, 352
Bayly, 25, 49, 99, 157, 183, 184, 297, 476
Bayne, 217, 255, 363, 394
Beale, 30, 37, 83, 110, 200, 250, 365, 370, 384
Beall, 16, 29, 90, 110, 122, 169, 268, 282, 284, 292, 320, 386, 418, 444
Bean, 29, 87, 107
Beard, 19, 94, 223, 266, 355, 454
Beardsley, 29, 365
Beatson, 124
Beatty, 50, 72, 445
Beauchamp, 131
Beauharnais, 243
Beaumont, 244
Bechnel, 79
Beck, 166, 435
Becker, 166, 318
Becket, 145
Beckett, 29
Beckham, 270, 271, 471
Beckwith, 283, 473
Beddinger, 18
Bedford, 335
Bedinger, 70
Bee, 118, 284, 288, 292
Beecher, 63, 256
Beekman, 363
Beell, 159
Beers, 243
Beetly, 340
Beirne, 164
Belden, 17, 23, 60, 65, 195
Belknap, 375
Bell, 25, 29, 83, 122, 127, 184, 261, 264, 283, 291, 363, 429, 433, 477
Belle Vue, 185
Belleview, 241
Bellinger, 271

Bellow, 262
Belmont, 10
Belmonte, 259
Belt, 15, 30, 86, 99, 160, 173, 239, 242, 394
Beltzhoover, 455
Bender, 72, 104
Benedict, 59
Benezett, 30
Benguerel, 74
Benham, 78, 96, 164, 169, 204, 288, 293, 368, 370, 375, 425
Benjamin, 29
Bennefiel, 59
Bennet, 475
Bennett, 17, 41, 113, 157, 207, 209, 214, 258, 337, 374, 438, 479, 481
Benson, 57, 95, 176, 253, 270
Bentley, 11, 60, 93
Benton, 92, 138, 165, 203, 226
Bentz, 207
Berg, 29
Bergershausen, 29
Berill, 166
Berkeley, 2
Berkley, 455
Bernard, 362, 393, 424
Berret, 153, 184
Berrett, 30
Berrian, 29
Berrien, 374
Berry, 30, 53, 73, 148, 157, 162, 184, 199, 238, 259, 296, 319, 339, 367, 392, 402, 431, 451, 463, 467, 476
Berryman, 88, 113
Besancon, 245
Beshe, 88
Bessau, 447
Bessent, 106
Best, 179, 227
Bestor, 30, 80, 92
Bett, 29
Bevans, 156, 435
Beverage, 340

Beveridge, 393
Beverley, 318
Bias, 30
Bibb, 205, 270
Bickel, 172
Bickley, 30
Biddle, 173, 190, 214, 238, 276, 449
Bidwold, 220
Bielaski, 181
Bier, 375
Bigelow, 29, 83, 214, 238, 321, 336, 337
Bigler, 1
Bilesola, 339
Bilisoly, 343
Billing, 133, 211, 225
Billings, 233
Billon, 416
Billups, 325
Bingham, 78
Binney, 80, 227
Birch, 378, 433, 461
Birchett, 260
Bird, 30, 112, 165, 200, 232, 252, 320, 363, 371
Birdsall, 104, 166
Birkhead, 30
Bishop, 183, 296, 416
Bissell, 119, 283, 369
Bisselle, 270
Bitner, 71
Bittinger, 139
Black, 119, 124, 266, 276, 293, 309
Blackburn, 404, 416, 421, 479
Blackford, 96, 101, 263, 270, 333, 336, 391, 396, 398, 404
Blacklock, 85
Blackman, 3
Blackwell, 340
Blagden, 30, 152, 253, 318, 451
Blain, 373
Blair, 96, 101, 138, 165, 220, 297
Blake, 125, 217, 248, 249, 374, 375, 387, 389, 477, 482

Blakely, 352
Blanchard, 148, 250
Bland, 315, 384
Blarck, 82
Bledsoe, 226
Bleecker, 9, 158
Blight, 418
Blinn, 220
Bliss, 210, 285, 467
Block, 228
Block Island, 436
Blodget, 56, 66
Bloomer, 331
Blooming Rose, 170
Blount, 263
Blous, 159
Blow, 401
Blowers, 323
Bloxham, 112, 212
Blue, 57, 70
Blunt, 283, 411
Boarman, 30, 110, 368
boat **David Seigle**, 313
boat **J Lambirc Washington**, 347
Boatwright, 11
Bodisco, 231
Boggs, 374, 479
Bogue, 180
Bogus, 265
Bohannon, 269, 343
Bohlayer, 217
Bohn, 279
Bohrer, 29, 235, 369, 376, 461
Boland, 457
Bollman, 79, 401
Bolton, 101, 273
Boltzell, 443
Bomford, 29, 462
Bonaparte, 91, 143, 309
Bond, 9, 29, 30, 283, 419
Bonell, 467
Bonesteel, 166
Bonneau, 284
Boom, 261

Boomer, 416
Boone, 29, 30, 53, 179, 183, 209, 306
Boorland, 210
Booth, 24, 139, 175, 186, 401
Boothe, 62
Boothy, 352
Boots, 17
Bordley, 413
Boreland, 68
Borgia, 449
Borland, 28, 93, 205
Borremans, 30
Borroughs, 223
Bosce, 30
Boss, 29, 166, 185, 252, 405, 472
Bosse, 30
Boswell, 253, 394
Boteler, 17, 113, 148, 162, 191, 216, 244, 322, 352, 358, 399
Botta, 142, 143
Bottom, 337, 344
Bottsford, 220
Bouic, 330
Bourke, 266
Bourne, 210, 362
Bouttillier, 338
Boutwell, 335
Bowen, 28, 29, 30, 166, 253, 275, 290, 331, 373, 375, 451
Bowens, 282
Bower, 29
Bowers, 91, 229, 369
Bowes, 53, 60, 61, 192
Bowie, 29, 177, 219, 238, 263, 270, 319, 392, 415, 445
Bowles, 413
Bowling, 306
Bowman, 27, 104, 119, 148, 166
Boxer, 257
Boyce, 104, 230, 240, 336, 337, 342, 344, 357, 371, 393, 397
Boyd, 82, 207, 274, 359, 420, 449
Boyer, 57

Boyle, 17, 29, 155, 209, 223, 245, 369, 388, 389, 409
Boyles, 154
Boyne, 452
Brachett, 121
Bradbury, 300
Braddock, 91
Bradford, 17, 20, 192, 209, 268, 374, 467
Bradfute, 120
Bradish, 401
Bradley, 29, 30, 53, 69, 94, 107, 108, 109, 115, 173, 183, 191, 232, 242, 252, 263, 264, 270, 309, 314, 412, 415, 436, 472
Brady, 109, 124, 157, 280, 327, 369
Bragg, 45, 96, 204, 293
Brainard, 76
Braine, 148, 375
Branat, 29
Branch, 262
Brand, 103
Brandebury, 269
Brandt, 250, 384
Brannan, 388, 389
Brant, 138, 456
Brasher, 425
Bratten, 349
Braxton, 315
Bray, 142
Breck, 258, 283
Breckenridge, 29
Brecker, 317
Brecknall, 265
Breemater, 273
Breese, 160, 239, 256, 273, 375
Brehm, 126
Brennahan, 71
Brennan, 418, 460
Brenner, 235
Brent, 29, 30, 216, 270, 341, 357, 374, 407, 415, 456
Brereton, 16, 29, 30, 75, 182, 278, 370
Breslyn, 210

Brett, 107
Brevoort House, 198
Brewer, 8, 216, 304
Brickey, 343
Brickhead, 155
Bridewell, 427
Bridge, 210
Bridges, 56
brig **Ann C Pratt**, 382
brig **Bainbridge**, 52
brig **Conde de Villanueva**, 193
brig **Dolphin**, 163
brig **Falmouth**, 14
brig **Gen Armstrong**, 109
brig **General Armstrong**, 328
brig **Grey Eagle**, 182
brig **Jennette**, 306
brig **Porpoise**, 210
brig **Two Friends**, 141
brig **Vesta**, 420
brigantine **Advance**, 388
Briggs, 184, 185, 340, 354, 356, 358, 366, 393, 401, 431, 480
Brigham, 9, 248
Brigham Young, 74
Bright, 29, 183, 209, 384
Brightwell, 442
brig-of-war **Dolphin**, 177
Briley, 398
Brindle, 450
Brinley, 158, 224, 301
Brintnall, 27
Brinton, 48
Brisco, 161
Briscoe, 30, 31, 55, 270, 366, 371
Brittingham, 343
Britton, 96
Broader, 446
Broadhead, 53
Brock, 164, 214
Brockenbrough, 386
Brodbeck, 29
Brodean, 39
Brodhead, 96, 101, 128

Brodt, 308
Brog, 276
Bromfield, 309
Bromwell, 259
Bronaugh, 418
Bronsell, 389
Bronson, 326
Brook, 415
Brook Farm, 129
Brooke, 18, 41, 125, 156, 162, 173, 223, 231, 236, 273, 316, 366, 375, 411, 430, 474
Brookes, 320
<u>**Brookeville Academy**</u>, 480
Brooking, 74
Brooks, 15, 30, 49, 75, 247, 271, 288, 289, 290, 346, 389, 428, 451, 464
Broom, 238
Broome, 306
Brotherton, 284
Broughton, 319, 325, 343, 362
Brown, 7, 11, 15, 18, 20, 23, 25, 29, 30, 46, 48, 60, 70, 80, 83, 85, 91, 93, 94, 98, 99, 110, 111, 117, 142, 146, 151, 157, 158, 170, 174, 177, 179, 184, 185, 197, 203, 220, 221, 227, 229, 230, 237, 238, 253, 254, 260, 261, 269, 297, 308, 313, 337, 340, 344, 350, 364, 386, 399, 411, 414, 416, 418, 425, 443, 450, 467, 468, 475
Brownell, 73, 146, 369
Browner, 51
Browning, 30, 47, 50, 73, 224, 325
Brownley, 371
Brownson, 268
Bruat, 478
Bruce, 29, 195, 220, 368, 369, 415
Brumbaugh, 414
Brune, 415
Bruniham, 354
Brush, 110, 145

Bryan, 30, 157, 159, 172, 199, 214, 219, 235, 258, 268, 281, 326, 327, 438
Bryant, 29, 234, 243, 352, 393, 458
Buchanan, 214, 238, 261, 322, 373
Buck, 78
Buckey, 29, 220, 280, 314, 330, 349
Buckingham, 174, 183, 252, 276
Buckley, 472
Buckly, 268
Buckner, 270, 284, 285, 290, 343
Buckney, 374
Bucks, 265
Budd, 416
Buel, 70, 351, 430, 449
Buell, 20, 28
Buffington, 279
Buford, 63, 380
Bujac, 202
Bulger, 164, 333, 430, 431
Bulins, 331
Bull, 334
Bullard, 416, 421
Bullitt, 116
Bullock, 58, 479
Bullus, 368
Bunting, 125, 268
Bunton, 467
Bunyan, 477
Burbridge, 304
Burch, 29, 30, 40, 85, 298, 450
Burche, 29, 30
Burchell, 263
Burchsted, 148
Burdett, 259
Burford, 29
Burgess, 235, 236, 253
Burghalter, 455
Burgoyne, 460
Burgwyn, 94
Burhan, 343
Burheene, 197
Burk, 338
Burke, 26, 164, 266, 444

Burling, 207
Burloch, 166
Burnetson, 146
Burnett, 35, 315
Burnett Farm, 395
Burnham, 69, 393
Burns, 106, 270, 271, 305, 370, 401, 451, 455, 479
Burr, 29, 98, 101, 211, 252, 333, 407, 471
Burrell, 202
Burris, 222
Burroughs, 249, 252, 460
Burrows, 261
Burt, 62, 80
Burton, 72, 93, 197, 238
Burtt, 17, 209
Busey, 30, 125, 173, 217, 333, 382
Bush, 6, 53, 60, 66, 277
Busher, 29, 252
Bushnell, 323
Butcher, 340
Butler, 29, 30, 48, 59, 61, 81, 88, 99, 104, 114, 130, 166, 194, 207, 208, 236, 276, 287, 289, 295, 365, 391, 402, 412, 416, 421, 453
Butlers, 402
Butterfield, 409
Buttle, 29
Button, 176, 473
Byington, 30, 470
Byng, 109
Byrens, 369
Byrne, 13, 30, 114, 156, 185, 188, 261, 394, 457
Byrum, 15

C

Cabaniss, 305
Cabel, 285
Cabell, 285
Cabot, 31
Cadwallader, 150
Cady, 379, 407

Caffey, 21, 60, 74, 196
Cahill, 66
Cahoe, 31
Cain, 316, 348
Calahan, 310
Calbraith, 95
Calcraft, 41
Caldwell, 21, 74, 144, 207, 253, 264, 310, 321, 366
Calhoun, 274, 306
Calhous, 19
Callaghan, 215, 277
Callahan, 31, 183
Callan, 31, 42, 99, 197, 220, 351, 367
Callinghan, 242
Callis, 78
Calvert, 24, 94, 184, 250, 300, 353
Camden, 347
Cameron, 20, 184, 311, 341
Cammack, 386
Camp, 20, 84, 340, 343, 352, 372
Campbell, 11, 20, 31, 52, 54, 80, 100, 102, 104, 130, 138, 161, 163, 183, 184, 233, 262, 272, 279, 280, 312, 315, 326, 340, 364, 375, 455, 467, 483
Canary, 310
Canby, 57, 70, 96, 290
Cannon, 31, 271, 339, 393
Capers, 58
Caperton, 26, 312, 357
Capps, 339
Capry, 370
Carbery, 31, 42, 67, 175, 184, 237, 253, 276, 451
Cardwell, 59
Carell, 135
Carey, 16, 220
Carker, 31
Carlin, 284
Carline, 222
Carlisle, 31, 41, 199, 263, 314, 401, 412
Carll, 78

Carlos, 140, 143
Carlton, 480
Carmichael, 262
Carnahan, 471
Carner, 70
Carother, 224
Carothers, 335, 341, 364, 396, 460, 463, 474, 475
Carpender, 368
Carpenter, 73
Carr, 31, 59, 120, 122, 171, 235, 282, 286, 288, 291, 374
Carreco, 30, 31
Carrey, 380
Carrico, 31
Carrington, 13, 112, 141, 148, 382
Carrol, 31
Carroll, 30, 31, 70, 84, 185, 192, 219, 227, 253, 265, 317, 379, 382, 414, 415, 418, 434
Carson, 416
Carter, 2, 14, 68, 70, 131, 156, 182, 246, 267, 273, 317, 369, 372, 374, 375, 383, 393, 425, 480
Carusi, 31, 125, 232, 255, 270, 432
Carver, 196, 335
Cary, 310
Case, 14, 28, 70, 374, 410, 416, 421
Casey, 74, 96, 212, 283, 292, 323
Cash, 147
Casler, 391
Casper, 207
Cass, 140, 263
Cassel, 267
Cassels, 422
Cassilis, 18
Cassin, 368
Castin, 59
Castle, 72
Castle Haven, 202
Castor, 396, 439
Cathcart, 31, 202
Catholic Cathedral, 245
Catlet, 179

Catlin, 108
Caton, 8, 16, 31
Catts, 360
Caughy, 188
Caulfield, 262
Caulk, 132, 160
Causin, 31, 45, 185, 313
Cavalier, 304
Cavanaugh, 127
Cavenagh, 4
Caverley, 300
Cedars, 234
Cenhors, 21
Cenhouse, 21
Cesarovitch, 136
Chaddock, 113
Chalfant, 447
Chaloner, 357
Chalsey, 213
Chamberlain, 1, 17, 87, 166, 209, 219, 467
Chambers, 84, 284, 311, 353
Chambliss, 121
Chamers, 328
Champion, 46, 183, 262
Champlin, 368
Chance, 155
Chancellor, 169, 175
Chancey, 295
Chandler, 31, 148, 169, 352, 356, 369, 375, 424, 467
Chapen, 377
Chapin, 142, 173, 178, 285
Chaplin, 170, 400
Chapman, 6, 12, 30, 51, 70, 78, 159, 164, 196, 208, 279, 286, 292, 349, 375, 424
Chappel, 421
Chappell, 149, 216, 307, 416
Chappin, 31
Charles, 30, 69
Charlton, 179, 340
Chase, 65, 70, 86, 96, 193, 301, 357, 376, 468

Chason, 141, 444
Chatard, 71, 374, 425
Chauncey, 368, 408
Chauncy, 114
Chauvenet, 116
Chearney, 354
Cheever, 30, 87, 179, 231, 273, 305, 376
Chenault, 150
Cheney, 277, 468
Cherry, 354, 392
Chesney, 415
Chester, 30, 416
Cheston, 141, 198
Chew, 259
Chichester, 238
Chickering, 464
Childers, 253
Childress, 153, 276
Childs, 156, 196, 204, 214, 228, 258, 322, 428, 437
Chilolmwood, 298
Chilton, 206, 259, 263, 301, 408
Chipman, 83, 259
Chirholm, 335
Chisholm, 355, 362, 393
Chism, 31
Choate, 139
Chouteau, 205, 407, 416, 421
Christian, 12, 60, 66, 95, 325
Christopher, 353
Chubb, 112
Church, 214, 258, 278, 437
Churchill, 71, 376
Cilley, 375, 467, 468
Cipperley, 429
Cissel, 234
Cissell, 251
Clack, 393
Clagett, 15, 83, 216, 224, 318, 451
Claghorn, 403
Claiborne, 427
Clampett, 217, 363
Clampitt, 386

Clampton, 103
Clanton, 450
Clapdore, 163
Clapham, 250
Clapier, 169
Clapsdale, 59
Clare, 266, 309
Claridge, 113
Clark, 24, 30, 31, 43, 52, 53, 57, 61, 66, 70, 83, 96, 111, 176, 177, 193, 198, 206, 217, 228, 233, 250, 260, 274, 275, 284, 295, 319, 329, 381, 382, 384, 398, 419, 421, 450, 454, 467, 475
Clarke, 30, 31, 42, 79, 80, 112, 116, 117, 123, 144, 158, 159, 161, 178, 184, 240, 246, 254, 263, 271, 288, 293, 294, 313, 338, 360, 383, 392, 417, 418, 443, 454, 468, 475, 479
Clarkson, 18, 89, 447, 458
Clary, 17, 82, 209, 271
Claude, 219
Claughton, 91
Claxton, 266
Clay, 88, 92, 373
Clayvell, 349
Clear, 370
Cleary, 285, 425
Clement, 415, 440
Clement XIV, 432
Clements, 30, 53, 156, 170, 184, 217, 271, 389
Clemson, 188
Cleveland, 339, 379
Clingman, 262, 392
Clinton, 4, 118, 187, 423
Clitch, 455
Clitz, 160
Clopper, 330
Clopton, 2
Closkey, 31
Clouth, 467
Clover Hill, 145
Clubb, 178, 207

Clutter, 2
Clymer, 6, 314
Coad, 270
Coale, 233
Coates, 468, 475
Cobb, 17, 31, 209, 315, 446
Cobbs, 226
Cobett, 72
Coburn, 31
Cocheu, 397
Cochran, 24, 30, 31, 61, 63, 305, 377, 451, 460
Cochrane, 383
Cocke, 203, 343, 368
Coddington, 30
Coe, 25, 359, 398
Coes, 22
Coffee, 122, 185
Coffey, 70
Coffin, 233
Cogswell, 438
Cohen, 387
Coit, 214
Coke, 419
Colbert, 30
Colburn, 214, 258, 437
Colcord, 290
Cole, 11, 30, 41, 70, 89, 259, 270, 313, 377, 384, 394, 402, 438
Cole Brook, 258
Coleman, 17, 180, 209, 224
Colemen, 31
Colhoun, 368
Colison, 86
Collard, 74
Collier, 84, 246, 354
Colligan, 14
Collings, 72
Collins, 17, 30, 31, 58, 125, 129, 178, 182, 191, 224, 297, 353, 427
Collison, 424
Colmesnil, 94
Colquitt, 177
Colson, 160, 224, 301

Colston, 348
Colt, 402, 453
Coltman, 30, 99, 235, 386
Columbus, 78
Colvin, 102
Com'g, 123
Combs, 31, 79
Compton, 288, 290, 294, 409
Comstock, 214, 258, 437
Conaffee, 451
Condict, 211
Congressional Burial Ground, 465
Congressional burying-ground, 164
Congressional Cemetery, 57, 128, 255
Congressional Grave Yard, 7
Conlan, 306, 454
Connecticut Courant, 16
Connell, 31, 222, 336, 337, 344, 480
Connelly, 31
Conner, 44, 285, 368, 404, 421
Connolly, 31, 105, 115, 173, 372, 455
Connor, 53, 58, 60
Conolly, 30, 265
Conover, 374
Conrad, 83, 418
Conroy, 30
Considine, 16
Constable, 340, 343, 393, 401
Converse, 467
Conway, 2, 92, 277, 405, 472
Coody, 14, 195
Cook, 8, 71, 93, 126, 153, 279
Cooke, 18, 72, 93, 288, 289, 343, 379, 415, 458
Cookman, 371
Cool Spring Farm, 60
Coolidge, 145, 228, 271, 287, 289, 376, 439
Coombe, 30, 31
Coombs, 125, 263
Coons, 113
Coon-skin tract, 257
Cooper, 115, 228, 294, 300, 317, 459, 479

Coote, 99
Copeland, 128
Copley, 77
Copp, 397
Coppee, 205, 283, 290
Cora, 460
Corbett, 246, 360
Corbin, 131, 132, 253
Corbitt, 161
Corcoran, 31, 86, 156, 183, 461
Corcuero, 47
Corday, 243
Cordery, 63
Corey, 480
Corley, 212, 284
Cornell, 93
Cornwell, 375
Corral, 445, 446
Corse, 31
Corwin, 273
Cory, 52
Cosby, 121, 291
Cosgrove, 54, 55
Coskery, 42
Cost, 332
Costa, 45
Coste, 31
Costello, 242, 251
Coster, 383
Costigan, 30, 31
Costigin, 265
Costin, 31
Costlow, 455
Cottage, 152
Cotterell, 323
Cotterill, 1
Cotton, 60
Cottrell, 343
Couch, 283, 290
Coulter, 98
Councill, 246
Count de Bruhl, 441
Count de Solms, 441
Cousin, 14

Coutte, 435
Couzins, 416
Covel, 75
Cow Island, 216
Coward, 19, 43
Cowling, 406
Cowman, 9
Cox, 30, 31, 86, 96, 108, 127, 128, 142, 148, 152, 165, 263, 308, 315, 320, 325, 361, 431, 449, 466, 469, 476
Cox's row, 246
Cox's Row, 325
Coxe, 70, 73, 191, 425
Coxen, 31
Coyle, 99, 183, 184, 411
Cozzens, 208, 214
Crabb, 375
Craig, 9, 74, 87, 130, 173, 228, 254, 263, 285, 310, 398, 450, 467
Craige, 262
Craighead, 382
Craighill, 281
Craik, 370, 440
Crain, 239
Crainard, 166
Craine, 351
Cramer, 280
Crampsey, 215
Crampton, 319
Cranch, 31, 54, 203, 316, 342, 397, 406, 447
Crandall, 142, 478
Crandell, 247, 465
Crane, 88, 99, 235, 246, 355, 447, 453, 473
Crate, 394
Cratty, 112
Craven, 31, 273, 276, 355, 371, 402
Craver, 279
Crawford, 31, 314, 377, 454, 463
Craycroft, 353, 402
Creager, 49
Creaser, 157

Creed, 415
Creighton, 425
Cripps, 407
Crittenden, 99, 123, 315, 329, 383
Crocker, 214, 332
Crocket, 415
Croggan, 472
Croghan, 227
Crome, 31
Cronin, 365
Cronise, 146
Crooks, 400
Cropley, 153, 314, 408
Crosby, 17, 18, 117, 296
Crosman, 403
Cross, 30, 98, 101, 121, 134, 145, 188, 420, 468
Cross Roads Tavern, 318
Crossen, 418
Crossman, 273
Cross-Roads Farm, 49
Crough, 59
Crown, 31, 99
Croysdale, 297
Crozet, 285, 294
Cruger, 358
Cruikshanks, 235
Cruise, 215, 218
Cruit, 49, 459
Crump, 31, 112, 212, 335
Crutchett, 31
Cruttenden, 31
Cryer, 31, 46
Cryss, 243
Cudlip, 30, 446
Cudman, 203
Culver, 23
Culverwell, 341
Cumberland, 443
Cumberland, Md, 223
Cummer, 197
Cummin, 99
Cumming, 118, 293, 395
Cummings, 58, 151, 189, 375, 479

496

Cummins, 80, 207, 240, 436, 461
Cummiskey, 266
Cunningham, 54, 55, 238, 301, 346, 354, 357, 370, 373, 424
Cunninghan, 417
Curran, 316, 384
Currie, 468
Currier, 156
Curry, 59, 107
Curson, 49
Curtain, 108
Curtass, 222
Curtin, 325
Curtis, 30, 31, 199, 234, 311
Curtiss, 230, 283
Curwen, 205
Cushing, 166
Cushman, 94, 101, 214, 231, 316, 322, 376
Custis, 3, 93, 183, 189, 440, 441
Cutter, 73
cutter **McLean**, 460

D

D'Tweedy, 358
Dade, 162
Daggett, 48, 383
Dahlgreen, 221, 374
Dailey, 112, 207
Daily, 208
Dainese, 38
Daingerfield, 360
Dale, 11, 32, 54, 55, 189, 352
Daley, 32, 393
Dallam, 336, 337, 344, 427
Dallas, 57, 83, 375, 387, 449
Dalton, 32, 301
Daly, 346
Dana, 17, 209, 287, 289
Danby, 160
Daniel, 2, 202, 317, 327
Daniels, 375, 410
Dannell, 271
Dant, 32, 224

Darby, 90
Darcantel, 368
Dardenne, 11
Dargan, 111
Darnall, 364
Darnes, 220
Darran, 378
Dart, 88, 199
Dashiell, 9, 125, 155, 170, 188, 202, 223, 239, 261, 371, 385, 394, 397, 454
Daudler, 353
Daunas, 387
Davant, 282, 439
Davenport, 56, 279, 357
Davey, 129
David, 151, 294, 421
Davidge, 42, 127
Davids, 306
Davidson, 32, 63, 141, 220, 222, 375, 420
Davies, 262
Davis, 8, 13, 14, 15, 16, 27, 31, 32, 33, 38, 42, 44, 57, 61, 67, 81, 99, 112, 113, 117, 127, 142, 151, 152, 156, 168, 173, 179, 183, 184, 199, 208, 209, 213, 214, 215, 217, 218, 225, 228, 235, 236, 250, 252, 256, 265, 269, 270, 283, 286, 288, 302, 317, 319, 341, 342, 358, 361, 363, 375, 384, 408, 409, 420, 422, 424, 427, 436, 445, 451, 464, 468, 474, 481
Davison, 347, 388, 394
Davy, 210, 442
Davys, 220
Daws, 467
Dawson, 60, 63, 99, 207, 299, 304, 314
Day, 20, 32, 125, 169, 188, 189, 211, 231, 253, 279, 283, 307, 312, 388, 394, 410, 427
Dayton, 31, 32, 230, 416, 421, 425, 453
de Agao, 193

De Besane, 402
de Boilleau, 226
De Boye, 232
De Castro, 355
De Forrest, 92
De Gayzucha, 329
De Grasse, 383
De Haven, 220, 375
De Kalb, 24, 460
De La Forest, 129
de Lagnel, 113
de Lesseps, 462
de Medici, 275
de Montholon, 407
De Peane, 305
De Puy, 102
De Quincy, 50
De Rothschild, 140
de Saussure, 122
De Saussure, 286
De Selding, 370
De Soto, 78, 84
de St Andre, 337, 344
de Ste Marie, 87
de Treville, 74
De Treville, 96
De_ios, 31
Deakins' Hall, 77
Deale, 125, 230, 239
Dean, 101, 150, 166, 263, 308
Dearing, 288, 289
Deas, 31, 75, 228, 410
Debar, 305, 311
DeBell, 327
Debile, 184
Deblois, 350
DeBow, 94
DeBree, 375
Debust, 433
DeCamp, 32, 374, 425
Decapry, 402
Decatur, 29, 192, 359, 368, 466
Decker, 186, 187
Dedrick, 314

Deeth, 446
Degenhart, 43
DeKalb, 195
DeKrafft, 31, 375
Delachaise, 468
Delacroix, 468
Delancy, 209
Delaney, 17, 101, 447
Delano, 229, 406
Delany, 139, 364
Delaway, 185
Delius, 31
Dell, 247, 462
Dellett, 463
Demenou, 331
Dement, 32, 110, 142, 143
Democrats of Louisiana, 244
Dempsey, 87
Denby, 159
Dendall, 434
Deneal, 88
Deneckerl, 255
Denham, 99, 179, 461
Denison, 102, 467
Denmaree, 317
Dennett, 53, 60, 61
Denney, 359
Dennis, 67, 74
Dennison, 51, 250, 467
Denniston, 250, 374
Denniz, 210
Denny, 227, 228
Densley, 32
Denson, 110
Dent, 31, 32, 119, 284, 292, 364, 432, 449
Deny, 434
Derby, 437
Derelin, 62
Dermott, 267
Derrick, 259, 361, 412
DeRussy, 377
Desaules, 100
DeSelding, 31

Deshler, 118, 292
Deuno, 218
Devall, 382
Develin, 47
Devereux, 271, 278, 363
Devers, 183
Devine, 267
Devire, 224
Devlin, 32, 142, 341, 345, 393, 468
Devoy, 309
Dewdney, 32
Dexter, 228, 394
Dey, 199
Dibbrel, 346
Dibbrell, 343
Diberl, 343
Dibrell, 393
Dick, 214, 258, 395, 414, 470
Dickens, 76
Dickenson, 32
Dickerson, 66, 70
Dickessey, 338
Dickey, 229, 468
Dickins, 31, 184
Dickinson, 3, 148, 213, 366
Dickson, 49, 101, 135, 219, 246
Diety, 32
Diffenderffer, 148
Digges, 32, 63, 162, 306
Dignum, 468
Dillard, 301
Dillaway, 160
Dilliard, 370
Dillon, 17, 206
Dillord, 401
Dilworth, 458
Dinkle, 383
Dinsmore, 56
Disher, 32
Disney, 21
Divine, 235
Dix, 216, 263, 314, 349
Dixey, 357

Dixon, 32, 238, 248, 252, 314, 346, 384
Doane, 280
Dobbin, 158, 250
Dobbyn, 384
Dodd, 340
Dodge, 30, 72, 166, 181, 235, 285, 327, 329, 436
Dodson, 17, 56, 60, 88
Dogan, 431
Doggett, 475
Dogherty, 280
Dolan, 371
Doland, 63, 93
Doleberte, 329
Dolsen, 42
Domenichino, 217
Domercq, 60, 196
Don, 468
Donahoe, 343
Donaldson, 107
Donegru, 305
Donelan, 4, 259, 371, 416, 442, 448, 457
Donelly, 183
Donelson, 281
Donheen, 311
Doniphan, 32, 435
Donn, 32, 91, 183, 185, 399, 461
Donnahoo, 142
Donnel, 6
Donnelly, 159, 366
Donoghue, 184, 270, 430
Donohoo, 32
Donohough, 318
Donovan, 89
Doolittle, 272
Dordan, 197
Dorman, 325
Dornin, 373
Dorr, 59
Dorrance, 244
Dorsett, 185
Dorsey, 44, 109, 380, 394, 480

Doten, 467
Doubleday, 282, 283
Dougherty, 184, 299
Doughty, 236
Douglas, 32, 105, 173, 293, 366, 434
Douglass, 27, 32, 120, 217, 305, 306, 363, 420
Doury, 235
Dove, 17, 155, 184, 209, 235, 252, 343, 358, 374, 384, 393
Dovilliers, 19
Dowdell, 315
Dowell, 335, 431
Dowling, 32, 146, 175, 307, 332, 408
Downer, 32
Downing, 99, 143, 260, 263, 359
Downman, 238
Downs, 19, 73, 203, 278
Dowre, 340
Doyle, 32, 34, 59, 101, 184, 304, 346, 354, 369, 393
Dozier, 134
Drake, 26, 64, 88, 99, 167, 420
Draper, 444
Drayton, 374, 403
Drew, 15, 101
Drewry, 393
Driggs, 81
Driscoll, 113, 309
Driver, 202
Drum, 380
Drummond, 250
Drury, 99, 101, 175, 256, 277, 434, 451
Drynan, 224
Drysdale, 287, 289
Du Barry, 74
Du Pont, 214, 238
Duane, 281
Dubois, 421, 437
DuBois, 214, 258
Dubose, 95
Duckett, 8
Duddington, 415

Dudley, 27, 118, 330, 380, 411
Duehay, 400
Duer, 14, 43, 194
Duff, 32
Duffin, 187
Duffy, 66, 74, 137
Dufief, 32, 92
Dufour, 50, 106
Dugan, 11, 60, 64, 95, 371
Duhamel, 164, 314
Duke, 249
Duke of Rutland, 461
Duke of Wellington, 210
Dulaney, 461
Dulany, 32, 299, 312, 360, 369
Duley, 32
Dulin, 32
Dumaresq, 350
Dumaresque, 350
Dummer, 83
Dummett, 439
Dummitt, 122
Dunbar, 104, 107, 354, 432
Duncan, 81, 156, 204, 213, 270, 274, 295, 310, 358, 365, 423, 430, 444, 475
Duncanson, 249, 386
Dundas, 54
Dunham, 119, 313
Dunkel, 11
Dunlap, 441
Dunlevy, 266
Dunlop, 55, 62, 69, 142, 190, 253, 281, 451, 456
Dunmore, 45
Dunn, 334, 370, 427, 467
Dunnington, 61, 184, 231, 376
Dunovant, 288
Dupont, 374
Duran, 454
Durkin, 52
Durr, 32
Durst, 102
Dusenbery, 294

Dusenbury, 203
Dustin, 468
Dutton, 15
Duval, 134, 256
Duvall, 21, 127, 150, 216, 336, 346, 375, 423, 435
Dwight, 365
Dyer, 31, 32, 53, 59, 72, 85, 96, 192, 367, 453
Dyott, 337
Dyson, 237, 323

E

Eagan, 183
Eagle, 121, 374
Earl, 71, 225, 278, 336
Earl of Buchan, 441
Earle, 398, 414
Easby, 32, 414
Eastman, 94, 111, 467
Easton, 270
Eastwood, 182
Eaton, 24, 28, 70, 102, 129, 178, 183, 187, 361, 375
Eayres, 357
Ebbs, 340
Ebeele, 416
Eberbach, 97
Eberle, 421
Eberll, 416
Ebney, 181
Echols, 305
Eckard, 81, 188, 378
Eckel, 32
Eckhardt, 459
Eckloff, 269, 433
Edd, 95
Edders, 210
Eddy, 101
Edelen, 271, 476
Edelin, 32, 288, 289, 451
Edes, 99, 351, 426
Edgar, 105, 383
Edge, 85

Edil, 79
Edmondston, 99
Edmonston, 20, 26, 157, 199, 295, 373, 472
Edmunson, 9
Edson, 145, 166, 233
Edwards, 3, 10, 27, 32, 80, 92, 166, 210, 235, 314, 315, 378, 468, 471
Egan, 65
Eggleson, 375
Eggleston, 125
Ehney, 175
Ehrmaunhout, 216
Eignbrodt, 32, 127
Eld, 461
Elda, 470
Eldridge, 151, 212, 415, 433
Elgar, 418
Elkins, 124
Ellaville, 22, 133, 250
Ellery, 369
Ellicott, 32, 63, 103, 191, 219
Ellin, 182
Elliot, 32, 33, 74, 138, 214, 283, 467
Elliott, 32, 70, 258, 263, 315, 396
Ellis, 32, 172, 173, 184, 211, 239, 254, 358, 386, 403, 444, 454, 467
Ellmore, 309
Ellsworth, 325, 378
Elmsbury, 239
Elvans, 233
Elwell, 235
Elwyn, 11, 94
Elyotte, 131
Embrich, 166
Emerick, 32
Emerson, 256, 313
Emery, 159, 209, 217, 378, 451
Emig, 326
Emmert, 32, 148, 431, 472
Emmons, 11
Emory, 89, 96, 123, 281, 290, 291, 415
Emperor Nicholas, 135, 136

Empson, 88
Endicott, 42
England, 225
Engle, 373, 399, 425
Engles, 159
English, 32, 119, 201, 284, 292, 351, 374, 427, 456
English Channel, 430
Ennis, 59, 164, 175, 184, 307, 363, 387, 408, 430
Enroughty, 323
Entwistle, 178
Erben, 231, 301, 376
Erie, 173
Erskine, 150, 226
Erving, 32
Erwin, 12, 19, 59, 77, 195
Esch, 129
Eskridge, 335, 355, 381, 393
Eslin, 352
Espey, 32, 142, 215, 235
Espinosa, 445
Espy, 51
Essex, 172, 271
Estabrook, 303
Estcourt, 265
Estep, 10
Esterly, 51
Estop, 32
Estrampes, 149
Etchison, 267, 306, 310, 450
Etchitson, 222
Etting, 32
Eva, 412
Evan, 461
Evans, 32, 46, 121, 126, 158, 173, 183, 208, 250, 253, 263, 273, 285, 291, 304, 347, 353, 380, 381, 384, 394, 431
Eve, 70, 193, 271
Evens, 24
Everett, 49, 103, 275, 322
Eversfield, 273
Ewell, 247

Ewing, 32, 59
Exchange Hotel, 359
Eyre, 251

F

Fabens, 343
Fagan, 107
Faherty, 63, 181
Fairbanks, 59, 139
Fairchild, 227
Fairfax, 224, 287, 289, 301, 374
Fairfield, 229
Fales, 236
Fallan, 15
Falling, 73
Fallon, 41, 325
Falls, 219, 355
Fanning, 33, 162, 210
Farant, 263
Faribault, 46
Faris, 110
Farish, 47
Farley, 95
Farmer, 237, 371
Farmington, 173
Farnham, 33, 462
Farnhan, 217
Farnum, 70, 213
Farquhar, 316
Farr, 162
Farragut, 32, 369, 373
Farrar, 75
Farrell, 33
Farring, 446
Farrington, 11
Farwell, 394
Fassett, 210
Fatham, 262
Fatherly, 339
Fauk, 84
Faulkner, 16, 394
Faunce, 32, 33, 113
Fauntleroy, 157, 261
Favier, 32, 148, 202, 271, 426, 431

Favre, 430
Fay, 28, 370
Fearson, 42, 99, 175
Febrey, 9
Federal Constitution, 356
Fedorowna, 136
Feiner, 407
Felch, 24, 60, 86, 87
Felix, 186, 246
Felker, 48
Fellows, 397
Felson, 124
Fendall, 163
Fennay, 467
Fentress, 354
Fenwick, 33, 99, 262, 306, 341, 389, 432
Ferdinand, 100
Feret, 346, 393
Ferguson, 1, 2, 31, 185, 224, 252, 253, 301, 345, 366, 367, 369, 370, 393, 431
Ferrall, 266, 270
Ferret, 352, 353
Ferris, 368, 429
Ferry, 111
Fessenden, 382
Field, 83, 121, 263, 291
Fields, 436
Fien, 249
Fierer, 59
Fill, 233
Fillebrown, 375
Fillmore, 77, 190, 387, 452
Finch, 32, 405
Finckel, 59
Findlay, 51
Findley, 470
Finger Rings, 10
Finier, 402
Fink, 379
Finkman, 183
Finley, 12, 96, 193, 337, 357, 412
Finnall, 194

Finnegan, 421
Finotti, 223
first book published, 165
Fischer, 33
Fish, 32, 433, 452
Fisher, 32, 149, 151, 175, 178, 205, 215, 217, 301, 307, 338, 363, 412
Fisk, 337, 351, 357
Fiske, 335, 352
Fisler, 305
Fitch, 263, 426
Fitz, 420
Fitzclarence, 6
Fitzgerald, 33, 134, 139, 243, 251, 350, 353, 369, 411, 473
Fitzhugh, 156, 346, 376
Fitzpatrick, 2, 11, 59, 178, 184, 212, 227, 261, 306, 323, 363, 379
Flagg, 369
Flanagan, 354
Flanigan, 28
Flannen, 99
Fleas, 353
Fleeas, 355
Fleet Hill, 175
Fleetwood, 114
Fleming, 120, 284, 293
Flemming, 33
Fletcher, 4, 32, 33, 98, 110, 119, 164, 472
Fliess, 401
Fling, 467
Flinn, 225, 340
Flint, 32, 33, 165, 183, 184, 368
Flint's Hotel, 368
floating ice, 74
Flournoy, 94, 110
Flowers, 18, 23
Flusser, 375
Flynn, 23
Foal, 2
Foedorovna, 135
Foertsch, 207
Foley, 409, 450

Follett, 439
Folsom, 331, 439, 474
Foncannon, 420
Font Hill, 356
Foos, 259
Foote, 214, 238, 448, 483
Forbes, 340, 343, 394
Force, 33, 79, 80, 183, 296, 413
Ford, 1, 99, 177, 220, 312, 397, 444
Foreman, 93
Forest, 246
Forest of PG, 273
Forest Retreat, 329
Forman, 262, 454
Forney, 102, 118, 184, 285, 293, 438, 452
Forrest, 32, 33, 80, 84, 258, 325, 328, 331, 369, 375, 448
Forster, 246
Fort Atkinson, 466
Fort Bliss, 123
Fort Boyer, 409
Fort Brooke, 483
Fort Clark, 406
Fort Columbus, 427
Fort Davis, 334, 354, 370
Fort Dodge, 102
Fort Duncan, 339
Fort Erie, 48
Fort Gibson, 157, 195
Fort Harney, 191
Fort Hill, 306
Fort Kearny, 408
Fort Laramie, 407, 408
Fort Leavenworth, 176, 206, 222, 254, 261, 294, 295
Fort McHenry, 246, 266, 268, 277
Fort McIntosh, 427
Fort Meigs, 329
Fort Mills, 51
Fort Monroe, 143
Fort Moultrie, 444
Fort Myers, 483
Fort Pierre, 222, 346, 465

Fort Plain, 171
Fort Riley, 319, 322, 376, 458
Fort San Carlos, 420
Fort Sarpy, 254
Fort Simon Drum, 483
Fort Snelling, 195
Fort St Pierre, 198
Fort Steilacoom, 26
Fort Tejon, 396
Fort Union, 254
Fort Washington, 189
Fort Wayne, 104
Fort Yuma, 204
Fortier, 15
Fortress Monroe, 345
Forust, 428
Foster, 88, 143, 250, 269, 375, 383, 384, 466
Fowble, 142
Fowle, 263
Fowler, 33, 84, 92, 105, 170, 232, 247, 265, 367, 444, 462
Fowlkes, 412
Fox, 18, 53, 87, 106, 220, 227, 249, 280, 409, 411
Foxwell, 183
Foy, 24, 68, 179, 392, 401, 464
Fraeler, 32
Frailey, 72, 459
Frampton, 219
France, 436
Frances, 306
Francis, 3, 54, 385
Francisco, 149, 345
Frankenberger, 32, 155, 445
Frankland, 328
Franklin, 42, 158, 184, 187, 188, 212, 220, 222, 237, 253, 328, 341, 363, 374, 388, 420, 451, 479, 480
Franklin Row, 454
Franz, 167
Franzoni, 33, 41
Fraser, 119, 169, 251, 417, 461
Frasier, 389

Frazer, 9, 284, 292, 345
Frazier, 33, 338
Frederick, 91, 207, 270
Free, 202
Freedley, 214
Freedly, 258, 437
Freely, 210
Freeman, 11, 42, 228, 233, 288, 289, 346, 355, 481
Freer, 255
Fremont, 26, 92, 138, 313, 450
French, 13, 26, 33, 56, 64, 88, 93, 94, 154, 173, 183, 217, 228, 246, 254, 261, 263, 272, 277, 278, 290, 301, 314, 374, 415, 425, 443, 459, 461, 464, 476
Frere, 404
Frey, 180
Freyhold, 114
Frick, 300
Friebus, 251
Friend, 69, 424
frig **Columbia**, 47, 130, 145
frig **Congress**, 228, 273
frig **Constitution**, 16, 17, 209
frig **Macedonian**, 339
frig **Merrimac**, 415
frig **Mississippi**, 160
frig **Mohawk**, 339
frig **Potomac**, 301
frig **Powhatan**, 397
frig **United States**, 466
Frink, 445
Fristoe, 80, 227, 253
Frost, 72
Frush, 330
Fry, 342, 375
Frye, 33, 35, 46
Fugett, 252
Fugitt, 33, 327
Fullalove, 142
Fuller, 178, 217, 324, 448, 473
Fulmore, 33
Fulton, 357

Funk, 65
Funsten, 360
Furgerson, 310
Furness, 342
Furse, 33
Fusting, 265, 266
Fyffe, 212, 220, 389
Fyffee, 375

G

Gaddis, 250, 384
Gadsby, 33, 365
Gaffin, 402
Gage, 208
Gagliati, 433
Gahan, 33
Gaines, 43, 49, 235, 468
Gainsboro, 217
Gaither, 18, 33, 76, 161, 253
Gale, 57, 60, 80, 415
Gales, 82, 184
Gallagher, 265, 271, 328
Gallaher, 3, 148, 237, 348
Gallant, 33
Gallaway, 318
Galligan, 112
Gallop, 413
Galt, 159, 183, 370
Gamble, 149, 300, 307, 375, 467
Gannell, 252
Gansevort, 374
Gant, 324
Gantt, 198
Gardiner, 86, 180, 305, 432
Gardner, 19, 29, 44, 61, 71, 117, 147, 209, 222, 230, 245, 246, 283, 285, 293, 296, 330, 333, 355, 373, 479
Garesche, 305, 438
Garet, 424
Garey, 260
Garibaldi, 190
Garland, 83, 231, 285, 301, 376
Garman, 243
Garner, 287, 289, 435

Garnett, 33, 121, 178, 179, 204, 230, 282, 284, 285, 288, 291, 293, 346
Garrard, 121, 291
Garrett, 15, 32, 33, 218, 271
Garrettson, 185
Garrison, 362
Garth, 173
Garther, 323
Garvin, 46
<u>Gas in the kitchen</u>, 245
Gaskill, 403
Gaskins, 361
Gassaway, 143, 216, 220
Gaston, 33
Gatcher, 185
Gates, 9, 197, 212, 232, 373, 423
Gatton, 423
Gaulden, 99
Gault, 370
Gauntt, 339
Gautier, 266, 343, 426
Gawler, 367
Gawronski, 413
Gay, 33, 160, 214, 227
Gaylord, 428
Geary, 447
Gedney, 368
Geiger, 243
Geisinger, 368
Gelbardt, 401
Genan, 33
Genet, 187
Gennelli, 147
Gentry, 94, 197
George, 107, 212, 276
Gereche, 33
Gerhard, 449
<u>German Reformed Church</u>, 314
<u>German Yagers</u>, 244
Gerrard, 58
Gerrish, 24
Gerry, 9, 158
Gethrell, 358
Gevers, 366, 436

Gherardi, 148, 375
Ghier, 21
Ghiselin, 285
Gibbean, 106
Gibbon, 1, 70, 108, 261
Gibbons, 47, 66, 390
Gibbs, 212, 304, 312, 347, 385, 449, 455, 475
Gibs, 166
Gibson, 2, 10, 33, 79, 148, 168, 183, 228, 304, 314, 317, 323, 325, 339, 345, 369, 375, 480
Giddings, 59, 71, 94, 234
Gideon, 178, 184, 451
Gieslin, 353
Gifford, 455
Gihon, 159
Gilbert, 59, 85, 220, 419
Gilchrist, 96, 101, 263
Gildemeister, 8
Giles, 97, 315
Gillan, 311
Gillem, 282
Gillespie, 337, 344, 357, 359, 399, 432
Gillett, 259, 470
Gilliam, 271
Gillies, 33
Gillis, 369, 374, 375
Gilliss, 33, 264
Gillmore, 247
Gillum, 421
Gilman, 126, 199, 235, 253, 305, 394, 412, 420, 445, 451
Gilmer, 166, 251
Gilmor House, 387
Gilmore, 102, 219
Giotto, 90
Girardeau, 94
Giraud, 357
Gittings, 451
Givenny, 89, 164
Gladding, 113
Gladman, 33

Gladmon, 82, 331
Glaize, 391
Glantz, 150
Glassell, 231, 375
Glasson, 369, 463
Gleason, 385
Glebe Farm, 257
Glen House, 362, 412
Glen Owen, 452
Glendy, 374
Glennon, 71
Glenroy, 179, 207
Glens, 166
Glentworth, 403
Glenwood Cemetery, 9, 10, 23, 162, 169, 225, 233, 305, 459
Glisson, 374
Glover, 24, 81, 88, 102, 132
Glynn, 368
Gobeens, 33
Godard, 213
Goddard, 33, 42, 180, 271, 351
Goddin, 63
Godey, 179
Godfrey, 33, 340, 343, 389
Godfroy, 266, 280
Godman, 41
Godon, 374, 425
Godwin, 113, 371
Goff, 43, 56, 335
Goggin, 47
Goheen, 125
Goins, 23
Gold, 394, 467
Golding, 451
Goldsboroug, 415
Goldsborough, 33, 373, 374, 415, 425, 482
Goldsmith, 233
Goldthwaite, 270
Gomery, 477
Gomez, 210
Gonzales, 314
Gooch, 352, 353, 401

Good Luck, 336
Goodall, 135
Goode, 287, 289
Goodfellow, 389
Goodman, 79
Goodrich, 257, 351, 352
Goods, 269
Goodwin, 33, 210, 249
Gooseman, 370
Gorbutt, 295
Gordan, 393
Gorden, 238
Gordon, 33, 64, 67, 113, 173, 214, 225, 250, 259, 286, 292, 355, 370, 384
Gore, 70, 423
Gorgas, 281
Gorham, 376
Gorman, 252
Gortschakoff, 303
Gosline, 186
Goss, 99
Gott, 216
Gough, 306
Gould, 79, 482
Gouldin, 126
Gouverneur, 104, 386
Gove, 118, 288
Gracie, 284
Grady, 102
Graeff, 395, 400
Graff, 165, 395
Grafton, 299, 369
Graham, 1, 53, 59, 64, 70, 72, 75, 142, 152, 156, 194, 210, 248, 253, 261, 287, 289, 301, 356, 368, 435, 449, 466
Grainger, 41
Grammer, 33, 99, 199, 221, 243, 321, 475
Grampus, 104
Granberry, 354
Granbury, 354
Grand Lodge of Va, 153

Grandison, 251
Granger, 48, 172, 188, 383
Grannis, 311
Grant, 153, 303, 313
Grason, 22
Gratiot, 198, 205, 249, 407
Grattan, 346
Gratz, 94
Grave, 396
Graves, 262, 406
Grawson, 311
Gray, 14, 33, 44, 155, 176, 258, 369, 375, 416, 421, 425, 448, 467
Grayson, 33, 57
Greathouse, 195
Green, 3, 33, 148, 160, 183, 185, 203, 230, 237, 266, 286, 289, 321, 328, 347, 361, 368, 374, 387, 412, 422, 425, 431
Green Springs, 296
Greene, 106, 170, 210, 332, 375
Greenleaf, 33, 54
Greenleaf's Point, 125, 161
Greenough, 42, 377
Greenwell, 33, 419
Greenwood, 128, 463
Greer, 223, 316, 375
Gregg, 33, 214, 258, 325, 437
Gregory, 213, 229, 415
Greneaux, 11, 244
Grenough, 435
Gretsche, 107
Grever, 118
Grey, 287, 289
Griff, 64
Griffin, 131, 142, 361, 419, 469
Griffing, 52, 60, 89, 166
Griffith, 11, 60, 93, 125, 140, 266, 319, 361
Griffiths, 77
Grigg, 317
Griggs, 41
Grigsby, 454

Grimes, 13, 94, 223, 252, 271, 312, 357, 436
Grimsley, 455
Grindall, 33
Grinder, 33, 46, 451
Gripenschutz, 67
Griswold, 163, 177, 199, 416
Groenveldt, 33
Groff, 33
Gross, 17, 137, 270
Grosvenor, 131
Grots, 99
Grover, 280, 292
Groves, 220, 221
Grow, 263
Grozelier, 76
Grubb, 72, 185
Grundy, 99
Grymes, 253
Guest, 46, 52
Guevall, 53
Guffin, 222
Guilding, 213
Guinand, 278
Guion, 255
Guise, 59
Guiton, 174
Gunnell, 33, 95, 159, 388
Gunnison, 51
Gunton, 69, 80, 99, 150, 169, 235, 312
Gurley, 150, 202, 213, 223, 263, 274, 305, 336, 373, 380, 455
Gurney, 417
Gusling, 263
Guterson, 133
Guthrie, 59, 119, 272
Guttenson, 93
Guttesnson, 33
Guy, 89, 392
Guydot, 131
Gwaltney, 80
Gwin, 68, 375
Gwinn, 153
Gwyan, 306

Gwynn, 53, 79, 306, 340, 343

H

H M S **Pemborke**, 423
Ha ja-on-gueh, 238
Habersham, 375, 421
Hackett, 223
Hackney, 127
Hadden, 74
Hadel, 395, 400
Hagadorn, 396
Hagar, 433
Hager, 235, 244
Hagerty, 73, 196, 224
Haggarty, 242
Haggerty, 53, 60, 199, 264
Haight, 372
Hain, 199
Hains, 467
Hainson, 113
Haldeman, 280
Hale, 274, 389
Haley, 220
Haliday, 34, 185, 252
Hall, 33, 34, 82, 124, 150, 155, 162, 166, 197, 212, 220, 234, 256, 281, 324, 336, 354, 356, 359, 365, 368, 369, 412, 417, 462, 467, 468, 472
Halleck, 92, 331, 387
Haller, 324, 457
Hallett, 346
Halley, 429
Halliday, 367
Halligan, 34
Halloway, 254
Hallowell, 264
Halsen, 393
Halsey, 68, 308, 398
Halson, 343, 401
Halston, 345, 346
Hamadinger, 95
Hambleton, 219
Hambureys, 353
Hamer, 70, 74
Hamersly, 342
Hamil, 127
Hamill, 361
Hamilton, 77, 102, 105, 112, 125, 144, 154, 198, 224, 251, 252, 265, 266, 267, 274, 283, 290, 301, 356, 375, 414, 465, 476
Hamlin, 159, 312
Hammer, 353
Hammett, 252
Hammond, 9, 137, 140, 219, 245, 326, 331, 343
Hampton, 34, 385
Hancock, 113, 184, 285, 330, 426, 438
Hand, 375
Handy, 252, 335, 336, 341, 369, 374, 396, 402, 424, 458
Hanewinckel, 237
Haney, 34, 44
Hanna, 483
Hannegan, 336, 338
Hanney, 34
Hanning, 43
Hanrahan, 343
Hansbrough, 373
Hansell, 93
Hansen, 70
Hanson, 34, 39, 48, 115, 125, 214, 219, 322
Hanway, 81
Haps, 48
Harbaugh, 157, 397
Harbell, 467
Hardasctle, 415
Hardcastle, 134, 288, 289
Hardee, 96, 282, 291
Hardesty, 149, 259, 307
Hardin, 88, 150
Harding, 193, 287, 289, 439
Hardy, 60, 231, 315, 394
Hare, 375
Hargis, 415
Hargrave, 59
Harkes, 394

Harkness, 34, 252, 253, 413
Harlan, 256, 315, 338
Harley, 400
Harman, 24, 405
Harmon, 235, 405
Harmony, 375
Harnett, 335
Harney, 379, 380, 407, 408, 465
Harper, 48, 57, 59, 72, 77, 180, 319, 482
Harrell, 369
Harrelson, 17
Harringon, 175
Harrington, 59, 104, 175, 263, 470
Harris, 8, 18, 34, 51, 70, 84, 117, 297, 301, 309, 315, 353, 374, 375, 380, 385, 403, 406, 416, 421
Harrison, 25, 34, 73, 79, 118, 120, 137, 183, 186, 235, 253, 288, 293, 339, 369, 439, 451, 475
Harrover, 183, 230
Harry, 335
Harshman, 235
Harsteine, 212
Harstene, 388
Hart, 33, 88, 171, 254, 340, 375, 412, 416
Hartley, 180, 220
Hartman, 448
Hartstein, 220
Hartsteine, 129
Hartstene, 374, 389
Hartsuff, 283, 483
Hartt, 422
Hartwell, 121, 194, 439
Hartz, 214, 258, 438
Harvard, 315
Harvey, 73, 99, 120, 146, 233, 235, 371, 378, 411
Harvie, 294
Harwood, 343, 352, 354, 374
Haskell, 193, 220, 394, 448
Haskins, 2, 56, 148, 356, 378
Haslan, 338

Haslap, 40
Hassell, 213
Hassler, 31
Hastings, 4
Hatch, 94, 102, 269, 414
Hathaway, 332
Hatley, 312
Hatton, 340, 343, 346, 371, 393
Hauptman, 395
Haven, 102
Havener, 209
Havenner, 33, 113, 204
Havens, 442
Haviland, 259, 430, 482
Havsham, 142
Haw, 101, 175, 235
Hawkes, 390
Hawkins, 145, 324
Hawks, 139
Hawley, 125, 448
Hawthorne, 363
Haxall, 2
Haxton, 375
Hay, 83, 172
Haydon, 371
Hayes, 94, 270, 389, 482
Haymaker, 258
Hayman, 34
Hayman, 285, 290
Hayne, 80, 219, 359, 434
Haynes, 303, 480
Hays, 1, 34, 46, 110
Hayward, 183, 333
Haywood, 101, 336, 337, 450
Hazard, 17, 147, 173, 209, 276, 374, 425
Hazel, 165, 320
Hazen, 214, 258, 438
Hazle, 34
Hazleton, 341
Hazlett, 166
Hazlup, 388
Hazzard, 156
Heacock, 426

Head, 210, 468
Head Hog Island, 333
Headley, 34
Heally, 379
Health report, 207
Heard, 49
Hearne, 415
Hearns, 254
Heart, 87
Heartwell, 7
Heath, 154
Heaton, 46
Hebb, 278
Hecht, 308
Hedley, 63
Heeskill, 297
Heileman, 375
Heine, 160
Heineken, 347, 371
Heintzelman, 283
Heiskell, 239, 314, 386, 409, 439
Heisley, 59
Helfenstein, 1
Hellen, 34, 147, 361
Heller, 112, 125
Hemans, 50
Heminger, 14, 48, 96
Hempstone, 270
Henderson, 16, 59, 190, 301, 325, 340, 341, 374, 376, 436, 455
Hendle, 416
Hendly, 33
Hendren, 451
Hendrick, 383
Hendricks, 305
Hendrickson, 59
Heneage, 43, 57
Heneiker, 336
Hening, 8
Henley, 24, 264
Hennegan, 25
Hennessey, 66
Henning, 34, 300
Henriques, 301

Henrity, 198
Henry, 59, 88, 89, 134, 157, 168, 220, 368, 375, 415, 420, 431, 439
Henry VIII, 478
Henshaw, 145, 182, 184, 233, 252
Hepburn, 34, 142, 400
Herald, 33
Herbert, 34, 273, 444, 478
Hercus, 205
Herington, 467
Herman, 49, 161
Hermon, 99
Herndon, 1, 108, 224, 301, 374
Herold, 250, 384
Heron, 34
Herring, 27, 388, 415
Herrity, 34
Herron, 92, 203, 244, 271, 311
Hersel, 355
Hersey, 481
Heslep, 77
Hess, 59, 325
Hester, 181, 231, 375
Heth, 284, 288, 292, 380
Hetzel, 33
Hetzell, 34
Hevener, 326
Hevner, 24
Hewitt, 306
Hewlett, 265
Heyward, 403
Hibbard, 405
Hibbs, 33, 472
Hickey, 13, 183, 270, 271, 323, 444
Hickman, 34, 87
Hicks, 2, 33, 34, 43, 61, 70, 271, 345, 435
Hieskell, 224, 255, 301
Higdon, 306
Higgins, 83, 284, 330, 343, 346, 393, 401, 410, 436
Higham, 210
Highlands, 456
Hight, 122, 286, 293, 380

Higton, 451
Hikok, 396
Hilbus, 357, 400
Hilde, 145
Hildeburn, 77
Hildreth, 309
Hildt, 125, 215, 397, 413, 473, 476
Hill, 18, 63, 80, 108, 110, 111, 132, 150, 183, 184, 210, 214, 253, 258, 273, 298, 300, 385, 386, 414, 429, 438, 467, 468
Hillard, 208
Hilleary, 34, 170, 200, 353
Hillman, 392
Hillon, 396
Hills, 265, 384
Hillyer, 56
Hilsman, 8
Hilton, 145, 252
Hindman, 34
Hinds, 274
Hines, 33, 34, 71, 299, 328, 445
Hingerty, 148
Hinkley, 17
Hinman, 194
Hinton, 20, 62, 68, 242
Hintze, 355
Hintzelman, 147
Hirst, 125
Hiss, 203
Hitchcock, 11, 222, 374, 407, 416, 439
Hitchinson, 468
Hitten, 126
Hitz, 50, 357, 400
Hixson, 63
Hoard, 273
Hoban, 34, 329
Hobbins, 464
Hobe, 124
Hobin, 280
Hobson, 262
Hodge, 329

Hodges, 15, 34, 46, 53, 72, 180, 188, 191, 212, 284, 310, 343, 373, 388, 424, 464
Hodgins, 18
Hodgkinson, 89
Hoe, 184
Hoey, 215
Hoff, 244
Hoffman, 34, 56, 62, 93, 232, 265, 406, 407, 436
Hog Island, 381
Hogan, 12, 34, 48, 195, 237, 251, 259, 405
Hoge, 274
Hogg, 129
Hohing, 34
Holabird, 206, 283
Holbein, 478
Holbrook, 93, 219
Holcomb, 147, 369
Holcombe, 93, 479
Holden, 196, 340, 346, 354
Holker, 70
Holland, 31, 34, 106, 108, 110, 160, 165, 251, 269, 281, 352
Holliday, 282, 371
Hollingshead, 101, 347, 405, 414
Hollingsworth, 12
Hollins, 34, 45, 84, 373, 425
Hollister, 166, 256
Holman, 70
Holmead, 33, 34, 142, 146, 155, 235, 261, 275, 361, 366, 405, 408, 412, 428, 443, 451
Holmes, 17, 25, 34, 94, 168, 209, 285, 468
Holohan, 9
Holroyd, 384
Holsman, 384
Holstein, 95
Holstin, 14
Holt, 11, 87
Holtz, 215
Holtzman, 29

Holy Cross, 268
Homans, 33
Home Hill, 419
Homer, 295
Homes, 104
Homiller, 271
Hommell, 398
Honeywell, 59
Honsum, 279
Hood, 287, 360
Hooe, 34
Hooff, 41
Hook, 8, 25, 126, 166, 320, 367
Hooper, 135
Hoople, 70, 196
Hoover, 33, 34, 64, 75, 117, 125, 145, 184, 243, 276, 279, 308, 339, 373, 475
Hope, 123
Hopkins, 44, 90, 166, 272, 273, 309, 385, 415, 425, 454
Hopkinson, 94, 441
Hopper, 396
Horbach, 252
Hord, 83
Horlbeck, 348
Horn, 107
Horner, 94
Horning, 33
Horry, 359, 434
Horsey, 415
Hosmer, 123, 249
Hotchkiss, 308
Houchins, 356
Houck, 300
Hough, 88, 125
Houston, 34, 175, 249, 297, 375
Houzam, 33
Howard, 2, 33, 59, 96, 133, 155, 188, 193, 207, 209, 263, 327, 336, 337, 344, 347, 364, 420, 438, 476, 478
Howdall, 34
Howe, 34, 76, 126, 131, 175, 283, 311, 352, 380, 401, 407, 408, 482

Howell, 313
Howes, 342
Howison, 93, 192
Howland, 282, 332
Howle, 45
Howlett, 34
Hoye, 461
Hubbard, 89, 154, 202, 268, 387
Hubbs, 34
Huber, 34
Huchings, 353
Hudgen, 325
Hudgins, 113
Hudry, 17
Hudson, 283, 348, 374, 380, 425
Huey, 214
Huff, 218
Huger, 78, 104, 166, 449
Huges, 64
Huggins, 133, 203, 229
Hughes, 34, 60, 89, 96, 101, 106, 150, 167, 192, 245, 275, 280, 325, 378, 409, 418, 429
Hull, 215, 249, 373, 415
Hulse, 17
Hume, 358, 421, 424
Hummonds, 8
Humphreville, 454
Humphrey, 26, 195
Humphreys, 33, 34, 86, 304
Humphries, 273, 344
Hunnewell, 406
Hunt, 9, 17, 33, 34, 60, 107, 210, 249, 250, 263, 283, 284, 292, 369, 374, 452, 463
Huntemuller, 218
Hunter, 50, 52, 59, 65, 106, 113, 134, 149, 150, 230, 280, 284, 298, 369, 377, 402, 418
Huntington, 80, 181, 227, 396
Hurdle, 271
Hurley, 34, 252
Hurst, 312, 368
Hurt, 262

Husband, 54
Hushe, 163
Hussey, 43, 266, 467
Hutchenson, 57
Hutchins, 24, 110, 166
Hutchinson, 19, 34, 68, 178, 211, 467
Hutchison, 25, 187
Hutter, 403
Hutton, 330
Hyacinth, 68
Hyatt, 253, 450
Hyde, 300
Hyen, 102
Hyland, 153
Hyler, 115
Hyman, 337

I

Iansbee, 468
Iardella, 430, 431
Iddins, 8
Iglehart, 155, 414
Ihler, 45
Ihrie, 169, 250, 287, 289
Immaculate Conception, 14
Immanuel, 100
Ingersoll, 166, 336, 337, 344
Ingle, 34, 253, 310, 359
Inglis, 210
Ingman, 316
Ingraham, 113, 148, 163, 374, 449
Ingram, 67, 323
Inman, 368
Iowa, 401
Ireland, 425
Ironside, 51
Irvin, 116
Irving, 53, 60, 64, 95, 446
Irwin, 20, 34, 375
Isaac, 47, 391
Isaacs, 273
Isemann, 17
Iseuring, 166
Isherwood, 60

Israel, 15, 78, 125, 157, 170, 209, 231, 327, 400
Isthmus of Suez, 462
Italian Hill, 223
Iverson, 122
Ives, 26, 281, 340
Izard, 101, 317

J

Jackson, 1, 22, 34, 35, 75, 77, 95, 153, 165, 243, 284, 285, 300, 340, 353, 356, 358, 368, 385, 393, 402, 412, 415, 425, 427, 429, 439, 445, 453, 464, 465, 481
Jacob, 138, 344
Jacobi, 35, 110
Jacobs, 34, 76, 308
Jakeman, 325
James, 14, 22, 34, 35, 266, 272
Jameson, 13, 432
Jamesson, 368
Jamieson, 133, 209, 270, 333
Jamison, 115, 183, 272
Janes, 446
Janin, 382
Janney, 145, 157
Jarbo, 295
Jarboe, 34, 62
Jardin, 202, 426
Jardine, 148, 431
Jarvis, 261, 368
Jay, 14, 35, 443
Jecko, 416
Jeffers, 385
Jefferson, 88, 172, 178, 217, 302, 315
Jeffrees, 421
Jeffrey, 83
Jemison, 87, 94
Jenckes, 181
Jenifer, 35, 121, 314, 475
Jenkens, 35
Jenkins, 102, 141, 265, 266, 322, 374, 432
Jenks, 150, 161

Jennens, 131
Jenning, 393
Jennings, 21, 35, 131, 328, 409, 410
Jermon, 245
Jerome, 383
Jervis, 344
Jesse, 262
Jesup, 228
Jewell, 112, 116
Jewelle, 127
Jewett, 80, 126, 227, 315
Jillard, 184
Jillson, 227
Johns, 4, 7, 56, 226, 262
Johnson, 6, 7, 24, 34, 35, 44, 46, 51, 52, 53, 56, 60, 61, 64, 68, 86, 88, 89, 96, 99, 102, 112, 121, 128, 130, 137, 157, 159, 160, 163, 166, 172, 177, 178, 183, 189, 193, 210, 220, 242, 247, 252, 253, 259, 261, 267, 280, 292, 297, 302, 312, 314, 315, 343, 348, 353, 357, 370, 375, 393, 397, 399, 400, 424, 428, 447, 455, 464
Johnston, 26, 96, 163, 188, 232, 281, 282, 285, 291, 368, 373, 469
Joice, 451
Joliffe, 452
Jolly, 45
Jones, 3, 5, 9, 12, 26, 31, 34, 35, 45, 51, 56, 60, 62, 74, 88, 94, 95, 98, 99, 113, 123, 124, 138, 156, 160, 166, 172, 173, 180, 185, 190, 191, 207, 209, 214, 235, 243, 253, 255, 269, 273, 283, 285, 287, 290, 300, 303, 307, 310, 316, 317, 318, 325, 328, 332, 334, 335, 339, 340, 368, 370, 374, 375, 390, 393, 398, 413, 415, 422, 442, 453, 468, 472
Jopes, 339
Jopman, 126
Jordan, 6, 58, 247, 358, 461
Jordon, 35, 166, 392
Josefovna, 136
Joseph, 210
Joslyn, 457
Jost, 34
Jouett, 375
Jowle, 401
Joy, 34, 179
Joyce, 35, 146, 184, 223
Joyner, 88
Joynes, 415
Judkins, 430, 475
Judson, 419
Junta, 149
Jurdine, 356

K

Kahl, 395
Kamehameha, 100
Kanally, 320
Kane, 107, 142, 212, 220, 336, 337, 338, 341, 357, 388, 389, 419, 424
Karreck, 442
Kay, 337
Kays, 173
Keally, 83
Kearny, 119
Keating, 53, 168
Kebby, 468
Keck, 346
Kedglie, 35
Keech, 446
Keefe, 217
Keefer, 104, 137, 183, 231, 433
Keegan, 271
Keeler, 481
Keeling, 325
Keen, 260, 328
Keenan, 191, 255, 266
Keene, 22, 236, 295, 342, 431
Keese, 347
Keighler, 239
Keirnan, 35
Keith, 68, 240, 295
Kell, 160, 375
Keller, 133, 227, 442

Kelley, 17, 35, 71, 337, 344, 357, 395
Kellogg, 99, 118, 166, 292, 398, 439
Kelly, 35, 118, 148, 170, 233, 306, 309, 336, 337, 373, 384, 467, 472
Kelton, 284
Kemble, 268
Kemp, 21, 361
Kemper, 430
Kempt, 66
Kempton, 228
Kendall, 35, 77, 165, 181, 197
Kendrick, 170, 420
Kengla, 271
Kennara, 467
Kennard, 415, 468
Kennedy, 3, 18, 35, 56, 60, 76, 114, 142, 159, 175, 178, 215, 218, 219, 235, 242, 354, 367, 373, 374, 380, 412, 423, 455, 472
Kennon, 51, 375
Kenrick, 216, 245
Kent, 88, 167, 309, 336, 337, 344
Kenyon, 247
Kerfoot, 270
Kerns, 266
Kerr, 29, 43, 51, 64, 77, 175, 262
Kersey, 86
Kesley, 35, 174
Kessler, 295
Ketcham, 53
Ketchen, 159
Ketchum, 88
Kettell, 454
Key, 7, 13, 33, 35, 93, 113, 125, 146, 173, 183, 190, 209, 350, 371, 377, 414
Keyes, 125, 465
Keys, 170, 232, 276
Keyworth, 13, 77, 183
Kibbey, 185, 469
Kibby, 158
Kickhoffer, 184
Kidder, 381, 468
Kidwell, 141, 151, 180, 235, 271

Kieckhaefer, 271
Kiger, 68
Kilbourn, 443
Kilgour, 330
Kilhour, 158
Killen, 147
Kilty, 369
Kimball, 74, 173, 467
Kimberly, 375
Kimble, 424
Kimmel, 414
Kinckle, 479
King, 12, 15, 35, 71, 74, 94, 132, 135, 157, 159, 168, 183, 211, 221, 235, 265, 270, 275, 280, 296, 336, 337, 350, 363, 369, 384, 403, 410, 416, 417, 430, 434, 464, 466
King Ferdinand VII, 143
King Wm III, 315
Kingdom, 371
Kinney, 35, 273, 280
Kinnicutt, 94
Kinsey, 268, 294
Kip, 68
Kirby, 77, 243, 356, 373
Kirk, 88, 297, 316, 400
Kirkland, 123, 293
Kirkwood, 184, 430, 445
Kirkwood House, 445
Kissane, 129
Kitchen, 23
Kite, 11
Kleiber, 53, 126, 166, 252, 462
Kleine, 126
Kleiss, 384
Kloman, 184
Klopfer, 350
Knapp, 11
Kneeland, 106
Kneller, 217
Knickerbocker, 56
Knight, 13, 35, 61, 71, 91, 173, 333, 376, 454
Knipe, 59

Knoll, 35
Knolton, 468
Knot, 225
Knowles, 200, 216, 373
Knox, 167, 365, 369, 380
Kohl, 251
Kohlert, 221
Komer, 126
Koones, 35, 92, 316, 331
Koran, 275
Krafft, 35, 366, 378, 405, 433, 445
Kraft, 35, 411
Kuhn, 35
Kurtz, 35, 228

L

La Branch, 77
La Follett, 60
La Follette, 11
Labranche, 46
Lacey, 35
Lackey, 124, 366
Lackland, 416
Lacy, 180
Ladd, 111, 244, 468
Ladde, 405
Lafayette, 79, 245, 326, 439, 441
Lafollett, 93
Lafontaine, 49
Lafonte, 90
Laframbeau, 346
Lahm, 338
Laight, 35
Lakeman, 357
Lakemeyer, 410, 434
Lalande, 248
Lallouette, 155
Lally, 327
Lamar, 59
Lamb, 90, 343, 403
Lambert, 224, 319, 429, 431
Lamden, 114
Lamennais, 243
Lanahan, 125

Lanas, 47
Lancaster, 35, 270
Lancelott, 259
Landing at Jamestown, 163
Landon, 391
Landrican, 108
Lane, 94, 131, 148, 299, 392, 416, 468
Laney, 22
Lang, 93
Langdale, 59
Langdon, 162
Langfit, 84
Langfitt, 149
Langley, 186, 467, 468
Langton, 433
Lanhan, 397
Lanhart, 35
Lanier, 160, 425
Lanman, 7, 374, 425
Lansdale, 177, 198, 308, 364
Lansdowne, 441
Lansing, 273
Lantz, 164
Lapham, 26
Laporte, 140, 479
Larabee, 64
Laramee, 167
Lardner, 70, 224, 301
Lare, 35, 413
Larken, 380
Larkin, 17, 36, 209, 374, 388
Larned, 29, 49, 108, 228
Larner, 236, 252, 325
Larson, 220
Lash, 102
Laskey, 178
Lassell, 13
Lasselle, 209
Latham, 36, 42, 88, 262, 343, 394
Lathan, 394
Latimer, 368
Latimre, 333
Latly, 326
Latrobe, 248

Latta, 456
Laub, 66, 70, 265, 266
Laurence, 246
Laurenson, 157
Laurent, 87
Laurie, 35
Lauxman, 170
Law, 36, 54, 158, 210, 261, 273, 374
Lawrence, 11, 35, 192, 220, 264, 321, 413, 482
Lawrenson, 351
Laws, 159, 220
Lawson, 11, 36, 77, 102, 228, 403
Lay, 106, 219, 272
Layton, 416
Lazell, 214, 258, 438
Lazelle, 427
Lazenby, 36, 163, 234
Lazzele, 164
Le Case, 47
Le Caze, 14, 191
Le Compte, 368
Lea, 263, 301, 317, 469
Leach, 9
Leachman, 60
Leakin, 442
Leamy, 403
Lear, 35, 287, 289, 441
Learned, 373
Lease, 146
Leavitt, 111
Leber, 125
Leckie, 36
Lecky, 47
Lecompte, 143
Lecompton, 319
Lee, 35, 96, 115, 131, 156, 160, 172, 177, 184, 195, 198, 202, 214, 215, 228, 233, 252, 253, 265, 281, 287, 290, 291, 296, 320, 339, 361, 374, 375, 437, 469, 479, 482
Leech, 73
Leeds, 312, 338
Lefevre, 35

Leguori, 383
Leigh, 315
Leiper, 332
Lelaway, 252
Lemmon, 388
Lengair, 380
Lenox, 11, 25, 35, 183, 227, 278, 279, 280, 310, 320, 345, 470
Lenthall, 35, 229
Lentz, 14
Leonard, 51, 172, 235
Lephard, 35
Lepreux, 294
Lerock, 182
Leslie, 328
Lester, 60, 126, 335
Letcher, 262
Letmate, 71
Levell, 222
Levely, 88
Lever, 220
Levy, 368, 373, 406, 427, 469, 470, 472
Lewis, 2, 17, 32, 35, 36, 44, 66, 80, 83, 100, 102, 124, 157, 158, 164, 167, 184, 200, 207, 209, 210, 215, 229, 252, 253, 263, 278, 284, 340, 353, 368, 369, 375, 381, 384, 387, 393, 398, 416, 442, 443, 450, 480
Lex, 274, 403
Leyburn, 77
Leyden, 322
Libbey, 35, 139
Libby, 173
Liberty, 150
Licklider, 79
Lieb, 166
Lieber, 472
Liederkerke, 433
Lieper, 419
Lightell, 35
Lightfoot, 131, 140, 370, 451
Lightner, 49, 67
Ligon, 131

Lilliendahl, 126
Limeburner, 151
Lincoln, 224, 336, 337, 344, 384
Lind, 296
Linderman, 200
Lindsay, 35, 87, 130, 277, 347, 398, 469
Lindsey, 235
Lindsley, 35, 155, 206, 302
Lindsly, 35
Lingo, 416
Linkins, 378
Linn, 115, 116, 166, 463
Linthicum, 220, 451
Linton, 84, 133, 141, 184, 225, 264, 417
Lippett, 253
Lippitt, 70, 262, 274
Lipscomb, 235, 347
Lisberger, 45, 301
Litle, 35
Little, 35, 86, 92, 111, 152, 157, 174, 201, 231, 237, 252, 259, 338, 467
Little Thunder, 379, 408
Littlefield, 11, 64
Littlejohn, 416
Littleton, 397, 475
Litzenberry, 235
Livermore, 416
Livingston, 32, 54, 55, 63, 167, 210, 231, 286, 289, 312, 374, 376, 380, 464
Lizear, 145
Llangolen, 176
Lloyd, 183, 217, 269, 306, 356, 394, 398, 406, 447, 449
Loch Willow, 451
Locke, 26, 447
Locker, 162
Lockery, 25, 35, 76, 111, 172, 320
Lockey, 35
Lockwood, 71, 81, 261, 368
Locust Grove, 361
Lodge, 35

Logan, 35, 146, 160, 179, 187, 222, 230, 449
Lomax, 448, 469
Lombard, 138, 379
Lombardi, 35
Long, 47, 99, 102, 284, 368
Long Meadow, 27, 186
Long Old Fields, 15, 70, 162
Longfellow, 113, 436
Looby, 89, 164
Loomis, 126, 207
Lopedo, 123
Loranger, 57
Lord, 128, 134, 207, 252, 279
Loring, 277, 288, 293, 334
Lorino, 419
Lorman, 447
Louden, 35
Loudon, 442, 462
Loughborough, 175, 187, 235
Loughead, 102
Loughery, 455
Loughney, 52
Loup, 266, 277
Love, 122, 368
Lovejoy, 170
Lovelace, 13, 405
Loveland, 344, 347, 371
Lovell, 176, 180, 212, 220, 375, 389
Lovett, 239, 401
Low, 369
Lowe, 115, 121, 159, 233, 240, 242, 287, 291, 453
Lowell, 468
Lower Gisboro, 474
Lowndes, 318, 373
Lowrey, 175, 181, 246, 253
Lowry, 60, 160, 368, 374
Loyall, 231, 273, 357, 376
Lucas, 16, 35, 418
Luce, 375
Lucket, 385
Luckett, 81, 226, 471
Lueber, 147

Lugenbeel, 284, 292
Lugenbeil, 119
Lujan, 266
Lukins, 337
Lull, 273
Lumin, 170
Lumpkin, 36, 96, 101
Lumsden, 125
Lundy, 36
Lunsford, 73
Lunt, 36
Lusby, 253
Lusher, 165
Lutz, 12, 193
Lyall, 379
Lyddane, 49, 318
Lyell, 76
Lygon, 131
Lykes, 36
Lyle, 280
Lyles, 82, 252
Lyman, 249, 457
Lynan, 323
Lynch, 1, 16, 31, 70, 73, 76, 81, 142, 143, 154, 172, 180, 219, 235, 278, 369, 421
Lyndall, 36
Lynde, 288, 290, 438
Lynn, 115, 167
Lyon, 65, 96, 167, 193, 317, 375, 396
Lyons, 23, 235, 468
Lyttle, 6

M

Macdonald, 82, 160
Macey, 37
Machell, 246
Mack, 261
Mackall, 12, 36, 178
Mackay, 192, 267
Mackey, 37
Mackie, 259
Maclay, 371
Macleod, 401

MacLeod, 255
Macomb, 342
Macomber, 301
Mactier, 185
MacWilliams, 378
Madan, 271
Madder, 104
Maddox, 265, 327, 448
Mademoiselle Rachel, 246
Madigan, 273, 369
Madison, 79, 114, 139, 355
Maffitt, 369
Magar, 36
Magaw, 333, 375
Magee, 100, 207
Magill, 391, 461, 464
Maginn, 182
Magle, 168
Maglennen, 469
Magraw, 57, 123
Magruder, 8, 10, 47, 62, 73, 84, 103, 117, 162, 178, 179, 184, 201, 216, 217, 219, 222, 235, 237, 239, 273, 282, 321, 365, 366, 374, 463, 476
Maguire, 36, 112, 156, 183, 230, 270
Mahan, 59
Maher, 256, 371
Mahers, 326
Mahon, 463
Mahoney, 399
Mahony, 326, 458
<u>Maine Giant</u>, 60
Maitland, 167
Major, 52, 270
Makibben, 447
Malbon, 271
Mallaby, 369
Mallet, 14, 47, 191
Mallett, 36, 180
Mallory, 213, 340, 345, 447
Malone, 211, 253
Malvern, 7
Mandt, 135
Mangenn, 427

Mangum, 405
Mangun, 269
Manierre, 256
Mankin, 390
Mankins, 380
Mann, 357, 451
Manners, 231
Manning, 310, 319, 340, 343, 368, 425
Mantle, 52
Mantz, 36
Maples, 426
Marberry, 220
Marbury, 143, 153, 167, 169, 189, 208, 234, 431
Marceron, 37, 158, 384, 469
March, 160, 369
Marchand, 374
Marchant, 65, 169
Marcy, 273, 300
Mardis, 37
Marin, 369
Marion, 167, 359, 434
Markell, 36
Markland, 352
Markoe, 259
Marks, 67, 132, 244, 247, 355, 411, 442
Markwood, 36, 37, 449
Marlow, 36, 319, 472
Marr, 9
Marriott, 104, 167
Marrisetti, 340
Marsh, 1, 18, 20, 60, 75, 81, 126, 167, 358, 364, 396
Marshal, 355
Marshall, 37, 54, 64, 71, 93, 118, 142, 162, 169, 256, 260, 284, 285, 292, 296, 297, 306, 315, 325, 332, 352, 353, 355, 402, 442
Marshfield, 106, 130
Marston, 12, 44, 374
Martin, 23, 28, 36, 37, 66, 67, 72, 104, 159, 167, 172, 180, 185, 210, 226, 233, 252, 256, 268, 280, 295, 349, 415, 423, 468, 477
Martinet, 234
Martinez, 266
Maryman, 165, 191, 320
Maser, 325
Masi, 36, 57, 183, 268, 272, 275
Mask, 320
Maskell, 263
Mason, 15, 18, 22, 36, 92, 107, 115, 194, 222, 248, 348, 368, 413, 418, 424, 425, 452
Mason & Dixon Line, 248
Masonic Hall, 100
Massasoit Guards, 330
Massey, 36, 105, 207, 398, 443
Massi, 270
Mather, 88, 214
Mathews, 36, 266, 315
Mathias, 297
Matranga, 433
Matterson, 167
Matthews, 156, 253, 306, 372, 481
Mattingly, 18, 37, 99, 106, 172, 180, 247, 306
Maubourg, 326
Maughan, 169
Maul, 340
Maupin, 226
Maury, 36, 58, 60, 67, 88, 108, 160, 183, 214, 238, 368, 436, 474
Maxcy, 37
Maximilian, 136
Maxwell, 168, 231, 301, 376, 412, 426
May, 36, 43, 65, 133, 158, 171, 269, 270, 282, 381, 438
Mayberry, 272
Mayhew, 443
Mayhugh, 309
Maynadier, 118, 228, 291
Maynard, 87, 184, 432
Mayo, 17, 209, 237, 301, 328, 375
Mayorga, 427
Mayson, 405

Maywood, 23
McAlister, 169
McAllister, 421
McAlwee, 428
McAram, 174
McArann, 369
McArthur, 121, 284, 292
McBee, 253
McBlair, 36, 158, 184, 374
McBride, 36, 159
McCabe, 345, 468
McCafferty, 316
McCall, 229, 287, 289
McCalla, 169, 173
McCallen, 19
McCallion, 314, 456
McCandless, 36
McCann, 198, 375
McCardle, 156, 453
McCarron, 418
McCarthy, 36, 233
McCarty, 14, 36
McCaslin, 102
McCathran, 87, 233, 250, 384, 455
McCauley, 174, 214, 238, 243, 252, 374, 375, 400
McCauly, 373
McCauslin, 224
McCaw, 151
McCay, 197
McCeney, 344
McCerren, 11, 60, 92, 191
McChesney, 36
McClay, 336, 337
McClean, 416
McCleary, 379
McClellan, 80, 81, 146, 281, 291
McClelland, 36, 51, 122, 270
McClery, 207, 236
McClintock, 39, 73, 310
McCloskey, 227, 313
McCluney, 240
McClure, 260
McCollum, 183, 375

McComb, 250, 364, 384
McConchi, 36
McConnell, 20, 305
McCord, 186
McCorkle, 336, 337, 375
McCormack, 220
McCormich, 155
McCormick, 36, 42, 43, 46, 59, 60, 70, 73, 87, 150, 178, 184, 430
McCoskey, 42
McCoy, 82
McCrabb, 16, 28
McCracken, 36
McCrea, 176, 206, 231, 254, 273, 376
McCree, 246
McCreery, 9, 104, 158, 167
McCue, 308
McCulloh, 51, 96
McCullom, 428
McCullough, 119, 204, 286, 293, 416, 421
McCullum, 13
McCurdy, 83
McCutchen, 36, 185, 263, 363
McCutcheon, 217
McDaniel, 327, 341
McDermott, 132, 174
McDermut, 374
McDevitt, 394
McDonald, 82, 107, 177, 253, 314, 379, 472
McDongas, 466
McDonough, 17, 252, 369, 425, 466
McDowell, 19, 97, 138
McDuell, 373
McElfresh, 230, 335, 425
McEniry, 183
McFadden, 345, 477
McFaddin, 340
McFadin, 71
McFalls, 125
McFarlan, 272, 341
McFarland, 37, 167, 253, 276, 340
McFerran, 17, 70

McFerren, 438
McGarr, 306
McGarrity, 270
McGarvey, 16, 89, 164
McGary, 375
McGeary, 389
McGee, 36, 125, 217, 252, 297
McGill, 26, 170, 179, 227, 240, 430
McGinn, 301
McGinnis, 197
McGinty, 372
McGlaughlin, 249
McGlue, 36, 253
McGowan, 103, 140, 167
McGown, 103
McGrann, 36
McGrath, 5
McGraw, 70
McGregor, 205, 247
McGuffy, 274
McGuiny, 203
McGuire, 161, 184, 185, 203, 253, 280, 299, 431, 443, 479
McGunnagle, 328
McGunnegle, 237, 375
McHenry, 20, 415
McIlhany, 170
McIlvaine, 249
McIntire, 11, 60, 93, 208, 286, 458
McIntosh, 73, 104, 122, 167, 211, 293, 333
McIntyre, 36, 167, 461
McKaig, 273
McKean, 183, 185, 373
McKee, 93, 125, 266
McKeever, 422
McKelden, 147
McKenna, 2, 142, 410
McKenney, 392, 451
McKenzie, 138
McKeon, 36
McKibben, 244
McKibbin, 120
McKim, 37, 117

McKin, 253
McKinley, 315
McKinstry, 374, 387
McKissack, 192, 239
McKnew, 37, 235, 252, 279
McKnight, 36, 37, 70
McLane, 11, 60, 196, 396
McLaughlin, 36, 61, 93, 95, 115, 266, 366, 369
McLauley, 398
McLean, 306, 438
McLellan, 194
McLelland, 142
McLemore, 24, 74
McLennan, 306
McLeod, 148, 201
McMahon, 88, 171, 192
McManners, 52
McMaster, 348
McMeekin, 297
McMilan, 43
McMillan, 11
McMim, 244
McMinn, 37
McMullen, 45, 239
McNab, 118, 210, 435
McNairy, 367
McNally, 167, 239, 287, 364, 446
McNamee, 36, 174, 303
McNaughton, 127, 235
McNeill, 164, 387
McNeir, 3, 175, 235
McNenny, 173, 276
McNerhany, 250, 384
McNiel, 136
McNutt, 380
McO'Blennis, 103
McPeak, 37
McPherson, 37, 46, 47, 84, 87, 235, 253, 366, 394, 400
McPiers, 37
McQuade, 207
McRae, 36, 42, 460
McRay, 176

McWilliam, 36
McWilliams, 36, 271, 341
Mead, 59, 95
Meade, 49, 56, 57, 77, 178, 226, 235, 262, 263, 369, 449, 451
Meads, 273
Means, 243
Mears, 12
Measher, 429
Measury, 468
Mechlin, 73
Mechling, 285
Medenhall, 380
Medical College, 100, 211, 269
Meehan, 36, 186, 472
Meek, 89, 386
Meem, 250
Mees, 33
Megallon, 314
Mehegan, 354
Meiere, 261
Meincke, 56
Meister, 314
Melvin, 185, 421, 455
Mendell, 281
Menschifoff, 302
Menser, 353
Mercer, 64, 160, 286, 369, 373
Merchant, 69, 246, 347, 360, 439
Meredith, 336, 337, 344
Merman, 36
Merrick, 7, 101, 109, 219, 263, 456
Merrifield, 121, 287, 288, 294
Merrill, 14, 58, 65, 74, 214, 257, 258, 404
Merritt, 102, 416, 477
Merriweather, 94
Merryman, 36, 414
Metcalfe, 329
Meteer, 210
Methodist, 334
Metropolitan Railroad, 313
Mettrigger, 82
Meung, 21

Meyer, 311, 354
Meyler, 1
Michie, 296
Mickun, 36
Middleton, 13, 36, 66, 92, 98, 112, 155, 174, 184, 208, 210, 233, 388, 389, 435, 443
Mierson, 402
Milbourne, 101
Milburn, 36, 37, 233, 474
Miles, 36, 53, 60, 142, 217, 227, 270, 306, 425
Miller, 36, 37, 54, 68, 81, 87, 88, 102, 117, 120, 139, 148, 178, 194, 209, 217, 234, 263, 270, 274, 306, 311, 332, 346, 355, 366, 368, 371, 382, 395, 400, 401, 418, 442, 451, 456, 458, 466
Milligan, 113
Millington, 365
Mills, 31, 36, 94, 95, 97, 102, 167, 215, 330, 365, 418, 439, 463
Milstead, 480
Miltimore, 107
Milward, 131
Min, 115
Minard, 11
Minchin, 171
Minnegerode, 169
Minor, 226, 296, 299, 374, 375, 422
Minot, 101, 145, 305
Mintas, 343
Minter, 121
Mir, 70
Miranda, 123
Mirick, 145, 316
Mish, 160
Mishler, 167
Misrain, 10
Missroon, 214, 238, 374
Mitchell, 5, 12, 36, 37, 48, 61, 66, 70, 88, 93, 104, 167, 180, 188, 192, 212, 225, 243, 252, 329, 363, 374, 375, 398, 400, 403, 451, 472, 481

Mitford, 50
Mixon, 254
Mockabee, 113, 180
Mockbee, 224, 334
Moeller, 369
Moffett, 171
Mohler, 36, 450
Mohun, 30, 157, 184, 235, 248, 427
Moise, 181, 197, 244
Molesworth, 116
Molesworthy, 419
Molina, 56, 58
Monagan, 59
Monaghan, 80
Monatt, 468
Monroe, 87, 125, 284, 290, 315, 360, 386
Montague, 210, 263, 270
Montgomery, 26, 100, 102, 163, 215, 306, 352, 470, 473, 477
Montholon, 407
Montpelier, 233, 471
Montrose, 235
Moody, 138, 300
Mooers, 319
Mooney, 37, 264
Moore, 20, 26, 28, 37, 48, 62, 64, 67, 89, 93, 102, 124, 137, 145, 199, 205, 208, 220, 225, 232, 261, 265, 269, 271, 272, 282, 283, 290, 298, 309, 310, 315, 324, 355, 364, 391, 394, 402, 403, 406, 411, 416, 430, 436, 464, 467
Moores, 369, 467
Moors, 9, 70
Moran, 22, 36, 308, 333, 372
Morant, 133
Morarity, 89
More, 68
Morehead, 4, 8, 315
Moreira, 270, 271
Moreland, 36, 37, 73, 109, 304
Morelion, 36
Morell, 83

Moreno, 270
Morff, 380
Morfit, 36, 169, 475
Morgan, 13, 14, 27, 37, 69, 74, 97, 102, 183, 184, 224, 226, 263, 266, 301, 327, 337, 369, 374, 409, 423, 452
Morhiser, 268
Morison, 114, 329
Morland, 53
Mormons, 260
Morrell, 77
Morrill, 467
Morris, 2, 9, 11, 12, 37, 53, 54, 60, 62, 66, 75, 93, 112, 192, 283, 284, 330, 352, 358, 369, 375, 383, 384, 401, 406, 418, 441
Morrisett, 343
Morrison, 74, 157, 235, 288, 289, 312, 357
Morriss, 481
Morrissey, 115
Morrow, 37, 106, 221, 277, 287
Morse, 88, 181, 353
Morsel, 382
Morsell, 28, 37, 109, 113, 142, 281, 407
Morson, 2
Mortimer, 265, 455
Morton, 37, 51, 94, 116, 389
Morton View, 455
Morven, 140
Morvin, 360
Mosby, 265, 480
Moscrop, 36
Moseley, 154, 155
Mosely, 37
Moses, 36, 285, 290
Mosher, 102, 239, 328
Moss, 54, 233, 458
Moss' farm, 296
Mott, 416, 421
Moulder, 36, 189, 244
Moulon, 70

Moultrie, 219
Mount Airy, 131, 231, 233
Mount Henry, 185, 188
Mount Oak, 312
Mount Pleasant, 318, 378
Mount Vernon, 272, 352, 358, 400, 403, 440, 441
Mount Vesuvius, 211
Mount Washington, 362
Mountain House, 323
Mountz, 152, 178
Mouton, 244, 479
Mower, 289
Mowry, 283
Moxley, 36, 99, 271
Moyer, 87
Mudd, 36, 127, 224, 306
Muebet, 305
Muerant, 262
Muir, 164
Mulberry Grove, 475
Muld, 323
Mullan, 283
Mullard, 398
Mullen, 479
Muller, 246
Mullican, 53
Mullikin, 9, 281, 312, 449
Mullin, 47
Mullins, 286, 474
Mulloway, 102
Mulloy, 183, 209, 236
Muncaster, 126, 201
Munck, 481
Mundell, 261
Munder, 183
Munford, 2
Munoz, 394
Munro, 57
Munroe, 54, 99, 178, 210
Munster, 135
Muntz, 473
Murat, 143, 243, 398
Murck, 36

Murdaugh, 375
Murdock, 67, 234, 428, 468
Murilla, 217
Murphey, 67, 145
Murphy, 123, 142, 179, 186, 215, 240, 310, 323, 432, 444, 451, 468
Murray, 11, 99, 118, 167, 261, 262, 266, 270, 369, 372, 391, 412, 426, 474, 477
Muse, 42, 374
Mustin, 249
Myer, 36, 227, 464
Myers, 36, 45, 53, 83, 120, 167, 210, 233, 273, 292, 343, 354, 368, 422
Mygatt, 375

N

N H Gaz, 16
N Y Historical Society, 401
Nabrega, 210
Nachimoff, 304
Nailor, 37, 475
Nairn, 179, 459
Nairy, 37
Nalley, 137
Nalls, 463
Napier, 11
Napoleon, 151, 190, 309
Napper, 197
Narine, 394
Nash, 137, 317, 343, 393, 434, 445, 475
Nasihyth, 402
Nat'l Eating House, 361
Navy Yard, Wash, 250
Naylor, 11, 15, 25, 37, 97, 148, 185, 188, 218, 253, 278, 279, 280, 310, 320, 327, 423, 431, 470
Naysmith, 403
Neal, 127, 204, 306, 339, 467
Neale, 37, 266, 270
Needles, 132
Negus, 214
Neilson, 6, 44, 84

Nelson, 53, 83, 109, 137, 153, 155, 158, 162, 183, 189, 219, 267, 284, 288, 292, 315, 467
Nenning, 182
Nesmith, 394
Nessler, 210
Neumann, 170
Nevers, 186
Neville, 368
Nevins, 259
Nevitt, 75, 174, 197
New Hampshire Veterans, 467
new steam-engine, 42
Newbold, 337, 357, 371
Newby, 286
Newcomb, 43
Newcomer, 415
Newell, 212, 220, 368, 389, 423, 468
Newhall, 310, 390
Newham, 351
Newington, 466
Newlin, 403
Newman, 37, 49, 108, 271, 375, 453
Newton, 93, 210, 215, 371
Nicholas, 189, 368
Nicholls, 37, 119, 237, 258, 404, 437
Nichols, 111, 172, 214, 268, 372
Nicholson, 37, 54, 146, 160, 207, 272, 274, 276, 277, 347, 351, 367, 373, 415, 425
Nickel, 88
Nicolaievna, 136
Nicolaivitch, 136
Nicolay, 126
Niles, 231, 477
Nimmo, 354
Ninon, 54
Nippes, 74
Nippins, 59
Nixdorf, 37
Nixon, 90
Noah, 113
Noble, 25, 87, 174, 203, 228, 267, 273, 369

Nock, 77, 88
Noerr, 412
Nohrden, 67
Noland, 23, 257, 318, 369
Nones, 113
Norgan, 207
Norment, 389, 444
Norris, 22, 37, 42, 86, 130, 167, 207, 282
Norse, 37
North, 233, 304, 394
Northampton, 161
Northrop, 41
Northup, 394
Norton, 59, 301, 312
Norwood, 69, 237, 238, 310
Nosay, 343
Nourse, 61, 100, 123, 249, 299, 347, 370
Nowell, 107
Nowton, 271
Noyes, 37, 100, 207, 235, 304, 308, 356
Nuckolls, 392
Nunn, 358
Nunnally, 2
Nuth, 6
Nutt, 150, 183, 468
Nuttrill, 15
Nye, 433

O

O'Bannon, 437
O'Brian, 58, 346
O'Brien, 210, 243, 251, 306, 360, 412, 418
O'Connor, 37, 170
O'Doherty, 182
O'Donnell, 37, 270
O'Donnoghue, 94, 271
O'Farrel, 295
O'Ferrall, 37
O'Flaherty, 416, 421
O'Hallaron, 210

O'Hara, 120
O'Hare, 432
O'Harra, 37
O'Kane, 341, 371
O'Leary, 183
O'Neal, 92, 248
O'Neale, 37, 126, 413
O'Neil, 157
O'Neill, 16, 271
O'Phelan, 338
O'Sullivan, 79
O'Toole, 429
Oak Hill, 27
Oak Hill Cemetery, 208, 276, 344, 403
Oak Mount, 299
Oakendale, 257
Oakes, 120, 282, 291
Oakland, 180
Oakley, 375
Ober, 185, 250, 384
Obermuller, 402
Obregon, 455
Ochiltree, 369
Odell, 349
Offut, 53, 137
Offutt, 13, 149, 152, 216, 307, 361, 408, 412, 426, 445
Ogden, 88, 231, 233, 319, 322, 327, 368, 376, 439, 446
Ogier, 68
Ogle, 278
Oglethorpe, 421
Ohlsen, 389
old age, 460
Oldenburg, 338
Olive, 211
Oliver, 43, 68, 177
Olmstead, 369
Olney, 74, 457
Oren, 338
Orendorf, 265
Orme, 37, 114, 163, 178, 217, 235, 253, 265, 357, 367

Orr, 94
Osborne, 24, 37
Osbourn, 178
Osbourne, 380
Osgodby, 260
Osgood, 207
Ostrander, 113
Otis, 106, 286, 292, 377
Ott, 423, 451
Otterback, 376, 454
Otto, 48
Ould, 98, 101, 426
Ouseley, 423
Owen, 30, 37, 184, 229, 231, 375
Owens, 99, 183, 352, 354, 458
Oyster, 235

P

Paaneah, 10
Pacetti, 266
Pacetty, 106
Packer, 337
Packsood, 141
Packwood, 444
Padget, 188
Padgett, 250, 384
Page, 37, 134, 154, 159, 169, 172, 214, 234, 238, 315, 340, 356, 368, 374, 419, 464, 468
Page's wharf, 389
Pagenstecher, 396
Pages, 108
Paige, 20, 70, 222
Paillard, 426
Paine, 262, 368, 450
Pairo, 99, 100, 223, 451
Palmer, 48, 57, 58, 67, 70, 120, 147, 185, 191, 215, 230, 282, 287, 288, 289, 291, 320, 335, 368, 396, 439, 444, 457, 468, 471
Pancoast, 37
Papedick, 407
Papendick, 402
Paradeda, 215

Pargene, 116
Parham, 163, 456
Paris, 392
Parish, 371
Park, 432
Parke, 183, 193
Parker, 2, 14, 37, 38, 59, 70, 102, 108, 167, 183, 199, 203, 234, 237, 253, 298, 319, 328, 332, 340, 355, 368, 369, 374, 375, 389, 401, 413, 417, 448, 467, 468, 473, 476
Parkes, 467
Parkhurst, 207
Parkins, 450
Parkinson, 123, 439
Parks, 12, 124, 169, 218
Parr, 478
Parrish, 48, 256
Parrott, 148
Parry, 98, 310, 409
Parsens, 184
Parsons, 14, 37, 65, 137, 149, 194, 227, 233, 371, 465, 467
Parvin, 338
Patem, 343
Patrick, 202
Patten, 467
Patterson, 12, 64, 71, 108, 119, 147, 193, 237, 249, 283, 291, 298, 360, 380, 446, 449
Pattison, 83
Patton, 1, 38, 110, 135, 273, 338, 467
Pattridge, 468
Paudeen, 115
Paul, 7, 85, 317
Paulding, 224, 234, 250, 301, 374
Paull, 398
Paulovna, 136
Paulowna, 135
<u>Pay for Gen Scott</u>, 414
Payne, 1, 38, 98, 114, 127, 270, 297
Paynter, 464
Peabody, 135
Peachy, 331

Peaco, 95, 306, 310, 450
Peacock, 14, 399
Peake, 384
Peale, 75, 96, 193, 403, 440, 441
Pearce, 285, 369
Pearson, 37, 38, 157, 309, 369, 374, 425, 473
Pease, 214, 258, 438
Peavy, 467
Pebworth, 343
Peck, 13, 37, 125, 168, 183, 209, 269, 314, 368, 425, 439, 456
Pecke, 250
Pedro, 143
Peebles, 481
Peerce, 113, 177, 252, 311
Peete, 343
Pegram, 263, 282, 398
Pegran, 397
Peirce, 413
Pelissier, 246
Pelot, 231, 376
Pender, 286, 292
Pendergast, 398
Pendergrast, 70, 163, 177, 214, 238, 373, 375
Pendleton, 166, 184, 263, 474
Penington, 107, 482
Penn, 278
Penney, 319
Pennington, 167, 295, 369
Penrice, 271
Pepper, 13, 43, 184, 363, 398, 463
Percival, 368
Percy, 409
Peregoy, 396
Perene, 305
Perkins, 18, 38, 78, 122, 403, 416
Perrie, 84, 87, 300, 473, 476
Perrier, 316
Perrine, 72
Perrone, 326

Perry, 6, 37, 70, 95, 160, 191, 208, 216, 217, 235, 238, 253, 369, 374, 395, 425, 461
Peter, 37, 220
Peterbaugh, 207
Peters, 3, 38, 217, 256, 263, 322, 345, 363, 466
Peterson, 11
Petigru, 368
Petit, 271
Petrie, 330
Pettibone, 88, 202
Pettigru, 219, 425
Petty, 64, 461
Peugh, 38, 252
Pew, 357, 371
Peyton, 173, 244, 473
Pharaoh, 10
Phelps, 28, 37, 41, 46, 47, 56, 68, 93, 105, 125, 137, 139, 143, 157, 163, 170, 203, 221, 230, 260, 300, 337, 344, 357, 360, 374, 375, 380, 384, 413, 447
Phenix, 375
Phifer, 121
Philip, 38, 158, 264, 374
Philips, 81, 250, 270, 271
Phillippe, 143
Phillips, 21, 37, 38, 53, 60, 179, 200, 226, 239, 243, 256, 325, 338, 384, 457, 481
Philp, 108
Phinney, 220, 390, 394
Phipps, 310
Pianozi, 190
Pickens, 148
Pickering, 374, 425
Pickett, 119, 249, 285, 293
Pickrel, 37
Pickrell, 135, 151, 211, 271, 443, 477
Pierce, 25, 173, 175, 224, 235, 276, 318, 342, 409, 444
Piermont, 64
Pierpont, 3

Pierson, 20
Piggot, 397
Pigott, 76
Pike, 238, 468
Pilgrims, 180
Pillsbury, 162, 457
Pinckney, 80
Pine, 441
Piney Point, 180, 216, 314
Pinkarton, 250
Pinkney, 374, 463
Piseros, 77
Pitcher, 118
Pizzini, 270, 271
Plain, 431
Plant, 37, 173, 333
Platt, 38, 368, 410
Pleasant Plains, 443
Pleasanton, 67, 145, 282, 290
Pleasants, 249
Pleasonton, 57, 101
Plowden, 42, 270, 415
Plowman, 99, 396
Plummer, 111, 285
Plumsill, 38
Plympton, 285
Pocahontas, 78
Pock, 399
Poe, 270, 391, 409
Poinsett, 148
Pointer, 88, 93
Poisal, 125
Poland, 249
Polk, 12, 18, 127, 165, 182, 259, 322, 353, 380
Polkinhorn, 184, 255, 371, 410
Pollard, 27
Pollock, 25, 83
Pomeroy, 309
Ponsonby, 116
Pook, 250, 384
Pool, 26, 59, 70
Poole, 115, 186
Poor, 160, 161, 374, 381, 425, 467

Poore, 94
Pope, 14, 116, 182, 374
Porcher, 14, 194, 219, 261
Porter, 9, 70, 73, 104, 167, 272, 273, 299, 312, 317, 323, 338, 369, 417, 450, 460
Portman, 74, 160
Posey, 207, 265, 271
Poshner, 267
Post, 416
Poston, 252, 405
Potentini, 466
Potter, 17, 83, 167, 220, 236, 270, 320, 467, 468
Potts, 210, 475
Poulson, 11
Poulter, 398
Poussin, 217
Powel, 441
Powell, 20, 38, 68, 78, 84, 115, 167, 172, 176, 194, 224, 232, 244, 257, 287, 289, 294, 301, 358, 374, 375, 444, 472
Power, 14, 37
Powers, 5, 37, 83, 102, 183, 194, 262, 343, 429
Praeda, 210
Prather, 38, 432
Pratt, 37, 38, 54, 164, 259, 357, 382
Pray, 24
Prentiss, 221, 233, 374
Prescott, 336, 337, 344
Preston, 38, 53, 60, 93, 147, 192
Prettyman, 232, 480
Prewitt, 12
Price, 103, 164, 220, 261, 266, 374
Priddy, 88
Priest, 394, 464
Prince, 284, 285, 292
Pringle, 263, 337, 357
Prioleau, 43
privateer **Chasseur**, 43
Proctor, 140, 371, 468
propellar **Arctic**, 220
propeller **Arctic**, 212, 389
propeller **Montezuma**, 323
propeller **Oregon**, 159
Prospect Hill, 21
Protestant cemetery, 128
Prout, 31, 37, 38
Provest, 37
Provost, 183
Prudhomme, 271
Pugh, 207, 305, 325, 447
Puig, 70
Pulizzi, 287, 290, 439
Pullin, 207
Pullman, 199
Pumphrey, 99, 178, 185, 203, 215, 217, 451
Pumroy, 274
Pupo, 37
Purdon, 401
Purdy, 253, 261, 274, 335
Purl, 37
Pursell, 411
Purviance, 165, 219
Puryear, 262
Putnam, 19, 66, 70, 196, 362, 372, 406
Putney, 467
Pyne, 104, 111, 204, 239, 276, 348, 428
Pyne-y-oh-te-mah, 194
Pywell, 90

Q

Quackenbush, 374
Quail, 385
Quarle, 435
Queen, 23, 112, 210, 306, 375
Queen Isabella, 143
Queen Mary, 315
Queen Victoria, 6, 151, 478
Quick, 393
Quigenfeuse, 345
Quigley, 142, 451
Quimby, 467
Quin, 113

Quinan, 438
Quinette, 416
Quinn, 38, 369

R

Rabe, 270
Radcliff, 208, 253, 280
Radcliffe, 416
Radford, 374, 437
Rady, 267
Radyieninski, 123
Radziminski, 286
Raglan, 212, 261, 302
Rahin, 249
Rainey, 375
Raley, 38, 107
Rall, 58
Rallston, 70
Ralston, 435
Ramsay, 108, 126, 287, 289
Ramsey, 11, 60, 61, 73, 93, 95, 368
Ranal, 167
Rand, 312
Randal, 286, 354
Randall, 24, 38, 44, 219, 256
Randle, 480
Randolph, 38, 129, 137, 144, 173, 233, 261, 288, 289, 315, 343, 361, 373
Randoph, 211
Ransom, 163, 286, 287, 289, 291
Ranson, 177
Ransour, 167
Raoul, 59
Raoult, 317
Ratcliff, 373
Ratcliffe, 355
Rathbone, 428
Rathman, 304
Ratrie, 38, 103, 482
Ravens, 210
Rawlings, 90, 187, 252, 422
Rawlins, 305, 331
Ray, 38, 210, 254, 349, 373, 404

Rayner, 238
Read, 64, 181, 188, 265, 340, 368, 369, 387, 439
Read, 438
Reade, 262
Reading, 38
Ready, 38
Reardon, 17
Reaver, 42
Reavis, 226
Rector, 101
Recus, 399
Red Sulphur Springs, 164
Reddall, 259
Redden, 482
Reddick, 51
Redfern, 38, 184
Redford, 14
Redin, 1, 135, 148, 158, 199, 314, 431, 456
Redman, 38, 377
Reed, 18, 59, 159, 185, 187, 188, 190, 210, 213, 222, 252, 255, 370, 380
Reeder, 254, 277, 296, 299
Reeler, 38
Reese, 13, 81, 94, 125, 183, 184, 209, 225
Reeve, 2
Reeves, 64, 338
Reichenbach, 350
Reid, 38, 49, 109, 259, 262, 328, 369, 471
Reilly, 63, 157, 389
Remily, 38
Renshaw, 375
Reopel, 68
Revel, 353
Reyburn, 73
Reynolds, 11, 38, 103, 113, 120, 122, 182, 283, 286, 288, 293, 368, 426
Reyworth, 77
Rhea, 325
Rhind, 369, 480
Rhodes, 85, 369, 387

Rice, 42, 53, 60, 75, 93, 107, 192, 270, 303
Rich, 70, 157, 284, 300, 366, 369
Richard, 59
Richards, 199, 306, 350, 367, 413
Richardson, 11, 60, 61, 89, 93, 95, 113, 220, 235, 277, 341, 385, 391, 416, 426, 439, 460, 467, 473
Richey, 125, 411, 455
Richmond, 137
Richter, 88
Ricker, 467
Ricketts, 167
Riddick, 286, 354
Riddle, 57, 191, 274, 466, 467
Rider, 38, 85, 252
Ridgeley, 380
Ridgely, 57, 66, 108, 116, 236, 253, 374, 394
Ridgeway, 92, 336, 337, 344
Ridgway, 11, 60, 110, 201
Ridout, 44
Rigdon, 38
Riger, 367
Riggles, 327
Riggs, 18, 38, 86, 175, 237, 279, 300, 396, 451
Rigoleto, 133
Riley, 9, 13, 38, 104, 155, 159, 167, 170, 183, 184, 210, 243, 276, 298, 310, 314, 371
Ring, 369
Ringgold, 47, 368
Riopel, 52
Ripley, 77
Ritchie, 38, 148, 163, 368, 378
Ritnour, 167
Rittenhouse, 15, 92, 403, 474
<u>Rittenhouse Academy</u>, 317
Ritter, 38, 137
Rivas, 446
Rivers, 219, 413
Rives, 315, 353
Rizer, 371, 402

Roach, 19, 38, 180, 313, 395, 427, 431, 456
Roan, 53, 60
Roane, 315
Robb, 150
Robbins, 392, 442
Robert, 352
Roberts, 38, 152, 167, 172, 323, 335, 413, 416, 425, 427, 436, 447
Robertson, 3, 80, 97, 242, 252, 282, 321, 381, 382, 393, 441
Robespierre, 243
Robey, 38, 85
Robie, 160
Robinson, 43, 69, 71, 82, 85, 102, 134, 153, 167, 183, 217, 229, 252, 253, 262, 270, 283, 301, 326, 332, 335, 354, 369, 380, 382, 394, 398, 446, 455, 467, 468
Roby, 467
Roche, 23, 112, 141, 178, 184, 248, 324
Rochelle, 375
Rock, 63, 171
Rock Hill, 356, 411
Rockwell, 263
Rocky Hill, 441
Roctor, 427
Rodbird, 38
Rodgers, 9, 17, 38, 125, 158, 264, 321, 366, 374
Rodier, 38, 233
Rodman, 14, 74, 281
Rodrigues, 210
Roe, 375
Rogers, 43, 57, 64, 90, 94, 100, 113, 145, 158, 209, 213, 290, 323, 390, 462, 468
Rolande, 369
Rolando, 397, 398
Rolfe, 9, 482
Rollings, 18
Rollins, 165, 467
Romain, 104

Roney, 158, 374
Ronkendorff, 425
Rooker, 57, 70
Rooney, 51
Roosevelt, 230
Rootes, 42, 374
<u>Rosalie</u>, 334
Rose, 3, 59, 157, 281, 340, 345
Rosedale, 230
Ross, 38, 210, 219, 232, 255, 421, 456, 481
Rossell, 118
Roth, 307
Rothschild, 328
Rothwell, 15, 23, 37, 38, 80, 110, 218, 238, 379
Roulhac, 478
Routh, 27
Rover, 408
Rowan, 89, 322, 374
Rowe, 48, 184, 353
Rowecroft, 267
Roy, 283, 284
Royal, 43
Royall, 121
Roye, 176
Rozier, 343
Rudd, 17, 209, 270, 373
Rudder, 393
Rudolph, 46, 59
Ruff, 217, 354
Ruffin, 262
Rugby Academy, 114, 329
Ruger, 290
Rugg, 167
Ruggles, 17, 38, 51, 80, 214, 227, 258, 303, 437
Rumbold, 416
Rumery, 11
Rundell, 467
Ruoff, 234
Rupp, 168, 205, 428
Ruppell, 183

Rush, 336, 337, 338, 341, 342, 344, 418
Rusk, 94
Russ, 443
Russell, 38, 57, 61, 64, 70, 73, 163, 196, 232, 242, 280, 375
<u>Russian railroad</u>, 312
Russum, 215
Rutherford, 160, 223, 379
Rutlidge, 70
Ryan, 202, 482
Ryder, 333, 380
Rye, 38
Ryland, 38
Ryne, 141
Rynex, 346
Rywell, 45

S

Sables, 481
Sack, 27
Sacket, 282
Sackett, 121, 291
Sacramento, 48
Sacrey, 99
Sage, 39, 135
Sailly, 47
Saker, 210
Salazar, 123
Sale, 362
Saler, 416
Salisbury, 347, 388
Salter, 368
Samestay, 25
Sample, 83
Sampson, 347
Samsctag, 55
Samson, 18, 24, 41, 80, 86, 88, 172, 309, 358, 365
Sanchez, 123
Sanders, 266, 306, 353, 479
Sanderson, 160, 184, 298, 395
Sandford, 171
Sandiford, 269

Sands, 38, 39, 215, 374, 415, 474
Sandy, 173
Sanford, 59, 192, 481
Sanger, 250, 384
Sansbury, 77
Santa Anna, 332
Santer, 39
Santos, 153
Sargeant, 289, 338, 449
Sargent, 119, 125, 263, 264, 287, 289, 292, 467, 468
Sartori, 369
Sasscer, 72
Sauer, 39
Saul, 390
Saunders, 38, 46, 48, 253, 335, 353, 368, 460
Saur, 112
Saurbeck, 338
Saut Canal, 249
Sauve, 271
Savage, 12, 70, 72, 192, 271, 394, 441
Sawtelle, 284
Sawyer, 20, 368, 468
Sax, 334
Saxton, 283
Sayers, 203
Scaggs, 327, 451
Scales, 262
Scanlon, 333
Scarburgh, 263
Scarritt, 11, 51, 88, 89
Sceitz, 168
Schaer, 1
Schaffer, 244, 287, 289
Schank, 279
Schaub, 39
Scheel, 325
Schell, 402
Schenck, 9, 191, 239, 263, 374
Schermerhorn, 334
Schiebler, 365
Schley, 219, 351
Schlosser, 125

Schmidt, 126, 306
Schnebley, 38
Schneider, 395
schnr **A G Brown**, 52, 83
schnr **A G Pease**, 307
schnr **Adrian**, 180
schnr **Black Dog**, 413
schnr **Brandywine**, 480
schnr **Conductor**, 318
schnr **Devothea Haynes**, 276
schnr **Effort**, 67
schnr Emma, 273
schnr **Fairview**, 419
schnr **Henry Plantagenet**, 52, 83
schnr **J Fennimore Cooper**, 116
schnr **J H Holmes**, 67
schnr **J Holmes**, 172
schnr **John Clark**, 176
schnr **Little Tour**, 180
schnr **Oregon**, 193
schnr **Scituate**, 94
schnr **Sea Gull**, 73
schnr **Seagull**, 74
schnr **Shark**, 16
schnr-of-war **Bermuda**, 45
Schoeph, 174
Schofield, 328
Schoolcraft, 188
Schoolfield, 345
Schoonmaker, 59
Schott, 382
Schough, 392
Schreiden, 254
Schreiner, 477
Schriver, 45, 398
Schroeder, 3, 140
Schubart, 389
Schulenburg, 416
Schultz, 72
Schwartz, 38, 54, 55
Schwartzman, 209
Schwarzman, 183, 244
Sciferline, 399
Sclater, 325

Scloo, 457
Scofield, 283
Scollay, 394
Scot, 452
Scott, 9, 28, 39, 63, 64, 80, 88, 93, 110, 167, 178, 185, 203, 228, 242, 265, 297, 301, 306, 315, 339, 372, 375, 404, 407, 409, 414, 418, 477, 479
Scoville, 4, 107
Scrivener, 39, 99, 172, 461
Scrivner, 142
Scroggin, 39
Scroyer, 445
Scudder, 151
Seabrook, 71, 77
Searle, 87, 192
Sears, 9, 88, 322
Seat, 11, 51
Seaton, 82, 99, 168, 179, 219, 227, 236
Seaver, 174
Secard, 301
Seccomb, 309
Sedgwick, 204, 283, 286, 291
Segars, 153
Sehisano, 362
Seibel, 38
Seibert, 39
Seitz, 39
Selden, 38, 39, 340, 343, 345, 359, 360, 361, 362, 365, 368, 369, 375, 393, 401, 412, 438, 446, 452
Seldens, 161
Seldon, 169, 353
Selfridge, 374, 425
Selkirk, 81
Semmes, 26, 39, 99, 155, 180, 184, 231, 270, 294, 361, 374, 375, 451, 480
Semple, 273
Sengstack, 38, 275
Serene, 341
Sergeant, 79, 287, 294

Sergler, 247
Servoss, 170
Sessford, 321
Seufferle, 335
Sevenfoot Knoll, 134
Severance, 49
Sewall, 39, 67, 139, 369
Seward, 229, 460
Sewell, 59, 213
Seymour, 139, 210, 448, 464, 478
Shaaf, 121, 293
Shaaff, 7, 284, 288, 289
Shackelford, 4
Shadd, 38
Shadforth, 262, 338
Shakespeare, 10
Shaler, 18
Shankland, 338
Shanks, 39, 99, 198
Shannon, 314, 412, 462
Sharbut, 22
Sharp, 23, 233, 323, 375
Sharpe, 200
Sharpless, 441
Sharpley, 340, 345
Sharratts, 39
Sharretts, 443
Shattuck, 88
Shaughnessy, 27
Shaw, 46, 52, 145, 262, 368, 393, 466
Shayer, 217
Shea, 153
Sheahan, 43
Shearman, 246
Sheckell, 38, 183, 209
Sheckells, 38
Shedd, 88, 185, 468
Shedden, 237
Sheffey, 226, 299
Shekel, 13
Shekell, 184, 272, 352
Sheldon, 256
Shelley, 91
Shenig, 44

Shepard, 70, 262
Shepherd, 15, 38, 90, 227, 261, 369
Sheppard, 222, 389
Shepperd, 231, 261, 286, 294, 295, 376
Sheriff, 207, 296
Sherman, 38, 264, 436
Sherrett, 426
Sherrod, 58
Sherwood, 11, 123, 452
Shew, 389
Shield, 99
Shields, 39, 198, 215, 242, 275, 345, 355, 368, 412, 416, 421, 455
Shiffner, 262
Shinn, 61, 431
ship **Aina**, 56
ship **Alert**, 151
ship **Arago**, 263
ship **Ariel**, 348, 357
ship **Asia**, 443
ship **Atrato**, 45
ship **Beacon Light**, 151
ship **Canon**-20, 409
ship **Colchis**, 306
ship **Cortes**, 420
ship **Dartmouth**, 275
ship **Decatur**, 103
ship **Devonshire**, 156
ship **Donald McKay**, 151
ship **Falmouth**, 128, 316
ship **Fanny Giffney**, 138
ship **Francis A Palmer**, 156
ship **Frolic**, 339
ship **George Turner**, 194
ship **Great Republic**, 151
ship **Griminesia**, 319
ship **Independence**, 132, 264
ship **Isabella Jewett**, 186
ship **James Baines**, 151
ship **James Cheston**, 141, 167, 444
ship **James Foster**, 156
ship **Jamestown**, 340
ship **John**, 264, 413
ship **John Adams**, 264
ship **John Jay**, 105
ship **King Lear**, 151
ship **La Lucie**, 329
ship **Levant**, 98
ship **Lexington**, 215
ship **Lightfoot**, 342
ship **Living Age**, 176
ship **Marathon**, 141
ship **Mayflower**, 322
ship **Merrimack**, 229
ship **Moses Taylor**, 228
ship **North Caro**lina, 167
ship **Peacock**, 193
ship **Pickering**, 65
ship **Potomac**, 224
ship **Preble**, 237, 328
ship **Romance of the Seas**, 350
ship **Saranac**, 98
ship **Thomas Dallett**, 408
ship **Three Bells**, 20
ship **Two Friends**, 167
ship **Vandalia**, 116
ship **Vincennes**, 474
ship **Virgin**, 420
ship **Warren**, 339
ship **Wasp**, 339
ship **West Point**, 156
ship **William Penn**, 384
ship **Wm Layton**, 153
Shipley, 91, 146
Shippen, 159, 163, 177
ships **Cyane & Levant**, 16
ships **Raritan & Dale**, 339
ships **Raritan & Vandalia**, 64
ships **Sophie & Childers**-18, 409
Shiras, 228
Shock, 442
Shoemaker, 42, 102, 167, 174, 235, 276, 312, 357
Short, 43, 103
Shorter, 25, 38, 45, 111, 315
Shoup, 258
Shreve, 70, 371

Shrewsbury, 370
Shrives, 152
Shrock, 4
Shubart, 214
Shubrick, 80, 214, 238, 314, 383
Shugert, 154, 157, 160, 162, 262, 268, 296, 300, 311, 397
Shulze, 9
Shunck, 276
Shuster, 363, 393
Shutter, 221
Shyne, 112
Sibley, 39, 89, 94, 256
Sibrey, 39
Sickels, 469
Sier, 260
Sikes, 254
Silence, 38
Sill, 199
Silvers, 398
Silverter, 393
Simmers, 325
Simmes, 278
Simmons, 59, 91, 99, 229, 280, 369, 451, 458
Simms, 38, 39, 77, 83, 132, 184, 209, 212, 219, 220, 261, 311, 389
Simonds, 252, 368
Simons, 59, 468
Simonson, 151
Simonton, 15, 130
Simpson, 39, 158, 285, 353, 397, 437, 454
Simpton, 43
Sims, 67, 157, 372
Sinclair, 340, 343, 374
Singleton, 371
Sinon, 39, 89
Sioussa, 114
Sirian, 273
Sisson, 39
Sister de Sales, 298
Sister Mary Serena, 304
Sister of Charity, 367

Sisters of Mercy, 298, 383
Skaggs, 186
Skerrett, 231, 301, 375
Skidmore, 132, 233, 479
Skinner, 340, 368, 415
Skirving, 362
Slade, 255
Slamm, 429
Slater, 252, 429
Slaughter, 48, 401
Slavin, 57, 70
Sleight, 331
Slevin, 266
Sleyter, 11
Slicer, 44, 113, 125, 225
Slidell, 165, 208
Slifer, 24
Slight, 15
Slingland, 56
Slingloff, 207
Sloan, 147, 167, 177
Sloat, 368
Slocum, 180, 283, 420
Sloo, 454
sloop of war **Saratoga**, 205
sloop **Rattler**, 397
sloop **St Louis**, 163
sloop **Venture**, 192
sloop-of-war **Albany**, 9, 158
sloop-of-war **Constellation**, 261
sloop-of-war **Falmouth**, 128, 194
sloop-of-war **Peacock**, 21
sloop-of-war **St Louis**, 148
sloop-of-war **Wasp**, 65
Sloup, 214
Sly, 481
Small, 38, 167, 214, 258, 339, 340, 352, 420, 437
Smalley, 59
Smallwood, 38, 39, 162
Smead, 286, 294
Smith, 1, 5, 13, 18, 23, 28, 36, 38, 39, 49, 53, 59, 61, 62, 64, 65, 67, 70, 73, 75, 80, 83, 91, 95, 96, 101, 109,

111, 112, 113, 116, 120, 123, 132, 135, 138, 143, 144, 146, 148, 151, 159, 161, 163, 167, 172, 174, 184, 192, 196, 203, 208, 212, 217, 218, 219, 220, 222, 224, 226, 227, 228, 235, 248, 251, 254, 256, 257, 262, 264, 265, 270, 271, 272, 273, 275, 279, 282, 284, 285, 288, 290, 291, 293, 295, 300, 301, 304, 306, 312, 315, 319, 320, 324, 327, 330, 335, 336, 337, 341, 342, 344, 353, 354, 355, 363, 364, 365, 368, 369, 370, 373, 374, 375, 383, 385, 386, 387, 388, 389, 399, 402, 405, 406, 414, 424, 425, 431, 432, 434, 442, 446, 448, 457, 459, 460, 466, 467, 472, 482
Smoot, 8, 39, 80, 89, 151, 219, 250, 368, 384, 460
Smull, 39, 451
Snead, 355, 422
Snelling, 43, 117, 285, 288, 293, 335, 439
Sniffin, 59
Snow Hill, 53
Snowden, 39, 464
Snyder, 25, 39, 108, 110, 112, 233, 379, 479
Society of Friends, 432
Society of Jesus, 432
Soldiers-1812, 3, 13, 236
Sollers, 266, 306
Solomon, 352
Somerville, 249, 251, 414
Sommers, 317
Sommerville, 39
Song of Hiawatha, 436
Sontag, 389
Soper, 319
Sorey, 353
Soria, 147
Sorley, 252
Sosa, 270
Sothoron, 15, 142, 218

South Carolina Historical Society, 219
Southall, 317
Southerland, 163
Southey, 100
Southoron, 39, 72
Soza, 210
Spaffford, 249
Spalding, 63, 71, 160, 184, 367
Sparks, 11
Sparrow, 475
Spates, 304, 364
Spaulding, 3, 18, 227
Speake, 125, 400, 462
Spear, 4
Speck, 421
Spedden, 231, 261, 375
Speiden, 39, 160
Spelman, 453
Spence, 44
Spence's Mill, 44
Spencer, 23, 155, 191, 243, 287, 289
Spicer, 361
Spiller, 142, 156
Spillman, 170
Spindle, 256
Spofford, 468
Spohn, 391
Spooner, 248
Spotswood, 253
Spottswood, 56
Sprague, 41, 47, 87, 202, 322
Spratt, 340, 353
Spratts, 83
Spretson, 375
Sprigg, 146, 161, 353, 435
Spriggs, 141
Springman, 39
Squibb, 159
St Andre, 336, 448
St Arnaud, 302
St Clair, 229, 360
St Mary's Female Institution, 306
Stabler, 38
Staff, 71

Stafford, 20, 424
Stainback, 246
Standifer, 67
Standish, 474
Stanford, 113
Staniford, 78, 143
Stanley, 27, 46, 87, 122, 146, 245, 261, 282, 286, 291, 334, 447
Stanly, 369, 406
Stanton, 231, 261, 264, 271, 376, 427
Stanwood, 420
Stapleton, 317
Stark, 54, 55, 61, 261, 326, 387, 393
Starke, 73, 343
Starr, 462
Stavely, 169
Steadman, 20
Steam Fire Engine, 426
steamboat **Fanny Fern** to Thos H Stuart, 66
steamboat **Martha Washington**, 173, 277
steamboat **Salem**, 187
steamer **America**, 264
steamer **Arctic**, 165
steamer **Ben Bolt**, 416
steamer **Curtis Peck**, 377
steamer **Derwent**, 45
steamer **Dresden**, 94
steamer **Elm City**, 335
steamer **Fanny Fern**, 77
steamer **Franklin Pierce**, 67
steamer **G W P Custis**, 330
steamer **General McDonald**, 307
steamer **Georgia**, 355, 358
steamer **Golden Age**, 207
steamer **H D Bacon**, 94
steamer **Hancock**, 50
steamer **Hetzel**, 333
steamer **Illinois**, 249
steamer **James Adger**, 324
steamer **James Robb**, 94
steamer **Jas Robb**, 449
steamer **John Hancock**, 116

steamer **Joseph Whitney**, 464
steamer **Keystone State**, 180
steamer **Merrimac**, 205
steamer **Michigan**, 18, 372
steamer **Minnesota**, 451
steamer **Nashville**, 159
Steamer **North Carolina**, 366
steamer **Ottawa**, 65
steamer **Pacific**, 159
steamer **Plymouth Rock**, 230
steamer **Powhatan**, 180, 240
steamer **San Carlos**, 420
steamer **San Francisco**, 20, 119
steamer **San Jacinto**, 209
steamer **Star of the West**, 427
steamer **Tagus**, 340
steamer **Texans**, 67
steamer **Thomas Collyer**, 352
steamer **Thomas H Stewart**, 77
steamer **Uncle Sam**, 130, 391, 427
steamer **Union**, 388
steamer **Wm Knox**, 165
steamship **America**, 461
steamship **City of Pittsburgh**, 463
steamship **Hermann**, 27
steam-ship **Mississippi**, 167
steamship **Pacific**, 433
steamship **San Francisco**, 9, 26
steamship **Sierra Nevada**, 428
steamship **Winfield Scott**, 20
Stearns, 466
Steart, 264
Steaten, 353
Stebbins, 327
Stedman, 70
Steed, 241
Steedman, 374
Steel, 180, 207, 213, 225
Steele, 24, 25, 125, 159, 369, 380, 417
Steen, 438
Steene, 65
Steer, 157, 481
Steiger, 39
Steigruff, 271

Steiner, 80, 158, 227, 300
Stelberg, 257
Stellwagon, 374
Stephen, 103, 449
Stephens, 160, 215, 254
Stephenson, 74, 389, 429
Steptoe, 96, 171, 283, 292
Sterett, 368
Sterling, 39, 43
Stettinius, 39
Steuart, 291, 414
Stevens, 70, 88, 99, 181, 183, 207, 252, 263, 269, 281, 362, 369, 467
Steward, 73
Stewardson, 449
Stewart, 16, 38, 39, 99, 105, 110, 122, 124, 138, 154, 159, 170, 207, 219, 227, 235, 236, 253, 263, 276, 300, 332, 336, 349, 368, 375, 406, 435, 448
Stickney, 39
Stikes, 354
Stillings, 385, 417, 430
Stillwell, 231, 375
Stimpson, 11, 72
Stinchcomb, 39
Stinson, 467
Stith, 438
Stockett, 2, 215
Stockton, 12, 17, 59, 122, 194, 285, 293, 347, 437
Stockwell, 46
Stoddard, 252, 273, 277, 334, 374
Stoke, 39
Stokes, 371, 467
Stoll, 146
Stollenwerck, 142
Stone, 17, 45, 157, 195, 197, 219, 246, 271, 313, 375, 378, 416, 431, 434, 460
Stoneman, 120, 282, 291
Stoop, 39
Stoops, 26, 99, 187
storeship **Bounding Billow**, 17

Storey, 455
Storm, 252
Storms, 247
Storrow, 253
Storrs, 346
Story, 230, 377, 409
Stothard, 90
Stott, 38, 39, 383, 451
Stoughton, 336, 337
Stout, 374
Stover, 11
Stowe, 262
Stownell, 75
Strader, 11, 87
Straes, 467
Strafford, 96
Strange, 163
Strangford, 231
Stratton, 335
Streaks, 170
Stribling, 108, 214, 238
Stricklin, 127
Stringfellow, 254, 280
Stringham, 361
Strohm, 249
Strong, 39, 76, 238, 253
Struly, 355
Stuart, 52, 123, 177, 178, 184, 194, 210, 217, 224, 226, 262, 266, 286, 291, 302, 341, 375, 381, 396, 440, 441, 458, 461
Stubbs, 259
Stump, 210
Sturdevant, 162
Sturgeon, 259
Sturgis, 70, 122, 215, 282, 291, 322
Sturgiss, 17
Stuyvesant, 401
Suddeway, 353
Sufferie, 39
Suit, 134, 399
Sullivan, 17, 19, 39, 93, 111, 166, 183, 249, 416, 418, 419, 421, 439
Sulphur Springs, 265

Summer Hill, 137
Summers, 59, 70
Sumner, 63, 96, 199, 282, 291
Sumpter, 434
Sumter, 359
Sunderland, 76, 80, 140, 163, 224, 264, 364, 365, 412, 420, 459
Sunnyside, 444
Suphis, 10
Surrat, 303
Surratt, 306
Suter, 114, 328
Sutherland, 261, 386, 387
Sutten, 213
Sutton, 174, 218, 259, 279
Swain, 39, 59
Swaine, 118, 292, 438
Swan, 125, 210
Swann, 38, 169, 327, 461
Swart, 172
Swartwout, 374
Swayze, 17, 209
Sweeney, 27, 184, 307, 341, 452
Sweeny, 39, 40, 92, 146, 175, 222, 381, 408, 410, 474
Sweet, 167, 363, 390
Sweetman, 449
Sweitzer, 121, 293, 437
Sweney, 137
Swentzel, 179
Swett, 77, 394
Swift, 158, 368
Swiss, 102
Swope, 315
Sword, 341
Sykes, 437
Sylva, 210
Sylvester, 87, 168, 319, 325, 340, 345, 346, 352, 357, 393, 394, 401
Symington, 479
Symmes, 118, 288, 293

T

Tabbs, 168
Taber, 167
Tackett, 256
Tacon, 419
Tafft, 317
Tait, 168, 183, 209
Talbert, 8
Talbot, 167
Talbott, 315
Talburt, 116, 133
Talfourd, 50
Taliafero, 40
Taliaferro, 11, 253
Taney, 377
Tanner, 90, 451
Tansill, 20, 56
Tardy, 167
Tarrant, 340
Tarsill, 160
Tasistro, 259
Tasmania, 478
Tatam, 422
Tate, 2, 13, 67
Tatem, 319, 340
Tattnall, 273
Tay, 91
Tayloe, 34, 35, 39, 99, 131, 132, 231, 233, 383
Taylor, 2, 4, 12, 30, 39, 40, 43, 44, 51, 79, 108, 129, 138, 140, 148, 163, 167, 178, 184, 204, 220, 231, 235, 253, 257, 265, 282, 287, 288, 289, 301, 302, 317, 325, 343, 355, 357, 368, 369, 371, 374, 376, 385, 397, 398, 409, 416, 425, 431, 435, 436, 443, 463, 466
Tazewell, 2, 315, 340
Teasdale, 421
Tebbs, 297, 448
telegraphic, 150
Teltzer, 155
Temple, 73, 158, 346, 479
Ten Broeck, 120, 288, 293
Ten Eyck, 168, 271
Tenant, 110

Tennallytown, 15, 256, 332
Tennella, 85
Tenney, 40
Tenny, 235
Terado, 106
Terrell, 260
Terrett, 17, 209, 212, 374
Terry, 142, 372
Tervin, 70
Tesson, 380
Thatch, 481
Thatcher, 374
Thaw, 149
Thayer, 39, 170, 317, 383
The Cottage, 84
The Home Farm, 304
The Iron Ore Field, 63
The Last Judgment, 81
The Octagon, 383
<u>**The Tent of Washington**</u>, 189
Thecker, 321
Therrell, 442
Thom, 226
Thomas, 13, 24, 39, 44, 47, 57, 82, 85, 100, 102, 113, 125, 160, 167, 168, 184, 204, 210, 214, 224, 228, 250, 253, 258, 283, 286, 292, 301, 316, 334, 369, 380, 394, 437, 452, 454
Thompson, 2, 13, 15, 16, 20, 39, 57, 62, 78, 81, 90, 94, 109, 126, 147, 160, 163, 164, 167, 178, 220, 233, 253, 256, 263, 269, 276, 286, 294, 335, 339, 340, 374, 390, 401, 410, 420, 438, 444, 451, 457, 463, 468
Thompson's Island, 275
Thomson, 133, 167, 177
Thorburn, 368, 375
Thorn, 19, 40, 264, 302, 303
Thorndike, 452
Thornley, 364
Thornton, 11, 39, 369
Throckmorton, 40
Thruston, 39, 53, 115, 219, 224, 232, 472

Thumb, 214
Thyson, 390
Tibbald, 60
Tiber creek, 363, 410
Tickner, 436
Tidball, 118, 292, 438
Tierney, 271
Tige, 248
Tilden, 48
Tilghman, 39, 56, 133, 154, 266, 415
Tillinghast, 231, 400
Tilotson, 467
Tilton, 413
Timan, 227
Tine, 334
Tingwell, 398
Tinkler, 327
Tippett, 47
Tirado, 114
Titus, 91, 323
Tochman, 137
Todd, 9, 40, 88, 157, 209, 217, 222, 281, 314, 340, 379, 380
Toddy, 323
Toland, 449
Toler, 153
Toll, 39, 181
Tollver, 163
Tolmie, 298
Tolson, 99, 191, 216, 218, 442, 451
Tomer, 396
Tomkins, 40
Tomlin, 85
Tompkins, 268, 401
Tongue, 52, 127
Toombs, 100, 140, 302
Torbert, 214, 258, 438
Torrence, 28, 70, 88, 193, 207
Torreyson, 225
Totten, 43, 52, 132, 188, 228, 374, 427, 437
Totterdill, 422
Toucey, 158
Toughey, 39

Toupe, 409
Tower, 281
Towers, 13, 173, 183, 209, 217, 227, 352
Towles, 9, 199, 217, 448
Towner, 235
Townley, 85, 301
Townsend, 159, 349, 355, 385, 429
Townshend, 85, 463
Tracy, 118, 287, 396
Trader, 278, 325
Tradu, 305
Trainor, 306
Trapple, 343
Travers, 40, 44, 67, 330
Travis, 120, 150
Treadwell, 334
Treass, 200
Treat, 101
Tredway, 412
Tree, 38
Tretler, 47, 68, 217
Triay, 364
Trigg, 142
Trimble, 394
Trine, 13, 137
Trippe, 445
Trook, 40
Trout, 153
Trowbridge, 417
Truair, 254
True, 410
Trueman, 39
Trugien, 335, 339, 341, 401
Truman, 209
Trumbo, 266
Trumbull, 78, 440
Trunnell, 442
Truxton, 375, 376
Tschiffely, 382, 477
Tuck, 111
Tucker, 39, 40, 105, 130, 131, 173, 179, 250, 253, 254, 295, 301, 335, 374, 384, 425, 447, 468, 472

Tuckerman, 367
Tufts, 255
Tully, 278
Tunis, 364
Tunstal, 339
Tunstall, 370, 371, 393, 401
Tuomy, 416
Turmen, 166
Turner, 25, 39, 45, 65, 115, 125, 151, 152, 201, 214, 218, 249, 258, 270, 361, 369, 374, 472
Turnhill, 267
Turpin, 145
Turton, 217
Tustin, 40, 411
Tuthill, 463
Tuttle, 111
Tutwiler, 62
Tweady, 40
Tweedy, 140, 297
Twyman, 475
Tyler, 42, 83, 155, 220, 265, 306, 309, 315, 401, 466
Tyson, 174, 204, 264, 365

U

Ullmann, 454
Umberfield, 123
Umpqua tribe, 185
Uncle Phil, 186
Underhill, 12, 56, 93
Underwood, 48, 236, 315, 339, 379, 439
Updyke, 360
Upham, 86, 139, 419
Upperman, 99
Upshur, 158, 251, 362, 364, 374, 393, 401
Urbana Female Institute, 295
Utermehle, 301
Utica Female Academy, 309
Uttermuehle, 319
Uttermuhle, 151, 319

V

Vail, 153
Valentine, 142, 263
Valle, 421
Vallejo, 63
Vallett, 266
Van Beethoven, 168
Van Bokkelen, 44
Van Brunt, 374
Van Buren, 42, 283, 290, 294, 414, 424
Van Camp, 214, 258, 437
Van Dieman's Land, 478
Van Dorn, 120, 285, 293
Van Dyke, 220
Van Hall, 10
Van Ingen, 208
Van Ness, 40, 87, 193, 244, 257, 423
Van Noast, 119
Van Patten, 211
Van Paxen, 40
Van Pelt, 115, 116
Van Rennselaer, 212
Van Rensselaer, 460
Van Reswick, 40
Van Voast, 292
Van Wart, 60
Van Willies, 217
Van Wyck, 210, 249
Van Zandt, 375
Vanaman, 351
Vance, 311
Vanch, 402
Vandeburg, 399
Vanderbilt, 167, 413
Vanderheuvel, 54
Vanderlyn, 78
Vandiver, 59
Vanhorn, 333
Vannerson, 76
Vanpelt, 471
Vansant, 159, 416
Vanzandt, 163, 177
Varden, 298

Varnell, 171, 380
Varnum, 368
Vasquez, 14
Vass, 22, 133
Vaublancum, 28
Vaudevelde, 430
Vaughan, 26, 369, 370
Vaulx, 405
Vecey, 40
Vedder, 45
Velasquez, 217
Venable, 69, 133, 217
Verdi, 133
Vermilion, 422
Vermillion, 360
Vernet, 217
Vernon, 40
vessel **Franklin Pierce**, 46
vessel **Hermes**, 409
vessel **J H Holmes**, 46
Vidsea, 215
Viedt, 183
Villalva, 75
Villard, 26, 40
Villepigue, 286
Villipigue, 282
Vincent, 14, 47, 191, 437
Viner, 1
Viney, 87
Vineyard, 102, 391, 435
Vinton, 214, 263
Vivans, 40
Vocell, 106
Volcker, 73
Vollenhoven, 33
Von Gluemer, 114
Von Herringen, 478
Von Itzstien, 403
Voorhees, 40, 49, 368
Vowell, 40

W

Wabon, 278
Waddell, 375, 418

Wade, 153, 297, 435, 480
Wadsworth, 40, 275, 436
Wafer, 440
Waful, 280
Wager, 93, 369, 470, 472
Wagler, 65
Wagner, 317, 330
Waheman, 263
Waiger, 266
Wailes, 40, 114, 134, 482
Wainwright, 163, 177
Wait, 369
Waite, 213, 227, 424, 451
Wakefield, 40
Wakeman, 264, 383, 433, 454, 481
Wakemanites, 481
Walbach, 65, 70, 88, 266, 369
Walch, 247
Walcutt, 369
Walden, 311
Waldersmidt, 398
Waldo, 210, 305
Waldron, 17, 42, 209, 311
Wales, 263, 420
Walhe, 369
Walke, 357
Walker, 17, 40, 65, 85, 96, 101, 146, 158, 161, 169, 171, 175, 176, 217, 235, 243, 251, 256, 261, 284, 286, 292, 309, 314, 315, 322, 341, 374, 375, 419, 420, 425, 445, 446, 456, 459, 461, 463, 467, 468, 469
Wall, 40, 41, 160, 182, 328, 354, 392, 411, 433, 460, 463
Wallace, 70, 98, 102, 139, 346, 451, 464, 467, 468, 475, 477
Wallach, 40, 138, 155, 162, 169, 178, 183, 184, 216, 232, 314, 389, 390, 456, 461, 472, 476
Wallard, 40
Waller, 40, 88
Wallford, 41
Wallingsford, 40, 184
Walls, 37, 320

Waln, 54
Walsh, 70, 99, 138, 229, 379, 415
Walter, 41, 413
Walters, 40, 353, 367, 370, 401
Walton, 91, 208, 394
Wanderstrand, 89
Wandestrand, 62
Wannall, 101
Ward, 40, 41, 76, 92, 102, 140, 141, 145, 152, 157, 159, 207, 231, 237, 256, 266, 267, 271, 273, 297, 328, 376, 389, 405, 412, 416
Warder, 335
Ware, 20, 70, 263, 415
Wareham, 411
Warfield, 185, 236
Waring, 63, 117, 237, 325
Warley, 374
Warmley, 181
Warner, 44, 110, 151, 167, 183, 387
Warren, 43, 101, 179, 208, 306, 378, 380, 416
Warren Academy, 273
Warrenton Female College, 455
Warriner, 27, 411
Warring, 271
Washburn, 263
Washington, 40, 41, 54, 61, 70, 78, 106, 132, 168, 181, 187, 189, 268, 272, 333, 352, 358, 400, 402, 440, 441, 447, 473
Waterbury, 151
Waters, 13, 41, 42, 75, 109, 137, 142, 221, 223, 254, 380, 412
Waterson, 297
Wathen, 259
Watkins, 3, 274, 423, 428, 432
Watmough, 17, 48, 66, 209, 375
Watson, 40, 68, 69, 77, 138, 142, 166, 182, 230, 253, 271, 307, 369, 425, 458, 477, 481
Watt, 149, 393
Watters, 375
Watterston, 40

Watts, 51, 94
Waugh, 99, 142, 366, 383, 385
Way, 71
Wayland, 472
Wayne, 16, 106, 228
Wayson, 201, 217, 363
Weadle, 297
Weatherford, 66, 70
Weathers, 71
Weaver, 41, 324, 333, 375, 378
Weaversville Mills, 81
Webb, 32, 86, 117, 118, 120, 160, 163, 167, 179, 183, 214, 230, 232, 258, 263, 288, 293, 361, 396, 425, 427, 437, 472
Webber, 286, 287, 288, 294
Webster, 26, 27, 47, 51, 79, 91, 106, 130, 147, 266, 269, 371
Weddell, 457
Weed, 40
Weeden, 40
Weedon, 129
Weeks, 14
Weems, 188, 255, 421
Wehsheim, 92
Weightman, 64, 236
Weir, 78, 339
Weir's Cave, 450
Weitzel, 258
Welch, 41
Welcker, 281
Weller, 16
Wellesley, 210
Wellford, 462
Wellington, 66
Wells, 17, 42, 112, 155, 190, 233, 374, 443, 472
Welsh, 74, 158
Weltzel, 214
Wendall, 71
Wendell, 66
Wentworth, 82, 94
Werner, 98
Wesley, 167

Wessells, 222
West, 41, 227, 312, 338, 348, 358, 369, 375
Westcott, 273
Weston, 480
Westwood, 125
Wetherford, 88
Wetherill, 274
Wetzell, 271
Weymouth, 137
Whalen, 40
Whaley, 25, 53, 71, 77, 129, 253
Wharton, 115, 288, 289, 294, 380
Wheat, 12, 40, 61, 161, 226
Wheatley, 198, 312, 357
Wheaton, 122, 338
Wheeden, 384
Wheelan, 40, 227, 337
Wheeler, 40, 43, 157, 184, 202, 214, 247, 252, 258, 307, 315, 354, 365, 371, 411, 437, 450, 475
Whelan, 142, 170, 336, 342, 361
Whipple, 11, 21, 281, 390, 394, 410
Whitaker, 59, 310
Whitall, 185
White, 2, 9, 11, 13, 40, 41, 53, 66, 78, 87, 99, 134, 141, 145, 150, 175, 184, 191, 208, 210, 229, 248, 250, 252, 271, 273, 275, 318, 332, 340, 348, 368, 384, 387, 388, 416, 420, 430, 433, 444, 450, 451, 459, 475
White Sulphur Springs, 301
Whitehead, 113, 280, 303, 353, 354, 358, 393
Whitely, 97
Whiteman, 339
Whitfield, 94, 102, 110
Whithead, 352
Whiting, 94, 108, 121, 174, 212, 220, 240, 360, 369, 374, 389
Whitlock, 297
Whitman, 220
Whitmore, 40, 41, 99, 167, 235, 371, 451

Whitney, 40, 199, 253, 361
Whittell, 389
Whittier, 88
Whitting, 352
Whittingham, 204, 280
Whittle, 340, 343, 467
Whittlesey, 188, 198, 221, 225, 452, 459
Whittlesy, 272
Whitwell, 158, 469
Whitworth, 270
Whorton, 41
Whyte, 266
Wickliffe, 244, 288, 289
Wicks, 170
Wiger, 266
Wight, 186, 317, 381
Wigston, 147
Wike, 19
Wilbur, 247
Wilcox, 158, 327, 374, 403
Wilde, 244
Wilder, 59, 93, 166
Wildgoss, 413
Wilgus, 17
Wilhelm, 345, 424
Wilhelmina, 135
Wilkerson, 40
Wilkes, 20, 40, 374
Wilkies, 154
Wilkins, 122, 286, 293
Wilkinson, 152, 212, 220, 259, 297, 368, 450, 477
Willard, 174, 179, 184, 245, 341, 373, 383
Willcoxen, 217
Willett, 252, 404, 418
Willey, 11
Williams, 9, 11, 16, 17, 40, 41, 46, 51, 61, 66, 102, 118, 128, 160, 163, 167, 168, 179, 182, 199, 201, 208, 210, 220, 228, 231, 236, 247, 249, 250, 260, 261, 263, 283, 286, 289, 290, 292, 297, 301, 309, 328, 334, 343, 348, 349, 353, 363, 370, 375, 397, 420, 422, 427, 431, 432, 437, 439, 449, 451, 470, 471
Williamson, 40, 87, 117, 154, 159, 201, 260, 358, 369, 419, 420, 460
Williman, 219, 393
Willis, 258, 398, 415
Willitt, 112
Willmuth, 273
Willner, 40
Wills, 165, 364, 370, 415
Willson, 405
Wilmer, 15, 472
Wilroy, 353
Wilson, 2, 40, 41, 50, 59, 77, 80, 91, 129, 160, 167, 183, 186, 188, 202, 207, 210, 213, 220, 222, 233, 252, 253, 256, 278, 305, 319, 328, 355, 373, 375, 382, 388, 396, 446, 451
Wiltberger, 40, 225, 298
Wimer, 166, 174, 416
Wimsatt, 40
Winans, 274, 299, 312
Winchester, 87, 210
Winder, 40, 41, 119, 126, 283, 292
Windsor Forest, 256
Wing, 299
Wingard, 449
Wingate, 41, 88
Wingenroth, 50
Winn, 53, 60, 66, 111, 452
Winner, 363
Winper, 45
Winship, 290, 380, 465
Winslow, 262, 374
Winston, 315, 345
Winter, 127, 183, 270
Winterbottom, 456
Winters, 41
Wintersmith, 315
Winthrop, 275, 296, 322, 377
Wirt, 40, 184, 219
Wise, 40, 99, 197, 207, 252, 255, 264, 410, 431, 476

Wishart, 18, 195
Wiswel, 214
Witherbury, 67
Witherell, 287
Withers, 39, 40, 296, 305, 360, 412
Wittenaur, 32
Witter, 290
Wix, 134
Wm & Mary College, 315
Wolfe, 253
Wolff, 125
Wollard, 252
Wood, 7, 28, 40, 41, 66, 72, 121, 122, 142, 157, 202, 225, 228, 251, 252, 282, 291, 373, 375, 429, 448
Wood Lawn, 442
Woodbridge, 83, 309, 410, 439
Woodbury, 397, 411
Woodeard, 353
Woodfin, 59
Woodhull, 64, 224, 301
Wooding, 481
Woodis, 319, 325, 333
Woodlands, 330
Woodlawn, 191
Woodruff, 26, 119, 137, 380, 470
Woods, 117, 120, 245, 263, 292, 302, 319, 376, 380, 438
Woodson, 256, 335
Woodward, 41, 68, 89, 101, 114, 240, 250, 266, 336, 346, 354, 384, 462
Woodworth, 11
Wool, 165, 194, 465
Woolard, 271
Wooley, 51
Woolsey, 368
Wooster, 89, 449
Wootten, 365
Wootton, 281
Worden, 231
Wordsworth, 50, 90, 100
Wormley, 40, 153
Worrell, 345
Worth, 47, 65, 396

Worthen, 59
Worthington, 41, 44, 94, 117, 237, 266, 415
Wortley, 461
Wotherspoon, 145, 207
Wray, 246, 260
Wren, 93
Wrenn, 343
Wright, 41, 48, 96, 98, 126, 144, 152, 158, 183, 205, 261, 279, 281, 282, 284, 292, 305, 312, 313, 350, 362, 380, 436, 441, 442, 455
Wroe, 41
Wroe, 41, 179
Wurdeman, 413
Wurtmuller, 442
Wyatt, 8, 393
Wyckoff, 239
Wyman, 98, 237, 328
Wymann, 428
Wynne, 480
Wythe, 169, 315

Y

Yard, 165, 374
Yardella, 41
Yarnall, 400
Yarrington, 26
Yates, 94, 155
Yea, 262
Yearnes, 243
years 1792-93, 328
Yeatman, 41, 347
Yeemans, 102
Yellott, 219
yellow fever, 66, 72, 316, 317, 323, 325, 332, 340, 343, 346, 354, 355, 356, 360, 362, 366, 367, 370, 377, 385, 393, 401, 405, 428, 430
Yeo, 355
Yosti, 416, 421
Yough, 468
Youlee, 271

Young, 6, 11, 39, 41, 53, 70, 74, 77, 99, 112, 150, 170, 171, 178, 227, 259, 266, 278, 313, 336, 345, 358, 362, 368, 369, 374, 375, 394, 425, 451, 467
Younger, 41, 297
Yturbide, 230

Z

Zantzinger, 38, 368
Zellers, 41
Zemp, 443
Zimmerman, 130, 310, 358, 387, 453

Other Heritage Books by Joan M. Dixon:

National Intelligencer *Newspaper Abstracts Special Edition: The Civil War Years Volume 1: January 1, 1861-June 30, 1863*

National Intelligencer *Newspaper Abstracts Special Edition: The Civil War Years Volume 2: July 1, 1863-December 31, 1865*

National Intelligencer *Newspaper Abstracts 1856*

National Intelligencer *Newspaper Abstracts 1855*

National Intelligencer *Newspaper Abstracts 1854*

National Intelligencer *Newspaper Abstracts 1853*

National Intelligencer *Newspaper Abstracts 1852*

National Intelligencer *Newspaper Abstracts 1851*

National Intelligencer *Newspaper Abstracts 1850*

National Intelligencer *Newspaper Abstracts 1849*

National Intelligencer *Newspaper Abstracts 1848*

National Intelligencer *Newspaper Abstracts 1847*

National Intelligencer *Newspaper Abstracts 1846*

National Intelligencer *Newspaper Abstracts 1845*

National Intelligencer *Newspaper Abstracts 1844*

National Intelligencer *Newspaper Abstracts 1843*

National Intelligencer *Newspaper Abstracts 1842*

National Intelligencer *Newspaper Abstracts 1841*

National Intelligencer *Newspaper Abstracts 1840*

National Intelligencer *Newspaper Abstracts, 1838-1839*

National Intelligencer *Newspaper Abstracts, 1836-1837*

National Intelligencer *Newspaper Abstracts, 1834-1835*

National Intelligencer *Newspaper Abstracts, 1832-1833*

National Intelligencer *Newspaper Abstracts, 1830-1831*

National Intelligencer *Newspaper Abstracts, 1827-1829*

National Intelligencer *Newspaper Abstracts, 1824-1826*

National Intelligencer *Newspaper Abstracts, 1821-1823*

National Intelligencer *Newspaper Abstracts, 1818-1820*

National Intelligencer *Newspaper Abstracts, 1814-1817*

National Intelligencer *Newspaper Abstracts, 1811-1813*

National Intelligencer *Newspaper Abstracts, 1806-1810*

National Intelligencer *Newspaper Abstracts, 1800-1805*

www.ingramcontent.com/pod-product-compliance
Lightning Source LLC
Chambersburg PA
CBHW060907300426
44112CB00011B/1381